PRINCIPLES OF EDUCATIONAL AND PSYCHOLOGICAL TESTING

PRINCIPLES OF EDUCATIONAL AND PSYCHOLOGICAL TESTING

Second Edition

FREDERICK G. BROWN
Iowa State University

HOLT, RINEHART AND WINSTON
New York   Chicago   San Francisco   Atlanta
Dallas   Montreal   Toronto   London   Sydney

Library of Congress Cataloging in Publication Data

Brown, Frederick Gramm.
    Principles of educational and psychological testing.

    Bibliography: p. 479
    Includes indexes.
    1. Educational tests and measurements.   2. Mental
tests.   I. Title.
LB1131.B72   1976   371.2'6   75-42004
ISBN 0–03–089051–9

PREFACE

Like many other textbooks, this one was written because I held a particular view of how a course in educational and psychological testing should be taught. This approach, stressed in the book, is to emphasize the logic of psychological measurement. By "logic" I mean *why* psychological measurement proceeds as it does. Such an approach implies that we must ask such questions as: Why do we want to measure certain characteristics and not others? Why must tests be reliable, valid, and standardized? Why are certain assumptions made when measuring achievement, abilities, and personality characteristics? Consideration of these "why" questions leads directly to the "how" questions, those dealing with the techniques and methods of test construction and makes discussion of the latter more meaningful.

If I had to state one overall goal for the book it would be this: to provide the reader with the necessary background so that he or she can make an informed, intelligent evaluation of a test whenever the need arises. Because each testing situation is unique, one cannot say that a particular test is good or bad. Rather one must combine a knowledge of the situation with knowledge of the principles of psychological measurement (presented in this book), and then make a reasoned evaluation of the potential usefulness of the test in that particular situation. Stated differently, my goal is for the reader to learn what questions to ask when evaluating a test.

I have also emphasized the applied aspects of testing by stressing how tests can be used when making educational and vocational decisions to better promote the development of each individual. This emphasis, in part, reflects my training as an applied psychologist. More importantly, applied aspects of testing are stressed because most readers will be consumers and users of tests rather than test developers or researchers.

The reader may ask how this book differs from other textbooks on educational and psychological testing. To me, the major differences are: (1) the emphasis on the logic of psychological measurement; (2) the use of specific tests as examples to illustrate important points and concepts rather than the provision of a catalog of existing tests; (3) the sequential development of topics from consistency, to validity, to scores and norms, to the construction of various types of tests; and (4) the emphasis on certain concepts—for example, incremental validity, base rates, decision-making accuracy, homogeneity—that are treated only briefly in other books.

As with the previous edition, I have drawn the majority of my illustrations from educational testing. This emphasis was selected because of the important role tests play in the educational process, and because I have found that students are better able to relate these examples to their own experiences.

Persons who have used the first edition of the book will be interested in the changes that have been made. Although many parts of the book will look familiar, it has been completely rewritten. My goal was to make the book a better teaching tool while, hopefully, retaining the best features of the first edition. Some of the more noticeable changes include (1) division of the material into more, and shorter chapters; (2) the providing of overviews through the use of introductory chapters and brief organizers for each section; (3) inclusion of a chapter on the applications of tests in educational, counseling, and industrial settings; (4) the updating of information on specific tests, current research, and thinking; (5) expanded coverage of teacher-built tests; and (6) an increased emphasis on using tests for purposes other than selection and discrimination between students—for example, the discussion of criterion-referenced and mastery testing.

Several comments on stylistic matters. First, references to the literature have been cited only to give background when the point discussed is controversial, to give credit to persons developing a new technique or approach, and to help the reader locate sources that treat the topic in more depth. The annotated Suggested Further Reading section at the end of each part also serves the last function. Second, I have tried to explain all statistical concepts both in words and formulas. Third, although I am well aware of the concern over possible sex bias, I have made no conscious attempt to balance the use of masculine and feminine pronouns or to otherwise confront this issue in a stylistic sense. The reader should note, however, that many of the important contributions discussed in the book were made by female psychologists, among them A. Anastasi, S. B. Anderson, S. L. Bem, G. C. Gleser, J. Loevinger, and L. Tyler.

While writing a book is a lonely task, it is one to which many people have contributed. The first edition was completed during a year spent at the Center for Advanced Study in the Behavioral Sciences, where the aid of O. Meredith Wilson, Jane Kielsmeier, and Preston Cutler, as well as my classmates, was invaluable. My students and colleagues at Iowa State, as well as several users of the first edition, provided many helpful suggestions that have been incorporated in the revision. Gwen Ethington eased my task considerably by translating my drafts into a polished, typed manuscript. The editors at Holt and Dryden—particularly Roger Williams, Siebert Adams, David P. Boynton, Richard Owen, and Kathleen Nevils—have provided the necessary encouragement (and prodding) and much valuable professional advice. And, most importantly, appreciation and gratitude go to my wife Barbara for her continued support and encouragement; and to Jeff, Kirk, and Danny, who were always interested in the progress of their "favorite author," even when it meant that he had to work rather than be with them.

Ames, Iowa   Frederick G. Brown
January 1976

CONTENTS

PART I

MEASUREMENT IN PSYCHOLOGY AND EDUCATION

People differ. But in what ways? How large are these differences? What are the practical implications of these differences? These are the sorts of questions to which this book is addressed. We shall attempt to answer these and other related questions by focusing on the process by which individual characteristics are measured. Although we shall emphasize educational and psychological tests, most of what we say applies equally well to any other process for measuring human characteristics.

We shall begin in this first part of the book by doing three things: defining and explaining the basic terms and concepts in testing and measurement, presenting an overview of the test construction process, and reviewing the prerequisite statistical concepts.

Chapter 1 focuses on two concepts: test and measurement. A test is viewed as a method for systematically observing a person's behavior. This approach has several important implications. First, as any test is only a sample of all possible items or behaviors, whether the test items adequately sample the wider range of possible items becomes of prime concern. Second, most testing procedures compare one person's performance with that of other people, rather than with an absolute scale. Thus, psychological measurement is relative, being concerned primarily with differences between people. Third, because we are trying to measure people's behavior, we must always be concerned that we are, in fact, measuring the characteristic that we presume to be measuring.

As tests are measuring instruments, the concept of measurement will be explored in some detail. Basically, measurement is the process of assigning numerical values to a person's performance in accordance with specified rules. You will see that using different rules results in different types of measurements. We shall also contrast measurement and evaluation; the basic distinction is that measurement answers the question "how much?" whereas evaluation is concerned with the question "how good?"

Chapter 2 gives an overview of the test construction process. A unifying thread in this chapter is that tests may serve as samples, signs, or predictors. Some tests are samples, in the sense that the test items are but a sample of all possible items in a particular area or domain. For example, a comprehensive final exam samples your knowledge of the material covered in a course. Other tests function as signs, in that they point out the nature of the characteristic we are attempting to measure. For example, the abilities and skills measured on an intelligence test help define what is meant by intelligence. Other tests serve as predictors. In this case we are interested in a test because it predicts some nontest behavior. An example is a college admissions test used to predict how well students will perform academically in college.

The remainder of Chapter 2 presents an outline of the process of constructing tests. Throughout our discussion we shall emphasize the need for standardized procedures—that is, the need for all persons to take the same items under the same conditions and to have their performance evaluated using the same methods and standards. Without standardization, scores of different individuals cannot be compared directly.

Since many of the basic concepts in testing and many of the theories underlying testing have a statistical base, Chapter 3 will review some basic descriptive statistics. Starting with simple tabular and graphic methods of illustrating distributions of scores (frequency distributions), we shall next show that to describe a score distribution we need measures of the average level of performance (central tendency) and the scatter or dispersion of the scores (variability).

Because scores from several tests cannot be compared unless performance is expressed on a common scale, we next describe a method for making this transformation to standard scores. Finally, we shall consider the correlation coefficient, which provides a technique for describing the relationship between two sets of test scores. These few fundamental concepts will provide the basis for all statistical methods used in the book.

1

THE NATURE
OF PSYCHOLOGICAL
MEASUREMENT

That people differ in numerous ways is apparent even to the most casual observer. Some people are short, others tall; some are blond, others brunet; some can run 100 yards in less than 10 seconds, others take 15 seconds or longer. People not only differ in physical appearance and skills, but also vary in psychological abilities and personality characteristics. Some people find math easy, whereas others are unable to cope with simple calculations; some people prefer constant companionship, but others prefer to be alone; some people emerge as leaders, but others are content to follow.

Because of these wide variations, the study of individual differences has been a continuing focus of interest in psychology. Part of this interest reflects our natural curiosity about our fellowmen—about what they are like and how they behave. Thus, in psychology, most terms used to describe people refer to characteristics that vary widely between people, such as intelligence, aggressiveness, mathematical ability, mechanical interest, and introversion, to name but a few. These differences also have important practical significance; perhaps the most obvious is that different skills and abilities are required for success in various occupations.

For the psychologist a major problem is how to describe the nature and extent of these individual differences precisely and accurately. Although in everyday conversation we may refer to one person as being "smart" and another as "dumb," such gross distinctions are not sufficient for the psychologist. He is concerned with such questions as: What is meant by intelligence? How can the various levels of intellectual ability be defined? How can intelligence be measured? What variables are related to, or predictable from, intelligence test scores? In this book we shall describe the methods psychologists use to develop instruments that help provide answers to such questions. Although there are many methods that might be used, such as observations, rating scales, work samples, and performance measures, we shall focus on psychological tests. In our opinion, they represent the best approach yet developed for measuring psychological characteristics.

Trait Theory

There are a myriad of ways of describing the behavior and characteristics of individuals. One investigator, for example, has identified over 40,000 terms that have been used to describe people. Obviously, to deal with such a large number of concepts is impractical. Thus psychologists have attempted to reduce the number of descriptive terms to a more manageable number. The primary approach that has been used is trait theory (see, e.g., Anastasi, 1948, 1970).[1]

A trait can be defined as a cluster of interrelated, or intercorrelated, behaviors. That is, a trait is a term that describes a group of behaviors that tend to occur together. It is an abstraction, a construct, rather than an objective, tangible reality. The typical procedure for identifying traits is to have a group of people respond to a large number of items, then statistically analyze the data to find which items cluster together. For example, we might administer a questionnaire covering a large number of vocational and avocational activities and ask people to respond by indicating whether they like or dislike each activity. Suppose that people who say they like to repair their own car also say that they like to work with power tools, would like to have a home workshop, enjoy working with their hands, like to see how machines work, and like to read *Popular Mechanics*. We have now identified a trait that we might label "mechanical interest." Similar procedures could be used to identify other cognitive and personality traits.

To be useful as descriptive constructs, traits must be relatively stable over time and in different situations. If a person's behavior is not consistent, then predictions of his behavior and reactions from situation to situation and from time to time will be inaccurate and of little use. Although most ability and cognitive traits are quite stable, personality characteristics tend to fluctuate more widely. In fact, some

---

[1]Literature references are to the bibliography at the end of this book.

psychologists (e.g., Mischel, 1968) have suggested that personality characteristics are so situation-specific that a trait view of personality is inappropriate.

Because of the relative stability of most characteristics, many people think that traits are genetically determined. Although differences between people may have a strong genetic basis (see, e.g., Burt, 1972; Jensen, 1969), it is not necessary to conceive of traits as being genetically based. An alternative view (Ferguson, 1954) conceives of traits as overlearned habits, as methods of behaving and reacting that have been so well learned that the person reacts similarly in many situations. Thus, in Ferguson's view, consistency in behavior results from reliance on habitual reaction modes, not because reaction patterns are genetically determined.

Another important point is that traits are inferred from behavior patterns. They are not directly measured tangible personal characteristics. In other words, psychological measurement is always indirect. Consequently, we are always faced with the question of whether we are actually measuring what we intend to measure. Perhaps an example will make this subtle distinction clearer. Probably no term causes more confusion and debate than intelligence. Much of this misunderstanding occurs because people think of intelligence as a fundamental, genetically based quality of a person (and often as one determining his worth as an individual). Viewed this way, such questions arise as: Do tests measure intelligence? Are there racial differences in intelligence? However, if we define intelligence as the ability to solve certain classes of intellectual problems, many of these emotion-laden questions become irrelevant.

The Relative Nature
of Psychological Measurement

Adopting a trait approach has another important implication: Psychological measurement is relative rather than absolute. Almost without exception, we compare the performance of one individual with that of other individuals, not with an absolute standard. In essence, we have a continuum of behavior and try to place each individual at the appropriate place along the continuum. Thus we must look at many varying degrees of a characteristic (trait), and our measurement will always be with reference to some comparison group.

Although the trait approach has some disadvantages, other possible approaches have even more serious weaknesses. One alternative approach would be to adopt a typology, to describe people as belonging to one of several qualitatively distinct classes. This approach must be rejected because human characteristics tend to vary continuously, rather than falling into neatly defined classes. For example, can you make a clear distinction between blonds and brunets? Thus, any division into types would be arbitrary. Another alternative would be to compare each individual to an absolute standard. However, in psychology and education, absolute standards seldom exist. Even when we appear to have absolute standards, closer examination usually reveals that these standards are normative. For example, to say a child can read at a "third grade level" might seem to imply an absolute standard. However, "third grade level" can only be defined in terms of the typical performance of third grade students, which is a relative standard.

DEFINITION OF "TEST"

The term "test" is one of those common words that everyone feels he understands and therefore seldom takes time to define precisely. However, if the procedures for constructing tests are to be understood, a definition must be attempted. We shall define a *test* as *a systematic procedure for measuring a sample of behavior*. This definition can best be understood by considering the implications of the various components of the definition.

The phrase "systematic procedure" indicates that a test is constructed, administered, and scored according to prescribed rules. Test items are systematically chosen to fit the test specifications, the same or equivalent items are administered to all persons, and the directions and time limits are the same for all persons taking the test. The use of predetermined rules for evaluating (scoring) responses assures agreement between different persons who might score the test.

Using standard procedures serves to minimize the possible influence of irrelevant personal and situational variables on test scores. For example, instructions about how to respond when uncertain of the proper response decrease individual differences in guessing behaviors. Another reason for standard procedures is to enable scores of different persons to be compared directly. If two individuals responded to different items, or had different amounts of time to complete the same items, we could not compare their scores. Thus, using standard procedures permits direct comparisons between individuals.

A second crucial term is behavior. In the strictest sense, a test measures only test-taking behavior—that is, the responses a person[2] makes to the test items. Thus, as mentioned previously, we do not measure a person directly; rather, we infer his characteristics (traits) from his responses to test items. If the behaviors exhibited on the test adequately mirror the construct being measured, the test will provide useful information. If the test does not adequately reflect the underlying characteristic, inferences made from test scores will be in error.

Third, a test contains only a sample of all possible items. No test is so comprehensive that it includes every possible item that might be developed to measure the behavior domain.[3] One could think of exceptions, such as an addition test covering every possible combination of two one-digit numbers, but these exceptions are rare and generally trivial. Thus any particular test is better thought of as a sample of all possible items.

Because a test contains only a sample of all possible items, two problems arise. First, we must be assured that the items included on the test are a representative sample of all possible items. The second problem involves the question of whether a

[2]In the earlier edition of this book, the definition stated that a test measured an individual's behavior. I now believe that this restriction may be too limiting, as it does not provide for tests in which several persons work together to produce a response or for tests in which individual responses are pooled to obtain a description, such as instruments designed to describe college environments. In most situations, however, tests measure characteristics of individuals.

[3]A behavioral domain is the hypothetical pool of all possible items covering a particular area. When speaking of this pool of possible items, we shall use the terms domain, universe, and population interchangeably.

person would obtain the same score if he responded to a different sample of items drawn from the same domain. In other words, would he obtain the same score on an equivalent form of the test? The former is the validity problem, the latter the problem of reliability.

Finally, a test is a measuring instrument. Because the concept of measurement is central to the development of many topics in this book, the process of measurement will be explained in some detail in the next section.

Before leaving our definition of "test," however, it should be noted that nothing in the definition requires that one particular format (for example, paper and pencil) be used, that the test taker makes specific preparations for the test, or that he even be aware he is being tested. Although a test taker generally is aware he is being evaluated and often prepares for a test, by study and review, these are not necessary conditions.

MEASUREMENT

A psychological test is a measuring instrument. But what is meant by measurement? Measurement is the description of data in terms of numbers (Guilford, 1954). More precisely, measurement has been defined as the assignment of numerals to objects or events according to rules (Stevens, 1951). In the context of testing, this definition could be restated: Measurement is the assignment of numerals to behavior according to rules. Therefore, measurement of any characteristic involves the utilization of certain procedures (operations), according to specified rules, that result in the assignment of numerical values to a person's performance. Implicit in the definition is the idea that these numerical values will be expressed on a well-defined scale. In other words, we have a continuum measuring some dimension, and our goal is to place each person at the proper place on this continuum.

Physical and Psychological Measurement

With physical dimensions the measurement process is relatively straightforward (see, Astin, 1968; Faller, 1967). Generally, there are commonly accepted operations and prescribed rules to follow, as well as well-defined scales on which to express the results. Consider how you would measure the length of this book. You would obtain a ruler, place one edge of the book at the zero point of the ruler, then read the scale point corresponding to the other end of the book. This set of operations gives the length of the book. Here our scale probably would be inches.

Measurement of psychological characteristics is, unfortunately, not so simple. However, the same steps are followed as with measurement of physical dimensions. Suppose that we are interested in the rate at which people read. We could define reading speed in terms of "words read per minute." The problem now becomes to specify a set of procedures for measuring reading rate. One obvious method would be to have each person read a standard passage for a set amount of time. By counting the number of words read and dividing by the number of minutes spent reading, we would obtain a measure of words read per minute. This procedure would be directly analogous to measuring length.

There are other factors, however, that must be considered when measuring reading rate. For one, the difficulty of the reading passage will affect the reading rate. Thus, the obtained rate will be meaningless unless we know the nature and difficulty of the material read. The length of the reading period may also be important. If it is so long that the reader becomes fatigued or bored, the rate may decrease. Moreover, the testing conditions might also have an effect; for example, the reading rate would probably be lower in a noisy room than in a quiet one. In addition, what is meant by "reading" would have to be clearly defined. The point is, of course, that although physical and psychological measurement involve the same procedures, more variables must be controlled in psychological measurement if meaningful measurement is to occur.

Measurement Scales

To understand the preciseness of psychological measurement, we must consider the nature of the scale used. Depending on the mathematical and logical assumptions made, several types of scales are possible. These scale levels are hierarchical in that the higher-level scales meet all the assumptions of the lower-order scales plus additional ones characteristic of their particular level. From lower to higher order, from simpler to more complex, the scales are called nominal, ordinal, interval, and ratio.

Nominal scales   Measurement on a nominal scale is simply assigning persons to qualitatively different categories. The fundamental operation is determining whether two persons are members of the same category or class; that is, whether they possess some common characteristics. For example, people can be classified as male or female, or voters as Republican, Democrat, or Independent. If desired, numerals can be assigned to each group. Thus, males might be coded 1 and females 2; or Republicans 1, Democrats 2, and Independents 3. On a nominal scale, numerals are used for identification only, to denote membership in a certain class; they do not imply magnitude. Measurement on a nominal scale is of limited usefulness, as it only allows for classification, whereas in most instances we are interested in some estimation of magnitude.

Ordinal scales   Ordinal scales rank people on some dimension. For example, we could rank schoolchildren in order according to their height, from tallest to shortest. If Charles is the tallest, then Eric, and then George, we can also say that Charles is taller than George. However, we cannot say how much taller one child is than another; we can only compare their relative heights. Thus, on an ordinal scale we have classification (two children can be the same height) and magnitude (some children are taller than others), but we have said nothing about the size of the measurement scale units.

In many situations, ranking is sufficient. If we want to select the 25 best math students from a class of 100, we have only to give a math test and identify the 25 highest scorers. We do not need to know how much higher they scored than the rest of the class; we only need to know that they obtained the highest scores. In general, when we are interested in selecting only a top (or bottom) group of people, ranking will suffice.

Interval scales   On an interval scale, a difference of a certain magnitude means the same thing at all points along the scale. In other words, the score units can be shown to be equivalent at all points on the scale.[4] Thus, an interval scale involves classification, magnitude, and of equal-sized units. Consequently, the crucial operation in the development of an interval scale is to establish that we do have equal-sized units. We must be able to show that a given interval on the scale, say a particular 5-point difference, is equivalent to a 5-point interval at any other place on the scale.

Psychologists are interested in obtaining interval scales for two reasons. First, on an interval scale scores can be transformed in any linear manner. This means that we can add or subtract a constant, or multiply or divide scores by a constant, without destroying the relationship between scores. Consequently, scores on one scale can be converted to a scale employing different units. This means that scores on several tests can be transformed to a common scale, thus allowing us to directly compare performance on different measures. The second reason for preferring an interval scale is that most widely used statistics assume an interval scale of measurement.

Ratio scales   The fourth level of measurement is the ratio scale. In addition to equal intervals, ratio scales also have a meaningful zero point. Since a meaningful absolute zero point is virtually impossible to define for most psychological characteristics (consider, for example, how to define "zero intelligence") and since interval scales are sufficient for most purposes, we shall not be overly concerned with attempting to develop tests that measure on ratio scales. It should be noted, however, that a new approach to measurement (Rasch, 1966) appears to provide a definition of a meaningful zero point.

What Level Is Psychological Measurement?

In a sense, measurement is only a game we play (Kerlinger, 1973, Chapter 25). The object of the game is to produce a correspondence between the measurement and "reality"; the greater the correspondence, the better the measurement. In this view, the critical consideration is whether one type of scale corresponds more closely to reality than another. In particular, our concern is usually whether interval scales are an adequate representation of reality.

An example   The problem can perhaps be clarified by an example. Suppose that we are interested in students' mathematical ability. One way we could determine ability

---

[4]Strictly speaking, the requirement is for equal-sized intervals (differences between scale points) rather than units; hence the designation "interval scale."

is by administering a well-constructed test covering basic mathematical skills. The obvious index of ability would be the score a student makes on the test, say, the number of items he answers correctly. Now, let us further suppose that the test consists of 50 items of varying difficulty. Can we say that a 5-point difference at any part on the scale is equivalent to a 5-point difference at any other portion on the scale? To use a specific example, is the difference between scores of 10 and 15 equal to the difference between scores of 45 and 50?

From one point of view, every point (that is, every item answered correctly) could be considered equal to every other point. Thus, the answer to our question would be ''yes, the difference between 10 and 15 is equal to the difference between 45 and 50.'' A little reflection, however, might lead one to conclude that the difference between scores of 45 and 50 is greater than the difference between scores of 10 and 15. One reason would be that to answer all items correctly (that is, to improve from 45 to 50) probably requires answering an additional five difficult items, whereas improving from 10 to 15 most likely involves answering an additional five relatively easy questions. If we accept this reasoning, then we would conclude that we do not have equal intervals on our scale.

The distinction between these two interpretations is whether we make any inferences over and above the operation of counting the number of items answered correctly. The first approach, called operational, makes no such inferences. In essence, it equates improvement with score changes. The second approach suggests we must also consider the psychological difficulty involved in improvement at different score ranges. This latter view involves a ''reality'' that includes psychological components.

Obtaining an interval scale   Although there is no doubt that psychological tests measure on an ordinal scale, most psychologists prefer that test scores be on interval scales. Fortunately there are several ways to proceed *as if* the assumptions of an interval scale have been met, even if we cannot prove that we have an interval scale.

One procedure was used in the example: defining variables in terms of test scores. In this approach we make no inferences about postulated underlying abilities; thus it has a certain mathematical purity. However, it can lead to some psychological absurdities. Another approach is to transform scores statistically to a scale having equal units. The most common transformation is to standard scores, which clearly represent an interval scale (see Chapter 3). This approach is analogous to pulling oneself up by one's own bootstraps.

The third, and probably most common, approach (see, e.g., Ghiselli, 1964; Nunnally, 1967; Kerlinger, 1973) is a pragmatic one. Although the details of each author's argument vary, all agree on two points: (1) Although test construction procedures do not guarantee interval scales, they at least approximate them; and (2) treating test scores as if they were on interval scales produces useful results. In short, we assume an interval scale and proceed as if we had one. If the results of our data analyses make sense, we have added confidence that the assumptions were not far wrong.

Measurement and Evaluation

A common confusion in psychological testing is the failure to make a clear distinction between measurement and evaluation. Measurement answers the question: how much? That is, measurement provides a description of a person's performance; it says nothing about the worth or value of the performance. However, when we interpret a person's performance, we usually place some value or worth on it. At this point we are going beyond description. We are attempting to answer the question: how good? This is evaluation.

Perhaps an example can illustrate the difference between measurement and evaluation. Suppose that I give a 50-item test to my class. John Jacobs asks me how he did, and I reply that he obtained a score of 36. His test score is a measurement, a description of his level of performance. He then asks me what grade he received, and I reply that a 36 is a B. Now I have made an evaluation because I have made a judgment of how good his performance was. In other words, the objective description of his performance (his test score) is a measurement; my subjective judgment of its quality (the grade) is an evaluation.

USES OF TESTS

Anyone reading this book has taken numerous tests. During your school career, you probably have taken one or more exams in each course as well as several scholastic aptitude tests and standardized achievement test batteries. When applying for college, you may have taken either the College Entrance Examination Board's Scholastic Aptitude Test (SAT) or the American College Testing Program (ACT) battery. Some readers also may have taken tests as part of a job application or during educational or vocational counseling.

How many tests are administered annually is not known, and probably never will be. Mehrens and Lehmann (1969) estimated that over 200,000,000 commercially published tests are sold each year. Since commercially published tests represent only a minority of test usage (certainly, teacher-built tests are much more common), the number of tests administered every year undoubtedly is in the billions.

Let us consider briefly some of the major purposes for which these billions of tests are administered.

Three Ways of Looking at Tests

In the broadest sense, tests measure the nature and extent of individual differences. If a test measuring a given trait is administered to a group of people, we can determine how each person ranks on that characteristic. If one individual takes several tests, we can describe his relative performance on several dimensions. When a number of tests are administered (under a variety of conditions) to large samples of persons, we have a means of studying the nature and range of human abilities and personality characteristics.

Applied versus theoretical uses   Most frequently, tests are used to supply data that aid in making practical decisions. The decision may involve individuals (for example, who should be hired for a particular job, or which students should be admitted to medical school) or some hypothesis (for example, that students learn more if taught in homogeneous ability groups). Inasmuch as a test is only one element in the decision-making process, the adequacy of the decision will also depend on other considerations, such as how adequately the problem is formulated, whether all important factors are taken into account, and how the data are interpreted and used. Thus, accurate test information is a necessary but not sufficient condition for good decision making.

In addition to serving as decision-making aids, tests can also aid in the development of psychological and educational theories. Theories in psychology and education, like those in other disciplines, involve both laws and constructs. One way of defining constructs is by tests. Thus, a theory might involve a construct called anxiety, which could be measured by a psychological test. Or, if a theory implied that more learning would occur under certain conditions, a test might be used as a measure of learning. In these cases, tests are used not to solve an applied problem, but rather to help define a theoretical construct of interest.

Descriptive versus predictive uses   In some situations, tests are used to provide descriptions of an individual. For example, tests are frequently administered during counseling to provide a client with an objective description of his abilities, skills, interests, or personality characteristics. In other situations, we may want to obtain a description of a particular population. For example, we might want to describe the ability levels of students attending Androscoggin College. In turn, we might use these normative data to compare a particular student's abilities to other students attending that college.

Purely descriptive data are generally of limited usefulness. In most situations we want to know what outcomes can be predicted from test scores. For example, although a student might be interested in knowing how his ability compared to that of other students attending the same college, it would be more helpful to know what success a student of his ability level might expect in college—for instance, what sort of grades he might be expected to obtain. To make such statements requires data regarding how accurately the test predicts the desired outcome—in this case, grades.

Maximal versus typical performance   A third distinction to keep in mind is between tests that measure maximal performance and those that measure typical performance. On tests of maximal performance the test taker attempts to make the highest possible score; the goal is to measure the limits of his abilities. Generally speaking, all achievement, aptitude, and ability tests are maximal performance measures. In contrast, typical performance measures attempt to assess a person's usual or habitual reactions and behaviors. Here we are interested not in what he can do or whether he knows how to react; rather, we are interested in his usual reaction or behavior. As might be expected, most personality, interest, and attitude tests are typical performance measures. Although this distinction is important primarily in classifying types of tests, it does have implications when interpreting test scores, for often there is a discrepancy between what a person knows or believes and how he acts.

Tests as Decision-Making Aids

There are several classes of situations in which tests are used as decision-making aids. Perhaps the most common is selection—either in academic settings (for example, admission to professional schools) or in business and industry. In the *selection* situation there are more applicants than can be accepted (or hired), and a decision must be made as to which ones will be accepted. The role of the test is to identify the most promising applicants—that is, those with the greatest probability of success. In the simplest case, the decision is either accept or reject. However, there can be more than two possible decisions; for example, a college may accept a student, accept him if he meets certain additional requirements, or reject him. Commonly, the organization doing the selection is interested only in those accepted; they want to maximize the proportion of persons selected who will succeed. They have, at most, limited interest in those persons who are rejected.

In *placement* there are several individuals and several alternative courses of action; for example, there may be several academic tracks, training programs, or jobs, and each person is to be assigned to one alternative. The goal is to match individuals and alternatives in an optimal manner. Examples include using tests to assign recruits to occupational specialities in the armed services or college freshmen to various levels within a sequence of French courses.

Diagnosis involves comparing an individual's performance in several areas in order to determine relative strengths and weaknesses. Generally, diagnostic procedures are instituted when an individual is having difficulty in some area. Once the areas of disability are identified, a program of remediation can be undertaken. Thus a diagnostic reading test might provide scores in phonetics, word meaning (vocabulary), sentence meaning, paragraph meaning, and reading rate. Here the goal would be to identify the student's particular weaknesses and strengths. Once the specific area of disability is identified, a program of remedial help can be arranged.

In psychological research, tests are often used for *hypothesis testing*. For example, one might hypothesize that anxiety would have a detrimental effect on performance of intellectual tasks. We could then run studies comparing performance on intellectual tasks under various anxiety conditions, using a test to measure anxiety level. Studies of this nature have, in fact, demonstrated that under certain conditions anxiety does have a detrimental effect on intellectual performance (see, e.g., Sarason et al., 1960).

Tests can also be used for *hypothesis building*. This use is illustrated by surveys and the use of tests in counseling. Suppose that a survey shows that persons living in a certain part of the United States score lower on intelligence and achievement tests than persons of comparable age and education in other states. Why? Several hypotheses could be developed. One is that the people living in that particular area are innately less intelligent. Another is that the results reflect differences in the quality of education. A third hypothesis might attribute the effects to socioeconomic and cultural differences. These hypotheses could then be checked by further studies.

The counselor, or therapist, often uses test results to build hypotheses about his clients. Suppose tests show that Clarence, whose father is an engineer, has excellent scholastic aptitude, is interested in literary and artistic activities, is submissive, and has conflicts with authority figures and a problem with family relationships. He is now enrolled in engineering and is failing. From the test data the counselor might hypothesize that Clarence is in engineering because of parental pressure. Unable to confront his parents directly with his dislike for engineering, he has chosen the indirect method of failing his courses. This hypothesis could then be checked through further interviews.

Another use of tests is in *evaluation,* as exemplified by classroom examinations. If properly analyzed, an achievement test not only gives an indication of differences between students, it also indicates which topics the students understood and which areas they had difficulty comprehending. If the student has the opportunity to review his examination, he can also determine his strengths and weaknesses and evaluate the effectiveness of his own preparation. Although classroom examinations and other academic achievement tests are usually used to evaluate students, they may also be used to evaluate the instructional method or the teacher.

All of these uses involve some decision. In selection, the decision is whether to accept or reject an applicant; in placement, which alternative course of action to instigate; in diagnosis, which remedial treatment; in hypothesis testing, the accuracy of the theoretical formulation; in hypothesis building, which further testing or information is needed; and in evaluation, what grade to assign to a student or how effective the procedure may be. The prime question in each case is not whether tests are accurate or inaccurate, but whether they contribute to making better decisions.

Attitudes toward Psychological Tests

Paradoxically, people hold extreme views regarding the efficacy of psychological tests (Brim et al., 1969; Goslin, 1967). On the one hand, there are a large number of people who overestimate the accuracy of tests. They tend to see test scores as providing almost perfect indications of a person's abilities and personality characteristics. These people think that if a test shows Johnny's IQ to be 120, then he is more intelligent, and should do better in school, than Sam, whose IQ is only 117. Or if Chuck's score on a mechanical comprehension test is relatively low, these people would discourage him from becoming a mechanic, neglecting the fact that he rebuilt the engine on his car. This view of tests is comforting, as it provides an easy way to make decisions; there is no need to weigh a variety of factors, just do what the test scores indicate.

On the other hand, there is another large group of persons who feel that psychological tests are essentially useless. These people argue that relying on tests will, in many cases, result in making wrong decisions; thus tests should not be used. This argument is buttressed with examples: the boy who was told that he lacked the ability to complete college, but who later became a successful physician; the company president who "failed" the employment test of his own company; the sullen "genius" who obtained a low score on the intelligence test because he rebelled against being asked to submit to the test.

Another view is that tests are undemocratic and an invasion of privacy. Proponents of this view argue that certain characteristics, usually some aspect of personality, should not be considered in making decisions about individuals. Their argument is frequently in terms of "what ought to be" rather than what "is." That is, they assume that certain personality characteristics ought not to be related to success and that if the empirical evidence indicates such a relationship exists it is only because some component of the situation produces a spurious relationship. Besides, they argue, a person's personality and attitudes are his own business and should not be considered in practical decision making.

As is usual in many controversies, neither extreme view accurately represents the situation. Psychological tests are by no means perfect, and no reputable psychologist will say they are. Yet even though tests do contribute to incorrect decisions in individual cases, there is a body of evidence that shows that, in a variety of situations, tests do a better job than other available evaluation methods. This point is often overlooked. In making practical decisions the important question is which of the available procedures, including tests, allows us to make the most correct decisions.

2

TEST CONSTRUCTION: AN OVERVIEW

The procedures used to construct tests are designed to ensure that the test attains its desired goals and purposes. This is accomplished through application of the measurement principles discussed in Chapter 1. Although the exact process will vary, depending upon the type of test, a general sequence of test construction steps can be identified. These include specifying the purpose of the test, constructing and pretesting items, assembling the final form of the test, standardization, and analyzing the test scores. In the construction of any specific test some of the steps may be omitted, the order of the steps may vary, or several steps may progress simultaneously. Yet a general sequence can be identified (see Figure 2.1).

This chapter will present an overview of the process of test development, showing in broad outline how the several steps fit together; the individual steps will then be considered in detail in following chapters. Throughout the discussion you should keep in mind that the process of test development is both a science and an art, uses both statistical and logical reasoning, and balances practical with theoretical considerations. The goal is to develop an instrument that is as technically sound as possible within any practical constraints.

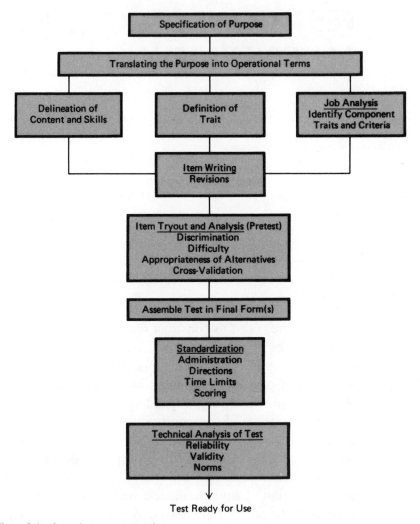

Figure 2.1   Steps in test construction.

Two obvious, though often overlooked, points should be stressed before we begin our discussion of test construction. First, in many situations a test is only one of several possible methods for obtaining the desired information. For example, if we want to measure a high school student's knowledge of mathematics, we might administer a test. Alternatively, we might use his grades in mathematics courses or ask his teachers to rate his knowledge. If some other method for obtaining the desired information is more accurate or practical, it should be used in preference to a test.

Second, there are published tests available in most areas (Buros, 1974a). Thus, we often can use an existing test rather than construct a new one. The advantages of using an existing test are, of course, the savings in time and labor to construct the test and the availability of prior information regarding the effectiveness of the test and the meaning of scores. The major disadvantage is that there may not be any published tests that are optimal for the particular situation.

Tests As Representing

The functions of psychological tests can be viewed from several perspectives. In Chapter 1 we discussed several possible classifications of tests. Another classification scheme, which will aid in understanding the test construction process, distinguishes between tests that represent and tests that predict. In this view, a test is a representation when the test items are similar to the behaviors we are interested in measuring; a test is a predictor when the focus is on some nontest behavior we wish to predict.

To illustrate the concept of a test as representing, let us suppose, for example, that we wanted to measure children's ability to add three-digit numbers. We could ask a child to solve every possible problem involving the addition of two three-digit numbers; however, this would result in an extremely lengthy test. Instead, we could select a sample of problems and ask the child to solve them. On the basis of his performance on these problems we could infer how well he would have done on the entire range of possible problems. The accuracy of our inference would depend on how well we sampled the items comprising the test from the potential pool of items. If by some quirk of sampling we selected many easy items, we would overestimate his ability; if hard problems were overrepresented, his ability would be underestimated. The method of item selection, however, is clear. We systematically sample items from the total pool of potential items. The sample of items included on the test therefore represents the domain of possible items.

Although achievement tests, such as arithmetic and vocabulary, provide the clearest examples of a test as representing, this concept can also be applied to other areas. Suppose that we wanted to measure the honesty of grade school children. One possible way would be to select a sample of situations in which a child has an opportunity to demonstrate his honesty, or lack of it, and observe whether in these situations he is, in fact, honest. We might allow the child to correct his own test paper, allow him to see the answers to an upcoming exam, or provide an opportunity for him to smuggle a valuable object out of the classroom. From observing his behavior in this sample of situations, we could then make inferences about his honesty.

Goodenough (1949) has made a further distinction within the class of tests that represent. She distinguished between tests as samples and tests as signs. The primary basis of her distinction is the clarity with which one can define the behavioral domain being sampled. In her classification, a test is a sample when the items are drawn from a clearly defined universe; a test is a sign when the universe is open-ended and not completely defined. The implication of the term "sign" is that the test points to, or signals, the nature of the universe being sampled. Thus tests that are samples can be viewed as describing the domain, tests that are signs as explaining the domain.

The idea of a test as a sign can be clarified by two examples. Consider creativity, a widely used, but seldom clearly defined, concept. One approach to studying creativity might be to develop a test of abilities and problem-solving styles that appear to measure creative ability. We could then relate scores on these measures to other indices of creativity, such as ratings by expert judges, winning prizes for creative accomplishments, or succeeding in occupations requiring creative skills. If such studies show that scores on our test do relate to these outcomes, we have helped define what is meant by creativity. In essence, our test has served as a sign that indicated the presence of creative abilities.

Or consider intelligence. One way to define "intelligence" is by the types of tasks included on intelligence tests. Using the concept of tests as signs, the oft-quoted phrase, "intelligence is what an intelligence test measures" is not just a circular definition. Rather it points out that performing well on the tasks included on an intelligence test is a sign that the person is intelligent.

In general, the sampling concept is most appropriate with achievement tests, in which the content and skills to be measured are usually clearly specified. When measuring constructs used in psychological theories, however, the domain is usually incompletely defined. Here conceptualizing tests as signs seems more appropriate.

Tests As Predicting

In many situations we are interested in a test because scores on the test enable us to predict how a person will perform in a qualitatively different situation. For example, although a college admissions test may include many vocabulary items, we are not directly interested in the student's vocabulary; rather we are interested in a student's vocabulary score because it predicts how well he will do in college. The focus is on what is predicted, not on the predictor. We are concerned with the student's test performance only because it predicts some other behavior or characteristic of interest. Thus, whether the test items adequately sample a particular domain is of little consequence.

The essential element in a predictor test is that the test scores relate to the behavior of concern (the criterion). Inasmuch as the selection of items for such a test is based upon the accuracy with which the item predicts the external behavior, items that seem to have no logical relationship to the behavior under consideration may be included on the test. For example, an interest inventory might include an item asking whether the person likes to play golf. Logically, this item may have little relationship to any vocational choice except possibly that of a professional golfer. However, if liking golf can be shown to be related to interest in certain occupations, this item would be included on the test because it would predict interest in those occupations.

Representing versus Predicting

The distinction between tests as representing or predicting refers to whether the test items and the relevant nontest behavior are similar or different. If the test and nontest behavior are essentially similar, the test is said to represent the relevant behavior; if they are different, the test is said to be a predictor. The process of test development will vary depending upon whether the test is to function as a sample, sign, or predictor. When the test is constructed to be a sample, items will be chosen by systematically sampling from a defined universe, and evaluation will consist of determining the adequacy of sampling. On the other hand, when a test is a predictor, the crucial step will be empirically establishing that a relationship exists between the item and behavior being predicted.

The distinction is not a clear dichotomy, since the same test can be both a sample and a predictor. To illustrate, a test might be developed by sampling concepts taught in high school mathematics. When administered to entering college freshmen, this test might be used to predict academic success in an engineering curriculum. Thus the same test serves both a sample (of achievement in high school mathematics) and as a predictor (of success in engineering). However, the process of test construction will vary depending on the test's primary function. If the primary goal is to develop a test that measures achievement in mathematics, representative sampling from the universe of math problems will be the *sine qua non* for item selection; if predictive accuracy is primary, sampling representativeness[1] will be subsidiary to predictive power as a basis for item selection. Thus, even though the test may serve both purposes, one or the other will be stressed in the test construction process.

THE TEST PURPOSE

From a pragmatic view, the test constructor has two major decisions: to determine the test's content and its format. That is, he must determine what behaviors, knowledge, or skills the test will cover, and how items will be presented. Before he can make these decisions, however, he must ask two prior questions: "What are the intended uses of the test?" and "What group will take the test?" The answers to these two questions will both set constraints and suggest how to proceed with the test construction process.

The question of purpose is preeminent. Most commonly, a test is developed for some combination of purposes and uses, rather than for a single purpose. Although this purpose usually is at least implicitly defined, an explicit and comprehensive statement of the purposes is highly desirable, if not essential. For example, the purpose of the College Entrance Examination Board's Scholastic Aptitude Test (SAT) is described as follows:

[1]A test used as a predictor is a sample of behavior, in the broad sense, since the items on the test are only a sample of all the items in the domain.

Because secondary schools differ greatly in their courses, academic standards, and grading practices, college admissions officers need some standard measure of ability when they compare the applications of candidates from different schools.

The SAT is a three-hour objective test designed to provide a standard measure of the verbal and mathematical abilities of candidates for college admission. The verbal sections of the SAT will test your ability to understand the relationships between words and ideas and to comprehend what you read. The mathematical sections will test your ability to understand mathematical symbols and to use them in solving problems. (College Entrance Examination Board, 1971, pp. 5–6)

Note that this statement not only explains the purpose of the test but also delineates the content of the test.

The other major consideration is the composition and characteristics of the group for which the test is intended. Here the test constructor must take into account such variables as the test takers' age, intellectual level, education, socioeconomic and cultural background, and reading level. Which variables will be relevant in a specific circumstance will, of course, depend upon the type and purposes of the test. For example, since the SAT is designed for applicants to American colleges and universities, the large majority of persons taking the test will be high school juniors and seniors, who are 16 to 18 years old and will have been exposed to a common core of educational experiences. Thus they will be more homogeneous than the general population in their level of intellectual development. Therefore, the items in the SAT are designed to be of appropriate difficulty and coverage for this particular group.

Test Content

In order to proceed with the building of the test, the test constructor must translate the test purposes into operational terms. That is, he must specify the operations he will use in constructing the test. This specification again covers two major areas—content and format.

Tests that represent   With achievement tests, the first step is to delineate the content and skills covered by the test.[2] A test might cover the sonnets of Shakespeare, the laws of permutations, the social and economic factors in the rise of the Nazi party, or the principles of achievement test construction. The content may be further specified by reference to particular materials; for example, in a classroom exam, content might be defined by reading assignments and the material covered in lectures. In addition to specifying the content, the test constructor may also specify the skills to be tested (for example, knowledge, applications, analysis, evaluation).

If the test is being developed to measure a particular psychological trait or characteristic, the test constructor's job is somewhat different. First he must define, as explicitly as possible, the trait being measured. Then he must indicate the behaviors through which the trait will be manifested. That is, he will describe the observable behaviors, skills, or abilities that are indicators of the trait being measured.

[2]An alternative approach, which is becoming more common, is to design tests to measure attainment of a specified list of behavioral objectives. This approach will be discussed in Chapters 13 and 14.

Tests that predict   When a test is being developed to serve as a predictor, the first step is to make a systematic analysis of the performance we are attempting to predict. In other words, a job analysis is conducted. The results of this analysis should indicate an appropriate criterion measure and identify those traits and behaviors that are necessary for satisfactory performance.

A criterion is a measure of success, that is, the behavior the test is designed to predict. What constitutes successful performance must be defined and an index of success specified. For example, success as a relay assembler might be defined as the number of units assembled per hour, success as a salesman by volume of sales, success as a student by grade point average. An adequate criterion measure must actually measure successful performance and be free from any bias.

Another goal of the job analysis is to identify those behaviors, and hence the traits, that appear to be related to success on the job. If a job involved installing small springs in the mechanism of a watch, the test constructor might hypothesize that finger dexterity was a necessary ability; if a job component was keeping inventory, he might hypothesize that arithmetic ability would be a prerequisite; if the job was cutting floor tiles to fit irregularly shaped floor areas, spatial visualization might be involved. Having hypothesized what abilities, skills, or traits are necessary to perform the job, the test constructor can then select items that measure these abilities and skills.

Test plans   The vehicle used to specify the coverage of a test is the test plan. A test plan is nothing more than a table showing the topics to be covered and the skills to be measured by the test, along with the relative emphases to be given each content-skill category. A simple example of a test plan, for a unit on descriptive statistics, is shown in Figure 2.2. Note that the content areas to be covered are listed on one axis and the skills to be measured on the other axis. The percentages within the cells indicate the proportion of test items that will be devoted to each topic. These proportions should reflect the relative importance of each area. A test plan for a longer or broader test would, of course, be much more extensive.

TEST ON DESCRIPTIVE STATISTICS

	Concepts	Computation	Interpretation
Distributions	10%	10%	5%
Central tendency	10%	10%	5%
Variability	15%	5%	5%
Correlation	15%	0%	10%

Figure 2.2   Example of a test plan.

A test plan serves two purposes. In the item-writing stage, it indicates how many and what sort of items need to be written. Later, we can compare the actual distribution of items on the final form test to the proportions suggested in the test plan, and thereby determine whether the test items do, in fact, adequately sample the domain.

Test Formats

The test constructor must also determine the manner in which the items will be presented. Will he use a paper-and-pencil test or will some apparatus be needed? Will the test taker have only to recognize the correct response, as in multiple-choice items, or will he have to produce the correct response? What emphasis will be given speed of responding? Some of the common test formats are listed below.

SOME COMMON DIMENSIONS OF TEST FORMATS

1. *Alternative versus free response.*   On an alternative response item, the test taker selects the appropriate response from among several alternatives, as in multiple-choice, true-false, or matching items. In free response items, the test taker supplies a response, as in completion, short answer, or essay questions.
2. *Speed versus power test.*   In a speed test the items are usually very simple, but there is a stringent time limit; thus the score is an index of speed of response. A power test is composed of items of varying difficulty, and has a time limit that allows completion of all items. Thus the score reflects the level of difficulty of item the test taker can answer.
3. *Maximum performance versus typical performance.*   On maximal performance tests the test taker is instructed to attain the best score he possibly can. On typical performance tests we are interested in his usual or habitual performance. In general, achievement and ability tests are maximum performance measures, whereas personality tests are typical performance measures.
4. *Paper and pencil versus performance.*   This distinction refers to how test items are presented and responses made. Performance tests often involve manipulation of some object or apparatus.
5. *Group versus individual administration.*   Group tests can be administered to more than one individual at a time, thus are usually paper-and-pencil tests. Individual tests can be administered to only one person at a time, and may be either performance or oral tests.
6. *Structured versus projective.*   In a structured test the stimuli and subject's task are clearly specified; in a projective test the stimuli and task are ambiguous. Structured tests are often called objective, even though this distinction more properly refers to scoring procedures (see pp. 31–33).

Any test will combine several of these dimensions; that is, the test may be a speeded paper-and-pencil test using recognition items. In addition, a test may include several different item types; for example, classroom tests often include both alternative choice (such as multiple-choice, true-false) and free response (such as short answer, essay) items.

As in most instances, any item can be presented in several formats; one problem is to select the "best" format. Two considerations aid in deciding between possible formats: the characteristics of the group to be tested and practical factors.

The role of the composition of the group tested can be illustrated by the practice of administering tests orally to young children and persons with limited reading skills and using tests with minimal verbal content with persons having language deficits. Practical considerations are exemplified by the use of multiple-choice items in nationwide college admissions tests, where, because of the volume of tests administered, the only feasible method of scoring is to use high-speed electronic scoring machines.

CONSTRUCTING THE TEST

Item Writing

Having made these preliminary decisions, the test developer is now ready to start writing[3] items. Again, he has several options as to how to proceed. Consider the sources that might be used in developing individual items. For a classroom exam the teacher can use textbooks, reading assignments, lectures, and class discussions as sources of items. In contrast, on achievement tests developed for use in a variety of schools, item writers consider not just one text, but several widely used texts; not the opinions of only one teacher, but those of a variety of teachers and curriculum experts. Personality inventory items are usually suggested by personality theories, by terms and phrases used to describe personality, by statements found in clinic records, by statements people use to describe themselves, and even by items on other personality inventories.

The process of developing good items is one of writing, editing, tryout, and revision. These steps are then repeated until a satisfactory item is developed. Consider, as an example, tests developed by test publishers. Groups of specialists, working from the test plan, write items to cover the designated content-skill areas. To start, several times as many items are written as will be needed, since many items will be eliminated by succeeding analyses. The first drafts of items are then reviewed and edited, both by the original item writers and by other persons. Editing involves correcting ambiguous wording, strengthening weak alternatives, and eliminating duplicate and otherwise unusable items.

Item Tryout and Analysis

Items that survive this initial screening are next combined into one or more forms of a pretest. These pretests are then administered to a sample of persons similar to those who will take the completed test. For example, for an achievement test, pretests would be administered to students of the same grade level and having the same subject matter background as those the test is designed for. The goal of pretesting is to obtain information on how students react to the items. This evidence

---

[3]Although we will use the term "item writing" to refer to the process of constructing test items, some items (such as those on performance tests) may involve nonverbal components, and thus, strictly speaking, are not written.

will consist of both qualitative comments, such as perceived ambiguities in the items, and quantitative indices of the difficulty and discrimination power of the items.

The item difficulty is the percentage of people who correctly answer an item. Knowing the item difficulties is important if the test constructor wants to compose a test of a given difficulty level. For example, a difficult test might be desired if the test is designed to select students for advanced training or education. Although the concept of difficulty makes sense with items having correct answers (maximal performance tests), its meaning may not be so clear on items where there are no "correct" answers, such as on personality tests. With typical performance items, however, we may desire a certain response pattern (for example, percent agreement with a statement).

The most important index is the item discrimination power. This statistic indicates the extent to which the item measures what it is designed to measure. Ideally, an external criterion measure would be available, so that it could be empirically determined whether people who answered an item correctly also obtained high criterion scores. In practice such outside measures frequently are not available. As a substitute, the total score on the test is used as a criterion measure and responses to individual items are compared to the total score to determine whether persons who obtain higher test scores answer the item correctly more often than persons obtaining lower test scores. When this occurs, the item is said to discriminate. Note that discrimination in this situation refers to making distinctions between persons having greater or lesser knowledge or skill in the area measured by the test.

On typical performance measures, the analogous procedure is to determine whether responses agree with the responses of a designated criterion group; for example, items in a measure of "dominance" would be compared to the responses of people who, by some independent method, have been identified as being dominant.

The third type of information obtained from an item analysis is the number of persons selecting each alternative response to an item. Alternatives that are very infrequently, or never, chosen need to be revised since they do not contribute anything to the item's effectiveness.

In specific situations, other analyses may be performed. If the test is designed to measure a single, homogeneous trait, some measure of the interrelationships between items will be needed. Or, if speed is important, an analysis of the effect of various time limits will be made.

Because statistics derived from different samples will vary due to sampling errors, item analyses are often conducted on two independent samples. This process, called cross-validation, decreases the probability of making decisions based on statistics that reflect only chance fluctuations rather than true differences.

Assembling the Test

The next step is to prepare the final form, or forms, of the test. The results of the item analyses are used to select those items that provide the best discrimination, are of appropriate difficulty, and have no weak alternatives or ambiguities. This selection requires balancing and compromising in that it may be necessary to include less discriminating items in order to ensure the desired content balance. If equivalent forms of the test are built, the test constructor has the further task of equating the forms in terms of content, difficulty, and discrimination power, and along other relevant dimensions.

After any final editorial changes have been made, the test is printed. Now, for the first time, the test exists as a distinct entity. At this point we have a collection of good items but not necessarily a good test. Whether the test will be good or mediocre depends on its standardization and on further technical analyses.

ANALYSES OF THE TEST

Standardization

In testing, our goal is to obtain as accurate an estimate of the test taker's performance as possible. Accurate estimation in psychological testing, as in other scientific procedures, depends upon control of errors—that is, minimizing the influence of factors irrelevant to the purposes of the testing. This is accomplished by making the test situation as similar as possible for all individuals.

The process of developing these controls is called *standardization*. Standardization means various things to different authors. All agree that standardization implies that the same (or equivalent) items are presented to each test taker and that there are specific rules for administering and scoring the test. Other authors would add the requirement that performance norms be available. The definition of standardization adopted in this book will include only the requirements of common item content and standard administration and scoring procedures. In other words, standardization will refer to the procedures for obtaining scores, not the provision of data necessary to interpret scores.[4]

Content   The first essential element is a common set of items that are administered to all test takers. Unless all persons are tested using the same (or equivalent) items, their performance cannot be directly compared, since the results will be based on different item samples. Because much of the previous discussion has focused on how this standard set of items is developed, no further comments seem necessary at this point.

Administration   Even if the same items were administered to all test takers, scores would not be comparable unless they were administered under the same conditions. Total comparability is, of course, impossible, inasmuch as a test will be administered to different persons, at various times and places, and by different examiners. However, much extraneous variability can be eliminated by using prescribed directions for administering the test, standard time limits, and objective scoring methods.

[4]Although any test meeting these criteria could properly be called a "standardized test," the latter term usually refers to commercially published tests that are standardized and also provide normative data.

Two sets of directions are usually required: one for the test taker and one for the test administrator. The former should explain, as clearly and simply as possible, how the test taker should respond to the items. These directions are printed at the beginning of the test,[5] preferably on a separate page, and may range from the simple one-sentence directions on a classroom exam to more complicated statements on standardized exams (see Figure 2.3). Directions to the test taker should indicate how to select a response, how to mark the response (for example, in the test booklet or on a separate answer sheet), and the time limits. On many tests the directions will also include a statement about how to respond when uncertain (guessing). Usually, it is also desirable to include several sample items. Inclusion of sample items is essential if the item format may be unfamiliar to the test takers.

Figure 2.3   Examples of test directions.

A. *Directions for a classroom exam (multiple-choice items)*
   For each item, select the correct alternative and mark its letter in the appropriate place on the answer sheet.

B. *Directions for an aptitude test**

I. VOCABULARY

Each test word, in capital letters, is followed by five possible answers. The correct answer is the word which *means most nearly the same* as the test word. Make a *heavy* line with your pencil between the pair of dotted lines at the right which are lettered the same as the correct answer. EXAMPLE:

FREQUENT: A) always   B) often
         C) never   D) very   E) soon

A B C D E

"Often" means most nearly the same as "frequent," so a heavy line has been made between the dotted lines at the right under B.

Mark an answer for every word. If you don't know the meaning of a word, make the best choice you can.

You will have *three minutes* to work on this test.

DO NOT TURN THE PAGE UNTIL YOU ARE TOLD TO DO SO.

---

*From E. E. Cureton et al., *The Multi-Aptitude Test.* New York: The Psychological Corporation, 1955.

[5]If a test has several sections (subtests) requiring different directions, separate directions should be included at the beginning of each section.

Directions for the test administrator are printed in a separate manual. These directions include those given to the test taker, with a further explanation of their ramifications. These directions will also include details about such things as the arrangement of the testing room, distributing test materials, timing, and scoring. There should also be instructions on how to handle problems and questions arising during the testing session.

One salient aspect of any testing procedure is time limits. In many instances, time limits are partially dictated by practical constraints, such as the length of class periods. Preferably, however, time limits should be determined by psychometric considerations and the purpose of the test.

Most typical performance measures are administered without time limits. However, when measuring abilities or achievement, speed is often a factor of some concern. A continuum for describing tests, based on the role that speed plays in performance, can be established. At one end are pure power tests, tests in which each individual is given unlimited time to respond to items arranged in order of increasing difficulty. Scores, therefore, indicate the number of items answered correctly —or, stated differently, the difficulty level attained. At the other extreme are time limit, or speed, tests. On speed tests the items are so simple that anyone could correctly answer them, given sufficient time. However, time limits are set so that few, if any, persons can finish. Scores thus reflect differences in speed of response, not difficulty.

Most tests fall between these two extremes. A rule of thumb, often used with achievement and ability tests, is to set time limits so that approximately 90 percent of the test takers can finish within the time allowed. If, in addition, items are arranged in order of increasing difficulty, most people will be able to complete all items that they can answer correctly. The administrative advantages of this procedure are obvious.

Scoring   The third element in standardization is objective scoring. Objectivity means agreement between two or more competent (trained) scorers. Ideally, the agreement between different scorers should be perfect; in practice, especially with free response items, agreement will be less than complete. One rule of thumb is to consider scoring objective if the average agreement between pairs of trained scorers is 90 percent or higher. Only if scoring is objective can differences between scores be attributed solely to differences between test takers.

Although a myriad of scoring techniques are available, from hand scoring to high-speed electronic scoring machines, the requirements for objective scoring can be reduced to three basic steps. The first is immediate and unambiguous recording of responses. Whether the test taker makes a mark on an IBM answer sheet, writes a letter, a word, a number, a phrase, or an essay, or answers orally, his response should be recorded immediately and completely. This permanent record avoids possible distortions due to memory loss, and provides the basis for classifying responses.

The second requirement is a list of standard or correct responses, a scoring key. For a multiple-choice exam this key would include the number or letter of the

Figure 2.4   Example of a scoring manual: Wechsler Adult Intelligence Scale.

SCORING CRITERIA AND SAMPLE ANSWERS: VOCABULARY

In general, any recognized meaning of the word is acceptable, disregarding elegance of expression. However, *poverty of content* is penalized to some extent; indication of only a vague knowledge of what the word means does not earn full credit. Responses to words 1-3 are scored 2 or 0, while all the other words are scored 2, 1 or 0. The following are general principles for scoring responses to the Vocabulary items.

2 Points

1. A good synonym.
2. A major use.
3. One or more definitive or primary features.
4. General classification to which word belongs.
5. Several correct descriptive features which are not precisely definitive but which cumulatively indicate understanding of the word.
6. For verbs, definitive example of action or causal relation.

1 Point

1. A response that is not incorrect but which shows poverty of content.
2. A vague or inexact synonym.
3. A minor use, not elaborated.
4. Attributes which are correct but not definitive or not distinguishing features.
5. Example using the word itself, not elaborated.
6. Correct definition of a related form of the word, e.g., "haste" instead of "hasten," "obstruction" instead of "obstruct."

0 Points

1. Obviously wrong answers.
2. Verbalisms, e.g., "Repair a car," when no real understanding is shown after inquiry.
3. Responses which show great poverty of content or are very vague even after questioning.

For the specific items, a general criterion for scoring is shown for every word at the 2-point level, followed by several sample answers. In some instances, a general criterion is given for 1-point and 0-point responses together with examples. For other items there is no appropriate generalization at these levels of credit beyond those provided by the general scoring principles, and only sample answers are given. Of course, these lists contain only a few of the many responses that are possible or that subjects will give. They are intended, however, to supplement dictionary definitions and the general scoring principles in such a way as to facilitate the task of scoring this test accurately.

Figure 2.4   (continued)

SAMPLE ANSWERS; VOCABULARY*

1. Chair

   2 points — a piece of furniture to sit in; to conduct a meeting
   to sit in . . . to sit on . . . sit on when eating
   1 point — furniture made of wood
   0 points — sitting down . . . soft object . . . be at a meeting

2. January

   2 points — first month of the year
   a month . . . first month . . . cold winter month
   1 point — after December . . . starts year . . . New Year's is January 1
   0 points — a Roman God

3. Construct

   2 points — to build or devise something; something built systematically
   to build . . . erect something . . . put together using a plan
   1 point — construct a building . . . make . . . process of building
   0 points — divide . . . tighten, draw together . . . helpful

   *To preserve the security of the test actual WAIS items were not used. The hypothetical items used are similar to the WAIS vocabulary items and the format of the scoring manual identical to the WAIS manual.

correct response to each item; for short-answer items, it would be a list of the correct responses and acceptable variations; for an essay item, it might be an outline of the points to be covered. For a personality inventory, the key will designate the responses that are indicative of the presence (or absence) of the trait or characteristic being measured. If various responses are to receive different weights, these weights should be indicated on the key.

The third requirement is a procedure for comparing the test taker's responses to the key—that is, a procedure for objectively classifying responses. On alternative-choice items, such as multiple-choice items, this procedure is straightforward and obvious. When the scorer's judgment may be a factor, as when grading essay exams, detailed directions for assigning scores need to be developed. An excellent example of scoring specifications is provided in the manual for the Wechsler Adult Intelligence Scale (see Figure 2.4). This scoring manual provides illustrations of acceptable responses and allowable variations. The scorer compares an individual's responses to the examples provided in the scoring manual, then assigns each response the score of the most nearly comparable sample response. Although this procedure does not insure perfect agreement between scorers, it does make scoring objective.

Psychometric Analysis

Application of the procedures discussed above will insure only one thing—that an individual's score will reflect his abilities or personality characteristics, not the peculiarities and vicissitudes of the testing situation. They provide no answer to the larger questions: How consistent are scores on the test? What does the test measure? What inferences can be drawn from scores on the test? How can the test scores be interpreted? These questions can be answered only by further analyses. These will be discussed briefly below. Their importance, however, is indicated by the space devoted to them in later chapters of the book, not by their emphasis here.

Reliability Unless a test measures consistently, little faith can be placed in the accuracy of the test scores. That is, an individual should obtain approximately the same scores on another administration of a test. Without consistency, testing would be analogous to measuring with a rubber ruler. Different results would be obtained on each occasion (measurement), depending on how much the ruler was stretched.

Estimating the degree of consistency of measurement, called the *reliability* of the test, requires either administering the test twice, administering equivalent forms of the test, or analyzing the internal structure of the test. As a practical matter this means that the test constructor must obtain a representative sample of subjects, apply one of the procedures mentioned, and calculate a reliability coefficient. Because different types of reliability data will be appropriate in different situations, the test constructor must collect various types of reliability evidence on diverse samples (see Chapters 5 and 6).

Validity The most important characteristic of a test is its validity—that is, the extent to which the test measures what it is designed to measure. Without evidence of the validity of a test, we do not know what the test actually measures; thus we cannot give meaning to, or interpret, the test scores.

Since the items comprising the test were selected partially on the basis of their discrimination power, we are assured that the test scores will have some validity. But as the whole (the test) may be more than a sum of its parts (the items), it is necessary to collect validity data utilizing the test in its final form. This means using the test in several situations, with a variety of groups, and determining its effectiveness (see Chapters 7 and 8). Because validity is situation-specific, collecting validity data is essentially an endless process. The test constructor's obligation is to provide sufficient data to ascertain what characteristics the test measures and/or what criteria it predicts.

Normative data Test scores by themselves have little, if any, meaning. They attain meaning only when an individual's score is compared with scores of other persons who have taken the test. By comparing an individual's score with those of other persons in a specified population (called the norm group) we obtain an indication of his relative performance compared with that of others in the same population. Thus the test constructor must collect data showing the performance of a relevant group of persons. Because, in most instances, we want to compare the individual's scores to several different groups, the test developer must provide data for various norm groups. And, as scores on psychological tests are generally expressed on scales other than raw score scales, the test constructor also must develop appropriate scales for expressing the test scores (see Chapters 10 and 11).

We have indicated that if the test is to be applied to more than one group, normative data will be needed, for each group, since every group will vary, in some way, from any other group. So, too, additional validity and reliability data must be obtained, inasmuch as a test that is valid (or reliable) in one situation will not necessarily be valid in another, even highly similar, situation. Thus collecting information about a test is a continuing process, which must be pursued as long as the test is used.

3

SOME
BASIC
STATISTICS

In order to understand many of the concepts in educational and psychological testing, it is necessary to know some basic descriptive statistics. Descriptive statistics summarize and describe a set of data in quantitative terms. The use of such indices has several advantages: observations are more objective; results can be reported more precisely and in finer detail; and communication is facilitated. In addition, using summary statistics is more economical than reporting masses of data.

In this chapter we shall explain and illustrate several basic statistical concepts, including raw and transformed scores, frequency distributions, measures of central tendency and variability, standard scores, and correlation. All statistics used in this book will be variations of these concepts.[1]

[1]The reader who desires a more detailed discussion of the statistics described in this chapter can consult any introductory statistics book (e.g., Edwards, 1974; Young & Veldman, 1972). Also, because we are interested in developing an understanding of statistical concepts rather than computational skill, we shall use only examples using ungrouped data.

Raw and Transformed Scores

Scores obtained directly from test performance are called *raw scores* (and will be symbolized by X). On maximal performance tests, the raw score usually is the number of items answered correctly; however, other measures can be used, such as the number of errors, the sum of points on various items, the time taken to complete the test, or a rating. On typical performance tests, such as personality inventories, the raw score is obtained in a slightly different manner. Here items are generally keyed to represent the dominant response of some defined group. A person's raw score will be the number of items answered in the keyed direction. Thus on either maximal or typical performance tests the raw score is derived directly from test performance.

Raw scores as composites   Most tests are composed of a number of independent items. Hence the raw score is usually a composite formed from the various item scores. This is true whether one overall score is obtained or the test is divided into several subtests or scales. The principles involved are the same whenever we obtain a composite score, be it a subtest or total score.

Most frequently, test scores are unweighted composites of the individual item scores. That is, each item is given equal (unit) weight:

$$X_c = I_1 + I_2 + \cdots + I_k \tag{3.1}$$

where X_c is the composite (test) score and I_1 through I_k are the scores on the k items comprising the test. For example, if a 50-item multiple-choice test were administered with each item scored 1 or 0 (for correct or incorrect), each person's total (composite) score would be the number of items he answered correctly.

It is also possible to weight the individual items differentially. For example, when items are worth different number of points, the composite score would be obtained by the formula

$$X_c = b_1 I_1 + b_2 I_2 + \cdots + b_k I_k \tag{3.2}$$

where X_c is the test (composite) score, I_1 through I_k are the scores on the individual items, and b_1 through b_k are the weights (i.e., points) assigned to each item.

Transformed scores   Raw scores are frequently transformed to other scales to facilitate analysis and interpretation. Scores resulting from such transformations are called derived, or transformed, scores. The most common transformations involve adding or subtracting a constant and/or multiplying or dividing by a constant:

$$X' = a + bX \tag{3.3}$$

where X' is the transformed score and a and b are constants.[2] Such a transformation is a *linear transformation* because the original (raw) and transformed scores will be related in a linear manner, and the relationship between comparable pairs of scores will be the same in each scale.

[2] The constant a is an intercept constant, which changes the mean of the scale; b is a slope constant, which changes the standard deviation. (The mean and standard deviation will be explained later in the chapter.)

Discrete and Continuous Scores

Another important distinction is between discrete and continuous measurement. On a discrete scale, scores can fall only at distinct points along the scale. The number of persons in a room and the number of points scored in a football game are both discrete scores. On a continuous scale, scores can fall at any point along the scale, the only limitations being the precision that the measurement techniques allow and/or the precision desired from the measurement. Thus, the dimensions of a room might be described in feet, in feet and inches, or even in fractions of inches. Although test scores are discrete, they usually are treated as if they were continuous, the assumption being that more precise distinctions could be made if necessary.

DESCRIBING SCORE DISTRIBUTIONS

Usually we are concerned with the scores of a group of persons. In the first part of this section we shall describe some simple tabular and graphical methods for summarizing and presenting test data from a group of individuals. However, even these methods are somewhat clumsy; it would be useful to have one number that would summarize the performance of a group. We shall see that we really need two numbers—one to describe the average level of performance and one to indicate how widely scattered the individual scores are around this average value. The latter portions of this section will thus describe the common indices of the central tendency and variability. We shall use one (hypothetical) set of data to illustrate the computation of these statistics.

Frequency Distributions

Suppose that we administered a nine-item quiz to a class of 30 students and their scores were as follows:

4 8 3 0 8 2 4 5 5 6 7 4 3 5 2 3 6 7 1 5 6 7 6 4 5 9 4 5 1 6

This arrangement tells us little except that there were 30 scores and that the range of scores was from 0 to 9 points. However, we could obtain a clearer picture if the scores were presented in a table showing how many people obtained each score. Such a table is called a *frequency distribution*. To illustrate, using the scores in our example:

Raw Score (X)	0	1	2	3	4	5	6	7	8	9	Σ
Frequency (f)	1	2	2	3	5	6	5	3	2	1	30

In the table X = the raw score, f = the frequency of each score, and Σ means "the sum of." Note also that Σf = the total number of scores (n).

This distribution could also be shown graphically by plotting the frequencies for each score. This can be done either as a *frequency polygon* (see Figure 3.1a) or a *histogram* (see Figure 3.1b).

Although distributions of test scores often approximate the normal (symmetrical bell-shaped) curve, a variety of other distributions are occasionally encountered. For example, if a test were very easy, scores would cluster at the high end of the scale and

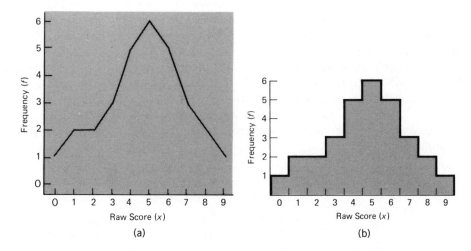

Figure 3.1   Examples of (a) a frequency polygon and (b) a histogram.

tail off toward the low end; conversely, on a difficult test, scores would bunch at the low end. These two distributions are called *negatively* and *positively skewed,* respectively. These, and several other possible distributions, are depicted in Figure 3.2.

Central Tendency

It is usually desirable to have one number that represents the average score of the group, a measure of central tendency. The three commonly used measures of central tendency are the mode, the median, and the mean.

The *mode* is the score that occurs with the highest frequency. In our example the mode is 5, since this score occurs more frequently ($f = 6$) than any other single score.

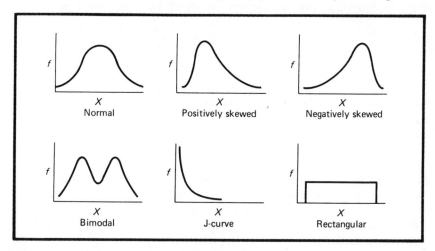

Figure 3.2   Shapes of common statistical distributions.

The mode is used with nominal data and when scores are so highly skewed that one value predominates. For example, the modal age of children entering first grade is 6, as almost all children who enter first grade are six years old.

The *median* is the score that divides the distribution in halves; the score above and below which 50 percent of the scores fall. In our example, the median is 5 because the point that divides the distribution in half—the point between the 15th and 16th scores—is a score of 5. The median is the appropriate measure of central tendency when data are in ranks or when the presence of a few extreme scores is likely to distort an arithmetic average.

The mean   The most useful measure of central tendency is the mean. The mean (symbolized $\bar{X}$) is nothing more than the arithmetic average:

$$\bar{X} = \frac{\Sigma X}{n} \tag{3.4a}$$

To compute the mean, we sum all the scores (ΣX) and divide by the number of scores (n). In our example,

$$\Sigma X = 4 + 8 + 3 + \cdots + 1 + 6 = 141$$

and

$$\bar{X} = \frac{\Sigma X}{n} = \frac{141}{30} = 4.7$$

The mean could also have been computed from the frequency distribution using the formula:

$$\bar{X} = \frac{\Sigma f_i X_i}{n} \tag{3.4b}$$

where f_i = the number of scores in a particular class (X_i). That is, multiply each score by its frequency, sum the products, and divide by n. In our example,

$$\Sigma f_i X_i = (1)(0) + (2)(1) + (2)(2) + \cdots + (1)(9) = 141$$

and

$$\bar{X} = \frac{141}{30} = 4.7$$

which is the same value that was obtained using Equation (3.4a).

Variability

Two score distributions may have the same mean, but in one distribution the scores may be closely bunched around the mean while in the other the scores vary widely (see Figure 3.3a), or two distributions may have the same variability but different means (see Figure 3.3b). Thus, to describe a distribution a measure of variability is also needed.

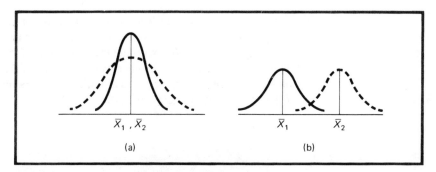

Figure 3.3   Examples showing need for measure of dispersion as well as of central tendency: (a) same mean, different dispersion; (b) same dispersion, different means.

The standard deviation   Measures of variability indicate the dispersion of scores around a given point; usually the mean. The most commonly used index is the standard deviation. The standard deviation (s) is the square root of the average squared deviation of the scores from the mean:

$$s = \sqrt{\frac{\Sigma x^2}{n}} \qquad\qquad (3.5a)$$

where x is a deviation score ($x = X - \bar{X}$).

To avoid transforming raw scores (X) to deviation scores (x), an equivalent raw score formula is usually used in any computations:

$$s = \frac{1}{n}\sqrt{n\Sigma X^2 - (\Sigma X)^2} \qquad\qquad (3.5b)$$

In our example, $\Sigma X = 141$, $n = 30$, and

$$\Sigma X^2 = (4)^2 + (8)^2 + (3)^2 + \cdots + (6)^2 = 803$$

Substituting in Equation (3.5b), we obtain

$$s = \frac{1}{30}\sqrt{(30)(803) - (141)^2} = 2.2$$

The standard deviation gives an index of how widely the scores are dispersed about the mean; the larger the standard deviation, the more widely scattered the scores.

Interpreting a standard deviation   Why the particular formula given by Equation (3.5a) is used is unimportant for our purpose. Instead, a working knowledge of the meaning of s can be attained by reference to the normal curve. In a normal distribution, there is a specifiable relation between the proportion of cases falling within certain score limits and the standard deviation.[3]

Some major benchmarks are presented in Figure 3.4; a more complete set of

---

[3]The normal distribution is a mathematical concept, not an empirical one. We shall use it only as a working model, not as an exact representation.

relationships can be found in Appendix A. Figure 3.4 shows that, in a normal distribution, 68 percent of the scores will fall within plus or minus one s of the mean. Similarly, the range $\pm 2s$ (more precisely, $\pm 1.96s$) will include 95 percent of the scores, and $\pm 3s$ will include almost all the scores. Another way of looking at the relationship is that, for example, 84 percent of the scores will fall below the point $\overline{X} + 1s$ and 97.5 percent of the scores will fall below the point $\overline{X} + 2s$.

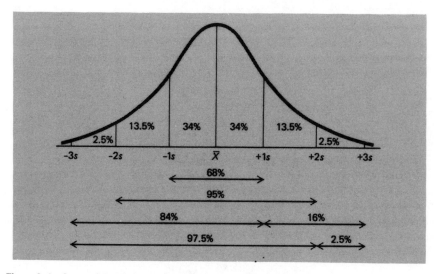

Figure 3.4   Some of the main relationships in a normal distribution.

Applying these relationships to our example, the following relations would be expected to hold:

68 percent of the scores will fall between 2.5 and 6.9; that is,

$$\overline{X} \pm 1s = 4.7 \pm 2.2$$

and

95 percent of the scores will fall between 0.3 and 9.1; that is,

$$\overline{X} \pm 2s = 4.7 \pm 2(2.2)$$

Comparing the obtained frequencies to the expected frequencies will indicate whether the empirical distribution approaches a normal distribution.

The variance   The square of the standard deviation (s^2) is the *variance:*

$$s^2 = \frac{\Sigma x^2}{n} = \frac{1}{n}\left(\Sigma X^2 - \frac{(\Sigma X)^2}{n}\right) \tag{3.6}$$

All terms have been defined previously. The variance is a measure of the total amount of variability in a set of test scores. The variance has the important property of additivity, which the standard deviation does not. Because variances are additive, the proportion of variability in a set of test scores that is attributable to each of several variables (or their interactions) can be determined. Thus statements about the relative influence of each variable can be made. In other words, the total amount of variability in a set of test scores (s^2) can be broken down and distributed among several effects. This property makes the variance a useful statistic for conceptualizing certain properties of tests (such as reliability and validity) and for determining the effects of varying conditions on test performance. Thus, in many statistical analyses we shall use the variance. However, when describing the variability of a set of scores we shall use the standard deviation.[4]

Standard Scores

Raw scores are frequently transformed to other scales to facilitate analysis and interpretation. Such scores are transformed, or derived scores. One type of derived score, the standard score, is particularly useful. A *standard score* (z) expresses a person's performance in terms of his deviation from the mean in standard deviation units:

$$z = \frac{x}{s} = \frac{X - \bar{X}}{s} \qquad (3.7)$$

As can be seen, the distribution of standard scores has a mean of 0 and a standard deviation of 1.

Standard scores have several advantages. First, they measure on an interval scale. By expressing performance in terms of standard deviation units, we have transformed raw scores to a scale with equal-sized units. Second, use of standard scores allows us to compare scores from several tests directly, even those having different means and/or standard deviations. Why this is so can be seen by examining Equation (3.7). In the numerator, by subtracting the mean from each score, we have, in essence, corrected for any differences between means. Then, dividing by the standard deviation we have corrected for any differences in standard deviations.

A third advantage of standard scores lies in their relationship to the normal distribution. Previously we described how a standard deviation could be interpreted in relation to the hypothetical normal distribution. Comparing that discussion to Equation (3.7), you can see that it makes no difference whether we express scores in terms of standard scores or standard deviations from the mean; that is, a z score of $+1.0$ is one standard deviation above the mean, a z score of -2.0 is two standard deviations below the mean, and so on. Thus the relations shown in Figure 3.4 hold for standard (z) scores, as well as for standard deviations.

Appendix A, "Areas of the normal curve," shows the relationships between the cumulative normal distribution and z scores in units of .05 standard score points. You should become familiar with this table and learn how to use it. To give but one

---

[4]Note that the standard deviation is expressed in the same units as raw scores, whereas the variance is not.

example, if a student's z score were 1.40, we would know that his score was 1.4 standard deviations above the mean and that 91.2 percent of the scores in the distribution were lower than his score (see column C) and 8.8 percent were higher (column D). Note that these relations hold regardless of the mean and standard deviation of the original distribution; however, how accurate they are will depend on how closely the original distribution approaches normality.

CORRELATION

The other important concept is correlation. A *correlation coefficient* is a measure of the relationship (literally the co-relation) between two sets of data. In testing, the correlation will generally be between two sets of scores collected on the same persons—for example, between scores obtained on two administrations of the same test, or between scores on a college entrance exam and grades in college.

The Correlation Coefficient

There are several different measures of correlation. The one most frequently used in psychological testing is the *Pearson product-moment correlation coefficient* (r). This coefficient is a measure of linear relationship; other correlation measures are based on nonlinear models (see Figure 3.5). So if we use r as a measure of correlation, and the relationship is not linear, the correlation coefficient (r) will underestimate the degree of relationship present.

The logic of the correlation coefficient can best be seen if scores are expressed as standard scores. If the two variables correlated are designated X and Y, and their corresponding standard scores as z_X and z_Y, then the correlation between X and Y will be:

$$r = \frac{\Sigma z_X z_Y}{n} \tag{3.8a}$$

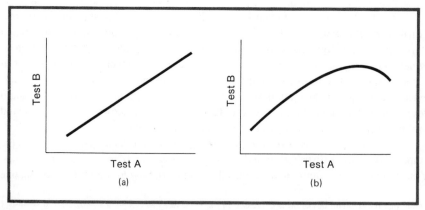

Figure 3.5 Linear and curvilinear relationships: (a) linear; (b) curvilinear.

where n = the number of *pairs* of scores (each pair being derived from a different individual). From Equation (3.8a) you can see that if corresponding standard scores (z_X, z_Y) are both large and have the same sign, the value of r will be large and positive; if both are large but have opposite signs, r will be large but negative; if both are small or some pairs have positive signs and others negative signs, the value of r will approach zero.

There are a number of alternative formulas for r. Two raw score formulas that have certain computational advantages are:

$$r = \frac{n\Sigma XY - (\Sigma X)(\Sigma Y)}{\sqrt{n\Sigma X^2 - (\Sigma X)^2}\ \sqrt{n\Sigma Y^2 - (\Sigma Y)^2}} \qquad (3.8b)$$

and

$$r = \frac{\Sigma XY/n - (\bar{X})(\bar{Y})}{s_X s_Y} \qquad (3.8c)$$

The cross-products term (ΣXY) is obtained by multiplying the two scores for each individual, then summing across all individuals. In this book, X will usually represent the independent variable (predictor) and Y the dependent variable (criterion).

Interpretation of r   The value of r can range from $+1.00$ to -1.00. The absolute value of the coefficient tells the strength of the relationship; the greater the absolute value, the greater the correspondence between the two sets of scores. Thus when $r_{XY} = 1.00$, scores on Y are completely predictable knowing scores on X. If $r_{XY} = 0.00$, the relationship between pairs of scores is random and no better than chance. The sign of the coefficient tells the direction of the relationship; thus coefficients of $+.68$ and $-.68$ represent equal degrees of predictability.

The relationship summarized by the correlation coefficient can also be shown by *scatterplots* of the test scores. If there is a high correlation, the scores will cluster around a straight line (in an elliptical pattern if scores on both variables are distributed normally). The orientation of the plot in relation to the axes indicates whether the coefficient is positive or negative (see Figure 3.6).

There are a number of ways to interpret r. We have already mentioned two: as representing the strength of the relationship between two variables and in terms of the accuracy of predicting one variable from another. Perhaps the most broadly applicable method is to interpret the squared correlation coefficient (r^2) as the proportion of variability in one set of scores that is shared in common with, or can be attributable to, the other variable. Thus if $r = .50$, r^2 will equal $.25$ ($.50^2$), and we can say that 25 percent of the variability in one measure is associated with (or attributable to) variation in the other measure.

It cannot be overemphasized that r indicates only the degree of relationship between two variables; it does *not* indicate causation. If variables X and Y are highly correlated, there are at least three possible explanations: (1) X causes Y, and thus changes in X result in changes in Y; (2) Y causes X, and thus the changes in X reflect changes in Y; or (3) X and Y are both influenced by some other variable. In other words, a correlation coefficient is never a sufficient basis for inferring causation.

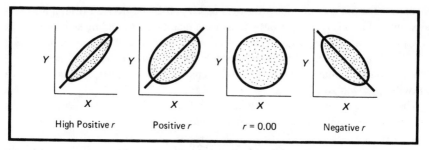

Figure 3.6   Scatterplots of test scores, indicating degree of correlation.

An Example

Suppose that two arithmetic tests (X and Y) were administered to 10 students[5] and their scores were as follows:

Individual	A B C D E F G H I J		
Test X	9 6 5 2 5 7 1 5 8 6	$\Sigma X = 54$	$\Sigma X^2 = 346$
Test Y	8 7 5 4 6 5 3 4 8 7	$\Sigma Y = 57$	$\Sigma Y^2 = 353$

The scatterplot of the scores is shown in Figure 3.7. Since the scores fall close to a straight line and high scores on one test are associated with high scores on the other, the value of r should be high and positive.

To calculate r, we first find the means and standard deviations of the two tests. Test X:

$$\bar{X} = \frac{\Sigma X}{n} = \frac{54}{10} = 5.40$$

$$s_X = \frac{1}{n}\sqrt{n\Sigma X^2 - (\Sigma X)^2} = \frac{1}{10}\sqrt{10(346) - (54)^2} = 2.33$$

Test Y:

$$\bar{Y} = \frac{\Sigma Y}{n} = \frac{57}{10} = 5.70$$

$$s_Y = \frac{1}{n}\sqrt{n\Sigma Y^2 - (\Sigma Y)^2} = \frac{1}{10}\sqrt{10(353) - (57)^2} = 1.68$$

Next we find the sum of cross-products (ΣXY). This is obtained by multiplying each individual's two scores, then summing over all individuals:

$$\Sigma XY = (9)(8) + (6)(7) + \cdots + (6)(7) = 341$$

[5]Normally we would not compute a correlation with so few cases. We are doing so here only to simplify our presentation.

Substituting into Equation (3.8c), we obtain

$$r = \frac{\Sigma XY/n - (\overline{X})(\overline{Y})}{s_X s_Y} = \frac{341/10 - (5.40)(5.70)}{(2.33)(1.68)} = 0.85$$

This value for r indicates that approximately 72 percent of the variance in scores $(.85^2)$ is common to the two tests; the other 28 percent represents variance unique to each test.

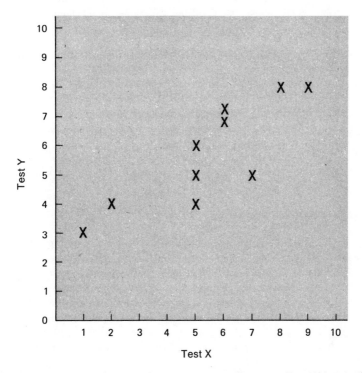

Figure 3.7   Scatterplot showing relationship between scores on tests X and Y (see text).

A Final Note

If you understand the statistics described in this chapter you should have no trouble with the statistics used in the remainder of the book. All further statistics will be either applications to specific cases or variations of these basic concepts. Hopefully, your instructor will provide several examples or practice problems. If not, you should work through several examples to check your understanding of these methods.

SUGGESTED FURTHER READING FOR PART I

Anastasi, A. On the formation of psychological traits. *American Psychologist,* 1970, *25*, 899–910.

A review of the major approaches to studying the nature and development of traits.

Brim, O. G., Jr., Glass, D. C., Neulinger, J., & Firestone, I. J. *American beliefs and attitudes about intelligence.* New York: Russell Sage Foundation, 1969.

Report of a large-scale study of students' experience with attitudes and toward ability tests.

DuBois, P. H. *A history of psychological testing.* Boston: Allyn & Bacon, 1970.

A brief history of educational and psychological testing, from antiquity to the present.

Educational Testing Service, *ETS builds a test.* Princeton, N.J.: Educational Testing Service, 1965.

A pamphlet presenting an overview of the process a test publisher goes through when constructing a standardized test.

Glaser, R. Instructional technology and the measurement of learning outcomes. *American Psychologist,* 1963, *18*, 519–521.

Distinguishes between measurement that compares individuals to each other (norm-referenced measurement) and measurement that compares an individual to a standard (criterion-referenced measurement).

Goslin, D. A. *Teachers and testing.* New York: Russell Sage Foundation, 1967.

Survey of teachers' attitudes toward and use of standardized tests; companion to the Brim et al. book (see above).

Guilford, J. P. *Psychometric methods.* (2d ed.) New York: McGraw-Hill, 1954.

Chapter 1 presents the theory of psychological measurement, emphasizing the postulates underlying the various measurement scales.

Jones, L. V. The nature of measurement. Chapter 12 in R. L. Thorndike (Ed.), *Educational measurement.* (2d ed.) Washington, D.C.: American Council on Education, 1971.

A readable description of the nature of psychological measurement.

Kelly, E. L. *Assessment of human characteristics.* Belmont, Calif.: Brooks/Cole, 1967.

Chapters 1 to 3 present a very readable overview of the assessment process, especially personality assessment; stresses what is assessed and how; good description of the trait approach.

Kerlinger, F. N. *Foundations of behavioral research.* (2d ed.) New York: Holt, Rinehart and Winston, 1973.

Chapter 25 is a brief, clear description of the measurement process. Chapter 3 describes the role of constructs, variables, and definitions in psychological theory.

Wallace, J., & Sechrest, L. *The nature and study of psychology.* Itasca, Ill.: F. E. Peacock, 1973.

Chapter 3 is another good, brief overview of the role of measurement in psychology.

PART II

CONSISTENCY AND VALIDITY

Having briefly surveyed the process of test construction, we now turn to a discussion of the procedures for evaluating the quality of the instrument we have developed. Here there are two basic questions: First, how consistently does the test measure? That is, would an individual receive the same score if he took the test at another time or on a different form of the test? This is the question of reliability or *consistency*. The second question is two-pronged: What does the test measure? And how accurately does it measure it? This is the *validity* question. Both consistency and validity are properties of the test, not individual scores. However, unless we know what characteristic a test measures, and unless the test measures this characteristic consistently, we cannot interpret individual scores accurately.

The framework that will be used to introduce the concepts of consistency and validity is based on measurement errors (Chapter 4). Two types of errors are of prime concern—random errors and systematic (constant) errors. Random errors are introduced whenever some variable produces inconsistency in test performance from situation to situation (for example, from one test administration to another). Identification and control of these random errors is, therefore, basic to the concept of reliability of measurement. Constant errors are ones that produce systematic effects on performance but are irrelevant to the purposes of testing (for example, the effects of speed of responding). Constant errors are crucial in the determination of validity.

Within this framework, reliability (Chapter 5) can be defined as the proportion of variability in a set of test scores that represents ''true'' differences between people; that is, the proportion not attributable to measurement errors. Three sources of measurement error will be discussed in detail: errors inherent in the test, primarily those due to item sampling; errors associated with the conditions of the test administration; and errors resulting from fluctuations in characteristics of the individual. As each error source will have its greatest influence under different circumstances, several types of reliability estimates are possible: consistency over time (the coefficient of stability); consistency over test forms (the coefficient of equivalence); and consistency over both time and test forms (the coefficient of stability and equivalence). We shall show that in each case an appropriate index of reliability, the reliability coefficient, is the correlation between scores on two administrations of the test. We shall also discuss procedures for determining reliability when only one form of a test is administered, a method for determining the amount of error in an individual's test score, and the factors that influence reliability coefficients.

Chapter 6 focuses on the internal consistency, or homogeneity, of tests. Here we shall be concerned with the question of whether all items on a test measure the same trait or characteristic. This topic is treated separately from the other measures of reliability to emphasize that a different question is asked (Are the items homogeneous?) and thus different information is obtained. In discussing homogeneity we shall utilize the domain sampling theory. This approach hypothesizes that for any trait there is a hypothetical population (domain) of items that measures the trait. Any test is conceived as being composed of a random sample of items from this domain. We shall then develop several indices of homogeneity.

The discussion will conclude with a consideration of several alternative approaches to consistency.

Consistency, though necessary, is not a sufficient basis for interpreting scores; we need to know what trait the test measures and/or what outcomes it predicts. This is the validity question, the central question in any measurement procedure. As with consistency, there are various methods for estimating validity, each of which addresses a somewhat different question. We shall discuss three general classes of validity estimates. In criterion-related validity (Chapter 7) the main question is the degree of relationship between test scores and a measure of some important extratest behavior, the criterion. We shall present several methods for determining this relation using the selection situation as an example: validity coefficients (the correlation between test and criterion scores) and indices of decision-making accuracy (how many correct decisions will be made using the test).

Chapter 8 focuses on two other types of validity: content validity and construct validity. Content validity is concerned with how representatively the test items sample the universe (domain) of behaviors we are interested in measuring. For example, how well do the items on a classroom examination sample the material and skills taught in the course?

Construct validity focuses on the trait being measured by the test. Here the major question is: What psychological trait (construct) is being measured by the test? We shall see that the evaluation of construct validity proceeds by an accumulation of evidence. This explanation of construct validity will be clearer if the reader keeps in mind that the procedures utilized to determine construct validity are basically those used in the general scientific method and that the goal is to clarify the meaning of the construct measured by the test.

Chapter 9 is concerned with combining scores into composite scores. Some of the techniques we shall discuss combine data from various tests in order to arrive at a more valid prediction; others combine scores in order to summarize a set of data. In other words, some combinations are developed for predictive purposes and others for descriptive purposes. Another important distinction is between compensatory and noncompensatory methods. Compensatory methods allow high levels of one skill to make up, or compensate, for deficiencies in other important areas; noncompensatory models require an individual to attain a given level of performance on each measure. A third distinction has to do with the statistical characteristics of the data and the method of forming a composite. Here we shall be concerned with such factors as whether the data are qualitative or quantitative and whether the various tests are equally or differentially weighted. Six methods of combining scores will be discussed in detail: clinical judgment, rational methods, multiple cutoff, multiple regression, discriminant analysis, and factor analysis. In addition, several other methods will be mentioned briefly.

The unifying concept underlying our discussion of composites scores is incremental validity. That is, the validity of a component element in a composite should be evaluated by its contribution to the composite, rather than its validity when used as the sole predictor. In other words, a test is useful to the extent that it provides additional information to what is otherwise available.

When reading this part of the book you should constantly keep in mind several general points. First, consistency and validity are both generic terms; thus they can be evaluated by several different methods. The choice of method will depend on the particular question you want to answer or what sources of error must be controlled. Second, reliability and validity are characteristics of the test; they tell us about the quality and effectiveness of a test for a group of people. Therefore, we cannot say, for example, that a test is an accurate predictor for a given individual, we can only say that a test predicts accurately for a designated group of people. Finally, consistency and validity data are always obtained from a particular group of people taking the test under a particular set of circumstances, with the results being evaluated by a one of several possible methods. In other words, consistency and validity are always situation-specific. There is no such thing as *the* reliability or *the* validity of a test.

4

CONSISTENCY, VALIDITY, AND MEASUREMENT ERROR

Having defined what is meant by a test and described how tests are constructed, we now turn to the question of what is a "good" test. From the psychometric viewpoint, a test must possess two characteristics if it is to be considered a good measuring instrument: the test must be reliable and it must be valid. By reliable we mean how consistently the test measures whatever it measures; that is, a test is considered reliable if it measures consistently. By valid we mean how accurately the test measures whatever it is designed to measure. A test is valid to the extent it measures a particular construct and does not measure extraneous variables.

One way of looking at the concepts of reliability and validity is to consider the variables that influence test scores. Any variable that produces inaccurate scores can be viewed as introducing *error*. Although several classes of errors can be identified (Helmstadter, 1964), two are of particular importance: unsystematic (random) errors and systematic (constant) errors. By *random errors* we mean inconsistencies in test scores from occasion to occasion. For example, giving a test with two different time limits might produce different scores for the same individual. Reliability is concerned with determining the degree of inconsistency in scores attributable to random (unsystematic) error sources.

Systematic errors are ones that produce effects irrelevant to the purpose of the testing, albeit consistent effects. To illustrate, on any test where the individual must read the test items, reading speed and comprehension may affect his performance. The influence of this variable is systematic in the sense that a good reader will always have an advantage. However, reading ability represents error if it is irrelevant to what we are trying to measure. Thus, if we were trying to measure a person's knowledge of history, and the test items were complexly worded, the test would measure both knowledge of history and reading ability. In this example, reading ability would introduce irrelevant variability. Validity is concerned with determining how much of the test performance is due to relevant variability (that is, the variable we are trying to measure) and how much represents irrelevant variability (that is, the effects of irrelevant variables).

We can approach the discussion of reliability and validity on either a statistical or practical level; that is, with the statistical theory underlying these concepts or the practical problem of making tests more reliable and valid. In our presentation we shall emphasize the latter approach. However, we shall also introduce you to the rudiments of the statistical theory of test scores.

CONSISTENCY

The problem of consistency of measurement has been likened to the money problem: it is only the lack of it that causes any trouble (Kerlinger, 1973). If we can be assured that a test measures consistently, we have no cause for concern. But since human behavior, including test-taking behavior, tends to fluctuate from time to time and situation to situation, we have to be concerned with consistency in test scores. Furthermore, any test contains only a sample of all possible items and is administered at a particular time. Thus, the sampling of items, the circumstances of the test administration, and the characteristics of the test taker may introduce error into the measurement.

The need for consistency of measurement may be so obvious that you have not thought about it, at least in the terms that we are concerned with in psychological testing. Most of the measurements we make are of physical characteristics (such as length, weight, speed, volume), which can be measured with high precision (little variation) from occasion to occasion. However, such precision does not occur in psychological measurement because test scores are more readily influenced by extraneous conditions. For example, you probably have had the experience of getting a higher than expected mark on an exam because it just happened to stress the areas you had studied most thoroughly. Or you may have obtained a lower than expected mark because there was a heavy emphasis on material that you had skimmed over. Or, another time, you may have felt that your performance was adversely affected because you were not feeling well on the day of the test. Or you may, in your haste, have mismarked an answer sheet, thus obtaining a lower score. In each of these cases you may have felt that the test was not a measure of your true ability. In these circumstances, you implied that if the test content were changed, or the test was administered under different circumstances, your score would have been a more accurate reflection of your ability. It is such concerns that have caused psychologists to study the consistency of their measurements.

The generic term given to the problem of consistency of measurement is *reliability*. When studying reliability we are basically interested in two sets of questions. The first set involves the degree of consistency of test scores: What is the relationship between scores obtained under varying testing conditions? How many points would a person's score change upon retesting? How close is an individual's obtained score to his "true score"? Does the test measure consistently enough that it can be applied in practical situations? The second set of questions revolves around the causes of discrepancies between test scores: What factors produce inconsistent scores? What is the relative magnitude of their effects? How do they operate? Traditionally, the study of reliability has placed more emphasis on the first set of questions, concentrating on the development of methods for making more precise estimates of the degree of consistency of measurement.

The Basic Equation

The fundamental concepts of reliability theory can best be presented by introducing the idea of a "true score." A *true score* can be defined as the score that a person would obtain if the measuring instrument (test) measured without error. Since this definition is rather circular, many people prefer an alternative definition: The true score is the score an individual would obtain if he took all the items in the domain. This second definition is often stated another way: A true score is the person's average score on a large number (theoretically, infinite) of equivalent forms of a test.

Each of these definitions states, in essence, that the score a person obtains on a test is a function of both his true score and the error involved in the measurement. Expressed as an equation:

$$X = T + E \tag{4.1}$$

where X is the obtained, or observed, score; T, the hypothetical true score; and E, the measurement error.

The measurement error term (E) represents the contribution of any variables that produce inconsistencies in measurement. This error component can be either positive or negative. If it is positive, the person's true score will be overestimated by his obtained score; if negative, his true score will be underestimated. Two assumptions are made about error. First, if averaged over many administrations of the test, or over a group of people, the average error will be zero. Second, true scores and measurement error are independent (uncorrelated). These assumptions are merely saying that error effects are random.

Equation (4.1) shows the relation between observed scores, true scores, and measurement error for a particular individual. But because reliability is a property of a test, not of an individual's score, we need an analogous equation for a group of persons. We can write this equation

$$s_X{}^2 = s_T{}^2 + s_E{}^2 \qquad (4.2)$$

or the variance of observed scores $(s_X{}^2)$ equals the variance of the true scores $(s_T{}^2)$ plus error variance $(s_E{}^2)$.

Reliability Defined

Equation (4.2) shows the relationship between obtained scores, true scores, and error, but does not define reliability. *Reliability can be defined as the ratio of true variance in a set of test scores to the total, or obtained, variance:*

$$r_{XX} = \frac{s_T{}^2}{s_X{}^2} \qquad (4.3)$$

where r_{XX} is the reliability of the test, $s_T{}^2$ the variance of true scores, and $s_X{}^2$ the variance of the obtained scores.

Note that Equations (4.2) and (4.3), in contrast to Equation (4.1), involve a set of test scores, not the score of one individual. This means that reliability refers to consistency within a set of measurements. From our knowledge of the degree of inconsistency (the reliability) of a set of test scores, we can infer the extent to which an individual's score will vary. However, reliability is a property of the set of test scores, not of an individual's score.

The reader who understands the equations and definitions is probably now saying, "Fine; but since you can never know a person's true score, or precisely define error, what have you?" And he has put his finger on an important point: One can never determine reliability precisely; one can only estimate it from a set of obtained data. Certain of the concepts in the equations—true score, true variance—cannot be directly measured; they can only be estimated. Thus, reliability is a construct, a hypothesized property of test scores.

To show how we make these estimates, consider Equation (4.2):

$$s_X{}^2 = s_T{}^2 + s_E{}^2$$

which states that the variance of the obtained scores $(s_X{}^2)$ equals the variance of the true scores $(s_T{}^2)$ plus error variance $(s_E{}^2)$. If we divide both sides of the equation by $s_X{}^2$, we have

$$\frac{s_X{}^2}{s_X{}^2} = \frac{s_T{}^2}{s_X{}^2} + \frac{s_E{}^2}{s_X{}^2} = 1.00$$

Since reliability was defined, in Equation (4.3), as

$$r_{XX} = \frac{s_T{}^2}{s_X{}^2}$$

we can make the appropriate substitutions and, alternatively, define reliabilty as

$$r_{XX} = 1 - \frac{s_E^2}{s_X^2} \tag{4.4a}$$

or

$$r_{XX} = \frac{s_X^2 - s_E^2}{s_X^2} \tag{4.4b}$$

Inasmuch as both s_X^2 and s_E^2 can be derived from a set of test scores, Equation (4.4) provides the basis for estimating the reliability of a test.

The relationships between true variance, observed variance, error variance, and reliability are shown in Figure 4.1.

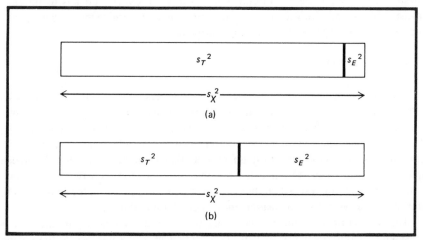

Figure 4.1   Reliability as the proportion of true variance: (a) a highly reliable test (small s_E^2); (b) an unreliable test (large s_E^2).

Types of Reliability

We can calculate several types of reliability estimates, depending upon which error sources are of greatest concern. Often we are interested in the stability of performance over time—that is, consistency between scores on a test and on a retest administered at a later date. In these cases we are calculating a coefficient of stability. At other times we are interested in the correspondence between scores on two, presumably equivalent, forms of a test. In this case, our estimate will be a coefficient of equivalence. We can also combine these two procedures and determine the consistency of scores between two forms of a test separated by a time interval. This gives us a coefficient of equivalence and stability.

Another group of reliability estimates focuses on the consistency of performance over items comprising the test—that is, the internal consistency of the test. Here we are, in essence, trying to determine whether all items on the test measure the same trait or characteristic. For several reasons, we shall consider these estimates separately from those described in the previous paragraph, and refer to them as indices of homogeneity.

Before discussing the various types of consistency in detail (in Chapters 5 and 6) we shall consider the various potential sources of error in test scores.

SOURCES OF ERROR

The goal in psychological testing is to have the observed scores reflect the true scores with as little error as possible. In order for obtained scores to approximate true scores, variables that influence observed scores but not true scores must be controlled or their influence minimized. In other words, our goal is to minimize measurement error. Conversely, we are attempting to maximize true variance in test scores—in essence, trying to maximize reliability.

Error Defined

Error can be a rather elusive concept to define. As indicated above, error is any effect that is irrelevant to the purposes and/or results in inconsistencies in measurement. Thus, if there are differences between John's scores on two equivalent forms of a mechanical aptitude test administered two months apart, and mechanical aptitude is assumed to be consistent over time, then some factor has introduced error into the measurement. Or, if Ellen obtains different scores on two (presumably) comparable spelling tests, then the particular sample of items on the two forms has introduced error into the measurement of her spelling ability.

This definition of error is two-pronged. It indicates that a variable can be considered as introducing error if it (1) is irrelevant to the purpose of the testing, and/or (2) produces inconsistencies in scores from one situation to another. In studying reliability we are concerned with variable errors, factors that produce discrepancies between scores on repeated administrations of the test. The other part of the definition, the relevancy aspect, is primarily concerned with systematic error and will be discussed as an aspect of validity. Suffice it to say, if an irrelevant variable produces a constant or systematic change in test scores, its effect will not be detected in a reliability analysis because it produces no inconsistencies in scores.

Although the particular error factors present in a given situation will vary with the group being tested, the type of test, and the testing conditions, certain common sources of error have been identified (Thorndike, 1951). Some errors result from the test itself, primarily variations resulting from the particular sampling of items included on a specific form of the test. A second class of error variables relates to the conditions of the particular test administration, such as the physical situation, directions, distracting factors, and errors in timing. A third class of error variables involves changes within the test taker. These may be long-term effects resulting from education, maturation, and changes in environment, or they may be relatively short-term fluctuations in mood, health, or attention.

Errors within the Test

The entire test construction process is designed to minimize errors attributable to the test per se. However, any aspect of a test that causes a test taker to respond to an item on bases other than knowledge of the ''correct'' or appropriate response may introduce error. Thus, ambiguity in the wording of an item, or in specifying the procedures for responding, may produce unstable responses. Difficult items that require the test taker to guess may introduce errors. Restrictive time limits, which encourage hasty reading and responding, frequently produce unstable performance. And the length of a test also influences reliability, with longer tests generally being more reliable.

The major source of inconsistency within the test, however, has to do with the sampling of items that comprise the test. This effect is clearest when we have several equivalent forms of the test. In order to be truly equivalent, test forms must be matched, item by item, on content and difficulty, and the distributions of test scores must be similar. These requirements are straightforward, but in practice such equivalence is difficult to attain, coming only as a result of exceedingly careful item construction and analysis. If several forms of the test do not yield equivalent scores, error has been introduced into the measurement, since the test taker would obtain different scores depending upon the particular sample of items (that is, form of the test) administered.

Errors due to item sampling can also occur within a single form of a test. Such errors are of particular importance when the test is designed to measure a single trait or characteristic. If the test is to measure a single trait, every item on the test should measure that trait, and nothing else. However, for various reasons, most items are not pure measures of a single trait. Even if they were, different test takers might not react similarly to any given item (for example, any particular math problem will be easy for some persons, difficult for others). Thus, the choice of the particular items included on a test becomes a potential source of error.

The Test Administration

As psychological tests have become more common, and administrative procedures more standardized, errors attributable to test administration conditions have probably decreased. However, because misunderstanding of directions, mismarking of answer sheets, mistakes in timing, and unforeseen interruptions and other distractions do occur, it is essential that the test administrator be alert to conditions that might result in inaccurate scores. These errors are most likely to occur in tests with complex procedures or directions, when very large groups are tested, in situations in which the test administrator has considerable leeway in setting the testing conditions (such as individually administered tests), and when tests are administered to young children or other persons who are unfamiliar with testing procedures.

Some examples of disruptions of administrative procedures that the author has experienced include having his watch stop during a timed section of the test; having the air conditioning fail and thus produce almost intolerable ventilation; having a custodian use the testing room as a passageway when emptying trash cans; having the microphone used for giving directions go "dead"; finding test booklets and answer sheets misprinted; having to deal with persons caught cheating; and having a student suffer an epileptic seizure. In each instance the test administrator must handle the immediate situation so as to produce minimal inconvenience and distraction to the other persons, estimate whether the disturbance was serious enough to result in inaccurate scores, and, when necessary, make plans for retesting.

Of the three sources of error, those concerned with the test administration are probably easiest to control or minimize. This is because experience with testing has resulted in the development of detailed instructions for administering (and scoring) tests. These instructions minimize error by outlining specific procedures for the test administrator to follow, thereby reducing irrelevant variability. Thus, unless there is some compelling reason for altering procedures, the test administrator should always follow the instructions exactly as printed in the manual.

Error may also be introduced in the scoring of the test. As mentioned in Chapter 2, scoring errors can be minimized by objective scoring methods, such as the utilization of electronic scoring machines to score multiple-choice exams. Under these conditions scoring errors should be negligible. On essay tests and other free response tests, scorers may disagree, thus producing large error effects. On these tests, an index of interscorer agreement (reliability) is essential.

The Test Taker

The sources of error that are the most difficult to control are those inherent in the test taker. Even when we have equivalent forms of a test, standardized administration and scoring procedures, and ideal testing arrangements—in short, model testing conditions—there still will be errors in test scores resulting from inconsistencies attributable to the test taker. Some of these result from pervasive, long-term changes in individuals; others reflect transient factors associated with a particular test administration (see Table 4.1). Although it is obvious how specific short-term influences, such as illness or attention, will affect reliability, it is not always clear whether changes in more pervasive characteristics introduce variable or constant errors. In the remainder of this section, we shall consider some of the important personal variables, stressing how they operate and how they can be controlled or their effects minimized.

Motivation   Earlier we made a distinction between maximal performance and typical performance measures. This distinction is made by the test developer, who communicates the desired emphasis to the test taker through the test directions. Thus the directions on aptitude and achievement tests generally stress trying one's best, selecting the correct answer, and answering as many questions as possible. Conversely, the directions on personality and interest inventories stress that there are "no correct answers" and that the person should respond according to his own feelings and usual behaviors.

Measurement errors will be introduced if a particular person, or subgroup of

TABLE 4.1   Sources of error in test scores*

1. Lasting and general characteristics of the individual
   A. Level of ability on traits which operate on a number of tests
   B. General skills and techniques of taking tests
   C. General ability to comprehend instructions
2. Lasting but specific characteristics of the individual
   A. Level of ability on traits required on *this* test
   B. Skills specific to particular form of test items
   C. "Chance"; whether individual knows the particular item
3. Temporary but general characteristics of the individual
   A. Health
   B. Fatigue
   C. Motivation
   D. Emotional strain
   E. General test-wiseness
   F. Understanding of the mechanics of testing
   G. External conditions (ventilation, lighting, etc.)
4. Temporary and specific characteristics of the individual
   A. Comprehension of the specific test task
   B. Specific techniques of dealing with particular test materials
   C. Level of practice on specific skills involved
   D. Momentary set for a particular test
   E. Fluctuations of memory
   F. Fluctuations of attention
5. Systematic and chance factors in the test administration
   A. Testing conditions (e.g., clarity of instruction, adherence to time limits)
   B. Scoring unreliability and/or bias
6. Factors not otherwise accounted for
   A. "Luck," guessing

*Adapted from R. L. Thorndike, 1951, Table 8: Possible sources of variance in scores on a particular test.

people, has a different motivation than do the majority of the test takers. Whenever this occurs, there is the question of whether the test results are comparable to those of other people or whether similar results would be obtained under different testing conditions. For example, most people view an achievement test as a situation calling for maximal performance, since our society stresses doing one's best. However, in certain segments of the population, particularly the lower socioeconomic classes, this achievement drive does not operate as it does in middle- and upper-class children. Thus, even though a test is designed as a measure of maximal performance, some children may have little motivation to do well, and may even respond randomly. An analogous situation occurs when a personality inventory is given as part of a selection process. Although the employer may be interested in the applicant's typical performance, the applicant may feel that it would be to his advantage to make a good impression. Thus, for the applicant, the testing situation becomes a maximal performance situation (showing his best possible profile) rather than presenting a picture of his typical behavior.

These examples show that atypical motivational patterns may manifest themselves in several ways. If a systematic bias is introduced, one that operates in a constant manner on repeated testings, scores might be less valid but not necessarily less consistent. If a test taker's motivation produces haphazard and erratic responding (as in the first example) there will be both a systematic effect (underestimation of the person's ability) and a variable error; only the latter would decrease reliability.

Learning, development, and education   Every test measures what the test taker has learned throughout his lifetime. In fact, the purpose of testing usually is to assess the level of developed skills in a certain area. Thus variations in test scores due to general learning experiences or development changes, for the most part, produce constant errors and are of little direct concern in determining reliability.

There are, however, several situations where learning experiences are important. One is when an individual receives specific coaching for a test while other test takers have undergone no special preparation. A second case occurs when, in the time intervening between two testings, some people receive special education or training while others do not. In these circumstances scores on the second administration of the test will reflect both what was tested on the first administration and what was learned between administrations. Since test takers will have received varying amounts of relevant training, their scores will be affected differentially, and the correlation between scores on the two administrations (reliability) will decrease.

Experience with tests   A fundamental assumption in testing is that the persons taking a test have had, at least within broad limits, equal exposure to the materials covered by the test and to the procedures and skills involved in taking tests. Although knowledge of the extent of each person's exposure to the material covered by the test is vital for an accurate interpretation of any test score, the question of familiarity with the procedure and skills of testing is more crucial when considering the consistency of measurement. Because we are concerned with consistency of performance, we need to be assured that test scores are accurate indices of the trait measured and not distorted by the test takers' inability to fathom the format of the test.

Any time a new item format[1] or a new procedure for responding (for example, a different type of answer sheet) is introduced, there is the possibility of misunderstanding, and consequently of introducing error into the measurement. Thus, practice problems and illustrations should be included whenever a new, or uncommon, test format or response mode is used. In most circumstances, this small amount of practice will be sufficient to insure that the item format does not produce extraneous variability. For persons with very limited exposure to testing, more

[1]New, as used here, means new to the person taking the test.

extensive practice may be needed. Several test publishers have published kits (see, e.g., Bennett and Doppelt, 1967) to aid such persons in developing their test-taking skills. In any case, the test administrator should always ascertain that everyone understands the test procedures before the test is administered.

A reverse phenomenon also occurs. Some persons have developed their test-taking skills into a fine art. These people, who are said to be "test sophisticated," are experts in understanding the subtler aspects of testing—for example, in detecting nuances that indicate correct answers and in knowing how to make the optimal use of their time. Through application of these skills, they frequently receive higher scores than persons with equal ability but less well-developed test-taking skills (see, e.g., Rowley, 1974).

Test anxiety   Some people get very tense, nervous, and upset at the prospect of taking a test or an examination. Frequently these are people who do not thoroughly understand testing procedures and/or are unsure of their own abilities. Since excess anxiety has a detrimental effect on performance and often produces erratic performance, test anxiety can contribute to measurement error (Wine, 1971). Minor cases of test anxiety can usually be alleviated by giving a clear explanation of the purposes of the testing and by ensuring that the person is familiar with the testing procedures—for example, by utilizing practice problems. Both approaches decrease anxiety by reducing unknown conditions. In more severe cases, special testing arrangements or counseling may be needed.

Coaching   The effect of coaching on test scores is frequently misunderstood. Many people feel that test scores can be fairly readily altered by coaching. However, a series of studies (College Entrance Examination Board, 1965) has found that coaching generally results in only negligible improvement in scores on college entrance exams. Coaching is likely to be effective only if the person is quite naive regarding test procedures, has little knowledge of the subject matter, or if the coaching reduces test anxiety. Even under these conditions, coaching does not necessarily produce significant increases in scores. The increases that do occur often can be attributed to a *practice effect,* which generally occurs whenever a test is taken a second time.

The crucial question is whether coaching increases the person's knowledge of the area covered by the test or only increases his test score. The former outcome should both increase the person's test score and provide long-term benefits to the individual; the latter only produces inaccurate measurement.

Physiological variables   We all have bad days. Tests taken when we are ill or fatigued may yield different results than tests taken when we are healthy and alert. Or, on a long test, the test taker may become bored and suffer momentary lapses of attention, thus decreasing his performance. Although evidence tends to indicate that when motivation remains high, fatigue and illness do not influence test performance significantly, the tester should be alert to the potential effect of these variables. If there is any indication that performance may have been affected by physiological or psychological disturbances, the safest procedure is to readminister the test under more favorable conditions.

There are, of course, a myriad of other conditions and factors that can result in inaccurate or inconsistent test scores. We have only briefly mentioned some of the major ones. Others will be mentioned as we discuss the various types of tests.

VALIDITY

The previous sections of this chapter have focused on the consistency of measurement, the precision with which a test measures whatever it measures. The basic problem was to identify variables that produce inconsistency in scores and estimate the magnitude of their effect. We now turn to the questions of (1) what the test measures, and (2) how well the test measures what it does measure. These two questions are the fundamental issues of validity.

Test scores have meaning only when they are related to other psychologically meaningful variables. Although theoretically it would be possible to develop a perfectly reliable test whose scores were not correlated with any other variable, the test would be of no practical usefulness since scores on the test would relate to nothing other than scores on another administration of the test. Such a test would measure with high consistency but no validity.

Validity Defined

Validity, like consistency and reliability, is a generic term given to a class of closely related concepts and procedures. Thus, validity can be defined on various levels and in various ways. The flavor of the concept can be conveyed by the types of questions that validity analyses seek to answer: What traits are measured by the test? Does the test measure the trait it is designed to measure? What percent of the variance in the test score is attributable to the variable that the test measures? What can be predicted from the test scores? Does the test supply information that can be used in making decisions?

Because the determination of validity may involve diverse questions and procedures, validity, like consistency, will always be situation-specific. That is, under differing conditions, using different samples and/or methods of analysis, different results will be obtained. Thus one can legitimately speak only of the validity of the test under certain specified conditions. To say that one test is more valid than another is meaningful only if the statement means that the test has been found to be valid in a wider variety of situations or for a greater number of purposes.

Whereas reliability was defined by the proportions of true and error variance, *validity is defined as the proportion of true variance that is relevant to the purposes of the testing*. Relevant, as used here, means attributable to the variable[2] that the test measures. The variable that the test measures may be a trait or attribute or some

---

[2]A test may, of course, measure more than one relevant variable. We shall use the singular case, however, for two reasons: first, to avoid the awkward phasing, "variable or variables"; and second, because it is frequently desirable to construct tests that measure only one trait (see Chapter 6).

independently observed measure. Therefore, the validity of a test is defined either by (1) the extent to which the test measures a hypothesized underlying trait, or construct, or (2) the relationship between test scores and some extratest criterion measure.

This definition of validity can be shown through the use of equations. Equation (4.2) stated that the total variance in a set of test scores equaled true variance plus error variance:

$$s_X{}^2 = s_T{}^2 + s_E{}^2$$

Defining validity as the proportion of relevant variance implies that true variance can be divided into two components: relevant variance and other reliable, but irrelevant variance; that is,

$$s_T{}^2 = s_V{}^2 + s_I{}^2 \qquad (4.5)$$

Where $s_V{}^2$ is the relevant (valid) variance and $s_I{}^2$ is the irrelevant but reliable variance. In other words, the stable (reliable or true) variance in test scores is composed of two components: that attributable to the variable the test measures (relevant or valid variance) and that attributable to other sources (irrelevant reliable variance).

If Equation (4.5) is substituted into Equation (4.2), we obtain

$$s_X{}^2 = s_V{}^2 + s_I{}^2 + s_E{}^2 \qquad (4.6)$$

or, in words, the variability in a set of test scores is determined by the valid variance, variance attributable to reliable but irrelevant sources (i.e., constant errors), and measurement error variance. It can be seen from Equation (4.6) that as error variance decreases (that is, as the test becomes more reliable), the proportion of potentially valid variance increases. However, because the remaining systematic variance may be either relevant or irrelevant, low error variance does not guarantee high validity (see Figure 4.2); thus low error variance (i.e., high reliability) is a necessary, but not sufficient, condition for high validity.

Relationship of reliability and validity   The distinction between reliability and validity is based on what is considered error. In reliability, we are concerned with random or unsystematic errors. In validity, error is introduced whenever our test measures any variable that is irrelevant to the purposes of the testing; here we are concerned with systematic errors. Equations (4.5) and (4.6) show these relationships.

The relationship between reliability and validity can also be shown by the *correction for attenuation* which indicates the effect of using unreliable measurements on the correlation between two measures. It can be shown (see, e.g., Nunnally, 1967) that the maximum correlation between two measures is

$$r_{XYmax} = \frac{r_{XY}}{\sqrt{r_{XX}}\sqrt{r_{YY}}} \qquad (4.7)$$

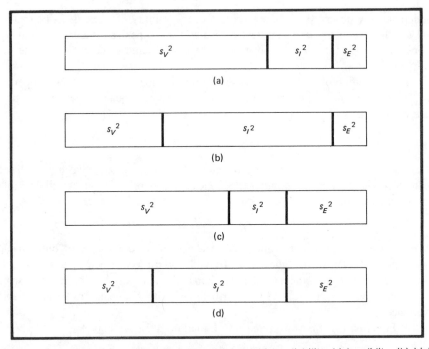

Figure 4.2   Relationship of reliability and validity: (a) high reliability, high validity; (b) high reliability, low validity; (c) low reliability, relatively high validity; (d) low reliability, low validity. In each diagram, s_V^2 refers to the valid variance, and s_I^2 refers to nonvalid but stable variance.

where r_{XY} is the correlation between the two measures, and r_{XX} and r_{YY} are the reliabilities of the two measures. If we assume that the theoretical correlation between the two measures is perfect ($r_{XY} = 1.00$), Equation (4.7) becomes[3]

$$r_{XY} \leqslant \sqrt{r_{XX}} \qquad\qquad (4.8)$$

Equation (4.8) states that the validity of a test cannot exceed the square root of its reliability; or, in more general terms, the valdity of a test will always be limited by its reliability.

Types of Validity

Although there are many possible classifications of types of validity, we shall follow the Standards for Educational and Psychological Tests (APA, 1974) and treat validity as falling into three major classes: criterion-related validity, content validity, and construct validity. The basic characteristics of the three types are summarized in Table 4.2 and briefly described in the following paragraphs.

Criterion-related validity   One frequent use of psychological tests is to predict an individual's future performance on some significant variable (the criterion). For

---

[3]This is because r_{YY}, and consequently $\sqrt{r_{YY}}$, will be less than 1.

TABLE 4.2   Summary of differences between content, criterion-related, and construct validity

Content validity
    Question asked: How would the individual perform in the universe of situations of which the test items are a sample?
    Evaluation: By estimating the adequacy of sampling.
    Orientation: Toward the task or behavior, the test process.
    Example: A classroom exam sampling the content of a given unit of the course.

Criterion-related validity
    Question asked: How well do scores on the test predict status or performance on some independent measure?
    Evaluation: By comparing scores on the test with scores on the independent (qualitatively different) measure.
    Orientation: Toward the criterion, the predicted variable.
    Examples: Using a scholastic aptitude test to predict college grade average; using a mechanical aptitude test to predict success as an automobile mechanic; using a personality inventory to predict which automobile drivers will have accidents.

Construct validity
    Question asked: What trait does the test measure?
    Evaluation: By accumulation of evidence as to what the test does and does not measure.
    Orientation: Toward the trait being measured by the test.
    Examples: Developing a test to define a trait such as intelligence or creativity.

example, we might want to predict the grade averages of prospective college students or the job performance of workers. The basic question in these situations is: How well do scores on the test predict performance on the criterion? An index of this predictive accuracy is a measure of the validity of the test.

Note that the most important aspect of the situation is the criterion, hence the label criterion-related validity. What is of ultimate interest is the individual's performance on the criterion variable; the test score is important only in that it predicts the criterion. Thus the major concern in constructing the test will be to select items that predict the criterion. Here the test operates as a predictor, rather than as a representation or sample.

Content validity   In other situations, the test user wants to know: How would the individual perform in the universe of situations of which the test is but a sample? For example, the typical classroom exam samples an individual's knowledge in a variety of areas; scores on this sample of items are then used to make inferences about the student's knowledge of the total domain covered by the exam. Since the test represents a well-defined domain, the test content will closely parallel the tasks constituting the domain under study, and performance on individual items—both the accuracy of the response and the process used to answer the item—will be of primary interest.

Because this type of test requires making inferences from a sample to a domain, evaluation of the content validity of a test will be in terms of the adequacy of the item sampling. Since no quantitative index of sampling adequacy is available, evaluation will necessarily be a rational, judgmental process.

Construct validity   A third use of psychological tests is in the study of psychological traits and their manifestations. Here the basic question is: What trait does the test measure? Knowing what trait, or traits, a test measures allows the test to be used for studies of individual differences and for the development of psychological theories. The focus of construct validity, therefore, may be on the test or the trait; the trait emphasis, however, is preeminent.

Construct validation proceeds by an accumulation of evidence as to what trait the test does, in fact, measure. Evidence may be accumulated in various manners and from various sources, including studies of content and criterion-related validity. As evidence accumulates, the trait-test relationship is clarified and the trait definition becomes sharper. As with content validity there is no single quantitative index of the construct validity of a test, evaluation being a judgmental process.

In the discussion that follows we shall treat each class separately, although, as we shall see, they are interrelated. Moreover, evidence on all three types of validity will generally be appropriate in evaluating any test.

Given this overview, the next five chapters will consider consistency and validity in more detail. Our major concern will be with the methods used to obtain data on the consistency and validity of a measure, and what conclusions and inferences can be drawn from this information. We shall begin, in Chapter 5, with a discussion of reliability indices.

5

RELIABILITY

Having briefly discussed the variables that produce error in test scores, we now turn to the problem of measuring the amount of error in measurements—that is, to the estimation of the degree of consistency of measurement. In our discussion we shall make a distinction between two types of consistency. Although the two types are related, both conceptually and statistically, it is useful to treat them separately. In this chapter we shall discuss consistency over time and over forms of a test; these estimates will be referred to as *reliability* estimates. Reliability is concerned with the question: How consistent would a person's performance be if he took another form of the test (equivalence) or if he took the same test at a different time (stability)?

In the next chapter we shall be concerned with the question of whether all items on a test measure the same variable. This is the question of *internal consistency* or *homogeneity*. Homogeneity is concerned with the question: Do all items on the test measure the same characteristic?

Reliability Coefficients

Most indices of reliability are expressed as a correlation coefficient, and, thus, are called reliability coefficients. A reliability coefficient is nothing more than the correlation between two sets of scores obtained from the same sample of people, and used as an index of consistency of measurement. It can be shown (see, e.g., Nunnally, 1967; Stanley, 1971) that a reliability coefficient derived in this manner is equivalent to reliability as defined earlier; that is,

$$r_{XX} = r_{XT}^2 = \frac{s_T^2}{s_X^2} \tag{5.1}$$

where r_{XX} is the reliability coefficient, and r_{XT} is the correlation between true and obtained scores.

Since the square of a correlation coefficient indicates the proportion of shared variance in two measures, Equation (5.1) states that a reliability coefficient indicates the proportion of variance in test scores that represents "true" differences between individuals. This, of course, is the definition of reliability.

The particular value obtained for any reliability coefficient will depend upon the group being tested and the sources of error that influence the scores. Thus, there is no such thing as *the* reliability of a test. Rather, there will be many reliability coefficients for any test—as many as there are different conditions for estimating the reliability.

Note, too, that a reliability coefficient is a measure of the amount of inconsistency; it does not indicate the causes of this lack of consistency. It tells how much the scores may be expected to vary, not why they vary. Thus, if we have reliability coefficients for two tests, obtained under similar conditions, we can tell which of the two tests measures more consistently. But without further analyses we cannot know why one test measures more accurately than the other.

TYPES OF RELIABILITY ESTIMATES

Many psychological characteristics are assumed to be relatively stable over time; scores on measures of these characteristics should not vary greatly over time. Therefore, one possible measure of reliability is the correlation between repeated measures (that is, between a test and a retest). Such an estimate is referred to as a *coefficient of stability*. Remember, also, that any test contains only a sample of all possible items. Hopefully, scores would be consistent from one sample of items to another—that is, from one form of the test to another. Thus, a second type of reliability estimate refers to consistency over forms of a test. This measure is referred to as a *coefficient of equivalence*. We could also combine these two procedures by administering equivalent forms of a test separated in time. A reliability estimate obtained in this manner would be a *coefficient of equivalence and stability*.

All of these procedures require two administrations of a test. However, in some situations only one form of a test is administered—for example, the typical classroom examination. Here we have two alternatives. One is to determine the internal consistency of the test (see Chapter 6). The other is to split the test artificially into two parts and calculate the correlation between scores on the two parts. These latter estimates are referred to as *split-half reliability*. Let us now look at each of these procedures in more detail.

Stability

For tests measuring psychological traits assumed to be relatively stable over time (for example, most aptitudes and abilities and many personality characteristics), we would like some evidence of stability of scores. In addition, whenever test scores are used in decision making involving long-range plans (for example, aptitudes and interests), a measure of the stability of test scores over time is essential. Even for characteristics that vary over time, knowledge of the degree of stability of test scores over short periods is usually desirable.

The paradigm for the coefficient of stability is quite simple. The test is administered, a period of time elapses, and the same test is readministered. We then compute the correlation between scores on the test and the retest (see Table 5.1, steps 1 and 2, for an example):

$$\text{TEST} \xrightarrow{\quad \text{time} \quad} \text{RETEST}$$

Because the procedure consists of a test followed by a retest, the coefficient of stability is also referred to as *test-retest reliability*.

The time interval between testings can vary from several minutes to several years. Thus, different values of the reliability coefficient will be obtained depending on the time between testings. If we were to plot the relationship between the magnitude of the reliability coefficient and the time between test administrations we would usually find that reliability decreases over time. Of course, it is not time per se that causes the changes in scores, it is the experiences of the individual between testings.

Several assumptions are made when we compute a coefficient of stability. The first, and most crucial, assumption is that the characteristic being measured by the test is stable over time. This assumption leads to a certain ambiguity and circularity, for if the trait is assumed stable but the test-retest reliability estimate is low, we cannot determine whether our assumption of the trait's stability was in error or extraneous conditions produced the lack of consistency. Conversely, if we assume that the trait is unstable but our reliability estimate is high, we do not know whether the assumption was in error or some systematic bias was producing a spuriously high correlation. Thus, the meaning of a coefficient of stability can only be interpreted within the context of our full range of knowledge of the trait being measured by the test.

Second, we must assume no differential forgetting or practice effects. When a test is repeated, especially after a short interval, some people may remember their responses or learn something about the technique of taking the test. In either case, if one person's score is influenced more than another person's score, reliability is lowered. Third, no differential learning should occur between the two adminis-

TABLE 5.1   Calculation of the coefficients of stability, equivalence, and stability and equivalence

(1) Assume that two (equivalent) forms of a 16-item test were administered to a group of 20 persons on a total of three occasions—Form A on March 1, Form B also on March 1, and Form A again on May 1. These administrations will be referred to as A_1, B_1, and A_2, respectively. Scores were as follows:

Subject

	A	B	C	D	E	F	G	H	I	J	K	L	M	N	O	P	Q	R	S	T
A_1	15	14	13	12	12	11	11	10	10	10	10	10	9	9	9	8	8	7	6	5
B_1	16	14	14	12	13	10	11	11	10	10	9	10	8	9	9	8	7	7	6	6
A_2	15	14	16	15	13	12	11	13	12	12	10	11	11	11	10	9	10	7	8	8

The summary statistics were as follows:

Test	ΣX	ΣX^2	$\bar{X}$	s	Cross-products (ΣXY) A_1	B_1	A_2
A_1	199	2101	9.95	2.46	—	2118	2375
B_1	200	2144	10.00	2.68		—	2397
A_2	228	2714	11.40	2.40			—

(2) *Coefficient of stability*. The coefficient of stability is the correlation between scores on two administrations of the same form of the test, separated by a time period—in this example the correlation between A_1 and A_2. Using as the formula:

$$r_{XX} = r_{(A1)(A2)} = \frac{\Sigma(X_{A1})(X_{A2})/N - (\bar{X}_{A1})(\bar{X}_{A2})}{(s_{A1})(s_{A2})}$$

Substituting in the data from the example and solving,

$$r_{(A1)(A2)} = \frac{2375/20 - (9.95)(11.40)}{(2.46)(2.40)} = .90$$

This is the coefficient of stability.

(3) *Coefficient of equivalence*. The coefficient of equivalence is the correlation between scores on parallel forms of the test, administered with a minimal time lag between testing—in the example, the correlation between A_1 and B_1:

$$r_{(A1)(B1)} = \frac{\Sigma(X_{A1})(X_{B1})/N - (\bar{X}_{A1})(\bar{X}_{B1})}{(s_{A1})(s_{B1})}$$

Substituting in the data and solving,

$$r_{(A1)(B1)} = \frac{2118/20 - (9.95)(10.00)}{(2.46)(2.68)} = .97$$

(4) *Coefficient of equivalence and stability*. This coefficient is the correlation between two parallel forms of the test administered at different times—in the example, the correlation between B_1 and A_2:

TABLE 5.1 (continued)

$$r_{(B1)(A2)} = \frac{\Sigma(X_{B1})(X_{A2})/N - (\bar{X}_{B1})(\bar{X}_{A2})}{(s_{B1})(s_{A2})}$$

Substituting in the data and solving,

$$r_{(B1)(A2)} = \frac{2397/20 - (10.00)(11.40)}{(2.68)(2.40)} = .91$$

(5) *Interpretation of the coefficients.* The very high value ($r = .97$) obtained for the coefficient of equivalence, plus the similarities in means and standard deviations, indicate that forms A and B are, in fact, parallel forms. As both stability indices were also high ($r \sim .90$), the trait tested evidently is quite stable, at least over a period of two months. Note also that there is some practice effect operating (i.e., the mean on A_2 is higher than the mean on A_1).

trations. For example, suppose that the same test is given as a pretest at the beginning of a course unit and also as a posttest after the unit is completed. If students learned different amounts during the unit, the pretest-posttest correlation will reflect these differential learning effects, and reliability will be decreased.

Because a coefficient of stability involves two administrations of the test, any variable that influences performance on one administration but not the other will also reduce the correlation. Examples include errors in timing or interruptions during the testing session. Thus, any errors associated with a specific administration of the test will affect the test-retest reliability. So, also, will day-to-day fluctuations in mood, health, and motivation. If the time between testings is relatively long, differential training or learning may become a factor. Item sampling does not affect the coefficient of stability since the same test form (i.e., the same collection of items) is used on both administrations.

Equivalence

Because any test contains only a sample of all possible items, a number of parallel forms of the test can be constructed. Parallel forms cover the same content, use the same types of items, and are of equal difficulty. Such parallel forms are needed whenever retesting with the same test is not feasible nor desirable. For example, you have probably worked "logic" problems—such as deducing how a person could be murdered in a sealed room. In these problems, once you find the solution you usually remember both the solution and the method for obtaining it. If the same problems were presented again you would immediately know the answer and would not have to repeat the deductive steps. If such a test were administered more than once, performance on the second administration would involve memory, not problem-solving abilities. Analogously, many math and science problems that are useful because they present a new situation, upon repetition present only a routine calculation exercise.

When we have equivalent forms, the reliability question becomes: How consistent are scores on the two forms of the test? To determine the equivalent forms reliability we would administer one form (Form A) of the test and then, with a minimum time lag,[1] administer a second form (Form B) . Correlating the scores on the two forms gives a coefficient of equivalence (see Table 5.1, sections 1 and 3, for an example). Diagrammatically the procedure would be:

$$\text{FORM A} \xrightarrow{\text{minimal time}} \text{FORM B}$$

In practice, to counterbalance any effects due to order of administration, half of the group would be administered Form A followed by Form B and the other half Form B followed by Form A. Because the procedure involves use of equivalent, or parallel, forms of the test, this method is also called *parallel forms reliability*.

The primary assumption when computing a coefficient of equivalence is that the forms are, in fact, equivalent. This means that they are equivalent not only in content, format, and length, but also in difficulty (that is, they have similar means) and variability (that is, they have similar standard deviations). To the extent that these conditions are not met, the coefficient of equivalence will give a distorted estimate of reliability.

In this method, inconsistencies in scores can be attributed primarily to differences in item sampling (that is, test forms). Since the two forms of the test are given close together in time, long-term fluctuations are eliminated. However, short-term fluctuations in the test taker's mood or differences in administration of the two forms are not entirely controlled. Thus, a pure measure of equivalence is not obtained. However, the major source of variance will be the difference between items on the two forms of the test.

Stability and Equivalence

If alternative forms of a test are available, it is possible to determine reliability by a combination of the two preceding methods. The procedure would be to administer one test form (Form A), allow a period of time to pass, then administer the other form (Form B):

$$\text{FORM A} \xrightarrow{\text{time}} \text{FORM B}$$

The coefficient of stability and equivalence will be the correlation between the two sets of scores. As with equivalent forms reliability, the experimental design would involve some people taking Form A first, others taking Form B first. (See Table 5.1, steps 1 and 4.)

Since all the factors that operate to produce inconsistencies in scores in the test-retest paradigm plus all the factors that produce inconsistencies in the parallel forms design can operate in this design, we would expect the greatest inconsistency in scores (that is, the lowest reliability coefficients) using this method of estimating reliability. Thus the coefficient of stability and equivalence will provide the most rigorous test and give the lower bound (lowest estimate) of reliability.

---

[1]Theoretically, the two forms would be administered simultaneously. Since this is impossible, the two forms are administered as close together as is feasible, generally within a few days of each other.

Split-half Reliability

In some situations it is not possible to use either equivalent forms or stability indices of reliability. For example, a teacher typically will not administer alternative forms of a classroom test (even if he had time to construct several forms), nor will the same exam be repeated at a later date. Nevertheless, some estimate of reliability may be needed. Fortunately, several methods are available for estimating reliability in these situations. One common method involves splitting the test into two equivalent halves—hence the designation split-half reliability.

As with the coefficient of equivalence, two independent halves are needed. Unless there is some systematic bias (such as alternating types of items or the response to one item being dependent on the response to a previous item), this split can usually be accomplished by using the odd-numbered items as one form and the even-numbered items as the other. In other words, for each test we would obtain separate scores for the odd- and even-numbered items. The correlation between these two scores gives an estimate of reliability.

One problem with this procedure is that each score is based on only half the items in the original test. Since reliability is dependent on test length (see below), the reliability estimated from the correlation between odd and even items will be lower than the reliability expected from a test of the original length. To estimate the reliability of a test of the original length we can use the *Spearman-Brown formula:*

$$r_{XX} = \frac{2r_{hh}}{1 + r_{hh}} \qquad (5.2)$$

where r_{hh} is the split-half reliability coefficient and r_{XX} is the estimate of the reliability of the test of the original length. The equation estimates the reliability of a test of the original length from the split-half reliability.

The general case of the Spearman-Brown formula is a very useful formula:

$$r_{kk} = \frac{kr_{XX}}{1 + (k - 1)r_{XX}} \qquad (5.3)$$

where k is the ratio (increased length to the original length), r_{XX} is the reliability of the original test, and r_{kk} is the estimated reliability of a test k times as long. This formula allows us to estimate the reliability of any longer, or shorter, test. Moreover, by solving for k we can also determine how much a test would have to be lengthened to reach a desired level of reliability.[2] One note of caution is necessary:

[2]To illustrate, suppose that we have a ten-item test whose reliability is .50 and we want to estimate what the reliability would be if the test were increased to 30 items. Here $k = 3 = 30/10$. Applying the Spearman-Brown formula, the reliability of a 30-item test would be:

$$r = \frac{3(.50)}{1 + (3 - 1)(.50)} = \frac{1.50}{2.00} = .75$$

If we wanted to know how long the test would have to be to obtain a reliability of .90, we would solve for k as follows:

$$.90 = \frac{k(.50)}{1 + (k - 1)(.50)}$$

Doing the algebra, we find that $k = 9$. Thus we would need a 90-item test; that is, we would have to add 80 items to our original ten.

This formula is appropriate only when the new items are drawn from the same pool as the original items.

The Spearman-Brown formula assumes that the variability of the two halves of the test are equal. An alternative formula (Guttman, 1945) does not make this assumption:

$$r_{XX} = 2\left[1 - \frac{s_a{}^2 + s_b{}^2}{s_X{}^2}\right] \tag{5.4}$$

where s_a and s_b are the standard deviations of the two subtest scores and s_X is the standard deviation of the total score. Other formulas are presented by Thorndike (1951) and Stanley (1971).

A split-half reliability estimate is interpreted like a coefficient of equivalence. Because the two forms (halves) are, in essence, administered simultaneously, only short-term fluctuations will influence reliability. An illustration of the computation of a split-half reliability coefficient is shown in Table 5.2.

TABLE 5.2   Calculation of split-half reliability

(1)   Form B of the test described in Table 5.1 was split into two halves—odd- and even-numbered items—and each half scored separately. Scores were as follows:

	A	B	C	D	E	F	G	H	I	J	K	L	M	N	O	P	Q	R	S	T
Odds	8	8	7	6	6	5	6	5	5	5	4	6	4	4	5	4	3	4	3	3
Evens	8	6	7	6	7	5	5	6	5	5	5	4	4	5	4	4	4	3	3	3
Total	16	14	14	12	13	10	11	11	10	10	9	10	8	9	9	8	7	7	6	6

(Subject)

The summary data were:

	ΣX	ΣX^2	$\bar{X}$	s	
Odds	101	553	5.05	1.47	$\Sigma X_o X_e = 532$
Evens	99	527	4.95	1.36	
Total	200	2144	10.00	2.68	

(2)   The split-half reliability is computed by correlating scores on the odd-numbered items (o) with scores on the even-numbered items (e):

$$r_{XX} = r_{oe} = \frac{\Sigma X_o X_e / N - (\bar{X}_o)(\bar{X}_e)}{(s_o)(s_e)}$$

Substituting in the data and solving:

$$r_{oe} = \frac{532/20 - (5.05)(4.95)}{(1.47)(1.36)} = .80$$

The value, $r = .80$, is the uncorrected split-half reliability coefficient.

TABLE 5.2 (continued)

(3) As each half of the test contained only eight items, and the full test contained 16, we can use the Spearman-Brown formula to estimate the reliability of a 16-item test:

$$r_{XX} = \frac{2r_{oe}}{1 + r_{oe}} = \frac{2(.80)}{1 + .80} = .89$$

The value, $r_{XX} = .89$, is the *corrected* split-half reliability coefficient.

(4) We could also estimate the split-half reliability using the alternative formula:

$$r_{XX} = 2\left[1 - \frac{s_a^2 + s_b^2}{s_X^2}\right] = 2\left[1 - \frac{s_o^2 + s_e^2}{s_X^2}\right]$$

$$= 2\left[1 - \frac{(1.47)^2 + (1.36)^2}{(2.68)^2}\right] = .88$$

Note that the two formulas produce essentially the same value for r_{XX} (.88 and .89) and that these values approximate the value found for the coefficient of equivalence.

FACTORS INFLUENCING RELIABILITY COEFFICIENTS

In discussing the various reliability coefficients we have mentioned several sources of error which influence the magnitude of the obtained correlation. We noted that the coefficient of stability and equivalence generally gives the lowest estimate of reliability because more factors have a chance to influence scores. Conversely, the corrected split-half correlation generally yields the highest estimate because the least number of factors have a chance to operate. However, there are other factors that can influence the reliability coefficient.

Range of Scores

Reliability coefficients, like all correlation coefficients, are influenced by the range of the score distribution. As variability decreases, the correlation coefficient decreases; as variability increases (that is, the scores become more heterogeneous), the coefficient will increase.

As an example of how this relationship is important, assume that you want to know how reliably you can estimate the spelling ability of fourth grade students. The manual for the test you are planning to use gives the reliability for a sample of fourth through sixth graders. This reliability coefficient is likely to be higher than one obtained using only fourth grade students. The logic is shown in Figure 5.1, which shows that a change of 1 point will be relatively larger when compared to the distribution of scores within a grade than when compared to the distribution of the combined group. Thus, reliability coefficients derived from the more heterogeneous combined group will overestimate the reliability for the more homogeneous group

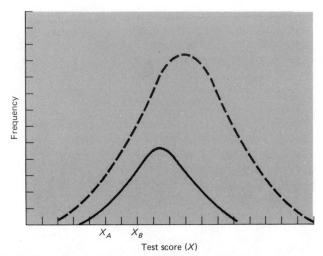

Figure 5.1   Reliability and score distributions. Note that a given distance $(X_a–X_b)$ encompasses a greater range within the fourth grade distribution (solid line) than within the combined fourth–sixth grade distribution (dashed line). This means that error will be higher, and reliability lower, in the fourth grade distribution.

of fourth grade students. A much better indication of the reliability for your purposes would be obtained by calculating the reliability coefficient on a sample of fourth grade students. Or, in general, whenever the reliability reported is for a group that is more heterogeneous than the group of direct concern, it is likely to be an overestimate.

Test Length

A second factor influencing the reliability coefficient is the length of the test. Adding more items, provided that they are equally reliable, will increase the reliability of the test. This can be seen readily if you consider increasing length as essentially producing a wider range of scores. The effect of increasing test length can be determined by the Spearman-Brown formula (Equation 5.3). Thus, an unreliable test can often be made more useful by increasing its length. A point of diminishing returns occurs fairly rapidly, however, and adding large numbers of items will not automatically produce large increases in reliability.

Test Difficulty

There is no simple relationship between the difficulty of the test and its reliability. Nor is there a simple relation between the level of performance of a group and reliability. However, whenever the range of scores is reduced, reliability will be also reduced. Thus, if the test is too difficult or too easy for a group, the range of scores will be narrowed and reliability reduced. This implies that to maximize reliability, the level of difficulty of a test should be such as to produce the widest possible distribution of scores.[3]

A specific problem occurs when the test is so difficult that testees repond to many items randomly—for example, by guessing. When a person responds randomly we cannot place any confidence in his scores, especially scores on individual items. If only a few people respond randomly, their scores will be consistently low (that is, on a test and a retest or on both forms) and reliability will be slightly, but not seriously overestimated. However, if many people guess or otherwise respond randomly, differences from test to test will be attributable primarily to randomly distributed error factors, and the reliability coefficient will approach zero.

Speededness

Speed is a fourth factor that can influence reliability. In fact, split-half reliability is inappropriate when speed is a major factor in test performance. To illustrate, assume that you give a 100-item test of simple arithmetic facts to fourth graders. The problems are ones that, with sufficient time, the students would get correct. However, by setting a restrictive time limit, such that not everyone can finish, we produce a speeded test. Under these circumstances, a child who completes 90 items will probably get 90 correct, 45 even and 45 odd; a child who finishes 80 items will get 80 correct, 40 even and 40 odd; and so forth. Thus each child will get the same score (with the exception of a few errors) on both halves. In this situation the split-half coefficient will be spuriously inflated.

An analogous situation occurs whenever speed plays a part in determining scores on a test. One way to minimize the problem is to use methods that are less influenced by speed, such as equivalent forms reliability. If alternative methods are not feasible, one can estimate the proportion of variance attributable to speed. At this point let it suffice to warn you that reliability coefficients obtained from one administration of a highly speeded test are overestimates and should be taken with a grain of salt.

INTERPRETATION OF A RELIABILITY COEFFICIENT

Having discussed potential sources of inconsistency in test scores and the methods for estimating reliability, we must now face two interrelated questions: How is a reliability coefficient interpreted? And, what constitutes an acceptable level of reliability? In attempting to answer these questions, three considerations must be kept in mind. First, the reliability of a test as estimated by one technique, in one situation, and with one sample will not be the same as an estimate obtained with a different technique, in a different situation, or with a different sample. Thus, we shall always be interpreting a specific reliability coefficient, not making statements

[3]It can be shown (see, e.g., Nunnally, 1967) that the widest distribution of scores will be obtained using items where the probability of obtaining the correct response is .50—that is, when half the group answers the item correctly (or in the keyed direction).

about *the* reliability of the test. Second, a reliability coefficient is only an estimate of the magnitude of inconsistency in test scores; it does not indicate, except indirectly, the causes of the inconsistency. Third, reliability is not the be-all and end-all of psychological measurement; it is not an end in itself but rather a step on a way to a goal. That is, unless test scores are consistent, they cannot be related to other variables with any degree of confidence. Thus reliability places limits on validity, and the crucial question becomes whether a test's reliability is high enough to allow satisfactory validity.

With these considerations in mind, we will briefly discuss three ways of interpreting reliability coefficients: (1) as the correlation between obtained and true scores; (2) by comparing the reliability of a given test to the reliability attained by other tests of the same type; and (3) as an index of the amount of error in individual scores.

Correlation between True and Obtained Scores

Earlier we defined reliability as the ratio of true score variance to obtained score variance; see Equation (4.3). We also stated that the reliability coefficient was equal to the squared correlation between obtained and true scores; see Equation (5.1). Thus, a reliability coefficient can be interpreted in terms of the proportion of variance in the obtained scores which represents variation in true scores. For example, if $r_{XX} = .90$, we can say that 90 percent of the variability in obtained scores is due to differences in true scores and only 10 percent is due to errors of measurement.[4] At the extremes, if $r_{XX} = 1.00$, there is no error of measurement, all variability being true score variance; if $r_{XX} = .00$, all variability reflects errors of measurement.

In short, the reliability coefficient tells us what proportion of the variance in obtained scores is due to differences in true scores and what proportion is measurement error. More precisely, since reliability is specific to each testing situation, a reliability coefficient indicates the extent of measurement error obtained when a given form of a test is administered to a particular sample of people under a specified set of conditions.

Comparative Reliability

A second method of interpretation is to use the reliability of existing tests as a guideline or minimum standard. Since many measures of aptitudes, achievement, and abilities have reliabilities of .90 or higher (often as high as .95), tests in these areas should be expected to have at least this degree of reliability. Measures of personality, interest, values, and other less objectively measured characteristics generally have reliabilities of .80 to .85 or higher, at least over short time periods.

---

[4]Note that although a reliability coefficient is a correlation coefficient, it is the one case in which we do not have to square the coefficient to obtain the percent of variance. This is because the reliability coefficient is the squared correlation between true and obtained scores; see Equation (5.1).

Thus, from a pragmatic point of view, the reliability of any test should be compared to the reliabilities attained by similar tests. The danger of this approach is, of course, that attainment of the present norm becomes the final goal, rather than being viewed as a minimum standard.

Error in Individual Scores

When interpreting individual test scores the most important question is: How much would this person's score be expected to change on retesting? In other words, what is the error of measurement for this particular individual? The magnitude of measurement error will, of course, be proportional to the reliability of the test.

One way of approaching this question is to consider how the person's rank within a group would change on retesting. If a test measured without error (that is, if r_{XX} were 1.00), then every person would keep the same relative position (rank) on retesting. However, if r_{XX} is less than 1.00, as it always is, then there will be changes in rankings between tests. Thorndike and Hagen (1961, 1969) have provided charts that show how relative ranks will change as reliability changes. To give but one example, suppose that two individuals' scores place them at the 75th and 50th percentile on a test (that is, they scored higher than 75 percent and 50 percent of the group, respectively). When the test's reliability is .60, there is about one chance in three that these two individuals would reverse positions on a retest; however, when $r_{XX} = .95$, there is only one chance in 50 that they will change positions. In other words, the higher the reliability, the less change in relative position.

Summary

Our discussion of the interpretation of a reliability coefficient can be summarized by answering three questions: (1) What is an acceptable level of reliability for a test? Ideally, tests would have perfect reliability ($r_{XX} = 1.00$); in practice, we should insist on reliability coefficients at least as high as those found for other similar tests and, hopefully, improve on this standard. (2) Can we speak of "*the* reliability" of a test? Only hypothetically, since a reliability coefficient is always specific to the sample being tested, the testing situation, and the method used to calculate the reliability coefficient. (3) Is there any meaningful way of comparing the reliabilities of various tests, of speaking of one test as being more reliable than another? Only if by "more reliable" we mean that one of the tests has demonstrated higher reliability in a wider variety of testing situations.

ERROR IN INDIVIDUAL SCORES

A reliability coefficient is an index of the consistency of a set of test scores over time or test forms. Thus it provides evidence essential to evaluate the test. It does not give a direct indication of the amount of variability (error) expected in an individual's test score. In many practical situations, however, we are interested in the degree to which an individual's score may be expected to vary on retesting. Suppose for example, that a school psychologist administers the Wechsler Intelligence Scale for Children (WISC) to a child who obtains an IQ of 116. He knows that the child would probably not obtain exactly the same score on retesting, and wonders how much variation can be expected if the child were retested. This is the question we now address.

The Standard Error of Measurement

Our problem, in technical terms, is to estimate the person's true score and the magnitude of the error component. As described earlier in Equation (4.1), measurement theory postulates that any obtained score is a function of the true score plus some error:

$$X = T + E$$

Because of measurement errors, we know that on some occasions the obtained score will be higher than the true score, sometimes the true scores will exceed the obtained score, and occasionally the two scores will be equal. In other words, the obtained score may overestimate, underestimate, or equal the true score.

Hypothetically we could test a person an infinite number of times, and compute the mean and standard deviation of the distribution of his (obtained) scores. In this hypothetical distribution, the mean would be the individual's true score and the standard deviation would be an index of the magnitude of the errors of measurement. This procedure is obviously unfeasible. An estimate of error variance can be made, however, by using the performance of a group of subjects on two administrations of the test as a substitute for repeated testing of the same individual. When we do this, the differences in individuals' scores on the two tests are errors of measurement. We could then develop a distribution of these error scores. The standard deviation of this distribution is the *standard error of measurement*.

It can be shown (see, e.g., Magnusson, 1967) that the standard error of measurement can be estimated directly from obtained test scores by using the formula:

$$s_m = s_X \sqrt{1 - r_{XX}} \qquad (5.5)$$

where s_m is the standard error of measurement, s_X is the standard deviation of the distribution of obtained scores, and r_{XX} is the reliability coefficient for the test. Thus, knowing the standard deviation of the obtained scores and the reliability of the test, we can estimate the magnitude of error in individual scores. Table 5.3 shows an example of the computation of the standard error of measurement.

There are several pesky problems with using s_m as an estimate of error in individual scores. First, since there are many possible estimates of the reliability of the test, there will also be many possible estimates of s_m. This problem can be alleviated by using the reliability estimate most appropriate for the particular situation of interest. For example, if we are interested in the stability of an individual's score over a six-month period, we would use as the reliability estimate a coefficient of stability computed with a six-month interval between testings. Second, this

TABLE 5.3   Computation and interpretation of the standard error of measurement

(1) For illustrative purposes we shall use data from the reliability example presented in Table 5.1. We shall use scores on the first administration of Form A and use the coefficient of stability as our reliability estimate. The mean $(\overline{X}_{A1})$, standard deviation (s_{A1}), and reliability coefficient (r_{A1A2}) were

$$\overline{X} = 9.95 \qquad s_X = 2.46 \qquad r_{XX} = .90$$

(2) To compute the standard error of measurement (s_m) for this example use Equation (5.5):

$$s_m = s_X\sqrt{1 - r_{XX}}$$

Substituting the appropriate values into the equation and solving for s_m:

$$s_m = 2.46\sqrt{1 - .90} = .78$$

(3) Suppose that an individual scored 12 on Form A of the test and we want to know the 95 percent confidence limits for his true score. The limits are

$$X \pm 1.96s_m$$

and, substituting in the values from the example,

$$12 \pm (1.96)(.78) = 12 \pm 1.53 = 10.47 - 13.53$$

we can say that the probability is .95 that the true score for an individual with $X = 12$ is between 10.5 and 13.5 points—or, rounded off, between 10 and 14.

estimate assumes that s_m is the same at all score levels—that is, that s_m is the same for high scores as for low scores. This is not the case. However, the standard error of measurement as computed above is an index of the *average* error of measurement throughout the entire score range. If more precise estimates are needed, more complicated procedures are needed (see e.g., Lord, 1957, or Magnusson, 1967).

Interpretation of s_m

Since s_m is a standard deviation (the standard deviation of the distribution of errors of measurement), it can be interpreted as any other standard deviation. In this situation, the mean will be the true score (X_T) and the standard deviation, s_m. Reference to Appendix A shows that an obtained score (X) will fall within plus or minus one standard error of measurement $(\pm 1.00s_m)$ of the true score (X_T) in approximately 68 percent of the test administrations, and within $\pm 1.96s_m$ of X_T in approximately 95 percent of the administrations (see, e.g., Hays, 1973). In other words, the standard error of measurement is an index of the expected variability of obtained scores around the true score. And, as a corollary, s_m can be used to estimate the amount of change in scores expected on retesting.

The test user, however, approaches the problem of estimation from the other direction; that is, he knows the obtained score (X) and wants to estimate the true score (X_T). He wants to know the range of score values that will, with a given probability, include the true score. He may select any probability level but generally the 95 percent confidence level is used. Selecting this level insures that the range of scores will include the true score in 95 percent of the instances.[5]

It can be shown that the probability is .95 that the true score will fall within the following range:

$$(X - 1.96s_m) \leqslant X_T \leqslant (X + 1.96s_m) \qquad (5.6)$$

In other words, the probability is approximately .95 that X_T falls within $\pm 1.96s_m$ of the obtained score (X). The range of values encompassing the true score is called the *confidence interval,* and the boundaries of the interval are called the *confidence limits.* Confidence intervals and confidence limits have an attached probability level; thus the range of scores, $X \pm 1.96s_m$, is referred to as the 95 percent confidence interval for X_T, and the boundaries of the range, $X + 1.96s_m$ and $X - 1.96s_m$, are called the 95 percent confidence limits.

Application of these relationships tells the test user two things: the amount of variability (difference in scores) to be expected on retesting and the range within which the true score will probably fall. To illustrate, consider a child who obtains an IQ of 116 on the WISC. Assume that $s_m = 3$ IQ points on the WISC. Using the 95 percent confidence level, we would expect that his score on retesting would be within approximately 6 points ($1.96s_m = 1.96 \times 3 = 5.9$) of his obtained score. Similarly, we can say that this true score probably ($p = .95$) lies between 110 and 122 (that is, $X \pm 1.96s_m = 116 \pm 5.9 = 110.1 - 121.9$ or, rounded off, 110–122). We say *probably* because if we use the 95 percent confidence interval, the true score will fall outside this range in approximately 5 percent of the instances.[6] (For another example, see Table 5.3.)

Exact Scores versus Ranges

The standard error of measurement has a very important function: It forces us to think of test scores as ranges or bands of scores and not as exact points. The obtained score on the test (X) will be the best available estimate of the person's true score (X_T); but, because of measurement error, it is not an exact indicator. How precise an estimate of the true score any given obtained score will be is indicated by the magnitude of s_m and, indirectly, by the reliability of the test. Since r_{XX} never is 1.00, *test scores must be thought of as ranges, or bands, not as precise points.* The larger the s_m (or the lower the reliability), the more imprecise is our measurement and the wider this range. If we constantly think of scores as ranges, rather than points, we will avoid the habit of overinterpreting small differences between scores.

[5]We could, of course, use any confidence limits; however, 95 percent is the most common.

[6]Although some statisticians would claim that it is not completely accurate to make such statements when estimating X_T from X, McHugh (1957) has shown that doing so generally will not introduce any large amounts of error.

6

HOMOGENEITY AND SPECIAL PROBLEMS IN RELIABILITY

In this chapter we shall continue our discussion of the consistency of psychological measurement, focusing on four additional areas. First, we shall consider the concept of homogeneity, or the degree to which the items on a test are interrelated and measure a single trait or characteristic. We shall discuss next the problems that arise when several test scores are considered simultaneously—that is, the reliability of subtests and difference scores, and the measurement of change. Third, we shall briefly present several alternative approaches to consistency. Finally, the problems involved in obtaining information on the relative influence of various error sources will be discussed.

HOMOGENEITY

In Chapter 5 we discussed the concept of reliability as consistency over time (stability) and as consistency over different forms of a test (equivalence). We did not consider the interrelationships among the various items that comprise a test—that is, the internal consistency of the test. Although split-half reliability might be considered a measure of internal consistency, we classified it as a special case of equivalence, differing from other measures of equivalence only in that the designation of the two forms occurs after the test is administered.

However, as was noted previously, there also are measures of consistency that focus on the interrelations between items within a test. Because the interpretation of these measures is somewhat different from the interpretation of other reliability indices, we have chosen to consider them separately. We shall use the term "homogeneity" to refer to consistency estimates that are primarily concerned with the internal structure of the test.

Homogeneity Defined

Analyses of internal consistency seek to determine the degree to which the test items are interrelated. In operational terms, are the scores on individual items intercorrelated? If the scores on the various items comprising a test intercorrelate positively, the test is homogeneous. Thus, homogeneity can be defined as consistency of performance over all items on a test (Loevinger, 1947; Anastasi, 1961). As a corollary, given a homogeneous test, knowing how a person performs on one item allows us to predict how he will perform on other items.

Note that the emphasis is on performance (scores), not on the content or format of the items. Thus, if item scores are intercorrelated positively, the test is homogeneous, regardless of the item content. Conversely, even if all items seemingly measure the same trait, but are not intercorrelated positively, the test is heterogeneous. The homogeneous-heterogeneous distinction is, of course, not a dichotomy but a continuum.

To some authors, the concept of homogeneity has a further implication, that of *unidimensionality*. Unidimensionality means that the test measures only one variable (trait) rather than a combination of variables. If a test is homogeneous, we might presume that all the items measured a common characteristic. However, it is conceivable that every item on a test might measure the same combination of traits and, thus, the items might be highly intercorrelated. Conversely, if a test is not homogeneous, the items, or certain subgroups of items, measure different characteristics. Therefore, homogeneity is a necessary, but not sufficient, characteristic of a test designed to measure a unitary trait.

Although we have defined homogeneity as consistency over all items on a test, the concept can be applied to subtests or clusters of items within the test. The appropriate level of analysis will depend upon the structure of the test and the purposes of the analysis. Thus, it is possible that a heterogeneous test may be composed of a number of subtests or clusters of items that are, within themselves, highly homogeneous.

Domain Sampling Theory

The concept of homogeneity can best be understood through an approach to testing called the *domain sampling theory* (Nunnally, 1967). This approach assumes that associated with every trait is a hypothetical domain of items that measure that particular construct. All the items in the domain are presumed to measure a "common core"; that is, each item, to some degree, measures the trait in question. To develop a test, we would randomly sample items[1] from this domain. Thus, any test can be conceived of as a random sample of items from the domain. And, by repeated sampling of items from the domain, we can develop any number of parallel tests that measure the construct of concern.

It would also be possible, at least theoretically, to determine the correlations between pairs of items in the domain (r_{ij}, where i and j represent individual items). We could also determine the average correlation ($\bar{r}_{ij}$) between the items in the domain. Since any test is a random sample of items from the domain, an individual's score on the test (item sample) will be an estimate of his true score (X_T).

By making certain other assumptions, the most important of which is that each item measures the common core to the same degree, it can be shown that the correlation between scores on any item and the true score equals the square root of the average interitem correlation:

$$r_{iT} = \sqrt{\bar{r}_{ij}} \tag{6.1}$$

where r_{iT} is the correlation between an item score and the true score and $\bar{r}_{ij}$ is the average interitem correlation. If we square both sides of this equation and substitute r_{ii} for r_{iT}^2 we obtain:

$$r_{ii} = \bar{r}_{ij} \tag{6.2}$$

where r_{ii} is the item reliability. In other words, the reliability of an item can be expressed in terms of the average intercorrelation between that item and every other item in the domain.

So far we have been talking about items; however, the same relationships hold for tests because in the domain sampling theory a test is a random sample of items. Thus we can also express Equation (6.2) as:

$$r_{XX} = \bar{r}_{XX'} \tag{6.3}$$

or the reliability of a test (r_{XX}) is equal to the average correlation ($\bar{r}_{XX'}$) of that particular test with all other randomly parallel tests drawn from the same domain. These equations form the basis of analyses of internal consistency. Note that this approach is based on specified theoretical notions rather than on the relationship between empirically constructed test forms.

[1]In practice, items are rarely selected randomly; rather they are selected to meet certain content and statistical requirements—for example, by their difficulty.

Measures of Homogeneity

A reliability coefficient was described as an index of consistency over time or forms of a test. Measures of homogeneity are indices of a test's internal consistency; they indicate the degree to which the test items intercorrelate. Both are summary statistics; however, they vary in their concern with the internal structure of a test. Homogeneity indices place primary emphasis on the internal structure, particularly the relationships between the items comprising the test, whereas reliability indices focus on the (correlation between) test scores.

Many measures of internal consistency are derived from one basic formula:

$$r_{kk} = \frac{k\bar{r}_{ij}}{1 + (k - 1)\bar{r}_{ij}} \tag{6.4}$$

where k is the number of items comprising the test. Equation (6.4) states that reliability can be expressed in terms of the average interitem correlation. As should be obvious from this formula, a test will be more homogeneous when the average interitem correlation is high—that is, when the items tend to measure the same trait.

Coefficient alpha   One well-known measure of homogeneity, which can be derived from the previous equation, is Cronbach's coefficient alpha (Cronbach, 1951):

$$r_{kk} = \frac{k}{k - 1}\left[1 - \frac{\Sigma s_i^2}{s_X^2}\right] \tag{6.5}$$

where k is the number of items on the test, Σs_i^2 is the sum of the variances of the item scores, and s_X^2 is the variance of the test scores (that is, the scores on all k items). Coefficient alpha can be interpreted as the average correlation between a test and another test of the same length drawn from the same domain.

Kuder-Richardson formulas   Another widely used index of homogeneity is the Kuder-Richardson formula 20 (Kuder and Richardson, 1937; Richardson and Kuder, 1939). This formula can be considered as a special case of coefficient alpha when the items are scored dichotomously (that is, either correct or incorrect). Although Kuder and Richardson developed several formulas, the most useful one is their formula 20 (K-R 20):

$$r_{kk} = \frac{k}{k - 1}\left[\frac{s_X^2 - \Sigma p_i q_i}{s_X^2}\right] \tag{6.6}$$

where

$$
\begin{aligned}
k &= \text{the number of items on the test} \\
s_X^2 &= \text{the variance of (total) scores on the test} \\
p_i &= \text{the proportion of people passing an item} \\
q_i &= 1 - p_i = \text{the proportion failing an item}
\end{aligned}
$$

Another formula (Kuder-Richardson 21) assumes all items to be of equal difficulty; as this assumption seldom holds, K-R 21 is less useful, even though computationally simpler. An example of the application of K-R 20 is given in Table 6.1.

TABLE 6.1   Computation of an index of internal consistency

As Coefficient Alpha and Kuder-Richardson formula 20 are equivalent with dichotomously scored items, we will illustrate the computation of K-R 20.

(1) Suppose that a ten-item test was administered to ten persons. Each item was scored either 1 or 0; 1 for a correct response, 0 for an incorrect response. The results were:

Subject	1	2	3	4	5	Item 6	7	8	9	10	X
A	1	1	1	1	1	1	1	1	1	1	10
B	1	1	1	1	1	1	1	1	1	0	9
C	1	1	1	1	1	1	1	0	1	0	8
D	1	1	1	1	1	1	1	1	0	0	8
E	1	1	1	1	1	0	1	0	0	1	7
F	1	1	1	1	1	1	0	1	0	0	7
G	1	1	1	1	1	0	0	1	0	0	6
H	1	1	1	1	1	0	0	0	1	0	6
I	1	1	1	1	0	1	0	0	0	0	5
J	1	1	1	0	0	1	0	0	0	0	4
Σ	10	10	10	9	8	7	5	5	4	2	70

$$\bar{X} = 7.00 \qquad s_x^2 = 3.00$$

(2) The proportion passing each item (p_i) is simply the number of people passing the item (n_{pi}) divided by the total number in the sample ($n_t = 10$). The number failing the item (q_i) equals $1 - p_i$. These data are shown below:

Item	1	2	3	4	5	6	7	8	9	10
n_{pi}	10	10	10	9	8	7	5	5	4	2
p_i	1.0	1.0	1.0	0.9	0.8	0.7	0.5	0.5	0.4	0.2
q_i	0.0	0.0	0.0	0.1	0.2	0.3	0.5	0.5	0.6	0.8
$p_i q_i$	.00	.00	.00	.09	.16	.21	.25	.25	.24	.16

The figure needed for the formula, $\Sigma p_i q_i$, is the product $p_i q_i$ summed over all ten items:

$$\Sigma p_i q_i = 0.00 + 0.00 + 0.00 + 0.09 + \cdots + 0.16 = 1.36$$

(3) Substituting in the formula

$$r_{kk} = \frac{k}{k-1}\left(\frac{s_x^2 - \Sigma p_i q_i}{s_x^2}\right) = \frac{10}{9}\left(\frac{3.00 - 1.36}{3.00}\right) = .61$$

If test items are heterogeneous, the value of r_{kk}, as computed by either coefficient alpha or K-R 20, will be lowered. The formula is also inappropriate for speeded tests, since item variances[2] will be accurate only if each item has been attempted by all persons. Inasmuch as these indices are based on data obtained from a single administration of a test, only errors attributable to short-term (that is, item-to-item) fluctuations in the individual are present. Thus the primary error source is noncomparability of items.

Factor analysis   An approach to determining the homogeneity of a test, factor analysis, is considered by some writers (e.g., Lumsden, 1961; Keats, 1967) to be the best method. Factor analysis is a statistical technique for determining the minimum number of constructs (factors) necessary to account for the interrelations among a group of variables. In terms of homogeneity, if one factor is sufficient to account for the variation in performance on all items, then the test is homogeneous; if more than one factor is necessary, then the test is heterogeneous in composition. As the process of factor analysis is complex and there are a variety of computational approaches to the analysis, we shall consider only the general logic of the procedure here.

To factor-analyze the item structure of a test we would start with a matrix showing the scores of each individual on each item. We would next construct a matrix of the intercorrelations among the items. This matrix of item intercorrelations would then be factor analyzed. This procedure, in essence, forms composites, or combinations, of scores and indicates how many composites (factors) are needed to explain the intercorrelations among the original variables—in this case, the items. If one common factor explains the correlations, the test is homogeneous; if more than one is needed, the test is heterogeneous. Finding more than one factor, though indicating that the test is not homogeneous, is not necessarily a disaster since we can develop subtests from clusters of items that are homogeneous, or eliminate items not relating to the major common factor, thus obtaining a pure (homogeneous) measure.

Hoyt reliability   Whether a test is internally consistent can also be determined through the framework of another statistical technique, analysis of variance (Hoyt, 1941). In this approach, the total variance in a set of test scores is apportioned to three sources—differences between people, differences between items, and differences due to the interaction between people and items. True score variance is estimated from the differences between people (mean square for persons) and measurement error variance from the person by item interaction. In analysis-of-variance terms, reliability is

$$r_{XX} = \frac{MS_{\text{persons}} - MS_{\text{persons} \times \text{items}}}{MS_{\text{persons}}} \qquad (6.7)$$

[2]The term Σpq in K-R 20 is the item variance component and is equivalent to Σs_i^2 in the coefficient alpha formula.

where $MS_{persons}$ is the mean square (variance) associated with differences between people and $MS_{persons \times items}$ is the mean square associated with the persons-by-items interaction. Rather than going into more detail, let it suffice to say that this reliability estimate is interpreted as any other internal consistency measure. The reader desiring further information and examples is referred to Hoyt's article or to Kerlinger (1973).

Other measures of homogeneity   A number of other measures of homogeneity have been proposed (see, e.g., Lumsden, 1961; Loevinger, 1947; Horst, 1966; Magnusson, 1967). However, no single measure seems to be generally accepted. One reason is the divergence of opinion as to an exact definition of homogeneity. Some authors consider a test homogeneous if the items are highly intercorrelated, whereas others add the requirement that the test must measure only one factor. Still others (e.g., Loevinger, 1947; Keats, 1967) make further restrictions. With such differences of opinion, it is no wonder that homogeneity is often relegated to limbo in discussions of measurement and testing.

Homogeneity and Psychological Theory

With the lack of agreement on the definition and an appropriate index of homogeneity, and with the neglect of the concept by many writers and test constructors, the reader might well ask why the emphasis here on the concept of homogeneity. The answer is quite simple: Homogeneous tests are necessary in order to develop an adequate psychological theory.

What constitutes a theory is a matter of debate among philosophers of science. Rather than discuss the technicalities of these arguments here, we shall adopt Kerlinger's definition.

> A theory is a set of interrelated constructs (concepts), definitions, and propositions that present a systematic view of phenomena by specifying relations among variables, with the purpose of explaining and predicting the phenomena. (Kerlinger, 1965, p. 11.)

The aspect of this definition that is central to our discussion is that a theory includes defined constructs. In psychological research constructs are frequently defined by, or inferred from, scores on psychological tests. Unless the tests used to define these theoretical constructs are homogeneous, we do not have "pure" measures of the constructs. Defining theoretical constructs and making inferences from test scores would be simpler if each test measured only one construct. Development of homogeneous tests would also probably reduce the number of constructs—and, consequently, measures (tests)—needed, and thus allow the development of psychological theory to proceed more rapidly.

One final point. We have discussed homogeneity as an aspect of consistency of measurement. Homogeneity, especially in its relation to the definition of psychological constructs, is also a crucial aspect of validity (see Chapter 8). Thus, in one sense, homogeneity stands between reliability and validity.

SOME PRACTICAL AND THEORETICAL ISSUES

Before leaving our discussion of the consistency of measurement, we shall consider several areas of practical and theoretical concern. First, we shall discuss some problems that arise when more than one score is available. Next, we shall briefly present several alternative approaches to reliability. Finally, we shall further consider the sources of error that can influence test scores.

Multiple Scores

Our discussion thus far has assumed that only one score was obtained from each administration of a test. Frequently, however, several scores are obtained from a single testing, usually by dividing the test into subtests or scales.[3] Whenever this is the case, we must be concerned with the reliability of each individual subtest. Furthermore, when we wish to compare an individual's performance on various subtests, we must be cognizant of problems that arise because we are comparing two unreliable measures. As a third special case we shall look at situations in which our focus is on changing performance, not on consistency of performance.

Reliability of subtests   Although many tests yield only one score, others provide scores on several subtests. These subtest scores may be combined into a total score or they may be treated separately. For example, the College Entrance Examination Board's Scholastic Aptitude Test (SAT) is composed of two separately scored subtests, a Verbal test and a Mathematical test. The American College Testing (ACT) program battery, in contrast, consists of four parts—English, Mathematics, Natural Sciences, and Social Sciences—and also has a Composite score, based on the average of the four part scores. In both of these tests, any item appears on only one subtest and each subtest is administered as a separate unit. On personality inventories items for any given scale are usually randomly distributed throughout the test. A given item may be scored on several scales, and a composite score is seldom computed.

A problem occurs when subtest scores are summed to yield a composite score, and inferences drawn from individual subtest scores. If reliability data are available for each subtest, there is no cause for concern. Too frequently, however, reliability data are available for the composite score but not for subtest scores. We cannot imply that the subtests will be as reliable as the composite score, since subtests contain fewer items. Because reliability is dependent on test length, subtest scores will almost certainly be less reliable than the composite score.[4] Thus, the test user

---

[3]Although the terms "subtest" and "scales" both refer to clusters of items measuring a particular domain, "subtest" generally refers to items that are administered as a separate integral unit and, in contrast, a "scale" usually refers to groups of items that are scored together, but not necessarily administered as a unit. Tests of maximal performance usually involve subtests, whereas scales are more common on typical performance measures. Scores on either are treated similarly in all statistical computations.

[4]Since a subtest is generally composed of items from only one domain, the homogeneity of a subtest will generally be higher than the homogeneity of the composite score, which may cover several domains.

must always check to see whether reliability estimates are reported for each subtest. If no estimate is reported, he cannot be sure that the subtest possesses acceptable reliability.

Reliability of differences   In many circumstances we want to compare an individual's performance on two tests or subtests. For example, an elementary school teacher may want to know whether a student scored higher on the arithmetic or language sections of an achievement battery. Or a counselor may want to compare a student's quantitative and verbal abilities.

Since any score is somewhat unreliable, differences between scores will also be unreliable. The reliability of the difference between two test scores can be estimated by the following formula (Mosier, 1951; Stanley, 1971):

$$r_{j-k} = \frac{r_{jj} + r_{kk} - 2r_{jk}}{2(1 - r_{jk})} \tag{6.8}$$

where r_{j-k} is the reliability of the difference score $(X_j - X_k)$; r_{jj} and r_{kk} are the reliabilities of tests j and k, respectively; and r_{jk} is the correlation of tests j and k.

Since the reliability of a difference score will be lower than the average subtest reliability, the standard error of measurement will be larger. Also, the range of difference scores generally will be less than the range of scores on either test. Consequently, an apparently large difference in scores may be attributable only to measurement error. Thus, extreme caution must always be used when interpreting differences between scores.

Measurement of change   Up to this point we have emphasized that inconsistency in performance is undesirable because it represents measurement error. In many situations, however, we are more interested in changes in performance than in consistency. For example, the goal of any educational program is to produce changes in students' knowledge and skills. Or we might study changes in attitudes and values as a consequence of college experiences or personality changes resulting from counseling or psychotherapy. In these instances, stability of performance would indicate that the treatment or experience had failed to produce the desired change.

Most of the measurement problems that arise when studying change are beyond the scope of this book (see Harris, 1963; Cronbach and Furby, 1970). The general flavor of the problems can be illustrated by one specific problem, the unreliability-invalidity dilemma (Bereiter, 1963). Briefly, the problem is as follows. The paradigm for measuring change is similar to that for the measurement of stability—a pretest is administered, followed after some time period by a posttest. In measuring change, however, there are two major differences from the stability paradigm. First, some specific treatment or experience, designed to produce change, is usually interposed between tests. Second, the variable of major interest is the amount of change in performance—that is, the change score.

In this situation, if a test is sensitive to changes in performance, the test-retest reliability will be low. That is, as the test becomes more effective in identifying valid changes in performance, change scores will become less reliable. Thus the requirements of high reliability and high validity seem to be incompatible in this situation. If we attempt to increase validity (sensitivity to changes) reliability will decrease; if we increase reliability, the test may become less sensitive to change. Hence, the unreliability-invalidity dilemma.[5] (See, also, Overall and Woodward, 1975).

A related question concerns the processes used by the test taker in responding to the test items. To measure change directly the pretest and the posttest should tap the same domain. Yet, the intervening treatment may change the nature of the performance. For example, suppose we ask a student how many different combinations of faces can appear when tossing two dice. Before he had been exposed to the laws of combinations and permutations he might arrive at the correct answer empirically, by listing all possible combinations. After studying combinations and permutations, however, he might solve the same problem by applying the appropriate formula. Here, the item has remained unchanged but the process used to solve it has shifted.

Bereiter (1963) has attempted to show that the unreliability-invalidity dilemma is a pseudodilemma by arguing that the requirement that the pretest and posttest measure the same thing is an unnecessary assumption. Whether his analysis will hold up remains to be seen. The dilemma does, however, illustrate some of the complexity of studying change. It also suggests that the traditional views of consistency and reliability may need to be expanded or altered to handle new problem areas.

Alternative Approaches

In our discussion of consistency we have, for the most part, followed the classical view, utilizing a model involving three components: true scores, obtained scores, and measurement error. Actually we have considered two parallel models: a theoretical model based on true scores and an empirical model based on obtained scores.

The major divergence between our presentation and the classical view was in the treatment of internal consistency. The traditional view conceives of the various reliability estimates as falling on a continuum from consistency over large samples of items (test forms) to consistency over individual items. However, because measures of internal consistency are, logically, directed at a different question (the homogeneity of the test), we have emphasized their distinctiveness rather than their similarity to other approaches to estimating reliability.

Referring to the classical view of reliability implies that there are alternative approaches. Because the classical approach has been quite successful, both as a conceptual tool and as a guide to test development, it still dominates most discussions of the consistency of psychological measurement. However, because certain problems present difficulties to the traditional view, reformulations are constantly being advanced.

---

[5]If all persons in the group changed by the same amount (an unlikely occurrence), we would have both high reliability and high validity.

Cattell   Cattell (1964) has proposed what he considers to be a more basic set of concepts, grouped under the generic term "consistency." In his view, consistency covers three major areas, each distinguishable by the sources of error involved. He suggested that the term reliability be restricted to consistency over time, homogeneity be used to refer to consistency over items, and transferability be used when refering to consistency over people. The third aspect, transferability, requires that a test score have the same meaning in various groups; for example, for subjects of different ages or from differing socioeconomic levels. That is, a reading comprehension test could be said to possess the property of transferability only if it actually measured reading comprehension in diverse groups of subjects. If it measured reading comprehension in one group and recall of learned materials in another, the scores would not be transferable.

Cattell further subdivided his major categories. For example, he distinguished between types of reliability coefficients wherein the major source of error can be attributed to different test administrators or administrations, differences in scoring, differences in the way subjects react to the test (for example, practice effects), or various combinations of these factors. Believing that there must be an operational procedure for identifying any concept, Cattell provided formulas and calculating procedures for each type of consistency estimate.

Reliability as generalizability   A second reformulation is that of Cronbach and his colleagues (Cronbach, Rajaratnam, and Gleser, 1963; Gleser, Cronbach, and Rajaratnam, 1965; Cronbach et al., 1972). Their approach considers any observation (such as a test score) as being but one sample from a universe of possible observations. The conditions under which an observation is obtained can vary along many dimensions; for example, any test is administered at only one of many possible times, is composed of a particular sample of items, is administered by one of many possible administrators, and so forth. The major measurement problems are to determine, first, what effects these various sources of variation have on the specific observation, and second, how accurately the universe score (ideal score or true score) can be estimated from the observation (obtained score). Because the basic concern is with making inferences about a universe from an observation, the primary problem of consistency is the generalizability of the meaning of an observation.

In their papers, the authors derive formulas and consider experimental designs for various types of studies, both of generalizability (reliability or consistency) and of decision making (validity). Their designs have the important advantages of estimating the magnitude of the various error effects as well as providing generalizability indices. One index, the ratio of the expected universe score variance to the expected observed score variance, is directly related to reliability as it is traditionally defined (r_{XT}). Their approach also emphasizes the fact that there is no one reliability for a test, that reliability is situation-specific. It also provides a unifying framework by viewing the varying approaches to reliability as aspects of the problem of generalizability across observations.

Reliability as the signal/noise ratio   Directly related to the previous view is another approach: considering reliability in terms of the signal-to-noise ratio (Cronbach, 1970; Stanley, 1971). In this approach, each bit of information is seen as containing some true information (signal) and some erroneous information (noise). In order to provide useful data, any set of observations should have a high signal/noise ratio— that is, provide much more valid than erroneous information. If we consider but a single test item, the signal/noise ratio will be low. However, as we cumulate items the ratio will increase because of two factors. First, since each item measures a common core, additional information is provided not only by the individual items but also by the interaction (covariation) among items, thereby increasing the true information (signal). Second, as errors of measurement are random, their effects tend to cancel each other out. Thus, as we have shown previously, adding items to a test will result in a more reliable measure.

An index of the signal/noise ratio, as it applies to the consistency of measurement is provided by the ratios:

$$\frac{r_{XX}}{1 - r_{XX}} \quad \text{or (equivalently)} \quad \frac{r_{TX}^2}{1 - r_{TX}^2}$$

Thus, if the reliability of a test were .90, the signal/noise ratio would be .90/ (1 − .90) = 9.0; that is, the ratio of true to error variance is 9:1. Note also, with highly reliable tests, a slight increase in reliability produces a large change in the signal/noise ratio; for example, an increase in reliability from .90 to .91 changes the signal/noise ratio from 9:1 to 10.1:1. In this view, attempting to improve the reliability of even highly reliable tests may be a worthwhile endeavor.

Mastery tests   One current trend in educational measurement is the development of mastery tests. In contrast to the usual approach to test construction, which seeks to maximize individual differences, mastery tests specify one particular level of performance as the mastery (passing) level and categorize individuals only as either attaining or not attaining this predetermined performance level. Furthermore, in most mastery learning situations, the goal is for every individual to attain mastery. If all individuals, in fact, do attain mastery, there will be no variation in scores between individuals within a group. And, since there is no variability, the usual reliability formulas are not applicable.

This, of course, presents a dilemma to the test constructor: How is he to evaluate the consistency of measurement of a mastery test? There have been attempts to develop reliability indices for mastery tests (see, e.g., Livingston, 1972) but there is no agreement as to the appropriate method. Until such indices are developed, whenever we use a mastery test we must very carefully scrutinize the test construction process to see that our possible error-producing sources are controlled.

Error Components

The feature that all conceptualizations of the consistency problem share is that they are based on a classification of error sources. Although consistency is concerned with variable errors, as contrasted to constant or systematic errors (cf. Helmstadter, 1964), there are, as was seen in the previous section, several possible classifications of variable errors. How these classifications are organized is the basic difference between the various approaches to consistency.

There is, however, another aspect of the error components problem, which has been referred to only tangentially—that is, the question of the relative effect of various error sources in determining the (obtained) test score. We have mentioned that error may be introduced by the examiner, by the circumstances of the test administration, by the item sample, by scorer unreliability, by fluctuations in the test taker's attention, and by a myriad of other factors. What has not been discussed is the relative contribution of each of these factors in particular testing situations.

Although test constructors and users have been aware of these error sources, there has been relatively little systematic study of the magnitude of their effects. Partially, this has been due to the complexity of the problem, the fact that a variety of sources error operate in any testing situation. Furthermore, the various sources of error interact with each other, necessitating highly sophisticated experimental designs to partial out the effects of the various error sources. Here, designs such as those presented by Cronbach et al. would seem to be a particularly valuable tool.

Another reason for the scarcity of experimental studies is that test constructors have succeeded quite well, at least in the areas of achievement and ability, in developing tests that measure with a high degree of consistency. By using item selection and standardization methods that eliminate or control the major sources of error, tests with reliabilities of .90 or higher have been developed. Thus, to invest time and resources in detailed studies of error effects is an unprofitable venture.

There has been intensive study in certain areas—for example, on the effects of varying time limits, guessing, characteristics of the test administrator, and scoring procedures. Personal characteristics of the test taker have also come under study— for example, systematic biases in responding when unsure of the correct response. Because of the design of these studies, the relative contribution of each error factor and the magnitude of its effect has generally not been determined. How serious a shortcoming this is depends on one's point of view. If the goal of these studies is seen as identifying error sources and the conditions under which they operate, so that appropriate control procedures can be built into the tests, the studies have been productive. On the other hand, if the goal is to obtain a precise specification of all variables effecting test scores, with an estimation of the magnitude of their effects, these studies leave much to be desired.

These studies also point up another problem; it is not always easy, in practice, to classify the effects of certain variables as producing constant or variable errors. Certain events, such as mistiming or improper directions, obviously introduce only variable errors. Other variables, such as the person's knowledge or skill in the relevant content area, usually produce constant effects. However, when the tests are separated widely in time, differential learning and/or forgetting will occur between testing sessions. This differential learning produces instability in scores (error) and also may signify a permanent change within the individual.

When personality characteristics are considered, the water becomes even murkier. Should test anxiety be considered as producing only random variability, and thus be classed as variable error? Or is it a pervasive influence that will effect performance in a predictable way, thus operating as a constant error? Or, perhaps, individuals vary in a cyclical fashion on such personality and temperamental dimensions. If so, we could identify at least three components in test scores: a constant component (responses that remain unchanged over repeated administrations of the test), systematic variation (responses that vary but in a systematic, predictable manner), and random variation (error). The typical reliability study, involving at most two administrations of a test, would not allow this systematic variation to be isolated.

A BRIEF SUMMARY

To summarize our discussion of consistency of measurement, we should raise four questions that a test user should always ask himself before employing a test.

What sorts of consistency data are most relevant for my purposes? Am I interested in the stability of scores over time, the equivalence between two test forms, or whether all items on the test measure the same construct? Since there is no one single reliability for a test, reliability will always be situation-specific. Thus this question can only be answered in terms of each specific situation.[6]

What do the available data say about the reliability of the test? Ideally, reliability should approach 1.00; realistically, we should demand at least as high values as obtained by other tests measuring the same domain. This information should be available in the test manual; if not, the test user must collect his own data.

What do the reliability data imply regarding variability in individual test scores? This information is provided by the standard error of measurement. Again, these values should be presented in the test manual. Here an important point to remember is that individual tests scores should always be thought of as ranges, or bands, not as exact points. How wide the band will be depends on the size of the standard error of measurement and, ultimately, on the reliability coefficient.

Is a reliable test necessarily a useful test? No, for our main concern should always be with validity. However, reliability is a necessary, though not sufficient, prerequisite for validity.

[6]When analyzing group differences, rather than individual scores, error in individual scores will not be so crucial, as we will be averaging over many observations. Consequently, we can often tolerate a lower level of reliability when focusing on group differences than when interpreting scores of individuals.

7

CRITERION-RELATED VALIDITY

One very common use of tests is to predict future behavior. For example, scholastic aptitude tests are used to predict academic success in college and professional schools, aptitude and ability tests are used to predict job performance, and personality inventories have been used to predict who will have automobile accidents. In each of these situations the function of the test is to predict an individual's performance in some qualitatively different situation. The performance being predicted is called the criterion, hence the designation criterion-related validity.

Although we sometimes make a prediction to test a theoretical hypothesis, more often we are predicting some socially relevant outcome; that is, using the test to help make some practical decision. In our previous examples, the decisions would be which students to admit, whom to hire, and what insurance premium rate to assess. In each situation, the more accurately we can predict the outcome (criterion), the more useful the test will be.

The fact that these predictions can drastically alter a person's life makes an understanding of the process of criterion-related validity essential to any one using tests. The importance of this topic is further attested to by the fact that several federal laws and court decisions (e.g., *Griggs,* et al., *v. Duke Power Company; United States,* et al., *v. Georgia Power Company*) have made it very clear that psychological tests are an acceptable part of any selection process *only* if it can be demonstrated that the test scores do, in fact, predict preformance on some important component of the job. That is, a test's criterion-related validity must be demonstrated if the test is to be used as part of a selection process.

In this chapter we shall discuss the processes involved in determining the criterion-related validity of a test (or other measure). We shall illustrate the procedure in which only one predictor is used; multiple predictors will be discussed in a later chapter. We shall also emphasize the selection situation, referring only briefly to the more complex placement situation.

The Paradigm

A general paradigm for investigating criterion-related validity can be identified, regardless of the nature of the test and criterion. This procedure involves establishing the relationship between scores on the test and the criterion:

$$\text{TEST} \longrightarrow \text{CRITERION}$$

Because the test predicts the criterion, criterion-related validity is sometimes referred to as predictive validity. And, since determining criterion-related validity always involves collection of empirical data on the relationship between test scores and the criterion measure, some writers refer to it as empirical validity.

The designation criterion-related validity emphasizes the fact that the fundamental concern is with criterion performance. We are interested in the test scores because they predict some important external behavior. Thus the content of the test is of secondary importance, and the test items need bear no obvious relation to the criterion. What is vital is that the test has empirical validity—that the test scores can, in fact, predict criterion performance.

One further distinction should be made, that between predictive and concurrent validity (APA, 1954). *Predictive validity* refers to situations in which criterion data are collected at some future time:

$$\text{TEST} \xrightarrow{\text{time}} \text{CRITERION}$$

In other words, test scores actually *predict* criterion scores. In *concurrent validity* studies, however, the test scores and criterion data are collected at the same point in time. Here, since criterion scores are already available, the purpose is to determine whether test scores can be substituted for actually collecting the criterion data. For example, can scores on a personality inventory, administered by a clerk, be used in place of an examination by a psychiatrist to determine the degree of psychopathology? Obviously such a substitution would be valuable only if (1) there was a high degree of relationship between the test scores and the criterion measure (in our example, between a diagnosis made from the test and a psychiatrist's diagnosis) and if (2) use of the test is more efficient, or less expensive, than actually collecting the criterion data. Hence, concurrent validity is logically different from predictive validity in that it involves a substitution of the test for the criterion rather than a prediction of a criterion from the test. However, inasmuch as both are basically concerned with the empirical relationship between test scores and the criterion, they both may be considered as aspects of criterion-related validity (APA, 1966, 1974).

Predictive Validity and Decision Making

Implicit in the concept of criterion-related validity is the idea that tests are used as part of a decision-making process. When a scholastic aptitude test is used to predict college grades, the decision is whether to admit the prospective student; when a test is administered to a job applicant, the decision is whether he should be hired. In each situation there is a decision to be made, one that will be influenced by the individual's test score. The test will be valid to the degree that it improves the effectiveness of the decision making.

There are several aspects of the decision-making situation that merit specific attention. First, and most important, a decision must be made regarding the treatment of individuals. If every individual received the same treatment (for example, if all students were allowed to enter college or all applicants were hired), there would be no need for testing. Only when a decision must be made can a test provide any useful information.

Second, the relative weight or influence of test scores, as opposed to other sources of information, in determining the course of action, may vary tremendously between situations. In certain situations, decisions may be made solely on the basis of test scores; in others, test scores may be invoked only when a decision cannot be reached using other data. In every case, however, the relative weight given test scores in the decision-making process should be determined empirically, by gathering evidence regarding the unique contribution test scores make to decision-making accuracy. The point of view taken in this book is that *the proper measure of a test's criterion related validity is its contribution to increased prediction (decision-making) accuracy.*

Third, in each situation there is some outcome (the criterion), specified or implicit, that is regarded as the "desirable" outcome. The goal of the decision-making process is to select or assign individuals so as to maximize performance on this criterion. Because the validity of a test is judged by its relationship to the criterion, if the criterion measure does not adequately reflect the desired outcome, the decision-making process will be less effective. However, this decreased effectiveness will be attributable to deficiencies in the criteria, not in the test. For example, consider the use of grades as a criterion of success in college. If a test predicted grades accurately, it would increase the proportion of students admitted who would obtain high grades.[1] The test would not select students with other desired characteristics, unless these characteristics were correlated with grade-getting ability.

In most decision-making situations, criterion performance, not test scores, are of ultimate interest. If, however, our primary interest is to evaluate a test, criteria are important because they indicate the types of behavior the test measures and suggest practical uses for the test.

Finally, validity always involves decision-making accuracy for groups. Thus, logically, statements about the validity of a test always refer to a set of scores, not an individual score. Although inferences can be made about individual scores, the errors in individual predictions may be quite large. But inferences regarding the effectiveness of a test for groups of persons can be made with reasonable accuracy.

Criteria

If a test is designed to predict performance in an area, some standard or measure of performance must be identified; this is the criterion. For instance, what is the criterion of success as a college student? The most common approach is to use grade-point-average; but grades are only one, and not necessarily the best, criterion of academic success. Other criteria are also possible, such as amount learned (which is not necessarily the same as the amount possessed at the end of a given course), ability to apply what one has learned, ability to evaluate knowledge critically, ability to learn by oneself, or development of positive attitudes toward education and learning.

Thus talking about *the* criterion is an oversimplification, as several writers have pointed out (see, e.g., Dunnette, 1963; Ghiselli, 1956b; Weitz, 1961). In most situations multiple criteria are desirable. Choosing one criterion is simpler, but neglects much valuable information. How to combine several criteria into a meaningful composite, however, is a knotty problem. If the various criteria are highly related, using a combination of criteria will not improve decision making greatly, since all criteria are measuring essentially the same behavior. Conversely, if the various criteria are not interrelated, combining them may produce a hodgepodge since they measure different things.

Ghiselli (1956b) has also pointed out two other problems besides the problem of combining criteria. One revolves around the fact that criteria may change over time. What is a good measure of success at the present time may not be a good measure at some future time (see, e.g., MacKinney, 1967). For example, to succeed as a physician a person must be able to master formal course work; later his success is judged by his effectiveness in treating patients. The other problem relates to individual differences. Two persons may perform the same job in quite different ways, yet be rated as equally successful. For example, one football receiver may get

---

[1]This is an oversimplification, since several studies (e.g., Hills, 1963; Webb, 1959) have shown that instructors do not always change their grading standards to correspond to changes in the ability level of their students.

free by utilizing his speed, another by deceptive moves. Or one student may get high grades because he grasps material easily, whereas another succeeds only through long hours of studying. The psychologist analyzing job performance is thus faced with the dilemma of either accepting several methods of performance as being equally appropriate, thus complicating his methodology, or choosing one method and ignoring other approaches.

Characteristics of criterion measures   Strictly speaking, a distinction can be made between a criterion and a criterion measure (see, e.g., Astin, 1964). A criterion is the global concept of successful performance, what Astin calls the *conceptual criterion*. But, as in all measurement, this conceptual concept must be identified by an operational measure that can be utilized in determining the validity of a test. Thus, the conceptual criterion might be success in college, the criterion measure grade-point-average; the conceptual criterion success as a salesman, the criterion measure dollar volume of sales. In short, even an ideal conceptual criterion will be useless unless an adequate measure of the criterion behavior is available.

The most important characteristic of a criterion measure is its *relevance*. A criterion measure must actually reflect the important facets of the conceptual criterion. Thus grade-point-average will be a relevant measure of college success only if the characteristics considered indications of college success are reflected in the student's grade-point-average. Or, output will be a relevant criterion measure of job performance only if it directly reflects the individual's skill rather than some characteristic of the work situation. Establishing the relevance of a criterion measure involves rationally judging whether relevant dimensions of the conceptual criterion are represented by the criterion measure.

A criterion measure also should be *reliable*. The reason is obvious; if criterion performance varies from time to time or situation to situation, it cannot consistently relate to other measures, including predictors. The implications for selection of criterion measures are twofold: (1) factors that introduce measurement error must be controlled, for they influence criterion measures as well as predictors; and (2) criterion reliability can often be increased by obtaining a larger sample of behavior and/or sampling over several occasions.

A third requirement is *freedom from bias*. This problem is particularly crucial when the criterion measure is a rating. If a rater assigns a criterion score on bases other than actual performance, such as his general opinion of the worker, the criterion score will be biased. If judgmental criterion measures must be used, the best control against bias is to provide specific, concrete directions and descriptions of the characteristics to be rated; in short, to make the rating procedure as objective as possible.

Another common source of bias is criterion contamination. *Criterion contamination* refers to the situation in which a person's criterion score is influenced by a rater's knowledge of his predictor score. Suppose that we want to determine whether an intelligence test predicts English grades. If the teacher assigning the grade knows the students' IQs, her evaluation of students may be influenced by this knowledge. For example, a student may receive a lower grade because the teacher thinks, on the basis of his IQ, that he should have done better and thus should be reprimanded by a lower grade.

Criterion contamination can be avoided by not allowing the person making the criterion rating to see the predictor scores. Predictor scores can be collected and filed, criterion ratings collected, then related to the criterion. This procedure would ensure independence of predictor and criterion scores.

Finally, other things being equal, the best criterion measure is the one that has the most *practical advantages*—that is, one that is the simplest to use, and is readily available and inexpensive. It should be emphasized, however, that this is generally the least important consideration; relevance, reliability, and freedom from bias are more crucial determiners of the adequacy of a criterion measure.

Types of criterion measures   A wide variety of variables can be used as criterion measures. The most obvious are direct measures of output, performance, or persistence. In industrial and business settings, volume of sales, production, salary, advancement, number of customers serviced, or tenure on the job may be used. In academic settings, the criterion measure might be grades, level of education attained, or graduation from a program. In other situations, the criterion measure may be performance on a test. Examples include course examinations, tests given at the end of training programs, and tests to certify competency in certain professions (for example, CPA exams and tests in medical specialties). Where objective measures of output or performance are unavailable or inappropriate, ratings by supervisors or peers are often used as criterion measures. In other situations, the criterion measure might be membership in a defined group. For example, intelligence tests frequently use an age differentiation criterion; that is, items are considered valid if the proportion of children passing the item increases with age. Interest inventories are considered valid if they differentiate between persons in various occupations; personality tests if they differentiate between people with various syndromes; aptitude tests if they differentiate between successful and unsuccessful workers. Finally, statistically derived criteria, such as factor loadings (see Chapter 9), may be used.

Criterion measures can also be classified in many other ways. For example, criterion measures may represent qualitatively differing groups, such as occupations, or be on a continuum, such as output measures and grade averages. Or criterion measures may be naturally available indices, such as production records or tenure, or they may be artificially devised, such as course examinations. Then, too, criterion measures vary along an objectivity-subjectivity dimension from performance in athletic events to ratings of broadly defined traits. And, finally, criterion data may be provided by the individual himself, through his performance or a self-rating, or may be made by an external rater or judge.

A final note of caution. A major problem in test validation is failing to appreciate the fact that there is no such thing as *the* criterion. This implies that the validation process should relate test scores to a variety of criteria in a variety of situations. The caveat to the test user, therefore, is to consider carefully the criterion measures used in validating a test and to be aware of the limitations that use of these particular criteria impose on the interpretation of the test scores.

METHODS FOR DETERMINING CRITERION-RELATED VALIDITY

We now turn to a discussion of methods for assessing criterion-related validity. Four methods will be presented in detail: validity coefficients, group separation, decision-making accuracy, and utility. These methods all provide a quantitative index of the relationship between the test and the criterion. When presenting the various techniques, we shall use a selection situation with one predictor as an illustration. Although this is an unnatural and overly simplified situation, hopefully it will clarify the underlying logic of the validation process. More complex situations will be illustrated in Chapter 9.

Validity Coefficients

The most frequently used method for establishing the validity of a test is to correlate test scores with a criterion. The procedure involves five steps: (1) selecting an appropriate group to study; (2) administering the predictor test; (3) applying the relevant treatment; (4) collecting the criterion data; and (5) correlating test and criterion scores. In diagrammatic form:

$$\text{TEST} \text{------(TREATMENT)------ CRITERION}$$
$$\uparrow\text{------------ Correlation ------------}\uparrow$$

The resultant correlation, called a *validity coefficient* (r_{XY}), is a measure of how accurately criterion (Y) performance can be predicted from test (X) scores.

Since a validity coefficient is a correlation coefficient, any factor that influences a correlation coefficient will affect a validity coefficient. Two factors are particularly relevant. First, if the two variables are not linearly related, the magnitude of the correlation will be underestimated. Thus we should always determine whether the predictor and criterion are linearly related before computing a validity coefficient.[2] Second, the magnitude of a correlation depends on the range of individual differences. Thus anything that restricts the range of predictor or criterion scores will reduce the validity coefficient (see pp. 75–77).

An example   Suppose that a high school mathematics teacher finds that a certain proportion of his students have trouble in first-year algebra. He would like to identify these students so that they could take a different math course. He decides to run a study to see whether he can differentiate between students who experience varying degrees of success in algebra. Because he thinks that students who have

[2]There are methods for determining the correlation when the relationship is not linear (see, e.g., Hays, 1973).

trouble in algebra lack the ability to reason mathematically, he develops a short (eight-item) test of mathematical reasoning, which he administers to all students the first day of class. To avoid contaminating his data, he does not score the tests, but files them away for further use. At the end of the term, after grades have been assigned, he scores the tests. He decides to compute a validity coefficient to see whether the test is a valid predictor.

The scatterplot showing the relation between test scores and algebra grades is shown in Table 7.1 (step 1). Scores on the math reasoning test serve as the predictor; the criterion is algebra grades. For his analysis, he assigns a numerical value to each grade (from 4 for an A to 0 for an F). He then computes the necessary summary statistics (step 2) and the validity coefficient (step 3). He finds a value of .60 for his validity coefficient. Since the correlation is positive and moderately high, his belief that mathematical reasoning ability may be an important determiner of grades in algebra is confirmed. (Obviously, however, other factors are involved, since the correlation is not perfect.)

TABLE 7.1   Calculation of a validity coefficient

(1) A high school math teacher wants to determine whether scores on a short mathematical reasoning test predict grades in algebra (see text). The distribution of scores is:

		1	2	3	4	5	6	7	8
	A					2	8	7	7
Algebra	B			1	3	14	20	8	2
Grade	C	4	8	26	42	29	9	2	
(Y)	D	8	11	8	6	3			
	F	8	1	1	1	1			

Mathematic Reasoning Test (X)

(2) Coding grades on a five-point scale ($A = 4$, $B = 3$, etc.), the summary statistics for these data are:

$$\bar{X} = 4.30 \quad s_X = 1.79 \quad \bar{Y} = 2.15 \quad s_Y = 1.22 \quad \Sigma XY = 2534 \quad n = 240$$

(3) The validity coefficient will be the correlation between the scores on the mathematics reasoning test and the algebra grades. Using Equation (3.8c),

$$r_{XY} = \frac{\Sigma XY/n - (\bar{X})(\bar{Y})}{s_X s_Y} = \frac{2534/240 - (4.30)(2.15)}{(1.79)(1.22)} = 0.60$$

(4) The value $r_{XY} = .60$ is the validity coefficient. One interpretation is that 36 percent (i.e., $r^2 = .60^2 = .36$) of the differences in algebra grades are predictable from scores on the math reasoning test.

Interpretation of r_{XY}   There are several ways to interpret and evaluate validity coefficients. Probably the most common method is comparative: to use the test with the highest validity coefficient. Thus, if in a given situation, the validity coefficients are .40 for Test A and .50 for Test B, Test B would be adopted because it is more valid under these circumstances. What is considered a "good" validity, thus, will depend on the specific situation.

Validity coefficients can also be interpreted in terms of percent of variance in the criterion accounted for by differences in predictor scores. The percent of variance accounted for is obtained by squaring the correlation coefficient. Thus, if $r_{XY} = .60$, as in our example, we can say that 36 per cent of the variance (that is, $.60^2 = .36 = 36$ percent) is shared by the two measures, or that 36 percent of the variance in criterion scores is attributable to variations in predictor scores. Note that r_{XY} must be .71 if half of the variance in the criterion is to be accounted for by predictor scores.

Brogden (1946, 1949) has shown that when both predictor and criterion scores are expressed as standard scores, r_{XY} can be interpreted by comparing the average criterion score made by persons selected by the test to the average criterion score made by selecting the same number of persons on the basis of their criterion scores. To illustrate, suppose there are 100 applicants for 40 positions. The ideal procedure would be to allow all 100 applicants to work for a period of time, collect a measure of their performance, and retain the 40 best workers—"best" meaning those obtaining the highest criterion score. The average criterion score of these 40 workers would obviously be the highest average obtainable by any combination of 40 workers. But since this procedure is usually unfeasible, instead we administer a test and hire the 40 applicants who score highest on the test. The validity coefficient for this test will equal the ratio of the gain in average criterion performance of the 40 persons selected by the test (over the average of all workers) to the gain in average performance obtained by selecting 40 workers on the basis of the criterion performance itself. Thus if $r_{XY} = .50$, the workers selected by the test will have an average criterion score gain half that of a group selected on the basis of criterion scores. If $r_{XY} = 1.00$, the two groups are identical.

A fourth method of interpretation involves prediction errors. Before discussing this approach, we shall first introduce an example showing how to determine predicted criterion scores.

Predicted criterion scores   One advantage of the correlational approach is that knowing an individual's test score and the validity coefficient, a prediction of his expected criterion score can be made. The procedure is based on the fact the relationship summarized by a validity coefficient can also be described by a straight line, called a *regression line,* that best fits the data points. Such a line can be described by a *regression equation* of the form:

$$Y' = a + b_{YX}X \tag{7.1}$$

where Y' is the predicted criterion score; a is an intercept constant, to correct for differences in the means; b_{YX} is the slope, or regression constant, which indicates the rate of change in Y as a function of changes in X; and X is the score on the predictor. An example, using the previous data, is given in Table 7.2.

A regression equation can be calculated from a given set of data, then applied to individuals who are similar to the group used to derive the equation. For example, the equation derived in Table 7.2 could be applied to future classes. Then, knowing a student's score on the math reasoning test, we could predict his algebra grade and decide whether he should enroll in algebra or another class.

One further clarification is needed. What is predicted (Y') is the average criterion score made by persons with the same predictor score (X). The actual criterion scores of people with the same predictor score will vary; some people will obtain criterion scores higher than the average, and some lower. The discrepancy between actual and predicted criterion scores will be prediction error. Unless $r_{XY} = 1.00$, there will be some error in each prediction.

Prediction errors   The magnitude of the prediction errors is indicated by the *standard error of estimate* (s_{est}); that is,

$$s_{est} = s_Y \sqrt{1 - r_{XY}^2} \tag{7.4}$$

The standard error of estimate is the standard deviation of the distribution of prediction errors. If we have both predicted (Y') and actual (Y) criterion scores, we can obtain a measure of prediction error from the difference between these scores ($E = Y - Y'$). If we then plot the distribution of these error scores for all individuals in the group, the standard deviation of the resulting distribution will be the standard error of estimate.

The standard error of estimate can be interpreted like any other standard deviation. The probability is .68 that the actual criterion score will fall within $\pm 1 s_{est}$ of the predicted criterion score and .95 that the actual criterion score will fall within $\pm 1.96 s_{est}$ of the predicted criterion score. An example is presented in step 4 of Table 7.2.

TABLE 7.2   Predicted criterion scores and prediction error

(1)   To derive a regression equation, we first must determine the values of the two constants. Using raw scores, these formulas are:

$$b_{YX} = r_{XY} s_Y / s_X \tag{7.2}$$

and

$$a = \bar{Y} - b_{YX} \bar{X} \tag{7.3}$$

(2)   We shall use as an example the data from Table 7.1:

$\bar{X} = 4.30$ $s_X = 1.79$ $\bar{Y} = 2.15$ $s_Y = 1.22$ $r_{XY} = 0.60$

Substituting these values in the equations and solving, we obtain

TABLE 7.2 (continued)

$$b_{YX} = .60(1.22/1.79) = 0.41$$
$$a = 2.15 - (4.30)(.41) = 0.39$$

(3) Substituting these values into the regression equation, we find that

$$Y' = 0.39 + 0.41X$$

This equation can be used to obtain a predicted criterion score (Y') for any predictor score. For example, suppose that a student scores 6 on the math reasoning test. His expected algebra grade would be

$$Y' = 0.39 + 0.41(6) = 2.85$$

or, most probably, a B grade.

(4) For prediction errors we apply Equation (7.4) for the standard error of estimate, and obtain

$$s_{est} = s_Y\sqrt{1 - r_{XY}^2} = 1.22\sqrt{1 - .60^2} = 0.98$$

That is, the standard error of estimate is 0.98 points. We know that a person scoring 6 on the test has a predicted algebra grade of 2.85 (see item 3 above). The 95 percent confidence limits around this predicted score are as follows:

$$Y' \pm 1.96s_{est} = 2.85 \pm 1.96(.98) = 0.91\text{--}4.79$$

Thus, although our best estimate of his grade is 2.85 (a B), because our prediction is not perfect, the 95 percent confidence limits will extend over a broad range—from 0.91 to 4.79 or from an A to a D.* In fact, about all that we can say, using these confidence limits, is that it is very improbable that he will fail the course.

*In this example, as sometimes happens in practice, the theoretical confidence limits exceed the range of possible scores.

The value $1 - r_{XY}^2$, the ratio s_{est}^2/s_Y^2, and other variations (such as $1 - \sqrt{1 - r_{XY}^2}$) provide other methods of interpreting a validity coefficient. These indices all estimate reduction in prediction errors resulting from knowledge of the validity coefficient—that is, the degree of improvement over predicting the mean criterion value for all persons, regardless of their test performance.

Evaluation The correlational approach to validity has several advantages. It provides an index, the validity coefficient, which summarizes the relationship between the predictor and criterion over the entire range of scores. It allows us to predict an expected criterion score for each individual through the regression equation. Validity coefficients are also widely used, thus providing comparability between studies. Moreover, most of the analyses involving multiple scores are based on the correlational model.

There are also some distinct disadvantages. If the predictor-criterion relationship is not linear, special correlational methods must be applied. The greatest disadvantage in practical situations is that, with the exception of Brogden's procedure, it does not provide an index of the decision-making accuracy resulting from using the test. As will be shown later, the usefulness of a test, with given validity, will vary depending on the proportion of applicants selected and the proportion of persons judged successful. Thus, no index of decision-making accuracy is directly derivable from a validity coefficient.

Group Separation

A second method for determining validity is to see whether predictor scores differentiate groups defined by their criterion performance. As an illustration, we shall use our previous example and divide students into two groups: those who succeed in algebra (received an A, B, or C) and those who do not (received a D or F grade). Then we could compare the test scores of these two groups to determine whether there is a statistically significant difference in their test scores. In other words, do successful students obtain significantly higher test scores than unsuccessful students? This procedure is illustrated in Table 7.3. As can be seen, the two groups do have significantly different test scores.

TABLE 7.3   Validity by group separation

(1)   Using data from the previous example (Table 7.1), we shall define two subgroups: successful (those who obtained an A, B, or C in algebra) and unsuccessful (those who obtained a D or F). The relevant summary statistics are:

SUCCESSFUL $\bar{X}_s = 4.79$ $s_s^2 = 2.43$ $n_s = 192$
UNSUCCESSFUL $\bar{X}_u = 2.40$ $s_u^2 = 1.70$ $n_u = 48$

These values refer to the test scores of the two groups.

(2)   To find whether there is a statistically significant difference in the test scores of the two groups we shall use the t statistic. This procedure compares the difference in means to a measure of sampling error (see, e.g., Hays, 1973). Applied to our example:

$$ t = \frac{\bar{X}_s - \bar{X}_u}{\sqrt{(s_s^2/n_s) + (s_u^2/n_u)}} = \frac{4.79 - 2.40}{\sqrt{(2.43/192) + (1.70/48)}} = 9.19 $$

The table of significant t values indicates that this large a difference would occur by chance less than one time in a thousand ($p < .001$). Thus we can say that the test scores of successful and unsuccessful students were different; that is, the math reasoning test does predict success in algebra.

A problem with using group separation to indicate validity is that the statistical significance of the difference between group means is a function of the size of the groups. As group size increases, smaller differences in average scores become statistically significant. With large groups, as are often used in testing, small differences between average scores often will be statistically significant, but the test may be of little practical value in discriminating between groups. To avoid this shortcoming, we could determine the amount of overlap between the two distributions. Two possible indices are the percent of scores in one group that exceed the mean score of the other group and the percentage of area common to the two distributions (Tilton, 1937). To avoid misinterpretation, means, standard deviations, and a measure of overlap should be reported, as should the statistical significance of the difference in mean predictor scores. A statistically significant mean difference may or may not indicate a difference large enough to be of practical significance. However, if test scores do not discriminate between criterion-defined groups, the test is not valid.

Decision-making Accuracy

A decision maker is always interested in the accuracy of his decisions; he strives to increase correct decisions and decrease incorrect decisions. Therefore, one way to evaluate a decision maker's performance is to determine the proportion of his decisions that are correct (see Meehl and Rosen, 1955). Analogously, when tests are used as the basis for decision making, an index of their effectiveness is the proportion of correct decisions made. The most effective (valid) test is the one that produces the greatest proportion of correct decisions.

Indices of decision-making accuracy   To derive an index of decision-making accuracy, we must classify test scores into two or more independent categories, similarly classify the criterion data, and then compare the two sets of data. The division of criterion scores will be in terms of performance—for example, success or failure, acceptable or unacceptable. The division of test scores will be in terms of score levels. Actually, our classification of test scores is really in terms of predicted outcomes—for example, predict success versus predict failure—or in terms of the decision to be made—hire or not hire, admit or reject. Thus we will be comparing a predicted outcome to the actual outcome.

In the simplest case, where both predictor and criterion data are dichotomized, there will be four groups: persons predicted to be successful who were successful, persons predicted to be successful who were unsuccessful, persons predicted to be unsuccessful who succeeded, and persons predicted to be unsuccessful who were unsuccessful. In diagrammatic form:

Criterion Performance

Test Prediction:	Failure (−)	Success (+)
Success (+)	(A) MISS	(B) HIT
Failure (−)	(C) HIT	(D) MISS

We shall call correct decisions (predictions) hits and incorrect ones misses.[3]

[3]Other labels (such as false positives and false negatives) are sometimes used to identify these various groups. However, since they are adopted from other fields, they often confuse more than clarify.

One obvious index of decision-making accuracy would be the proportion of the decisions made that were correct (P_{CT}). In other words, the index would be the ratio of correct decisions (hits) to total decisions:

$$P_{CT} = \frac{\text{Hits}}{\text{Hits} + \text{Misses}} = \frac{B + C}{A + B + C + D} = \frac{\text{Hits}}{N} \tag{7.5}$$

where A, B, C, and D are the numbers of persons classified in each cell of the decision table, and N is the number of decisions made. This ratio (P_{CT}) can be used as an index of the validity of the test when validity is defined as decision-making accuracy.

Two aspects of this index deserve special note. First, the index takes into account all decisions made. Second, both correct and incorrect decisions are weighted equally. Note, however, that differential weighting of categories could be handled by assigning difference values (weights) to correct and incorrect decisions.

In some situations, another index of accuracy may be more appropriate. For example, an employer typically is concerned only with the success or failure of applicants he hires and not with the fate of persons he does not hire. A college admissions officer, too, is more concerned with the potential success of students who are admitted than of those students not admitted. In these situations, a more appropriate index of decision-making effectiveness will be the *positive hit* ratio (P_{CP}); the proportion of those selected who will be successful:

$$P_{CP} = \frac{B}{A + B} = \frac{\text{Number successful}}{\text{Number selected}} \tag{7.6}$$

This is the appropriate validity index when the goal of the selection procedure is to maximize the proportion of people selected who will be successful. Although it is recognized that incorrect decision will be made by not accepting some people who would have been successful, this category of decisions is considered less important and given no weight in the computation of this index.

Setting cutting scores   Thus far we have assumed that the test score that divided the acceptable (predicted successful) and unacceptable (predicted unsuccessful) groups was known. To determine the validity of a test, in terms of decision-making accuracy, however, we must find the optimal cutting score. This will be the test (predictor) score that separates the groups so as to produce the maximum number of correct decisions. When this is done, another statistic becomes particularly relevant: the selection ratio. The *selection ratio* is the proportion of applicants selected—that is, the number of persons selected divided by the number of applicants. Note that as selection becomes more stringent (that is, as a higher cutting score is used), the selection ratio becomes lower.

An illustration using various cutting scores is shown in Table 7.4, the data being that used in all examples in this chapter. Several trends can be noted from the data: (1) As the cutting score is set higher, the selection ratio decreases. This follows directly from the definition of the selection ratio. (2) As the cutting score is set higher, positive hits increase. In other words, there is an inverse relation between the selection ratio and positive hits. (3) As the selection ratio decreases, total correct decisions increase and then decrease.[4]

If our goal were to maximize positive hits, the cutting score would be set as high as possible. Using a stringent cutting score, however, results in a lower selection ratio; thus fewer persons are accepted. In the example, if we used a cutting score of 6, all applicants selected would be successful; however, 74 percent of the students would be rejected. If no set number of persons are to be selected, a low selection ratio presents no problem. If, however, there are a certain number of positions to be filled, as is often the case, there are two alternatives. The cutting score can be lowered, consequently decreasing validity, or we can attempt to attract a larger pool of applicants, thus increasing the number of acceptable applicants without lowering the cutting score or decreasing validity.

If the goal of the selection process were to maximize the total number of correct decisions, the optimal cutting score would fall in the middle range of scores. The reason is, of course, that as the cutting score is raised, the number of persons who would be successful but who are rejected increases, and, as the cutting score is lowered, the number of accepted persons who are unsuccessful increases. Only in the middle ranges of scores are these two outcomes balanced.

As with our discussion of prediction equations, the results obtained for the validity study will be applied to future situations. That is, we obtain data from one sample and apply the data to future samples. To the extent that future samples are unlike the validation sample, the results will not generalize.

Evaluation   The main advantage of the decision-making accuracy (selection efficiency) approach is that it closely parallels the ''real-life'' situation. Although a validity coefficient provides an index of the relationship between predictor and criterion scores throughout the entire score range, the decision-making accuracy approach is concerned with effectiveness at a specific decision point. Thus the model is a closer representation of ''reality'' than the correlational model. Other advantages include its computational simplicity and the ease of understanding.

A frequent criticism of this approach is that, due to the errors of measurement, it is unfair to people whose scores fall just below the cutting line. However, perhaps unfortunately, in any practical situation a select-reject line must be drawn at some point. A more telling criticism is that using groups (for example, accept-reject) rather than a continuum of scores reduces precision. The reply to this criticism would be that the precision of the regression approach is a false precision, because the critical question is accuracy at the decision point, not throughout the score range.

---

[4]These relationships hold when there is a positive correlation between predictor and criterion; they may not hold with other distributions.

TABLE 7.4   Decision-making accuracy using various cutting scores

(1)   The problem is to determine the validity of the math reasoning test as a predictor of algebra grades, using the decision-making accuracy paradigm. Again we shall consider obtaining an A, B, or C grade as successful performance and D or F grades as unsuccessful performance. Our data are as follows:

PREDICTOR (TEST) SCORE	CRITERION PERFORMANCE (ALGEBRA GRADE) SUCCESSFUL	UNSUCCESSFUL	TOTAL
8	9	0	9
7	17	0	17
6	37	0	37
5	45	4	49
4	45	7	52
3	27	9	36
2	8	12	20
1	4	16	20
Total	192	48	240

(2)   Consider, as an example, what happens when a score of 5 is used as a cutting score—that is, when we predict that students scoring 5 or above on the test will succeed in algebra.

Using this cutting score, the decision table will be as follows:

TEST PREDICTION	CRITERION PERFORMANCE Successful	Unsuccessful
Successful	108	4
Unsuccessful	84	44

Utility

One further method of evaluating the usefulness of a test will be considered, that of ascertaining the utility of a test. Utility is concerned with the analysis of the costs and benefits of various courses of action. Therefore, to use utility as an index of the validity of the test involves determination of the benefits attained and costs incurred by using the test.

To illustrate, consider a selection situation in which there is no concern with persons who are not hired. In this situation three classes of costs and benefits can be estimated: (1) the benefit to the company of hiring a worker who is successful; (2) the cost to the company of hiring a worker who later proves unsuccessful; and (3) the cost of the selection program. The calculation of each of these values is a complex cost-accounting procedure. For example, the benefits derived from hiring a successful worker will be a function of his productivity minus the costs of his salary, fringe benefits, equipment needed to perform his job, training costs, and other overhead costs. (A more through analysis might include such factors as expected job

TABLE 7.4 (continued)

The proportion of total correct decisions (total hits) will be

$$P_{CT} = \frac{108 + 44}{240} = \frac{152}{240} = .63$$

The proportion of positive hits will be

$$P_{CP} = \frac{108}{112} = .96$$

And the selection ratio will be:

S.R. = 108 + 4/240 = 112/240 = .47

(3) Applying the same procedure to all possible cutting scores:

CUTTING SCORE	PREDICT SUCCESSFUL		PREDICT UNSUCCESSFUL		P_{CT}	P_{CP}	S.R.
	Succ.	Unsucc.	Succ.	Unsucc.			
8	9	0	183	48	.24	1.00	.04
7	26	0	166	48	.31	1.00	.11
6	63	0	129	48	.46	1.00	.26
5	108	4	84	44	.63	.96	.47
4	153	11	39	37	.79	.93	.68
3	180	20	12	28	.87	.90	.83
2	188	32	4	16	.85	.85	.92
1	192	48	0	0	.80	.80	1.00

(4) Considering total correct decisions (P_{CT}), the optimal procedure would be to use 3 as the cutting score. Using this cutting score, $P_{CT} = .87$ since 208 of 240 decisions would have been correct. As this is higher than the base rate (192/240 or .80) for correct decisions, use of the test results in more correct decisions; that is, the test has some validity. Note, also, that if we use this cutting score, 83 percent of the students would have been allowed to enroll in the algebra class.

tenure, his influence on the productivity of other workers, and social costs and benefits associated with the employment of the worker.) Costs of hiring an unsuccessful worker would include such things as training costs and the expense of hiring a new worker to replace the unsuccessful one.

Let us assume, however, that the benefits of hiring a successful worker and the costs of hiring a worker who later proves to be unsuccessful can be established. Then utility could be calculated, using a formula of the form:

$$\text{Utility} = B(N_s) - C(N_u) - S \tag{7.7}$$

where B is the average benefit accrued by a successful worker; C the cost associated with hiring a worker who proves to be unsuccessful; N_s and N_u are the numbers of successful and unsuccessful workers hired, respectively; and S is the cost of the selection program. Although Equation (7.7) is highly simplified (cf. Cronbach and Gleser, 1957, 1965), it does show that for any selection program to have utility the gains obtained through testing must exceed the costs of the testing program.

In situations in which costs and benefits can readily be translated in exact values, such as dollars, a utility analysis will have the advantage of translating validity into units that are meaningful to the decision maker. However, in many situations exact values cannot be assigned to the various outcomes. For example, in most educational situations outcome values cannot be precisely determined. Although attempts have been made to apply the model in educational situations (for example, to determine the economic value of higher education), these applications do not include the intangible values of an education (such as a more satisfying life) and frequently must assign somewhat arbitrary values to certain costs and benefits.

INTERPRETING CRITERION-RELATED VALIDITY DATA

Having presented four approaches to criterion-related validity, we now turn to the interpretation of these validity data. First, we shall discuss factors that can influence the magnitude of the obtained validity index. Then we shall consider the question of the generalizability of validity data—the extent to which data derived from one situation can be applied to other situations.

Factors Influencing Validity Indices

Any variable that affects predictor (test) scores, the criterion measure, or alters the situation in which the validity data are collected, may influence a validity index. Many of these have been discussed earlier and, therefore, will not be considered here. However, three interrelated factors—the sample used to determine validity, the base rates, and the selection ratio—have such pervasive influence that they will be discussed in some detail.

The sample   As has been indicated previously, the composition of the sample used in a validation study will have an effect on the magnitude of the obtained index. Two dimensions of the sample are most crucial: its size and representativeness. As the sample size increases, measurement errors tend to counterbalance each other and more stable results will be obtained. Also, the larger the sample, the more likely that the obtained results will be statistically significant. As indicated in the discussion of indices of group separation, this is not an unmixed blessing. Yet, other things being equal, large samples are always preferable to smaller ones.

Of more importance is the representativeness of the group—that is, how the group was selected. The overriding requirement is that the group used in a validity study be one to which the test might reasonably be applied. Thus validation studies of college aptitude tests should use applicants for college, an industrial selection test should be validated using job applicants, and a verbal ability test for bilingual children should be evaluated using children who have been exposed to two languages.

Within this general requirement, there still remain several alternative sampling strategies (Cronbach, 1971). One approach is to include all members of the relevant group, or at least a random sample, in the validity study. Thus in an industrial selection situation the selection test would be administered to all applicants; all (or a random sample) would be hired, irrespective of their test scores, and allowed to work for a set period of time; criterion data would be collected; and the validity of the test would be determined. Although in many ways this is the ideal procedure, since data are collected along the entire range of predictor and criterion scores, it is often unfeasible. Because employers want immediate results from the selection procedure, and costs or facilities do not allow all applicants to be hired, some applicants are rejected. Inasmuch as the eliminated persons generally have lower ability, the range of individual differences is restricted by eliminating the lower end of the predictor scale.

A second design utilizes only "screened applicants"; that is, those people who have survived some initial culling. This initial selection may be made on the basis of the predictor variable (the test being validated) or another variable. In the latter case, if the variable used for screening is positively correlated with the test being validated, as is generally the case, individual differences on the predictor test will be reduced; if the two variables are independent, there will be no effect. Screening using the scores on the predictor test will, of course, reduce the range of scores. In either case, the most likely outcome is that the range of individual differences will be restricted, thereby reducing validity (see Dawes, 1975).

When viewed within the framework of decision-making effectiveness, this second design is appropriate when our concern is with positive hits; the first design is appropriate when the concern is with total hits. Although this second design does not allow us to calculate the predictor-criterion relationship throughout the entire score range, it closely reflects the practical situation.

A third sampling procedure is sometimes used. In this approach, presently employed workers are divided into groups on the basis of their criterion performance (for example, successful and unsuccessful workers). Tests are then administered to see what variables differentiate the groups. This design has several major shortcomings. First, only persons who have survived all screening procedures and persisted until the criterion data were collected will be included—certainly an unrepresentative group. Second, the skills or characteristics that differentiate the two groups may have developed on the job and not have been present when the groups were hired. Third, the skills needed to perform the job may be common to everyone on the job but seldom found in other groups. The design does not allow these variables to be detected. Thus, the approach should be used only in preliminary investigations and, even then, results must be interpreted with extreme caution. Either of the first two sampling methods is preferable. Needless to say, regardless of which design is chosen, the actual sampling of subjects must be random or representative so as not to introduce any further biases.

Base rates   We have previously stated that the most valid test was the one whose use resulted in the most correct decisions. However, a test that makes a large number of correct decisions, or has a high validity coefficient, still may not be a useful instrument. To understand why this is so requires consideration of another parameter, base rates. The *base rate* may be defined as the rate of occurrence of a phenomenon in an unselected population. In the selection situation, the base rate would be the proportion of people in an unselected group who would be successful. Actually, all groups probably are selected in some way, formally or informally, or by self-selection. Thus, in validity studies, the base rates more appropriately refer to the rate of occurrence of the phenomenon in the group selected by present procedures.

To be of use, a test must improve on the base rates; that is, it must make more correct decisions than would be made on the basis of the base rates alone. To illustrate, in our example (see Table 7.4) 192 out of the 240 students successfully completed algebra (that is, received an A, B, or C grade). Thus .80 was the base rate for successful performance. Using the optimal cutting score resulted in an improvement over the base rate (.87 compared to .80). Thus use of the test did, in fact, increase decision-making accuracy. Note, however, use of other cutting scores would have resulted in more errors than going with the base rate—that is, letting everyone take algebra.

The importance of base rates is particularly apparent when the phenomenon being predicted occurs either very frequently or very infrequently. In these circumstances, any prediction made on bases other than the base rates is likely to result in more errors than predicting the most likely outcome. Suppose, for example, that you want to identify people who will attempt to commit suicide. If only 5 persons in 1000 attempt suicide, and if you predict that no one will attempt suicide (even knowing that some people will) your accuracy rate will be .995, or 5 errors per 1000. Hence it is highly unlikely that a test will be useful in identifying potential suicides. Conversely, when selecting persons for a job that is so simple that 95 percent of the applicants can perform it adequately, the optimal selection strategy is to go with the base rates, to hire people as they apply. The reason, of course, is that no test can identify successful persons with greater than .95 accuracy, the accuracy obtained using the base rates. (For a further discussion, see Meehl and Rosen, 1955.)

Selection ratios   A third consideration is the selection ratio, the proportion of persons selected out of the number of applicants. If a predictor is positively related to the criterion, by being more and more selective we can increase the probability that any person selected will be successful. That is, we can select only from ranges of the population that have high probabilities of success; we can take the cream of the crop.

The effect of the selection ratio on selection effectiveness is illustrated in Table 7.5. This table shows that the effectiveness of the selection procedure can be increased in two ways: by increasing the validity coefficient or by decreasing the selection ratio. The former is shown by the increasing values as one goes down the columns; the latter by the increasing values as one goes across the rows from right to left. Thus even a relatively invalid test can be quite useful if the pool of applicants is large enough that we can use a low (stringent) selection ratio.

TABLE 7.5 The effect of the selection ratio on selection efficiency

					Selection Ratio						
Validity	.05	.10	.20	.30	.40	.50	.60	.70	.80	.90	.95
.00	.60	.60	.60	.60	.60	.60	.60	.60	.60	.60	.60
.05	.64	.63	.63	.62	.62	.62	.61	.61	.61	.60	.60
.10	.68	.67	.65	.64	.64	.63	.63	.62	.61	.61	.60
.15	.71	.70	.68	.67	.66	.65	.64	.63	.62	.61	.61
.20	.75	.73	.71	.69	.67	.66	.65	.64	.63	.62	.61
.25	.78	.76	.73	.71	.69	.68	.66	.65	.63	.62	.61
.30	.82	.79	.76	.73	.71	.69	.68	.66	.64	.62	.61
.35	.85	.82	.78	.75	.73	.71	.69	.67	.65	.63	.62
.40	.88	.85	.81	.78	.75	.73	.70	.68	.66	.63	.62
.45	.90	.87	.83	.80	.77	.74	.72	.69	.66	.64	.62
.50	.93	.90	.86	.82	.79	.76	.73	.70	.67	.64	.62
.55	.95	.92	.88	.84	.81	.78	.75	.71	.68	.64	.62
.60	.96	.94	.90	.87	.83	.80	.76	.73	.69	.65	.63
.65	.98	.96	.92	.89	.85	.82	.78	.74	.70	.65	.63
.70	.99	.97	.94	.91	.87	.84	.80	.75	.71	.66	.63
.75	.99	.99	.96	.93	.90	.86	.81	.77	.71	.66	.63
.80	1.00	.99	.98	.95	.92	.88	.83	.78	.72	.66	.63
.85	1.00	1.00	.99	.97	.95	.91	.86	.80	.73	.66	.63
.90	1.00	1.00	1.00	.99	.97	.94	.88	.82	.74	.67	.63
.95	1.00	1.00	1.00	1.00	.99	.97	.92	.84	.75	.67	.63
1.00	1.00	1.00	1.00	1.00	1.00	1.00	1.00	.86	.75	.67	.63

The figures in the table show the proportions of persons who will be judged successful when selection is made on the basis of a test of given validity and the base rate is .60 (Table from Taylor and Russell, 1939, p. 576).

Generalizability of Validity Data

It should now be apparent that *validity data are situation-specific*. That is, the results of any validity study are dependent upon the characteristics of the specific situation in which the data were collected. This statement has two important implications. First, a test will have not one, but many validities. Second, even though validity has been established in one situation, it cannot be assumed that the test will be equally valid in another, presumably comparable, situation. Thus, in any situation, adoption of a test must always be tentative until its validity has been established empirically. The need to evaluate a test independently for each specific use cannot be overstressed. In this author's opinion, using a test without evaluating its effectiveness is both poor practice and borders on the unethical.

In many situations, such as when trying to identify potentially useful tests or constructing new tests, some basis for generalizing validity data is needed. The first step is to establish that the validity obtained in a specific situation is, in fact, a good estimate of the relationship between the test and the criterion in that situation. Although control of the variables influencing test scores is essential, spurious results may be obtained if some variable that has been overlooked in the analysis influences the results. Thus, cross-validation and replication are needed.

Cross-validation Cross-validation refers to the process of determining a relationship from two or more samples independently drawn from the same population.[5] In validity studies this would involve establishing the predictor-criterion relationship on two separate samples drawn from the same population. Although computation of a validity index in two samples will not detect systematic effects, it will detect variable errors; that is, it will establish the reliability of the validity data. Thus the magnitude of chance errors, those associated with one sample, can be estimated and the data corrected accordingly.

Cross-validation, in the single predictor situation, would proceed as follows. Test scores and criterion data would be collected on one sample, r_{XY} computed, and a regression equation derived. A second sample would then be independently drawn from the same population. For each person in this second (cross-validation) group, the regression equation derived from the first sample would be used to calculate a predicted criterion score. Actual criterion scores would then be collected and the correlation between predicted and actual criterion scores calculated. This correlation should not differ markedly from the validity coefficient established on data from the first sample. If it does, we know that the first correlation was a poor estimate of the relationship. The coefficient calculated on the cross-validation sample will generally be slightly lower than the original correlation since chance factors that tend to maximize the original correlation will not operate in the cross-validation sample. Thus the cross-validated correlation is a better estimate of the true degree of relationship.

Validity generalization Cross-validation involves only one type of generalization—generalization over various samples drawn from the same population. However, we can consider generalization over at least five dimensions: predictors, criteria, situations, samples or populations of subjects, and methods of establishing validity.[6] Let us consider each dimension individually.

[5]Another related term is replication, which refers to repeating the study on another sample, not necessarily drawn from the same population. There are also other methods of doing cross-validation (see, e.g., Cronbach, 1971; Dawes and Meehl, 1966; Dunnette, 1966).

[6]In contrast to the definition of validity generalization sometimes used (generalization across populations), we shall use the term to refer to generalization across any relevant dimension.

Up to this point our discussion of validity has been concerned with only one test or predictor. Thus the question of generalizability over tests (predictors) may seem unnecessary. Yet we might ask such questions as: Do tests supposedly measuring the same trait or ability have comparable validity in a particular situation? Would validity be the same with a different item format? Or, within a given test, is the test valid at different score levels—that is, is the test as valid for persons scoring high as for persons obtaining low scores? Thus, on the predictor dimension, information is needed on generalization over comparable tests, item formats, and score levels.

We are also interested in generalizability over criteria. Earlier in the chapter we stressed that the idea of *the* criterion was a myth. However, as a practical matter, one or a few criteria are used in any study. The obvious question, then, is: Does the test predict the other possible criteria equally well? Since criteria involve a time dimension, one might also ask about the validity over various time spans. Or, analogous to the score level problem of predictors, what is the validity of the test at various criterion score levels? Can good performance be predicted as well as poor performance?

The various aspects of testing situations are far too numerous to mention. A few relevant points include: What is the generalizability over different examiners? Over different administration conditions? Over different instructions or sets to take the test? This latter point is especially crucial because validity may vary markedly depending on whether the test is structured as part of an experiment used for counseling or advising or is part of a selection procedure for a desired position or educational opportunity.

Of central importance is the generalizability over different groups of subjects. Here the important questions are: Over what age range is the test valid? For what educational levels? For what socioeconomic levels? Is the test valid for both men and women? In different parts of the United States, or in different towns or schools? For what range of jobs or companies? Because there is such a diversity among groups (for example, the applicants to Stanford or Harvard differ greatly from the applicants to South Siwash Tech), the limits of generalizability, or applicability, have to be established. Just because a test is designed for use with college freshmen does not mean that it will be valid at all colleges. The more important question is: In what types of colleges is the test valid? (See, e.g., ACT, 1972.)

Finally, by what method is the validity established? Unfortunately, the results obtained from the various techniques of measuring validity do not always agree. For example, it is possible to have a high validity coefficient but poor decision-making effectiveness. Or decision-making accuracy may be high but utility low. Thus one must also consider the method or index used when interpreting validity data.

At least three conclusions can be drawn from these comments on validity generalization. First, because validity is influenced by many variables, systematic collection of validity data is essential. Most validity studies reported in the literature have been conducted to justify use of a particular test (for example, the data provided in the test manual) or represent the hit-or-miss, shotgun approach of many investigators—each pursuing his own interests and specific problems. Although attempts have been made to summarize available validity data (e.g., Ghiselli, 1966;

Super and Crites, 1962), more studies that deliberately and systematically vary the relevant parameters to establish the limits of the transsituational validity of commonly used tests are needed.

Second, more adequate methods of summarizing and interpreting the results are needed. The development of a single summary index of transsituational validity is probably not possible. But the variables influencing a particular test and the effects of manipulating each can be specified. This specification would not only provide an estimate of the probable validity of the test in new situations, but would make drawing inferences about the meaning of the test score easier. In essence, one would have a miniature theory for each test.

Third, the discussion shows the close relation between the data and concepts of validity and those of consistency. Many of the relevant variables influencing validity generalization are the same as, or parallel to, those that influence the consistency of test scores. And, since reliability was measured by consistency over forms and occasions, and homogeneity was measured by consistency over items, so, too, consistency over tests and occasions—as well as over samples, criteria, and methods—is basic to validity. In both validity and consistency we are interested in generalizability, the only difference being in the number and nature of the dimensions over which generalizations are made. (For a more extensive discussion see Cronbach et al., 1972.)

Two Final Points

We have avoided an explicit discussion of the question that plagued the discussion on reliability—the question of how high is high, or, in more technical terms, what is an acceptable level of validity? Because of the situation-specific nature of validity, the variety of validity coefficients, and the multitude of factors that influence a validity coefficient, it is impossible to give one definite answer. At best one can set certain minimal requirements: (1) The cross-validated relationship between predictor and criterion scores must be statistically significant—that is, be more than a chance relationship. (2) Using the test must result in more correct decisions being made than would be made by resorting to base rates alone. (3) The test must possess some utility; it must result in some gain to the user. (4) The effectiveness of the test must be greater than other available decision-making tools; that is, the test should provide some unique information. If these requirements are not met (at least the ones that can be evaluated in the particular situation), use of the test is not justified.

Finally, although test results are ultimately used to make decisions about individuals, the validity of a test is established by determining its effectiveness for a group of persons. Because there is no logical link that allows group results to be applied unerringly to any individual member of the group, the effectiveness of a test must always be evaluated in terms of decisions made regarding the group collectively, not the decision made in an individual case. Although the decision made about John Jones is of utmost importance, with imperfect tests errors will be made in individual cases. Our goal is to minimize errors in individual cases. Yet, until the day arrives, it if ever does, when tests predict with perfect accuracy, some errors will be made in individual cases. When evaluating tests the appropriate question is not "Will errors be made in individual cases?"—a question that obviously can only be answered "Yes." Rather the crucial question is: "Will fewer errors be made in individual cases using the test or by using some other technique?"

8

CONTENT AND CONSTRUCT VALIDITY

In an earlier chapter we made a distinction between tests that represent and tests that predict. Our discussion of criterion-related validity focused on the latter type, tests that function as predictors. We now turn to the other class, tests that represent. Here our concern will be with tests that are used primarily to describe people's behavior and characteristics, rather than for predicting extra-test behavior.

Tests that represent, you will recall, can be further sub-divided into tests that serve as samples and those that serve as signs. A test is a sample when the items are drawn from a clearly specified content or behavioral domain. A test serves as a sign when the domain is open-ended; here the test helps point out the nature of the domain being sampled. This distinction, between samples and signs, has a parallel in the types of validity—content validity being the analog of tests as samples, construct validity of tests as signs. Thus, content validity focuses on the process of evaluating how adequately a sample of items (the test) samples the relevant domain. Construct validity, in contrast, focuses on the definition of the trait measured by the test, on the ability of the test to provide information concerning the nature of the trait.

CONTENT VALIDITY

A classroom teacher is constantly confronted with the problem of assessing his students' knowledge and/or skills. Usually he is interested in a relatively well-defined content area. If time permitted, he might administer an extensive examination, covering all important aspects of the subject matter, to each student individually. Obviously such a procedure, desirable as it may be, usually is unfeasible. Thus some substitute procedure must be devised, one that provides a valid estimate of each student's knowledge in a reasonable amount of time. Frequently the solution is to administer some sort of achievement test.

In these situations the variable of interest is the students' knowledge[1] of the subject matter domain. The test serves as a sample, or representation, of the content domain. Scores on the test are not ends in themselves; rather, they are used to make inferences about performance in the wider domain. In other words, the purpose of the exam is to provide an objective basis for making an inference about the students' knowledge of the material. Because he cannot ask every possible question, the teacher selects a sample of the possible items to serve as the test. On the basis of the student's performance on this sample of items, the teacher makes inferences about the student's knowledge of (all) the material in the unit. To the extent that the items are a good sample of the total pool of potential items, the inferences will be valid; to the extent that any bias is introduced into the item selection, the inferences will be invalid.

Definition of Content Validity

The basic question in content validity, therefore, is whether the items composing the test do, in fact, constitute a representative sample of the content domain of concern. Thus, content validation involves a determination of the adequacy of the sampling of items from the universe of potential items, and content validity is a "measure" of the adequacy of sampling. "Measure" is placed in quotes because, as will be seen below, determination of content validity usually is a judgmental procedure, which provides no quantitative index of validity.

Before considering the methods used to establish content validity, let us first consider some of the major implications of the definition.

The content domain   Content validity, as its name indicates, is concerned with the content of the test. Content means the substantive constituents of the materials, their factual and informational components. Therefore, on achievement tests the em-

---

[1]To avoid repeating the awkward phrase "knowledge or skills," we shall use these terms somewhat interchangeably. The reader should keep in mind, however, that a test may measure either knowledge or cognitive skills, or both.

phasis will be primarily on the subject matter covered (for example, the laws of permutations and combinations, the novels of Charles Dickens, measures of central tendency, irregular French verbs) and the processes used to answer the items. The mode of response will be of lesser importance.

The appropriate emphasis on the process (skill) dimension is a debatable issue. Some experts feel that since different persons may answer the same item using different processes (for example, the item "multiply 11 by 12" might involve computation by one child and recall of a learned fact by another), inclusion of process factors introduces unnecessary ambiguity. Other experts, however, feel that failure to consider process dimensions is both sterile and a poor educational practice. They would argue that the types of achievement tests that are so widely criticized (for example, tests composed solely of items testing factual recall) would never be developed if the test constructor considered process variables (see, e.g., Bloom et al., 1971).

The definition also implies that the boundaries of the content domain are well-delineated. Although some authorities would insist that content validity requires an explicitly defined, finite universe of items (cf. Bornmuth, 1970; Hively et al., 1968), most people interpret this requirement to mean that the test constructor must, as clearly as possible, specify what materials and skills the test is designed to cover. On achievement tests the content usually is specified by topical areas (for example, the theory of reliability, alcoholism in women), by the assignments covered, or by specification of behavioral objectives for a unit.

Although content validity is usually associated with achievement testing, there is no reason why the concept cannot be applied in other areas of psychological testing. For example, we could sample the various skills and abilities constituting mechanical aptitude or sample a person's reactions to different types of people to measure ethnocentrism. We could apply similar approaches in any area of educational and psychological testing, being limited only by our ability to specify the boundaries of the domain.

Representative sampling   The definition of content validity states that the test items must be a representative sample of the domain of possible content or behaviors. Note that the definition specifies *representative sampling,* not random sampling. Representative sampling means selecting items in proportion to their emphasis or importance. For example, in a typical instructional unit, some of the material repeats what has been learned previously, some is trivial or included as filler, and some is otherwise inappropriate for test items. These materials will not be included on the test. The test will include only material that, in the judgment of the test constructor, represents important content and/or skill dimensions. The test items, therefore, need not be representative of the total content of the course or unit, but only of the material judged to be relevant and important.

In test construction, the process of item sampling, given a pool of potential items, involves first dividing the content domain into a number of subcategories, each representing a relevant content area; then assigning a proportionate weight to each category; and finally sampling items randomly within each category until the required numbers of items are attained. In practice, the sampling in the last step is not random. One reason is that the items selected generally have to meet certain statistical requirements; for example, they should be of appropriate difficulty. Another reason is that a balance of content within each category may be desired. And, third, items sometimes are chosen to serve a specific function—for example, to be easy "warm-up" items or to test the limits of the best students' knowledge.

Note also that nothing in the definition requires the test to be homogeneous. Since even the most limited instructional unit usually involves a variety of content and skills, a requirement of high homogeneity would be both unrealistic and undesirable (cf. Ebel, 1968). A high degree of homogeneity within subareas may be desirable, but it is not necessary that the test as a whole be homogeneous. However, if we are concerned with the content validity of a test designed to measure some psychological trait or construct, high homogeneity is desirable.

Methods for Determining Content Validity

Content validity is determined by systematically comparing the test items to the postulated content domain. If the test items appear, to an expert judge, to represent the domain adequately, the test possesses content validity. This validation procedure is logical and rational, involving a judgment of the correspondence between the test and the underlying domain. As such, it has several drawbacks. First, no quantitative index can be used to describe the degree of relationship. Second, different judges may disagree as to the content validity of a test. Third, lack of clarity in the specifying of the domain will make judgments of content validity process difficult.

Several procedures have been suggested that would make the process more objective. As a starting point we could insist upon a well-specified definition of the content universe—a description that would delineate the domain, the relevant skills and knowledge, and the source materials used (if an achievement exam). Relevant subcategories could also be defined, and their proportionate emphases specified. In addition, the test constructor could specify what content and skills were being measured by each item. Finally, rating scales could be developed to measure the overall validity of the test and/or its quality along several relevant dimensions, such as coverage of content, coverage of skills, stress on important materials, and appropriateness of item format to content. Judges rating the content validity of a test could then go through the test, item by item, comparing his categorization of each item with the test constructor's, and making ratings on the summary rating scales.

Besides standardizing descriptive language, these ratings could also be analyzed statistically. For example, an index of agreement between two independent reviewers' ratings could be calculated. Here the extent of agreement would indicate the reliability of the judgments; the actual ratings would indicate the (content) validity of the test.

In practice, several of these steps are now used. The content domain is usually spelled out in some detail, and a classification of items by content and skill categories frequently is available.

Other methods for ascertaining content validity are also possible. Cronbach

(1971) has proposed that content validity could be evaluated quantitatively by correlating scores of two forms of a test, independently constructed from the same content domain.[2] If the correlation between forms were high, we would have presumptive evidence of content validity; if the correlation were low, at least one form would lack content validity. An alternative method is to pretest a group having minimal knowledge in the area covered by the test, exposing the group to a course or training program covering the relevant material, then administering a posttest. This procedure would indicate whether the test measured knowledge taught in the course rather than knowledge obtained by other means.

Specificity of content validity   In one sense, content validity is a general property of a test rather than being situation-specific. If the test constructor clearly defines the content domain and selects items to represent this domain, he either does or does not succeed (more precisely, succeeds to a certain degree) in attaining his goal. Although we may disagree with his definition of the domain, we must evaluate the test in terms of how well the test attains the specified goal, by how well the test represents the domain as the test constructor defined it.

In another sense, however, content validity is situation-specific. A test user will always apply a test in a specific situation to measure certain behaviors that he considers important. If the domain as defined by the user and as defined by the test constructor are congruent, there is no problem. If, however, the user defines the domain differently than did the test constructor, a conflict arises. Now the test is not a good representation of the domain as the user defines it, and thus will be less valid for his purposes. In this sense, content validity is situation-specific.

To illustrate, suppose that a standardized test is constructed to measure achievement in mathematics as traditionally taught in the upper elementary grades. Assume also that the test has well-constructed items that measure important concepts—in short, assume that the test has content validity as a measure of mathematics as traditionally taught in the upper elementary grades. If this test is used in a school system that teaches math in the traditional manner, it should be a valid measure of achievement. True, there may be some differences in emphasis and coverage due to the particular text used and teacher preferences, but, by and large, these will be minor differences. On the other hand, if the test is used in a school system which teaches the "new" math, some items will cover concepts that are not taught or emphasized and some of the concepts stressed in the new math will not be covered on the test. In this situation, the disparity in definitions of the content domain would be so great as to render the test inappropriate—in essence, to reduce its validity.

This illustration raises another point; that is, evidence of content validity, like other types of validity, must periodically be reviewed. Because knowledge expands, teaching methods change, and the placement of subjects in the curriculum varies,

---

[2]"Independently constructed" means built by two separate test construction teams working from the same definition of the content domain and following agreed-upon guidelines (such as number of items and time limits).

periodic review of the appropriateness of any test is needed. What is taught in the sixth grade today may be taught in the fourth grade next year, or not taught at all!

Face validity   Content validity is frequently confused with face validity. A test has face validity when the items *look like* they measure what the test is supposed to measure. That is, when a test taker looks at the items, they appear relevant to the purpose of the testing. Thus, a test containing items that ask the individual's reactions to such activities as basketball, geometry, selling as a career, and working with people would have face validity as an interest inventory but not as an intelligence test. In short, face validity is determined by a somewhat superficial examination of the test by the test taker, and considers only obvious relevance. Content validity, in contrast, is established by a thorough and systematic evaluation of the test by a qualified judge, and considers both subtle and obvious aspects of relevance.

Face validity may be an important consideration if the apparent relevance of the items influences the test taker's motivation. In some situations, particularly in employment testing, if a test lacks face validity, the test taker may not be motivated to do well, feeling that the test is irrelevant to the decision being made. In other situations, such as when measuring personality characteristics, a high degree of face validity may be undesirable because it may threaten the test taker and/or encourage him to dissimulate (bias his responses). Thus face validity, though not guaranteeing accurate measurement, may have an important influence on motivation and, therefore, on validity.

Evaluation

Content validity, as a concept and as a method, has both its strong points and limitations. The emphasis on evaluating the correspondence between the test items and the stated content, skill, or behavioral domain sampled both ensures care in item selection and requires careful specification of the domain to be sampled. Thus considerations of content validity are an essential aspect of the construction of any test. Content validity is clearly the most appropriate method for evaluating the validity of achievement tests (unless, of course, the achievement test is used primarily as a predictor). And content validity, as a concept, reminds us that our major concern is not with the test itself but with the inferences we draw about the student's performance in the broader domain from which the items were sampled.

The major limitation of content validity is, of course, the lack of quantitative indices that summarize the degree of validity. Lack of available quantitative indices hinders communication of information about the content validity of a test. As a first step we should attempt to develop clearly specified methods, techniques, and procedures for determining content validity and scales, or a set of standards that can be used to summarize and communicate the degree of content validity. Such procedures and scales are, in principle, attainable; however, as yet, they are not used.

CONSTRUCT VALIDITY

Any science must provide a theoretical framework to integrate and explain its data and provide direction for further work. One essential element of a theory is well-defined constructs. Frequently, in psychology, these constructs are operationally defined and measured by tests. Since neither criterion-related nor content validity have as their fundamental goal the understanding of the trait (construct) that a test measures, the original Technical Recommendation for Psychological Tests and Diagnostic Techniques (APA, 1954) put forth a new approach to validity, called *construct validity,* which focused on this issue. This approach was then further explicated in an article by Cronbach and Meehl (1955), who provided an extensive discussion of the logic and methods of construct validity.

The most recent revision of the Standards for Educational and Psychological Tests states: "construct validity is implied when one evaluates a test or other set of operations in light of the specified construct" (APA, 1974, p. 29). The previous edition stated that construct validation was to be used when

> The test user wishes to infer the degree to which the individual possesses some hypothetical trait or quality (construct) presumed to be reflected in the test performance (APA, 1966, p. 12).

Thus, construct validity is important whenever a test is designed to measure some attribute or quality (construct) that people are presumed to possess. Construct validity studies attempt to answer the questions: What psychological construct is measured by a test? How well does the test measure this construct? Thus the focus is on the construct,[3] the characteristic being measured.

Frequently, in psychology, constructs are not definable solely in operational terms. That is, the definition of a construct may include statements that, though anchored in observable data, contain elements that go beyond observable behaviors. Such definitions are often broader and more meaningful than definitions involving a mere rephrasing of empirical relationships. Thus construct validity is evaluated by an accumulation of evidence, and no single quantitative index of construct validity is possible. To determine the construct validity of a test, one must examine the entire body of evidence surrounding the test: what sort of items are included on the test, the stability of the test scores under varying conditions, the homogeneity of the test, its correlation with other tests or variables, the effects of experimental manipulations on test performance, and any other data that cast light on the meaning of test scores. By evaluating, sifting, and refining the evidence about the test, a clearer definition of the construct measured by the test emerges.

The process of construct validation can also be conceptualized as an attempt to answer the question: What proportion of the variance in test scores is attributable to the variable the test measures? That is, to what extent does performance on the test reflect the construct the test is designed to measure? Formulation of the problem in these terms is a useful conceptual and heuristic tool.

---

[3]A test may, of course, measure more than a single construct. We shall talk about a test measuring a construct since there are advantages to homogeneous, single-construct tests, and to avoid the awkward phrase "construct or constructs."

The Logic of Construct Validation

Before we consider the specific methods used to establish construct validity, it would be well to discuss the philosophic and logical bases of the idea of construct validity. Here, as throughout our discussion of construct validity, we shall rely heavily on the article by Cronbach and Meehl (1955).

In many ways the logic of construct validity, as well as its methods, are essentially those of the scientific method. One starts with a theory that includes a construct presumably measured by the test in question. From this theory certain predictions can be made about the relationships between variables. These predictions are then tested empirically. Depending on the results of the empirical check, the theory is supported or revised. Continual predictions, empirical tests, and theory revision serve to define the construct more precisely.

Another way of viewing the process is that construct validation involves building a miniature theory about a test. This theory building involves three steps. First, on the basis of his currently held theory about the test, the investigator derives certain hypotheses about the expected behavior of persons obtaining different scores on the test. He then gathers data that will confirm or disconfirm these hypotheses. On the basis of the accumulated data he decides whether the theory does, in fact, adequately explain the data. If it does not, he must revise his theory and repeat the process until a more adequate explanation is available. Since no one set of data ever provides a complete and unambiguous explanation, the process is one of continual reformulation and refinement.

With this general overview, let us now be more specific.

The nomological net   Any theory is comprised of a series of interrelated concepts, propositions, and laws. This system of interlocking laws is called a nomological network (Cronbach and Meehl, 1955). These laws may relate observable characteristics or behaviors to other observables, observables to theoretical constructs, or two or more theoretical constructs. The relationships expressed by the laws may be either deterministic (all or none) or probabilistic in nature. At some point all laws and concepts must be tied to observable behaviors. However, a given law or concept may not directly involve observables; it may be derivable from other laws and concepts, which, in turn, are directly tied to observables. The essential requirement is that the definition of a concept (or formulation of a law) can be traced back to laws or concepts that are anchored in observable data.

Clarification of the meaning of any concept in the network occurs by elaborating the network (that is, including more lawful relationships) or by making the existing relationships more specific and definite. Thus, many operations, even qualitatively different ones, can be used to measure a concept. Using data derived from psychological tests is one method of measuring a construct.

Several important implications arise out of this metatheoretical position. First, at some stage in the process of explicating the meaning of a construct, there must be observable data; often these data are test scores. Second, the process of inference (from the observable data to the meaning of the construct) must be public and explicitly specified; otherwise there is no means of checking the accuracy of the inference. Third, unless various users of the construct adopt essentially the same network, communication among investigators is not possible. This point is especially relevant in psychological research where the same label frequently refers to different constructs (for example, people mean different things by ''intelligence'') or different labels refer to the same construct (for example, divergent thinking and creativity sometimes are used to refer to the same construct).

Validation paradigm   The validation procedure implied by this view involves deducing testable hypotheses from the theory (nomological network), then collecting data to test these hypotheses. Therefore, when reporting construct validity data an investigator must clearly specify at least three things. First, what interpretation was proposed? That is, what construct is being investigated, how this construct is defined, and how the particular hypothesis tested in the study was derived from the relevant theory. Second, how adequately was the interpretation substantiated? Here the investigator should give an evaluation of the overall substantiation of his hypothesis and also indicate where the hypothesis was particularly well supported and where support was weak. Third, he must tell why he believes his claims were substantiated. This is done by giving details of the experimental procedure and the line of reasoning taken in making inferences from these procedures to the meaning of the construct.

Suppose that the results of an empirical study give us reason to believe that our hypotheses have been substantiated. What do the results mean? Certainly they do not "validate" or "prove" the entire theory, since we were dealing with only one portion of the theory. Instead, we retain our belief that the test measures the construct and can have more faith in our adoption[4] of the concept.

What of negative results, of the data failing to confirm our hypothesis or prediction? Here there are at least three possible interpretations. The test may not measure the construct. Or the theoretical framework may have been in error, thus allowing for an incorrect inference to be made. Or, perhaps, the design of the experiment did not permit an appropriate test of the hypothesis. Unfortunately, it is not always clear which of these three possibilities is operating in a specific instance. The third interpretation, faulty experimental design, is usually easiest to detect; the other two are more likely to be confounded. Therefore, failure to confirm a prediction indicates that some revision is needed in the theoretical network and/or the experimental procedure, but the exact locus of the failure is not always clearly identified. This ambiguous interpretation of negative results is an obvious drawback of the construct validation procedure.

Tests as signs   The picture we have presented, of a formalized theory involving well-defined constructs and a set of specified laws, is overly idealistic. Many psychological constructs and laws are vaguely and incompletely defined, and

---

[4]Cronbach and Meehl used the term ''adopt'' to emphasize the fact that a construct is never proved in an absolute sense, it can only be adopted as the best working definition.

systematic theories are relatively rare. Construct validation aids progress toward this ideal, however, because in addition to clarifying existing constructs and laws, validation studies may also point out relationships that heretofore have gone undetected. When this occurs, the test is serving as a sign; that is, it provides information that clarifies the nature of the behavioral domain of interest. This function also explains why some authors (e.g., Thorndike and Hagen, 1969) refer to construct validity as signifying; the test signifies the nature of the behavioral domain and, consequently, the nature of the construct.

Methods of Gathering Information Regarding Construct Validity

In construct validation, we simultaneously validate both the construct and the theory surrounding the construct.[5] Any evidence that bears on either the theory or the construct is thus relevant. Consequently, construct validity can be investigated by a wide variety of techniques, including the methods of content and criterion-related validity. These techniques can be classified in various ways (see, e.g., Cronbach and Meehl, 1955; Cronbach, 1971). In our discussion we shall group these techniques in five categories: intratest methods, interest methods, criterion-related studies, experimental manipulations, and generalizability studies. As with any classification, this one is somewhat arbitrary, and the categories are not completely independent. It does, however, illustrate the variety of techniques used to establish construct validity.

Intratest methods   One class of methods consists of techniques that study the internal structure of a test: its content, the processes utilized in responding to the items, and the relationships between items and/or subtests. Because these techniques are concerned solely with the internal structure of the test, they help circumscribe the domain measured by the construct but provide no evidence about relationships between the construct and other variables (that is, about the laws in the theory).

One source of evidence falling within this category is the *content validity* of a test. Specification of the behavioral domain sampled by the test serves to define the nature of the construct the test measures. For example, if when developing a test of ''verbal intelligence'' a test author describes the content universe as the ability to define words, reason by verbal analogies, and use words appropriately in sentences, he has defined his construct of ''verbal intelligence.'' Thus, the process of establishing the content validity of the test can also provide evidence regarding the test's construct validity.

On many tests we are also interested in the processes and skills individuals use

---

[5]Other writers (e.g., Birnbaum, 1974; Campbell, 1960) make a distinction between validating a theory and validating a construct. Campbell, for example, argues that psychological theories have not yet advanced beyond the stage of postulating important constructs and dimensions; thus construct validity is, for all practical purposes, concerned with validating constructs, since there are no well-specified theories surrounding these constructs.

when responding to items. Such information might be obtained by asking the test taker how he approached an item, observing his performance, or (statistically) analyzing his responses. For example, on a personality inventory, we might find that responses to the item "I frequently get angry when things do not go my way" are determined both by the test taker's actual behavior and the social desirability of responding positively. These *process analyses* identify the skills, abilities, and reaction tendencies the person brings to bear when responding. Knowledge of the basis for responding clarifies the nature of the construct by indicating which variables influence responses.

Another subclass of intratest methods is studies of the *homogeneity* of the test. Here one might derive a measure of internal consistency, such as coefficient alpha or a Kuder-Richardson coefficient. These homogeneity indices indicate whether the test measures a single trait or is multifaceted.

Intertest methods   This class contains methods that consider the interrelations among several tests simultaneously. In general, these methods are designed to indicate what features several tests share in common, or, from another viewpoint, whether the tests measure the same construct.

The simplest procedure, called *congruent validity,* is to correlate scores on a new test with scores on an established test; for example, new intelligence tests are usually compared to well-validated individual measures such as the Stanford-Binet or one of the Wechsler Intelligence Scales. If the correlation is high, the two tests measure the same construct, and scores on the newer test can be interpreted as scores on the older test. We can also infer that scores on the new test will relate to other variables in somewhat the same manner as scores on the established test. These statements hold only when the two tests are highly correlated. The lower the intercorrelations between the two tests, the less faith we can have in generalizing from one test to the other.[6]

A second possible approach would be to perform a *factor analysis* on a group of tests. Factor analysis is a statistical procedure for determining how many factors (constructs) are needed to account for the intercorrelations among a set of test scores. A factor analysis provides three relevant types of information: (1) how many factors are needed to account for the intercorrelations among the tests; (2) what factors determine performance on each test; and, (3) how much variance in the test scores is accounted for by the factors. (See Chapter 9 for a more complete discussion of factor analysis.)

From this analysis we can determine which tests share common variance and thus measure the same construct (factor). By investigating the content of tests

[6]Suppose, for example, that a new scholastic aptitude test (Test A) correlates moderately, say .50, with an established test (Test B). The fact that Test B predicts grades in a given curriculum cannot be taken as evidence that Test A will also predict grades in the same curriculum because the factors responsible for the low correlation between the tests may also predict the criterion. For example, if Test A is entirely verbal but Test B contains both verbal and quantitative items, and we are predicting grades in engineering, the inclusion of quantitative items on Test B may be the reason why it predicts engineering grades (and also why the intertest correlation is not higher).

loading[7] on the same factor, we can infer the nature of the construct being tapped. A factor analysis also shows the extent to which performance on each test is determined by the common underlying factor and the extent to which performance depends upon factors specific to that test.

Factor analysis is a commonly used technique for establishing construct validity. Many writers, in fact, designate *factorial validity,* defined as the loading of a test on a factor (construct), as a major type of validity. Thus, if this definition is used, the proportion of total variance in the test scores that is attributable to the factor can be used as an index of construct validity.

Closely related to the previous two approaches is Campbell's conception of *convergent validity* and *discriminant validity* (Campbell, 1960; Campbell and Fiske, 1959). Campbell states that validation usually proceeds convergently; that is, we attempt to establish that two instruments (tests) are, in fact, measuring the same construct. Factorial and congruent validity are two examples of convergent methods. But, according to Campbell, not only should a test correlate with other tests purporting to measure the same construct, it also should be uncorrelated with tests that measure different constructs. This is the divergent (discriminant) aspect of the dichotomy. Thus, scores on a test proposed as a measure of creativity should not be correlated highly with scores on an intelligence test. In other words, to be valid a test must measure a construct that is demonstrably independent of other established constructs.

Criterion-related studies   The nature and type of criteria that can be predicted by the test give an indication of the construct the test measures. Thus, data from criterion-related validity studies can provide information relevant to construct validity.

One common source of evidence is the ability of the test scores to separate naturally occurring or experimentally contrived groups (*group differentiation*). For example, scales on the Strong Vocational Interest Blank were constructed by contrasting the responses of persons in specific occupations with those of men in general. To construct a scale for physicians, Strong selected items that differentiated physicians from men in general; to construct a scale for real estate salesmen, he selected items that differentiated real estate salesmen from men in general. Or, to use a different illustration, a test proposed as a measure of creativity should differentiate between highly creative artists and persons whose artwork is stereotyped and mundane.

Conversely, groups can be constructed on the basis of their test scores (for example, those scoring in the upper and lower portions of the score distributions) and the distinguishing characteristics of the groups identified. These characteristics serve to define the construct. For example, Barron (1963) showed that graduate students who scored high on an Ego Strength scale were rated as being alert, adventuresome, determined, independent, (having) initiative, outspoken, per-

---

[7]The term "loading" refers to the correlation between the test and the factor. A high loading indicates that a test is a good measure of the factor—that is, a good measure of the construct.

sistent, reliable, resourceful, and responsible; low scorers were rated as being dependent, effeminate, mannerly, and mild. These descriptions give the flavor of the construct being measured by the test, thus defining its nature.

Validity coefficients also may provide relevant data. A test designed as a measure of scholastic aptitude should, of course, predict grades in academic subjects; a test of finger dexterity should predict success in an occupation, such as watch repairing, where fine movements are essential; a test of sociopathic tendencies should predict delinquency. Confirmation or disconfirmation of these predictions would strengthen or weaken, respectively, our confidence in the test as a measure of the purported trait.

Experimental manipulation   We can also obtain useful information by experimentally manipulating some variable and observing its effects on test scores or the relation between test scores and some criterion. For example, suppose that we define "test anxiety" as the fear of failure on examinations when results have significance for a person's self-concept. From this definition we could hypothesize that performance on an examination would be negatively related to test anxiety (that is, high anxiety produces poor performance) if the exam were structured as being important to the person (for example, used to make some decision about his educational future), but that test-taking anxiety and examination scores would be unrelated if the test were structured so as to produce no threat to the individual (for example, if the test were presented as part of a standardization project and the student responded anonymously). If such an experiment were conducted and scores on the anxiety test did have the predicted relationships with examination scores, we would have evidence that the test did, in fact, measure test anxiety.

The category of experimental manipulation also includes evidence on variations resulting from naturally occurring events. For example, if the definition of a trait (construct) implies that the trait is resistant to environmental effects and is stable over time, the coefficient of stability should be high. Note that here reliability data are used as validity evidence—another illustration of the close relationship between the two concepts. Or if intelligence is defined so as to imply that it will increase with age, then a test presuming to measure intelligence must show increasing scores with age.

Generalizability studies   Our fifth category is harder to delineate. Studies that fall into this category systematically study the test over a range of conditions or dimensions—for example, in a variety of populations (transferability) or with different administration conditions.

The clearest example of this approach is the *multitrait-multimethod matrix* proposed by Campbell and Fiske (1959). They pointed out that any test is really a trait-method unit; that is, any test measures a given trait by a given method. For example, the results obtained on a personality inventory may be attributable to the particular characteristics measured (the traits), or to the method of measurement (an inventory, rather than some other method), or to some combination of trait and method. If we studied different traits, or the same trait using a differerent method, we might obtain different results. Therefore, if we want to separate the relative contributions of trait and method components, we must study more than one trait and more than one method simultaneously. In essence, we are studying convergent and discriminant validity: convergent validity by looking at the correlations between the same traits measured by different methods; discriminant validity by looking at the correlations between different traits measured by the same method.

TABLE 8.1   An example of a multitrait-multimethod matrix

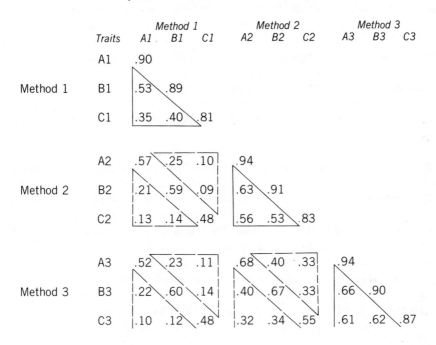

An example of a multitrait-multimethod matrix is shown in Table 8.1. This table shows the (hypothetical) correlations obtained when three traits (A, B, C) were measured by three different methods (1, 2, 3). The three traits might, for example, be dominance, social sensitivity, and self-assurance as measured by three methods: self-reports, projective techniques, and peer ratings. Or they might be measures of verbal comprehension, numerical reasoning, and general information as measured by a paper-and-pencil test, an individually administered test, and teacher's ratings. Any number and type of traits and methods can be utilized, with the number of traits not necessarily being equal to the number of methods. The three traits and methods used in the example were arbitrary choices.

The correlations in Table 8.1 can be divided into four categories. The correlations in the major diagonal are the reliabilities (measuring the same trait by the same method). The triangles outlined by dashed lines show the correlations between separate traits measured by different methods. The values within the triangles outlined by solid lines are the correlations across traits using a single method (measures of method variance). Finally, the values in the diagonals between the dashed triangles are validity coefficients. Validity, in this approach, means convergent validity, since the values show the correlations between the same trait measured by different methods.

Several lines of evidence from the matrix are relevant to validity. First, the validity coefficients should be significantly larger than zero and, hopefully, high enough to encourage further study. That is, different measures of the same trait should be positively correlated. Second, correlations between different methods of measuring a single trait (validity diagonals) should be higher than correlations between different traits measured by the same method (values in solid triangles). This means that trait differences should be more important than method differences. Third, validity coefficients should be higher than correlations involving both different traits and different methods (dashed triangles). The first point demonstrates convergent validity; the latter two are directed toward discriminant validity, showing that the interrelations between traits are not artifacts of the method of measurement used.

Two aspects of the multitrait-multimethod matrix approach deserve further mention. First, note that reliability is defined as the agreement between two measurements of the same trait using the same method, while validity is defined as the agreement between two measurements of the same trait using different methods. Thus the fundamental distinction between reliability and validity is in the similarity of the measurement methods. Second, this matrix provides evidence on possible method bias—for example, by showing the relationship between various traits measured using the same method. This evidence is not obtained in the usual validity study because each trait is measured by only one method, thus making it logically impossible to separate the effects of the trait, the measurement method, and their interaction. Only when multiple methods are utilized can we be sure that our results are attributable to trait differences, rather than being artifacts of the measurement method.

An Example of Construct Validation

Since the procedures utilized in construct validity are more complex than other methods discussed so far, it may be helpful to consider a detailed example of how evidence on construct validity might be gathered. As an illustration we have chosen Barron's development of his Ego Strength (ES) scale. This example was chosen because a variety of types of evidence were utilized; it represents a blending of theory and empiricism; and the process illustrates how the test served as a sign to point out the nature of the behavioral domain. (See Barron, 1963, Chapters 9 and 10, for further details.)

Barron's original goal was to build a scale that would predict which psychoneurotics would respond favorably to psychotherapy. He administered the Minnesota Multiphasic Personality Inventory (MMPI), a test consisting of about 550 personality items, to a group of patients prior to therapy. After therapy the group was divided into two groups: those rated improved and those rated as un-improved. With improvement as the criterion, an item analysis was conducted, and 68 items that discriminated between the two groups were selected for the ES scale. Odd-even reliability and a coefficient of stability were calculated and found to be of an acceptable level. Barron then did a content analysis by classifying the scale items into rational groups and attempting to summarize the content of the scale. On the basis of this analysis, and such other data as a study of adjectives rated descriptive of persons obtaining high and low scores on the scale, Barron postulated that the test measured something broader than response to psychotherapy; he called this trait "Ego Strength," and proposed a tentative description of the construct.

Barron next predicted that scores on the ES scale would be related in certain ways to other variables. He tested these relationships in various groups, and in most instances his predictions were confirmed. For example, he hypothesized that ES and measures of intellectual ability would be moderately positively correlated, and found such relationships ($r = .35$ to $.50$). He also correlated ES with characteristics exhibited in social interactions—self-confidence, drive, submissiveness—and found the correlation with variables such as tolerance ($r = .40$), ethnocentrism ($r = -.40$), and measures of psychopathology ($r = -.50$ to $-.60$). These relationships were viewed as supporting his interpretation of the ES scale. Barron also cross-validated the ES scale with three separate groups of psychotherapy patients, obtaining validity coefficients of .38, .42, and .54 in the three groups.

At this point Barron defined "Ego Strength" as a construct expressed in characteristics such as physiological stability and good health, a strong sense of reality, feelings of personal adequacy and vitality, permissive morality, lack of ethnic prejudice, emotional outgoingness and spontaneity, and intelligence.

From this definition certain implications and hypotheses were drawn, then tested in further studies using various groups of normal subjects. ES scores were related to a variety of variables including intellectual performance, spatial orientation, ability to play charades, performance in the Asch experiment, and courage under fire in the Korean War. A cluster analysis to determine the item groupings was also conducted.

Although far from exhausting the possible relationships and studies, and being collected in a somewhat unsystematic manner, these data all served to clarify the meaning of the construct "Ego Strength." In addition, they provided the basis for a set of laws relating Ego Strength to other concepts. Thus they are a good beginning for the continual process of validating the ES scale as a measure of the construct "Ego Strength."

Evaluation

Reactions to the concept of construct validity have ranged over the entire spectrum. Some writers (e.g., Loevinger, 1957) believe that the construct validity is the essence of validity and that all other concepts of validity can be subsumed under construct validity. At the other extreme are writers (e.g., Bechtoldt, 1959; Ebel, 1961) who vigorously attack the notion of construct validity, primarily on the grounds that it violates the canons of operationalism. Other psychologists approve of the idea but suggest some modifications. For example, Jessor and Hammond (1957) pointed out that the theory surrounding a construct plays an important part in test construction; thus the concepts and methods of construct validity should be applied to test construction as well as to validation. Campbell (1960) suggested that there are really two varieties of construct validity, *trait validity* and *nomological validity*, with the former focusing on the trait (construct) and the latter being concerned with the test as representing a term in a formal theoretical network.

Probably the greatest contribution the concept of construct validity has made is to focus attention on psychological tests as instruments of psychological theory. Thus tests are viewed in broader perspective than solely as tools to aid in practical decision making. Even when no formal theory is involved, construct validity forces the investigator to precisely define the trait being measured and to specify the relationships expected between test scores and other variables. It has also placed an emphasis on collecting a variety of data to support one's claims, rather than relying on only one technique or measure. Finally, it has suggested a systematic way to proceed with validation when "hard" data are not abundantly available.

Construct validity also has several disadvantages. Many persons have tried to pawn off sloppy evidence as indications of construct validity; this, however, is more a fault of the investigator than of the concept. Also, the necessary operational steps and procedures are not unambiguous. For example, negative evidence has several possible interpretations, and no clear indication is presented of which way to proceed after obtaining negative evidence. Third, there is no single summary index to describe the degree of validity. Although the proportion of variance attributable to the trait being measured would appear to be a simple quantitative index of construct validity, this value may vary between situations. Fourth, unless all parties agree upon the definition of the construct, the results of various studies will not be comparable. In psychology, where terms frequently are only vaguely defined, it is not unusual for the same term to be applied to different concepts, and the same construct to be given different names by different authors. Unless there is agreement on definitions of basic terms, the investigators will just talk past each other. And, finally, the process of construct validation as proposed by Cronbach and Meehl (1955), with its stress on the nomological network, may be unnecessarily complex. It may be that something more akin to Campbell's concept of trait validity will provide a more workable framework.

SOME POINTS OF INTEGRATION

We shall conclude our discussion of validity by emphasizing several points that were implied throughout the discussion. First, for any given test, any or all of the types of validity evidence may be relevant and desirable. For example, an achievement test typically is evaluated primarily in terms of its content validity. But because achievement tests frequently serve, at least implicitly, as predictors of success in the next unit or course in a sequence, criterion-related (predictive) validity may also be relevant. Or, to use another illustration, a test of divergent thinking could be evaluated in terms of its sampling of the various facets of divergent thinking (content validity), its ability to predict success in occupations or academic curricula requiring divergent thinking (criterion-related validity), and its role as a defining construct in a theory of intellectual organization (construct validity). Two important corollaries follow from this position: (1) *Validity will always be situation specific*. (2) *Any test will have many different validities*.

Second, although the various approaches to validity can be classified in numerous ways, there are basically two major questions asked in validity studies: (1) How effective is the test as a decision-making aid? (2) What is the nature of the variable measured by the test? Criterion-related validity data are generally used to evaluate the test's effectiveness as a decision-making aid. The question of the nature of the variable measured by the test is answered by evidence from studies of construct validity. In this framework, content validity can, without too many difficulties, be subsumed under construct validity since both are using tests to represent.

Third, although validity is usually discussed in connection with the final form of a test, the basic philosophy of validity plays an integral role in the test construction process. The pool of potential test items is composed of items that measure some important construct, sample some relevant content or behavioral domain, and/or are presumed to be predictive of the relevant criteria. Items are selected from this pool of potential items on the basis of their content or criterion-related validity. Items not meeting certain requirements dictated by the nature of the trait measured (for example, those that reduce homogeneity) are eliminated. Thus, the concepts and procedures of validity are an essential element in the test construction process.

Fourth, not all types of validity have been included in our discussion. In particular, two important types—synthetic validity and incremental validity—were not discussed. *Synthetic validity* (Balma, 1959) is the process of inferring validity in a specific situation from a logical analysis of job elements. The basic procedure involves three steps: identifying the essential elements in a job or groups of jobs, estimating the validity of tests in measuring these elements, and combining the elemental validities into a composite. This procedure, which is most commonly used in industrial and business settings, would appear most valuable in the initial stages of developing a testing program, where one is interested in identifying relevant criteria and potential predictors. Since the procedure is rational, but lends itself to empirical confirmation, synthetic validity would seem to be an aspect of criterion-related validity.

Incremental validity (Sechrest, 1963) stresses the fact that the validity of a test is determined by its unique contribution to predictive efficiency. In other words, a test is valid if it produces an increment in predictive accuracy. Inasmuch as the concept of incremental validity is easier to illustrate with multiple measures, it will be discussed in the following chapter.

Finally, we shall once again emphasize the relationship between reliability, homogeneity, and validity. Lack of reliability, in both the predictor and criterion, limits validity. Reliability and homogeneity data both were relevant information in construct validity. Taking a broad view, one could place reliability, homogeneity, and validity all under the tent of measures of generalizability (cf. Cronbach et al., 1972)—the fundamental difference between the concepts being the dimensions over which generalizations are made.

9

COMBINING
TEST SCORES

In previous chapters we have, with few exceptions, discussed only one test score at a time. This was done to simplify the presentation of the basic concepts. In practice, however, one seldom deals with only a single test score; generally scores are combined to arrive at a composite score or prediction. At least three types of combinations are frequently encountered: individual test items are combined into a scale, subtest, or test; scores on several subtests are combined into a composite score; and scores on several tests are combined to yield a composite description or prediction. Although these three problems involve different components, the logic and statistical methods involved are basically similar.

Types of Composite Scores

Every test is composed of a number of independent items. Various subgroups of these items may be combined to form scales or subtests, or all items may contribute to one overall test score. In each case, the total (test) score will be a composite of individual item scores. Although most scores are unweighted composites, with all items weighted equally, the individual items may be weighted differentially (see Chapter 3). Regardless of the weighting method used, unless he has some specific interest in individual items, the test user generally will work only with composite scores.

Some tests are composed of several subtests or scales, each of which yields a score. These scores may or may not be combined into a composite score. For example, the Strong Vocational Interest Blank reports scores for more than 50 occupations, but has no total score. On the other hand, the Wechsler Adult Intelligence Scale (WAIS) is composed of eleven independent subtests. Six subtests (Vocabulary, Information, Arithmetic, Comprehension, Similarities, and Digit Span) comprise the Verbal Scale, and the sum of the scores on these six subtests is reported as a Verbal IQ. The other five scales (Digit Symbol, Picture Completion, Block Design, Picture Arrangement, and Object Assembly) comprise the Performance Scale, and a Performance IQ is computed in an analogous manner. In addition, a Full Scale IQ is derived from performance on all eleven subtests.

Frequently several tests or predictors are utilized simultaneously. For example, when deciding which applicants to admit to college, the admissions officer may consider high school grades, scores on college aptitude tests, nonacademic accomplishments, and recommendations of teachers and counselors. Counselors in the U.S. Employment Service administer the General Aptitude Test Battery, a battery consisting of twelve tests measuring nine factors, which predict success in various occupations. In both of these situations, in order to arrive at a decision, the test user must somehow combine the test scores, taking into account the contradictions in the data as well as points where different data confirm and support each other.

Three Questions

Whenever test scores are combined, three interrelated questions must be asked. First, what methods can be used to combine the scores? Second, what is the optimal combination of scores? And third, how much and what kind of data (scores) are needed to produce an optimal combination?

The answer to the first question will depend primarily on the purpose of combining the test scores, on the type of decision to be made. The decision may require individuals to be ranked in order, or only that individuals be placed in broad groups (for example, acceptable or unacceptable). In other situations the primary question is which variables best differentiate between existing groups, rather than how to classify individuals most effectively.

Although certain characteristics of the data may influence the choice of a method, in general, types of data and method are independent. That is, the same set of data may be combined by different methods and/or to make various decisions. For example, combinations of the same aptitude, achievement, and interest test data might be used, even for the same individual, in a selection battery, for job placement, and for long-range vocational planning. Since these three uses ask different questions, and thereby require different answers, the method of combining scores might well be different in each situation. Yet all methods would utilize the same set of data.

The second question is essentially one of validity. Generally we are concerned with the combination of tests that yields the highest criterion-related validity; thus, the standards of criterion-related validity will be used to evaluate the composite. In situations where criterion-related validity is not the basic concern, evaluation will, of course, utilize other standards.

The third question is closely related to the other two, especially the second. When a combination of tests is used to predict a criterion, we generally start with the single best predictor, then add predictors until the validity of the composite no longer increases. If a test is added to a composite and validity does not increase, the test has provided no new information (and can be eliminated). Because we are interested in tests that add an increment to predictive accuracy, we are concerned with *incremental validity* (Sechrest, 1963). If a test does not add to predictive accuracy, it is tapping characteristics already measured by other predictors, and consequently tells us nothing that we do not already know. Thus, one important task will be to select variables that tap unique sources of information.

A parallel concern is the number of variables needed before a composite attains optimal predictive accuracy. Empirical studies show that the point of diminishing returns generally occurs quite rapidly. Rarely does inclusion of more than three of four variables increase predictive accuracy in any practical sense.

METHODS OF COMBINING TEST SCORES

In this section we shall consider the various ways that scores can be combined into a composite measure. In discussing the various methods, we shall not differentiate between combining items, subtest scores or test scores, since the logic and methods remain the same regardless of the unit of analysis.

As a framework for our discussion, let us first present some dimensions along which the techniques vary. (1) Scores contributing to the composite can be given equal weight or they may be differentially weighted. Differential weighting may be on a rational basis, or reflect the empirical characteristics of the data. (2) Some of the methods use categorical data, while others utilize continuous measurement. The measurement mode may be the same or different on the input and output sides. (3) The method of combination may be either statistical, rational, or intuitive. That is, the combination may be made according to a statistical model or on the basis of the psychologist's judgment. (4) The variables used may be either objective (for example, test scores or demographic information) or more subjective (for example, ratings). However, when data are combined statistically, numerical values must be assigned to all variables. (5) Some methods assume that low ability in one area can be compensated for by a high degree of another ability or skill. Other methods are noncompensatory, requiring persons to attain a given level on each variable. (6) The addition of the tests to the composite may be simultaneous or sequential; that is, variables may be analyzed simultaneously or in stages. (7) Some methods are predictive, having as their goal the optimal prediction of a criterion; others are descriptive, serving to summarize the data from diverse measures.

With these dimensions in mind, we now turn to a discussion of six widely used methods of combining test scores—clinical judgment, rational methods, multiple cutoff, multiple regression, discriminant analysis, and factor analysis—and several lesser known, but interesting, methods.

Clinical Judgment

Probably the most frequently used approach is to make an intuitive combination of test scores. A high school counselor, when discussing college plans with a student, generally does not utilize statistical predictions of the student's chances of success in each college being considered. Rather, he will consider the student's grades, scores on college admissions tests, teacher opinions about the student, and his knowledge of the various colleges, and make a summary statement (prediction), such as: "State University may be a little rough, but Northwest College offers the same program. You'll have a better chance of succeeding there." Or a clinical psychologist, reflecting on a client's scores on various scales of a personality inventory, might conclude: "The client is very depressed, emotionally unstable, anxious, and tends to act out his problems. Yet, since he has highly developed superego controls, I don't think that he will commit suicide." In both examples, the psychologist weighed the various factors subjectively and arrived at a conclusion or prediction.

The distinguishing characteristic of the clinical approach is that it is an individualized intuitive process. Regardless of the type of input data—objective, subjective, or both—the psychologist considers the diverse data and arrives at what, to him, seems to be the meaning of the data. The results of his deliberations may be a global statement ("This person is dishonest"), a specific prediction ("He will cheat on the final exam"), or an if-then statement ("If he feels that he cannot obtain an A any other way, he will cheat. If the probability of being caught is low, he will cheat."). He may also attach some degree of confidence to his judgment. The form of the judgment, and its specificity, will be determined by the purposes of the judgment and the willingness of the psychologist to be specific in his predictions.

How the psychologist combines data clinically has been extensively studied (see, e.g., Meehl, 1954, 1957; Holt, 1958; Hoffman, 1960; Goldberg, 1968; Kleinmuntz, 1975). Although the parameters are still not completely defined, the process goes somewhat as follows. When a psychologist looks at a test profile he considers several elements: the highest score or scores, the lowest scores, the general elevation of the profile (are the scores generally high or low?), the scatter (do the scores tend to cluster at one level, or are some high and some low?), the shape of the profile, and so forth. He also takes into account the unique features of the scores, characteristics of the individual that may influence the scores, and situational and environmental factors. He then combines the data, weighting the various factors according to what he thinks is their relative importance. This weighting is an implicit, perhaps unconscious, process. The net result is a prediction or description.

Validity   The usefulness of a clinical prediction must be evaluated by determining its validity. That is, the number of correct decisions made using the clinical approach must be compared with the number of correct decisions that would be made using other approaches. Unless the clinical approach can produce more correct decisions, make the same number of correct decisions more efficiently, or make different types of predictions than other methods, it is no more valuable. The validity of clinical predictions will be discussed in detail after a consideration of other types of methods for combining test scores. Suffice it to say here, the evidence for the superiority of clinical judgment is far from overwhelming.

Evaluation   Advocates of the clinical approach stress several presumed advantages. First, it allows for consideration of unique and/or configural patterns of scores. Since most of the statistical techniques involve linear combinations of variables or simple configurations, they are of limited usefulness. To understand and predict human behavior fully, one must take into account the highly configural nature of the interactions between variables, a task only trained human judgment can accomplish. Second, since statistical analyses are normative, they do not indicate how to handle atypical patterns. Because each individual is unique, normative statistical models are never completely applicable to any individual; hence sophisticated clinical analyses are needed. Third, even if normative data are applicable in a particular situation, statistical predictions must be overridden in certain circumstances. For example, Meehl (1954) cites a case of the highly predictable moviegoing behavior of an individual being disrupted by a broken leg. The clinician would argue that he could take this factor (the broken leg) into account and reverse the prediction, whereas a statistical formula would be unable to incorporate this new bit of data. In short, clinical prediction is most valuable when there are unique or novel patterns, when some special factor influences the prediction, and when the probabilities of occurrence (base rates) or one or more variables are very low.

In response, a statistically oriented psychologist would argue that the assumption of complex configural patterns has not been verified, that clinicians overemphasize atypical patterns or events, and that following the base rates or statistical predictions will lead to the better predictive accuracy. They view the clinician as operating as an inefficient computer, one that assigns less than optimum weights to the predictor variables. The weight of the evidence, at least as it pertains to the prediction of specific outcomes or behaviors, tends to support the statistician rather than the clinician.

Rational Methods

A second approach utilizes rational bases for combining test scores. The simplest approach would be to sum the scores of the individual variables (such as items, subtests, or tests) to arrive at a composite score:

$$X_c = X_1 + X_2 + \cdots + X_n \tag{9.1}$$

where X_c is the composite score and $X_1 \cdots X_n$ are the scores on the n variables making up the composite. Although Equation (9.1) appears to weight all variables equally, this procedure weights each variable in proportion to its standard deviation—the most variable test being weighted heaviest. Each variable can be weighted equally by changing all scores to standard scores (z scores) then combining them:

$$z_c = z_1 + z_2 + \cdots + z_n \tag{9.2}$$

Other rational weighting methods could also be used; for example, scores could be weighted by their reliabilities or by some rationally derived differential weights. All of these methods involve purely rational weighting based on an *a priori* conception of the ideal weighting procedure.

Validity   Again, the ultimate test is the validity of the predictions made using alternative weighting methods. When a small number of predictors is involved, differential weighting based on empirical relationships between variables generally results in more valid predictions and thus is preferred over rational weighting systems. With a large number of predictors, however, simple unit weighting generally is almost as valid as differential weighting and thus may be substituted, with little loss of precision, for the more complex differential weighting techniques. The prime example is the weighting of test items. Since a test generally includes a relatively large number of items, it seldom is necessary to use other than unit weights—1 point for a keyed (correct) response and 0 for other responses—for item scores. In fact, several tests that formerly used differential item weighting systems have moved to a unit weight system. For example, the Strong Vocational Interest Blank has changed from a −4 to +4 weighting system to a −1, 0, +1 weighting format (Strong and Campbell, 1966).

In summary, unless there is some compelling reason for using a rational weighting system, elements in a composite will generally be given unit weights or differentially weighted by a technique such as multiple regression (see below) which takes into account the empirical relationships among variables. The former approach is generally used to weight items, the latter to weight tests in a prediction equation. (See Wang and Stanley, 1970, for a review of weighting methods.)

Multiple Cutoff

In the discussion of criterion-related validity (Chapter 7), methods of determining an optimal cutting score were discussed. This cutting score was set so as to maximize the probability that persons scoring higher than the cutting score would succeed on the criterion task and those falling below the cutting score would not. The cutting score also served as the selection point; persons scoring above the line were accepted and those scoring below it rejected. Although, with psychological traits, discrimination is usually probabilistic, when considering other characteristics, such as physical abilities, one can conceive of cutting points that do, in fact, represent minimum standards that a person must attain if he is to succeed on the criterion task. For example, near-normal hearing is necessary for a telephone switchboard operator; jet pilots must be of a certain stature in order to reach important controls; a fire watcher in a national forest lookout tower must have acute vision if he is to spot fires.

The paradigm   Using a procedure analogous to that used with a single predictor, it is possible to develop cutting scores on two (or more) predictors operating jointly. The paradigm, using two predictors, is shown in Figure 9.1. If an individual's scores are above the cutting score on *both* variables, he is accepted; if his score on *either* variable falls below the cutting score, he is rejected. This paradigm can be generalized to any number of predictors. Regardless of the number of predictors, if a person's score falls below the cutting line on *any* variable, he is rejected; if he is to be accepted his scores must exceed the cutting score on *all* variables.

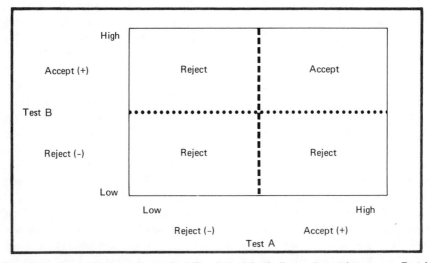

Figure 9.1   The multiple-cutoff paradigm. The dashed line indicates the cutting score on Test A, the dotted line the cutting score on Test B. The cells of the table show the decision based on both tests acting as joint predictors.

Several points about the multiple cutoff model should be noted. First, the model is noncompensatory. That is, poor performance (score) on one variable cannot be compensated for by superior performance on another variable. If a person obtained exceedingly high scores on all tests except one, but fell below the cutting score on that one, he would be eliminated. Therefore, this model is appropriate only when there is evidence that the variables are, in fact, noncompensatory. If the predictors are compensatory, and the multiple cutoff model is used, classification errors will be made.

Second, the model is most appropriate when there are definite cutting lines that differentiate persons having the necessary abilities from those who lack the relevant skills. In these circumstances the cutting line represents this minimal ability level. If there are no definite ability thresholds, the cutting scores can be set to maximize certain outcomes. In this latter situation, the several variables must be manipulated simultaneously to obtain the desired cutting scores; in the former case, cutting scores can be determined for each variable independently.

Third, the decision will be either to accept or reject. Each individual is placed in one of two categories: those meeting the minimum requirements and those not meeting the minimum standards.[1] Thus we obtain a pool of acceptable candidates, with no ranking of people within the pool. If we want to distinguish between minimally acceptable applicants (for example, rank them) we must use some other procedure.

Determining validity   The validity of predictions made using a multiple cutoff paradigm can be evaluated by determining the number of correct decisions made. As with the single predictor case, the criterion may be either total correct decisions or positive hits. The number of correct decisions must also be compared to the base rates, and to the number obtained by other techniques, to determine if multiple cutoff is the optimal strategy.

An example   An example of a multiple cutoff problem is presented in Table 9.1. Inasmuch as the predictor data are continuous, this example illustrates how cutting lines can be set on two predictors simultaneously so as to maximize the total number of correct decisions. Rather than presenting all possible cutting lines, we have included (in step 3) only those in the region of maximal selection efficiency.

Several comments should be made on this particular example. First, there was a large degree of self-selection among students, as can be seen by the skewed distribution of rank in the high school class (HSR). Second, students who did not complete the year are not included; these students generally had lower ability than those who completed the year. Both of these factors serve to reduce the potential effectiveness of any selection strategy. Third, the same maximal hit rate can be attained using only HSR; the math test (MATH) adds nothing to predictive efficiency. The reader is encouraged to confirm this statement by working through the problem.

Successive hurdles   In our discussion of the multiple cutoff methods, we have assumed that all predictor scores were obtained concurrently. In practice, however,

---

[1] It is possible to use more than two classifications—for example, accept, reject, hold for further information; or admit, admit on probation, reject.

TABLE 9.1 An example of the multiple cutoff method

(1) PROBLEM. To determine the optimal combination of cutting scores on two variables—rank in high school class (HSR) and a mathematics test (MATH)—to select students for a college of engineering.

SAMPLE. 660 freshmen engineering students in a midwestern university.

CRITERION. Grade-point-average (GPA) during the freshman year. This measure was dichotomized at GPA = 2.00, the minimal GPA needed for continuation in the program. Students obtaining a GPA ≥ 2.00 were considered acceptable, those with GPA < 2.00 were unacceptable.

VALIDITY. The total number of correct decisions (total hits) was used as a validity index.

(2) DATA. The data are listed in the table below. The first figure in each cell is the number of students with GPA < 2.00, the second figure is the number with GPA ≥ 2.00. (Note that HSR = 1 is the highest score and that greater values indicate a lower class rank.)

				MATH TEST					
HSR	0–24	25–29	30–34	35–39	40–44	45–49	50–54	55–65	Σ
1–5	*	0–2	1–4	2–10	2–11	1–16	0–23	1–28	7–94
6–10	*	1–5	1–3	1–17	2–22	0–28	1–25	0–12	6–112
11–15	0–2	1–0	2–7	1–13	4–17	1–12	3–7	1–5	13–63
16–20	1–2	2–2	2–10	2–12	6–13	6–9	0–4	1–6	20–58
21–25	1–2	2–2	3–5	5–5	5–13	4–12	2–10	*	22–49
26–30	3–1	2–3	2–13	5–5	2–6	1–4	2–4	0–1	17–37
31–35	3–3	2–2	8–5	4–6	3–1	1–3	0–6	*	21–26
36–40	3–2	2–2	0–5	5–2	1–1	2–3	*	*	13–15
41–45	2–0	1–3	5–3	2–3	3–4	2–1	*	*	15–14
46–50	2–3	3–0	1–2	2–1	2–2	*	*	*	10–8
51–60	7–4	1–0	2–1	*	1–0	*	0–1	*	11–6
61–99	12–3	6–0	1–1	*	*	*	*	*	19–4
Σ	34–22	23–21	28–59	29–74	31–90	18–88	8–80	3–52	174–486 = 660

*No cases in cell.

(3) ANALYSIS. To determine the optimal cutting score—ignoring the problem of the number of places available in the class—required considering the number of correct decisions made using a particular pair of cutting lines. If we choose, for example, the cutting lines HSR ≤ 35 and MATH ≥ 30, we would find that use of these cutting lines would result in 499 correct decisions—413 persons who were accepted and succeeded plus 86 rejects who would have failed.

predictor data are often collected sequentially. Rather than have all applicants take all predictors, only applicants who pass one go on to the next step in the sequence, the others being eliminated. Since the successful applicant must surmount a series of hurdles, the method is referred to as successive hurdles.

Table 9.1 (continued)

Varying the cutting lines in analogous fashion we find:

CUTTING SCORE		ACCEPT GPA		REJECT GPA		TOTAL
MATH	HSR	<2.00	≥2.00	<2.00	≥2.00	HITS
30	35	88–413		86–73		499
30	40	96–424		78–62		502
30	45	108–435		66–51		501
30	50	113–440		61–46		501
30	60	116–442		58–44		500
25	35	98–429		76–57		505
25	40	108–442		66–44		508
25	45	121–456		53–30		509
25	50	129–461		45–25		506
25	60	133–463		41–23		504

(4) INTERPRETATION.   The optimal selection procedure would be to require a combination of a MATH score of 25 or higher and an HSR of 45 or less. Using these cutting scores, 509 correct decisions would be made, an improvement of 23 (about 5 percent) over the base rates. The selection ratio, using these cutting scores, would be .87, or almost 9 of 10 applicants would be accepted. Because no great improvement in hit rate was attained, and refusing admission to a student who might succeed is certainly less desirable than admitting a student who later fails, one might well conclude that no cutting lines should be set, and the admissions policies be left unchanged.

(5) ADDENDUM.   It can be shown that the same maximum hit rate can be attained using HSR alone, and thus MATH adds nothing to predictive efficiency. The student who wishes to confirm the last statement can work out the problem for himself.

To illustrate this method, consider the case of a company recruiter hiring college graduates to work as production engineers in an automobile manufacturing plant. His first requirement may be that an applicant majored in mechanical engineering; this is the first hurdle. Only mechanical engineering majors are considered further; all other applicants are eliminated, regardless of their interest in or aptitude for the job. As a second step, or hurdle, the applicant has an on-campus interview with the recruiter. Those whom the interviewer rates favorably go on to the next step; those with unfavorable ratings are eliminated. Suppose the next step is a test battery. Again, some applicants pass and others fail, further reducing the pool. The final hurdle is an interview with their prospective supervisor at the job site. Those who receive an acceptable rating are offered positions; the others must look elsewhere. Note that only those persons who passed all hurdles were offered a job; all others were eliminated at the point where they failed to meet a requirement. This sequence is diagrammed in Figure 9.2.

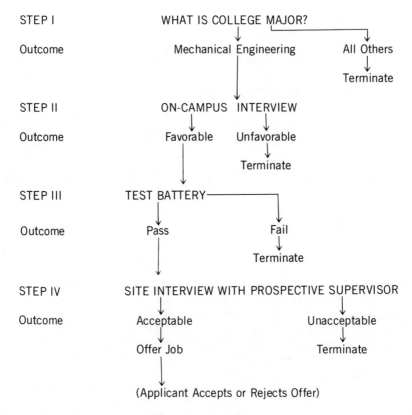

STEP I

Outcome

WHAT IS COLLEGE MAJOR?

Mechanical Engineering   All Others

Terminate

STEP II

Outcome

ON-CAMPUS INTERVIEW

Favorable   Unfavorable

Terminate

STEP III

Outcome

TEST BATTERY

Pass   Fail

Terminate

STEP IV

Outcome

SITE INTERVIEW WITH PROSPECTIVE SUPERVISOR

Acceptable   Unacceptable

Offer Job   Terminate

(Applicant Accepts or Rejects Offer)

Figure 9.2 An example of a sequential selection strategy.

If a sequential selection procedure is to have the maximum validity, the most valid predictor should be used first, followed by the next most valid predictor, and so on. Although the last step would utilize the least valid predictor, the pool of surviving applicants is the best possible pool, given the validity of the predictors. Thus the validity of the selection procedure will be only slightly affected by the use of a poorer predictor at this point.

In practice, the order of presentation of the predictors is usually determined by practical and economic considerations, rather than their validity. As it is more economical to send one recruiter to a university to interview 50 students than to send 50 students to the company plant for interviews, the on-campus interview will usually be conducted before the plant interview, regardless of the validity of the two interviews. Similarly, relatively simple and inexpensive selection methods, such as application blanks and tests, are often administered early in an employment procedure. The more costly and time-consuming, though not necessarily more valid, selection methods occur later in the sequence and are applied only to those that have survived the first hurdles. In this way the total cost of the selection process is minimized.

Evaluation   The multiple cutoff method is applicable whenever minimum cutting scores can be established on certain crucial variables. Because the model is noncompensatory, high performance on one variable cannot compensate for deficiencies in other areas. The model is appropriate for sequential selection strategies and when the variables combine in a nonlinear manner. The model is also compatible with a decision-making approach to validity. In addition, its computation ease and ready interpretability are desirable features.

The model also has several disadvantages. By the use of classes rather than continuous measurement, some precision is sacrificed. Unless there are definable minimal standards (cutting scores), people who would have succeeded through utilization of a compensatory skill or ability will be eliminated. Also, the technique provides a pool of acceptable candidates, not a rank ordering, and thus does not provide the information necessary for selecting from the pool those persons with the greatest probability of success.

Multiple Regression

The multiple cutoff method assumed no compensation between predictors; however, in most situations involving psychological variables some degree of compensation does occur. One student may study long hours to compensate for his lesser ability or weaker background in a course, while another student, possessing a more facile mind and retentive memory, studies hardly at all; or two workers may attain the same production level, one by working rapidly and producing a large number of both acceptable and defective units and the other by working slowly but rarely spoiling a unit. In both of these situations a high degree of one skill or ability compensates for a relative weakness in another relevant areas.

The paradigm   In situations in which compensation between abilities is the rule, multiple regression is the most frequently used model for combining scores. Multiple regression is similar to the regression procedure described previously, except that more than one predictor is used.

The basic logic of multiple regression can best be illustrated by the *multiple regression equation:*

$$Y' = a + b_1X_1 + b_2X_2 + \cdots + b_nX_n \qquad (9.3)$$

where Y' is the predicted criterion score, $X_1 \cdots X_n$ are the scores on the X predictor variables, $b_1 \cdots b_n$ are weights assigned each predictor, and a is a constant to correct for differences in predictor and criterion means.[2] Each predictor receives a weight proportional to its contribution to predictive accuracy.

To illustrate the compensatory nature of the model, consider a case with two predictors. In this situation the regression equation will be of the form

$$Y' = a + b_1X_1 + b_2X_2 \qquad (9.4)$$

---

[2]Equation (9.3) and the other regression equations in this chapter are in raw score form. Analogous equations could be written for standard scores.

Since a, b_1 and b_2 are constants, the only values that can vary are the test scores, X_1 and X_2. Various combinations of scores on X_1 and X_2 can produce the same predicted criterion score (Y'). Suppose that the actual equation was

$$Y' = 10 + 2X_1 + 3X_2$$

In this case the same Y' might be obtained by scoring high on Test I (such as 35) and low on Test II (such as 5), scoring low on Test I (5) but high on Test II (25), or scoring in the middle ranges on both tests (20 and 15, respectively).

Figure 9.3 depicts the multiple regression model for a two-predictor problem. The exact placement and slope of the lines depend on the relative contributions of each predictor variable. The compensatory nature of the model should be obvious from the figure.

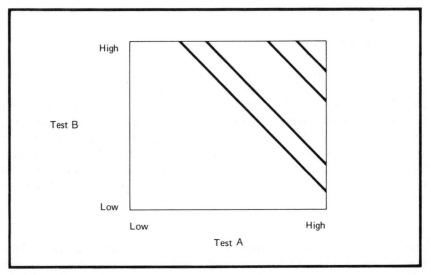

Figure 9.3 The multiple regression paradigm. Every point on a given line represents an equivalent predicted score; the closer the line to the upper right hand corner, the higher the predicted score.

Multiple regression analysis   Since the computational details of multiple regression analysis are quite complex, they will not be discussed in detail here; instead, only a general description of the procedure will be given. (The reader who is interested in the details of multiple regression analysis should consult Kerlinger and Pedhazer, 1973.)

The input data for the analysis are the means and standard deviations of the predictors and the criterion, and a correlation matrix showing the correlations between all pairs of variables. The analysis consists of solving a series of simultaneous equations, a task usually done by computer. This analysis weights the predictors so as to obtain the weighted combination of test scores that predicts the criterion with the least error. The output has two components of prime interest: (1) a regression equation indicating the weights assigned to the various predictors; and (2) a *multiple correlation coefficient, R,* which indicates the correlation between the predictors (considered as a composite) and the criterion measure.

Several aspects of the analysis merit special mention: (1) Because the analysis is based on a linear model, it is appropriate only when relationship between the predictors and the criterion is linear. (2) Theoretically, any number of variables can be used as predictors. (3) The method allows for a determination of the statistical significance of the contribution of any variable. Thus variables that contribute no significant variance can be eliminated, and the regression equation can be based on only those variables that add to predictive accuracy. (4) In general, variables that contribute to predictive accuracy will be those having high correlations with the criterion and low correlations with other predictors. These are variables that predict some significant, unique aspect of the criterion performance.

Validity   In the multiple regression model, validity can be looked at from two angles: the validity of the overall prediction and the validity of each component predictor. The validity of the composite prediction is indicated by the magnitude of the multiple correlation coefficient, R. The square of this correlation, R^2, gives the proportion of variance in the criterion accounted for by the predictors. The validity of each individual predictor can be evaluated by determining its incremental validity—that is, by asking: Does this predictor contribute any unique variance? Does it increase predictive accuracy over and above the level attained when it is not included in the multiple correlation? If a predictor does not increase R significantly, it can be eliminated. Thus variables that are correlated with the criterion may not be included in the prediction (regression) equation if they measure characteristics already tapped by another variable. In practice, two to four predictors generally are sufficient to reach maximal predictive accuracy.

An example   An example of a multiple regression analysis is shown in Table 9.2. The problem is predicting college grades from high school performance and test scores. The analysis was done by a *stepwise* procedure. In this procedure the best predictor is included first; then we add the predictor that in combination with the best predictor increases R the greatest amount. The next predictor included is the one that in combination with the first two adds the greatest amount to R; and so on. We terminate the analysis when additional variables no longer significantly increase the multiple correlation coefficient. The computational steps are not shown in the table, only the summary data for each step. However, inspection of Table 9.2 shows that several of the points mentioned previously hold: The variables included in the regression equation are those having high correlations with the criterion and low correlations with the previously added variables. Not all predictors were included in the prediction equation. Since the data in Table 9.2 are the same as the data in Table 9.1, the differences in the two approaches can be seen by comparing the two tables.

TABLE 9.2 Example of multiple-regression

(1) PROBLEM. Scores on seven predictors—two scholastic aptitude tests (ACT, MSAT), a test of reading speed (RS) and comprehension (RC), an English test (ENGL), and a math test (MATH)—plus the student's rank in his high school class (HSR) were used to predict grade point average (GPA) during the freshman year. The sample consisted of 660 freshmen in the College of Engineering at a midwestern university.

ANALYSIS. Analysis was done on a computer using a stepwise multiple regression procedure (see text).

(2) THE INPUT DATA. The input data consisted of the means and standard deviations on all variables, plus the matrix of intercorrelations among the variables:

Variable	$\bar{X}$	s	GPA	HSR	ACT	MSAT	RS	RC	ENGL
GPA	2.317	.625							
HSR	21.4	17.0	−.544						
ACT	26.1	3.3	.444	−.621					
MSAT	52.2	12.4	.384	−.553	.760				
RS	40.4	9.2	.237	−.313	.497	.456			
RC	28.5	9.3	.327	−.431	.675	.661	.844		
ENGL	186.3	28.5	.390	−.589	.705	.741	.468	.594	
MATH	40.5	10.9	.471	−.592	.681	.598	.374	.481	.591

Note that HSR is scaled so that a score of 1 is the highest possible score, and 100 the lowest; thus HSR correlated negatively with other variables. GPA is on a scale where A = 4, B = 3, and so on.

(3) STEP 1. The first step selected the single best predictor, HSR:

$$R_{\text{GPA,HSR}} = .544$$

The regression equation, using only HSR, is

$$\text{GPA}' = 2.74523 - .01998\,(\text{HSR})$$

where GPA' is the predicted GPA. Note also, that the important fact is the magnitude of the correlation between HSR and GPA, not the sign of the correlation.

(4) STEP II. The second step selected the variable, MATH, that in combination with HSR gave the highest value of R:

$$R_{\text{GPA,HSR+MATH}} = .574$$

Table 9.2 (continued)

and the regression equation is

$$GPA' = 2.10372 - .01499 \,(HSR) + .01321 \,(MATH)$$

(5) STEP III.   The next step selected the variable, ACT, that in combination with HSR and MATH gave the highest R; that is,

$$R_{\text{GPA,HSR+MATH+ACT}} = .577$$

and the regression equation is

$$GPA' = 1.79550 - .01408 \,(HSR) + .01115 \,(MATH) + .01423 \,(ACT)$$

(6) STEPS IV–VII.   These steps added the remaining variables in order; since none of the variables increased R more than .01, they were not added to the regression equation.

(7) SUMMARY.   The results can be summarized by showing R, R^2, and the increase in R produced by each additional variable.

Variables	R	R^2	Increase in R
HSR	.544	.296	.544
MATH, HSR	.574	.330	.030
ACT, MATH, HSR	.577	.333	.003
All variables	.578	.334	.001

The analysis showed that the asymptote of predictive accuracy was reached using three of the seven variables, and that using only two variables resulted in essentially as accurate prediction as using three predictors.

Evaluation   An advantage of the multiple regression method is that a predicted criterion score can be derived for each individual. This is done by substituting his test scores in the regression equation. Thus individuals can be ranked according to their predicted criterion performance. Another advantage is that, because of the compensatory nature of the model, various combinations of ability patterns are equally acceptable. An index of predictive accuracy (R or R^2), is provided, along with an estimate of prediction error (the standard error of estimate). Finally, the selection of the variables to be included in the regression equation, from among all possible predictors, is objective.

The disadvantages are several. First, the computational labor is tedious, an objection mitigated by the availability of computers. Second, having a predicted criterion score may give an aura of exact predictability when, in actuality, the predicted criterion score is really a best estimate—the mean of the distribution of criterion scores for all individuals having the same predictor scores. However, the standard error of estimate can be computed for R in a manner analogous to that for r. Third, the model is inappropriate when compensation among abilities cannot be assumed and when the predictor-criterion relation is not linear.

Discriminant Analysis

In both the multiple cutoff and multiple regression models, scores on a number of predictors were combined to predict some criterion performance. That is, the basic question was: Which individuals will perform better on the criterion? In other situations another question may be more central: What group does the individual most closely resemble? Instead of a selection problem we now have a classification or placement problem. One method of attacking this problem is discriminant analysis.[3]

The paradigm   In the preceding paragraph the basic question of discriminant analysis was phrased in terms of comparing an individual to a group. Actually that question presupposes another question: What variables differentiate between the groups? That is, before we can say which of several groups an individual most closely resembles we must first know what variables differentiate the groups. Thus the first step is to construct an index to differentiate between the groups.

To illustrate, suppose that we want to develop a method to help college freshmen decide which of various curricula—engineering, business, the physical sciences, the social sciences, or the humanities—they should enter. One possibility is to develop an index that indicates which curricular group a student most closely resembles. To do this we could collect a variety of data on members of each group—their abilities, interests, personal characteristics, and the like. We could then run a discriminant analysis to determine whether the curricular groups were, in fact, different, and which variables contribute to the difference—that is, which variables best discriminate between the groups. If a combination of variables, a discriminant function, that differentiated the groups could be found, it could be applied to assess the similarity of any individual to each of the curricular groups.

To recapitulate, discriminant analysis is directed at two problems: (1) determining the combination of variables that best differentiates between defined groups and, once this function is known, (2) classifying individuals in terms of their similarity to the various groups. In order to accomplish these ends, the analysis establishes a function (combination of variables) that maximizes the differences between groups while minimizing the differences within groups.[4] In the ideal situation each subgroup would be distinctly different from every other one, but each would be composed of a homogeneous subgroup of persons. In practice, of course, such ideal separation does not occur; instead, the groups overlap in varying degrees.

Although discriminant analysis can be applied to any number of groups and variables, its logic can be illustrated using two groups and two variables. Figure 9.4 shows the distribution of scores for two groups on two variables (Test I and Test II). These distributions have been projected on a third axis (labeled Y), which is the discriminant function. The basis for determining this function is beyond the scope of

[3]Other terms are used interchangeably with discriminant analysis—for example, discriminant function analysis, multiple discriminant analysis.

[4]In variance terms, we are attempting to maximize between-groups variance and minimize within-groups variance.

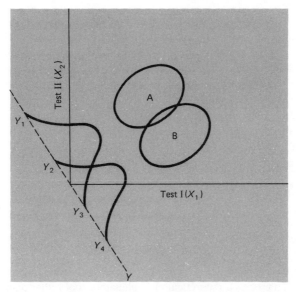

Figure 9.4 The discriminant analysis paradigm. The ellipses represent the distributions of scores within the two groups, A and B. The dashed axis, labeled Y, is the discriminant function. Persons falling in the range between Y_1 and Y_2 would be classified in Group A, those falling in the range between Y_3 and Y_4 would be classified in Group B. Those falling between Y_2 and Y_3 cannot be classified unambiguously; however, the closer they fall to Y_2, the more similar they are to Group A. (See text for further discussion.)

this book; suffice it to say that it is based on an optimal combination of the scores on the two variables. Because there is overlap between the groups on each test, discrimination must be made on the basis of a combination of scores from the two measures.

Discriminant analysis can readily be adapted to fit the selection paradigm. The necessary condition is that the groups represent classifications on the criterion measure—for example, successful and unsuccessful carpenters, college graduates and dropouts. A discriminant analysis would be performed, and if, for example, the applicant more closely resembled successful carpenters than unsuccessful ones, he would be hired.[5]

Validity   The validity of the discriminant analysis will be evaluated in different ways, depending upon which of the two aspects of the problem is being investigated. When considering whether groups can be differentiated, the appropriate index of validity will be the proportion of the variance accounted for by the discriminant function. The greater the proportion of variance accounted for, the higher the validity. When considering the question of the similarity of an individual to the various groups, an appropriate index would be the proportion of correct classifications made—the hit rate.

[5]Because of the complexity of discriminant analysis, no example will be presented. (The interested reader should see, e.g., Borgen and Harper, 1973.)

Evaluation   One advantage of discriminant analysis is that it answers a different type of question, the question of the similarity of an individual to a group. Moreover, a person can be compared to several groups simultaneously. Thus, a discriminant analysis not only indicates which variables differentiate between groups; it also provides a practical classification aid. By casting the criterion variables in terms of categories of success, it can also be utilized in selection problems. A disadvantage is its computational complexity, which makes it more suitable for research projects and large-scale personnel programs than for the occasional user. Also there are several statistical artifacts that influence classification accuracy in an undesirable manner (see, e.g., Tatsuoka, 1973).

Factor Analysis

The techniques discussed earlier in this chapter have combined test scores for prediction or classification purposes. Factor analysis, in contrast, combines scores to reduce the number of variables and/or summarize data. The goal of factor analysis is to have one variable, a factor, replace several diverse measures. Thus, its usefulness is primarily as a theoretical or explanatory tool rather than as a practical decision-making aid.

The paradigm   Factor analysis is a statistical technique for determining the minimum number of constructs (factors) necessary to account for the intercorrelations among a set of variables. Its goal is to find clusters of variables that measure the same factor. This clustering process serves to reduce the number of explanatory concepts needed in the system. A factor is nothing more than a particular linear composite formed from some of the original variables.

The input data for a factor analysis consists of a correlation matrix showing the intercorrelations between t tests. This correlation matrix is then factor-analyzed by one of a variety of methods (see, e.g., Harman, 1967; Nunnally, 1967; Child, 1970), the details of which need not concern us here. The factor analysis transforms the correlation matrix into a factor matrix, which shows the correlations between the test scores and the underlying factor scores. Since the number of factors will be less than the number of tests $(f < t)$, the factor matrix will be smaller than the correlation matrix.

A factor analysis provides three types of information: (1) The number of factors needed to account for the correlations among the tests. (2) The *factor loadings*—that is, the relative weight of each factor in determining the performance on each test. Factor loadings are correlations between the test and the factor (composite). (3) The *communality*, or total amount of variance in the test scores accounted for by common factors. A common factor is a factor that two or more variables share in common.

In other words, factor analysis answers three questions: How many factors account for the performance of the test? What are these factors? And, how much variance in each test is accounted for by the common factors? Factor analysis is similar to the techniques discussed previously in that scores are combined to arrive at a composite; it differs in that its purpose is to reduce the number of explanatory concepts.

An example   An example of a factor analysis is shown in Table 9.3. This example has been chosen for illustrative purposes, and presents a highly simplified, perhaps unrealistic, example. However, for illustrative purposes its clarity and simplicity are virtues. As can be seen in the example, the six separate tests measure but two factors, which we have called verbal and numerical. Thus, we could substitute two factors (constructs) for the six separate measures.

TABLE 9.3   Example of a factor analysis

(1) PROBLEM.   To factor analyze the correlations between six tests to find (a) the number of factors accounting for performance on the tests, (b) the loadings of each test on each factor, (c) the proportion of variance in each test accounted for by the common factors, and (d) the nature of the factors.

(2) DATA.   Suppose we have the following correlation matrix:

	V	R	S	N	AS	AT
V	—	.72	.63	.09	.09	.00
R	.72	—	.57	.15	.16	.09
S	.63	.57	—	.14	.15	.09
N	.09	.15	.14	—	.57	.63
AS	.09	.16	.15	.57	—	.72
AT	.00	.09	.09	.63	.72	—

Inspection of the data reveals that there are two clusters of tests: one composed of tests V, R, and S; the other composed of tests N, AS, and AT.

(3) ANALYSIS.   If the correlation matrix (above) is subjected to a factor analysis using Thurstone's centroid method, with rotation, the following factor matrix will be obtained:

TESTS	I	II	III	h^2
V	.86	.00	.03	.74
R	.83	.09	.11	.71
S	.75	.10	−.09	.57
N	.10	.75	−.09	.57
AS	.09	.83	.11	.71
AT	.00	.86	.03	.74

The figures within the table represent the *factor loadings,* the correlation between test and factor scores. Thus the figure .86 in the upper left corner is the loading of Test V on Factor I. The far right column, labeled h^2, gives the *communalities,* or common factor variance. The communality for Test R was obtained as $h^2 = (.83)^2 + (.09)^2 + (.11)^2 = .71$; communalities for the other tests were similarly obtained.

TABLE 9.3 (cont.)

(4) INTERPRETATION.   The answers to our original questions would be:
  (a) *Number of factors.* Two clear factors emerged, I and II; since III represents essentially zero correlations, it is not an interpretable factor.
  (b) *Factor loadings.* These are shown in the factor matrix. Tests V, R, and S load significantly on Factor I; tests N, AS, and AT load on Factor II.
  (c) *Communalities.* These are shown in the right hand column. Four of the tests—V, R, AS, and AT—have over 70 percent of their variance explained by the common factors. The other two have over half of their variance attributable to the common factors.
  (d) *Nature of the factors.* This cannot be determined without knowing the composition of the tests. Given that V is a vocabulary test, R a reading test, S a test of synonyms, N a test of numerical reasoning, and AS and AT arithmetic tests, it would be evident that Factor I was a *verbal* factor and Factor II a *numerical* factor.

[Note of caution. This example is based on fictitious data given by Kerlinger (1965, Chapter 36). Factor analyses of actual data would be more complex, probably involve additional tests, and would not present such clear-cut, readily interpretable results.]

Evaluation   One advantage of factor analysis is the reduction of a larger number of diverse measures to a smaller number of purer measures. In addition to reducing the number of constructs (and, hopefully, the proliferation of tests) and providing evidence on the correlation between factors, the procedure should clarify the nature and definition of the construct by showing that various tests measure the same concept. In situations in which pure measures of a given trait (that is, homogeneous tests) are required, factor analysis of the items might be an appropriate step in the test construction process. Finally, though not completely objective, factor analytic procedures are replicable by other investigators.

Several criticisms of factor analysis are often heard. One common criticism is that nothing comes out of a factor analysis that doesn't go into it; that is, a factor will not be found unless tests measuring that factor are included as input data. Although this is undoubtedly true, this criticism also pertains to any other type of analysis, a fact that is sometimes overlooked. Second, one may get different results depending upon which of several possible methods of factoring is used. A fundamental question here is whether to assume that the factors themselves are correlated (oblique factors) or are independent (orthogonal factors). This question can be resolved only by determining which procedure provides the most explanatory power. Finally, there is the labeling problem. Since naming a factor is a subjective process, and the results of a factor analysis are frequently not clear-cut, the proper label for the factor is not always evident. In these circumstances, different names may be assigned to factors, thus creating more confusion than clarification.

Factor analysis can be applied to other problems than identifying traits. For example, a factor analysis could be conducted over people, rather than over tests. This procedure would group individuals by their similarities, rather than grouping tests (Cattell, 1952).

Other Methods of Combining Scores

In this section we shall briefly present several other methods of combining scores. As each method is of particular value in certain circumstances, they are worthy of some, albeit brief, mention.

Configural scoring   Configural scoring refers to combining scores so as to consider patterns of responses rather than only simple linear combinations. A classical example of configural scoring is the paradox presented by Meehl (1950). Suppose that two true-false items are administered to 50 schizophrenic and 50 normal subjects. If half of each group responds true (T) and half false (F) to each item, both items, considered individually, will have zero validity. We would predict, therefore, that the validity of the composite score on the two items will also be zero. Suppose, however, that all normals answered both items in the same way (either TT or FF) and all schizophrenics were inconsistent in their responses (responded TF or FT). If this situation obtained and if the pattern of responses were considered (that is, the two items were scored configurally), the configuration would have perfect validity for discriminating between normal and schizophrenic subjects.

Because of the possibility of such dramatic increases in validity through configural scoring, and the predisposition to believe that human behavior is complexly and configurally determined, a fair amount of research on configural scoring has been conducted. However, simpler scoring techniques generally have been found to be as valid as configural scoring. These results are at least partially attributable, no doubt, to the fact that using large numbers of items compensates for interactions among items and because, in many cases, the configurations used have had no firm theoretical base.

Profile analysis   The analog of configural scoring, when considering test scores, is profile analysis. Earlier in the chapter, we presented an illustration of an intuitive profile analysis performed by a clinician. In addition to such subjective combinations, a number of objective techniques for profile analysis have been developed. For example, Cronbach and Gleser (1953) developed a general distance function (D^2) to measure the differences in scores between test profiles. The measure used, D^2, is essentially the sum of squared difference between corresponding scores on two profiles.

Other profile analysis techniques are based on characteristics of the test profile. One approach, which has been widely used with the Minnesota Multiphasic Personality Inventory (MMPI), is to consider "high-point" codes. This approach ranks the various scale scores in order of magnitude and classifies the persons on the basis of their (one or two) highest scores. The modal characteristics of persons having this high-point code are attributed to any individual obtaining this high-point code. Although utilizing a simple ordinal classification method, studies (e.g., Meehl, 1959) have shown this method to be as valid as more complicated profile analysis techniques.

Moderator variables   Moderators are variables that identify subgroups of persons who are differentially predictable. For example, if a different pattern of scores is predictive for males and females, then sex is a moderator variable in the situation. Or, if different patterns of scores predict academic success for black and white children, then race is a moderator variable.

An example of the development of moderator variables is provided by Ghiselli's studies of predictability (Ghiselli, 1956a, 1960a, 1960b, 1963). The general model is as follows: First, using traditional regression procedures, a predicted criterion score was obtained for each individual in the sample. Then each person's predicted criterion score was compared to his actual criterion score, and a discrepancy score (difference between predicted and actual criterion score) was obtained. If the absolute value of this discrepancy score is small, the individual is predictable; if its absolute value is large, the individual is unpredictable. The next step is to find a variable that correlates with the discrepancy score. This variable, the moderator variable, is usually identified by empirical analyses. The moderator variable is then used to identify predictable and unpredictable persons in future samples. If the predictive battery is applied only to people classified as predictable by the moderator variable, then the validity of the selection procedure can be increased. This increased predictive accuracy is obtained at the cost of a reduction in sample size, since unpredictable people are eliminated from further consideration. Ghiselli has found this technique, which is based on the assumption that there is a general trait of predictability, to be useful in an industrial selection situation. Other investigators have found it to be useful in academic situations.

The moderator approach can also be applied to other problems. For example, the technique can be utilized to determine which of two tests is more predictive for an individual (see, e.g., Brown and Scott, 1967; Ghiselli, 1960b). This procedure increases validity and eliminates the necessity for administering the same test to all persons.

Multivariate techniques   One of the blessings wrought by computers is the feasibility of using statistical techniques whose complex computational procedures previously rendered them inapplicable. The availability of computers has opened the possibility of using multivariate analyses that consider several predictor variables and several criterion variables simultaneously. Because using multiple criteria generally is desirable, such analyses are an improvement over simpler models that related several predictors to one criterion measure. For example, we might want to study the relationship of children's intelligence, family background, subject matter achievement, social skills, emotional development, and nonclassroom accomplishments to their academic performance, leadership, and reputation among their peers. Or we might want to study the pattern of study techniques characterizing students enrolled in different curricula, knowing that students in different curricula have differing abilities, interests, values, and personality characteristics. Such studies are amenable to multivariate analyses. Because of the relative newness and complexity of such techniques, they have not yet been widely used in psychological and educational testing. The mathematically sophisticated reader who is interested in pursuing this area should consult sources such as Kerlinger and Pedhazur (1973) and Darlington et al. (1973).

COMPARISON OF METHODS

Prior to discussing the various methods of combining test scores, we listed seven dimensions along which the techniques varied. We shall now use three of these dimensions—the situations in which each technique is most appropriately used, the nature of the input and output data, and validity—as bases for comparing the methods.

Comparisons along some of the other dimensions are so obvious that they need only brief mention here. For example, it should be evident that clinical judgement involves intuitive combinations of data; the rational methods utilize *a priori* weights; and the other methods—multiple cutoff, multiple regression, discriminant function, and factor analysis—all use empirically derived weights. It should also be evident that, except for certain rational weighting schemes, all techniques employ differential weighting.

Areas of Use

The techniques of combining scores can be dichotomized into predictive and descriptive methods. That is, our goal might be either to predict a criterion behavior more accurately or to summarize diverse data in order to make a general descriptive statement. Predictive uses can be further broken down into two classes: selection problems, where the goal is to identify the best or acceptable candidates in a pool of applicants; and placement (classification) problems, where the goal is to assign individuals optimally to treatment conditions.

In the selection situation, tests are usually combined by either the multiple cutoff or multiple regression methods, the particular method chosen being a function of the type of input data and whether the desired outcome is a ranking or a pool of applicants. Generally, multiple regression will be used unless the input data are not continuous, noncompensatory traits are used as predictors, or the predictor-criterion relation is not linear. If any of these three conditions holds, the multiple cutoff method will be more appropriate. Discriminant analysis and clinical judgment can also be structured to fit the selection situation. Rational combinations could also be used, but they almost always will be less valid than combinations based on differential weighting.

In many situations, a sequential selection strategy will be more efficient or less costly than other strategies. For example, the successive-hurdles variation of the multiple cutoff methods was designed for just such situations. Clinical judgment can, of course, also be readily adapted to sequential strategies. In addition, a combination of methods can, and often is, used. For example, the first stage in a selection procedure may be an interview. Here the interviewer reaches a decision on the basis of his clinical judgment. The next step may be a test battery in which a decision is made from scores combined by multiple regression or multiple cutoff procedures. And so on. Thus several different techniques may be used sequentially, with a different technique being utilized at each stage in the process.

Discriminant analysis is clearly suited for the classification situation, inasmuch as it provides an indication of the person's similarity to several groups. The multiple regression model can be adapted to the classification problem by developing separate regression lines for each treatment condition and assigning each individual to a treatment group so as to maximize predicted criterion scores. Figure 9.5 illustrates this procedure with two groups. Suppose that Treatment A is a traditional physics course, Treatment B is a modern physics course, and scores on a scholastic aptitude test and grades in math courses were used as predictors. Using a composite formed from these two predictors, we could develop separate regression lines for each course. Then, students having higher aptitude and better grades in math courses would be assigned to the modern physics course and other students would be assigned to the traditional course.[6]

All of the methods provide descriptive information as all combine diverse data to arrive at an overall summary score or prediction. However, factor analysis and discriminant analysis yield the clearest examples of methods that provide descriptive information. Factor analysis serves this function by summarizing the results of various tests and identifying the underlying factors (the hypothetical constructs) that account for performance on a variety of tests. Discriminant analysis, by identifying the variables that differentiate between various groups and describing how the groups differ, gives a clearer idea of the nature of the groups.

Data Characteristics

The methods also differ in the type of data acceptable as input and in the mode of data output. Because the type of data influences the choice of method, the data requirements of each method will be briefly reviewed. First, input data. The clinical method, because of its flexibility (or lack of rigor, if you prefer) accepts any type of input data—subjective or objective, qualitative or quantitative, discrete or continuous. All other methods require quantitative data; even data that are subjectively based, such as ratings, must be scaled prior to analysis. All the statistically based methods, with the exception of multiple cutoff, assume that the predictor data is on a continuous scale; multiple cutoff is adaptable to discrete classes. Thus, in most instances, continuous quantitative data are needed.

The output mode also varies. Again, the clinical method allows any manner of output; the only restriction is the ability of the clinician to express his judgment in a particular mode. Multiple cutoff methods partition the subjects into classes—for

---

[6]This is an example of an aptitude-treatment interaction study (Cronbach, 1967; Cronbach and Snow, 1975; Bracht, 1970; Berliner and Cahen, 1973).

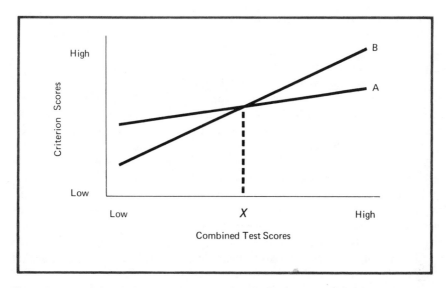

Figure 9.5   Multiple regression applied to the classification problem. Suppose that Treatment A is a traditional physics course and Treatment B is a modern physics course. Students whose composite scores fall to the left of the dashed line would be assigned to traditional physics (Treatment A) and those whose scores fall to the right would be assigned to a modern physics course (Treatment B). The lines A and B, designating the two treatments, are the regression lines showing the predicted course (criterion) performance.

example, acceptable or unacceptable, select or reject. The other methods provide a ranking on a continuous scale: multiple regression giving a predicted criterion score, factor analysis giving correlations between test and factor scores, and discriminant analysis giving the degree of similarity of an individual to a group. Of course, in discriminant analysis and multiple regression, if one is willing to divide the output scores at some point (or points) along the scale, the output can be expressed in terms of class membership. For example, in multiple regression a point on the criterion scale may be designated as the minimal acceptable criterion performance; this score divides individuals into two classes: those predicted to surpass this level and those whose predicted performance is below this level.

Finally, it should be reiterated that all methods, except factor analysis, make predictions about, or give descriptions of, individuals or groups. Although the data utilized in a factor analysis is based on the test performance of individuals, the primary concern involves characteristics of tests and the factors tapped by the tests. Using these data to describe persons is one step removed. However, it is possible, as was pointed out earlier, to factor-analyze people rather than tests.

Validity

Since the value of any test is indicated by its validity, it would be inappropriate to leave our discussion of combining test scores without further consideration of the validity of the various methods of combining test scores. When considering combinations of test scores, validity can be viewed from three angles: the validity of the composite, the validity of the elements comprising the composite, and the comparative validity of the various methods.[7]

The need for cross-validation is particularly crucial when combining several measures, since measurement errors may cumulate, rather than canceling each other out; consequently, the composite may contain large amounts of measurement error. Because of this error, multiple correlation coefficients (and other multiple measures) are subject to large shrinkage (that is, decrease in magnitude) upon cross-validation. A cross-validated R, consequently, is a more accurate estimate of the true degree of relationship than a noncross-validated measure.

In addition to validity, utility must also be considered. Since use of additional predictors will, undoubtedly, increase both direct and indirect costs, and since the increment in predictive accuracy generally drops off rapidly with additional predictors, the costs associated with obtaining additional predictor data may well overbalance any benefits attained by using an additional predictor. Thus use of fewer predictors may result in lower validity but higher utility.

With these considerations in mind, let us now look at the validity of the various methods.

Validity of the composite   Inasmuch as the purpose in combining several test scores is to increase validity, an essential requirement is that the validity of the composite should be significantly greater than the validity of any single test or predictor. If the validity of the composite is not higher than that of the most valid element, then building a composite has been a fruitless exercise. As a corollary, a test should not be added to the composite unless it adds to predictive accuracy; that is, unless it has incremental validity. Thus any composite may not utilize all possible predictors, but will only include those predictors that contribute unique information. It should go without saying that the composite should also predict more accurately than the base rates or other possible selection methods.

The statistic used to evaluate validity will depend upon the method used. In multiple regression, R (or R^2) is an appropriate index of validity. In the multiple cutoff model, or when multiple regression is applied to a classification problem, the hit rate will be an appropriate validity index. Alternatively, a measure of average criterion performance may be used with both the multiple regression and multiple cutoff models. When discriminant analysis is used to differentiate between groups, the percent of variance accounted for is the best index; when it is used to classify individuals, the proportion of correct classifications (hit rate) will be an appropriate index. Since factor analysis is used to reduce the number of variables, the proportion of variance accounted for by the common factors will provide an index of validity (factorial validity).

Validity of components   The validity of the component elements in a composite can be assessed in several ways. At the simplest level we can look at the correlation

---

[7]In the discussion that follows, we shall assume that all necessary experimental controls have been instituted in the validity studies and that the empirical results have been cross-validated.

between a single predictor and the criterion or the hit rate attained using only a particular test. However, these approaches assume that each predictor is used in isolation, when, in fact, it is part of a composite. An appropriate index, therefore, must assess the contribution of the individual test to the predictive efficiency of the composite. In short, we are interested in the incremental validity of the predictor, the ability of the predictor to contribute unique information (see, Hoffman, 1962).

To illustrate, consider the multiple regression model. Using a stepwise model (as in our example), we first selected the variable that was the best single predictor. (The validity of this test as a part of the composite is identical to its validity when used as the sole predictor.) Next, we selected the predictor that, in combination with the first, resulted in the highest R. The incremental validity of this predictor was represented by the increase in R (or alternatively R^2) obtained by adding it to the first predictor. This value will be a function of the test's validity as a predictor of the criterion (zero-order validity) and its intercorrelation with the first predictor. We then added, as the third predictor, the variable that, in combination with the first two, resulted in the greatest increase in R. And so on, until addition of more predictors results in no further significant increase in R. For each predictor the crucial value was its incremental validity—the increase in R resulting from including the variable in the composite.

This method can be applied in an analogous fashion to the multiple cutoff situation. The only difference is that validity would be evaluated by the increase in the hit rate rather than the increase in the multiple correlation coefficient.

Some people claim that incremental validity gives a misleading picture of the contribution of predictors added after the first predictor. Consider, as an example, a test that has high validity when used as the only predictor, but correlates highly with the first predictor and thus adds little to the multiple prediction. They feel that evaluating the contribution of this predictor in incremental terms implies that the test is less valid than it is. If, however, one takes the view, as does this author, that the validity of the composite is the prime concern, then the contribution of any predictor must be evaluated in terms of its contribution to the composite—that is, in terms of its incremental validity. A more damaging criticism of incremental validity is the fact that the contribution of the first (best) predictor is usually assessed by comparing its validity (R or hit rate) to chance (or zero validity) when it should be evaluated by determining its improvement over the base-rate validity. Thus, rather than underestimating the contribution of subsequently added predictors, the error usually is to overestimate the contribution of the first predictor.

Comparative validity   Since the various models are based on different assumptions, are used in different situations, and express their results in different terms, it is difficult to compare the effectiveness of two or more techniques applied to the same problem. There are, however, two situations in which comparisons can readily be made: comparing the multiple cutoff and multiple regression models in the selection situation, and comparing clinical and actuarial predictions.

Consider first the cutoff and regression methods. Here, the method whose assumptions best fit the situation will yield the higher validity. If there is compensation between predictor variables and the relation between predictors and the criterion is linear, the multiple regression model will be more valid; if the predictors are noncompensatory, or if the predictor-criterion relationship is not linear, then the cutoff model will be more valid. Where both models can be applied, the regression model is generally more valid.[8]

Another problem that has been extensively studied is the comparison of clinical and actuarial predictions. Actuarial prediction includes all models based on a statistical combination of test scores. The controversy over the relative merits of these two approaches was given its original impetus by Meehl (1954). In his book, *Clinical vs. Statistical Prediction,* Meehl surveyed the available evidence and concluded that although clinical predictions may have certain unique functions, in those situations in which both clinical and statistical predictions have been compared statistical (actuarial) prediction has always been equally or more accurate than clinical predictions.

In the years following publication of this book, there have been a number of articles concerning the clinical-actuarial issue. Some have emphasized the logic of the two approaches, concluding that the two types of prediction are appropriate in different situations. For example, clinical prediction is claimed to be appropriate when an "open-ended" prediction needs to be made, actuarial prediction is appropriate for predicting specific observable criteria. Other studies have compared clinical and actuarial predictions in various situations, such as academic achievement, job performance, psychiatric diagnosis, response to various treatments, and so forth. The weight of the evidence is that when a specific circumscribed outcome is to be predicted, the actuarial approach is usually as good as, if not better than, the clinical prediction. This is not unexpected, since the statistical techniques are designed to minimize prediction errors and weight each predictor optimally. The best that an individual making a clinical prediction can hope for, unless he can identify a relevant variable not considered in the equation, is to duplicate the optimal weighting of the formula. In addition, even if a clinician identified a salient variable, this variable could be incorporated into a new statistical prediction formula, thus retaining the advantage for the formula.

---

[8]Whenever continuous scores are classified into groups, some precision is lost and thus validity is lowered.

SUGGESTED FURTHER READING FOR PART II

American Psychological Association. *Standards for educational and psychological tests.* Washington, D.C.: American Psychological Association, 1974.

Pages 25 to 55 present and explain the standards for reliability and validity studies. All test users should read this discussion.

Cronbach, L. J. Test validation. In R. L. Thorndike (Ed.), *Educational measurement.* (2d ed.) Washington, D.C.: American Council on Education, 1971.

An excellent, comprehensive discussion of the concept of validity and the methods of obtaining validity data.

Cronbach, L. J., & Meehl, P. E. Construct validity and psychological tests. *Psychological Bulletin,* 1955, *52,* 281–302.

The classic paper on construct validity.

Fincher, C. Is the SAT worth its salt? *Review of Educational Research,* 1974, *44*, 293–305.

An example of a large-scale study designed to evaluate the validity of a particular test.

Helmstadter, G. C. *Principles of psychological measurement.* New York: Appleton, 1964.

Chapters 2 to 6 cover reliability and validity, using the different types of measurement errors as an organizing framework.

Hills, J. R. Use of measurement in selection and placement. In R. L. Thorndike (Ed.), *Educational measurement.* (2d ed.) Washington, D.C.: American Council on Education, 1971.

Thorough discussion of the practical and statistical problems in using tests in placement and selection. Also includes descriptions of illustrative studies.

Kerlinger, F. N. *Foundations of behavioral research.* (2d ed.) New York: Holt, Rinehart and Winston, 1973.

Includes excellent brief chapters on reliability (Chapter 26) and validity (Chapter 27).

Lavin, D. E. *The prediction of academic performance.* New York: Russell Sage Foundation, 1965.

A review of attempts to predict academic performance from ability, personal, and social variables; includes suggestions for future research directions. Relatively nontechnical.

Magnusson. D. *Test theory.* Reading, Mass.: Addison-Wesley, 1967.

Chapters 10 to 12 present a brief mathematical treatment of validity and prediction as applied to selection and classification problems; a clear mathematical presentation.

Psychological Corporation. Test Service Bulletins. New York: The Psychological Corporation.

These are brief, very readable descriptions of practical problems encountered by test users. See particularly numbers 37 ("How effective are your tests?"), 44 ("Reliability and confidence"), 45 ("Better than chance"), 47 ("Cross-validation"), 50 ("How accurate is a test score?"), and 59 ("Restriction of range").

Sechrest, L. Incremental validity. *Educational and Psychological Measurement,* 1963, *23*, 153–158.

Author points out that a test should be evaluated in terms of the amount of unique information it provides.

Wine, J. Test anxiety and direction of attention. *Psychological Bulletin,* 1971, *76*, 92–104.

Review of research that attempts to answer the question: What do anxious people do that interferes with their performance on tests?

PART III

INTERPRETING TEST SCORES

In the first two parts of this book we have focused on the construction and evaluation of measuring instruments (tests). We now turn to the topic of most concern to the majority of people who use tests—that is, how to interpret test scores. We have purposely delayed our discussion of scores until this point. Our reasoning is simple; unless we know what a test measures, and how accurately it measures, we cannot interpret test scores with any degree of confidence or accuracy.

The problems involved in interpreting scores fall in two general areas. First, we must develop scoring procedures and scales that are both meaningful and statistically sound. Usually this requires transforming raw scores (that is, scores derived directly from the test) to another scale. Thus much of our discussion will revolve around the advantages and limitations of various possible score scales. Our second problem is how to communicate the maximum amount of usable and meaningful information to the test taker or user. This topic will be approached both by illustrating several methods of presenting scores and by discussing how to interpret scores and communicate the meaning of scores to other people.

In our presentation we shall classify scores into three broad categories based on the standard of comparison used when interpreting scores. The first category involves scores that are interpreted by comparison with the performance of other people. These scores, called *norm-referenced,* are expressed, either directly or indirectly, in terms of a relative ranking within some comparison group. In the second category are scores that express performance in terms of degree of mastery of a defined content or skill domain. Here the comparison is not with other people, but with the content covered by the test. These scores are referred to as *content-referenced* because they tell whether or not (or to what degree) the person has mastered the relevant content. The third category, *outcome-referenced* scores, includes those scores where performance is expressed in terms of level of performance on an external criterion. Outcome-referenced scores have the advantage of combining validity and normative data.

Chapter 10 focuses on norm-referenced scores. Since norm-referenced scores involve comparisons among people, we shall first tackle the question of what is a relevant comparison (norm) group, emphasizing the dimensions to be considered when developing or evaluating a norm group. We shall then proceed to a discussion of the major types of norm-referenced scores, starting with the simplest, and probably most common, type of score, the percentile rank. Percentile ranks indicate a person's relative ranking in a norm group in percentage terms. We shall see that for many purposes a scoring scale that has equal-sized units is desirable. Thus we shall next discuss a type of scale that has these interval properties: standard scores. Standard scores express a person's performance in terms of his deviation from the mean in standard deviation units. This method of expressing scores has another advantage: It allows us to place scores from different tests on a common scale—an important consideration when we want to compare scores on several tests. A third type of norm-referenced scores is developmentally based, reporting performance as either age or grade equivalents. The chapter will conclude with examples of various methods for presenting normative data.

In Chapter 11 we shall discuss content-referenced and outcome-referenced scores. With content-referenced scoring systems we have two major problems: specifying the content and/or skill domain and defining a scale that directly indicates the student's degree of mastery in content terms. As might be expected, content-referenced scores are most appropriate for testing mastery of academic subjects. We shall see that developing content-referenced scores is difficult and that many content-referenced scores have, at least implicitly, a normative basis. We shall also emphasize that content- and norm-referenced scores are really just two ways of looking at the same performance; thus, both types of scores may be used on the same test.

Outcome-referenced scores are most appropriate when using tests to predict some extratest behavior, as in selection or placement situations. Since outcome-referenced scores incorporate validity data directly into the test interpretation process, the first step will always be to collect the necessary validity data. Only after this step is completed can we be concerned with methods for presenting scores. We shall discuss two types of outcome-referenced scores: one that indicates the prob-ability of various outcomes (expectancy tables) and one that makes a prediction of the level of criterion performance. In our view, outcome-referenced scores, by incorporating validity data into the test interpretation process, have much to rec-ommend them over the other types of scores, particularly norm-referenced scores.

After discussing several problems in score interpretation (imprecise scores, equating scores on different tests, and difference scores), this part of the book will conclude with some suggestions for communicating test results to other people. Obviously, we cannot make you an expert in test interpretation; this comes only through practice and knowledge of human development and counseling techniques. What we will do is present some useful guidelines for interpreting scores. These guidelines can be summarized briefly: First, make sure the person knows what his scores mean and how they will be used; and second, allow him to react to the information presented, so as to clarify their meaning and implications.

10

NORM-REFERENCED SCORES

Most readers of this book will probably never determine the reliability or validity of a test. However, at some time in your life you will probably have occasion to interpret scores on psychological or educational tests. This may be in your professional role as a teacher, counselor, or personnel manager, or when interpreting scores on tests that you or your children have taken. Thus, in this section, we will discuss the "hows" and "whys" of developing and interpreting test scores.

Before we discuss the various types of scores, it would be well to consider what information is derived from test scores. An individual's score on any test will always be a function of three conditions: his genetic makeup, his learning and experiences prior to the testing, and the conditions of the testing situation. All three will play a part in determining his performance. Although it is difficult to separate the genetic and experiential components, standardizing testing conditions ensure that a person's performance will reflect his abilities and characteristics, not the particular testing situation.

Another, perhaps more fruitful, way of looking at test scores is in terms of the conclusions that can be drawn from them. Three questions are preeminent: Where is the person now? How did he get there? What are the implications for his future behavior? In other words, we are interested in the individual's current performance, the factors that have caused him to perform at that level, and what he might be expected to do in the future. If we view test scores only from the first perspective—where he is now—we interpret test scores only as a measurement of present status. However, this is a limited view since the same test score obtained by two people may mean different things depending on their prior experiences. For example, a high score on a vocabulary test might have different implications if obtained by a child whose parents were college professors or by a child from the depths of Appalachia. Thus, in order to make meaningful interpretations, we must take the individual's experiences prior to the test into account.

The third question—What are the implications of the score?—is, of course, an aspect of validity. Although it may be interesting to know how an individual scores on a test in comparison to some group, we usually want to know what the score implies about his future behavior. To make this prediction (interpretation) we must have validity data. In short, *meaningful interpretation of test scores requires both means of expressing scores (that is, a scale) and validity data indicating what the test measures.*

Raw Scores

After a test is administered, an individual's responses are compared to a *key* to obtain his score on the test. On achievement and ability tests, the keyed responses are the correct answers. On interest and personality inventories, the keyed responses are usually the predominant choices of a particular criterion group. Other performance measures can also be used as scores—for example, the number of errors, the sum of points on various items or problems, the time taken to complete the test, or a rating. Any such score obtained directly from the test is called a *raw score*.

Raw scores are seldom meaningful in and by themselves. Only when a test covers an explicitly defined domain, and when an absolute standard of performance is available, does a raw score have meaning. Otherwise, a raw score must be compared to the scores of comparable individuals or to some defined standard, or expressed in terms of some outcome or criterion. Each of these approaches requires transforming raw scores to a different scale. Since the new scale is derived from the raw scores by a statistical transformation, they are called *transformed* or *derived scores*.

Derived Scores

There are a number of possible ways of classifying derived scores (see, e.g., Angoff, 1971a; Lyman, 1971). In our discussion we shall use three broad classes: norm-referenced scores, content-referenced scores, and outcome-referenced scores.

Norm-referenced scores   Most frequently, an individual's performance is compared to the scores of other individuals in a relevant reference group, the *norm group*. The norm group is composed of people who share certain characteristics with the individual. For example, on a classroom examination the norm group will be other persons taking the same course; on an intelligence test, children of the same age; on college admissions tests, students planning to attend college. Thus developing norm-referenced scores involves: (1) identifying a relevant comparison group; (2) obtaining the test scores of members of this group; and (3) converting raw scores to a scale that expresses performance as a relative ranking within this norm group.

The use of norm-referenced scores emphasizes that psychological measurement is relative rather than absolute. As mentioned earlier, in educational and psychological measurement absolute scales or standards seldom are available. Also, in most situations, differences between individuals are more important, or at least more interesting, than similarities. Both of these factors argue for expressing performance in comparative terms; that is, on norm-referenced scales.

Content-referenced scores   Although psychological and educational measurement generally is norm-referenced, this approach often does not provide the desired information. Consider a parent talking to his child's third grade teacher. The teacher reports that Dan's arithmetic skills place him in the top 10 percent of his class. This is a norm-referenced interpretation and gives the parent some valuable information. However, the parent might well ask, "What arithmetic skills has Dan mastered?" Here the parent is asking for a description of his child's performance in terms of the content he has mastered, not in terms of his performance relative to his classmates.

This example illustrates a second method of reporting performance, in terms of content mastery. That such scores are valuable, particularly in educational settings, should be obvious. However, development of content-referenced scores has proceeded slowly. One reason is that this approach requires a precise specification of the content (and skill) domain; this task is difficult except in very circumscribed areas. For example, it is relatively easy to delineate the domain "addition of two-digit numbers" but more difficult to circumscribe the domain "ability to solve algebraic equations." The second problem is defining an acceptable mastery level. At first glance it might appear easy to specify the level of mastery expected in arithmetic from a third grader, given a description of the domain. However, a little thought should indicate that the only nonarbitrary way to do this is in terms of what skills third graders typically master; this, of course, would be a normative approach.

Outcome-referenced scores   A third possibility is to express performance in terms of a predicted outcome or behavior. That is, rather than interpreting an individual's score on a college admissions test by saying that he scored higher than 78 percent of the freshman class, we would say that he would be expected to obtain B grades. Or, when interpreting an interest inventory, we might say that a person's interests were similar to physicians'. In both examples, we have interpreted test scores, not as a relative ranking within a group, but in terms of some important outcome or criterion behavior.

Outcome-referenced scores have one important advantage over other types of scores: They incorporate validity data into the test interpretation. That is, the interpretation is essentially a prediction of future behavior. In order to make this prediction, we need validity data indicating what behaviors can be predicted from test scores. Usually, of course, these will be criterion-related validity data. Although this approach requires more work, in that validity studies must be conducted and their results incorporated into the score interpretation procedure, it should result in more meaningful interpretations.

To summarize, *norm-referenced scores* report performance in terms of the individual's relative ranking within a comparison group, *content-referenced scores* report performance in terms of the content or skills mastered, and *outcome-referenced scores* report performance in terms of a prediction of future behavior.[1] With these distinctions in mind, we now turn to a more detailed discussion of each type of score. Since norm-referenced scores are most commonly used, they will be discussed first. And since interpretation of norm-referenced scores always is in relation to a norm group, we shall consider the process of building norm groups before presenting the various types of norm-referenced scores.

NORM GROUPS

On most tests, scores are interpreted by comparing an individual's performance with that of others in the norm group. The norm group provides a basis for comparison by showing the scores of a standard, defined reference group. Potentially, there are a number of possible norm groups for any test. Since a person's relative ranking may vary widely, depending on the norm group used for comparison, the composition of the norm group is a crucial factor in the interpretation of norm-referenced scores. Thus, when developing norms, the first question is: What are the various possible norm groups?

From the test developer's viewpoint, this question becomes: In what populations will the test be used? The norm groups should be chosen to represent these populations. If the test is designed to assess high school seniors' aptitude for college work, the norm group should consist of high school seniors planning to attend college. If the test is designed to measure the personality characteristics of adolescents, the norm group would consist of a cross section of adolescents. If the test is designed to measure the reading readiness of kindergarten students, the norm group should consist of kindergarten students who have not begun reading instruction. Since most tests are designed for use with various groups, more than one norm group generally will be needed.

The test user looks at norms from a different vantage point. His primary question is: Which of the available norm groups is most appropriate? Again, several norm groups may be relevant. For example, when counseling a high school student who plans to study engineering in college, a counselor might compare the student's scores on a scholastic aptitude test with those of other high school students planning

---

[1]A more common approach is to consider two major types of scores: norm-referenced and criterion-referenced (Glaser, 1963). Criterion-referenced scores correspond to what we are calling content scores.

to attend college, with those of entering freshmen at the universities the student is thinking of attending, and with those of freshmen engineering students at the universities the student is thinking of attending.

For both the test developer and the test user the crucial consideration is the composition of the norm groups. For aptitude and achievement tests, the appropriate norm group usually consists of present or potential competitors. For tests of broad abilities or personality characteristics, norm groups are usually composed of people of the same age or educational level. Of course, in any particular situation a variety of dimensions may be used to define the norm group—such as sex, age, grade or educational level, occupation, geographic region, socioeconomic status, race.

Requirements for Norm Groups

The test developer or user must consider several factors when constructing or evaluating norm groups. The first requirement is that *the composition of the norm group be clearly defined*. Although the general specifications of the norm groups will be dictated by the purposes and uses of the test, within this range there is a variety of potential norm groups. Therefore a concise, yet clear, description of the nature and characteristics of each norm group is necessary. A statement that a norm group is composed of ''5000 college freshmen'' is insufficient. Even the following statement provides only a minimal description:

> The norm group consists of entering freshmen, male and female, enrolled in liberal arts curricula at land-grant universities.

Some questions we might ask are: What is an ''entering freshman''? What curricula are subsumed under ''liberal arts''? What are ''land-grant universities''?

If a norm group is composed of people in a particular job or occupation, the title of the job should be given along with its code in the *Dictionary of Occupational Titles,* the job duties should be specified, and the type of business or industry, its geographic location, the years of experience of the workers, and other relevant information should be included. For achievement tests, the basic information should include the grade level of the students, the type of school, socioeconomic and other demographic data, and the student's experience in the subject matter area being tested.

Frequently various subgroups within a population perform differentially on a test. If subgroups exhibit different levels or ranges of performance, then separate norms should be constructed for each subgroup. For example, men generally perform better than women on tests of mechanical aptitude, whereas, conversely, women score higher than men on clerical aptitude tests; therefore, separate normative data for men and women are usually provided on these tests. Variables that frequently are related to test performance, and thus may constitute the basis of separate norm groups, include sex, age, education, socioeconomic status, intelligence, occupation, geographic region, race, and amount of special training.

In most instances a norm group consists of a sample drawn from the relevant population rather than the entire population. Thus a second requirement is that *the norm group must be a representative sample of the designated population.* For example, if a test is designed for use with junior high students, it should include proportionate numbers of students from each grade level, urban and rural areas, various races, both high and low socioeconomic areas, various areas of the country, and so forth. Failure to obtain a representative sample will bias the norm data and make interpretation of scores more difficult. Since norm data are easier to obtain from certain groups (for example, it is easier to obtain data from high socioeconomic status suburban schools than from ghetto schools, and easier to collect a sample of college students than 18-year-olds who are working), the possibility of biased sampling is ever present.

Implicit in the previous paragraph is a third requirement: *The sampling procedure must be clearly described.* To return to our previous example, the description of the sampling, and thus of the norm group, might be:

> The norm group consisted of 5000 entering freshmen tested in the first week of classes in September 1975; 250 students (125 male and 125 female) were randomly selected from students enrolled in liberal arts curricula at each of 20 universities randomly selected from among all land-grant institutions.

As with the description of the population, the more precise and comprehensive the description the better.

A fourth requirement is that *the norm groups be based on a sample of adequate size.* What constitutes "adequate size" is hard to define precisely. However, since the amount of sampling error varies inversely with sample size, the larger the sample the better. Certainly it is not unreasonable to expect national norms on standardized tests to include several hundred cases in each sampling cell. However, the need for large samples, which provide more stable estimates, must be tempered by the requirement of representative sampling. That is, obtaining scores from a smaller, more representative sample is generally more desirable than a set of scores from a larger but vaguely defined group. (See Angoff, 1971a, for a discussion of the procedures of developing norm groups.)

A final consideration is the recency of the norms. With rapid changes in education and job requirements, norms that were developed a number of years ago may no longer be appropriate. Since certain concepts are now being introduced at lower grade levels, the present-day student has been exposed to more and different materials than his counterparts of previous years. Some job requirements have changed radically, as have the skills of the workers. Thus *norms should be updated periodically* and old norms looked upon with appropriate skepticism.

Local Norms

A test user may find that none of the available norm groups fits his purposes. Or he may want to utilize a more limited norm group than those presented in the test manual, which are usually rather broad in scope. For instance, a classroom teacher may want to compare the performance of her students to other students in her class or in the local school system. In this situation, one solution is to construct *local norms.*

Developing local norms is simple and straightforward (Ricks, 1971). Since norm tables are basically frequency distributions, the procedure involves obtaining scores for all people in the local group (or a sample of this group), compiling a frequency distribution, and calculating derived scores (see below). With the data processing equipment now available this is an easy job, even with large numbers of people; done by hand, the task is far from overwhelming.

The main advantage of local norms is, of course, that they allow for comparisons between a person and his immediate associates. Because each class, school, or company is in some ways unique, its members will differ from the members of the norm groups listed in the manual. Since the test performance of the local group may be different from the national norm groups, reliance on the latter may lead to improper inferences when interpreting scores. For example, the students in any particular class or school will not have had the same educational experiences as students in the national norm group. The local students will probably also differ from the national norm group on factors related to school achievement, such as abilities or socioeconomic background. When such differences occur between local and national norm groups, a local norm group may represent a better standard of comparison. Of course, a test user can use both local and national norms, and thus extract the maximal amount of information from the test scores.

The advantage of local norms—providing a more immediate comparison group—is also its major weakness. Although local norms provide information relevant to immediate local decisions, they do not allow for interpretations in a broader context. For example, data from local groups may be most valuable in helping a student decide whether to take Geometry A or Geometry B; they will be of limited use in counseling the student about a career in mathematics. In the latter case, broader norms will provide better information.

Our discussion of norms can best be summarized by paraphrasing several general principles formulated by Seashore and Ricks (1950). They suggest that one should: (1) use well-defined norms groups and avoid vaguely defined people-in-general norms; (2) use separate subgroup norms whenever populations differ and combine groups only when the combination makes sense; (3) report all useful norm data (that is, provide norms on various groups); (4) develop and use local and special group norms; (5) make all normative data available to other test users; and (6) use the available normative data when interpreting scores.

NORM-REFERENCED SCORES

In this section we shall discuss four classes of norm-referenced scores: percentiles, standard scores, developmental scales, and ratios and quotients. For each score we shall consider its rationale and computation, cite its advantages and limitations, give an example, and describe how it is interpreted.

Percentiles

Probably the most widely used method of expressing test scores is percentile ranks. *The percentile rank for a score is defined as the percentage of persons in the norm group who obtain lower scores.* Thus, a percentile rank of 78 indicates that 78 percent of the people in the norm group obtained lower scores; a percentile rank of 5 indicates that only 5 percent of the norm group obtained lower scores. In other words, a percentile rank indicates the person's relative ranking in percentage terms. The important point is that percentile ranks involve percentages of people. This is in contrast to percentage scores, which express performance in terms of percent of content mastered; that is, a percentage score of 78 means that the student correctly answered 78 percent of the items.

Computation of percentile ranks   To develop percentile ranks requires determining what proportion of people in the norm group score below a particular score. The first step is to prepare a frequency distribution. Next we find the number of persons who scored lower than the particular score in question (the cumulative frequency). Dividing this number by the total number of scores in the sample gives the proportion of cases falling below the score (the cumulative proportion). Multiplying this proportion by 100 converts scores to percentile ranks.

Actually the procedure is not quite so simple. The reason is that we can use the proportion of people scoring *lower than* a given score or the proportion scoring *at or below* a given score. In other words, the cumulative frequency can be defined in terms of the lower limit of the score interval or the midpoint of the score interval.[2] We shall use the latter approach. An example of the calculation of percentile ranks is given in Table 10.1.[3]

Interpretation of percentile ranks is straightforward. All you have to remember is that a percentile rank indicates the number of people out of 100 who scored lower than the score in question. To illustrate, in our example (Table 10.1), a raw score of 25 was equivalent to a percentile rank of 31. Thus a student who scored 25 on the American College Testing Program (ACT) scored higher than 31 percent of his classmates and lower than the other 69 percent.

Percentile ranks can also be obtained using graphic procedures. For example, we could plot the cumulative frequencies and obtain a curve, called an *ogive.* From this curve we could read percentile ranks directly. Figure 10.1 illustrates how this is done, showing that a raw score of 25 is equivalent to a percentile rank of 31. This rank is the same as that obtained through the tabular method (see Table 10.1).

Percentile points   When determining percentile ranks we found the proportion of individuals who scored lower than a given test score. Sometimes, however, we want to know what test score divides a distribution into certain proportions; for example, we might want to identify the top 20 percent of students so that they could be placed in an accelerated section of a course. To do this we must find the test score corresponding to a percentile rank of 80. This can be done by finding the cumulative proportion associated with the percentile rank, then finding the point on the raw

---

[2] A third approach is sometimes used, wherein percentiles are defined in terms of the percentage of people who obtain a given score or lower. The differences between the three approaches will be relatively small when there is a wide range of scores. However, when the range of possible scores is narrow, there will be relatively large differences between percentile ranks computed by different methods.

[3] For other methods of computing percentiles see Ebel (1972) or Angoff (1971a).

TABLE 10.1   Computation of percentile ranks

The following steps illustrate the procedures for computing percentile ranks. The data used are the ACT Composite scores for a sample of 177 entering freshmen women in a midwestern liberal arts college.

Computational steps

(1) Prepare a frequency distribution of the scores.

(2) Find the cumulative frequency (*CF*) to the lower limit of each score. This is the sum of all scores below the score in question. For example, the *CF* for a score of 23 is: $1 + 3 + 12 = 16$, the number of students scoring 22 or lower.

(3) Find the cumulative frequency to the midpoint of the score interval (CF_{mp}). This is obtained by adding one-half the number of scores in the interval to the *CF*. For example, for a score of 23:

$$CF_{mp} = 16 + (.5)(14) = 23.0$$

(4) Find the cumulative proportion (*CP*) by dividing CF_{mp} by *N*, the total number of scores. For a score of 23:

$$CP = \frac{23.0}{177} = .130$$

(5) To find the percentile rank (*PR*), multiply *CP* by 100. Again, with a score of 23,

$$PR = (.130)(100) = 13$$

A percentile rank of 13 means that 13 of every 100 students (13 percent) scored lower than 23 on the ACT and 87 of every 100 (87 percent) scored higher.

X	f	CF	CF_{mp}	CP	PR
32	4	173	175.0	.989	99
31	7	166	169.5	.958	96
30	17	149	157.5	.890	89
29	22	127	138.0	.780	78
28	18	109	118.0	.667	67
27	28	81	95.0	.537	54
26	15	66	73.5	.415	42
25	22	44	55.0	.311	31
24	14	30	37.0	.209	21
23	14	16	23.0	.130	13
22	12	4	10.0	.056	6
21	3	1	2.5	.014	1
20	1	0	0.5	.003	<1

score scale corresponding to this cumulative proportion. The point on the score scale corresponding to the desired percentile rank is called a *percentile point*.

To illustrate, let us find the raw score, in our example, that divides the top 20 percent of the distribution from the remaining 80 percent. From Table 10.1 we can see that a raw score of 30 has a *CP* of .890 and a raw score of 29 has a *CP* of .780; interpolating, we find that a raw score of 29.2 is equivalent to a percentile rank of 80. Therefore, students scoring higher than 29 would be in the top 20 percent of their class and would be eligible for the accelerated section.

Note that we also could have utilized the graphical procedure to obtain the percentile point. Or, if, as in our example, we only wanted to find one cutting line, we could have just counted off the top 20 percent of the scores (in the example, the top 35 scores). Generally, however, we are interested in several percentile points. For example, we might want to develop a norm table (see below) which, instead of showing the percentile rank for each raw score, showed what raw score was needed to obtain various percentiles' ranks—such as 90, 80, 70, and so on. In this case we would compute percentile points.

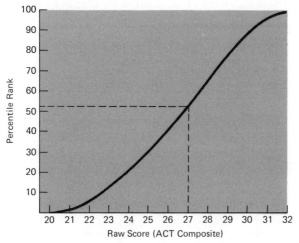

Figure 10.1 Graphical method of obtaining percentile ranks. (*Note:* By drawing perpendiculars to the axes we find that a raw score of 27 is equivalent to a percentile rank of 54.)

Deciles   Percentile points divide a score distribution into 100 equal parts. In many circumstances, however, such fine distinctions are not needed, and dividing the distribution into a smaller number of segments may be sufficient. Of the possible divisions, tenths are most frequently used. The score points dividing the distribution into tenths are referred to as deciles. Since deciles divide the distribution into ten equal segments (by cutting it at the 10th, 20th, . . . , 90th percentile points), computing deciles is the same as computing the 10th, 20th, . . . , 90th percentile points. In essence, deciles provide a ten-step ranking scale, with each step containing 10 percent of the scores. Traditionally, the lowest tenth (percentile ranks 1–10) is referred to as the first decile, the next tenth (percentile ranks 11–20) is the second decile, and so on.

Evaluation   The major advantage of percentiles is the ease of interpretation. Knowing a person's relative ranking in a relevant comparison group is, to most persons, a simple, readily comprehensible, and meaningful index of performance.

Also, for many purposes, ranking within a group is sufficient; thus more complex transformations are not needed.

Percentile ranks have two major limitations. First, being on an ordinal scale, they cannot legitimately be added, subtracted, multiplied, or divided. This is not a serious limitation when interpreting scores, but it is a serious liability in statistical analyses. A second limitation is of more concern to the test user. Percentile ranks have a rectangular distribution, whereas test score distributions generally approximate the normal curve. As a consequence, small raw score differences near the center of the distribution result in large percentile differences. Conversely, large raw score differences at the extremes of the distribution produce only small percentile differences (see Figure 10.2). Unless these relations are kept in mind, percentile ranks can easily be misinterpreted; in particular, seemingly large differences in percentile ranks near the center of the distribution tend to be overinterpreted.

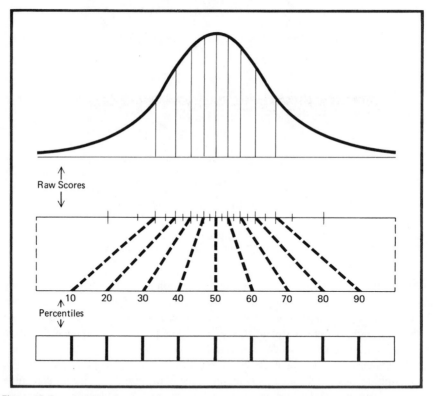

Figure 10.2   Relationship between distributions of raw scores and percentile ranks.

Standard Scores

Percentile ranks measure on an ordinal scale. For several reasons, but particularly when statistical analyses are being performed on test scores, it would be desirable to have scores expressed on an interval scale—that is, to have a scale with equal-size units. Standard scores possess this property.

A *standard score (z) is the deviation of a raw score from the mean in standard deviation units:*

$$z = \frac{X - \bar{X}}{s} \qquad (10.1)$$

Since the basic scale unit is the standard deviation, such scores are referred to as standard scores.

Several properties of standard scores (z scores) should be noted: (1) They are expressed on a scale having a mean of 0 and a standard deviation of 1. (2) The absolute value of a z score indicates the distance of the raw score from the mean of the distribution. The sign of the z scores indicates whether the raw score falls above or below the mean; scores above the mean will have positive signs; scores below the mean, negative signs. (3) Inasmuch as standard scores are expressed on an interval scale, they can be subjected to the common algebraic operations. (4) The transformation of raw scores to standard scores is *linear.* Thus the shape of the distribution of z scores is similar to the distribution of raw scores. If the raw score distribution is normal, so will be the distribution of z scores; if the raw score distribution is skewed, so will be the distribution of z scores. (5) If the distribution of raw scores is normal, the range of z scores will be from approximately -3 to $+3$.

To avoid decimals and negative values, z scores are usually transformed to yet another scale. This transformation is of the form:

$$Z = A + Bz \qquad (10.2a)$$

where Z is the transformed standard score and A and B are constants.[4] Since the addition of, or multiplication by, a constant does not destroy the relationships within the scale, relationships between z scores will be the same as between raw scores.

Although any constants can be used, the recommended procedure (APA, 1974) is to use the transformation:

$$Z = 50 + 10z \qquad (10.2b)$$

In essence, this transformation transforms scores to a scale having the mean of 50 points and a standard deviation of 10 points. Other transformations can be made, using any mean and standard deviation that are appropriate and desirable. In all cases, scores are rounded to whole numbers.[5]

An example of the computation of standard scores is given in Table 10.2.

Normalized standard scores   The transformation of raw scores to standard scores described above was a linear transformation; thus the shape of the distributions of z scores and raw scores will be the same. If the distribution of standard scores is normal, standard scores can be converted directly into percentile ranks. This transformation can be made using a table of areas of the normal curve, as given in

---

[4]Note that this is the equation for a straight line, where B is the slope constant and A the intercept constant. As applied to our problem, A will transform the mean and B the standard deviation.

[5]These transformations also have the advantage of eliminating decimals and negative values (for example, on the 50, 10 scale, the expected range of scores will be approximately 20–80).

TABLE 10.2   Computation of standard scores

The following steps illustrate the computation of standard scores. The data are those used in Table 10.1.

Computational steps

(1) Compute the mean and standard deviation. For these data you will obtain $\bar{X} = 26.54$ and $s = 2.76$.

(2) For each raw score, find the deviation score (x), which is the raw score minus the mean. For example, when $X = 25$:

$$x = 25 - 26.54 = -1.54$$

(3) Find z for each score. Remember, $z = x/s$. For $X = 25$,

$$z = \frac{-1.54}{2.76} = -0.56$$

The z score expresses the raw score in terms of standard deviation units from the mean. Our example indicates that a raw score of 25 is 0.56 standard deviation below the mean.

(4) To eliminate decimals and negative numbers, we transform z scores to another scale. The recommended transformation is to a scale with mean of 50 and standard deviation of 10. This can be accomplished using the formula $Z = 50 + 10z$. Applied to our example, with $X = 25$,

$$Z = 50 + 10(-0.56) = 50 - 5.6 = 44.4, \text{ or } 44$$

Our scores are now expressed on a standard score scale with mean of 50 and standard deviation of 10 points.

The computational routine is tabulated as follows:

X	x	z	Z
32	5.46	1.98	70
31	4.46	1.62	66
30	3.46	1.25	62
29	2.46	0.89	59
28	1.46	0.53	55
27	0.46	0.17	52
26	−0.54	−0.20	48
25	−1.54	−0.56	44
24	−2.54	−0.92	41
23	−3.54	−1.28	37
22	−4.54	−1.64	34
21	−5.54	−2.01	30
20	−6.54	−2.37	26

Appendix A. This transformation is possible because in a normal distribution there is a specifiable relationship between standard scores (z scores) and the areas within the curve (that is, the proportion of cases falling between any two points).

Even when raw scores are not normally distributed, we can make an *area transformation,* and force scores into a normal distribution. Scores derived in this manner are called *normalized standard scores;* the word "normalized" indicates that scores have been forced into a normal distribution. In order to normalize scores, there must be some basis for assuming that scores on the characteristic being measured are, in fact, normally distributed. If scores cannot be assumed to be normally distributed, forcing them into a normal distribution only distorts the distribution. Therefore, normalized standard scores are computed only when an obtained distribution approaches normality, but, because of sampling errors, is slightly different. This situation frequently occurs in standardization of tests on large, heterogeneous samples. Table 10.3 illustrates the procedure used to derive normalized standard scores.

As with all standard score scales, any arbitrary mean and standard deviation can be used. Again, the recommended procedure is to transform scores to a scale with a mean of 50 and a standard deviation of 10 points. Of course, other constants can be used if the situation warrants.

Other standard scores   When normalized standard scores are reported on a scale with a mean of 50 and standard deviation of 10, they are frequently called *T scores.* This usage may cause some confusion, since *T* scores were originally defined with reference to a particular norm group (McCall, 1922)—not in a generic sense. Moreover, some people use the designation "*T* score" to refer to any transformed standard score system, normalized or unnormalized. Most frequently, any normalized standard score system with a mean of 50 and standard deviation of 10 is called a *T* score system (Lyman, 1971).

Another well-known variety of standard score is the *stanine,* stanine being an abbreviation for "standard nine." The stanine scale is a nine-step standard score scale with 5 as the mean and a standard deviation of 2 points. Each of nine score categories, except for the two extreme categories, is one-half standard deviation wide (see Figure 10.3). Utilizing one-digit scores has certain advantages; for example, stanines can be punched into one column of an IBM card. However, like any other system that reduces the range by grouping, it sacrifices some precision in favor of simplicity.

Interpretation of standard scores   A z score of 1.00, a Z (or T) of 60, and a normalized standard score of 60 all indicate that the raw score is one standard deviation above the mean of the distribution. Similarly, a z of -1.50, a Z of 35, and a normalized standard score of 35 all represent a score one and one-half standard deviations below the mean. Thus, standard scores indicate an individual's relative position in terms of standard deviations from the mean.

For a person unfamiliar with the concept of the standard deviation, such an interpretation will, at best, be vague. However, when using normalized standard scores, or when the distribution of linearly transformed standard scores approaches normality, standard scores can be converted into percentile ranks with reference to the normal curve. Thus, a standard score of 60 is equivalent to a percentile rank of 84 and a standard score of 35 is equivalent to a percentile rank of 7. These relationships between standard scores and percentile ranks hold regardless of the nature

TABLE 10.3   Computation of normalized standard scores

The following steps illustrate the computation of normalized standard scores. The data are those used in the previous examples (Tables 10.1 and 10.2).

Computational steps

(1)   For each raw score find the cumulative proportion (*CP*) using the procedures described in Table 10.1.

(2)   In the Table of Areas of the Normal Curve (see Appendix A), find the *z* score comparable to this *CP*. For scores above the median (*CP* > .500) use the column labeled "Area of the Larger Proportion"; for scores below the median (*CP* > .500) use the column labeled "Area of the Smaller Proportion." This gives the *z* score that cuts the distribution into the desired proportions. We shall refer to this value as *z'* to distinguish it from *z* scores computed by a linear transformation (as in Table 10.2). To obtain values of *z'* you may have to interpolate.

(3)   Again, we shall transform scores to another scale. And, again, we shall use one with a mean of 50 and a standard deviation of 10 points; that is, $Z' = 50 + 10z'$.

The computational routine is tabulated as follows:

X	CP	z'	Z'
32	.989	2.29	73
31	.958	1.73	67
30	.890	1.23	62
29	.780	0.77	58
28	.667	0.43	54
27	.537	0.09	51
26	.415	−0.21	48
25	.311	−0.49	45
24	.209	−0.81	42
23	.130	−1.13	39
22	.056	−1.59	36
21	.014	−2.20	28
20	.003	−2.75	22

Note: If the distribution is normal, normalized standard scores (*z'* or *Z'*) will have the same value, within rounding errors, as the comparable linearly transformed standard scores (*z* or *Z*, respectively). If the distribution is not normal, the comparable values will differ.

and content of the test. Thus, normalized standard scores and Z scores can be converted to and interpreted as percentiles. When interpreting tests to people unfamiliar with standard scores, you will probably want to use a percentile-based interpretation.

Evaluation   Since standard scores express test scores on an interval scale, they are valuable when further statistical analyses are necessary; as, for example, when

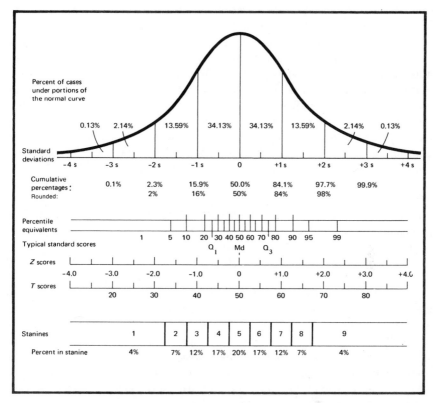

Figure 10.3 Relationship of several common scoring scales. These relations hold only when scores are normally distributed. (Adapted from H. G. Seashore, *Methods of Expressing Test Scores*. New York: The Psychological Corporation, Test Service Bulletin No. 48, 1955.)

several scores are to be combined into a composite measure. In addition, normalized standard scores permit reference to a standard distribution (the normal curve) and direct conversion to percentiles, thus simplifying interpretation.

Another advantage of standard scores is that they allow for direct comparison of scores on two or more tests or scales. Transforming scores into standard scores corrects for differences in means and standard deviations of the various distributions, thereby placing scores on the various tests on the same scale. In other words, a given z score represents the same relative position in the two distributions regardless of the mean and standard deviation of the original distributions. To illustrate, suppose that Test A has a mean of 40 and a standard deviation of 20, Test B has a mean of 50 and a standard deviation of 10, and that Johnny scored 70 on Test A and 65 on Test B. Converting to standard scores, we would find that his z score was the same ($+1.50$) on both tests:

$$\text{Test A: } \frac{70 - 40}{20} = 1.50 \qquad \text{Test B: } \frac{65 - 50}{10} = 1.50$$

Thus, even though his raw scores differed on the two tests, his standard scores were the same, and therefore he fell in the same relative position on both tests.

Standard scores, being statistically more complex and less familiar than percentiles, are harder for the layman to understand. Also, standard score systems utilize different means and standard deviations, and scores are often referred to only as standard scores, with no distinction made between normalized and linearly transformed scores. Therefore, the test user must always ascertain the scale values used in the particular scale and whether the scores are normalized or a linear transformation of the raw scores. Finally, normalizing standard scores forces the scores into a normal distribution. This procedure is justified to smooth out sampling errors; otherwise it will only distort the shape of the distribution.

The relationship of percentiles and several commonly used types of standard scores is shown in Figure 10.3. This figure shows the relationships when the distribution of raw scores is normal; naturally, the relationships would be different in nonnormal distributions.

Developmental Scales

Many abilities, skills, and characteristics develop in a systematic manner over time. For example, a child's ability to read increases with age and with additional years of schooling. So, too, do most other intellectual abilities and skills. Because these abilities increase systematically, score scales can be developed that compare an individual's performance to that of the average person of various developmental levels. On these scales, an individual's score indicates the developmental level that his performance typifies. As might be expected, developmental scales generally report performance as an age or grade equivalent.

Age scales   Alfred Binet, around the turn of the century, conceived of the idea of measuring mental growth by comparing a given child's performance with that of the average child of various age levels. He first identified intellectual tasks (items) that discriminated between children of various ages—that is, items on which performance varied systematically with age. Each item was then placed at the age level at which the majority of children could successfully complete it. For example, if the majority of eight-year-olds could answer the item "What is nine times nine?" but fewer than half of the seven-year-olds can, then this item would be included at the eight-year-old level. By developing a number of appropriate items for each age level, Binet constructed a scale that assessed the level of mental development of children. The score a child received was the age level that his performance best typifies. Such a score is referred to as a *mental age*.

All age scales are developed using essentially the same reasoning and procedures. Age scales assign a score to an individual by comparing his performance to the *average* child of various ages. For example, if a child can correctly answer the items commonly answered by ten-year-olds, but fails most of the items at higher age levels, his age score would be ten.[6]

[6]In practice, age scores are usually reported as years and months. Thus, an age score of 10-5 means that the individual obtained the same score as the average child who is 10 years and 5 months old.

Note that a fundamental assumption of age scales is that the characteristic being measured increases systematically with age. Thus the essential elements in an age scale are: (1) a set of items that discriminate between persons of different ages; (2) a norm group, composed of a representative sample of persons of different ages, that provides the basis for assigning an item to a particular age group; and (3) a scale for reporting performance. A hypothetical example of how items would be assigned to age levels is given in Figure 10.4.

When skills vary systematically with age, age scores are straightforward and easy to interpret. However, when the rate of development varies from year to year, age scores are difficult to interpret due to differing amounts of growth between years. (That is, unit sizes are not equal.) For example, most intellectual abilities develop rapidly, and at a fairly constant rate, throughout childhood but the rate of

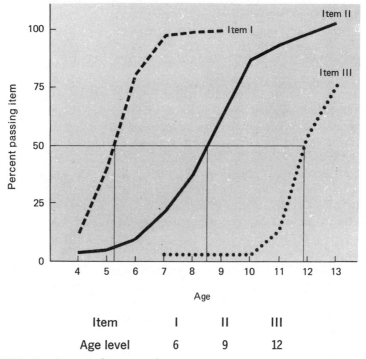

Item	I	II	III
Age level	6	9	12

Figure 10.4   Development of an age scale.

growth begins to decelerate during adolescence. Therefore, the amount of increase in, say, reading comprehension, will be less between the ages of 17 and 18 than between ages 7 and 8. Thus, a difference of one year in age scores will have different implications at various ages. Furthermore, since performance will be affected by education or general life experiences, what is "normal" for a given age under certain circumstances may not be "normal" under different circumstances. For all of these reasons, age scales are most appropriately used with younger children growing up in rather typical surroundings; for adults and children from restricted or atypical environments, age scores will be less meaningful.

Grade scales   An analogous type of score is the grade-equivalent score. Rather than comparing an individual's performance with that of persons of different ages, grade scales compare his performance with average student performance in various grades. Thus, if Jeremy's grade equivalent on an arithmetic test is 3-5, his performance is comparable to that of the *average* student in the fifth month of the third grade. (Because growth continues throughout the year, grade scores are reported as months within grade.[7]) The procedures for selecting items and assigning scores are directly analogous to those used on age scales except that grade levels are used instead of age levels.

Like age scores, grade-equivalent scores are appropriate only when the characteristic being measured varies systematically between grade levels. Moreover, one must assume equivalent educational experiences. To illustrate, suppose that a junior high level mathematics test consisting of 75 items—50 arithmetic and 25 algebra items—is administered in the sixth month of school. Suppose also that the average score for eighth grade students is 40 and for ninth grade students 50, and that algebra is taught only in the ninth grade. Albert, an eighth grade student, takes this test and obtains a raw score of 50—the average score for ninth grade students. What does this score mean? Albert probably obtained his score by being extremely accurate on the arithmetic items, whereas the average ninth grade student obtained the same score by correctly answering some of the arithmetic and some of the algebra items. In other words, Albert and the average ninth grade student both obtained the same scores but correctly answered different items. Thus Albert's knowledge of mathematics is not necessarily equivalent to that of the average ninth grade student, because he has not studied algebra.

Besides being dependent on the material taught at various grade levels, grade scores also reflect the composition of the normative group. We have already mentioned that students' educational experiences must be similar to the experiences of students in the norm group. In addition, some schools have nongraded programs or require children to repeat a grade if their performance does not meet certain minimal standards and accelerate students if their development clearly surpasses that of their classmates. In these situations any grade will include some students who are older and others who are younger than children who have advanced from grade to grade in accordance with normal promotional policies. To control for such diversity, some test publishers use *modal age grade norms*. These norms are based on samples that include only students who are in the grade typical for their age level. Students who are accelerated or retarded a year or more are eliminated from the norm groups, thereby providing a better estimate of the performance of the typical child in a given grade. When interpreting grade-equivalent scores, therefore, one must take into account not only the material taught but also promotion policies.

---

[7]A 10-month school year is usually assumed. Thus, for example, in third grade, grade-equivalent scores can range from 3-0 to 3-9.

There is one other problem with grade-equivalent scores. Scores are developed for a sample of grades and, by definition, half of the students in the highest grade will score above average for that grade. What grade equivalent should they be assigned? The usual procedure is to assign scores extrapolating to higher grade levels. But here we run into the same problem as with age scores—that is, slower rates of development in years. Thus the extrapolated scores are often somewhat inaccurate.

Evaluation   The advantages of developmental scales are: (1) they report scores in readily understandable units—in terms of age or grade equivalents; (2) they provide a direct comparison with the performance of a student's peers; and (3) they provide a basis for intraindividual comparisons and the study of growth over time. Their main disadvantages are: (1) they are appropriate only when the characteristic measured changes systematically with age, thus being limited mainly to use with younger children; (2) they are influenced by the composition—that is, previous education and experiences—of the norm group; (3) scale units at various ages or grade are not equal; and (4) extrapolations from one grade or age level to another are risky. In short, age and grade scales cannot be interpreted as unambiguously as superficial consideration might suggest.

Because of this problem in interpreting grade-equivalent scores, many people prefer to use *percentile ranks within grades* rather than grade scores. In this approach an individual's score is expressed as his relative ranking (percentile rank) within a particular grade level. Thus, in our example, Albert's score might fall at the 95th percentile rank for eighth grade students.

Ratios and Quotients

There have been numerous attempts to develop scales that use the ratio of two scores. Probably the best known of these is the intelligence quotient (IQ). On Binet's original intelligence test, scores were expressed on an age scale. As his test was used, some psychometricians pointed out that a mental age of 10 could have differing meanings and implications if it was obtained by a child of 8, a child of 10, or one of 15. Consequently they suggested that the rate of mental development should be measured as well as the level of development (that is, the mental age). The intelligence quotient, defined as the ratio of the child's mental age to his chronological age, was proposed as an index of the rate of intellectual development:

$$IQ = \frac{\text{mental age}}{\text{chronological age}} \times 100 \qquad (10.3)$$

As can be seen from this formula, a child whose intellectual development is average for his age (that is, one whose mental age equals his chronological age) will obtain an IQ of 100, children whose mental development is more rapid than average will obtain scores over 100, and those whose development is slower than average will obtain IQs below 100. The more the rate of development deviates from the average, the farther the IQ will fall from 100.

An IQ computed in this manner is a *ratio IQ*. On the major American revision of the Binet test—Forms L and M of the Stanford-Binet—the distribution of IQs tended to have a standard deviation of about 16 points. However, these standard deviations varied from about 12 to 20 IQ points at different age levels (Terman and Merrill, 1937). Because of nonequivalent standard deviations, and the fact that intellectual growth does not increase linearly with increasing age, ratio IQs are no longer used on major intelligence tests. Instead, normalized standard scores based on a representative sample of the population at each level are now used. These scores, called *deviation IQs,* have a mean of 100 and a standard deviation of 15 (Wechsler scales) or 16 (Stanford-Binet) points at each age level.

The IQ measures the rate of general intellectual development. In educational testing, one frequently encounters measures that purportedly indicate the rate of educational development or achievement. These go by various names, such as *educational quotients* or *achievement quotients*. These indices are all ratios that use as their numerator some measure of achievement and as the denominator chronological age, a measure of intellectual ability, or grade placement. The purpose of such ratios is to compare a person's actual achievement to his expected achievement (as estimated from his age, grade, or intelligence). These quotients have two major drawbacks. First, the ratio of two unreliable scores will be less reliable than either individual measure. Thus the quotient will, typically, be a statistically unsound measure. Second, comparing a measure of achievement to one of intellectual ability assumes that achievement is determined solely by intellectual ability. This assumption is both constricting and inconsistent with empirical facts. In this author's opinion, achievement quotients based on the comparison of achievement test scores to measure intellectual development can best be ignored.

METHODS OF PRESENTING NORMATIVE DATA

Earlier in this chapter we discussed the construction of norm groups and the development of the various types of norm-referenced scores. We now turn to the techniques of summarizing and presenting normative data.

Conversion Tables

The simplest, and most basic, technique for presenting normative data is the *conversion table* or, as it is sometimes called, the *norm table*. A conversion table shows the raw scores and equivalent derived scores—be they percentiles, standard scores, or any other type of score—for a particular norm group. The conversion table thus enables the test user to convert a raw score into a derived score or to find the raw score equivalent of a given derived score. The essential elements of a conversion table are (1) a list of raw scores, (2) a corresponding list of derived scores, and (3) a description of the norm group.

An example of a conversion table is shown in Table 10.4. This table (which is derived from the data in Table 10.1 and 10.2) gives the percentile rank and standard

TABLE 10.4   Example of a norm (conversion) table

Percentile Rank and Standard Score Equivalents on a
College Aptitude Test

Raw Score	Percentile Rank	Standard Score
32	99	70
31	96	66
30	89	62
29	78	59
28	67	55
27	54	52
26	42	48
25	31	44
24	21	41
23	13	37
22	6	34
21	1	30
20	1	26

$N = 177$ freshman female liberal arts majors at a midwestern university.

score equivalents of the Composite score on the ACT college aptitude test for a group of freshmen women in a liberal arts curriculum. To read the table we need only to consider scores in a given row. Thus, if a student's raw score were 27, her percentile rank would be 54 and her standard score 52. We could interpret her score by saying that, compared to freshmen women in liberal arts at this university, she was .2 standard deviation above the mean (standard score = 52) or that her score exceeded that of 54 percent of the students (percentile rank = 54) in the curricula.

There are several aspects of this interpretation that are worth emphasizing. First, the score was interpreted by comparison to the scores of a particular norm group; in this case, freshmen women in the liberal arts curriculum at a particular university. To compare her performance to that of other groups would require other norm tables. Second, scores were expressed both as percentiles and as standard scores. In other cases, the conversion table might include only one type of derived score. Third, the derived scores in the conversion table give only the student's relative performance within the norm group; they give no direct evidence of the outcomes that might be associated with a particular test score. If we know that the test scores predict some relevant outcome, we can make some inferences from her scores. For example, if the test predicts college grades, we can infer that the higher her ranking (test score) the higher the grades she will probably attain.

Conversely, if there is no validity evidence, the data in the conversion table will tell only the student's relative ranking within the group—and nothing more. This latter point cannot be overstressed. Too often the availability of normative data is taken as a license to interpret performance on the test as indicative of probable high performance on some criterion. *Without validity data, conversion tables only translate raw scores into another type of score.* Even with validity data, criterion performance can only be inferred from normative data. That is, raw scores are converted to relative performance measures, not expressed in outcome terms. There is, as we shall see later, no reason why normative data cannot be expressed in outcome terms.

Complex Conversion Tables

Frequently data from several subtests (or scales) or from the various tests in a single battery are presented in one conversion table. When such data are to be interpreted, one caution is paramount: Unless the same norm group is used, scores

TABLE 10.5   Example of a conversion table showing norms for several subtests

Scale score	English	Math	Social Studies	Natural Science	Composite
35		99			
34		95		99	
33		90	99	96	
32		84	97	91	99
31		76	93	83	97
30		66	86	75	92
29	99	56	79	65	84
28	97	46	72	55	74
27	93	36	62	45	62
26	87	28	54	34	50
25	79	22	45	25	39
24	69	18	35	19	29
23	59	14	27	15	21
22	48	11	21	11	14
21	37	8	16	8	9
20	28	6	12	6	6
19	20	4	8	5	4
18	14	3	6	3	2
17	9	2	5	2	2
16	5	1	3	2	1
15	3		3	1	
14	2		2		
13	1		1		

Table shows the percentile equivalents on the four subtests (plus composite) of the American College Testing Program (ACT). Sample was 2087 entering freshmen at a midwestern university.

will not be directly comparable, since they will be based on different samples. If the data are based on a common norm group, as they should be, this type of conversion table provides a method for directly comparing the performance of an individual on various tests or subtests.

Table 10.5 illustrates a conversion table that presents the normative data for the several subtests of the ACT. It can be seen that the same raw score (scale score) results in widely different percentile ranks on the various subtests. Conversely, to obtain equivalent percentile ranks on the various subtests would require quite different scale scores.

On other occasions we might use a conversion table to show the performance of several distinct groups on a single test. An example of such a table is shown in Table 10.6. This table provides two types of information. First, since it presents derived scores for several groups, the test user can compare an individual's scores to several relevant norm groups simultaneously. And, second, the table also allows comparisons to be made of the performance of diverse groups. That is, by observing the derived score equivalents of various raw scores we can infer which norm group is "tougher." For example, in Table 10.6, College D represents the "toughest" norm group because a given raw score will have a lower percentile equivalent in College D than in any other group. Conversely, College C is the "easiest" norm group since the percentile equivalents are generally highest. Or, to view the results in a different manner, a raw score of 28 will be equivalent to a percentile rank of 82 in College C, 65 in College E, 55 in College A, 52 in College B, and 35 in College D. These findings, of course, reflect the differences in mathematics background and ability of students who elect to enter the various colleges. As such, the conversion table not only provides useful normative data, but it also indicates the characteristics (in this example, mathematics ability) of the students in the various norm groups.

One note of caution. If we are to compare various groups directly (as in Table 10.6), the scores must have been obtained under equivalent conditions. If, for example, the test was administered as a selection test in one college and as an advising aid in another, the motivation of the two groups might have differed. Thus the results would not be comparable. Of course, any differences in sampling in the various groups would make comparisons tenuous.

Profiles

For some people, visual or graphic presentations facilitate understanding of sets of scores. A *test profile* serves just this need. Basically, a profile is nothing more than a graph on which a series of test scores are plotted. All scores are plotted on the same scale using norms derived from a common group. The profile shows at a glance the configuration of the individual's scores on the various tests, indicating the relative position of his several scores. A typical test profile is shown in Figure 10.5.

Several rules must be followed if the profile is not to present a misleading picture. First, the same norm group must be used for each test. If diverse norm groups are used for the various tests, the scores, being based on different groups,

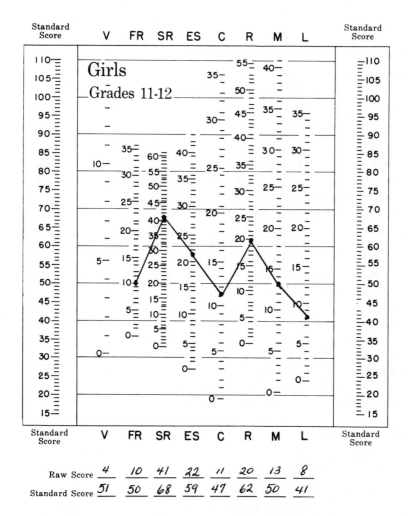

Raw Score   4   10   41   22   11   20   13   8

Standard Score   51   50   68   59   47   62   50   41

Figure 10.5 Illustration of a test profile. Reproduced by permission. Copyright © 1957 by The Psychological Corporation, New York, N. Y. All rights reserved.

will not be directly comparable. Second, all scores must be plotted on the same scale; that is, all scores should be expressed as percentiles, or as a particular type of standard score. Corollary to this second point is the need for using dimensions that do not exaggerate small differences or compress large differences. This latter prob-

TABLE 10.6   Example of a conversion table showing the performance of several norm groups on the same test

Score	A	B	College C	D	E
36		99		99	
35	99	98		97	
34	96	94	99	92	99
33	94	88	98	86	97
32	90	81	96	77	94
31	82	74	95	67	90
30	72	66	92	57	84
29	62	58	87	45	75
28	55	52	82	35	65
27	50	44	76	26	59
26	43	36	67	17	52
25	35	29	59	11	44
24	28	24	53	8	36
23	20	18	45	5	29
22	14	13	38	3	24
21	11	11	30	2	19
20	8	7	24	1	14
19	6	4	17		10
18	4	3	13		7
17	3	2	9		4
16	1	1	5		2
15			3		1
14			2		
13			1		
N	177	486	340	528	307

Table presents percentile equivalents of ACT mathematics test scores for five colleges within the same university. (See text for explanation.)

lem can be minimized if a third rule is followed; that is, build into the profile some index of error. Since all tests are, to some extent, unreliable, and since differences between test scores are even more unreliable, insignificant differences between scores are prone to be overinterpreted. One interesting attempt to minimize the danger of overinterpretation (used by the Psychological Corporation on their Differential Aptitude Tests) is to construct the profile so that a difference of a certain measurable distance on the profile represents a significant difference between two scores; the user thus can quickly ascertain which pairs of scores differ significantly. An alternative approach is to report scores as *bands,* rather than exact scores, with differences between scores being significant only if the bands do not overlap.

Normal Percentile Charts

One of the best ways of presenting test profiles—a method that both guards against overinterpretation and simplifies interpretation—is by the use of normal percentile charts. A *normal percentile chart* is a profile in which the scores are reported in percentile ranks, but the dimensions of the scale are drawn to correspond to a standard score (*z*) scale. That is, the distances on the score (vertical) axis are equal to *z* scale units and corresponding percentile ranks are placed along this scale. In other words, percentile ranks are superimposed on a standard score scale. The normal percentile chart provides the advantages of both percentiles and standard scores, more accurately reflects the relationship of raw scores to percentiles, and minimizes the chances of misinterpreting differences between percentiles. An

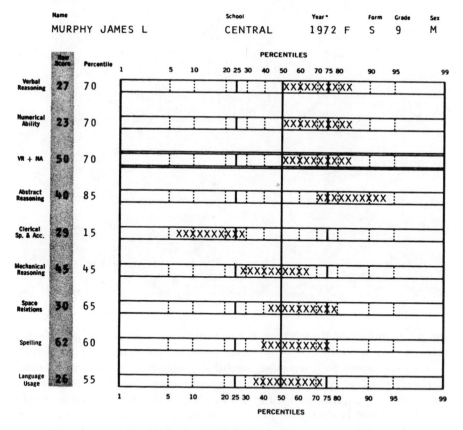

Figure 10.6 Example of a normal percentile chart. The profile form is derived from Differential Aptitude Tests (The Psychological Corporation). Note that the vertical axis is scaled in standard score units with percentile ranks superimposed on this scale. Reproduced by permission. Copyright © 1961, 1963 by The Psychological Corporation, New York, N. Y. All rights reserved.

example of a normal percentile chart is illustrated in Figure 10.6. Note that on the normal percentile chart the differences between percentile ranks are smaller near the center of the distribution and larger at the extremes. Thus, the distribution of percentile ranks more clearly parallels the distribution of raw scores. As a result, the test interpreter is not as likely to overinterpret small differences near the center of the distribution.

A Final Note

Throughout this chapter we have emphasized that norm-referenced scores only indicate a person's relative position compared to some relevant norm group. Unless there is some validity data, or absolute performance standard, our interpretations are limited to statements relating to test performance alone. They do not tell us about potential performance on some outside criteria. In the next chapter we shall discuss those situations in which an individual's test performance is interpreted by being compared to some defined standard (content-referenced scores) or in terms of criterion performance (outcome-referenced scores).

11

CONTENT - AND OUTCOME-REFERENCED SCORES

Several years ago, Glaser (1963) made an important distinction between norm-referenced and criterion-referenced tests. On norm-referenced tests, performance is interpreted by comparing a given individual's score to that of a relevant comparison group. Thus, interpretation involves a statement of the person's relative ranking within a norm group. All the scores discussed in the previous chapter were norm-referenced. Scores on criterion-referenced tests, in contrast, are interpreted in terms of specified performance standards. That is, an individual's performance on a test is compared, not to the performance of other people, but to some standard of proficiency or mastery of the material covered by the test. Usually, this standard is defined in terms of degree of mastery of the test material—that is, in terms of the test content. We will refer to such scores as *content-referenced*.

There is, as we have mentioned earlier, yet another possibility. When we know the relationship between test scores and an external criterion, we can express performance directly in terms of criterion (or outcome) performance. Hence, the name *outcome-referenced* scores. In this case we are interpreting scores in terms of predicted criterion performance. To derive such scores we first determine the relationship between test scores and a criterion measure, and then use this information to make a prediction about an individual's expected criterion performance. This predicted criterion performance then becomes the means of expressing and interpreting an individual's performance. In essence, we are directly incorporating validity data into the test interpretation process. The advantages of such a procedure should be obvious.

In this chapter we shall discuss the various ways of expressing content-referenced and outcome-referenced scores. We shall then consider several recurring problems in test score interpretation. Finally, we shall give some suggestions for interpreting test scores and communicating information about test performance to the test taker or to other interested persons.

CONTENT-REFERENCED SCORES

Developing content-referenced scores involves two major steps. The first is specifying the content and/or skills domain covered by the test. The second is generating a scale on which test performance can be reported. Although both of these requirements are attainable, at least theoretically, when one turns to the practical situation he finds both steps involve complex, if not insoluble, problems.

Consider first the problem of specifying the domain. This would seem to be a rather straightforward task, in that all you have to do is circumscribe the content or skills you wish to measure. In certain cases, this is not difficult (see, e.g., Bornmuth, 1970; Hiveley, Patterson, and Page, 1968; Block, 1971, 1974). For example, we can easily specify certain basic arithmetic operations (such as addition, subtraction, multiplication, division) and, without too much trouble, we can also delimit the range of problems to which these operations will be applied—say, whole numbers of no more than four digits. As we proceed to more abstract or less well-defined subject matter areas, the problem becomes more complex. Try to define the domain of algebraic problem solving, Civil War history, or reading comprehension. You will soon see that adequately describing the domain is no easy task.

One approach that has been gaining favor in educational circles (see, e.g., Mager, 1962; Payne, 1974) is to specify behavioral objectives for each unit (that is, domain). A behavioral objective, you will recall, is a statement describing what behaviors students will be expected to perform, and under what conditions and to what level of proficiency. The universe of behavioral objectives, in essence, defines the domain. This approach, of course, assumes that an exhaustive list of objectives can be developed for each unit of instruction.

Moving from a domain defined strictly by content into domains defined by intellectual skills further complicates the picture. Here we must first define the intellectual skills, and then develop exercises to measure these skills. Perhaps the most ambitious attempt to specify intellectual skills is Bloom's *Taxonomy of*

Educational Objectives (Bloom et al., 1956). Bloom classified intellectual skills from simple to complex, as knowledge, comprehension, application, analysis, synthesis, and evaluation. In a later book (Bloom et al., 1971), Bloom and his co-workers provided numerous illustrations of items that measure these different skills in various subject matter areas. (Any person interested in writing test items that measure more than retention of facts would profit from reading this book.)

It should now be clear that adequately defining a domain is not an easy task. Since this book focuses on testing, rather than curriculum, we shall not belabor the point further. Suffice it to say that without an adequate specification of the content and/or skill domain, all that follows will represent only the meaningless assignment of numbers to some vaguely defined type of performance.

Types of Content-Referenced Scales

Let us assume that we have, at least to a minimally acceptable degree, specified the domain to be measured. Our second problem is to develop a scale for reporting test performance—a scale that will communicate the test taker's level of performance in terms that relate to content mastery. Again, we shall see that this is not so simple as it might appear at first glance.

Mastery scores   Perhaps the simplest approach is to specify one passing or mastery score—that is, indicate the minimal level of proficiency we will accept. If a person attains this score (or a higher one), we say that he has mastered the material. The implication, usually, is that if he attains this mastery level, he can proceed to the next unit of instruction; if he does not attain it, he is assigned further practice and/or remedial work. In other words, the mastery (passing) score is the minimal level of performance needed to proceed to the next level.

How is this level set? Usually, somewhat arbitrarily. Although there is some debate, generally it is in the range of 80 to 90 percent correct responses (Bloom, 1971). The assumption is that persons performing at this level have mastered enough of the material so that they will be able to complete the next unit in the sequence successfully. Ideally, we would have empirical evidence that the designated proficiency level was, in fact, the minimal level needed to pursue further work in the area. Although there is some evidence that 80 to 90 percent is an appropriate level, in most cases the level is chosen arbitrarily, rather than on the basis of empirical evidence.

Note that we are interested only in whether he attains this designated standard or not. That is, we are interested only in a pass-fail decision. If the mastery level is set at 85 percent, a score of 98 percent correct will be treated the same as a score of 85 percent, and score of 36 percent the same as a score of 84 percent.

Percent correct   Any time we dichotomize scores, as with mastery scores, we lose some information. Thus, rather than using only pass-fail scoring, we might report scores on a continuum of mastery. A simple index would be the percent of items answered correctly:

$$\text{Percent correct} = \frac{\text{number items correct}}{\text{total number of items}} \times 100 \qquad (11.1)$$

This score, obviously, tells what proportion of the test items the individual answered correctly.

Because of their computational simplicity and apparent meaningfulness, percentage correct scores have a certain appeal. A little reflection, however, suggests that things are not so simple. For one thing, a percent score will not have meaning unless "percent of what?" can be defined. Strictly speaking, we are talking of percent of test items answered correctly; by implication, we are talking of the percent of the domain mastered. But unless the test items representatively sample the domain, and unless the domain is clearly described, we find ourselves taking a percent of some unknown area.

Another factor of concern is the difficulty of the test items. A given score, say 75 percent, would mean different things on a difficult or an easy test. If the test items do, in fact, represent the behaviors in the relevant domain, there is no problem; some domains may be more difficult to master than others. However, if the item sample is not representative, the difficulties of the items included on the (particular) test are of importance. Then, too, we must consider that two persons can attain the same score by answering different items correctly. Again, if we consider every item to be of equal value, there is no problem; if not, the same percent score may have different implications for different people.[1]

Content standard scores   Ebel (1962) proposed what he calls *content standard test scores*. The word "content" implies that the scores are based directly on the tasks that make up the test—that is, its content. By "standard" Ebel means both that scores must be expressed on a common scale (such as percent correct) and, more important, that the process of test construction, administration, and scoring are standardized. Ebel also stresses that content scores are not substitutes for normative scores, but rather that content and normative scores should be utilized in conjunction with each other.

Obviously the crucial steps in constructing any content standard scale are to specify the content domain and the scale clearly. Given these specifications, one could interpret scores in content terms. Alternatively, the interpretation process could start with the total score on the test. By specifying the types of items answered correctly or incorrectly by the "typical" person attaining each score level, an individual's scores could be interpreted. This interpretation would indicate the skills or difficulty of problems solved by persons at this score level.

---

[1]This problem is not unique to percentage scores, only more obvious. On any scoring scale, the same total score does not necessarily mean that two persons made the same response to each item.

Rating scales   In some circumstances we are more interested in a person's ability to carry out a process or produce a product than his ability to answer questions about material. One example is handwriting. When children are being taught to write, the goal is the development of a legible writing style. Other examples can be found in industrial education, art, and music. When we are concerned with products or performance, the important skills and proficiency levels cannot be specified in terms of answering questions. Instead, we usually have to develop a rating procedure that indicates level of proficiency, either for the total product or process or on the various component steps.

Often only a normative rating is used—for example, when a letter grade is assigned to a speech or musical performance. However, we could also develop content-referenced scales. To illustrate, again consider handwriting. One approach that has been used is to have judges rate the quality of samples of children's handwriting. Various levels of quality, from illegible to legible, are identified, and samples of handwriting typifying the various levels are included as standards for comparison. To rate the quality of a child's handwriting, the teacher would compare his handwriting to the standard samples. The child's score (rating) would be the level that best corresponds to the quality of his handwriting.

Evaluation

The major advantage of content-referenced scores is, of course, that they describe performance in terms of the level of content or skills the individual has mastered. That is, they indicate what a student knows and can do, rather than his relative ranking in a norm group. In most educational and training programs, this is the most useful type of evidence. For example, it is more useful for a teacher to know that Johnny can multiply whole numbers and decimals but cannot cope with fractions than for her to know that his multiplication skills are better than those of 60 percent of sixth graders. Only if she knows what skills he has and has not mastered can she adequately prescribe instruction.

Another point is implicit in the previous paragraph; that is, content-referenced scores are applicable primarily when achievement is being measured. The reason is that with aptitudes or personality characteristics it is difficult to define the relevant domain. In most achievement areas we can, at least in principle, identify the important knowledges and skills.[2]

Another problem concerns how we define proficiency levels. Previously we mentioned that mastery scores are usually determined arbitrarily, although they could be developed empirically. If you asked a teacher how he determines an appropriate passing score, he would probably say: "By the level of performance I expect of a child in this grade." But how does he know what level to expect? The only way, other than using some ideal standard, is to consider what skills children in that grade typically master. This, of course, is a normative interpretation. Similar

---

[2] Another way of saying this is that content-referenced scores are appropriate whenever a test serves as a sample (tests that represent). They are less appropriate with tests that predict or serve as signs.

arguments can be advanced with all types of criterion-referenced scores. In other words, content-referenced scores generally have at least an implicit normative base.

This fact should not dissuade us from using content-referenced scores. Rather, it points out that content-referenced and norm-referenced scores are but two ways of looking at an individual's performance. In some circumstances, one or the other approach may provide more information; in many situations, both content- and norm-referenced scores may provide valuable information. For example, we may want to know if Mike has mastered the basic arithmetic operations (a content-referenced approach) and also how his arithmetic skills compare to those of other children in his grade (a norm-referenced interpretation). There is no reason why both types of scores cannot be used, even on the same test.

OUTCOME-REFERENCED SCORES

Throughout the discussion of scores we have emphasized that unless we have evidence that the test is valid, we can compare a person's performance only with that of other people who take the test; we cannot generalize beyond the test or make predictions about how the person could behave in other situations. Thus, it would be desirable to have a method of incorporating validity data directly into the test interpretation process. This is most apparent when we use tests for predictive purposes. Here our primary concern is with the criterion; test scores are of interest only because they predict the criterion. If we could make our predictions directly in outcome (criterion) terms, they would be simpler and more useful.

If we have both validity and normative data, we can combine the two, but our path is more circuitous. To illustrate, suppose that we know that a measure of Economic Drive validly predicts success as a life insurance salesman (success being defined as the amount of insurance sold). We can now say that the higher the Economic Drive score, the greater the amount of insurance we expect the applicant to sell. That is, we can say that an applicant scoring, say, 28 on the test will probably sell more than an applicant who scores 20. However, it would be more useful if we could say that a person's scoring 28 on the test averages $600,000 worth of sales per year. Outcome-referenced scores express test results in this manner.

Thus, there are two requirements for developing outcome-referenced scores. First, we must have validity evidence relating scores on the test to an important criterion measure. (These data would be collected using the procedures discussed in Chapter 7.) The second requirement is for a method of presenting and interpreting test scores that incorporates the relationship between test scores and criterion performance. We shall discuss several methods of presenting outcome-referenced scores, beginning with the most commonly used method: expectancy tables.

Expectancy Tables

An *expectancy table* is simply a table that shows the percentage of people with a given predictor score (or range of predictor scores) who obtain each of various criterion scores (Schrader, 1965). An example of an expectancy table with one predictor is shown in Table 11.1. This table shows the probability that students with various scores on a college admissions test (the ACT) will obtain a given grade point average during their first term in college. This table allows us to make a prediction of a student's chances of obtaining various grade point averages. That is, we can say that 89 out of 100 students with ACT scores of 28 will obtain at least a C (2.0) average and 34 out of 100 will attain a B (3.0) average or higher. Thus, we have more relevant information than if we just compared the student to a norm group and found that his score was at the, say, 79th percentile. In short, expectancy tables skip the intermediate step of derived scores, and report scores directly in outcome (criterion) terms.

TABLE 11.1 Expectancy table for predicting first quarter college grades from a college aptitude test

Test raw score	Grade-point average		
	≥3.0	≥2.0	<2.0
32–	93	99+	1
30–31	58	97	3
28–29	34	89	11
26–27	19	75	25
24–25	14	63	37
22–23	5	52	48
20–21	4	49	51
18–19	2	44	56
16–17	3	36	64

A more complex expectancy table, in which two variables are used jointly to predict grade point average, is shown in Table 11.2. The data in Table 11.2 are the same as those in Table 11.1 except that high school rank has been added as a second predictor. To interpret an individual's score, find the cell at the intersection of the row corresponding to his test score and the column corresponding to his high school rank. The figures in this cell indicate the probabilities of obtaining various criterion scores. To illustrate, 92 out of 100 students with a test score of 28 and a high school rank in the third 10 percent obtained at least a C average and 16 out of 100 attained a B average or higher.

Constructing an expectancy table Construction of an expectancy table is relatively simple. First, predictor scores and criterion scores must be collected, divided into categories, and the frequency of each combination of predictor and criterion scores determined. These frequencies are then converted to percentages (or proportions) and a table constructed. (An illustration is given in Table 11.3.) Expectancy tables also can be constructed using regression equations, a procedure that gives a smoother distribution of scores than does the empirical distribution.[3]

TABLE 11.2 Expectancy table for predicting first quarter college grades from a college aptitude test and high school rank

Test raw score	High school rank (in tenths)						Seventh –Tenth
	First	Second	Third	Fourth	Fifth	Sixth	
30–	82–98–2	26–93–7					
28–29	52–94–6	21–89–11	16–92–8	30–80–20	7–47–53		
26–37	37–93–7	18–81–19	9–65–35	5–66–34	17–52–48	*–36–64	
24–25	35–93–7	19–70–30	4–61–39	13–49–51	3–37–63	*–40–60	8–16–84
22–23	17–95–5	7–63–37	4–61–39	3–41–59	3–40–60	*–32–68	6–25–75
20–21	22–78–22	4–67–33	5–50–50	3–43–57	5–52–48	*–36–64	*–45–55
18–19			*–31–69	*–38–62	6–45–55	8–41–69	*–33–67
–17					*–20–80		4–26–74

The numbers within the cells represent the chance in 100 of attaining at least a 3.0, at least a 2.0, and below a 2.0 grade-point average, respectively. Where a cell is blank, there were too few cases for a stable estimate to be made; an asterisk (*) indicates less than one chance in 100. The probabilities are based on observed frequencies, unsmoothed by theoretical considerations, and thus show some reversals in trends.

Evaluation   The major advantage of expectancy tables is that, by incorporating validity data, they enable test scores to be interpreted in terms of expected outcomes. In many circumstances this type of interpretation is more useful than a relative ranking. For example, a prospective college student may be more interested in knowing his chances of attaining a B (or a C) average at a particular college than knowing how his rank compared with that of other prospective students. The fact that his test score places him at the 55th percentile does not tell him whether this indicates almost certain academic success, a 50-50 chance of success, or probable failure.

Expectancy tables, also, have several disadvantages. In order to present the data in tabular form, both predictor and criterion scores are grouped, thereby sacrificing some precision. Also, unless the sample is very large, some cells will contain few cases, and thus provide unstable estimates. Even with a large number of cases, unless there are exact and meaningful cutting points, any classification system will be somewhat arbitrary. (In Tables 11.1 and 11.2, a C (2.0) grade average was selected because it was the minimum GPA needed for continuation.) Finally, when we have more than two predictors, several tables will be needed to present the data.

[3]Data from an expectancy table could also be presented graphically, with bars of different lengths corresponding to the probability of each outcome.

TABLE 11.3   Construction of an expectancy table

The following steps illustrate how to construct an expectancy table. We shall use as an example the scores of 100 job applicants. The predictor data are scores on a short test of terms used in the occupation; the criterion (outcome) measure is a rating of job performance by a supervisor. Both predictor and outcome data must be classified into categories. This is generally done to get meaningful categories that contain enough cases to permit stable estimates. We shall divide the outcome data into two categories—rated successful and unsuccessful—and the predictor scores into seven levels: 0–2, 3, 4, 5, 6, 7, and 8–10. This latter division ensures, with one exception, that there will be 10 cases at each level (A larger number of cases in each cell would be desirable; however, with a total sample of 100 cases, larger groups are unfeasible).

Within each predictor level score, the frequency of each outcome is then determined. This will result in a table of the form:

		Outcome		
		1–3	*4–8*	
		Unsucc	*Succ*	Σ
	8–10	0	15	15
	7	1	14	15
	6	5	13	18
Test	5	9	11	20
scores	4	9	3	12
	3	9	2	11
	0–2	9	0	9
	Σ	42	58	100

Within each predictor level, find the proportion of cases having each outcome. For example, for test score = 3, 9/11 or 82 percent of the cases have an outcome score in the range 1–3 and 2/11 or 18 percent are in the 4–8 range. Repeat for each predictor score level.

Construct the final form of the expectancy table using as the cell entries the chances in 100 (i.e., the percentage of cases) that a given test score is associated with a given outcome. For our example the table would be:

Chances (in 100) of being rated successful as a function of predictor test scores

	Job rating	
Test score	*Unsuccessful*	*Successful*
8–10	0	100
7	7	93
6	28	72
5	45	55
4	75	25
3	82	18
0–2	100	0

Expectancy tables also clearly illustrate a dilemma that plagues psychological testing: how to apply group data to an individual. The figures within the cells of an expectancy table show the probability of various levels of criterion performance *given* the predictor score. These data are derived from groups and directly interpretable only for groups. For example, if the probability of success on the job is .63 for applicants having a particular predictor score, then an employer can expect 63 percent of the applicants that he hires who have this particular predictor score will be successful. When considering a specific individual, however, difficulties are encountered. Any individual will either succeed or fail; that is, for an individual the probability is either 1.00 (succeed) or 0.00 (fail). To say that an individual has a 63 percent chance of success is logically meaningless. Thus, when interpreting data from expectancy tables to an individual, it must be stressed that the predictions are group averages. In other words, these data only give an estimate of the success of a group of people obtaining similar predictor scores.

Predicted Performance Level

Expectancy tables describe test performance in terms of the probability of various outcomes. Another possibility is to present the predicted outcome scores (criterion scores) for persons with various test scores. This could be done in either tabular or graphic form. In either case the procedure would be analogous to that for constructing expectancy tables. First, we would obtain test and criterion scores for a sample of people. Next, we would find the average criterion level performance of people obtaining each of various test scores. Then, we would construct a table or graph that presents this information.

Note that the table will show the *average* criterion performance associated with a given test score. The reported value will always be an average because since the correlation between test and criterion is not perfect, there will be a range of criterion scores associated with each test score.

The simplest procedure would be to determine the mean criterion score at each test score level. However, a more general solution can be made using the regression equations. In our discussion of validity coefficients we showed how regression equations can be developed; these equations give a predicted criterion score for any predictor score. To use this approach we first find the validity coefficient and the corresponding regression equation. Then, for each test score value we determine the predicted criterion score. These scores are the ones reported in the table.

Tabular methods   We mentioned that predicted scores can be presented in either tabular or graphical form. Consider first the tabular presentation. This case is similar to a conversion table; however, instead of presenting percentile equivalents of various raw scores, the table presents criterion performance equivalents of various raw scores. An example of such a table is shown in Table 11.4. This table shows the average freshman year GPA obtained by students having various ACT scores. From the table we can see that a student having an ACT score of 30 would have a predicted freshman year GPA of 2.95 and a student with an ACT score of 24 would have a predicted GPA of 2.29, and so on.

Graphic methods   We can also present the same information graphically. Figure 11.1 presents the same data as in Table 11.4, except in graphical form. The only advantage of the graphic presentation, with one predictor, is that the relationship may be more immediately obvious. A potential disadvantage is that the pattern presented is, at least to the casual viewer, dependent on the units used on the criterion score dimension. If the distance between points on the criterion scale is wide, the differences between various test scores will appear larger; if the distances are small, the differences between test scores will appear smaller.

TABLE 11.4   Example of an outcome-referenced conversion table: predicted grade-point-averages

ACT Composite	Predicted GPA
32	3.17
31	3.06
30	2.95
29	2.84
28	2.73
27	2.62
26	2.51
25	2.40
24	2.29
23	2.18
22	2.07
21	1.96
20	1.85

Data based on a sample of 330 entering freshmen at a midwestern college. The regression equation was:

$$GPA' = 0.11 (ACT) - 0.35$$

GPAs are reported on a four-point scale (A = 4, B = 3, and so on). Note also that predicted GPAs cover a narrower range than actual GPAs; this is a statistical artifact that could be corrected for, if desired.

The advantage of a graphical presentation is more apparent when we have two predictor variables. In this case we can show several levels of predicted criterion performance simultaneously. Consider Figure 11.2, which shows freshman year GPAs predicted from a combination of ACT test scores and high school class rank (HSR). Note that line C shows the various combinations of ACT and HSR scores needed to obtain a predicted C average; line B shows the combination needed for a predicted B average; and so on.

Figure 11.2 was developed in the following manner. First HSR, ACT, and GPA data were collected for a sample of students. We then found the regression equation for predicting GPA from ACT and HSR. To find the lines corresponding to a particular predicted GPA, we set one side of the equation equal to the predicted GPA. We then substituted various values of ACT into the equation and solved for HSR. This procedure told us what combination of ACT and HSR scores were needed to obtain the desired GPA. We then plotted the results on the graph. A graph developed in this manner is called a *nomograph*.

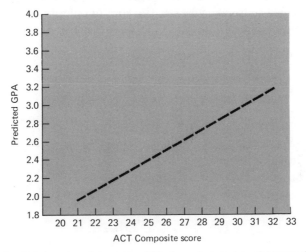

Figure 11.1   Predicted grade-point-average. This figure is based on the same data as used in Table 11.4.

Evaluation of Outcome-Referenced Scores

The major advantage of outcome-referenced scores is obvious: They allow us to interpret scores in terms of predicted criterion level performance. Whenever our concern is with prediction, outcome-referenced scores should be used. (Unfortunately, they rarely are.) Although, as we have indicated, it is possible to incorporate validity data into our interpretations in other ways, these ways are all indirect. And in test score interpretation, as in many other situations, the direct route is usually best.

If criterion data are not available, or if the criterion data are not inherently meaningful or of interest, then outcome-referenced scores are inappropriate. The first case is obvious, but the second may not be. To illustrate, personality tests are sometimes validated using ratings or judgments as a criterion measure. For example, one might validate a test of aggressiveness using teachers' ratings of children's aggressiveness as a criterion. To express such data in outcome-referenced terms would only give us a prediction of teacher's ratings—hardly an item of interest. In other situations involving personality measures, meaningful criterion data may be available. For example, scores on the occupational scales of the Strong Vocational Interest Blank have been validated using job tenure or occupational change as a criterion. In these circumstances, outcome-referenced scores could be used.

Another important consideration is the strength of the relationship between test scores and the criterion measures. We have only said that we need a valid predictor. But, there can be different degrees of validity. The higher the validity, the less error in our predictions; the lower the validity, the greater the error. Using average predicted criterion scores may mask this fact. The solution, of course, is to incorporate some index of error into our prediction and thus build it into the table. This margin would be based on the standard error of estimate. The result would be to report predicted (outcome) scores not as exact points, but as ranges.

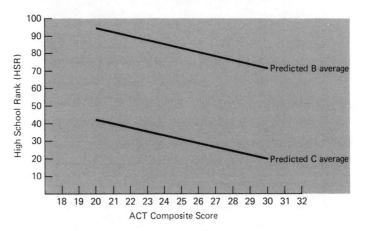

Figure 11.2 Grade-point-average predicted from high school rank and ACT composite scores. Data based on the performance of 455 freshmen at a midwestern college. The regression equation was:

$$GPA' = 0.38 + .02 \ (HSR) + .04 \ (ACT)$$

The lines in the figure are indicated equal predicted GPAs.

Finally, there is a practical point. Presentation of outcome-referenced scores is relatively straightforward when there are only one or two predictors. With more predictors the situation becomes complex, though not impossible. Consider the three-predictor case. Here we could either develop a graph that presented a three-dimensional view or we could develop a series of two-dimensional expectancy tables, one for each level of the third predictor. With more than three predictor variables, other approaches generally will be simpler. Fortunately, there are few situations in which the use of more than three predictors significantly increases predictive accuracy.

PROBLEMS IN SCORE INTERPRETATION

In this section we shall briefly consider three important problems that arise when interpreting test scores: (1) the sources of error that affect test scores; (2) equating scores from various tests; and (3) some problems involved when using several scores simultaneously.

Errors in Scores

Throughout this book we have emphasized that scores on psychological and educational tests contain some error of measurement. Now we shall indicate how these errors may affect score interpretations. In doing so we shall consider three sources of error: those due to unreliability, those due to invalidity, and errors attributable to improper generalization.

Unreliability   In our discussion of derived scores, we assumed that a given raw score could be directly transformed into an equivalent derived score. That is, test scores were treated as precise indicators. However, we also pointed out that since, in practice, tests are never perfectly reliable, test scores should be treated as ranges or bands rather than exact points. This means that one must always consider the standard error of measurement. Many test publishers have developed conversion tables or profiles that utilize a band approach to score interpretation. That is, derived scores are reported as ranges (bands) rather than as exact points. Even if the test publisher has not used this approach, the test interpreter should provide his own band interpretation to test scores. If exact scores are used, it should be with the understanding that such scores are not precise indicators but rather the best estimate that we have of the person's "true" score. In other words, a percentile rank of 55 should not be interpreted as the person's exact rank; rather it should be considered as the best available estimate of his rank.

Invalidity   An equally important source of interpretive errors is often overlooked: the invalidity of test scores or, worse yet, the lack of validity evidence. As has been pointed out previously, without evidence of validity normative data tell nothing more than the individual's relative ranking within a norm group. Yet, the very fact that normative data are available (regardless of the presence or absence of validity data) often provides a subtle temptation to interpret test scores *as if* validity data were available. If a test is labeled as a measure of mathematical aptitude, and if there are normative data available, it is only too easy to interpret scores on the test as if they predicted success in activities requiring mathematical ability. Or, if a test is labeled as a measure of introversion, and normative data are available, it is easy to say that a person scoring high on the test will be introverted.

Probably no other error occurs more frequently in the interpretation of psychological test data than to infer meaning of test scores from the title of the test and normative data, neglecting the fact that validity data supporting the interpretation are either nonexistent or fragmentary. To summarize what should now be obvious: *Normative data are not sufficient for accurate test interpretation; one also needs validity data.*

Generalizability   Frequently, none of the available norm groups are clearly appropriate for the individuals whose scores are being interpreted. To the extent that an individual differs from the norm group, errors of faulty generalization may be introduced into the test interpretation. Sometimes this problem can be overcome by developing local norms; other times, as in many counseling settings, such a procedure is not feasible. Thus, the test user should constantly be aware of the possibility of making improper generalizations from inadequate normative data.[4]

An analogous problem occurs with validity data, especially when we wish to predict some possible outcome. Here, again, there may be no available validity data that correspond to the particular situation and individual. Thus we often have to rely on the best available data—that is, data from the most comparable situation. Since each situation (for example, school, company) is in many ways unique, in these situations we always run the risk of improper generalizations. As with normative data, one possibility is to collect new validity data. If this procedure is unfeasible, we can only interpret scores with due caution.

Equating Scores

Test users sometimes encounter a situation similar to the following:

A high school student, Jimmy Jones, applies to Midwest State and Prestige U. As part of the application procedure to Prestige U he takes the XYZ College Aptitude Test. He also submits his scores on the XYZ Test to Midwest State. Unfortunately, Midwest State requires the ABC College Aptitude Test and asks Jimmy to submit scores on the ABC Test. Jimmy may well ask why scores on the XYZ Test cannot be substituted for scores on the ABC Test since both tests purportedly measure aptitude for college.

The basic problem in this situation is that of equating test scores; that is, of placing both scores on a common scale.

One fundamental distinction that must be considered is whether the tests are equivalent or merely comparable (Wesman, 1958). Scores on the two tests can be considered comparable if they represent the same relative standing in the same population. However, to be considered equivalent, the items on the tests must represent the same content domain; that is, the tests must be interchangeable in regard to content. It is at this point that most attempts to equate test scores get hung up, since two tests seldom measure identical domains, nor do they utilize the same norm groups.[5]

Equating methods   Suppose, however, that two tests sample the same domain. How can scores on the tests be equated? One common procedure is called the *equipercentile method* (see Angoff, 1971a; Jaeger, 1973). In this technique both tests are administered to the same sample, and raw scores (on both tests) are translated into percentile ranks. Then, using the percentile ranks as pivot points, a table of equivalent raw scores can be prepared. That is, if a raw score of 55 on Test ABC is at the 90th percentile rank and a raw score of 36 on Test XYZ is also at the

---

[4]Compare Cattell's concept of transferability discussed in Chapter 6.

[5]For example, the two most widely used college admissions tests—the ACT and SAT—cover quite different content/skill domains. In addition, since the two tests are, by and large, used by different types of colleges, their normative samples are not comparable.

90th percentile, scores of 55 on ABC and 36 on XYZ can be considered equivalent. To return to our example, if Jimmy Jones submitted a score of 36 on Test XYZ to Midwest State, the admissions officer could convert this score to a 55 on Test ABC and, thereby, have a basis for interpreting Jimmy's score.

An alternative procedure, which sidesteps the equivalence problem, would be to equate tests in terms of some outcome measure. That is, rather than using equal percentile ranks as the pivot point, equal outcomes could be used as the basis of equation (in the example, we might use equal college grade averages). This approach, besides sidestepping the content equivalence problem, has the advantage of incorporating validity data into the interpretation process.

Change and Difference Scores

Most of our discussion has been concerned with a single score. There are, however, at least two common situations in which we must consider more than one score. One is when we are concerned with repeated measurements over time (change scores). The other is when we want to compare scores on two or more tests, scales, or subtests. Both of these situations involve difference scores.

When measuring change we obtain scores on the same measure at several points in time, then calculate some index of change. Perhaps the most common illustration is measuring academic growth over time. Suppose, for example, that a school administers a standardized Reading Comprehension Test each October. If Mike's grade-equivalent score were 5–4 one year and 6–1 the next, we could say that he showed 7 months' growth. Since "normal" growth would be 10 months,[6] we might conclude that Mike showed less than normal growth in reading ability.

There are several problems with such an interpretation (even neglecting our concern with grade-equivalent scores per se). One is the large error of measurement due to the unreliability of difference scores. The other is that we do not usually know the distribution of growth scores. Although we can infer (from the score development procedure) that the average amount of growth will be 10 months, we do not know how many students improve by only 7 months. Such information would aid our interpretations.

The other common situation involves interpreting differences between several scores obtained at the same time. For example, a teacher might want to know whether Mary's verbal ability is better than her quantitative ability or whether Kirk's arithmetic computational skills are better than his problem-solving skills. Here again, we are confronted with the same problem—the unreliability of difference scores. Fortunately, it is possible to determine whether a given difference between pairs of scores is statistically significant. Some test publishers incorporate this information into their interpretive material, either (1) by reporting scores as bands, with nonoverlapping bands indicating significant differences, or (2) by stating that a difference of a certain number of points is statistically significant. Such practices should be encouraged. The important point is that unless we have evidence

---

[6]Remember, grade equivalent scores are based on a ten-month school year.

that the observed differences are true differences, we cannot imply that the person performed differently on the two tests or occasions. That is, unless we know that Mary's verbal ability is significantly higher than her quantitative ability, we cannot draw any conclusions about her verbal or quantitative skills. Because of the large error of measurement in difference scores, the difference needed for significance is usually larger than might be expected at first glance. Thus, we should always be cautious when interpreting difference scores so as not to draw conclusions from chance differences.

COMMUNICATING INFORMATION ABOUT TEST SCORES

In a broad sense, everything discussed thus far has been concerned with the interpretation of test scores. By this we mean that one cannot adequately interpret test scores unless he understands how tests are constructed and validated, as well as those concepts more directly related to scores and norms. But this knowledge only ensures that we can describe an individual's test performance. Often we are more concerned with the developmental and situational factors that led to the person's performance (see Glaser, 1972; Estes, 1974) or how he will react to and use information about his performance. These are the questions of greatest concern to teachers and counselors.

One point deserves particular emphasis, since it often leads to improper interpretations. It is easy to think of factors, either in the test taker's background or in aspects of the testing situation, that may influence an individual's performance. Usually, it is easier to identify factors that might interfere with performance, thus causing lower scores, than factors that will produce better performance. Combining this with our seemingly natural tendency to say good things about people and avoid the bad may result in a tendency to explain away poor performance—that is, to think of reasons why the person may have obtained a low score. In other words, we often overemphasize possible reasons for weak performance. This is not to imply that reasons for poor performance do not exist; they do. The point is that these reasons should be placed in proper perspective, so as not to present an excessively rosy picture to the test taker.

One way to avoid this problem is to separate the level of performance from the reasons for this performance, even though we know they are related. Consider an example. Many students from disadvantaged backgrounds, not having had the experiences of middle-class children, score low on achievement and ability tests. When interpreting their scores, we cannot neglect this fact. However, the student's level of performance may provide valuable information, regardless of why the score was obtained. For example, if a student's reading skills are poor he will probably experience difficulty in any class or situation that requires reading skills. This is the interpretation we make from his level of performance on the reading test. When considering how to improve the student's reading skills, however, knowledge of the relevant background factors becomes an important bit of information.

Some Guidelines

Even if the tester has the necessary technical background to interpret a test score, there is no guarantee that this information will be effectively communicated to the test taker. Thus, in this section we shall suggest several guidelines to aid you in communicating scores in such a way that the client[7] will understand their meaning. These suggestions will not make you an expert; hopefully, however, they will provide a starting point (for a detailed treatment see Goldman, 1971).

1. *Use language the client understands.* Testing, like other specialized fields, has its own vocabulary. Just because you understand a term doesn't mean that the client will. For example, you know what standard deviations and standard scores are; however, it is unlikely that the client will. Thus, you will have to explain standard scores in nontechnical terms; generally, using an interpretation involving relative position (that is, percentile ranks) will suffice. If in doubt, ask the client whether he understands. Better yet, ask him to tell you what your interpretation meant.

2. *Be sure the client knows what the test measures or predicts.* This is the validity question. Here again, we do not need a detailed technical explanation, just the major implications. For example, you don't need to give a client a short course on the construction of the Strong Vocational Interest Blank, but he should know that the Occupational scales compare his interests to people in that occupation and high scores mean that the person will probably stay in an occupation if he enters it. Another aspect might be called the *labeling problem.* To tell the client that a certain scale measures, say, Dominance will probably not be sufficient. You may well have to explain what the test constructor means by Dominance. This is particularly important with emotionally laden personality dimensions, such as Heterosexuality or Masculinity-Femininity.

3. If the scores are norm-referenced, *be sure that the student knows what group he is being compared to*. For example, a student's ranking on a college aptitude test, such as the ACT or SAT, will vary widely depending on whether he is being compared to a cross-section of high school seniors, students at a local community college, or students at a highly selective Ivy League school.

4. *Be sure the student recognizes that scores are only "best estimates."* Here we are referring both to unreliability and prediction errors (invalidity), as well as to the fact that validity data are based on groups, not individuals. The important point to be communicated is that the scores, or predictions, are "best estimates," and that there will also be some degree of error involved when considering an individual score. To do this without creating the impression that scores are so error-filled that they are worthless often involves treading a narrow path.

5. *Be sure the client knows how his scores will be used.* This is particularly important when tests are used in selection and placement. Our concern is with the

[7]We shall use "client" as an all-purpose term to refer to the person to whom the scores are being interpreted. The client may be either the person who took the test (for example, a student, counselee, therapy patient, or job applicant) or someone concerned with the test taker's scores (for example, his parents, an employer, a teacher).

role test scores will play in the decision-making process. Will the test scores be an important factor or will they be used only in borderline cases? Are there minimal cutting scores or is the process compensatory? Often this information is not available, particularly in counseling situations. However, we often have some information that may be useful. For example, suppose a student is thinking of applying for graduate work in Psychology at Old Ivy, and we know that the average GRE-Verbal score of students in this program is 700. If John Smith scored only 500 on the GRE-V, we can probably safely imply that his chances of acceptance will be low, even if we do not know exactly how much weight is placed on GRE scores by the admissions committee.

6. *Consider what the impact of knowing his test scores will be on the client.* Take the example in the previous paragraph. Will John be discouraged because his scores were low? Or, will it confirm what he already suspects about his abilities? Will it cause him to abandon some long-held plans? Or will it cause him to work harder to show that his score is not a true indication of his ability? In short, how will your interpretation affect the client?

Furthermore, how will you handle his reaction? Although we usually think of the possible upsetting reactions when scores are lower than the person expects, we must also be prepared for the opposite situation. If a student thinks he has only average ability, what will be the effect if he finds that his ability is quite high? How will he reconcile this with his previous self-image? These are the sorts of questions a test interpreter must be prepared to face.

7. Implicit in many of the previous guidelines is our final point: *Let the client be an active participant in the test interpretation process.* After all, the scores are his, not yours, and the decisions to be made will affect his life, not yours. Thus, at all stages of the process you should solicit his reactions, encourage him to ask questions, and help him reflect upon the implications of his scores. Although a test score is only one limited piece of information, finding out the score may set off a chain of events that drastically changes an individual's life. Thus, you must be assured that he thoroughly understands the meanings and implications of his scores. Unless the client is an active participant in the process, you may not be aware of how well he understands his scores.

SUGGESTED FURTHER READING FOR PART III

American College Testing Program. *Assessing students on the way to college.* Iowa City, Iowa: American College Testing Program, 1972.

Vol. 2 illustrates the variety of normative data and how it can be used in the educational process.

American Psychological Association. *Standards for educational and psychological tests.* Washington, D.C.: American Psychological Association, 1974.

Pages 17 to 24 and 64 to 73 present standards for administration of tests, development of scores and norms, and interpretation of scores. "Must" reading.

Angoff, W. H. Scales, norms, and equivalent scores. In R. L. Thorndike (Ed.), *Educational measurement.* (2d ed.) Washington, D.C.: American Council on Education, 1971.

A thorough description of the process of developing norms and scores for educational tests.

Angoff, W. H. Criterion-referencing, norm-referencing, and the SAT. *College Board Review,* Summer 1974, pp. 2–5; 21.

Points out that norm-referenced and criterion-referenced scores are not incompatible, rather they are just two different ways of expressing performance on a test.

Carver, R. P. Two dimensions of tests: Psychometric and edumetric. *American Psychologist,* 1974, *29,* 512–518.

Distinguishes between the use of tests to measure individual differences and their use to measure learning.

Davis, J. A. Nonapparent limitations of normative data. *Personnel and Guidance Journal,* 1959, *37,* 656–659.

Points out some factors which are often overlooked when evaluating and using normative data.

Glaser, R. Instructional technology and the measurement of learning outcomes. *American Psychologist,* 1963, *18,* 519–521.

On the distinction between norm-referenced and criterion-referenced scores.

Goldman, L. *Using tests in counseling.* (2d ed.) New York: Appleton, 1971.

Best and most comprehensive treatment of the role of tests in the counseling process.

Jensen, A. R. The effect of race of examiner on the mental test scores of white and black pupils. *Journal of Educational Measurement,* 1974, *11,* 1–14.

Considers the question of whether the race of the examiner effects the results obtained from tests.

Lyman, H. G. *Test scores and what they mean.* (2d ed.) Englewood Cliffs, N.J.: Prentice-Hall, 1971.

A brief, well-written book that describes the various types of test scores and provides suggestions for test interpretation. Excellent for the person who needs to interpret scores.

Popham, W. J., & Husek, T. R. Implications of criterion-referenced measurement. *Journal of Educational Measurement,* 1969, *6,* 1–9.

Discussion of the major differences between norm- and criterion-referenced measurement and the implications for test construction, evaluation, and use.

Psychological Corporation. Test Service Bulletins. New York: The Psychological Corporation.

See especially numbers 38 ("Expectancy tables: A way of interpreting test validity"), 39 ("Norms must be relevant"), 48 ("Methods of expressing test scores"), 53 ("Comparability vs. equivalence of test scores"), 54 ("On telling parents about test results"), 56 ("Double-entry expectancy tables"), and 58 ("Local norms: When and why"). Brief presentations with a practical flavor; designed for the test user.

PART IV

MEASURES OF MAXIMAL PERFORMANCE

Earlier we made a distinction between maximal and typical performance tests. On maximal performance tests we are interested in obtaining an estimate of the individual's best possible performance; on typical performance measures we are interested in usual or habitual behavior. Achievement, ability, and aptitude tests are maximal performance measures; personality tests are typical performance measures. In this section of the book we shall be concerned with maximal performance measures.

We will start by differentiating between three types of maximal performance measures—ability, achievement, and aptitude tests. Achievement tests measure the results of learning, usually learning in a relatively circumscribed area. Thus reference is to current status or to the past—to what has been learned. The typical classroom exam is an illustration of an achievement test. Aptitude tests, in contrast, are designed to measure what can be learned, given appropriate training; thus, they focus on future behavior. College admissions tests and employment tests used to hire workers are examples of aptitude measures. Ability tests fall between achievement and aptitude measures, being designed to measure current levels of skills or knowledge. They differ from achievement tests in that they measure the results of both formal and informal learning, and may cover both academic and nonacademic skills. All three types of tests measure what an individual has learned. They differ in the specificity of the prior learning and the uses made of test results.

In Chapter 12 we shall expand on these distinctions and discuss the underlying assumptions made when constructing and using each type of test. The remaining chapters in this section will consider each type of test in greater detail, emphasizing their construction and appropriate uses. In Chapter 12 we shall also make several other basic distinctions. One is between the norm-referenced and criterion-referenced approaches to measurement. Norm-referenced tests compare individuals with each other; thus, performance is usually interpreted in terms of a relative ranking. Criterion-referenced measures stress mastery of certain defined skills and content; that is, what the individual knows and can do. Scores on criterion-referenced tests are interpreted by indicating what skills and knowledge the individual has mastered. In this chapter we shall also consider the role of cultural influences on test performance, as exemplified by the attempts to build culture-fair tests.

Certainly the most commonly used tests are teacher-built classroom exams. In Chapter 13 we shall discuss classroom tests. We shall start by emphasizing the need for careful and thorough planning of the test, stressing that the teacher must always consider what he is testing and why. We shall describe several ways of ensuring that the test does, in fact, accomplish its intended purposes. After our discussion of test plans, we shall consider, in some detail, the various types of items encountered on classroom tests and present some guidelines for writing good items. The major point of this section is that each type of item has certain advantages and limitations; no one item type will work best in all situations. Thus the teacher should always consider what he is trying to measure, then choose the item type that will best attain his goals. We shall also consider the various ways that tests can be used to facilitate and improve instruction, emphasizing that tests have other, and more important uses, than just as a basis for assigning grades.

In many circumstances teacher-built tests are not adequate—for example, when measuring students' growth from year to year or when comparing several groups of students or instructional methods. In these cases, standardized measures of achievement are needed. Throughout the discussion, you should compare teacher-built and standardized tests, contrasting their advantages and limitations. Our discussion (Chapter 14) will consider the various types and uses of standardized achievement tests, stressing the implications for test construction and for the ways scores are interpreted and used. Our discussion will focus on three major classes of standardized achievement tests: survey tests, which provide a broad formative evaluation; tests used to facilitate the instructional process—for example, diagnostic, readiness, and placement tests; and tests that measure educational outcomes and vocational proficiency. Because any test is no better than the items comprising it, we shall also discuss techniques for selecting good items by the process of item analysis.

In the discussion of achievement tests we shall constantly be stressing three major points. First, a test will be no better than the planning that goes into it; thus, you should always consider what you want to test and why you are giving the test. Second, different types of items and tests are appropriate in various circumstances; no one type is best in all situations. Here, again, the message is clear: Select the type of items and/or tests that will best attain your objectives. Third, the major purpose of achievement testing is to facilitate and improve instruction. Thus, the value of an achievement test is determined by its contribution to improving instruction. At a minimum, this requires detailed feedback of the results of the testing, on an item-by-item basis, to both the teacher and the student.

The remaining two chapters of this part of the book (Chapters 15 and 16) will discuss aptitude and ability tests. We shall start with the broadest-range and historically most important test, the individual intelligence test, and then discuss other measures of general ability (group intelligence and scholastic aptitude tests), tests that measure several broad abilities (multiple aptitude batteries), and tests of specific abilities and aptitudes. Again, we shall stress the assumptions, construction, and uses of each type of test.

The main point to keep in mind when reading Chapters 15 and 16 is that all ability and aptitude tests measure developed abilities. That is, they measure the skills, knowledge and abilities that the person has learned throughout his life. Because past performance is often the best predictor of future performance, and because certain skills are needed to succeed in any academic and vocational setting, aptitude and ability tests do predict future performance. Thus, knowledge of a person's abilities can be very useful when educational and career plans are being made. However, any test indicates only the level of developed skills; that is, the test score is a description of the person's current performance on a certain set of tasks. What implications scores will have depend on a number of factors, the most important of which are the person's opportunity to develop the skills measured by the test and what role mastery of the skills has in determining (future) performance in the specific situation of concern. In short, scores on aptitude and ability tests should never be interpreted in isolation; we must always look carefully at the test taker's background and the characteristics of situations he is to enter.

12

APTITUDE, ABILITY, AND ACHIEVEMENT

On measures of maximal performance we are interested in obtaining an estimate of the person's best possible performance; on measures of typical performance we are interested in his usual or habitual performance. The set to respond to a testing situation, as either maximal or typical performance, is usually engendered by the test directions. That is, on measures of maximal performance, the test taker is instructed to "do his best," to "obtain the highest possible score." In contrast, on measures of typical performance the test taker is directed to express his usual or habitual reactions.

As might be expected, maximal performance measures involve situations where there are definite correct answers to the items. Thus this category encompasses tests that measure outcomes of educational or training programs (achievement tests), tests that measure a person's developed skills in an area (ability tests), and tests that indicate whether a person has the necessary skills and abilities to succeed in further work in an area (aptitude tests). Measure of typical performance are appropriate in areas where there are "no correct answers"; that is, when we want to know how a person typically behaves or reacts, not whether he knows the appropriate reaction for a particular situation. Personality, interest, and aptitude tests are examples of typical performance measures.

In this section we shall focus on maximal performance measures; typical performance measures will be discussed in the next part of the book.

Aptitude, Achievement, and Ability

As we have noted, maximal performance tests can be classified into three broad categories: aptitude tests, ability tests, and achievement tests. Although these three categories are not mutually exclusive, and although a particular test may serve more than one of these functions, there are enough differences in emphasis to consider these types of tests separately. We shall start with the type of test you are probably most familiar with, achievement tests.

Achievement   You undoubtedly have taken many achievement tests during your educational career. For example, classroom examinations clearly are achievement tests. So are the test batteries that you took during your elementary and secondary school days that measured your mastery of arithmetic and mathematics, spelling, history, natural sciences, reading, and other basic skills. Not only could you give other examples of achievement tests, you probably also could specify the types of items included on such tests—for example, questions measuring knowledge of specific facts, principles, and concepts; problems involving the manipulation of numbers and formulas; questions requiring you to draw conclusions from information contained in a reading passage; items requiring application of your knowledge to new situations; and, at least on classroom exams, essay questions requiring you to evaluate or integrate material.

A question remains, however: How can achievement tests be differentiated from other types of tests? Probably your first response would be that achievement tests measure what a person has learned. This is obviously true, but a little reflection will show that all tests measure what an individual has learned. You might take another tack and say that achievement tests assess mastery of academic subjects. Yet the written test that you took to obtain a driver's license was an achievement test. Or you might try to define achievement tests by the types of items included on the test or the processes used in responding to the items—recall of facts, reasoning, problem solving, and so forth. Yet anyone looking at two unlabeled tests, one measuring achievement and another scholastic aptitude, would be hard put to classify the tests correctly. Trying again, you might try to distinguish achievement tests by their uses. That is, if a test is designed to evaluate teaching or learning, it is an achievement test. However, there are instances where achievement tests are used primarily to predict future performance, since past performance is frequently the best predictor of future performance. In this situation the test would be functioning as a measure of aptitude, not achievement.

In this book a test will be classified as an achievement test if it measures learning that has occurred: (1) as a result of experiences in a relatively circumscribed learning situation, such as in a classroom or training program; and (2) when the frame of reference is on the present or past, that is, on what *has been learned*.

Aptitudes and abilities   Although most persons have had more exposure to achievement tests than any other type of test, if asked to give an example of a psychological test, the man on the street would probably cite an intelligence or aptitude test. "IQ tests" and "tests that tell you what you can do" have become known as the psychologist's stock-in-trade. We will consider a test to be an aptitude measure if: (1) it measures the results of general and incidental learning experiences; and (2) its frame of reference is toward the future. This is in contrast to an achievement test, which measures learning resulting from relatively specific experiences, and focuses on past learning. Another way of clarifying the definition of aptitude is to say that the learnings tapped by an aptitude measure reflect the individual's total life experience and that the goal of testing is to predict what can be learned in the future.

This latter point, that aptitude tests predict future learning, is the hallmark of the definition of aptitude. Most definitions of aptitude state that *aptitude tests indicate the ability to acquire certain behaviors or skills given appropriate opportunity* (see, e.g., English and English, 1958; Drever, 1964; Michael, 1960). Thus aptitudes are important because they indicate the probability that certain other behaviors will be acquired or learned. What is to be learned may vary from a complex intellectual skill, such as a foreign language or calculus, to simple motor or physical acts. Thus the definition of aptitude encompasses the ability to learn a variety of skills or behaviors, with the common thread being the ability to learn, not the type of skills learned.

To clarify our terminology, we should include a third concept: *ability*. *Ability indicates the power to perform a task.* This is in contrast to aptitude, which signifies the power to learn to perform a task. In other words, ability refers to a current state, aptitude to a future state. In this respect, ability is similar to achievement. However, ability and achievement differ in that achievement tests usually measure the outcomes of specific learning experiences, ability tests the results of more general or broad learning experiences.

In short, the major distinctions are that achievement refers to well-specified learning experiences and has a past or present reference; ability refers to broad learning experience and has a present reference; and aptitude refers to broad learning experiences and has a future reference.

ACHIEVEMENT TESTS

Achievement tests, as we have indicated, are designed to measure the knowledge and skills developed in a relatively circumscribed area (domain). This area may be as narrow as one day's class assignment (for example, computing the mean, the battle of Bull Run) or as broad as several years' study (such as high school mathematics or college French). In every case, however, we are attempting to measure what a person knows or can do at a particular point in time. Furthermore, our reference is usually to the past; that is, we are interested in what has been learned as a result of a particular course or experience or a series of experiences. Because it generally is not feasible to measure every bit of knowledge and every possible skill, the test items usually are only a sample of all the possible items in the domain.

Three Basic Assumptions

When we adopt this view of achievement, we are making certain assumptions about our measurements. The first is that the content and/or skill domain covered by the test can be specified in behavioral terms. Although some educators think that certain important aims of education cannot be specified behaviorally (for example, a positive attitude towards learning), if educational goals are not expressed in behavioral terms they cannot be measured. All this requirement really means is that the knowledge and skills to be measured must be specified in a manner that is readily communicable to other persons. As a corollary, *important* goals must be differentiated from peripheral or incidental goals. Because of time limitations, only certain outcomes can be measured; these outcomes should be the most important ones.

A second assumption is that the test does, in fact, measure these important behaviors rather than irrelevant considerations. This is an assumption of content validity. Consider an example used earlier, algebra word problems. To solve such problems requires several skills: being able to read the problem, to translate it into algebraic form, and to do the necessary arithmetic computations. If the test is designed to measure students' ability to solve algebraic word problems, we have no problem. If, however, we are only interested in students' ability to manipulate algebraic formulas, the test will also measure a skill (reading ability) that is irrelevant to the purposes of the testing. To cite another example, if the knowledge necessary to answer an item correctly could have been obtained outside the classroom, and the goal of the test is to measure what students have learned in a particular class, then the test will not be a true measure of learning that took place in that class. In short, we must always be sure that our test measures only those outcomes that we want to measure, not irrelevant factors.

The third assumption is that the test takers have had the opportunity to learn the material covered by the test. More specifically, if we want to compare students, they should have had equal opportunities for learning. This assumption is generally well met on classroom exams, since all students are in the same course and the instructor has specified what assignments will be covered on the exam. The problem of unequal educational experiences becomes an issue when dealing with standardized achievement tests. Because standardized tests are administered in a variety of schools, of necessity they cover material that is widely taught. To the extent that the subject matter taught in any particular school differs from that covered on the test, the students in a particular school will not have had equivalent experiences to those of the norm group. Consider an example with current significance. If an achievement test standardized on middle-class children is administered to children from a disadvantaged area, the normative data will be inappropriate, since the experience of the two groups has not been comparable. The scores of the children from the disadvantaged area, when compared to those of the norm group, will show how these children compare to their more privileged age-mates. The scores will not, however, tell how these children's performances rank in comparison to those of other children with similar educational backgrounds.

Types of Achievement Tests

There are various dimensions that could be used to classify achievement tests. One obvious basis is by content area. Some achievement tests measure knowledge of spelling, others arithmetic, others United States history, others chemistry, and so forth. The content area can be defined very broadly (for example, calculus, reading, American history) or narrowly (for example, economic causes of the Civil War; squaring a polynomial). Since the standard references, such as *Tests in Print* (Buros, 1974), the *Mental Measurements Yearbooks* (Buros, 1972), as well as many publishers' catalogs, utilize content classifications, a test user interested in a particular content area can readily locate the available tests.

Many academic achievement tests are batteries, measuring several major content areas rather than only one area. With these tests, an appropriate basis of classification would be by grade level; that is, some batteries are designed for primary grades, and others for upper elementary grades, junior high school, or high school. Many test publishers have integrated series of achievement batteries, each covering a different grade level, thus allowing a school system to obtain continuous measures of academic growth over a period of years.

Achievement tests can be viewed as serving one of three general functions: survey, diagnostic, and readiness. An achievement test acts as a survey when it provides an estimate of a student's overall level of performance in a content area. *Survey tests,* therefore, sample a broad range of content and generally yield only one total score. The typical classroom final exam is an illustration of a survey test. A *diagnostic test,* in contrast, attempts to assess relative strengths and weaknesses in important component skills. Thus diagnostic tests are divided into subtests, and scores are provided for each important component. For example, a diagnostic reading test might include subtests covering word recognition, word comprehension, vocabulary, rate of reading, story comprehension, identification of sounds, and syllabication. By studying the pattern of scores, the psychologist can determine the areas in which the individual needs remedial work. A *readiness test* indicates whether the individual possesses the skills needed to learn the material at the next higher level. By its emphasis on prerequisite skills, a readiness test resembles a diagnostic test; in its use to predict further performance, the readiness test serves as an aptitude measure. The most common examples of readiness measures are reading readiness tests, which are administered at the end of kindergarten or beginning of first grade, to determine whether a child has learned the skills necessary to start formal reading instruction.

Achievement tests can also be classified according to the mode of response utilized. Although most achievement measures are paper-and-pencil tests, some are performance tests. *Performance tests* require the student to demonstrate his skill— for example, by tuning an automobile engine, performing a physical feat, or playing a musical composition. Paper-and-pencil tests are further divisible into two broad classes: recall and recognition. On *recognition* tests several possible answers are included with the question and the student's task is to choose between alternatives; on a *recall* test, the student must construct an answer. Multiple-choice and true-false items illustrate the former, essay and completion items the latter.

Another major distinction is between standardized achievement tests and class-room, or teacher-made, tests. *Standardized* tests are constructed by test publishers, and are designed for use in a wide variety of schools. Thus their coverage is necessarily broad. That is, they include materials covered in many schools. This coverage is usually identified by consulting widely used textbooks and from the opinions of curriculum experts. Norms are generally national in scope. *Teacher-built tests,* in contrast, are constructed by the classroom teacher, or possibly by a committee of several teachers in the same school. The content area will be more circumscribed, being based on the curriculum of a particular course or school. And, because the test covers a narrower domain, materials will be covered in more detail. Scores will be interpreted with reference to the student's immediate competitors, his classmates.

Because of these differences, standardized and teacher-made tests have differing uses. Standardized tests are useful when the purpose of the testing is to compare students' performance in different content areas; to compare an individual student, class, or school system to a wider population; when comparing classes or schools with each other; and when measuring growth over a period of years. Teacher-made tests are used when determining whether specific curriculum goals have been met and when comparing students with their immediate peers, as in assigning grades.

A distinction that is becoming more prevalent in educational circles is that between *norm-referenced* and *criterion-referenced tests* (Glaser, 1963). Although there is no complete agreement on the meanings of these two terms, most writers base their distinction on the standard of comparison used to interpret performance. On norm-referenced tests, a person's performance is compared with that of other people; that is, we are interested in a relative ranking. Criterion-referenced tests, in contrast, focus on the mastery of a defined content/skill domain.[1] Thus, a person's score is compared with some standard of content mastery, not with scores of other people. Because many people think instruction should stress mastery of specified objectives, rather than comparisons among students, criterion-referenced tests have received more emphasis in recent years. We shall consider the implications of this distinction, especially as it applies to test construction, in the following two chapters.

[1]Criterion-referenced scores, as defined by Glaser, include both content-referenced and outcome-referenced scores; however, the obvious parallel is content-referenced scores.

Uses of Achievement Tests

We have already mentioned a variety of uses for achievement tests, and you can probably suggest other possible uses. We have also indicated that any given test can serve several functions simultaneously and, in the case of standardized tests, the same test may perform different functions for different users. Before turning to a more detailed discussion of standardized and teacher-made achievement tests, it might be useful to review the uses of achievement tests.

Student uses   The most important use of any achievement test, particularly teacher-made tests, is to provide *feedback to students* regarding the effectiveness of their learning. Learning cannot occur without knowledge of results; that is, without the student's knowing whether his responses were correct or incorrect. To be most effective, this feedback should be continual, as immediate as possible, and to specific responses. Ideally, the student should receive some feedback on each individual response. Unfortunately, exams[2] often occur infrequently, papers are returned days or weeks later, and feedback is in terms of an overall score or letter grade. Although frequent testing with detailed feedback is time-consuming, evidence supporting the value of such testing as a learning experience would seem to justify an increased emphasis on testing. This is particularly true if the feedback is presented in a manner that enables the student to identify and learn from his errors.

Many educators feel that tests *motivate students to study*. Thus, tests are frequently used to show the student how much he does *not* know, and, thereby, supposedly to stimulate him to study (see e.g., Goldberg, 1965a). Or the threat of a test may be used to ensure that students will study, and thus presumably learn, hopefully, the basic concepts of the course. (Often, however, only the material students know will be on the exam.) But data from learning experiments lead to the conclusion that tests most effectively stimulate study when they function as reinforcers, when they show students that they can learn the material. The moral is clear: Tests can stimulate learning, if used for their feedback and reinforcement value (see, e.g., Skinner,1968; Anderson and Faust, 1973).

Diagnostic and counseling uses of achievement tests are also primarily for the benefit of individual students. When achievement tests are used for diagnostic purposes, the goal is to identify the sources of the student's difficulty and indicate possible courses of remedial action. Determining the causes of a student's difficulty is only the first step; our ultimate goal is to plan a remedial program that will increase his skill in the area of concern. There are also times when achievement tests may be useful in the *counseling* process. For example, a discrepancy between a student's aptitude and achievement may give some insights into his interests, study habits, or motivation. Or achievement test scores may indicate gaps in the student's knowledge, and thus aid in planning an educational program. Finally, since past performance is usually the best indicator of future performance, achievement tests can be utilized to predict future academic success.

---

[2]This point applies to any method of assessing students' performance, not just exams.

Instructor uses   Not only should an achievement test furnish feedback to the learner, it should also provide *feedback to the instructor*. Unless an instructor obtains detailed knowledge of what the students have and have not learned, he cannot ascertain how well his objectives have been met and how effective his teaching has been. By studying the pattern of responses on each item, particularly incorrect responses, the teacher can identify gaps and misconceptions in students' knowledge. This analysis can also provide clues as to which aspects of the teaching led to incomplete learning, thus providing a basis for modifying instruction to ensure more effective learning.

It hardly needs mentioning that achievement tests are frequently used as a basis for *assigning grades*. Because teacher-made tests are designed to measure the attainment of the objectives of a particular course or unit, they are almost always better basis for assigning grades than standardized tests. Using achievement tests as the primary basis for grading assumes that the material on the tests represents the desired outcomes of instruction. Therefore, the content and format of the exams must reflect these outcomes. As many critics of "objective" (that is, multiple-choice, true-false) items have pointed out (e.g., Hoffmann, 1961, 1962), this is often not the case. Too often, tests are comprised of items that are easy to construct—items measuring only factual material—rather than items tapping application, integration, understanding, and evaluation skills (see Bloom et al., 1971; R. Anderson, 1972).

The teacher can use achievement tests in several other ways. A *pretest,* administered before instruction begins, can serve as a diagnostic device. By identifying the knowledge and skills that students already possess and areas in which they lack knowledge, instruction can be tailored to fit the needs of a particular individual or class. A teacher could also use an achievement test to *check on students' studying;* for example, he could give a quiz to determine whether students have read a required assignment. Such a test need only cover the major points of the assignment and may be very brief. Or a teacher can use an achievement test to *stimulate discussion* by administering the test and using the students' responses, or difficulties with the items, as the basis for discussion.

Administrative uses   Achievement tests frequently are used as *selection* tools—for example, when scores on the achievement tests on the Graduate Record Exam are used to select students for graduate work. Civil service exams are used to determine whether an applicant has the requisite job skills. When an achievement test is used as a selection device, the skills measured by the test should, in fact, be prerequisites for adequate performance.

In educational settings, achievement tests may be used to place students in courses. For example, when entering college you may have taken an achievement test in a language that you had previously studied and, on the basis of your performance, been assigned to a particular level or section of a language course. If a given subject is taught in different manners, an achievement test might be used to determine which section of the course each student should enter. In industrial, military, and business settings, achievement tests may be used to determine which of several positions best fits an individual's skills. In each of these examples, the function of the test is to aid in making *placement or classification* decisions.

Achievement tests are also used to determine whether a person has attained the minimal level of proficiency needed to engage in some activity. For example, driver's license examinations are achievement tests designed to establish that the applicant has the requisite skills to drive an automobile on public streets and highways. The written portion of the test establishes the applicant's knowledge of traffic laws; the performance part (driving test) establishes his ability to drive the car in traffic. Other examples of using achievement tests as *performance standards* include examinations for professional licenses (for example, for medical specialists, professional engineers, or certified public accountants); examinations given at the end of a training program in business and industry; preliminary exams for the doctorate; and examinations for credit or for testing out of a course.

Evaluation of instruction   Probably no other area is so filled with danger, or provides so many examples of the misuse of test scores, as the use of achievement tests to evaluate the effectiveness of teachers, curricula, or teaching methods. Because achievement tests do measure students' knowledge, and because a basic objective of education is the acquisition of knowledge, achievement tests do play an important role in the evaluation of instruction. The problem is that this evaluation process is not as simple or straightforward as some people seem to believe.

To discuss the problems involved in evaluating instruction would require an entire book (see, e.g., Gage, 1963; Wittrock and Wiley, 1970; Campbell and Stanley, 1963; S. Anderson et al., 1974; Astin and Panos, 1971; Travers, 1973). Suffice it to say that studies evaluating instruction must specify in detail the characteristics of the learners, the type of treatment or method used, and how the outcomes are measured. Furthermore, to conduct a "true" experiment, students must be randomly assigned to treatments (for example, teachers or instructional methods)—something that is usually not feasible in actual real-life settings. Other common problems include confounding variables (for example, having different teachers use different methods or materials), failing to apply a method or procedure consistently, and neglecting important variables (such as students' background knowledge or motivation). Thus, evaluations of instruction based on fortuitous collections of data—such as the results of yearly testing programs—usually should be taken with a grain of salt.

APTITUDE AND ABILITY TESTS

In addition to achievement tests, there are two other types of maximal performance tests: ability tests and aptitude tests. When we defined these terms earlier, we indicated that ability tests measured present status, whereas aptitude tests were designed to predict future performance. In many ways ability tests are similar to achievement tests. They differ in that ability tests generally cover relatively broad areas, measure learning done in a variety of settings, can measure skills other than specifically academic ones, and frequently involve performance testing. Because the basic assumptions and methods of constructing ability tests are similar to those for achievement tests, we shall not consider them in detail here, but wait until we discuss specific types of ability tests. However, since aptitude measures are based on different assumptions, we shall spend the remainder of this chapter looking at some assumptions and generalizations that underlie aptitude testing.

Some Basic Assumptions

When measuring aptitudes, we usually adopt a *trait-and-factor view* of human abilities. That is, human abilities are conceptualized as being organized and expressed through combinations of intercorrelated behaviors and responses. To say that someone has mathematical aptitude is, in essence, to say that he possesses a set of (intercorrelated) skills, abilities, and characteristics that enable him to learn mathematics. These skills, abilities, and characteristics *are* the aptitude. Thus an aptitude is a construct, a summarizing term, and not an entity. The trait-and-factor approach is also normative, in the sense that an individual's aptitude is compared with that of other persons rather than with an absolute standard. To say that Johnny has high aptitude for mathematics means that he can learn mathematics faster, with less effort, or to a greater level of complexity than the majority of his peers; to say that George has no aptitude for math does not mean that he cannot learn any math, but only that it will be more difficult for him than for most other persons.[3]

If a trait (aptitude) is to predict future performance, it must be relatively stable over time. This emphasis on stability has led many people to conclude that aptitudes are inherited characteristics that are unchanging throughout life. (Note such common expressions as a "God-given talent" or a "natural athlete.") There is no doubt that aptitudes do have genetic bases; there is also no doubt, however, that aptitudes also reflect prior learning and the interaction between genetic potentials and environmental (learning) effects. The apparent stability of aptitude measures, therefore, does not indicate that aptitudes are determined solely by genetic factors but rather is a reflection of the consistency of most individuals' life patterns. Given the proper set of circumstances, aptitudes can be drastically influenced by environmental and situational characteristics (see, e.g., Anastasi, 1958; Bloom, 1964; Hunt, 1961; Bayley, 1968; Vernon, 1971).

This finding should not be interpreted to mean that an individual's performance on a given task is determined solely by situational forces. In all situations, performance will be determined by the individual's aptitudes, environmental factors, and the interaction of the two. The importance of any single component will, of course, depend on the particular situation. When individuals do not vary widely in their relevant traits (aptitudes), performance differences will be determined primarily by environmental characteristics; when the group is heterogeneous and the situation remains quite stable, individual differences become more important (Herrnstein, 1971). The psychologist's task is to study the relative contribution of

---

[3] An alternative view, proposed by Carroll (1963), defines aptitude in terms of the time needed to attain an objective or master a skill. This view implies that most students can master a skill given sufficient time and appropriate instruction. In other words, Carroll defines aptitude as time needed to learn, not in terms of the level of difficulty or complexity of the material that can be learned (see, also, Bloom, 1974).

each set of variables and to formulate general laws that relate trait and environmental conditions to performance.

Our definition also stated that *aptitudes assess the ability to learn, given the opportunity to learn*. Hence, when we say that Johnny has an aptitude for art, we are actually predicting that Johnny will become a better than average artist *if* given proper training. There is no reason to believe that he will develop his artistic ability without the relevant training. Thus, our prediction from an aptitude test is that a certain combination of abilities and skills (the aptitude) coupled with appropriate training will lead to a certain behavior. Although the statement "aptitude plus training equals accomplishment" appears straightforward and simple, in actuality it is highly complex. For example, what do we mean by appropriate training? Is the same training appropriate for all individuals? Or is there an interaction between training and personal characteristics? Will the same training program produce different effects if introduced at different points in the individual's development? To what extent does the person's aptitude reflect his previous training? If the person fails to perform at the expected level, is this evidence of the inappropriateness or failure of the training?

Or consider that elusive characteristic called motivation. Aptitude tests, being tests of maximal performance, assume that the test taker is motivated to make a maximal score; if not, the meaning of the score is ambiguous. Also, since aptitude indicates the ability to learn a skill with training, we must assume that the student is motivated during training; if not, we cannot say whether the training failed because of lack of aptitude or lack of motivation. Given the aptitude and training, the individual must be motivated to perform.

Theories of Intellectual Structure

Aptitude testing generally presupposes, as mentioned above, a trait-and-factor approach to the structure of abilities. That is, we assume that intellectual functioning can be described by a number of basic dimensions (traits or factors) and the person's standing on each dimension. More precisely, we need to know the number of traits needed to describe a person, the nature of these traits, the relationships between these traits, and the person's score on a measure (test) of each trait.

The development of a theory of intellectual structure has occupied the attention of a number of psychologists. Their attack has been both empirical and theoretical, but generally it has been closely connected with intelligence testing and has utilized factor analysis as the primary research technique. Although research on the structure of the intellect has been proceeding throughout the twentieth century there is still considerable controversy as to the validity of the proposed models. To give a flavor of the various approaches, précis of several historically interesting and currently fashionable models are presented below.[4]

---

[4]In our discussion we shall consider only cognitive abilities. Many psychologists would prefer to include also personality characteristics that influence intellectual performance (such as learning styles and achievement motivation).

General intelligence theories   The simplest approach is to postulate that intelligence is a unitary ability, a single general capacity. This view holds that although intelligence may be expressed in diverse fashions or may be directed toward a variety of activities, basically it is a single ability. Any test that provides a single score (IQ) is, at least in a broad sense, representing a unifactor theory. However, since empirical data frequently suggest that a more complex model is needed, the unifactor approach is considered too simplistic by most present-day theorists. It should be pointed out, however, that as practical decision-making tools, tests utilizing a single IQ score have a long history of success (McNemar, 1964).

One type of general intelligence model is that of Spearman, who was the first person to propose a theory of intellectual structure based on statistical analyses of data from psychological tests. Spearman proposed a two-factor theory. The first factor was a general capacity or mental energy factor, which was basically a reasoning factor. In addition to this general factor (labeled *g*), each specific test was presumed to measure skills that were specific to that particular test. Hence, the second component included specific intelligences (see Figure 12.1a). Thus, although assigning primary importance to the general factor, the theory does recognize that other specific factors (and even other general factors) must be considered. The implication for measuring intelligence, however, is that the best test would be one saturated with general intelligence.

Group factors   The approach accepted by the largest number of U.S. theorists is a group factor theory. This approach assumes that the fundamental dimensions can be represented by a relatively small number of fairly broad common factors (see Figure 12.1b). Although the exact abilities (group factors) found in any specific study depend upon several variables (such as the tests used, the nature of the sample tested, and the method of analysis), the following factors have appeared with some regularity and have been confirmed by several investigators:

> *Space*. The ability to visualize geometric patterns in space
> *Perceptual speed*. Quick and accurate noting of details
> *Number*. Quickness and accuracy in simple arithmetic computations
> *Verbal comprehension*. Knowing the meaning of, and relationships between, words
> *Word fluency*. Ability to use many words
> *Rote memory*. Immediate recall of rote materials
> *Induction*. Ability to extract rules

To measure intellectual ability, therefore, one would administer a battery of tests, each of which measured one of the factors. Inasmuch as any given task or skill may require a combination of primary abilities, *any* intellectual task or skill can be represented by a weighted composite of the relevant group factors.

Hierarchical theories   The basic idea of this approach is that intellectual structure can be conceived of as a hierarchy, extending from one or more broad general

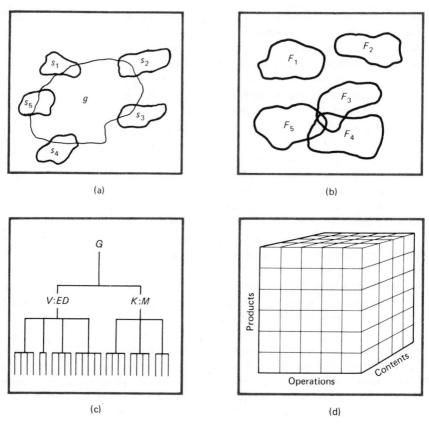

Figure 12.1   Models of intellectual structure: (a) Spearman's model; (b) a group factor model; (c) a hierarchical model (after Vernon, 1971); (d) Guilford's model (from *The Nature of Human Intelligence*, McGraw-Hill, Inc., 1967).

factors (general intelligence?), through group factors, to more and more specific factors. For example, Vernon (1971) has proposed a model (see Figure 12.1c) in which general ability (g) is at the apex of the hierarchy. This general factor is subdivided into two major group factors—a verbal-educational (V:ED) factor and a practical-mechanical (K:M) one. Each of these categories is further subdivided into group factors and then into more and more specific factors. For example, at a third level of the hierarchy, which represents minor group factors, we might find a spatial factor. At the next level, this factor might be further subdivided into three more specific factors, such as (1) the ability to comprehend spatial relations using the body as a point of reference, (2) the ability to manipulate mentally a series of visual objects through a sequence of motions, and (3) the ability to make left-right discriminations (cf. Michael et al., 1957). The hierarchical approach represents an intuitively satisfying collation of data and, since tests can be constructed to represent any level in the hierarchy, it is a useful tool for guiding test construction.

Guilford's three-dimensional model   Guilford (1956, 1959, 1967) conceives of intellectual functioning having three dimensions: operations, contents, and products (see Figure 12.1d). Operations are the processes involved in intellectual behavior; in Guilford's system these are cognition, memory, divergent thinking, convergent thinking, and evaluation. The contents of these operations may be figural, symbolic, semantic, or behavioral, and the products may be units, classes, relations, systems, transformations, or implications. Thus the model contains 120 cells (5 operations ×4 contents × 6 products), each of which represents a distinct factor that is measured by a separate test. For example, in Guilford's scheme, the verbal comprehension factor (vocabulary) becomes the ability to cognize semantic units. From the theorist's viewpoint, Guilford's precisely defined and integrated model has much to recommend it, including the advantage of being able to specify in advance the nature of currently unmeasured intellectual abilities.

The various models presented are both conceptual and heuristic devices. Since their comparative validity has not been determined, whichever model a particular investigator adopts will generally be a function of his individual preferences.[5] The most widely used individual intelligence measures (the Stanford-Binet and Wechsler scales) are based on a general intelligence model. The group factor theory is most clearly shown in the multifactor batteries such as the *Primary Mental Abilities* and the *Differential Aptitude Tests*. No test is explicitly derived from a hierarchial theory but Guilford has developed tests for many of the cells in his model.

It should be emphasized that not all test constructors have based their work on a particular theory of intellectual structure. In fact, the dominant approach has been an empirical one of attempting to predict a specific criterion with maximal accuracy. Thus, tests of scholastic aptitude have been developed not in accord with a prevailing theory of intellectual structure, but by including skills that previous research has shown to be predictive of academic success. Most tests of dexterities and physical skills were developed not to reflect a given theory, but rather to measure the components shown by job analyses to be important in the performance of certain types of jobs. In other words, empirical rather than theoretical considerations were preeminent.

Types of Aptitude and Ability Tests

In our previous discussion we referred to several different types of aptitude and ability tests. At this point it might be well to distinguish briefly between the major categories of aptitude and ability tests.

Probably the most well-known are *general intelligence tests* — what the man in the street calls "IQ tests." These are tests designed to obtain a broad, overall measure of a person's intellectual functioning. The original, and still most important, general intelligence tests are the individually administered tests, such as the

---

[5]The examples listed do not exhaust all possibilities; they are only the most common approaches. Other examples are tests based on Piaget's theory of intellectual development and Luria's theory of cortical functioning (Das, 1973; Das, Kirby, and Jarman, 1975).

Stanford-Binet Intelligence Scale and the various Wechsler Intelligence Scales. These *individual intelligence tests* all report performance in terms of an overall, or full-scale, IQ (intelligence quotient) even though they may contain various types of items (for example, both verbal and performance test). Thus they are based on a unifactor theory of intelligence.

Because individually administered intelligence tests require a trained administrator, and therefore are costly in terms of time and money, a number of *group intelligence tests* have been developed. In many ways, these tests are similar to the verbal portions of individually administered tests, but, of necessity, they are restricted to measuring skills that can be tested by a paper-and-pencil format. Thus they do not contain performance items. As might be expected, group tests are used in educational and industrial settings, where large numbers of people have to be tested. In contrast, individual tests are more appropriate when working intensively with single individuals, as in counseling or with children needing special educational programs.

Closely related to group intelligence tests are *scholastic aptitude tests.* The major difference between the two types of tests is that scholastic aptitude tests focus directly on skills that are necessary for success in formal educational settings. Thus, for example, although both group intelligence tests and scholastic aptitude tests might contain vocabulary items, only a scholastic aptitude test would include reading comprehension items. Furthermore, group intelligence tests are constructed to sample the various skills that make up intellectual ability; items included on scholastic aptitude tests are ones that predict future academic success.

Theorists who subscribe to a group factors theory of intellectual structure conceive of intellectual ability as being composed of a small number of relatively broad intellectual abilities. This view has led to the construction of *multiple aptitude (multiaptitude) batteries*. These batteries are integrated series of tests, each measuring one of the major group factors. For example, the *Differential Aptitude Test* contains separate tests measuring Verbal Reasoning, Numerical Ability, Abstract Reasoning, Mechanical Reasoning, Space Relations, (Perceptual) Speed and Accuracy, and Language Usage. Like group intelligence tests, multiaptitude batteries generally do include performance measures.

There are also a number of aptitude tests that measure a single specific ability. We will refer to these as tests of *special aptitudes*. Some of these tests measure special types of cognitive abilities, such as mathematical ability or creativity or divergent thinking. Others are designed to measure vocationally oriented aptitudes—such as tests of perceptual speed and accuracy, manual dexterity, and mechanical abilities. Others are designed to tap musical and artistic aptitude. As you can see, some special aptitude tests have their counterparts on multiaptitude batteries.

Another way to distinguish between aptitude tests is by their use. Some aptitude tests are used descriptively; others for predictive purposes.[6] When they are used

---

[6]This distinction parallels that made in Chapter 2 between tests as representing (descriptive uses) and tests as predicting (predictive uses).

descriptively, we are trying to obtain a view of a person's (or group's) abilities. A good example is the use of aptitude tests in counseling. Here tests are frequently administered to provide the client with information about his abilities, strengths, and limitations that he can then use in making decisions about his future career or educational plans. Although this use involves an implicit prediction (such as a client's chances of success in various careers or educational programs), the major goal is to provide a broad description of his abilities. In predictive situations, in contrast, the primary use of the test is to aid in making a decision about an individual. Examples include tests given for admission to college or professional schools and tests used to select among applicants for a position in business or industry.

Culture-Fair Tests

One of the assumptions underlying aptitude testing was that all test takers have had the opportunity to acquire the prerequisite skills. Yet we know that certain tests are unfair to certain individuals or groups—unfair in the sense that the individuals in question have had different experiences or would react differently to the testing situation than would the typical individual. As a consequence, the score of these individuals will not be comparable to those of other individuals.[7]

The problem of cultural influences on test performance has been studied for many years. Originally, investigators attempted to develop tests that would eliminate all effects of culture and, thus, presumably measure the individual's abilities more accurately. However, it soon became apparent that any attempt to develop completely *culture-free tests* was doomed to failure. Consequently, the emphasis in test construction has shifted to the development of *culture-fair tests*—tests that, though not eliminating cultural effects, attempt to control certain critical variables, thus making the test equally fair to all persons.

To accomplish this end, procedures must be developed to control the influence of variables that are important determiners of test performance but vary between cultures. An obvious example is language. Not only would a test written in one language be inappropriate for a person who does not speak that language fluently, but also words and phrasing have different connotations in different cultures. Therefore, a direct translation of a test from one language to another will not necessarily produce comparable tests. Another important dimension is speed. In our culture, responding rapidly is stressed and most persons will attempt to complete a test within the time limits. In other cultures, and within certain American subcultures, speed of performance is not highly valued. Use of a speeded test with these groups would produce ambiguous results. A third relevant facet is the role of competitive motivation. In this country, most children and adults attempt to do their best (that is, adopt a maximal performance motivation) even without explicit directions to do so. Yet, in cultures or subcultures where competition is not stressed,

[7]When we talk about different cultures, we are referring to both major culture groups (for example, American and Chinese) and differences between subcultures within a major group (for example, blacks and whites, or people of high and low socioeconomic status in the United States).

one cannot expect the test taker to have similar motivation. A fourth dimension of concern is the relative emphasis given to different content areas in different cultures. Even if several subjects are taught in various cultures, it cannot be assumed that they are given the same relative emphasis or have the same importance in all cultures (see, e.g., Husén, 1967; Thorndike, 1973).

Validation strategies   Regardless of the approach used in constructing a culture-fair test, unless it can be demonstrated that the test is fair and equally valid for various cultural groups, it cannot be said to have attained its purpose. One possible strategy is to develop, use, and validate the test in only one culture. Unless the test is applied to a different cultural group, no problems arise. If a test is needed to do a similar job in a different culture, a new test can be constructed within that culture. Such a strategy obviously sidesteps the basic issue.

A second possible strategy is to develop a test in one culture, then validate it in other cultures. If the test proves valid in a variety of cultures, it can be considered culture-fair. To expect a test to be valid in all cultures is undoubtably expecting too much; yet some generalizability across cultures is necessary. This strategy has frequently been applied. For example, many tests have been translated into foreign languages and used in foreign countries (see, e.g., Lonner, 1968). Another example is the application of scholastic aptitude tests to minority groups. Although many persons feel the scholastic aptitude tests are unfair to black Americans, particularly those coming from lower socioeconomic and disadvantaged backgrounds, data show that the tests predict academic success as accurately for blacks as for middle- and upper-class white students (see, e.g., Munday, 1965; Stanley and Porter, 1967; Cleary, 1968; Bowers, 1970; Thomas and Stanley, 1969). Needless to say, tests are usually more valid in the culture in which they were developed than in other cultures in which they happen to be applied.

One disadvantage of this second approach is that it does not consider the impact of culture-related variables during the test construction process. A third strategy focuses on the item selection process. By first identifying skills and content common to many cultures, and including on the test only items that measure these universal elements, one could develop a culture-fair measure. The effectiveness of the test construction procedure is subsequently checked by validation studies in a variety of cultures. The fundamental step in this procedure is the identification of skills and relationships that are common to a number of cultures. This requirement restricts the pool of potential items—for example, to characteristics of human beings and nonverbal tasks such as relationships between geometric objects and designs. But even these items may be heavily culturally loaded.

Examples of culture-fair tests   The *Goodenough Draw-a-Man Test* has frequently been used in cross-cultural studies. Since the task, drawing a figure of a man (or woman), involves content and skills that seem to be universal, the test would seem to be quite appropriate for cross-cultural studies. Yet data from cross-cultural studies show that scores on the test vary between cultural groups, with higher average scores occurring in cultures stressing skill in representational art.

Other tests that have been used in cross-cultural studies emphasize abstract reasoning, primarily through items that measure relationships among geometric and other nonverbal stimuli. For example, on the *Cattell's Culture Fair Intelligence Test,* one subtest requires the subject to choose the design, from among several alternatives, that best completes a sequence of designs. Another subtest requires the test taker to identify the design that does not belong to the class represented by the other designs in the series. *Raven's Progressive Matrices Test,* which was designed to measure Spearman's *g* factor, consists of geometric matrices of varying degrees of difficulty from which one section has been removed. The test taker must choose, from among six to eight alternatives, the element that completes the design. In each case, the relationship rather than the design is the important feature (see Figure 12.2).

Future directions   Many psychologists now feel that even the quest for a culture-fair test is illusory. If one eliminated all culturally relevant material, he would be

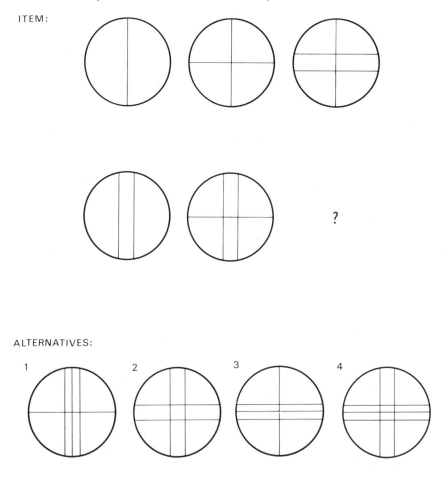

Figure 12.2   Example of an item similar to those on Raven's Progressive Matrices Test.

left with trivia. Furthermore, he would be unable to predict any socially meaningful criteria because criteria themselves are culturally laden. Consequently, as the social usefulness of a test increases, so too does the loading on culturally relevant variables. Thus we are caught on the horns of a dilemma. To complicate matters further, seemingly less culturally loaded materials, such as nonverbal items, have often proven to be as culturally loaded as verbal items. Thus it would seem that, rather than attempting to develop additional or better culture-fair tests, the research strategy now should be to concentrate on understanding the factors that produce different performance in various cultural groups.

13

CLASSROOM TESTS

All students are familiar with the ubiquitous teacher-made test. In fact, you may have already taken one or more tests on the material in this book. The distinguishing features of these tests were that they were constructed by the course instructor and covered only the material taught in this particular course or a unit within the course. These tests probably have never been, or ever will be, given to any other class; individual items, however, may have appeared on exams during previous terms or may appear on future exams. The primary purpose of the exam was probably for assigning grades, although the purpose may have been to provide feedback to you and the instructor regarding the progress of your learning.

This same process occurs in thousands of classrooms every day. In fact, it is rare when examinations are not an integral part of a course. Because any classroom examination is typically administered only once, to a particular class under a singular set of circumstances, the methods of constructing and evaluating teacher-made tests are somewhat different from the methods of constructing and evaluating standardized tests. Thus, we will consider teacher-built and standardized achievement tests separately.

Our discussion of the classroom tests will proceed in stages that parallel the process the teacher goes through in constructing and analyzing the test. Our presentation will be brief, illustrative, and evaluative; a detailed discussion of the process of building good test items must be reserved for other books (see, e.g., Ebel, 1972; or Bloom et al., 1971).

Planning a Classroom Test

The first, and most crucial, step in building a classroom test is to plan the test. The nature of the test, and even the decision to test at all, should follow from the instructor's educational philosophy and his goals for the particular course. These basic views will determine not only the nature of the testing, but also the frequency and timing of exams. For example, if an instructor uses tests only to assign grades, he will probably give a final exam and several unit tests. If, however, he believes the primary purpose of testing is to facilitate students' learning, he will use more frequent tests so as to maximize feedback.

The previous paragraph makes a distinction that is too often overlooked: Tests can be used either to measure the outcomes of learning or to facilitate the learning process. In technical terms, evaluations can be either formative or summative (Bloom et al., 1971; Scriven, 1967). By *summative evaluation* we mean those evaluations obtained at the end of a course (or unit) that are used to determine whether students have mastered the course objectives. This evaluation may be based on tests or other assessment procedures. In all cases, however, the concern is with obtaining an indication of the degree of learning or mastery.

Formative evaluation, in contrast, refers to evaluations made during the course of learning that provide evidence of the effectiveness of the learning process. As with summative evaluation, the evaluation may be based on tests or other information sources, such as worksheets, observations, and informal questioning. Formative evaluation may focus on the learner's progress and be used to prescribe instruction for the individual learner. At other times, the main emphasis is on evaluating the effectiveness of the instructional methods and materials; then if students are not learning, instruction should be changed. Of course, both purposes may be met concurrently.

Criterion-referenced tests   As we have stated several times, there are two approaches to the construction of achievement tests. One method is to define the objectives for a particular course or unit and then write items that measure attainment of these objectives. This is the criterion-referenced approach.[1] The other approach, which is probably more common, is to specify the content and skills

---

[1] Criterion-referenced tests are analogous to what we earlier referred to as content-referenced scores. Our use of criterion-referenced here follows the distinction between norm-referenced and criterion-referenced measurement (Glaser, 1963), which is currently widely used in education.

covered in the course or unit and then build a test that samples these content and skills. This is the norm-referenced approach. We shall first consider criterion-referenced tests.

In the criterion-referenced approach, the first step is for the instructor to specify the objectives (goals and desired outcomes) for the course. This specification should, of course, occur when the instructor plans the course, not when he starts to build the exam. He will probably have several broad goals (for example, students should be able to interpret test scores) and many specific objectives (for example, students can interpret percentile ranks). These objectives define the domain to be covered by the exam.

To be useful in planning examinations (as well as for planning instruction), objectives must be expressed in behavioral terms. By behavioral objectives we mean statements that indicate what the student will be expected to know or do, as well as under what conditions and to what level of proficiency (Mager, 1962). It is not sufficient to state that students will "understand percentiles." Rather we must state objectives in the form: "Given a conversion table, the student can find the percentile rank for any raw score and give a verbal description of the person's performance."

Once objectives have been defined, the instructor can write the test items. Since all objectives are presumably important, he will, testing time permitting, write one or more items for each objective. Although some writers seem to imply that different types of items are needed on criterion-referenced tests than on norm-referenced tests, the author has not found this argument convincing. What is crucial, however, is that the test items directly reflect the skills prescribed by the objectives. In other words, the difference is not in the types of items written, but why an item is included on the test.

Norm-referenced tests   The other approach to constructing classroom tests is to start by specifying what material is covered in the course or unit and then write items that sample this domain. On classroom tests, what materials will be covered on any exam usually are clearly specified by the teacher—that is, the assignments for the unit. When using this approach, the test constructor must be concerned with two dimensions. First of all, he must sample the various content areas. For example, an exam on test scores should include items on several types of test scores, not just questions about, say, standard scores. The second dimension—skills—is often neglected. By skills we mean the cognitive process used to answer the item: processes such as knowledge, comprehension, application, analysis, synthesis, and evaluation (Bloom et al., 1956). That is, we generally do not want a test to measure only retention of facts; we also want to see whether students can apply their knowledge and draw appropriate conclusions.

Specifying the important content and skills provides a basis for constructing a *test plan*. Table 13.1 is an illustration of a test plan for a hypothetical test on test scores. The vertical axis lists the major content areas to be covered. On any given test, the number of categories will depend upon the logical organization of the material and the length of the test; however, on a classroom test, five to ten categories will usually suffice. The horizontal axis lists the skills to be measured:

definitions, computation, and interpretation. The test plan thus outlines the content and skills to be covered, thereby directing attention to the type of items to be constructed.

TABLE 13.1   An example of a test plan: Test on types of test scores

		Skills		
Content areas		Definitions (30%)	Computation (50%)	Interpretation (20%)
Need for derived scores	10%	(1–2 items)	(2–3)	(1)
Content scores	10%	(1–2)	(2–3)	(1)
Percentiles	20%	(3)	(5)	(2)
Standard scores	20%	(3)	(5)	(2)
Developmental scores	10%	(1–2)	(2–3)	(1)
Ratios and quotients	10%	(1–2)	(2–3)	(1)
Comparison of types of scores	20%	(3)	(5)	(1)

The figures in parentheses indicate the number of items that would be devoted to each content/skill category on a 50-item alternative-choice exam.

The test plan is generally elaborated one step further by the assignment of weights to each category. These weights indicate the relative emphasis given to each topic and skill (see Table 13.1). These weights represent the teacher's judgment as to the relative emphases to be given each category; another instructor might, of course, assign different emphases. By multiplying the row weightings by the column weightings we can determine the proportion of items needed for each content/skill category. These proportions give an *approximate* picture of the composition of the test; approximate because some cells may not be meaningful or, for some reason the instructor may want to change the emphasis on certain areas. If all items are given equal weight, the proportions can be directly translated into the number of items required. For example, in Table 13.1 the number of items devoted to each content/skill category on a 50-item objective test, where each item receives unit weight, are indicated in parentheses. If the test items were assigned different weights, the percentages would indicate the relative weight to be given each type. Thus items dealing with the computation of percentiles would comprise 10 percent of the test; this might be one problem or several problems totaling 10 percent of the score (that is, 5 points on a 50-point test).

In summary, a test plan indicates not only the content and skills (or objectives) covered by the test, but also the relative emphasis to be given each content/skill category (or objective). Thus it provides a basis both for constructing items and for determining the content validity of the test.

Other Considerations in Planning a Classroom Test

The formal test plan, be it based on behavioral objectives or a content/skill analysis, indicates what will be covered on the test, with what relative emphasis.

This is a necessary first step. The test constructor, however, has to make several other important decisions before writing the test items. These decisions have to do with the length of the test, the format of the items, and the difficulty of the items.

Probably the first factor the teacher will consider is the *length* of the test. This is not because length is the most important factor, but because of practical constraints, which are often hard to overcome. The obvious one is the length of class periods. Usually, except for final exams, teacher-built tests are designed so that they can be completed within one class period (45–50 minutes). Often a teacher will give short quizzes that take only a few minutes.

Regardless of the length of the test, a fundamental question is the number of items that can be completed within the time limits. Since the purpose of a classroom test usually is to determine the extent of students' knowledge rather than speed of response, time limits should be set so that all, or almost all, students can finish the test. The time needed will, of course, vary with the number of items, the difficulty of the items, the length of the items, the age of the students, and many other variables. The author's experience suggests that students can answer about one multiple-choice question per minute. The time to be devoted to essay questions will depend primarily on the completeness of the response desired. The author has found that college students need a minimum of a half-hour to respond to any reasonably comprehensive essay question. Younger children, though writing shorter answers, take longer to compose and write their answers. How much time to allow students to answer essay items can be determined only by experience in a particular course.

A second important consideration is the *item format*. Which format to use will be determined, at least partially, by the objectives or skills measured. For example, if a teacher is interested in students' ability to marshal arguments to support a point of view, he will probably use essay items. If a music teacher wants to see whether a trombone player can sight-read a new composition, he will use a performance test. If a math teacher wants to measure students' ability to apply an analytic technique to a new situation, he will use problems.

In many instances, however, the teacher will have a choice between several item formats. To consider a trivial example, a geography test on state capitals might use multiple-choice items:

The capital of New York State is:

(a) Albany   (b) Buffalo   (c) New York City   (d) Rochester

or, alternatively, true-false items:

The capital of New York State is Albany. (TRUE   FALSE)

or the same knowledge could be tested by a completion item:

The capital of New York State is _____.

Since in many, if not most, circumstances alternative item formats may be appropriate, the choice between them will be made on the basis of other considerations—for example, time constraints or the teacher's preference for, or skill in, writing different types of items.

In selecting an item format, the teacher should also consider several other factors. Does he want to include a large number of short items or a smaller number of broader items? Does he want students to rely on recall or recognition to answer the items? Does he want to use only one type of item or several different types? If he uses several types, what sort of mix of item types will be optimal? And so on.

One factor that is often neglected is whether students will be allowed to use any aids when working on the test or will have to rely on their memory. A case in point is the open-book exam. If the purpose of an exam is to test students' ability to apply their knowledge to new situations or problems, an open-book exam should be considered. Proponents of open-book exams argue that they minimize anxiety associated with time pressure, permit a more comprehensive approach to a problem, and better reflect the realities of the nonacademic world. Opponents counter that people often have to make decisions under time pressures and on the basis of available (incomplete) information. They think the typical closed-book exam better represents this situation. Although neither type of exam is appropriate for all situations, the author feels that teachers should consider making more use of open-book exams.

Probably the major decision when choosing between item formats is whether to utilize a large number of specific items or a smaller number of fairly broad items. In other words, a choice between alternative-choice or short-answer items on one hand and essay questions on the other. The former procedure has the advantage of allowing for a more representative sampling of the material. The essay format concentrates coverage into certain areas, rather than providing representative coverage of all content areas, but covers these areas in greater depth. Therefore, from a sampling point of view, more shorter items are preferred. However, since the two approaches also differ on a variety of other dimensions (such as skills tapped, ease of construction, testing time, scoring ease, and bias), in choosing between the two formats the test constructor should realize that he will always be sacrificing one set of goals for another. For example, essay items sacrifice representative sampling in order to provide greater depth; with alternative-choice items, content sampling will be more representative, but certain skills will not be tested.

Another type of decision has to do with the *difficulty* of the items. Obviously, what is difficult varies with the type of course and characteristics of the students. Nevertheless, within any course a wide range of difficulty is possible. What level is appropriate will depend on the purposes of the testing. If a teacher gives a quiz to check on whether students have read an assignment, he can use items that will be very easy for anyone who has read the material. Easy items are also appropriate to identify students who are lagging behind their classmates and as "warm-up" items (items used at the beginning of a test to get students into the swing of the test and to build confidence).

If one adopts a criterion-referenced approach to testing, difficulty is, at least in one sense, irrelevant. In this approach, items are included on a test if they measure an important educational objective. Items will be included regardless of their difficulty. Ideally, at the end of instruction, every student will be able to pass every item. On the other hand, if many students fail an item (that is, the item is difficult) there was some fault in the instructional process—either poor teaching or teaching material that is too advanced for the students.[2]

If one uses a test to discriminate between students, a different set of criteria apply. It can be shown that items of medium difficulty—that is, items that 50 to 70 percent of the students can answer correctly—are optimal if we want to spread out the distributions of scores. Items that are very easy or very difficult are not as good as medium-difficulty items in this situation.

VARIETIES OF TEST ITEMS

After we have made the basic decisions regarding the format of the test, the next step is to construct the test items. In this section we shall discuss the more common varieties of test items. We shall describe the basic characteristics of each type and the common variations, provide examples, and discuss its advantages and limitations. We shall also provide some guidelines for writing each type of item.

Writing good items is a skill that is developed only by practice.[3] Even experienced item writers find it desirable to write many more items than will be included on the test. They then edit these items and select the best items, where "best" refers both to the quality of the items and to the fact that the items achieve the balance of coverage indicated on the test plan. Thus, if at all possible, you should always write more items than you plan to use.

One rule is preeminent when writing any type of item: *Write as clearly and simply as possible.* Use only terms that students will understand and eliminate all nonfunctional words. This not only will ensure that students will respond on the basis of their knowledge, rather than being distracted by irrelevant considerations, it also will usually allow more items to be included on the exams, thus increasing reliability and providing better content sampling.

The other aspect of item writing that deserves further consideration is the question of whether students will be asked to choose among given alternatives or construct their own answers. Several frequently used types of items (for example, multiple-choice, matching) require the student to select the correct response from among several alternatives, or indicate whether the information presented is correct or incorrect (true-false items). These items, called *recognition* or *alternative-choice* items, assume that a student's knowledge can be adequately measured by his ability to discriminate between correct and incorrect responses. Other items, called *recall* or *supply* items, require the student to actually construct a response. Examples include short-answer and completion items, essay questions, and math and physics problems. (A third general class of items includes cases in which the student must perform a feat, such as playing a musical instrument, baking a cake, painting a picture, or running the 100-yard dash; these items, not surprisingly, are called *performance* items.)

The relative merits of recall and recognition items have been widely debated.

---

[2]Of course, an item may also be difficult because it is constructed poorly, for example, ambiguously.

[3]Rather than providing numerous examples of good and poor items we suggest that you try your hand at writing items, using the suggested guidelines. If possible, administer them to some students and get their reactions. If this is not feasible, have your classmates or instructor evaluate your efforts.

Advocates of recall items stress that they provide a more difficult, and thus better, test of a student's knowledge. They also point out that most "real-life" situations require the construction or production of a response, not a choice among a set of clearly labeled alternatives. Advocates of recognition items stress the technical superiority of recognition items (for example, their higher reliability) and the fact that it has not been clearly demonstrated that use of recall items results in superior learning or better retention. Advocates of both positions would probably admit that students will use differing study habits depending on the type of item expected on the test (Jacoby, 1973; Rothkopf and Bisbiscos, 1967; Watts and Anderson, 1971).

The controversy is confounded by the failure to make a clear distinction between learning and testing. If the purpose of the testing is other than to facilitate learning (for example, to assign grades or for selection or placement), the critical consideration is whether the test validly measures the student's present level of achievement. The question of how the student attained this level of accomplishment is irrelevant. For example, if a (recognition) test requiring students to spot errors in sentence construction is highly correlated with the student's ability to construct good English sentences, as measured by more direct methods, then the recognition exam can be substituted for actually writing sentences. Note, we did *not* say that the ability to construct good sentences can be developed by identifying errors in other people's sentences; it may be that this ability can only be developed by having the student write sentences. What we did say was that the results of the learning process, however it occurred, can be measured by either technique.

Alternative-Choice Items

As mentioned above, one major class of test items is alternative-choice items. The distinguishing feature of all items that fall in this category—multiple-choice, true-false, matching—is that all possible responses are provided to the student. The student's task is to recognize the correct response, either by selecting among alternatives or indicating whether a statement is true or false. Providing all possible responses serves to standardize conditions and allows students to respond to more items in a given time period, thus increasing reliability. On the other hand, the possibility of misunderstanding a question is not eliminated. This problem is exacerbated by the fact that, except for rare instances, there is no opportunity provided for the student to explain his answer or comment on the question. In other words, the student must respond within the given alternatives and cannot supply his own interpretation or answer. (For a critique of multiple-choice items see Hoffmann, 1962.)

Multiple-choice   A multiple-choice item consists of a stem, which may be either a question or an incomplete statement, and a set (usually 4 or 5) of alternatives. The student's task is to select the alternative from among the distracters (incorrect responses), that correctly answers the question or completes the statement. For example:

> If two tests rank people in a given population in the same order, the tests are said to be:
>> (a) comparable   (b) equivalent   (c) homogeneous   (d) reliable

The stem of the item should present the problem in enough detail that there is no ambiguity as to the nature of the problem; the alternatives provide the basis for inferring whether the student possesses the desired knowledge.

Distracters on multiple-choice items often are chosen to represent the most frequent incorrect responses. Thus, one empirical method of obtaining distracters would be to have a sample of students respond to a recall form of the item and determine which wrong answers are most prevalent; these responses would be incorporated as distracters. Other methods of selecting distracters include use of common misconceptions, logical alternatives, and distracters that maximize item validity. (See Ebel, 1972; Cronbach and Merwin, 1955; Wesman, 1971.)

Although multiple-choice items have been criticized for testing only factual material, if properly designed they can be used to test complex intellectual skills (R. Anderson, 1972). For example, the ability to apply mathematical and statistical principles can be tested readily by a multiple-choice format:

> The mean on a test is 20 and the standard deviation is 5 points. Mike scores 13. If scores are expressed on a standard score scale having a mean of 50 and a standard deviation of 10, Mike's derived score would be:
> (a) 14   (b) 26   (c) 36   (d) 65

This item requires the student to go through the same sequence of steps that he would if the item were presented as a problem; the difference is that he selects among alternatives rather than supplying an answer. Another example of an item requiring application of knowledge is:

> A scholastic aptitude test consists of mathematics and vocabulary items. There is only one form of the test, and less than 10 percent of the test takers complete all items within the time limits. To estimate the reliability of this test, you would use:
> (a) coefficient alpha
> (b) a coefficient of equivalence
> (c) a coefficient of stability
> (d) Kuder-Richardson formula 20

Many other examples could be given (see, e.g., Bloom et al., 1971; Ebel, 1972; Payne, 1974), but the point is clear: Multiple-choice items can be used to measure complex reasoning skills.

Because a large number of multiple-choice items can be administered in a relatively short period, broad sampling of the domain is possible, and thus both reliability and validity are increased. Scoring of multiple-choice items is rapid and objective and items can be analyzed statistically, thereby providing data that can be used to improve item quality. A presumed disadvantage is their limited applicability (it is easier to write factual items than ones testing more complex skills); but, as indicated above, this is not an inherent limitation of the item format. Good multiple-choice items are, without doubt, difficult and time-consuming to construct. However, the high reliability and validity of good multiple-choice items makes this time well spent.

Several variations of the traditional multiple-choice format are sometimes encountered. One procedure is to base a series of multiple-choice items on one reading passage, diagram, chart, table, or other set of stimulus materials. This procedure permits one topic to be extensively probed, but may, as a consequence, sacrifice some sampling representativeness. When using sets of related items, the test constructor must guard against having the answer to one item be revealed by another item or having the response to one item hinge upon correctly responding to a previous item. In short, items should be independent, even when based on common stimulus material. Another variation allows the student to select any number of alternatives (from none to all) as being correct. This procedure, besides confusing many students, in essence changes a multiple-choice item into a series of true-false items. Thus, it has the advantages and disadvantages of the true-false format (see below).

Some guidelines for writing multiple-choice items are given in Table 13.2. These guidelines are only suggestions; all will be broken at one time or another. However, following these guidelines should result in simpler, clearer, and more valid items. Remember, too, that any guideline for writing items will be of less importance than the item content. Unless an item measures an important educational outcome it will be a poor item, regardless of how well it was written. Conversely, an item that tries to measure an important outcome will not succeed unless it is well written.

True-false   A true-false item is a declarative statement; the test taker's task is to determine whether the statement is correct or incorrect (true or false).

The mean is a measure of the dispersion of a set of test scores. (T F)

If a gas is heated within a container of constant volume, its pressure will increase. (T F)

In essence, the test taker judges the veracity of the statement. If any part of the statement is incorrect, the item is false.

Many people think that true-false items are restricted to factual content, to situations in which there is agreement as to the correct response. If *factual* refers only to recalling learned knowledge, this view of true-false items is incorrect, since there is no doubt that this format can be used to test applications and comprehension of principles (see the second example). As Ebel (1972) has convincingly argued, much knowledge is in the form of propositions (if-then statements), and propositional knowledge can readily be tested by true-false items. Nevertheless, responses are probably more affected by the item wording in true-false items than with other formats (see, especially, guidelines 3 and 6 in Table 13.3). Because of these limitations, true-false items are most appropriate with younger children (who are not as alert to the subtleties of language) and when a quick superficial estimate is needed—for example, to check on whether students have read an assignment.

True-false items are easily scored and relatively easy to construct, certainly much easier than multiple-choice items. (See Table 13.3 for guidelines.) And, since many items can be administered in a given time period, scores on true-false tests can

TABLE 13.2 Guidelines for writing multiple-choice items.

1. Write clearly, simply, and briefly. Eliminate nonfunctional words. Use only words whose meanings are clear to students.

2. The item stem should present the problem and all qualifying phrases. The stem should include all words that would otherwise appear in each alternative.

3. There should be one, and only one, correct response. This alternative should be clearly correct.

4. All distracters should be plausible and attractive to students who do not know the correct answer; yet they should be clearly incorrect. Distracters can be common misconceptions, frequent errors, or other plausible but incorrect information.

5. Alternatives should be homogeneous in form and grammatical structure. They should not overlap, be synonymous with each other, or otherwise be interdependent.

6. Whenever possible, use new situations and examples. Try to avoid repeating textbook examples or phraseology.

7. Each item should be independent. One item should not aid in answering another item on the test.

8. Avoid negatively stated items. Try to avoid using all of the above, none of the above, or some of the above (for example, A and B).

9. If an item includes controversial material, cite the authority whose opinion is used.

10. Avoid irrelevant clues to the correct answer provided by response length, repetition of key words, common associations, or grammar.

11. If alternatives fall in a logical arrangement (for example, alphabetically or by magnitude), list them in this order. Otherwise randomize the positions of the correct responses so that they do not fall into a pattern.

12. Try to have each item test only one central concept or idea.

be highly reliable and the content domain may be broadly sampled. On the other hand, the format may limit usage to certain types of content.

Probably the most common alternative format for true-false items is to require students to correct false statements. The major disadvantage of this procedure is that an item can be corrected in many ways, including a variety of trivial ways; for example:

> Item: Percentile ranks fall in a normal distribution. (T or F)
> Response: False
> Correction: Percentile ranks do *not* fall in a normal distribution.
> Intended correction: Percentile ranks fall in a rectangular distribution.

Thus the teacher is required to make decisions regarding the acceptability of any specific correction. A simpler correction procedure would be to have the student only identify the false element in the statement, not correct the statement.

Matching   Matching items consist of two parallel lists, one consisting of a series of stimulus words or phrases and the other containing a series of responses. The student's task is to match the appropriate response with each stimulus. A typical matching item might be:

> DIRECTIONS: The following items all refer to consistency of measurement. For each statement in the left column choose the method from the right column that is most appropriate. Each response alternative may be used once, more than once, or not at all.

1. Method used to determine the consistency of a classroom test	A. Stability
	B. Equivalence
	C. Stability and equivalence
2. Method whose results are most affected by the speededness of the test	D. Split-half
	E. Internal consistency
3. Method based on the intercorrelations among test items	
4. Method used to determine whether students' values change with college experience	

Note that this item could also be administered as four separate multiple-choice items; thus, in essence, a matching item is a series of multiple-choice items, covering a homogeneous content domain, with the same set of alternatives serving for all items.

Since matching items are essentially multiple-choice items, they have many of the same advantages, limitations, and uses as multiple-choice items. The major consideration in determining whether to use matching items is the amount of emphasis to be given the area covered by the matching item. Because the use of a matching item will necessarily involve devoting four or five items to a topic, disproportionate weighting will occur unless this great an emphasis is desired.

Several other cautions must also be considered with matching items. Unless a matching item covers a single content area, the student can break the item into subsections, thus reducing the number of possible responses for any given stimulus. Frequently one sees matching items with a dozen or more stems and responses, covering several distinct areas. This approach puts a premium on reading and sorting skills at the expense of knowledge. This problem could be eliminated by using several matching items, each covering homogeneous material. Another problem concerns the number of response alternatives. If the number of responses equals the number of stimuli and each response can be used only once, the student can correctly answer the final item by a process of elimination and/or will get at least two items wrong if he does not know the answer to one. These possibilities can be eliminated by providing more responses than stimuli or by allowing each response to be used more than once.

Table 13.4 gives some guidelines for writing matching items.

TABLE 13.3   Guidelines for writing true-false items.

1. Items should be based on significant facts, concepts, or principles. Items should deal with a single idea.

2. The crucial element in the statement should be apparent to the student. The truth of the statement should not rest on trivial details or trick phrases.

3. Express items clearly and simply in words whose meaning are definite and precise and known to the student. Include no more than one qualifying phrase. Use quantitative rather than qualitative terms whenever possible.

4. Statements should be clearly true or false, not partially true and partially false.

5. Avoid mere repetitions or minor variations on textbook wording. Do not create false items by inserting "not" in a statement from the text.

6. Avoid "specific determiners"—words such as always, never, or sometimes—which may provide clues to the correct answer.

7. Include approximately equal numbers of true and false statements. Make sure correct answers do not fall in a pattern.

8. When items refer to controversial material or to matters of opinion or value, cite the authority whose opinion is being used.

TABLE 13.4   Guidelines for writing matching items.

1. All parts of a single matching item should be homogeneous in content; that is, all should refer to dates, all to names, all to places, and so on. Be sure that the student knows the basis on which the terms should be matched.

2. If the two lists contain phrases of different length, have the longer phrases serve as stems and the shorter ones as responses.

3. Each list should contain no more than five to seven items. When possible, include one or two more responses than stems. Instruct students as to whether each response can be used more than once or only once.

4. Each stem should have one, and only one, response associated with it; that is, there should be only one correct response for each stem.

5. Arrange responses in a logical order—for example, alphabetically. Avoid response patterns.

Short-Answer and Completion Items

Alternative-choice items require recognition of the correct response. In most situations, the same material could also be tested using a format that requires students to supply the correct response. For example, the multiple-choice item illustrated on page 253 could also be written as a completion item:

If two tests rank people in a given population in the same order, the tests are said to be (*comparable*).

or as a short-answer item:

Two tests may be said to be comparable when (*they rank people in a given population in the same order*).

The distinction between a short-answer and completion item is mainly the length and format of response. A completion item usually requires the student to provide a one- or two-word response, often within the body of the item; a short-answer item requires him to respond to a question in a sentence or two.

Short-answer and completion items generally cover the same type of material as alternative-choice items. Since there is no definitive evidence that either recognition or recall items are better, which format is used depends upon the preferences, item writing skills, and educational philosophy of the instructor. For example, if an instructor thinks that students should be able to recall material, rather than just recognize correct responses, he will use short-answer or completion items. This format is also appropriate for younger children who are less likely to get confused with the mechanisms of responding than with a multiple-choice item. Also, it usually is easier and less time-consuming to compose a short-answer or completion item than to build a good multiple-choice item. (See Table 13.5 for guidelines for writing short-answer and completion items.)

The major disadvantage of this format involves scoring. Not only does scoring take longer than for recognition items, it requires some decision-making on the part of the scorer, and thus may decrease reliability. For example, in the item: "Reliability can be defined as _____," it is obvious that there are a large number of possible responses that will be wholly or partially correct. When scoring this item, the teacher would have to decide which responses were acceptable and how much credit would be allowed for each variation. Scoring can be made easier and more objective if the teacher prepares a scoring key prior to scoring the test. Even with a key, some students probably will give responses that are not on the key, and the teacher will have to use his best judgment in scoring these responses.

Several variations of the completion format are possible. Some teachers prefer to indicate the first letter of the desired response or the number of words in the desired response in an attempt to standardize responding; others feel that these

TABLE 13.5   Guidelines for writing short-answer and completion items.

1. Phrase items so that there is only one possible correct response (see guidelines 2 and 5).

2. Phrase items so that the student knows the type, length, and preciseness of the required response; for example, in items with numerical answers, the units in which the response should be expressed; if a listing, how many points to include.

3. Ask questions that can be completed by a word, phrase, or sentence.

4. Use new examples of illustrations. Avoid wording or examples taken directly from the text.

5. Before administering the test, prepare a key that indicates the correct response and acceptable variations. If partial credit is to be awarded, indicate what responses will receive partial credit.

6. On completion items omit key words, not trivia; place the blank near the end of the sentence; avoid overly mutilated items (preferably include only one blank, and never more than two blanks).

procedures provide too many clues to the correct response. Short-answer items also come in various formats. One obvious variation is the *definition item*. Definitions are usually presented as a list of words preceded by directions as to the required length and specificity of the response (definition). Or the student may be asked to indicate the importance of, describe, compare, or identify persons, places, events, or objects. In mathematics the student may be asked to provide formulas. In science courses the student may be asked to identify (by naming) a part of an animal or plant, a specimen, or a part of a device.

Essay Items

At some not clearly specifiable point, a short-answer item shades into an essay question. The distinction between the two types of items, however, is not solely in terms of their length; it also involves the function the item performs. Whereas short-answer items are best suited to measure factual knowledge, comprehension of principles, and the ability to identify and define concepts, essay questions provide a basis for evaluating the ability to organize, integrate, and evaluate knowledge. Responses to essay questions may also reflect students' attitudes, creativity, and verbal fluency—factors that may or may not be relevant to the purposes of the testing.

When constructing essay items, the teacher treads a thin line between making the question too general and making the question excessively detailed. For example, the essay item, "Discuss the concept of reliability," is so general that a student could take any of a number of approaches when answering. On the other hand, an essay question phrased:

> Define reliability. Give the basic formula in terms of true and error variance. Define the coefficient of stability, the coefficient of equivalence, and coefficient alpha. List the sources of error that enter into each of these methods. Give an example of a situation in which each type might be used.

is little more than a series of short-answer items. This question might better be phrased:

> Define reliability verbally and by a formula. Identify and differentiate between three types of reliability by indicating their paradigm, the influencing error sources, and their appropriate uses.

This third version is not as specific as the second, and also places a greater premium on the student's ability to compare and evaluate the various methods of estimating reliability.

A primary advantage of essay questions is that they assess certain skills—particulary organization, integration, and evaluation—more effectively than do other item formats. Because of the semistructured nature, the student usually can approach an answer from several equally valid angles, thus yielding a flexibility not found in other formats. As with other recall items, faking and guessing are minimized. The length of response allows the student to treat an area in depth. Although the ease of constructing essay items may be more apparent than real (see

Table 13.6), essay tests are easier to write than multiple-choice tests, if for no other reason than that fewer items are required.

The major disadvantage of essay items become readily apparent when scoring begins. To read and grade essay items is a time-consuming task. Since each response will be different, comparing students who used different information and approached problems from different angles is an arduous task. Consequently, it is not surprising that the reliability of grades assigned responses to essay questions—

TABLE 13.6   Guidelines for writing essay items.

1. The question should clearly define the task for the student (without being so specific or detailed so as to make the item nothing more than a series of short-answer items).

2. Be sure that the student knows the scope and direction of the answer required—for example, the length, amount of detail or facts to be included, and point value.

3. Use new examples and illustrations. The best essay items are usually ones that require students to apply their knowledge to new problems, examples, or situations.

4. Use questions that have clearly acceptable correct answers, rather than ones that measure opinions or attitudes. (This does not mean that there will be only one correct answer, only that the student should demonstrate reasoning rather than unsupported opinion.)

5. It is usually better to use a larger number of more specific questions (that can be answered briefly) than to include fewer, very broad questions.

6. Do not use optional questions unless you can accurately equate the scoring of responses to different questions.

7. Good phrases to use in essay questions include: compare and contrast, present the arguments for and against, give the reasons for, explain how (or why), give an example of, and so on.

8. Before administering the test, construct several "ideal" answers to each essay question. Since you will probably be awarding various amounts of partial credit, decide on how these points will be awarded.

from grader to grader, time to time, or question to question—is often unsatisfactory, even when scoring standards and procedures are clearly specified. Graders may also be influenced by irrelevant factors such as length of responses, quality of prose, or neatness and handwriting (see, e.g., Coffman, 1966, 1971; Klein and Hart, 1968). Finally, as mentioned previously, essay exams do not provide as representative a sampling of the content domain as does the same amount of time devoted to multiple-choice or other "objective" items.

Variations on the essay question include take-home tests, using a composition (such as a poem, test manual, or journal article) as a stimulus for an evaluation essay, book reviews, and term papers. All are basically only variations on essay exams.

TABLE 13.7   Guidelines for writing problem items.

1. Phrase items so the student is clear what is expected of him (what the task is), and in what form (for example, units or precision) the response should be made.
2. Include all necessary data and information in the item except, of course, information and skills that you expect the student to bring to bear on the solution. You may want to include some irrelevant data to see whether students can distinguish between relevant and irrelevant information.
3. Use new situations and examples rather than repeating those previously used. Be sure, however, that the examples refer to situations that students will be familiar with.
4. If you are interested in the process used in solving the problem, construct problems so that the student must go through all steps to attain the solution. Indicate to the student how much detail regarding the various steps he should supply in his response.
5. Make problems independent; that is, the response to one item should not determine the response to a following item. This does not mean that you cannot base several items on one set of data; only that you should try to avoid interdependent responses.
6. Make the wording as simple, clear, and direct as possible; remember, it is not a test of reading comprehension.

Problems

Certain subjects, particularly mathematics and sciences, often use problems as test items. Here the item describes a specific situation and gives some relevant data; the student's task is to solve the problem presented.[4] Usually this solution involves identifying the question asked and the relevant parameters and data, setting up an equation or an analytic procedure, then applying the procedure to the data to obtain a solution. For example:

An instructor administers a 50-item multiple-choice test to 200 students in an Introductory Psychology course. The mean is 37 and the standard deviation is 5 points. He grades on a curve and wants to give A grades to 16 percent of the students. What score will a student have to make to get an A?

To solve this problem the student must first recognize the general strategy, then apply the strategy to the specific data.[5]

Problems are obviously well suited to testing computational skills, mathematical

[4] In a problem there is a gap between the student's current level or state and where he needs to be to achieve a solution (Ausubel and Robinson, 1969). Often the gap occurs because the student has no well-practiced method of obtaining an answer. In all cases he must transform or reorganize the information at hand to arrive at a solution.

[5] In case you do not see the answer, here is how you get it: Since a z score of $+1$ separates the lower 84 percent from the top 16 percent of the distribution (see Appendix A), and a z of $+1$ is equivalent to a score one standard deviation above the mean, a student must score 42 (that is, $37 + 5$) or higher to get an A.

and scientific reasoning, and ability to apply knowledge to new situations. Although we generally think of problems presented on paper-and-pencil tests, the student may have to manipulate apparatus as, for example, in chemistry or physics experiments. Construction of problems is generally quite easy, since there are a large variety of possible items and the skills to be measured are well-specified (see Table 13.7). Scoring can be objective if attaining a correct answer is the sole consideration. If, however, (partial) credit is awarded for a correct approach marred by incorrect manipulations or computations, scoring may be less objective and reliable.

Performance Items

In many situations we are more interested in a student's ability to demonstrate his skill than in his ability to answer written questions. Many examples come readily to mind: tailoring a dress or making a soufflé (in home economics), assembling a carburetor (industrial arts), sight reading a musical composition (music), throwing a pot or painting a watercolor (art), being able to serve a tennis ball (physical education), or typing 40 words per minute. Other examples, which may not be so obvious, would include giving an extemporaneous speech, conducting an opinion poll, performing an engineering survey, conducting a counseling interview, or programming a computer. In each of these cases the student must demonstrate his ability by an actual performance; hence the label "performance items."

When preparing performance items, there is basically only one major guideline to follow: The task must be structured so that students know exactly what they are to do and under what conditions. The first part, knowing what to do, is usually specified by the instructional objective. In other words, the desired outcome serves to define the task. For example, asking the student to assemble a carburetor clearly defines the task for him. The other aspect, specifying the conditions, refers to such factors as the length of time the student is given to perform the task, what aids can he use (for example, whether he can use a schematic diagram to aid in his assembly of the carburetor), and any other variables that may affect his performance. In short, telling the student the desired outcome and the limiting conditions usually is sufficient to define the task.

Grading performance items presents more problems. In some cases the basis for evaluation may be obvious and objective—for example, the number of words typed per minute, the number of pushups a student can do, or whether the car runs with the carburetor installed. However, in many cases, evaluation may be more subjective. For example, what is the criterion for sight-reading a musical piece? Or, what is an acceptable tailored dress? In these cases, the instructor should do two things. First, he should define for himself, as clearly as possible, the bases of his evaluation and the standards he will use. Second, he should communicate these procedures and standards to the students so that they will know how their performance will be evaluated. Frequently this process will require breaking the task down into component skills and setting standards for each skill. (For a more complete discussion see Gagné, 1970, or Anderson and Faust, 1973.)

Performance items are well suited to a criterion-referenced approach to evaluation. That is, in many cases it will be relatively easy to determine whether the student has met the minimally acceptable standards (Can he assemble the carburetor? Can he throw a pot?) but more difficult to make finer distinctions. Thus a criterion-referenced approach, with stress on completing the task to a minimally acceptable level rather than comparing students, is frequently more appropriate.

ADMINISTERING, SCORING, AND ANALYZING THE TEST

Ideally, the teacher will have written more items than are needed. He can then select from this pool those items that are the best written, test important concepts, and produce a distribution of content and skills that parallels the test plan. More realistically, the classroom teacher will probably write only as many items as are needed.

Administering the Test

Most commonly, the test questions are duplicated so that each student will have his own copy of the test. However, other procedures may be used. For example, the teacher might read the questions, particularly when testing young children or other persons with limited reading skills; or items might be projected on a screen. This latter procedure places definite time restrictions on responding, but is an excellent method of presenting certain types of identification items—for example, identifying sites on a map, the artist or characteristics of a painting, or the parts of the body. Similarly, in a science class, the teacher might set up displays and ask students to identify designated characteristics. Or, in a highly automated system, items might be presented by computers and the students would respond directly on the computer console (see, e.g., Atkinson 1968, 1974; Glaser, 1968).

There are several important considerations when administering a classroom test. Several days prior to the test, the teacher should inform students of the test, its purpose, the content domain covered, and the test format and length. The test proper should include explicit directions as to the time limits, how and where to respond, and scoring. For example, on recall items the directions should indicate the length of response desired. If the item format changes within the test, a new set of directions may be needed. Of course, with older students, or when a test is similar to previous tests in the course, formal directions may be minimal. In any situation, however, the teacher should ensure that all students know what is expected of them.

The testing room should be quiet, well lighted and well ventilated, free from interruptions and distractions, and with enough space between seats so that students do not interfere with each other's performance. If special equipment is used (such as projectors or displays), each student should be able to see, hear, or have access to the materials. The teacher should also make provisions for handling special problems (such as students with hearing or vision problems) and for handling unforeseen interruptions and emergencies (such as illness, defective tests, fire drills) with a minimum of confusion. Here, no set of rules can be given; one has to rely on common sense.

Scoring the Test

The scoring procedures used will depend on the type of items. In all cases, however, scoring involves comparing each student's responses with a scoring key.

Recognition items may be scored either by hand (that is, by visual checking against the key) or by electronic scoring machines. Scoring by electronic scoring machines is faster and more accurate, but requires special answer sheets. The use of separate answer sheets, whether for electronic scoring or hand scoring, makes responding more complex and thus may confuse younger children.

The teacher must also assign weights to each item, a decision that should be made when planning the exam. For alternative-choice items, and most completion and short-answer items, the simplest procedure will usually be to award one point for each correct response (and 0 for incorrect answers). Problems, essays, and some short-answer items may be worth several points. If the teacher wants to award partial credit on items, he must clearly specify the bases on which partial credit will be awarded. The total points assigned for correct responses will generally be used as the (total) test score.

Correction for guessing   In some circumstances, when using alternative-choice items, a teacher may want to apply a correction for guessing. This correction subtracts a portion of the wrong responses from the correct responses. The general formula to correct for guessing is

$$\text{Corrected score} = R - \frac{W}{N-1} \tag{13.1}$$

where R is the number of correct responses, W the number of incorrect responses, and N the number of response alternatives per item. With true-false items the formula is

$$\text{Corrected score} = R - W \tag{13.1a}$$

since there are only two possible alternatives: true and false. For multiple-choice items with four alternatives, the formula is:

$$\text{Corrected score} = R - \frac{W}{3} \tag{13.1b}$$

These formulas assume that the student responds randomly when unsure of the correct response—a highly tenuous assumption in most cases.

To illustrate, consider a 50-item multiple-choice exam with four alternatives per item. Suppose that Mike answers 36 items correctly, 12 items incorrectly, and does not respond to 2 items. His score, corrected for guessing, would be

$$X_{corrected} = 36 - \frac{12}{3} = 36 - 4 = 32$$

Since there were 4 alternatives per item, the denominator of the correction term was 3; that is, $n - 1 = 4 - 1 = 3$. Note also that omitted items are not considered in the correction; that is, omitted items are not considered as wrong answers.

Whether correcting for guessing is a worthwhile expenditure of effort is a debatable point (see, e.g., Ebel, 1965; Davis, 1951, 1964). Proponents argue that correcting for guessing produces scores that better reflect students' true achievement levels and discourages the habit of wild guessing. Opponents argue that the ranking of students will be approximately the same whether or not scores are corrected, that guessing patterns are not random (as assumed by the correction formulas), that the probability of obtaining a high score by guessing is exceedingly small, that applying the correction makes scoring more cumbersome, and that the making of rational guesses under conditions of uncertainty may be a habit worth cultivating. Also, if all students attempt all items—as is usually the case on classroom exams—correcting for guessing will not alter rankings, but only reduce scores. It would seem that the burden of proof would fall upon proponents of correcting for guessing; in this author's opinion they have not as yet made a compelling case.

Scoring essay, problem, and performance items   We have already mentioned some of the problems involved in scoring and evaluating responses to essay, problem, and performance items. Some of these problems arise (particularly with essay and performance items) because of the length and/or complexity of the response. Others arise because with each type of item there is usually more than one correct answer or solution and/or more than one way to arrive at a correct response. Thus it is difficult to compare responses, and there is more room for subjective judgment. The net effect is to reduce the reliability of the scores assigned.

The practical problem, therefore, is to devise methods for making scoring more objective and reliable, and hence more accurate and valid. One way to attain these goals lies within the task (items). When the task is clearly defined, the range of response options will be limited; thus scoring can be more standardized and consistent. The danger is that we will go overboard; for example, if we structure a problem in too much detail it may no longer present a problem, since we have, in essence, told the student how to go about solving it. Or if an essay question is too specific, it may become nothing more than a series of short-answer items. In both of these illustrations, a task requiring higher-order intellectual skills has been reduced to one requiring lower-level skills. Thus we must tread a thin line between providing enough structure to produce some standardization of responses and providing so much structure that the nature of the item is changed.

A second approach lies in clarifying the bases for assigning scores. If the instructor analyzes the task (both its overall nature and component parts) and considers the possible alternative responses at each point, he will have a guide to use when scoring any given response. This analysis should also indicate the relative weight assigned each part and each alternative response. In practice this would mean that on essay items the instructor would write several sample answers; on problems he would have to work through the solution using various possible methods. The point is that the instructor, insofar as possible, should anticipate the various responses students will make and determine how he will score them. In addition, he must decide what emphasis to place on factors other than content or method used; for example, on an essay exam will he consider factors such as organization and writing style when assigning scores?

A third area in which standardization can be achieved is through the mechanics of the scoring process. Some procedures that I have found useful are to scan several papers before starting scoring to get a baseline view of the type and level of responses; grading a sample of papers twice to see if I am, in fact, grading consistently; and scoring papers anonymously so as not to be influenced by students' performance in other aspects of the course. Another important mechanism is to grade items one at a time; that is, first grade all answers to item 1, then all responses to item 2, and so on. Of course, using a predetermined key helps; however, I always find some unanticipated responses.

Needless to say, all of these approaches can be used on any test. The important point is to try to make your scoring as objective as possible by setting certain standards and prescribing certain rules, then following them consistently. My experience is that students recognize that some subjectivity is always involved in grading essay, problem, and performance items; all they ask is that the instructor consistently apply well-reasoned rules when scoring their papers.

Analyzing the Test

After a test has been administered and scored, the teacher may want to analyze the test to determine how effective an instrument he has constructed. Although in practice few teachers make systematic analyses of their tests, the feedback provided by such analyses will help improve test construction skills. In addition, these analyses provide information regarding the effectiveness of teaching and learning.

Analyses may be of (total) test scores or of individual items. When analyzing test scores we shall be concerned with their distribution, validity, and reliability. At the individual item level we shall be concerned with the difficulty and discrimination power of the items and the attractiveness of the various distracters.[6]

Score distributions   Usually the teacher looks at the distribution of scores obtained by the students taking the exam. Often this is done casually, prior to assigning grades. However, if the teacher computes the mean (which is a measure of the *difficulty* of the test) and actually plots the distribution of scores, valuable information will be provided regarding the test.

What do distributions tell us? A normal distribution, with the majority of the scores falling in the middle ranges and fewer scores falling at the extremes, provides good discrimination between students at either end of the distribution. This distribution generally is optimal when assigning grades. If the distribution is negatively skewed, with many students obtaining high scores and few obtaining low scores, the test was quite easy. This distribution would discriminate only between students with lesser degrees of knowledge. If the purpose of the test was to check whether students had read an assignment or mastered basic material, such a distribution would be expected. If the distribution is positively skewed, with few persons obtaining high scores, the test would be difficult. However, such a distribution might be found for a pretest over unstudied material. Or, if a posttest, it could indicate poorly constructed items or incomplete learning.

The mean also indicates the difficulty of the test. For tests designed to discriminate between students, a mean score between 50 and 70 percent is optimal. For mastery tests, an average score of 85 to 90 percent would be desired (Bloom, 1971). In all circumstances, discrepancies between the expected and actual mean scores may provide useful information for evaluating the test.

[6]Item analysis will be discussed in Chapter 14.

Consistency   Since the typical classroom exam has only one form and will be administered only once, there are only two methods of obtaining a reliability estimate: split-half and internal consistency.[7] When using the split-half method, an odd-even split will generally suffice, since items usually are positioned randomly. Of course, the Spearman-Brown correction formula must be used.

The other approach is to use a measure of internal consistency (for example, coefficient alpha or Kuder-Richardson 20). This approach, it will be remembered, assumes that all test items are drawn from the same domain. Although the knowledge and skills measured by the typical classroom exam are generally intercorrelated positively, whether they are so highly intercorrelated that they measure only one factor is problematical. Thus the assumptions of the internal consistency formula will be, at best, only approximated. On comprehensive exams, such as semester finals, the test content will probably be so diverse as to make internal consistency analyses inappropriate. (For an opposing view see Ebel, 1968.)

In fact, computation of any reliability coefficient may seem unnecessary to the classroom teacher. After all, he has only one form of the test and will use the results regardless of the test's reliability. True; however, viewed from a longer-range perspective, computation of reliability estimates will indicate what types of tests and items produce the highest consistency and, therefore, enable the teacher to improve his future tests by using similar test construction procedures.

Validity   With any achievement test, including classroom tests, content validity is the primary procedure for establishing validity. The basic procedure is to compare the skills and content covered by the items with the test plan. If the items reflect the emphases in the plan, and cover important rather than trivial material, then the test has content validity. This process, of course, assumes that the test plan is a fair representation of the content domain and/or instructional goals.

Sometimes the validity of a classroom test can be supported by other evidence. For example, when courses are sequential, the relationship between scores on an exam in one course and success in the following course could be determined. Or scores on classroom exams could be correlated with standardized achievement tests covering the same general content area. If external measures are unavailable, data from within the class can be used. For example, if test scores do not parallel the teacher's judgment of students' knowledge and ability, the validity of the test might be called into question. (These results might, of course, also reflect upon the teacher's judgmental ability.) The scores on an exam could be correlated with scores on other exams or assignments—for example, term papers and reports. We might even be interested in comparing test scores and students' judgment of their learning. All of these data sources provide, albeit somewhat incomplete and biased, evidence of the validity of the test.

Grading

This is not the place for an extensive discussion of grading and marking systems (see, e.g., Brown, 1971; Cureton, 1971; Dressel, 1961; Ebel, 1972). Since the

[7]Split-half and internal consistency estimates are inappropriate for speeded tests; however, most classroom tests are, or should be, power tests.

classroom teacher usually must operate within an institutionally defined grading system, the question of what grading system is "best" generally is moot. Thus we will only discuss several measurement-related aspects of grading that are important, regardless of type of marks assigned.[8]

First, grades should always be based on sufficient evidence. By "sufficient" we mean a large enough sample of each student's performance so that grades can be reliably assigned. In practice, this means basing grades on several exams and/or assignments; preferably measuring different abilities and skills. How many assignments, and what type, will vary between courses. What is important is that the tests and assignments representatively sample the domain—that is, that the grades have content validity. This implies that, whenever feasible, grades should be based on more than test performance (although test scores might be the most important determiner). In situations where evaluations must be based solely on test scores— for example, in large college lecture courses—the tests should sample different types of intellectual skills.

Because marks will be based on performance on several assignments, the instructor must decide how to combine the several scores. Since no external criterion measures are available, weighting will have to be on a rational—not empirical— basis. Thus, unless the instructor combines scores subjectively, he will have to assign relative weights to each score and transform all qualitative judgments (such as ratings of class participation) to a quantitative scale. To ensure that each variable (for example, test scores) receives the desired weights, he can translate all scores to standard scores, weight each variable appropriately, then form a composite (see Chapter 9). In practice, this procedure is often not followed. One reason is the amount of computational labor. The other is that if the distributions on all variables are relatively comparable, the relative rankings obtained by combining raw scores do not differ greatly from those obtained by combining standard scores.

Another problem is where to draw the cutting lines to separate the different grade categories. This is a tricky problem. Some instructors follow an arbitrary distribution, saying the top x percent will get A's (or whatever the top mark is), the next y percent will get B's, and so on. Other instructors insist that they mark on an absolute scale, comparing performance of each student to some, presumably well-defined, standard. Other instructors try to develop grading distribution using some external anchor—for example, the ability or previous grades of the students in the class (Ebel, 1972). Probably the most common procedure is to have certain expected percentages in mind, but apply these percentages flexibly depending on the performance of the particular class (for example, looking at natural breaks in the distribution). In short, there is no completely objective method available for assigning grades; subjective evaluations will always be involved.

AN EVALUATION OF CLASSROOM TESTS

What can we say in summary regarding classroom tests? Certainly it should be clear that effective instruction cannot occur without periodic evaluation and feedback—

[8]We shall not discuss grading individual exams and other assignments, because grading, at this level, serves no useful purpose. That is, the information needed to improve instruction and learning is provided by the test score and an analysis of errors, not by a letter grade.

that is, without some sort of testing. The question is the frequency and form of the testing or measurement.

There are four points in the instructional sequence where testing provides useful information. At the beginning of an instructional unit, a pretest may be used to determine students' level of mastery of prerequisite skills and knowledge, and the material to be covered in the unit. Instruction can then be adapted to fit students' present performance level. During instruction, the teacher can use various forms of formative evaluation to provide feedback on learning progress and, when necessary, to modify the instructional process. At the end of each unit, the teacher will probably use a summative evaluation instrument. Finally, later in the course or after a course is completed, students' ability to integrate, apply, and transfer their knowledge and skills may be measured, often through standardized tests (see Chapter 14).

One other important function of classroom testing is often overlooked. When we think of classroom testing, we usually first think of grading—that is, of evaluating students. However, classroom tests also provide information that is useful for evaluating and modifying instruction. One example, formative evaluation, was mentioned in the previous paragraph. The teacher can also use the results of an item analysis of his test to see what items students had difficulty with and what types of mistakes they made. This information can, then, provide a basis for modifying instruction.

On a more technical level, classroom tests do not meet all of the psychometric requirements prescribed in earlier chapters. They are standardized to the extent that a common set of items are administered to all students under identical conditions. Scores are compared to a common norm group: the class. The reliability of classroom tests is usually not computed, and in some senses is superfluous (see above). Validity is determined primarily by content validity, with evidence of empirical validity being derived only from sources internal to the test.

One issue that has caused a considerable amount of debate is the relative merits of alternative-choice and free response items—particularly multiple-choice and essay items. The resolution depends on the recognition that the two tests formats are complementary, not opposed. Exams including essay and other free response items (such as problem and performance items) will be most appropriate with small classes, when time pressures are minimal, when the subject matter is to be covered in depth, and when the skills to be tested include application, organization, integration, evaluation, or creativity. Alternative-choice items will be used with large classes, for broad content sampling, with time pressures, and when testing of recognition skills is sufficient.

In summary, the status of classroom examinations is, in many ways, contradictory. Even people who vigorously attack other types of testing generally concede that measurement of classroom achievement is essential to the educational process. Yet few teachers make the effort to increase their test-building skills or fully utilize tests as learning tools. Hopefully those of you who become teachers will take the time and make the necessary effort.

14

STANDARDIZED ACHIEVEMENT TESTS

In education, we frequently need information that can be obtained only from broad, standardized samples of student performance. Some common examples include measuring educational growth from year to year, comparing curricula or teaching methods, measurement of retention and transfer of skills, and placement of students in appropriate courses. In each of these situations, sufficient information cannot be obtained from teacher-built tests; hence, the need for standardized achievement tests.[1]

Rather than spelling out the differences between standardized and classroom achievement tests, we shall discuss the construction of standardized achievement tests, letting the reader compare and contrast the two types of tests. We shall describe the procedures that a test publisher might follow, since most standardized achievement tests are developed by professional test publishing organizations. Similar procedures would be followed, however, by anyone constructing such a test.

[1]Earlier we discussed standardization as an aspect of the test construction process (that is, common content, administration, and scoring). Standardized, as the term is used in this chapter, refers to tests that have these properties and, in addition, have performance norms available and have known (and high) consistency and validity. Usually, though not necessarily, such tests are developed by test publishers.

CONSTRUCTION AND STANDARDIZATION

Once the need for a test has been recognized, test construction is directed by an advisory committee consisting of curriculum and measurement experts. This committee establishes general guidelines for the test, for example: What type of test (for example, survey or diagnostic) is needed? What content and skills will be covered? With what relative emphasis? What is the appropriate age range? What should the length of the test be? What is the relationship between this test and other tests in the battery and/or on the market? What item formats should be used? How many scores or subtests are needed? And so on, through many more questions. Their decisions regarding these questions form the general plans and guidelines for the test.

Constructing the Test

The actual construction of the test is usually managed by curriculum experts working in conjunction with test construction experts employed by the publisher.

Figure 14.1 Examples of multiple-choice items measuring higher-level intellectual skills.

Courtesy of the Metropolitan Museum of Art, Gift of John D. Rockefeller, Jr., 1932.

In which of the following centuries was the piece of sculpture shown above most probably produced?

(A) The fifth century B.C.
(B) The fourteenth century A.D.
(C) The sixteenth century A.D.
(D) The eighteenth century A.D.
(E) The twentieth century A.D.

Figure 14.1 (continued)

Question 17

One method of obtaining "artificial gravity" in a space station is to have the station rotating about axis AA' as it revolves around Earth.

Side View

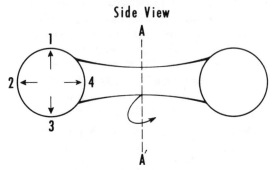

The inhabitants of the space station would call which direction "down"?

(A) Direction 1
(B) Direction 2
(C) Direction 3
(D) Direction 4
(E) Any one of the four, depending on speed of rotation

Question 22

The question below is followed by two statements, labeled (1) and (2), in which certain data are given. In this question you do not actually have to compute an answer, but rather you have to decide whether the data given in the statements are sufficient for answering the question. Using the data given in the statements plus your knowledge of mathematics and everyday facts (such as the number of days in July), you are to select answer

(A) if statement (1) ALONE is sufficient but statement (2) alone is not sufficient to answer the question asked,
(B) if statement (2) ALONE is sufficient but statement (1) alone is not sufficient to answer the question asked,
(C) if both statements (1) and (2) TOGETHER are sufficient to answer the question asked, but NEITHER statement ALONE is sufficient,
(D) if EACH statement is sufficient by itself to answer the question asked,
(E) if statements (1) and (2) TOGETHER are NOT sufficient to answer the question asked and additional data specific to the problem are needed.

If x is a whole number, is it a two-digit number?
  (1) x^2 is a three-digit number.
  (2) 10x is a three-digit number.

Figure 14.1 (continued)

European History and World Cultures Test

16. "To princes power is given on earth, but to priests power is given also in heaven. The former have power over bodies only, the latter have power also over souls. Therefore, to that degree by which the soul is more worthy than the body, by so much is the priesthood more worthy than the kingdom. Single rulers have single provinces, and single kings have single kingdoms; but Peter rules them all."

    Which of the following subscribed to the point of view above?

    (A) Henry II of England
    (B) Innocent III
    (C) The Apostle Peter
    (D) Leo I
    (E) Louis XIV of France

17. "All life is pain, pain caused by selfish desire, pain which can be relieved only by renouncing our desires and achieving complete forgetfulness of ourselves. This common fate of mankind makes brothers of men."

    The quotation above expresses the basic idea of

    (A) Buddhism
    (B) Confucianism
    (C) Islam
    (D) Shintoism
    (E) Taoism

Physics Test

Ability to interpret experimental data

17. A tuning fork vibrating at 500 vibrations per second in a certain gas produces waves in the gas whose successive rarefactions are 3.00 feet apart. The speed of sound in the gas could be calculated

    (A) only if the density of the gas were also known
    (B) only if the temperature of the gas were also known
    (C) only if both the density and the temperature of the gas were also known
    (D) only if the amplitude of the oscillation were also known
    (E) with no further information

Questions 18-21:

Figure 2

The graph in Figure 2 shows the velocity of a car as a function of time while the car moves along a straight track.

18. During the 7th second, the car is moving with constant

    (A) speed
    (B) velocity
    (C) acceleration
    (D) momentum
    (E) kinetic energy

Figure 14.1 (continued)

19. During the first 3 seconds, the car has an average acceleration of about

(A) $-\dfrac{8}{3}$ m/sec^2 (D) $\dfrac{4}{3}$ m/sec^2

(B) $-\dfrac{4}{3}$ m/sec^2 (E) $\dfrac{8}{3}$ m/sec^2

(C) 0 m/sec^2

European History and World Cultures Test and Physics Test. Reproduced by permission from *A Description of the College Board Achievement Tests.* Copyright © 1968 by College Entrance Examination Board, New York.

Although the steps will vary, depending on the nature of the test, a typical sequence would be: planning the test, writing the items, pretesting items, preparing the final form, collecting reliability and validity evidence, and developing normative and interpretive material (ETS, 1965).

Planning the test   One obvious difference between standardized and classroom tests is that the former, having been planned by more than one person, will reflect a compromise among points of view rather than the preferences and biases of only one person, the classroom teacher. Therefore, a standardized test will stress material that is widely taught—that is, presented in the most frequently used textbooks. Because the test will be administered to diverse groups, the content domain sampled will be broad and no topic will be covered in depth. The planners may also have a problem of articulation. Since many standardized achievement tests will be parts of a test battery, and designed for a particular grade level, each specific test must fit into the grade sequence and battery.

Given these boundary conditions, the engineering of the test plan is similar to that of a classroom test. The test constructors will generally use some form of the content/skills grid.[2] However, they will probably use more dimensions and define these dimensions more specifically than will the teacher building a classroom exam. In short, the process is the same, the difference being in the thoroughness of the specifications.

Item writing   Items are written by subject matter specialists or professional item writers, then reviewed by other subject matter and testing specialists. Proposed items are edited, revised and rewritten, reviewed again, and so on until an acceptable item is attained. Note that items are written and independently reviewed by subject matter experts;[3] the test specialists serve only as technical advisors. Thus, the test includes items testing material that educators think important—not, as is sometimes charged, material that psychometricians feel is important.

It should also be noted that although the classroom teacher can use a variety of item formats, standardized tests will generally utilize alternative-choice items. The reasons are several: more adequate sampling of content, speed and accuracy of scoring, and higher reliability. Since multiple-choice items offer more advantages

[2]Criterion-referenced tests are developed by writing one or more items for each behavioral objective.

[3]These experts are usually persons who teach the subject in secondary schools and colleges.

than other alternative-choice items, they are most widely used. The item writing task, thus, usually becomes one of writing multiple-choice items. Because of the importance of standardized tests, and the resources devoted to developing these tests, exceedingly sophisticated forms of multiple-choice items have been developed (see Figure 14.1 and ETS, 1963).

Many more items will be written than will be needed, often three or four times as many. The required number of items will then be selected from this pool, using pretest data to identify items displaying the desired characteristics. If more than one form of the test is being constructed, enough good items will be needed that the forms can be equated in content, difficulty, variability, and along other relevant dimensions.

Pretesting items   Although experienced item writers can construct items without obvious faults, there is no assurance that any given item will perform exactly as expected when administered to groups of students. Thus, preliminary forms of the test are administered to samples of students (similar to those that the completed test will be administered to) and relevant item statistics computed (see below, pp. 278–283. On the basis of these analyses, some items are eliminated, others are revised, and others are deemed acceptable as they stand.

Assembling the final form   When the final forms of the test are being assembled, several considerations must be balanced to produce a test with the desired characteristics. For example, the items should represent the various content/skill categories as outlined in the test plan; the number of items must be appropriate for the time limits; the test must be of the proper difficulty level; and a wide distribution of scores must be obtained. Moreover, these considerations apply to each form of the test and the various forms must be equated to each other. This balancing is an extremely delicate process, one that relies on both statistical data and rational judgment.

Finally, the test is again reviewed by subject matter and test construction specialists. After they have made any modifications, the test can be printed.

Psychometric data   Determining the psychometric qualities of the test is a continual process. For example, although some characteristics (difficulty, time limits) can be estimated from pretest data, students' response to the completed test may differ from their response to the pretests. Thus, analyses of completed forms of the test are needed. We are interested in the average score (for various groups) and the distribution of scores. The consistency of the test scores must be determined, particularly equivalent forms reliability if there is more than one form of the test. The validity of the test—always content validity, but often also criterion-related—must be established. Normative data must be collected. Although the process of test development is designed to ensure that the test will be adequate in these respects, empirical tests are needed to confirm the effectiveness of the test construction process.

The final step is to develop interpretive data and aids. One essential aid is a technical manual containing information on the test construction process—content/

skills domain, the basis of item selection, item statistics—as well as normative, validity, and reliability data. Adequate normative data is especially crucial. A variety of norm data should be available, in forms that are precise yet readily understandable by test users. To accomplish this end, the test publisher will usually provide a variety of interpretive aids—for example, explanatory material, report forms, profiles. Although development of these aids may appear rather pedestrian in comparison with the sophisticated statistical analyses of the psychometrician, the quality and clarity of these interpretive aids probably contribute as much, if not more, than any other factor to proper use and interpretation of test scores.

Technical Characteristics

Before discussing the major types of standardized achievement tests, let us review how the considerations of consistency, validity, and norms apply to standardized achievement tests. Our purpose here is only to set certain general guidelines, to provide a framework for evaluation. In evaluating any particular test, used for a specific purpose, the unique features of that situation must, of course, be taken into account. (For other discussions see, e.g., Ebel, 1972; Englehart, 1964; Thorndike, 1971a.)

Consistency   Any test must measure consistently and reliably. Previously (see Chapters 4–6) we discussed several methods of estimating consistency. However, some of these indices are of only limited usefulness with standardized achievement tests. For example, in education we are interested in retention of knowledge over relatively long time periods. Thus, one might think that a high degree of stability would be desirable. However, since differential learning (and/or forgetting) will occur between testings, a test that is sensitive to changes in knowledge will be unstable; that is, it will have a low coefficient of stability. But this instability would reflect true changes in ability, not error variance. Thus, stability estimates are inappropriate. Measures of stability and equivalence will, consequently, also be of limited value.

The typical standardized achievement test is broad and designed to measure a variety of abilities and skills. Although items may intercorrelate positively, the level of relationship is not such that the test can be considered homogeneous. Thus, for both rational and empirical reasons, measures of homogeneity generally will not be applicable. An obvious exception is subtests of diagnostic batteries. Here the goal is to measure the basic components of a skill or ability; hence, homogeneity will be a relevant consideration.

Thus we are left with two possibilities: measures of equivalence and split-half measures. The former is the more stringent measure, and thus is to be preferred. Needless to say, whenever an achievement test has more than one form, evidence of equivalent forms reliability is essential.

Two factors that may influence the magnitude of a reliability coefficient deserve special mention. The magnitude of a reliability coefficient, you will recall, varies with the group taking the test—more specifically, with the distribution of scores.

The more heterogeneous the scores, the higher the potential r_{XX}. Standardized achievement tests generally are applicable at several grade levels. Inclusion of several grade levels in the sample used to determine reliability will increase the heterogeneity of the scores, and consequently increase r_{XX}. In other words, reliability estimates based on multigrade samples will be inflated compared to single-grade samples. In most cases a more stringent, accurate, and useful estimate will be the reliability within a given grade level. Second, if the test is speeded and/or many students do not finish within the time limits, any internal consistency reliability estimate will be spuriously inflated. The most meaningful estimates of consistency are obtained when the test functions as a power test.

Validity   On achievement tests the behavior of inherent interest is that sampled by the test items. Thus the appropriate validity index is a measure of the adequacy of sampling—to wit, content validity. When establishing the content validity of any achievement test, two considerations are particularly relevant. First, the content domain must be clearly specified. Even though the test developers may have specified the content domain when constructing the test, this definition is not always transmitted, through the test manual, to the test user. However, in order to evaluate the content validity of a test, this specification must be made public. Second, any individual user may, of course, define the relevant domain differently than the test developers. That is, the test will be more or less appropriate for his particular situation and purpose, depending on the congruence between the two definitions of the content domain. The test user will have to judge the appropriateness of the test for his purposes. In other words, all estimates of content validity will be situation-specific.

In some circumstances, criterion-related validity evidence may be germane. For example, when a standardized achievement test is used in making selection or placement decisions, the proportion of correct decisions or the increase in average criterion performance would be an appropriate validity index. Construct validity is sometimes also relevant, particularly discriminant validity. Achievement tests, as other tests, should measure only the domain of immediate interest, not irrelevant but related variables. However, it is obvious that performance on many achievement tests is dependent on other factors, most commonly reading ability. A more subtle example is provided by Gagné (1967), who pointed out that tests measuring knowledge of principles typically cannot distinguish between persons who fail an item because they lack knowledge of the principle and those who fail because they lack knowledge of the concepts involved in illustrating the principle. The point is clear, most achievement tests are not ''pure'' measures of the purported domain.

Norms   Scores on standardized achievement tests may be interpreted using either norm-referenced or content-referenced standards. In the traditional norm-referenced approach, scores are reported as a relative standing within a group. However, since different groups will have different score distributions, various norm groups will be needed. With achievement tests these groups usually will represent different grade levels, geographic areas, types of schools, or groups of students differing in their previous curricular experiences. Because norm-referenced scores do not directly indicate an individual's degree of proficiency in the subject matter, it may also be desirable to provide content-referenced scores. Content-referenced scores, you will recall, describe what the student can do; that is, they describe his degree of proficiency. Although content-referenced scores have not been widely used, there is increasing demand for such scores (see, e.g., Bloom, 1971; Popham and Husek, 1969; Mehrens and Lehmann, 1973; Payne, 1974) and tests are being published that report scores in this manner.

ITEM ANALYSIS

Several times previously we have referred to the role of item analysis in test construction and for providing feedback regarding the effectiveness of instruction and learning. In this section we shall illustrate procedures involved in running an item analysis and look at some of the uses of item analysis. For a more detailed discussion of item analysis the reader is referred to Davis (1951), Ebel (1972), or Henryssen (1971).

Procedure

The exact procedures used in an item analysis will vary depending on whether we are dealing with a standardized test or a teacher-built test and whether we are using the analysis primarily to select good test items or to provide students feedback regarding learning. In all cases, however, we are interested in three types of information. First, we are interested in item difficulties—that is, the proportion of people who correctly answer an item. Second, we are interested in discrimination—whether the item differentiates between persons having greater and lesser amounts of knowledge. Third, we are concerned with the pattern of responses to the various distracters.

When running an item analysis we want to use enough subjects (tests) to provide stable estimates of item characteristics. On standardized tests there usually is no problem obtaining enough tests for analysis. Thus, we often select only a sample of the tests for analysis. One common procedure is to select 370 papers randomly, and then use the top 27 percent (that is, 100 tests) and bottom 27 percent in the analysis. On classroom tests, there may be a problem in obtaining sufficient responses. In these cases, especially when there are fewer than 100 students, we often break the distribution at the median and compare the upper and lower halves. This procedure provides a more stringent test by using all data, not just extreme scores. In either case, as we shall see below, we shall compare people who know more about the subject (that is, the high scorers) with those who know less (that is, the low scorers).

Indices

As mentioned above, we are interested in three types of analyses: item difficulties, item discrimination indices, and patterns of responses to distracters.

Quantitative indices can be derived for the first two cases. Although quantitative indices are possible when analyzing distracters, they usually are not used, particularly with teacher-built tests. There are numerous possible quantitative indices of item difficulty and discrimination powers, but we shall illustrate only several simple ones. In all our examples we shall use multiple-choice items; similar procedures could be used with other alternative-choice items and, with some alterations, even with recall items.

Difficulty   All item difficulty indices basically indicate what percent of people answer an item correctly. One possible method is to use all the tests (or the sample selected for analysis) and compute the number of people who answer the item correctly. Another procedure is to average the proportion (or percent) correct in the high and low groups:

$$\text{Item difficulty} = \frac{\text{P correct high} + \text{P correct low}}{2} \qquad (14.1)$$

When using this latter procedure we are assuming that the middle (unanalyzed) group responds halfway between the high and low groups.

Interpretation of item difficulty indices is not as straightforward as might appear on first blush. The reason is that the "absolute" difficulty of the item and (the degree of) students' learning are confounded. That is, an item may be easy because of something about the way the item was constructed (for example, the answer is obvious) or because students have learned the material thoroughly. Conversely, an item may be difficult because it is poorly constructed (for example, it is ambiguous), because the item covers intrinsically difficult material, or because students, for some reason, did not learn this material. Or the item may even be miskeyed. Thus, we always have to look at the wording of the items, and consider students' learning experiences and the structure of the subject matter when interpreting item difficulty indices.

Another important question is the optimal level of difficulty for an item. It can be shown, that if the goal of measurement is to maximize differences between students, items with difficulties of .5 are best.[4] Since there is little difference in discrimination power between items with difficulties of .5 and .7, a useful rule of thumb is to use items that 50 to 70 percent of the students can answer correctly. In some cases, however, we may want to use easier or more difficult items. For example, "warm-up" items, used at the beginning of a test to build confidence and get students used to the testing situation, should be easy; perhaps so easy that 90 percent or more of the students answer correctly.

Discrimination   The second index is the item discrimination index. Again there are various possible indices, all of which provide an index of how well an item dif-

---

[4]This is because variance will be maximized (since $s^2 = pq$, s^2 will be maximal when $p = q = .5$). Actually the variance of total scores depends on item intercorrelations as well as on their difficulties, and to discriminate at a particular score level, the .5 difficulty level will not always be optimal. (See Nunnally, 1967; Magnusson, 1967.)

ferentiates between students having greater and lesser amounts of knowledge of the relevant domain. Ideally, this differentiation would be made by using an external criterion. However, on achievement tests, such external indices generally are not available.[5] Thus the criterion generally used is the total score on the test—that is, the score on all the items (the total test score). This procedure assumes that the test as a whole is an adequate measure of the domain. Although this may seem like a tenuous assumption, empirical data support the use of this procedure (Horn, 1966; Ebel, 1968).

The problem, therefore, is to derive an index that measures this relationship. One procedure is to use the item-test correlation. That is, we can correlate scores on an individual item with (total) scores on the test. If students who score high on the test tend to answer the item correctly and those who score low answer incorrectly, the item-test correlation will be high. If there is no relation between answering an item correctly and the test score, the discrimination index will be zero. In other words, discriminating items will be ones that correlate highly with the total score. It is difficult to set an exact level, other than that the correlation be significantly greater than zero. However, a good rule of thumb would be to require r to be .20 or higher.

Another possibility is to compare the percent of students in the high and low groups answering the item correctly. The simplest index would be to look at the differences in proportions or percentages:

$$\text{Item discrimination} = \text{P correct high} - \text{P correct low} \qquad (14.2)$$

Here, again, we are looking for a high positive value. As a rule of thumb, we can say that any difference of 15 to 20 percent (.15–.20) or higher would indicate good discrimination.

Distracters   The third aspect of an item analysis concerns the pattern of responses to the various distracters. Obviously, one thing we are looking for is alternatives that do not attract any responses. These alternatives contribute nothing to the test, except to increase reading time. Here a rule of thumb is that an alternative should be eliminated or revised unless one of every 50 students (2 percent) select it. Other analyses are more subtle, but may provide useful information. For example, if an incorrect alternative is chosen by many students in the "high" group but few in the "low" group, it might suggest that this response is, at least in some aspects, also correct.

Since the three parts of an item analysis are obviously interrelated, we should always look at the total picture when considering an item. To illustrate, if an item is very easy or very difficult, it cannot discriminate well. Or, if an item is very easy, few people will choose any of the distracters. Whether this means the item is weak depends on our criteria; as mentioned earlier, an easy item might be used as a warm-up item. Or a teacher might include an item because it covers important

---

[5]External criteria may be available when selecting items for other types of tests. Items for scholastic aptitude tests can be validated by contrasting the responses of students obtaining high and low grades; items on an interest inventory can be validated by comparing responses of persons in various occupations.

material that he thinks should be tested; whether this item discriminates will be of secondary importance. Or, to give a final example, consider what response pattern would suggest that students guessed at an item. If responses reflected pure guessing, the item difficulty would be at the chance level (for example, .25 in a four-choice item), the item would not discriminate, and approximately equal numbers of people would select each alternative.

We should also mention that the typical item analysis provides more than item characteristic data. For example, the item analysis computer program at the school where I teach also gives the class mean, standard deviation, and variance; provides a Kuder-Richardson reliability index; prints a distribution of scores that includes frequencies, percentile ranks, and standard scores; provides a list of students (in order of social security or other identifying number); and prints out a list indicating the items each student answered incorrectly.

An Example

An example of an item analysis is provided in Table 14.1. This analysis is of several items from a student-constructed exam. Part I of the table shows the number of students who selected each alternative; the item difficulties (the column labeled "%R," for percent right) and the discrimination indices (item-test correlations, in the column labeled "CORR"). Part II shows the same data, using an item analysis conducted by dividing the group into the upper and lower halves. We will leave it as an exercise for you to interpret the results of the analysis of the various items.

Mastery Tests

On mastery (criterion-referenced) tests, item analyses are somewhat different. Since we expect (hope?) that most students will have mastered the objectives, on items administered after instruction most students will obtain the correct answer and there will be little variance in responses. Thus, the typical item analysis procedures will be inappropriate. Indices of item difficulty will still provide useful information, by indicating what skills students have and have not mastered. However, the usual item discrimination indices will not work. How, then, can we identify discriminating items? One possibility is to administer the same test both before instruction (as a pretest) and after instruction. Before students have studied the material, few students should obtain the correct answer; after instruction, most students should obtain the correct answer. Thus, a discriminating item will be one in which there is a large difference in the proportion of correct answers from pretest to posttest. This procedure has another advantage. If we select items which students cannot answer correctly before instruction but can after instruction, we have some assurance that the material was learned as a result of the instruction (unless, of course, students learned it elsewhere at the same time as the instruction). Needless to say, since most classroom teachers do not administer both pretests and posttests, this procedure is used most often with standardized achievement tests.

TABLE 14.1   An example of an item analysis.

ITEMS:
1. Incorrect choices on multiple-choice tests are called:
   (A) alternatives (B) distracters (C) relatives (D) deceivers
2. Which of the following is NOT an alternative-choice item?
   (A) true-false (B) short-answer (C) matching (D) multiple-choice
3. Difficult test items can best be used to:
   (A) challenge students to do better.
   (B) separate the better and average students.
   (C) let poor students know where they need help.
   (D) reinforce the better students.
4. A psychologist who strongly favors true-false items is:
   (A) Ebel (B) Bloom (C) Tyler (D) Ausubel

I. ANALYSIS OF TOTAL GROUP

Item	OM	A	B	C	D	%R	CORR
1	2	25	141^a	2	7	81	.31
2	0	6	170^a	1	0	96	.14
3	0	21	130^a	10	16	73	.39
4	5	45^a	41	39	47	25	.03

II. ANALYSIS BY HIGH-LOW GROUPS

Item-Group[b]	OM	A	B	C	D	%R	DIFF	DISCRIM
1-High	1	5	80^a	0	2	91	.80	.22
-Low	1	20	61	2	5	69		
2-High	0	0	88^a	0	0	100	.96	.08
-Low	0	6	82	1	0	92		
3-High	0	4	75^a	4	5	85	.74	.23
-Low	0	17	55	6	11	62		
4-High	2	23^a	19	20	24	26	.25	.02
-Low	3	22	22	19	23	24		

[a]Indicates correct answer.
[b]High group consists of 88 highest scores, low group the 89 lowest scores.

Uses of Item Analysis Data

We have already suggested several possible uses for item analysis data. Let us now review and summarize these uses.

One obvious use is to determine which items to include on a test. On standardized tests, this means trying out the items and using the item analysis data as a basis for selecting items for the final forms of a test. In general, we select items of appropriate difficulty that discriminate well. However, the procedure is not quite this simple. We also have to look at the intercorrelations between items (see, e.g., Nunnally, 1967; Magnusson, 1967) and, of course, we must be concerned with the content balance of the test. The classroom teacher usually is unable to try out items; however, he can keep a file of questions that have proved to be effective and use them on future tests.

Item analysis can also be used to improve items and item writing skills. If the test writer finds an item to be defective in some respect (for example, it is too easy or one distracter does not work), this is a signal for the item to be revised. This is one obvious reason for pretesting items. At a more general level, item writers, through experience, come to know what sorts of items work well and which items "bomb out." Thus by considering their past experiences (both mistakes and successes), they learn what characteristics (such as wording and types of problems) produce good items.

The results of an item analysis also provide useful information for improving instruction. The instructor can look at the items a student misses, identify weaknesses in his knowledge, and suggest appropriate remedial instruction. One application of this procedure has been suggested by Dunstan (1973). His item analysis program provides each student with a list of the items that he missed and indicates where (in the reading assignments) the material was covered. Thus, each student is directed to the appropriate source for remedial help.

The teacher can look at the results of an item analysis for his class and identify what items, or types of items,[6] many students missed and what ones they have mastered. He can then plan instruction accordingly—for example, by going over the material covered by items that many students answered incorrectly. By looking at the pattern of incorrect answers, he may also get some clues as to why students missed a particular item. Suppose, for example, that an item analysis of an arithmetic test shows that many of Ms. Piaget's fifth grade students had difficulty on items involving decimals. She could then spend more time teaching decimals. If, in addition, the item analysis showed that most wrong answers involved misplacing the decimal point, she could focus her instruction on this particular operation.

Fortunately, many test publishers will supply item analysis data, in addition to scores and normative data—for a small fee, of course. Given the potential value of such information for improving instruction and facilitating students' learning, expenditure of the necessary funds to obtain item analysis data would seem to be a worthwhile investment.

TYPES OF STANDARDIZED ACHIEVEMENT TESTS

Having discussed the process of constructing standardized achievement tests, we now turn to a discussion of the major types of standardized achievement tests. Somewhat arbitrarily we have divided our presentation into three major sections: survey tests and batteries, tests used to facilitate instruction, and measures of educational outputs.

---

[6]What skill is measured by an item should be indicated in the test manual. If not, the instructor can make his own classification of items.

Survey Tests

The most frequently used standardized achievemnent tests are survey tests. Survey tests, you will recall, broadly sample the content domain and are designed to provide an indication of a student's overall command of a given content domain. Usually only a single total score is reported. Some survey tests are built specifically for a particular subject, others are part of an integrated battery covering the major content areas.

In selecting or evaluating a survey test, several considerations are preeminent. First, the test items should representatively sample a defined content domain. (A prior requisite, of course, is that the domain be clearly specified.) On most survey tests the content universe will be quite broad, usually covering more than a single course. In defining the domain, test constructors have taken one of two approaches. Some emphasize command of the basic knowledge, concepts, and principles of a given subject matter area, whereas others stress general skills that are transferable to several subject matter areas. An example of the latter approach is the *Iowa Tests of Basic Skills,* which assesses broad fundamental skills such as vocabulary, reading comprehension, language usage, work-study skills, and arithmetic. Perhaps the clearest example of the skills approach is the Work-Study portion of the test. This portion of the test contains problems measuring the skills of map reading, reading graphs and tables, and the use of reference materials (such as dictionaries). These are skills that can be applied to a variety of subject matter areas.

With a test battery we are concerned not only with each test, but also with the adequacy of the coverage of the battery as a whole and with the interrelationships between tests within the battery. Ideally, an achievement battery would cover all important aspects of the curriculum; to use a facetious example, an elementary-level achievement battery that did not cover basic arithmetic operations would obviously be incomplete. The separate tests should measure distinct skills; if they are highly intercorrelated, they are measuring the same abilities.

A second requirement is that the test measure achievement in the relevant domain, not other abilities. This requirement may be harder to attain than might be expected. Certain broad skills that influence performance on survey tests—for example, reading comprehension and test-taking skills—can and should be minimized. Also, unless there is some overwhelming argument otherwise, a survey test should be a power test, since our objective usually is to measure the breadth and depth of students' knowledge, not the speed with which they can respond.

Preferably survey tests will measure not only the student's current status but also provide a basis for measuring growth. In practice, this is generally accomplished by an integrated series of test batteries, each covering several grade levels. Although a battery may not include exactly the same tests at each grade level, since different skills are emphasized at each grade level, there will be overlap from level to level, thus providing some basis for measuring growth.

The *Sequential Tests of Educational Progress (STEP) Series II* illustrate how an integrated test battery can operate. The STEP battery has forms at each of four levels of difficulty (for grades 4–6, 7–9, 10–12, and 13–14); at each level the same seven tests[7] are represented: English Expression, Reading, Mechanics of Writing, Mathematics Computation, Mathematics Basic Concepts, Science, and Social Studies. Equivalent forms are available at each level. Thus, by using a series of test batteries, covering various age levels, one can measure both current status and growth.

A fourth desirable feature is that scores be interpretable in both norm-referenced and criterion-referenced terms. Traditionally, norm-referenced scores have been stressed but, as pointed out earlier, criterion-referenced scores are often more meaningful educationally (Carver, 1974).

Implications for test construction   The considerations discussed in the preceding paragraphs, coupled with the requirements discussed in previous chapters, have several implications for the construction of survey achievement tests. (1) More than one test form should be available. For example, when measuring growth, equivalent forms allow retesting without using the same items. (2) Each level of the test should cover only a few grades, preferably no more than three. Because the skills and materials taught vary widely between grades, and students' skills change rapidly (especially at younger ages), tests serving a wide age (grade) range usually are inappropriate at one or both ends of the range.[8] (3) Since school curricula are constantly changing, a test must be periodically revised. (4) Scores should be expressed in meaningful units. Usually, the most appropriate norm-referenced scores will be percentiles within grades. In addition, content-referenced scores will be desirable and, as a basis for measuring growth, a continuous standard score system may be needed. (5) Normative data from a variety of groups, having distinctive characteristics, should be available.

Many standardized achievement tests meet these requirements quite well. There are a number of published tests (and test batteries) that cover a variety of content and skills, have equivalent forms at different age levels, have been periodically revised, are reliable, and provide a variety of normative data. In short, there are many technically adequate standardized achievement tests. The user's question, thus, should have to do with the importance of the material tested. That is, does a test measure the important skills and basic concepts of an area as he defines them? This can only be answered by an intensive analysis of the test and the curriculum.

Some examples   A brief description of a survey test battery is presented in Table 14.2; other, briefer examples are given in Appendix B. This listing is not intended to be exhaustive or to constitute a recommendation for these particular tests; rather it is to illustrate the variety of survey tests available. We shall not attempt to evaluate individual tests here, since a thorough evaluation would be too space-consuming besides being rather artificial, representing the author's evaluation of the test for a hypothetical use and population. It is suggested, rather, that the reader obtain copies of one or more standardized achievement tests and their manuals, and make his own

[7]The Mechanics of Writing and Mathematics Computations tests are not available at the college level.
[8]The test would be too difficult for many students in the lowest grades and too easy for many in the highest grades.

TABLE 14.2   An example of a survey achievement battery.

Test series: The Stanford Achievement Tests
Publisher: Harcourt, Brace and Jovanovich (1973)

Stanford Early School Achievement Test (K–grade 1.1)
  The Environment (social studies, science), Mathematics, Letters and Sounds,
  Aural Comprehension. Designed to measure what has been learned, not as a
  readiness test.

Stanford Achievement Tests (grades 1.5–9.5)
  Levels. Primary I (1.5–2.4), Primary II (2.5–3.4), Primary III (3.5–4.4),
  Intermediate I (4.5–5.4), Intermediate II (5.5–6.9), Advanced (7–9.5)
  Tests. The following tests are included:

Test	P1	P2	P3	I1	I2	Adv
Vocabulary	X	X	X	X	X	X
Reading Comprehension	X	X	X	X	X	X
Word Study Skills	X	X	X	X	X	
Math Concepts	X	X	X	X	X	X
Math Computation	X	X	X	X	X	X
Math Applications		X	X	X	X	X
Spelling	X	X	X	X	X	X
Language		X	X	X	X	
Social Science		X	X	X	X	X
Science		X	X	X	X	X
Listening Comprehension	X	X	X	X	X	

Test of Academic Skills
  Levels. Level I (9–10), Level II (11–13)
  Tests. Reading Comprehension, Math Concepts, Language

Items. See Figure 14.2
Scoring. By hand or machine
Scores. Percentile ranks, grade equivalents, stanines, scale scores. Profile
  provided for plotting scores.
Norms. On SAT, based on 275,000 students in 109 systems in 43 states. On
  TASK, based on 47,000 students from 29 states.
Validity. Basically content or curricular validity. Suggest compare content to local
  objectives.
Consistency. Report Kuder-Richardson 20, corrected split-half coefficients, and
  standard error of measurement. The reliability coefficients are generally .85 or
  higher.
Other services. Item analysis; diagnostic reading and arithmetic tests (two levels,
  2.5–4.5 and 4.5–8.5), modern math concepts test (two levels, 5–6, 7–9).
Suggested uses. Measure achievement level; cumulative measurement of
  growth; diagnosis of strengths and weaknesses; selection and placement;
  curriculum planning and evaluation; guidance.

For further information see Mehrens and Lehmann, 1975.

evaluation for a situation where he might conceivably use the test. After you make your evaluation, compare your evaluation to one in another source—for example, the *Mental Measurements Yearbook,* or Mehrens and Lehmann (1975). Such a process will be of greater value than any artificial evaluation that could be made here.

Some further examples of items from standardized achievement tests are shown in Figure 14.2. Although a representative sample of items obviously cannot be presented in so limited a space, the examples should give the reader a feeling for the types of items found in achievement tests. Here, again, there is no substitute for detailed study of the actual test materials.

Tests Used To Facilitate Instruction

Survey batteries are the most widely used standardized achievement tests; however, a variety of other types are also available. Some of these, such as diagnostic tests, readiness measures, and advanced placement exams, are used primarily in educational settings to aid in making particular types of educational decisions. In this section we shall consider tests used primarily to facilitate the instructional *process.* In a later section we will discuss tests that focus on the *outcomes* of the instructional process.

Diagnostic tests   In the teaching of any subject or skill, one encounters some students who have difficulty learning. Some students have trouble with many or all aspects of the material, whereas others seemingly falter over only one or two aspects of the material. However, in basic academic skills, such as reading or mathematics, these difficulties may affect learning in all academic areas. Diagnostic tests have been developed to pinpoint the causes of a student's learning difficulties.

A diagnostic test, therefore, must cover the component abilities necessary for successful performance. Before tests can be built to measure these component abilities the abilities must, of course, be identified. The identification of these component skills will be both an empirical or a logical undertaking. Regardless, several implications pertain. First, the skill must be such that dividing the overall performance into components does not destroy the nature of the total act; if it does, any partitioning of the skill will result in scores that will be of limited usefulness. Second, there will, necessarily, be several subtests or scales, each measuring a single component. Third, the various subtests should be homogeneous or, at least, measure combinations of skills that are, in some respects, inseparable. Fourth, the test battery should be inclusive; if certain fundamental skills are not measured, it will be impossible to ascertain the exact cause of a student's difficulty. Finally, the subtest scores should have implications for remedial work; that is, the appropriate form of remedial treatment should follow directly from the pattern of scores.

Diagnostic tests are most common in reading and arithmetic, primarily because both are fundamental educational skills that can be broken down into component skills (see Appendix B). For example, one diagnostic reading test provides four major scores—word recognition, oral reading, silent reading, and auditory

Figure 14.2 Examples of items on a standardized achievement test: the Intermediate II battery of the Stanford Achievement Test. (Copyright © 1973 by Harcourt Brace Jovanovich, Inc. Reproduced by special permission of the publisher.)

TEST 1: Vocabulary

STEPS TO FOLLOW

I. Listen to each sentence your teacher reads to you.
II. Choose the word from those below that *best* completes each sentence.
III. Look at the answer spaces at the right or on your answer sheet (if you have one).
IV. Fill in the space which has the same number as the word you have chosen.

SAMPLE

The name of a winter month is —

A 1 April   3 January
   2 October   4 June

TEST 2: Reading Comprehension

STEPS TO FOLLOW

I. Read each selection.
II. Read the questions that follow the selection.
III. Choose the *best* answer for each question.
IV. Look at the answer spaces at the right or on your answer sheet (if you have one).
V. Fill in the space which has the same number as the answer you have chosen.

SAMPLES

Joe is often quite tardy. This week, however, he has been on time every day.

A Joe is often —
   1 late   2 ill   3 tired   4 early

B This week he has been —
   5 worse   7 on time
   6 absent   8 late

TEST 4: Mathematics Concepts

STEPS TO FOLLOW

I. Read each statement or question.
II. Decide which answer is *best*.
III. Look at the answer spaces at the right or on your answer sheet (if you have one).
IV. Fill in the space which has the same letter as the letter beside your answer.

SAMPLE

A Which numeral has the greatest value?

   a seven   c eight
   b nine   d three

TEST 5: Mathematics Computation   Part A

STEPS TO FOLLOW

I. Read each mathematical sentence.
II. Decide which of these signs will make it true:
   > is greater than   < is less than   = is equal to
III. Look at the answer spaces at the right or on your answer sheet (if you have one).
IV. Fill in the space which has the same letter as the answer you have chosen.

SAMPLE

A $2 + 4$ ⬤ $4 + 2$

Part B

STEPS TO FOLLOW

I. Work each exercise.
II. Look at the possible answers beside each problem and see if your answer is here.
III. If it is, fill in the space at the right or on your answer sheet (if you have one) which has the same letter as your answer.
IV. If your answer is *Not Here*, fill in the space which has the same letter as the letter beside NH.

SAMPLE

B   25   a 97
         + 73   b 88
                     c 98
                     d 89
                     e NH

TEST 6: Mathematics Applications

STEPS TO FOLLOW

I. Solve each problem. Unless you are told otherwise, there is no sales tax.
II. Look at the possible answers under the problem. Is your answer here?
III. If it is, fill in the space at the right or on your answer sheet (if you have one) which has the same letter as your answer.
IV. If your answer is *Not Here*, fill in the space which has the same letter as the letter beside NH.

SAMPLE

A Susan lost 2 beads. She now has 8 left. How many beads did Susan have at first?

   a 4   c 6
   b 12   d 10
                e NH

Figure 14.2 (continued)

TEST 7: Spelling   Part A

STEPS TO FOLLOW (Questions 1-8)
  I. Read each group of phrases. Look at the under-
     lined word in each phrase. One of the underlined
     words is misspelled for the way it is used in the
     phrase.
  II. Find the word that is *not* spelled correctly.
  III. Look at the answer spaces at the right or on your
       answer sheet (if you have one).
  IV. Fill in the space which has the same number as
      the word you have chosen.

SAMPLE

A 1 <u>no</u> school today   3 a honey <u>be</u>
    2 <u>meet</u> at the bus   4 the two <u>dogs</u>

A ① ② ● ④

Part B

STEPS TO FOLLOW (Questions 9-60)
  I. Read each group of words.
  II. Find the misspelled word in each group.
  III. Look at the answer spaces at the right or on your
       answer sheet (if you have one).
  IV. Fill in the space which has the same number as
      the word you have chosen.

SAMPLE

B 5 cow   7 sky
    6 bagg   8 tell

B ⑤ ● ⑦ ⑧

TEST 8: Language   Part A

STEPS TO FOLLOW (Questions 1-42)
  I. Read each sentence.
  II. Look at the four different ways in which you can
      fill in the blank.
  III. Choose the best form to write in a school paper.
  IV. Look at the answer spaces at the right or on your
      answer sheet (if you have one).
  V. Fill in the space which has the same number as
     the answer you have chosen.

SAMPLES

A My teacher lives on ___
    1 Center street
    2 Center Stree
    3 center street.
    4 center Street.

A ① ● ③ ④

TEST 8: Language   Part C

STEPS TO FOLLOW (Questions 51-70)
  I. Read each group of words.
  II. Fill in, in the spaces at the right or on your answer
      sheet (if you have one), the space for:
      1 if the group of words makes *ONE* complete
        sentence with the addition of a period or ques-
        tion mark
      2 if the group of words makes *TWO OR MORE*
        sentences without changing or omitting any
        words
      N if the group of words is *NOT* a complete sen-
        tence.

SAMPLE

C It was raining
    a 1   b N   c 2

C ● ⓑ ⓒ

TEST 9: Social Science

STEPS TO FOLLOW
  I. Read each question.
  II. Choose the *best* answer.
  III. Look at the answer spaces at the right or on your
       answer sheet (if you have one).
  IV. Fill in the space which has the same number as
      the answer you have chosen.

SAMPLE

A Which one of the following is a continent?
    1 England   3 Mexico
    2 Africa   4 Canada   **A** ① ● ③ ④

TEST 10: Science

STEPS TO FOLLOW
  I. Read each question.
  II. Choose the *best* answer.
  III. Look at the answer spaces at the right or on your
       answer sheet (if you have one).
  IV. Fill in the space which has the same number as
      the answer you have chosen.

SAMPLE

A The sun is a —
    1 planet   3 comet
    2 star   4 meteor   **A** ① ● ③ ④

TEST 11: Listening Comprehension

Listen while I read the sample story. It says:

> After school, John went to the store. He
> took a loaf of bread home and then he
> went to Ken's home.

The question is: "After school, where did John go
first? 1 home, 2 the library, 3 the store, 4 Ken's
home." Which of the answers tells where John went
first?

① ② ● ④

comprehension—plus supplementary measures of rate of silent reading and phonics. Another measures word recognition, comprehension, vocabulary, rate of reading, story comprehension, and both oral and silent word-attack skills. Although these tests may not measure the basic components of reading in the ideal sense discussed above, use of subtests provides a more thorough understanding of a student's reading skills than a survey measure of reading speed and/or comprehension.

Interpretation of diagnostic tests should be done by a person who has a thorough grounding in testing, the learning process, and the subject matter covered by the test. The test interpreter must be knowledgeable of testing in order to place the psychometric characteristics of the test (for example, the intercorrelations between subtests, reliability of difference scores) in the proper perspective and to make sense out of patterns and profiles of scores. And, unless the interpreter understands the process of learning the skill (for example, reading or arithmetic), he will not be able to make meaningful suggestions for remedial programs. In most circumstances, these requirements mean that the test should be administered and interpreted by a school psychologist or a child clinical psychologist.

Readiness measures   Readiness tests, like diagnostic tests, are generally concerned with fundamental skills, particularly reading. The basic question to be answered by readiness tests is: "Does the student possess the necessary skills to succeed in a particular educational task?" In other words, is he ready to start to study a particular skill? Therefore, a readiness test is really a predictive or prognostic device. Hence validity is determined by its effectiveness in separating students who are ready for instruction in the relevant area from those who are not.

The first step in test construction, thus, is to identify the skills that are predictive of success. These skills may be of various sorts. In some instances, they may be general intellectual or physical abilities; for example, before a child can learn to read, his visual discrimination must be developed to a level at which he can discriminate between printed letters. In other instances, the indication may be possession of an appropriate fund of knowledge; for example, a student must be able to count before he can learn to add, and know the names of objects and meanings of words before he can learn to read. One can also conceive of attitudes and predispositions toward learning and attacking problems as being essential aspects of readiness.

Viewed in this framework, any pretest or aptitude test used to predict success in a course or educational program is a type of readiness measure. However, readiness tests are usually encountered at the preschool and kindergarten age levels, where the interest is in determining readiness to begin formal educational programs, particularly instruction in reading. Since readiness tests are designed for use with children who have not yet learned to read, they will, necessarily, involve nonverbal materials. Thus reading readiness tests usually consist of pictorial and symbolic materials administered with oral directions; the directions instruct the child to mark or otherwise indicate one of the objects pictured. (See Figure 14.3 and Appendix B.)

A. Student marks the object mentioned in a statement (story) read by the teacher (e. g, "Mary took her dog for a walk") Designed to measure simple sentence recall and listening discrimination.

B. Student marks picture of word that starts with same sound as stimulus picture (i.e., fish and finger start with same sound). Measures discrimination of sounds.

Figure 14.3 Example of items from a readiness test. From the communication skills section of "Instructional and Assessment Materials for First Graders" (prepared for Board of Education of the City of New York by the Educational Testing Service). Reprinted by permission of the Board of Education, City of New York.

One word of caution should be interjected regarding the use of readiness measures. Since these tests are typically administered to children whose test-taking skills are undeveloped, whose attention span is short, and whose emotional behavior is often erratic, the test results may well present a misleading picture of the child. Thus decisions about the child's readiness should never be based solely on tests; rather the test results should be supplemented by other information, such as observations by teachers and parents.

Advanced placement examinations   These examinations are designed to establish a student's competency (proficiency) in a given content domain, thus allowing him to be placed at an advanced level of a course, rather than repeating material that he has already mastered. Hence the label "advanced placement" exam. These examinations are typically administered at the college level and cover materials presented in widely taught courses. In essence, they are standardized course examinations.

The best known advanced placement exams are those administered by the Committee on Advanced Placement of the College Entrance Examination Board. At present, twelve exams are available in diverse subjects—including, for example, Chemistry, European History, French, Physics, Latin. Each examination is three hours in length and is predominantly essay questions; some exams, however, are supplemented by objective questions, and the modern language tests include listening comprehension sections. The exams are graded on a five-point scale by special committees of secondary school and college teachers. The results are sent to the college the student enters and the individual college decides whether to grant credit and/or advanced placement.

By providing a student with a means for demonstrating his competency in an area, advanced placement exams allow for flexibility in educational planning by allowing students to advance in accordance with their abilities, rather than be required to take courses that repeat material already learned. By combining the test development skills of a test publisher with local standards for interpreting scores, the *Advanced Placement Exams* provide the test user with the best of both worlds. It should be noted, however, that many colleges use other standardized tests, or locally constructed achievement tests, to serve the same placement and credit-awarding functions.

Measures of Educational Outcomes

The tests discussed in the preceding section all were designed for use in planning and facilitating instruction. In addition, there also are tests that are used to measure the results of formal and informal educational experiences—that is, to measure educational outcomes or outputs (Astin and Panos, 1971). Some of the tests are used to award credit for informal educational experiences. Others are used primarily in research evaluating educational programs. Still others are used to establish an individual's proficiency in an educational or occupational specialty. The common thread in all these testing programs is that they measure status; that is, they are summative evaluations, designed to determine whether an individual possesses certain essential knowledge and/or skills.

One example is the *College Level Examination Program* (CLEP), sponsored by the College Board. These examinations were developed to serve the college student who is following a nontraditional pattern (that is, a pattern other than high school immediately followed by college). Thus, they are used for such purposes as establishing the level of educational attainment of adults returning to college, who, through independent study or vocational experiences, have developed knowledge and skills equivalent to those taught in college-level courses. They can also be used to measure knowledge at a transition point—for example, at the end of the sophomore year of college or at the completion of junior college.

There are two types of exams: general and subject matter. The general exams measure achievement in broad areas of liberal arts (English Composition, Humanities, Mathematics, Natural Sciences, and Social Sciences–History) and are multiple-choice exams, 60 to 75 minutes in length. The subject examinations consist of a 90-minute multiple-choice section and an optional essay exam of the same length. The exams are designed to measure basic facts and concepts and the ability to apply these facts and concepts to the solution and interpretation of problems. Currently there are exams available for approximately 30 undergraduate courses.

Vocational proficiency tests   Although we generally think of achievement tests in connection with education, they are also used in industrial, military, and professional settings—for example, the tests given in training programs. These tests generally are comparable to classroom exams, but in on-going training programs involving large numbers of persons, as in the military and large corporations, the tests used may well be standardized. Achievement tests are also used for selection and placement in business and industry—for example, typing tests used in civil service exams. Achievement tests are also used as a basis for promotion in many civil service and military positions.

Achievement tests are also used for licensing or certification in certain professions—such as medicine, law, accounting, and engineering. Generally the examination is only one part of the licensing procedure, education and experience requirements also being used. The basic assumption when achievement tests are used for certification is, of course, that there are certain skills or knowledge that an individual must possess if he is to engage successfully in a given occupation or practice a particular profession. The achievement test serves as a mechanism for determining whether the individual possesses these competencies. Depending on the particular circumstances (for example, what occupation, whether the governing board is local or national) the examination may be informal and *ad hoc*, a standardized test, or, most commonly, something in between.

Proficiency exams are ideal for a criterion-referenced approach to measurement. The reasons are obvious. When establishing proficiency, we must first define what knowledge and skills the individual must possess. This is analogous to defining behavioral objectives for job performance. The test, then, can be constructed to sample these competencies.[9] Thus we have criterion-referenced measurement. A number of projects (for example, ETS's National Occupational Competency Testing Program; ETS, 1973) are now under way to develop such tests. Some of these projects focus primarily on minority group and disadvantaged workers, but others concern professions, such as teaching and counseling.

Research uses of achievement tests One final utilization of standardized achievement measures should be mentioned—that of assessing the achievement of broad samples of students as a basis for evaluating learning and instruction. An example is the International Studies of Achievement, in mathematics (Husén, 1967) and reading (Thorndike, 1973). In the mathematics study, a standardized paper-and-pencil mathematics achievement examination was administered to students in various countries to assess their proficiency in mathematics. A variety of other data (on the characteristics of the schools, students, and teaching methods) were also collected in an attempt to identify the factors that determined the level of mathematics achievement in the various countries. The reading study had a similar design.

Another illustration is the National Assessment of Educational Progress (Womer, 1970a, 1970b). This program involves the administration of achievement tests to a representative sample of U.S. children and adults. Tests in ten areas (literature, science, social studies, writing, citizenship, music, mathematics, reading, art, and vocational education) are being administered to students of four age levels (9, 13, 17, and young adult). The major purpose of the assessment is to ascertain the level of achievement in various curricular areas of U.S. students of different ages. Besides providing needed baseline data, periodic retesting will allow for identification of changes in the competencies of U.S. schoolchildren. The emphasis of the assessment is on competencies, and thus measurement is criterion-referenced and results are reported in terms of group averages (percent of students passing each item) rather than of individual students.

EVALUATION OF ACHIEVEMENT TESTS

Having discussed both teacher-built and standardized achievement tests, we shall now review some major points and provide some integration by looking at the major issues in achievement testing and evaluating the technical quality of standardized achievement tests.

Issues in Achievement Testing

Standardized achievement tests have been criticized from several quarters and for a variety of reasons (see, e.g., Hoffmann, 1961, 1962; Black, 1963; Skinner, 1968). One set of criticisms revolves around the fact that standardized achievement batteries rely almost exclusively on multiple-choice items. Critics point out that not

[9]For this reason, such tests are often referred to as competency-based tests.

only do multiple-choice items not measure certain important skills (for example, integration, evaluation, and creativity), but that the item format also has certain imperfections (for example, items may be ambiguous or penalize students with a greater depth of knowledge). The conclusion of many of these critics seems to be that multiple-choice questions should be replaced by a better type of item. What this new type of item would be often is not clear; presumably it would be some form of a free response item.

There are, however, two points that must be emphasized. For one, it is not feasible to conduct a large-scale testing program using free response items because of the grading problems (both time, and thus money, and score unreliability).[10] Second, there is the learning-testing distinction mentioned earlier. It is clear that the results of learning can be assessed by methods different from the method used when learning. Therefore, if the goal of testing is to measure what a student knows or can do, there is no reason why the test must involve the same procedures as the learning process. Critics who point out that the multiple-choice approach cannot produce certain desired learnings may be correct; however, it does not follow that the results of some of these learning experiences cannot be assessed with objective tests.

Another set of issues revolves around the questions of whether standardized tests determine the curricula and whether teachers teach to tests. This view presumes that teachers will be evaluated in terms of their students' performance. Thus, to make themselves look good, teachers will teach to the test, stressing the materials that they know (or presume) will be covered on the test and neglecting other equally important materials. Although some teachers, no doubt, try to teach toward tests, the incidence of such behavior is unknown but probably overestimated. In addition, the evidence from coaching studies would indicate that such attempts to influence scores are likely to be unsuccessful.

Note also that this view assumes that the test measures outcomes other than the important outcomes of education. In fact, one sometimes hears that standardized tests are worthless because they measure what test publishers are interested in, not what educators say are the important outcomes. Such arguments only betray the ignorance of their proponents because, as was mentioned earlier, the content of achievement batteries is determined by subject matter experts, not psychologists and test specialists. And, although test publishers may claim that their tests reflect classroom practices, they may, in fact, lead classroom practices. If they lead, then, in effect, they do determine curricula. But the overriding issue is not whether tests lead or follow classroom practices but whether the test content reflects important educational outcomes.

Still another aspect of the testing-curricula relationship is the proper use of achievement batteries in evaluating teachers, instructional methods, curricula, and school systems (see, e.g., Astin and Panos, 1971; Wittrock and Wiley, 1970). Because many studies using achievement tests to evaluate instruction have involved faulty design, teachers justifiably have negative attitudes toward such evaluations.

---

[10]There are exceptions—for example, the Advanced Placement Tests—in which essay items are used. However, even in this case, the grading problem remains.

The point that we would stress, however, is that such evaluations, when conducted according to the principles of good experimental design and used in conjunction with other relevant evidence, can provide an important source of data for evaluating educational programs. However, *ad hoc* comparisons of fortuitously collected data are generally of little, if any, value and may be detrimental.

A third issue in achievement testing is just beginning to arise (see Bloom et al., 1971; Block, 1971, 1974; Carver, 1974; Gagné, 1967; Glaser, 1963, 1972). Most of the tests that we have discussed are based on an individual difference or discrimination model. That is, the tests are built to maximize differences between individuals—that is, to discriminate between individuals. An opposing view holds that the function of achievement tests is to indicate whether the student has mastered certain important knowledge and skills. Thus, if the purpose of a unit of instruction is to teach students the proper uses of ''who'' and ''whom,'' the test should indicate whether they have learned this distinction. Items would be chosen to represent the variety of situations where the two words might be used—a procedure similar to the traditional model. But, in this view, if every student obtained 100 percent accuracy on the test it would only show that all students had mastered the material and that the teaching had been effective. The fact that the test did not discriminate among students with differing degrees of knowledge would be unimportant and irrelevant. In short, the testing goal is to obtain knowledge regarding mastery of the important subject matter, not to discriminate between students.

This criterion-referenced or mastery view, of course, assumes that there are basic units of knowledge and skills to be learned, that these can be identified, and that items can be constructed to measure them—assumptions that also hold for tests constructed in the traditional manner. It differs from the traditional model by denying that the criterion of discrimination between students has any relevance. The emphasis, in short, is on mastery, not individual differences.

Psychometric Properties

Of all the varieties of psychological and educational tests, standardized achievement measures have, by and large, attained higher standards of consistency, validity, and normative data than any other type of test. This is not to say that all standardized achievement measures are satisfactory; far from it. Rather, there are a number of standardized achievement tests on the market, particularly survey tests, that are highly reliable ($r_{xx} > .90$), have content and predictive validity, and provide normative data from representative samples of the population. Thus a potential user has a high probability of finding a carefully constructed and technically satisfactory achievement test.

Yet there are several ways in which standardized achievement tests could be improved. Consider, first, normative data. Although the task of collecting normative data is somewhat easier on achievement tests, because of the ''captive'' nature of the population being sampled (persons attending school), these data are likely to underrepresent lower socioeconomic and disadvantaged groups. And since the education of these children will probably be inferior to those of their more privileged contemporaries, the available normative data may be inappropriate for these groups. Second, scores are usually norm-referenced rather than content-referenced, even though the latter have certain advantages in educational settings. And, third, normative data are usually presented for national samples or samples designated in some gross manner (by geographic region, size of school), thus necessitating the construction of local norms.

One might also hope for more diversity in approaches to measuring achievement. Most standardized achievement tests are composed primarily of objective items presented in a paper-and-pencil format. Furthermore, all students take the same items in the same sequence. Consequently, skills that are not tapped by objective items are not measured and the flexibility in adapting a test to an individual may be limited.

The use of other types of items remains a problem due to the difficulties in scoring nonobjective items. Although a number of research projects being conducted attempt to objectify the scoring of essay exams (see, e.g., Coffman, 1966), and even to use computers to grade nonobjective items (Page, 1967), at present there is no feasible alternative to recognition items. Unless a new form of item is developed, evaluation of these other skills will have to be based on techniques other than standardized tests.

The other problem, adapting the test to the individual, appears closer to solution. One approach is to use that used by the College Level Exams, to design tests that can be used to evaluate nontraditional learning experiences. Another approach is to use *sequential testing* methods (see, e.g., Weiss, 1974). In this approach the answer an individual gives to one item determines which of several items will be presented next in sequence. Thus, for example, if we start with an item of a particular difficulty level, persons passing this first item would be directed to an item at the next highest difficulty level, whereas persons failing the item would be directed to another item of the same difficulty or even an easier item, depending on their response to the first item. In this way, the person's level of competence can be established with a minimum number of questions. The salient features of this approach are that the response to one item determines which item is administered next; there must be a logical framework for sequencing items, for example, by their difficulty; and individuals will go through different sequences of items. The procedure is similar to that used in a programmed textbook using branching methods. Although sequential tests have been presented in paper-and-pencil format, they are ideally suited for presentation by computer (see, e.g., Glaser, 1968; Atkinson, 1968). It seems a safe bet to assume that more computer-based sequential tests will be developed in coming years.

15

MEASURES OF GENERAL INTELLECTUAL ABILITY

Having discussed both teacher-built and standardized achievement tests, we now turn to other types of maximal performance measures—ability and aptitude tests. We shall not maintain any fine distinction between aptitude and ability tests since in many ways they are more similar than different. For example, at the operational level, both have similar content and formats. At a more theoretical level, both aptitude and ability tests serve as signs, since the domain being measured often is not clearly circumscribed. They differ primarily in their uses; that is, ability tests describe present status and aptitude tests predict future performance.

In our presentation we shall start with the broadest measures, tests of general intellectual abilities, then proceed to more and more specific measures. What we are calling general intellectual ability is what most people refer to as intelligence. But, as we shall see, there are other measures of general intellectual ability than intelligence tests. However, because of the prominence of the term "intelligence," it would be well to consider briefly what the term means.

What is Intelligence?

Intelligence is one of those terms that everyone thinks he understands yet few people can define precisely. My dictionary defines it as:

> a) the ability to learn or understand from experience; ability to acquire and maintain knowledge; mental ability. b) the ability to respond quickly and successfully to a new situation; use of the faculty of reasoning in solving problems, directing conduct, etc. effectively. (*Webster's New World Dictionary*, 1966, p. 760)

Note that this definition includes a variety of, albeit related, skills: the ability to learn or acquire knowledge, the ability to retain knowledge, reasoning ability, and the ability to respond to new situations. Note, also, that in each case intelligence is referred to as an ability, thus implying that it is a stable characteristic of the person (a trait).

Most people would probably say that this is a fairly accurate definition of intelligence. They might quibble about some aspects of the definition, or include other abilities, but, by and large, it would be satisfactory. Or if you asked a person how he would identify intelligent people, he would probably use criteria similar to those mentioned in this definition.

The same dictionary, however, includes a third definition of intelligence:

> c) in *psychology*, measured success in using these abilities to perform certain tasks. (*Webster's New World Dictionary*, 1966, p. 760)

This is a very important addition, and one that is often overlooked. Note what this part of the definition says. First, it says that intelligence is "measured success in using these abilities." What does this mean? It means that intelligence is an observable and measurable characteristic. Although we may postulate some underlying ability, we can only measure observable manifestations of the ability. That is, intelligence is indicated by the ability to perform. Perform what? Here the definition is not much help: It merely says "certain tasks." However, the implication is that only performance on certain types of tasks is considered to be a sign of intelligent behavior. Some indication of the sorts of tasks that fall under the tent of intelligence was provided in our discussion of theories of mental structure (in Chapter 12); our discussion in this chapter will further define the nature of these tasks.

To summarize, intelligence, to the psychologist, is the ability to perform certain types of tasks. This is the basis for one frequently heard definition: "Intelligence is what an intelligence test measures." As we shall see, the particular tasks have been selected because they provide useful information (for example, predict academic success), or meet certain theoretical criteria (for example, improve with age).

Why, then, is there so much controversy over intelligence tests? One reason is that people do not agree on what tasks should be considered as indications of intelligence. Thus, we frequently hear the complaint that intelligence tests do not measure certain abilities. For example, intelligence tests have been criticized because they emphasize convergent rather than divergent thinking. This argument is true, but it misses the point. The fact that intelligence tests do not measure creative abilities does not imply that creative abilities are unimportant; it only indicates that they must be measured by other types of instruments.

Another reason for disagreement is the confusion between the measured performance and the (hypothetical) underlying ability. If we conceive of intelligence as an index of performance on a certain set of tasks (one of many possible sets of tasks), there should be little controversy. However, most people think of intelligence in terms of the presumed underlying characteristics of the person. Furthermore, these underlying characteristics are seen as the cause of behavior. However, psychologists prefer not to think in this manner. They prefer to view intelligence as a description of the person's level of performance, not as a causal agent (see, e.g., Howe, 1972, Chapter 6).

Developed Abilities

The previous paragraphs should have made one point clear: Scores on an intelligence test are an index of the level of development of certain abilities. Similarly, all other measures of maximal performance can be considered indices of the level of developed skills. The emphasis on the word "developed" is deliberate, to imply that past learning and experience determine the present level of performance. Although test scores indicate the person's current ability, we often cannot interpret the meaning of the performance without knowing how he got there; that is, what opportunities did he have to develop proficiency in the skill?

If we are only interested in obtaining an index of the individual's current status (level of skill), there is no problem. Similarly, if we want to predict future performance, we have few problems; we just use the score as a predictor. However, when we want to understand the reasons for a person's performance the situation becomes more complex. Here we are interested in more than just the score obtained on a particular testing; we want to know why the particular score was obtained. As indicated previously, any score will be a function of the person's inherited potentials, his learning and experiences prior to testing, and the testing conditions. Usually the testing effects are controlled by standardization procedures. However, this may not always be the case—for example, if a maximal performance set is not adopted by the test taker. Then, too, we seldom, if ever, have any direct knowledge of the person's genetic potential. Usually, however, we do have some knowledge of the person's past experiences, at least his formal educational opportunities. This information can be of use in interpreting performance. If all test takers have had similar experiences, test scores should reflect differences in their abilities. If their past experiences differ widely (as, for example, when some test takers are from disadvantaged backgrounds), we must be more cautious when interpreting scores.

Implicit in the previous discussion is one further point. To say that a test measures developed abilities implies that the test taker may not have reached his maximal level of development; given further experiences or training, his ability may develop to a higher level. Whether he, in fact, will continue developing depends both on his prior experiences and the nature of further training. To illustrate, a child who comes from a home where reading and verbal skills are not stressed will probably score low on a vocabulary test; given further training, his score might improve greatly. Thus, his score would not reflect his potential. In contrast, when testing children who have had the opportunity to develop their verbal skills, the test can be a good measure of differences in ability.

In short, a test score indicates the test taker's level of performance of a particular skill at the time of testing; it measures his development to that point. To understand why his development (score) is at that level requires consideration of other factors—primarily his opportunities to learn the skill.

INDIVIDUAL INTELLIGENCE TESTS

Throughout the twentieth century, attempts to measure intellectual ability (intelligence) have played a preeminent role in psychological testing (J. Edwards, 1971; Goslin, 1963). In earlier years the idea of general intelligence held forth; during the past three or four decades attention has focused on the variety of intellectual abilities. However, measures of general intellectual ability are still widely used and, in spite of their theoretical deficiencies, have shown practical utility (McNemar, 1964; J. Edwards, 1975). Thus, we shall describe, in detail, the most important individual intelligence tests.[1]

The Stanford-Binet Intelligence Scale

The Stanford-Binet Intelligence Scale is the healthiest surviving direct descendent of Binet's original scale. Binet originally developed his test to identify slow learners in Paris schools. Using a definition of intelligent behavior that stressed the ability to take and maintain a definite direction or set, the capacity to adapt in order to obtain a given end, and the power of self-criticism, he developed a test that was first published in 1905 and later revised in 1908 and 1911. Although the test departed from then current practices along many dimensions, three aspects were of greatest import: (1) using complex tasks as test items; (2) using age standards; and (3) measuring general mental development rather than separate mental faculties.

Early forms   As the test became popular, several attempts were made to translate the test and adapt it for American usage. Terman's version, first published in 1916, and known as the Stanford-Binet, was most successful. Terman's test was an extension and improvement on Binet's scale and, in many respects, uses Binet's scale only as a point of departure. The 1916 version was important for several reasons. It was the first test to provide detailed administrative and scoring instructions, recognizing that variations along these dimensions could produce wide differences in scores. Second, the concept of the IQ was introduced. And, third, the

[1]For more detailed descriptions see J. Edwards, 1971, 1972, 1975; Terman and Merrill, 1960; Wechsler, 1958; Matarazzo, 1972.

need for securing a representative sample of subjects for standardizing the test was recognized.

In the 1937 revision, two forms of the test were constructed—L and M. Each form covered the age range from 2 years to adult and was standardized on more than 3000 children (ages 1½–18). Selection of items was based on three criteria: (1) The item measured behavior considered intelligent; (2) the percentage of children passing the item increased rapidly with age; and (3) the mean mental age of children passing and failing the item differed significantly. The 1937 (second) revision of the Stanford-Binet was undoubtedly the best measure of children's intellectual ability then available, but it suffered several technical limitations (in the composition of the standardization sample and the IQ distribution). The test was also heavily loaded with verbal materials, to the exclusion of items measuring other types of intellectual functioning, and the administrative procedure was time-consuming. But compared to the earlier form of the Stanford-Binet and other available intelligence tests, the 1937 revision sampled a wider range of abilities, covered a broader age range, and provided more detailed instructions for administration and scoring.

The 1960 revision   When making a decision regarding the desirability of revising an existing test, a test constructor must weigh the advantages of a revision—such as elimination of obsolete materials and utilization of new techniques—against the disadvantages of such a revision—such as the time and cost of the revision and the need to collect new normative, reliability, and validity data (Anastasi, 1968; Terman and Merrill, 1960). When faced with this question, the authors of the Stanford-Binet chose updating materials and rechecking item effectiveness rather than attempting a complete revision and restandardization. The result was the publication of a single scale, Form LM, incorporating the best items from Forms L and M.

Rather than an entirely new standardization sample, the data for the revision were based on the responses of approximately 4500 persons (ages 2½–18) who had taken Form L or M between 1950 and 1954. Although this sample was not a representative sample of American schoolchildren, and was drawn from only six states, care was taken to avoid obviously selective factors. Several analyses were run on each item. First, item difficulties were computed and items reassigned to appropriate age levels. Second, the percentages of children passing each item at each age level was determined and new growth curves developed. The correlations between item and total scores were computed and used as an index of internal consistency. Analyses were also conducted for several regional and socioeconomic classes to ensure that items did not discriminate unfairly against certain children. The content of some items was updated. A number of other special analyses were also performed. (See Terman and Merrill, 1960, or J. Edwards, 1972, for details.)

Form LM   Items[2] on Form LM are grouped into twenty age levels. At the youngest age levels, from ages 2 through 5, there is a separate set of items for each 6

[2]We shall use the term "item" to describe the tasks on the Stanford-Binet even though some tasks consist of a series of items and are actually more like subtests.

months; from age 5 through 14, there is a set of items for each year. In addition, there is an Average Adult plus three Superior Adult levels. At each level, except Average Adult, there are six subtests plus an alternate subtest. A given subtest may appear at only one age level or occur at several age levels, with different levels of proficiency being required for passing at different age levels. For example, the Vocabulary subtest appears at age levels VI, VIII, X, XII, XIV plus the four adult levels. At age 6, successfully defining 6 words constitutes success; at the Superior Adult III level, 30 of the 45 items must be correctly defined in order to pass the subtest.

The composition of the test can best be appreciated by actual study of the test items. To give a flavor of the items, Table 15.1 briefly describes the items at four age levels. Some of the distinct features of the test can be noted from this sample of items. Note that at Age II the test items involve sensory-motor skills, the ability to follow directions, and identification of objects and parts of the body; verbal and language skills play a minor role. By Age VI the tests are heavily weighted with verbal skills (Vocabulary, Analogies, Differences), and discriminations (Differences, Mutilated Pictures) and numerical concepts begin to appear. Age X again emphasizes verbal skills but many of the items now involve abstract concepts rather than relying on concrete experience (as at Age VI). By the Average Adult level the test materials are almost entirely verbal, symbolic, and abstract.

The Stanford-Binet must be administered individually and, because of the complexity of the testing procedures, requires a trained examiner. Testing begins at the age level at which "the child is likely to succeed, but not without some effort" (Terman and Merrill, 1960, p. 59). Typically this will be the age level immediately lower than the child's chronological age. Explicit directions for administering the items (for example, the exact wording to be used) are provided in the manual. The testing proceeds, alternating age levels, until every set of items from the highest age level at which all items are completed successfully (the *basal age*) through the lowest age at which all items are failed (the *ceiling or maximal age*) have been administered. Because testings continue until the basal and ceiling ages are reached, especially with brighter children the testing sessions are often quite long— frequently an hour and a half or longer.

Scoring   The correctness of each response is determined by comparing it to a list of correct responses in the test manual. Scoring is on an all-or-none basis, with no partial credit. Scores are translated into an age scale by assigning a certain number of months credit to each correct answer. These credits, when added to the basal age, give the *mental age* of the subject.

Because of certain problems (equating the distributions of IQs at various age levels and the nonlinearity of the mental growth curve), the 1960 revision uses deviation IQs rather than the ratio IQs used on previous forms (see Terman and Merrill, 1960, or Pinneau, 1961, for details). These deviation IQs are normalized standard scores with a mean of 100 and a standard deviation of 16 points. The use of deviation IQs ensures that any given IQ will represent the same relative position within any age level.

Thus there are two distinct, though related, ways of interpreting performance on

TABLE 15.1   Examples of items on the Stanford-Binet Intelligence Scale.

AGE II

1. Three-hole Form Board. Placing three geometric objects in form board.
2. Delayed Response. Identifying placement of hidden object after 10-second delay.
3. Identifying Parts of the Body. Point out features on paper doll.
4. Block Building Tower. Build four-block tower by imitating examiner's procedure.
5. Picture Vocabulary. Naming common objects from pictures.
6. Word Combinations. Spontaneous combination of two words.

AGE VI

1. Vocabulary. Correctly define six words on 45-word list.
2. Differences. Telling difference between two objects.
3. Mutilated Pictures. Pointing out missing part of pictured object.
4. Number Concepts. Counting number of blocks in a pile.
5. Opposite Analogies II. Items of form "Summer is hot; winter is _____."
6. Maze Tracing. Finding shortest path in simple maze.

AGE X

1. Vocabulary. Correctly define 11 words on same list.
2. Block Counting. Counting number of cubes in three-dimensional picture, some cubes hidden.
3. Abstract Words I. Definition of abstract adverbs.
4. Finding Reasons I. Giving reasons for laws or preferences.
5. Word Naming. Naming as many words as possible in one minute.
6. Repeating six digits. Repeat six digits in order.

AVERAGE ADULT

1. Vocabulary. 20 words correct.
2. Ingenuity I. Algebraic word problems involving mental manipulation of volumes.
3. Differences between Abstract Words. Differentiate between two related abstract words.
4. Arithmetical Reasoning. Word problems involving simple computations.
5. Proverbs I. Giving meaning of proverbs.
6. Orientation: Direction II. Finding orientation after a verbal series of changes in directions.
7. Essential Differences. Give principle difference between two related concepts.
8. Abstract Words III. Meanings of abstract adverbs.

the Binet. The *mental age* gives an indication of the level of intellectual development; the *IQ* indicates the relative rate of intellectual development (compared to agemates). Although both mental age and IQ are normative scores, being based on the performance of a standard sample of children, a mental age score can also be interpreted in terms of the type and complexity of tasks the child can perform.[3] In that sense, mental ages can be interpreted as a content-referenced score.

Consistency and validity   Data from extensive studies of Form L and M indicated that the coefficient of equivalence was generally .90 or higher with children aged 5 or older; other studies have shown test-retest reliabilities of similar magnitude (see J. Edwards, 1972). These levels of reliability can be translated in a standard error of measure of approximately 5 IQ points. In general, reliability is higher for older than younger children and for children having lower rather than higher IQs. The method of item selection, requiring each item to correlate with the total score, assures that the test will be homogeneous. And, of course, the method of deriving IQs assures that the average level of performance will remain constant from year to year.

Since the Binet can most appropriately be viewed as a sign of intelligent behavior, construct validity becomes the central issue. Here several lines of evidence are relevant. The authors state that intelligent behavior is exhibited in the solution of problems such as analogies, opposites, vocabulary, comprehension, similarities and differences, absurdities, completion of verbal and pictorial materials, and memory for rote and meaningful materials. Thus, there is an implicit definition of the content universe sampled, one that is heavily weighted with verbal reasoning abilities. The item selection criteria (age differentiation, internal consistency) also serve to define the construct of intelligence. Second, factor analyses have shown that performance on the Stanford-Binet reflects a general factor, verbal reasoning, but that other abilities (for example, memory, perception) influence performance at certain age levels. Finding a general factor should not be surprising as one criterion for items was that they correlated highly with the total score. Third, criterion-related validity studies have shown that Stanford-Binet IQs correlate with a variety of measures of academic accomplishment (for example, grades, years of education, teachers' ratings, achievement test scores) and that the correlations are usually slightly higher for verbal areas (for example, English, history, reading) than in mathematics and science areas.

In short, the Stanford-Binet is an accurate measure of the intellectual abilities, particularly verbal abilities, of school-aged children. Because of its technical quality, plus its historical importance, it has come to serve as *the* standard for measuring intelligence, the standard against which all other purported measure of intelligence must be calibrated. Thus the strengths and limitations of the Stanford-Binet approach to measuring intelligence are, to a considerable extent, reflected in many other instruments.

The Wechsler Scales

The Stanford-Binet has certain drawbacks as a measure of adult intelligence: The items were developed for children and some are inappropriate for adults; the

---

[3]For example, a child with a mental age of five would be expected to define simple words, identify parts of the body, fold a piece of paper into a triangle, draw a square, and note similarities and differences in line drawings of common objects.

mental age concept is of questionable utility with adults; and the normative data were collected on children, not adults. For these and other reasons, David Wechsler developed a scale for measuring adult intelligence, the Wechsler-Bellevue Intelligence Scale, first published in 1939. In 1955 this scale was modified and restandardized as the Wechsler Adult Intelligence Scale (WAIS).

Wechsler's approach   Several predominant considerations shaped Wechsler's tests. One was that the content and scoring procedures be appropriate for adults and that the normative data based on adult samples. Second, by defining intelligence as "the aggregate or global capacity of the individual to act purposefully, to think rationally, and to deal effectively with his environment" (Wechsler, 1958, p. 7), Wechsler adopts a general intelligence approach. This view is supported by the statement that the subtests are "different measures of intelligence, not measures of different kinds of intelligence" (Wechsler, 1958, p. 64). Yet, paradoxically, Wechsler also stresses using the test as a diagnostic instrument by using patterns of subtest scores as a basis for making inferences about the individual's intellectual and emotional status. Third, although the IQ is viewed as "a comprehensive statement about the person's overall intellectual functioning ability" (Wechsler, 1958, p. 156), an index of relative brightness compared to age peers, Wechsler also says that intelligence is not the mere sum of abilities tapped by the various subtests. Rather it is the configuration of abilities plus motivational and personality factors that produce intelligent behavior.

The WAIS   The Wechsler Adult Intelligence Scale (WAIS) consists of eleven subtests. Six tests (Information, Comprehension, Arithmetic, Similarities, Digit Span, and Vocabulary) form the *Verbal Scale;* the other five (Digit Symbol, Picture Completion, Block Design, Picture Arrangement, and Object Assembly) comprise the *Performance Scale*. All eleven tests make up the *Full Scale*. (See Table 15.2.)

Within each subtest, items are arranged and administered in (approximate) order of difficulty, with testing being discontinued after a prescribed number of consecutive failures. Some items have time limits; others are untimed. As with the Stanford-Binet, the WAIS is individually administered and requires a trained examiner, and instructions for administration and scoring are spelled out in detail in the manual. The testing session is generally shorter than on the Binet, usually lasting 45 to 60 minutes.

Items are scored by comparing the response to a list of acceptable response variations given in the manual.[4] Points are assigned on the basis of correctness and, on several tests, speed of response. On some tests, differing number of points are awarded depending on the quality of the response. Thus, in contrast to the age scale approach of the Binet, the WAIS is a *point scale* (as are the other Wechsler scales).

Raw scores on each subtest are converted to standard scores ($\bar{X} = 10$ and $s = 3$ points). Subtest standard scores are then summed and converted into three IQ scores: a Verbal IQ, a Performance IQ, and a Full Scale IQ. As test performance

[4]See Figure 2.4, pages 32–33.

TABLE 15.2 Description of WAIS subtests.

VERBAL SCALE

Information: 29 items that measure the range of the examinee's knowledge, retention of learned materials, and assess the examinee's cultural background. Items are of the form "Where does wool come from?" and "Who wrote *Paradise Lost?*"

Comprehension: 14 items measuring judgment and "common sense." Includes translation of proverbs and items of form "Why should children be warned against playing with matches?"

Arithmetic: 14 items testing concentration, arithmetic ability, and problem-solving skill. All items have time limits and are simple word problems; for example, "If I have $15 and earn $8 more, how much money do I now have?"

Similarities: 13 items measuring logical thinking and conceptual ability; a good measure of general intelligence. Items are of the form "In what way are a car and a boat alike?"

Digit Span: Tests attention and immediate memory by items requiring examinee to repeat series of digits either forward or backwards.

Vocabulary: 40 words of varying difficulty. Is the best single index of Full-Scale IQ; indicates range of knowledge and cultural background.

PERFORMANCE SCALE

Digit Symbol: Measures flexibility and ability for new learning through a task requiring the substitution of symbols for numbers. Speeded.

Picture Completion: 21 items that require examinee to tell what is missing in a picture of a common object. Measures perceptual ability, particularly ability to differentiate essential from unessential details.

Block Design: Examinee reproduces designs with colored blocks. Measures ability to analyze and organize. Good test for observing problem-solving strategy as well as distorted perception and visual-motor coordination. Generally considered best single performance test. Time limits.

Picture Arrangement: Requires examinee to arrange a group of pictures (similar to comic strip panels) to tell a coherent story. Measures ability to comprehend a total situation. Bonus points for rapid solutions.

Object Assembly: Task is to assemble pieces of a puzzle to form a common object. Speeded. Tests perceptual ability and persistence.

decreases with age, IQs are computed separately for several age groups;[5] hence, IQs indicate relative standing among age peers. The IQs are deviation IQs with $\bar{X} = 100$ and $s = 15$ (cf. the Stanford-Binet IQ), derived from a normative sample that, in essence, was a cross-section of the U.S. adult population.

[5]IQ conversion tables are presented (Wechsler, 1955) for the following age groups: 16–17, 18–19, 20–24, 25–34, 35–44, 45–54, 55–64, 65–69, 70–74, and 75 and older.

Consistency and validity of the WAIS   The Verbal, Performance, and Full Scale IQs are all highly reliable, with r_{xx} ranging from .93 for the Performance Scale to .97 for the Full Scale IQ (Wechsler, 1955). The corresponding standard errors of measurement range from 2.6 to 4 IQ points. When the WAIS is used as a diagnostic instrument, the questions of subtest reliability and the reliability of subtest difference scores become important. The subtest reliability coefficients range from the upper .60s (for Digit Span, Picture Arrangement, and Object Assembly) to around .95 (for Vocabulary), with the median being in the low .80s. Standard errors of measurement ranged from .7 to 1.7 scaled score points. The distribution of standard errors of differences between pairs of subtest scores had a median of three points, leading Wechsler to conclude: "Differences as large as five points may be unusual enough to be noteworthy" (Wechsler, 1955, p. 18). In other words, unless two subtest scores differ by five or more points, the difference may not be statistically meaningful and thus must be interpreted with caution. Unfortunately, Wechsler (1958) and others who use the WAIS as a diagnostic instrument have ignored this advice and have interpreted much smaller differences as being meaningful differences.

Items were selected for inclusion on the Wechsler scales by studying previous tests to determine what sorts of items best measured intelligent behavior, from clinical experience, and by trying out experimental items on groups having known characteristics. Wechsler has also presented a detailed justification of including each subtest as a measure of intelligence (Wechsler, 1955). Such procedures support the content and construct validity of the WAIS subtests. Although the exact magnitude depends on the group tested, correlations of .80–.85 between WAIS and Stanford-Binet IQs are often found. WAIS scores have also been correlated with a variety of educational and vocational criteria. The weight of the evidence would seem to support the notion that the WAIS measures intelligence.

One might also ask whether separate Verbal and Performance Scales are justified by the empirical evidence. Several types of evidence are relevant here. First, Verbal and Performance IQs usually correlate around .80, indicating that about two-thirds of the variance is common. Second, although scores on the verbal subtests generally correlate higher with the Verbal IQ than with Performance IQ (and vice versa for performance subtests), the difference in correlations are generally low—the median being less than .10. The third line of evidence, factor analysis data, is more complex. A general factor, best labeled general reasoning, is typically found. However, two other factors—a verbal comprehension factor and a nonverbal or performance factor—usually also appear, and a memory factor is sometimes found. To summarize, although there is some support for separate Verbal and Performance scales, the evidence is far from overwhelming. To consider the WAIS as a measure of general intelligence would not be incompatible with the empirical data.

The Wechsler Intelligence Scale for Children (WISC)   The original rationale for constructing the Wechsler-Bellevue, and later the WAIS, was to provide a measure of intellectual ability particularly appropriate for adults. Nevertheless, two tests for children have since been constructed as outgrowths of the adult scales. The first of these, the Wechsler Intelligence Scale for Children (WISC) was an extension, to lower age levels, of the Wechsler-Bellevue. The format of the WISC is similar to the adult scales and only one WISC subtest (Mazes) did not appear on the adult form. Many of the WISC scales were constructed by adding easier items to the adult scale and eliminating some of the more difficult items.

In 1974, a revised version of the WISC (the WISC-R) was published. As with the Stanford-Binet, this revision was more of a restandardization than a massive change. The same subtests were retained, but some items were revised and others were replaced with new items. A more representative normative sample was used for computing IQs. Perhaps the major change was shifting the age range; the WISC is now designed for children aged 6 through 16. As with the WAIS, the WISC-R IQs appear to be highly reliable ($r_{xx} = .90$ or higher). One other welcome addition is tables showing the number of points two subscales and verbal and performance IQs must differ before the difference can be considered significant (Wechsler, 1974, Tables 12 and 13).

Of particular interest is the relationship between WISC and Stanford-Binet IQ scores. Here two facts emerge. First, the two tests are highly intercorrelated, the modal correlation found in various studies being in the .80s. And, second, the range of IQs is greater on the Binet than on the WISC. Brighter children obtain higher IQs on the Binet and duller children score higher on the WISC. This, of course, reflects the difference in the standard deviations of the IQ distributions.

The Wechsler Preschool and Primary Scale of Intelligence   In 1967 another Wechsler scale, the Preschool and Primary Scale of Intelligence (WPPSI) was published. This test is designed for use at ages 4–6½, when the child is beginning his formal schooling and accurate measures of intelligence may play an important part in many critical educational decisions. As is typical of Wechsler's scales, the test was well standardized and the reliabilities of the Verbal, Performance, and Full Scale IQs are quite high, although, as might be expected when testing younger children, the reliability coefficients are slightly lower than those for the WISC and WAIS. The format and subtests are quite similar to the WAIS and WISC, but certain changes have been made (for example, including more nonverbal tasks) to make the test appropriate for preschoolers. In fact, about half of the WPPSI items also appear on the WISC. The goal of the WPPSI, however, is to include only items particularly appropriate to the 4–6½-year age range so that an accurate estimate of the child's intelligence can be made.

The Wechsler and the Stanford-Binet   Before proceeding to a discussion of other measures of general intelligence, it may be well to review and contrast the approach to measurement of intelligence exhibited by the Stanford-Binet and Wechsler scales. Although both are individually administered general intelligence measures, there are a number of major differences between the two scales: (1) The Wechsler tests are arranged and administered by subtests; the Binet by age levels. (2) The Wechsler tests include both verbal and performance tasks; the Binet is heavily verbal in content. (3) The Wechsler scales provide three IQs—Verbal, Performance, and Full Scale—plus ten subtest scores; the Binet provides one overall IQ plus a mental-age score. (4) The Binet is designed primarily for children of ages 2 to 18, but can be administered to adults; the WAIS was designed for adults (age 15 and over), but scales have been developed for children—the WISC-R for ages 6–16 and the WPPSI for ages 4½–6. (5) The Wechsler scales are point scales; the Stanford-Binet an age scale. (6) All subjects are administered identical subtests on the Wechsler scales; on the Stanford-Binet the content varies depending upon the age level. (7) Although both tests take changes in mental growth with age into account (see below), the Binet is primarily concerned with corrections for the differential rates of growth in childhood, whereas the WAIS corrects for the decline in intellectual performance with age. (8) There is greater emphasis on use of the Wechsler scales as diagnostic instruments.

OTHER MEASURES OF GENERAL INTELLECTUAL ABILITY

The Stanford-Binet and Wechsler are only two of the myriad of intelligence tests (Buros, 1974), albeit probably the two most important ones. Both are individually administered general intelligence tests and, in many ways, set the standards for measuring intelligence. However, there are other approaches: group tests, nonverbal or performance measures, tests designed for very young children, and scholastic aptitude tests. As we discuss these types of tests, you should consider how they are similar to and different from the individual measures.

Group Intelligence Tests

The original stimulus for the development of group intelligence tests was World War I, when the United States was faced with the task of mobilizing and organizing millions of men in a short time. Two tasks in particular, the screening out of men whose mental limitations made them unfit for military service and the identification of potential officer candidates, seemed to be appropriate areas for application of the techniques of the then developing field of mental testing. However, use of the available methods for assessing intelligence, individually administered tests like Stanford-Binet, was obviously not feasible. Fortunately a psychologist, Arthur Otis, was developing a group intelligence test and turned his materials over to the armed services. This material was the basis of the Army Alpha test, which became the grandfather of group intelligence tests.

In the 60 years since World War I, many intelligence tests have been developed (see DuBois, 1970, or Goslin, 1963). Group tests share certain common features. First, they can be administered to groups of people, not to just one individual at a time. Group administration permits more efficient testing of large numbers of persons and, because of less complex procedures, a highly trained professional administrator generally is not required. On the other hand, the test usually is administered with a time limit, direct observation of test-taking behavior is not feasible, and certain persons—for example, young children and other persons who cannot read—cannot be tested. Group tests are usually paper-and-pencil tests and use multiple-choice items.

This latter point, the restricted range of item types, is potentially the most serious limitation. Group intelligence tests typically are composed of several types of items: vocabulary, general information, arithmetic, and reasoning. In particular, they are often heavily weighted with vocabulary items, either in the traditional form or variations such as selecting the correct word to use in a sentence or analogies items. The emphasis on vocabulary items reflects the empirical finding that vocabulary is the best single index of intelligence. General information items (''The capital city of France is ————'' and ''The population of the United States is ————'') are included to probe the individual's range of knowledge. Arithmetic items generally involve only simple computations, certainly no more complex than basic algebra. Reasoning items may be either verbal or nonverbal analogies, number series (''What is the next number in the sequence 1, 2, 4, 7, 11, . . . ?''), or other similar items. By and large, group tests include only items that have proved to be valid indices of intellectual ability. The fact that these items (vocabulary, general information, arithmetic, reasoning) are valid indices no doubt reflects the high premium placed on verbal and symbolic tasks in our culture. (See Appendix B for a description of some group intelligence tests.)

Although group intelligence tests were originally designed to be economical substitutes for individual tests, and are still used in this manner, several varieties of group tests have assumed an existence of their own. For example, scholastic aptitude tests (see below) are designed to predict academic success. Other group intelligence measures are also used for industrial and business screening. These tests are generally short (often requiring only 15 to 30 minutes of working time), are constructed along traditional lines, and cover only the commonest components of intellectual ability. In both of these cases, the goal of testing is accurate prediction, rather than adequate sampling, of intellectual abilities. However, scores on these tests generally correlate highly with other measures of general intelligence.

Performance Tests

All of the intelligence tests discussed thus far have been composed wholly, or primarily, of verbal items, and all have relied on verbal directions. But there are several groups for whom verbal testing materials may present problems, such as persons being tested in other than their native language, the very young, the severely mentally retarded, and persons with visual or auditory handicaps. When testing these groups there is need for items that measure the ability to conceptualize, categorize, and do abstract thinking but that do not rely on verbal stimulus materials, response modes, and/or directions. Such tests are nonverbal or performance tests.

Performance tests consist of a variety of items. Some of the most common types are: *form boards,* in which the examinee must place cut-out objects in the corresponding hole on a board, usually within a time limit; *block designs*, in which the examinee reproduces a design using multicolored cubes (as in the Wechsler subtest); *mazes*, in which the examinee traces the shortest path through a maze; and *object assembly* or *puzzles*, in which the examinee must fit pieces together to make an object (as in Wechsler and Binet subtests) or complete a puzzle. Scores on performance tests usually correlate positively with scores on verbal measures of intelligence; however, the correlations generally are such that scores on the two types of tests can be substituted for each other.

The use of nonverbal and performance tests has been decreasing in recent years as, with increasing educational opportunities and decreasing immigration, verbal tests can be appropriately administered to a greater proportion of the population. Then, too, as in our culture measures of verbal ability have proved to be more useful, whenever there is a choice between verbal and nonverbal tests, a verbal measure usually is preferred. Thus, the use of nonverbal and performance tests is confined to testing the very young, the severely handicapped or retarded, and to obtain a "culture-fair" measure of ability.

Preschool and Infant Tests

The testing of infants (children less than 18 months old) and preschool children (ages 18 months to 5 years) present enough special problems to merit separate consideration. One obvious reason is that, typically, children do not learn to read nor write until they are in first grade (about 6 years old). Therefore, tests requiring reading skills are obviously inappropriate for preschool children (and even of questionable appropriateness in primary grades). Furthermore, most young children have not practiced the type of responses required on paper-and-pencil tests. Consequently, even the relatively simple task of making a mark to indicate one of several objects, which is the response format used on many tests at the primary level, may be beyond their grasp. Thus, preschool tests are usually performance tests or ones that require the child to respond orally to orally presented questions.

The typical preschool test, thus, will include some or all of the following item types: perceptual and motor skills (such as block designs, copying patterns or structures, or form boards), simple discriminations (identifying which object in a series is different, and telling how it differs), recognition of incongruities (indicating what is missing or out of place in a picture), naming parts of the body or common objects and/or indicating their function, following simple directions, and tests of immediate memory (for example, repeating words or digits, noticing what object in a group has been removed during a short period when the stimuli has been covered from the subject's view). For examples see Figure 14.3.

Infant tests typically involve assessment of gross and fine motor control, coordinated movements, ability to communicate in language and by other modalities (for example, through gestures or facial expressions), and social responsiveness. (See, e.g., Anastasi, 1968, Chapter 10.)

Most infant and preschool tests, explicitly or implicitly, utilize a developmental approach; that is, they include items measuring skills and abilities that typify children at various developmental stages. The developmental approach places tremendous importance on obtaining satisfactory normative data because if the norm group is not representative, any conclusions drawn about meaning of an individual's scores will be in error. Obtaining a representative sample of preschool children or infants is not an easy task since no single source, such as public schools, is available from which a representative sample of children can be drawn. Too often normative samples are composed of volunteers or drawn from special groups (such as children from a particular clinic)—sources that are likely to be biased in terms of parents' socioeconomic and educational levels.

The age of the examiness also presents certain administrative problems. With infants it may be necessary to observe spontaneous behavior, rather than relying on responses elicited by specific stimuli (items). Young children also have short attention spans, tire easily, may be shy or refuse to interact with the examiner, may prefer to play with the test materials rather than continue with the test, are easily upset, and may otherwise exhibit erratic behavior. Because they have limited conceptions of time, speeded items are generally inappropriate. In addition, scoring of infant and preschool tests often is not objective, frequently being based on ratings derived from behavioral observations. These factors serve to underscore the need for trained and perceptive examiners and to decrease reliability. This lower reliability of infant and preschool tests is well documented by the empirical data.

Because infant and preschool tests generally adopt a developmental approach, an age differentiation criterion can be applied as one approach to determining validity. A second approach would be to relate scores on infant and preschool tests to scores on established intelligence tests taken at later ages. The data from numerous studies show the correlation between scores on infant tests and adolescent or adult intelligence to be essentially zero (see, e.g., Bayley, 1968; McCall, Hogarty, and Hurlburt, 1972). However, correlations between scores obtained during preschool years sometimes correlate as high as .50 to .70 with adolescent IQs. The fact that preschool and infant tests do not predict later IQs with any greater accuracy should not be surprising if one considers the difference in item content between the tests at the various ages and the problems involved in obtaining reliable measures with young children.

Scholastic Aptitude Tests

Scholastic aptitude tests, as their name implies, are designed to predict performance in academic situations. They differ from general intelligence measures primarily by having a more limited focus, that of predicting academic performance. However, since basic intellectual skills are important determiners of success in most educational settings, it would be surprising if the content of scholastic aptitude tests differed markedly from that of general intelligence tests. And, in fact, they are so similar that even an expert would have difficulty categorizing many tests as being either general intelligence measures or scholastic aptitude tests. Yet because of their distinctive features, and the fact that they are the most widely used type of general ability measure, we shall consider scholastic aptitude tests in detail.

Basic features   The fact that scholastic aptitude tests are designed to predict academic accomplishment has several important implications. First, validity will be determined by how well the test predicts relevant academic criteria; that is, the model for evaluation is criterion-related validity. The emphasis on criterion-related validity leads to a second implication: Any item or type of item that predicts scholastic performance is acceptable. Thus, critics who argue against the use of multiple-choice items on scholastic aptitude tests (e.g., Hoffmann, 1962) are missing the point. If multiple-choice items predict academic performance, as in fact they do, they may be properly included in scholastic aptitude tests. This is not to say, however, that the criteria of academic success against which the tests are typically validated (for example, grade points) are without limitation. But this is another question. The standard of effectiveness of the test is how well it predicts the stipulated criterion—no more and no less.

What, then, are the criteria used to validate scholastic aptitude tests? The most obvious and widely used are grades—in specific courses or overall grade point averages. But other criteria are also possible, such as scores on achievement tests, teachers' ratings, completion of an education program, prizes or awards won, or rate of learning. However, for various reasons, validation studies have generally utilized criteria such as grades. Consequently, the tests often predict a particular type of educational accomplishment, grade-getting ability.

Although the content of scholastic aptitude tests is basically unrestricted, in point of fact, content is generally quite standardized. Among the most widely used item types are: *vocabulary,* or a variation such as analogies or sentence completion (selecting the proper word to complete a sentence); *reading comprehension,* where the student reads a paragraph and then answers questions based upon the information contained in the paragraph; *numerical ability,* tested through straight computation and/or word problems; measures of *abstract reasoning,* such as number series problems or nonverbal analogies; and *general information* items. The exact content will, of course, vary with the scope of the test and the age level of the students. For example, in the primary grades, before children have acquired any fluency in reading, vocabulary will be tested by picture vocabulary items, but at older ages more complex item forms, such as analogies, can be used.

Finally, consider the role previous learning plays on scholastic aptitude tests. Since the educational system is cumulative and past performance is usually the best predictor of future performance, it would be surprising if scholastic aptitude tests were not heavily loaded with skills developed by previous school learnings. And they are. However, to avoid being too closely tied to specific learnings and educational experiences, the tests concentrate on skills and materials that transfer to a wide variety of situations. Furthermore, whenever possible, items are constructed so that the student must apply his repertoire of knowledge and skills to new situations; specific information, if needed, is provided in the item content. For example, a reading comprehension item, even though it covers a topic new to the student, can test his ability to extract salient features from what he has read. Or a graph interpretation item, though presenting a student with data he has never previously encountered, can test his ability to interpret graphs. Thus previous learning may

Figure 15.1 Examples of items on scholastic aptitude tests. (All items in parts A and B reproduced from Otis-Lennon Mental Ability Test. Copyright © 1967, Harcourt Brace Jovanovich. Reproduced by special permission. Items in part C reprinted with permission from the College Entrance Examination Board, New York, from *A Description of the College Board Scholastic Aptitude Test,* 1967.)

A. Items from a primary level test

Identify the picture that is not like the other three.

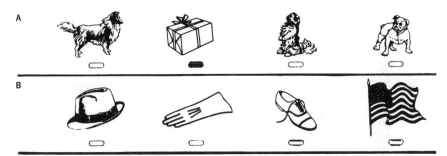

Picture vocabulary. Identify object teacher refers to — e.g., "Mark the thing we drink from." "Find the picture that shows two boys running."

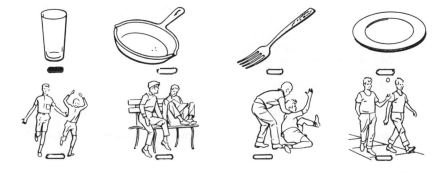

B. Items from a junior high level test

Practice Examples	*Sample Answer Spaces*

Eye is to **see** as **ear** is to –

   head   hear   talk   nose   cheek

X a b c d e ○ ● ○ ○ ○

A boy bought 3 pencils at 5¢ each. How much did the 3 pencils cost?

   5¢   10¢   20¢   25¢   none of these

Y f g h j k ○ ○ ○ ○ ●

○ is to ○ as ☐ is to –

☐   ☐   ○   ○   ▭

Z a b c d e ● ○ ○ ○ ○

Figure 15.1   (continued)

C. Sample items from a college admissions test

Verbal: Sentence completion and analogies

23. The Indo-European group of languages is a relatively junior member
     of the Old World linguistic family, evolving at a time when such
     languages as Sumerian and those in the Hamitic and Semitic groups
     were of respectable ------.

     (A) origin
     (B) antiquity
     (C) usage
     (D) size
     (E) fluency

24. Though he was romantic and sensual in his aesthetic philosophy, his
     life was one of ------.

     (A) disillusionment
     (B) abandonment
     (C) creativity
     (D) naïveté
     (E) austerity

25. Plato's insistence on the all-pervading domination of the state, exag-
     gerated though it be, is exaggerated on the actual lines of Greek
     practice, and ------ the ------ between their point of view and our
     idea of individual dignity.

     (A) evades . . inconsistency
     (B) prevents . . relationship
     (C) minimizes . . incongruity
     (D) indicates . . antithesis
     (E) resolves . . dispute

     In each of the following questions, a related pair of words or phrases
     is followed by five lettered pairs of words or phrases. Select the lettered
     pair which best expresses a relationship similar to that expressed in
     the original pair.

26. KNIFE:INCISION :: (A) bulldozer:excavation   (B) tool:operation
     (C) pencil:calculation   (D) hose:irrigation   (E) plow:agriculture

27. TORCH:LIBERTY :: (A) tray:waiter   (B) scales:justice
     (C) candle:poverty   (D) bars:punishment   (E) lever:power

28. ADVERTISEMENT:PURCHASE :: (A) defense:conquest
     (B) attitude:conviction   (C) electioneering:vote
     (D) offer:force   (E) attempt:achievement

Verbal: Reading comprehension

     The essential trick of the Renaissance pastoral poem, which was
     felt to imply a beautiful relation between rich and poor, was to make
     simple people express strong feelings in learned and fashionable

Figure 15.1   (continued)

language. From seeing elements of the two sorts of people combined
(5) like this the reader thought better of both; the best parts of each were
used. The effect was in some degree to combine in the reader or the
author the merits of the two sorts; he was made to mirror in himself
more completely the effective elements of the society in which he
lived. This was not a process that had to be explained in the course
(10) of writing pastoral poems; it was already shown in the clash between
style and subject, and to make the clash work in the right way the
writer had to keep up a firm pretense that he was unconscious of it.

The usual process for putting further meanings into the pastoral
situation was to insist that the shepherds were rulers of sheep and
(15) so compare them to politicians or bishops or what not; this piled the
heroic convention onto the pastoral one since the hero was another
symbol of his whole society. Such a pretense, no doubt, made the
characters unreal, but not the feelings expressed or even the situation
(as opposed to the setting) described. The same pretense is often
valuable in modern writing.

53. Which of the following is LEAST likely to be found in a Renaissance
pastoral?

(A) Serious intent
(B) The heroic convention
(C) Symbolism
(D) Elegance of expression
(E) Accurate depiction of social structures

54. In lines 17-19 the author finds it necessary to oppose the situation to
the setting because

(A) in pastoral poetry a possibly real situation is conveyed by unreal
characters in unreal scenes
(B) setting and situation are natural opposites
(C) the addition of the heroic convention makes the pastoral setting
an absurd situation
(D) situation and setting are the same in modern writing
(E) in pastoral poetry the pretense makes the setting even more real
than the situation

55. The author would say that of the following the LEAST artificial element
in pastoral poetry is the

(A) heroic convention
(B) characterization
(C) level of language
(D) underlying emotion
(E) pastoral convention

Mathematical

79. If $x(x - y) = 0$, which of the following is a correct conclusion?

(A) $x = 0$ (B) Either $x = 0$ or $x = y$
(C) $x = y$ (D) $x^2 = y$ (E) Both $x = 0$ and $x - y = 0$

Figure 15.1   (continued)

80. The area of one circle is nine times that of another. The circumference of the larger circle is how many times that of the smaller?

    (A) 3   (B) $4\frac{1}{2}$ (C) 6   (D) 9   (E) 18

81. A number n equals $\frac{3}{2}$ the average of the three numbers 7, 9, and t. What is t in terms of n?

    (A) $\frac{2n}{3} - 16$ (B) $\frac{4n}{3} - 16$ (C) $2n - 16$

    (D) $\frac{9n}{2} - 16$ (E) $\frac{n}{2} + 8$

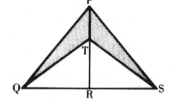

82. Triangle QTS above has base QS of 15 inches. If altitude RT is extended 4 inches to P, what is the area of QTSP?

    (A) 30 sq. in   (B) 60 sq. in.   (C) 90 sq. in.   (D) 120 sq. in.
    (E) 150 sq. in.

83. What is the average of the first 25 positive whole numbers?

    (A) 12   (B) 12.5   (C) 13   (D) 13.5   (E) 26

84. The houses on the east side of a street are numbered with the consecutive even integers from 256 to 834, inclusive. How many houses are there on the east side of the street?

    (A) 287   (B) 288   (C) 289   (D) 290   (E) 291

play a role in test performance by influencing problem-solving strategies as well as being reflected in knowledge of specific factual material.

Implications for test construction   Although many of the implications for the process of constructing a scholastic aptitude test should now be obvious, it would be well to emphasize several points. First, the primary basis for item selection should be the validity of the item in predicting external academic criteria. Second, the tests will, almost without exception, be paper-and-pencil tests. Furthermore, because the tests will be administered to large numbers of students, items will generally be cast in multiple-choice or other objective formats to facilitate scoring. In tests designed for primary grades, the student may respond in the test booklet rather than on a separate answer sheet, but the format still permits objective scoring. Third, most scholastic aptitude tests are part of a series, with tests at various age levels. The pragmatic problem is deciding how many age levels to include, where to divide the levels, and articulation between age levels. The age level problem is also reflected in the norms; the test constructor must obtain representative samples of students at each grade level. Because each level of the test will be used in several adjacent grades, and periodic testing will probably occur, provision of equivalent forms at each level is highly desirable.

Finally, scholastic aptitude tests will be power tests. On a power test, you will recall, scores reflect the complexity or difficulty of the items the student can correctly answer. Since the important dimension of academic performance is the complexity of the material that can be mastered, not speed of responding, validity will be higher when a power test is used as a predictor.

The preceding paragraphs, plus the discussion of general intelligence tests, should give you a good idea of the format and content of scholastic aptitude tests. Thus, rather than single out a particular test for detailed comment we shall only indicate the characteristics, levels, and content of a number of the widely used scholastic aptitude tests (see Appendix B) and illustrate some of the variety of items that appear on these tests (see Figure 15.1).

College admissions tests   One particular type of scholastic aptitude test, the college admissions test, has been the center of so much attention and debate in both the popular press and professional literature (see, e.g., Angoff, 1971b; McClelland, 1973; Black, 1963; Hoffmann, 1962; Lavin, 1965) that it is worthy of special comment. These tests—of which there are two major national batteries, the College Entrance Examination Board's *Scholastic Aptitude Test* (SAT) and the *American College Testing Program* battery (ACT)—are, as their name implies, designed to aid college and university admissions officers in evaluating the qualifications of applicants for admission. Prospective students take the ACT or SAT during their junior or senior year in high school, and scores are reported to colleges to which they have applied. Some colleges require (or recommend) the ACT, others the SAT, some accept both, and others do not require either test.

Although the ACT and SAT are both college admissions tests, they differ in both content and format. The ACT battery is composed of four tests: English Usage, Mathematics Usage, Social Studies Reading, and Natural Science Reading. A score is reported for each subtest and, in addition, the average of the four test scores is reported as a Composite score. The tests in the ACT battery are achievement oriented, emphasizing the ability to apply developed skills. For example, the Social Studies and Natural Sciences tests place primary emphasis on the ability to interpret material presented in reading paragraphs.

The College Board program, in contrast, makes a clearer separation between its aptitude and achievement tests. The SAT is a measure of scholastic aptitude and provides two scores: a Verbal score and a Mathematical score. No composite score is obtained. As with the ACT, all items are in a multiple-choice format. The Verbal section consists of antonym, sentence completion, analogy, reading comprehension, and general understanding (information) items. The Mathematical section includes word and computational problems in algebra, geometry, and basic arithmetic processes, the interpretation of graphs and charts, and logical reasoning items. In addition to the SAT, a series of achievement tests covering various subjects, and in some areas levels within subjects, are available in CEEB series.

One criticism of college admissions tests concerns the duplication of effort involved when students have to take both the ACT and the SAT because colleges they are applying to require different tests. Why, many people ask, cannot one test be substituted for the other? Or, phrasing this question in more technical terms: Can scores on the ACT and the SAT be equated? Although it is, of course, possible to equate scores statistically on the ACT and SAT, doing so will provide only comparable scores; the two tests cannot be considered equivalent, since they cover different content areas. And because they measure different content areas (and probably vary in difficulty), one or the other of the tests may be more appropriate for a given college or university.

A second criticism is that many important abilities are not tapped because of the multiple-choice format. This is no doubt true, but neither thoughtful psychologists nor test publishers claim that the tests measure all the important abilities. Rather they stress that test scores should be used only in conjunction with other evidence—such as grades, teachers' recommendations, and evidence of special skills and abilities—when admissions decisions are made. A related criticism holds that opportunities for higher education are too dependent on scoring well on college admissions tests, since colleges place undue emphasis on test scores. Individual schools vary in the reliance they place on tests from allowing test scores to determine admissions to virtually ignoring test scores. Here, again, we emphasize the need for validity studies that indicate how much emphasis should be placed on admissions tests in relation to other admissions criteria.

Finally, college admissions tests have been said to be unfair to persons from atypical, disadvantaged, and culturally limited backgrounds. Although individuals from these groups may, in fact, be penalized, the available data indicate that the tests predict as well for minority group students as for middle-class students (see, e.g., Munday, 1965; Stanley and Porter, 1967; Cleary, 1968; Thorndike, 1971; Darlington, 1971; Angoff and Ford, 1973; Cole, 1973; Cleary, Humphreys, Kendrick, and Wesman, 1975). However, these results may reflect the fact that minority group students suffer the same handicaps in the college situations as they do on the test. That is, since the same skills and abilities are needed for successful performance in college as are needed to obtain a high score on the test, the tests still predict success even though they may possibly be biased.

We should also mention that although we have mentioned only tests designed to aid in selecting undergraduates, there also are tests designed for assessing the qualifications of applicants for admission to graduate school (the Graduate Record Exam, the Miller Analogies Test) and to professional schools (the Medical College Admission Test, the Law School Admission Test), and for a variety of other educational programs.

It may be considered nitpicking to think of scholastic aptitude tests as distinct from group tests of intelligence. But since intelligence tests and scholastic aptitude tests are based on different philosophies (that is, the measurement of a general human trait versus prediction of academic success), rely on different types of validation (that is, construct versus criterion-related validity), and utilize different norm groups (that is, general population versus students), they can be separated in theory, if not in fact. The main criticism leveled at scholastic aptitude tests is that they do not cover all relevant educational skills, and thus predict only a limited range of educational outcomes. This criticism cannot be denied, but since the tests are designed to predict academic criteria, limitations of the test reflect limitations in criteria and point up the need for developing alternative criteria.

EVALUATION OF GENERAL INTELLECTUAL ABILITY TESTS

There is no doubt that a number of carefully constructed, well-normed measures of general intellectual ability are available to the test user. This is true whether one considers individual intelligence measures, such as the Stanford-Binet and Wechsler scales, or paper-and-pencil measures, such as the SAT and ACT. The amount of care of effort devoted to the construction of these tests, and the resultant technical sophistication, are models to be emulated. Procedures for administration and scoring are highly standardized. Available normative data are extensive and, generally, representative of the population the test is designed to serve. A possible exception is the representation of minority groups in normative samples. However, many tests currently include minority group members in normative samples and/or have developed normative data based on minority groups.

Consistency and Validity

The internal consistency of IQs on individual intelligence tests are very high; for both Wechsler and Stanford-Binet IQs they are in the .90s. Reliabilities on most group intelligence and scholastic aptitude tests are equally as high. These findings, coupled with the fact that the domains sampled by the tests are usually quite clearly specified, lead to the conclusion that there are tests that provide accurate indications of general intelligence or verbal reasoning ability.

Looking to a longer-range perspective, a different set of issues arises. Here the important concerns are: "How stable are measures of general ability?" and "Do measures of general ability predict socially relevant outcomes?" We shall consider each of these questions briefly.

The stability of the IQ   Here we are interested in such questions as: How stable is the IQ? What factors produce changes in the IQ? What is the relative magnitude of changes produced by the various factors? At what age levels are changes most likely to occur? Are changes systematic or random? Do certain aspects of intelligence fluctuate more, or more readily, than others? Are the scores of certain individuals more stable than others? All of these questions presume that intelligence is, in some degree, unstable. The basic question, consequently, is: Under what conditions and to what extent do intelligence scores vary?

Although earlier studies stressed the stability of the IQ, it is now recognized that the stability reflected the fact that most people experience relatively constant environmental conditions. As a consequence, environmental factors may not have a chance to demonstrate their effects fully. And since the greatest fluctuations in IQs occur with large changes in environmental conditions, environmental stability leads to stability in intelligence test scores. Moreover, the cumulative nature of intellectual development (and measurement) tends to produce artifacts that ensure a high correlation between successive IQ measures (J. Anderson, 1940). However, other data have shown that marked changes in IQ (20 IQ points or more) do occur under certain conditions.

What factors, then, produce greater than chance changes in the IQ? Some of the factors that may decrease intelligence are obvious: injury or illness, particularly if it effects the brain or central nervous system; and severe emotional trauma. Growing up in an extremely restricted or deprived environment may limit intellectual development. Conversely, the removal of an emotional block or provision of an especially stimulating environment or educational experiences may lead to increased intellectual growth. (For a further discussion see, e.g., Bloom, 1964; Hunt, 1961; Rohwer and Ammon, 1974).

The relationship between intelligence and experience can also be viewed in a slightly different manner (see, e.g., Jensen, 1968, 1969). Assume that the environment must provide a certain minimal amount of stimulation if normal intellectual growth is to occur. If this threshold of stimulation is reached, the person's intellectual development will proceed normally and consistently unless, of course, something occurs that reduces the effective environmental stimulation to below the threshold; at this point normal development will be retarded. Similarly, if the stimulation threshold is not reached during early years, mental development will be arrested. Because mental growth is most rapid in early childhood, and because all learning depends on previous learning, changes in environmental conditions will be optimally effective at this time; thus the stress on the importance of adequate intellectual stimulation in the earliest years (Bloom, 1964; Hunt, 1961). Because most persons grow up in environments in which the effective stimulation level is above the threshold and do not frequently experience major changes in environmental conditions, their mental development will be consistent. However, moving to or from a severely restricted environment can produce noticeable changes in the effectiveness of intellectual functioning—changes that will be reflected in the IQ.

Two further points should be briefly noted. First, the low correlations observed between measures of infant and adult intelligence are attributable to the unreliability of infant tests and to the fact that different skills are measured when testing infants and testing adults, as well as to the effects of intervening experiences. Second, we have been considering intelligence as a single general ability. This is not necessarily the case, nor perhaps is it even consistent with research evidence. Thus, for example, Cattell and his colleagues (Cattell, 1963, 1968; Horn, 1967) have suggested that intelligence can better be viewed as consisting of two general factors: fluid intelligence and crystallized intelligence. Crystallized intelligence has a heavy cultural component and is best measured by those subtests that traditionally are included in intelligence tests: vocabulary, numerical skills, and general and specific information. Fluid intelligence involves more perceptual and performance skills.

Since the relative contributions of fluid and crystallized intelligence to intellectual performance vary from person to person and situation to situation, and by developmental level, the stability of intellectual performance will depend on the role fluid and crystallized components play in the behavior measured.

Predictive validity   Another area that has been the subject of a large amount of research is the relationship between intelligence and socially relevant criteria, such as educational and vocational success. Binet's test, you will recall, was originally developed to identify slow learners—in essence, to predict academic success. Since Binet's time, innumerable studies have been conducted relating intelligence measures to a wide variety of educational outcomes (see, e.g., Goslin, 1963; Hills, 1971). Considering the diversity of tests, samples, and criteria used, the results of these studies have been amazingly consistent; the correlations between scores on general intelligence tests and measures of academic success generally fall in the .40–.70 range. Correlations are generally higher when the criterion is a standardized measure of achievement, in more academic and verbal areas, and with younger children. Intelligence scores are also related to the level of education completed. In short, measures of general intellectual ability predict a variety of academic criteria (McNemar, 1964).

There is also a tremendous body of literature dealing with the predictive validity of scholastic aptitude tests, particularly college admissions tests (see, e.g., Hills, 1971; Angoff, 1971b; ACT, 1972). Although there are wide differences between schools, the trend of the data indicates that scores on college admissions tests are related to measures of academic outcome, such as grades and graduation. In most situations, measures of previous academic performance (for example, high school grades) predict more accurately than the test scores. However, tests do add to predictive efficiency; that is, the test scores have incremental validity. As might be expected, the correlations are highest in the traditionally academic subjects, such as English, mathematics, and the sciences. In short, tests provide valuable information that cannot feasibly be obtained by other methods (Cleary et al., 1975).

The relationship of intelligence test scores to occupational success is also a controversial area. On the one hand there are studies, such as the famous Army studies (Harrell and Harrell, 1945), which have shown that occupations can be ranked in terms of the intellectual ability of persons working within these occupations. Then, too, it is well documented that occupational membership is closely related to educational attainment and that educational attainment can be predicted from intelligence test scores (see, e.g., Herrnstein, 1971). On the other hand, there are studies (e.g., Thorndike and Hagen, 1959; D. Hoyt, 1965) that show little relationship between ability and academic achievement and occupational success, at least when predicting relative success *within* an occupational group. Perhaps the best reconciliation of the present knowledge is that many occupations may have minimal intellectual requirements, but given the minimal level of intellectual ability, an individual's performance in an occupation will be determined by factors and abilities other than general intellectual ability.

Intelligence as a Construct

Any evaluation of general intelligence tests is, in many ways, an evaluation of the construct of general intelligence. There is no doubt that general intelligence tests reliably sample a certain constellation of abilities (vocabulary, fund of general information, numerical ability). However, the question remains as to whether the concept of general intelligence is a viable one.

There would, at first blush, appear to be many reasons for rejecting the notion of general intelligence. The tests themselves are composed of several different types of items, and factor analyses have confirmed the existence of a number of distinct intellectual abilities. True, these abilities tend to be positively intercorrelated, but not to the extent that one would subsume them all under one general ability. Other studies have shown that performance on general intelligence tests is a function of different sets of abilities at different age levels; again, an argument against the general intelligence view. Why, then, do psychologists persist in building general intelligence tests and use a single score, usually the IQ, to summarize an individual's intellectual abilities? One reason no doubt is historical tradition; the early tests used this approach, and their descendants have followed in their footsteps. But this is hardly a sufficient reason. More important is the fact that scores on general intelligence tests predict a variety of educational and vocational criteria. Furthermore, as we shall see later in the discussion of multiaptitude batterires, in the majority of situations prediction using multiple abilities has proven to be no more effective than predicting from a single index of general intelligence (cf. McNemar, 1964).

The debate over the concept of general intelligence also illustrates the distinction between basic research on the structure of abilities and application of knowledge gained to the technology of test construction. It would be hard to argue against the view that intellectual ability is best conceived of as a number of intelligences or, if you will, a number of quite distinct intellectual abilities. However, although test constructors have been able to develop tests measuring these abilities, the tests do not produce greater predictive efficiency than do general intelligence measures. Since general intelligence tests are more familiar to test users, more efficient, simpler to interpret, and as valid as multiaptitude batteries, many persons prefer to use general intelligence tests, even though they realize the theoretical limitations of such measures.

16

MEASURES OF APTITUDES AND ABILITIES

The tests discussed in Chapter 15 were designed to measure general intellectual ability (that is, intelligence), and described performance by a single summary score, such as an IQ. Many psychologists, however, think this conception is too simplistic, preferring to think in terms of cognitive abilities (in the plural), rather than just a single unitary ability. They point out that factor analytic studies have shown that even individual intelligence tests measure more than one ability. On a more practical level, the need to consider diverse abilities is also apparent. Educational psychologists are concerned with matching students' abilities with schools or courses; industrial psychologists are interested in placing workers in jobs that match their skills and abilities; counselors consider various abilities when helping their clients to make educational and vocational plans. In all of these situations, reliance on a single score would be unnecessarily restrictive; what is needed are measures of the various human abilities.

Test constructors have typically taken one of two approaches to measuring these diverse characteristics. Some have attempted to develop integrated batteries that measure a number of relatively broad abilities. That is, they have constructed test batteries that measure a small number, usually six to twelve, broad abilities. This is the multiaptitude approach. On the theoretical level this approach represents, at least implicitly, an adoption of a group factors approach to abilities. On a practical level, this approach recognizes that testing time will always necessarily be limited and that specific abilities can be clustered into groups. Thus, the optimal approach is to measure a small number of relatively broad abilities.

The other approach has been to develop individual tests for each specific ability. That is, rather than broadly measuring the range of an individual's abilities, the test constructor concentrates on one particular ability. Sometimes this is because his interests are confined to a specific area; for example, he may only be interested in studying, say, creativity or musical ability. In other cases a test may be developed in response to a particular demand; for example, if a job demands a particular skill, an industrial psychologist may develop a test of that particularly ability in order to aid in selecting workers. In either case, separate tests are constructed for each ability and no attempt is made to develop an integrated test battery.

In this chapter, we shall first discuss multiaptitude batteries, then consider tests of specific abilities, looking at tests measuring both cognitive and vocational abilities. The chapter will conclude with a discussion of some of the problems and emerging trends in the measurement of abilities.

MULTIAPTITUDE BATTERIES

Adoption of a multiaptitude approach has several important implications for the test construction process. First, a test battery, not just a single test, must be constructed. If there are a number of relatively broad, more or less independent, abilities and if we want a relatively complete picture of an individual's abilities, then a number of independent tests will be needed. Specifically, the test battery must contain as many tests as there are abilities to be measured. A second, perhaps corollary, implication is that each test should measure one, and only, one ability. Third, the normative data must permit intraindividual comparisons. Usually this means that identical normative samples must be used for all tests within the battery.

These implications can be translated into practical decisions that the test constructor must make. For example, is the test battery to be comprehensive (that is, measure all major abilities) or will it sample only several of the more important ones? A closely related issue is whether to measure ''pure'' factors or whether each test can be comprised of items measuring several closely related abilities. Test batteries taking the former approach can legitimately be referred to as *multifactor* tests; tests taking the latter approach are more properly called *multiaptitude* tests. Since there is evidence to suggest that the structure of abilities may not be the same at different age levels, the test constructor must also determine the optimal division of age levels. Since intraindividual comparisons will be made, high reliability and small standard errors of measurement must be attained.

As the tests within a multiaptitude battery will, hopefully, predict relevant and important criteria, the question of the proper method of combining test scores arises. In theory, any criterion can be predicted from a particular combination of factors (test scores); the empirical question is to determine the optimal weighting of the factors. Application of the multiple regression model allows the appropriate weights to be assigned to each predictor. Thus, the same basic set of predictors (test scores) can be used to predict each of several criteria, but each component will be differentially weighted when predicting various criteria.

The Differential Aptitude Tests

As our primary example of a multiaptitude battery we have chosen the Differential Aptitude Tests (DAT) published by the Psychological Corporation. This battery of eight tests was designed to serve as an aid in the educational and vocational guidance of students in grades eight through twelve. First published in 1947, with the latest revision in 1972 (Forms S and T), the DAT is probably the most widely used multiaptitude battery on the secondary school level.

The development of the DAT was guided by certain general principles. The two most important were that the test battery measure multiple abilities and that the test should be useful in educational and vocational guidance. In addition, the tests in the battery were to be independent. However, rather than measuring factorially defined constructs, the DAT measures constructs that were considered independent by counselors and other tests users. Inasmuch as the level of ability an individual possesses (not his speed of response) is usually the critical consideration, the tests are power tests. (The one exception is the Clerical Speed and Accuracy Test.)

The differential aptitude approach directly implies two other guiding principles: The test battery should yield a profile of ability scores, and adequate normative data must be provided. Three remaining principles derive from the intended use of the tests in the public schools: The test materials should be practical, the tests should be easy to administer, and alternate forms will be available.

In reviewing the guiding philosophy of the DAT, one can see the interplay of theoretical and practical demands and the necessity for tempering a purely psychometric approach with the requirements of developing an instrument that provides meaningful scores to students and counselors. In constructing the DAT the authors satisfied the essential psychometric requirements (of reliability and normative data) but never lost sight of the needs of the test user.

The tests   The DAT consists of eight separately administered tests. Three of the tests—Verbal Reasoning (VR), Numerical Ability (NA), and Abstract Reasoning (AR)—measure broad intellectual abilities. The items on VR and NA, in particular, are similar to items on many general intelligence and scholastic aptitude tests, whereas the AR items measure nonlanguage reasoning ability. The test authors realized that no clear distinction between ability and achievement can be drawn. However, to ensure that a common core of experience was tapped, items on VR and NA use materials commonly taught in U.S. schools. VR utilizes a special form of analogies item that requires students to use reasoning rather than mere associations (see Figure 16.1 for illustrations of DAT items). NA uses computation items, rather than word problems, to avoid contamination from irrelevant abilities. The authors propose using the combined VR and NA scores as an index scholastic aptitude; this combination (VR + NA) is the ninth score on the battery.

The other five DAT tests are more specific in content and function. Three of the tests—Clerical Speed and Accuracy (CSA), Mechanical Reasoning (MR), and Space Relations (SR)—would seem to be most valuable in vocational counseling. CSA is the only test in the battery placing primary emphasis on speed, measuring speed of performing a simple perceptual task. MR measures comprehension of mechanical and physical principles as expressed in familiar situations. SR measures the ability to visualize and mentally manipulate concrete materials. The other two tests—Language Usage (LU) and Spelling (Sp)—are both achievement tests. The authors justify their inclusion in the battery because "they represent basic skills that are necessary in so many academic and vocational pursuits" (Bennett, Seashore, and Wesman, 1966, pp. 1–9).

Figure 16.1 Examples of items on the Differential Aptitude Tests. Reproduced by permission. Copyright 1947, © 1961, 1962 by The Psychological Corporation, New York, N.Y. All rights reserved.

Verbal Reasoning
   Pick out words that will fill the blanks so that the sentence will be true and sensible.
   Example X. . . . . is to water as eat is to . . . .
      A   continue — drive   D   girl — industry
      B   foot — enemy   E   drink — enemy
      C   drink — food

   Example Z. . . . . is to one as second is to . . . .
      A   two — middle   D   first — two
      B   first — fire   E   rain — fire
      C   queen — hill

Numerical Ability
   Select the correct answer.
   Example X.   *Example Y.*

Add	13	A	14		Subtract	30	A	15
	12	B	25			20	B	26
	—	C	16			—	C	16
		D	59				D	8
		E	**none of these**				E	**none of these**

Abstract Reasoning
   Select the answer figure that completes the series begun in the Problem Figures.

   PROBLEM FIGURES   **ANSWER FIGURES**

Clerical Speed and Accuracy
   Mark the blank on the answer sheet corresponding to the underlined combination on the Test-Items.

Figure 16.1   (continued)

TEST ITEMS

V. <u>AB</u>	AC	AD	AE	AF
W. aA	aB	BA	Ba	<u>Bb</u>
X. A7	7A	B7	<u>7B</u>	AB
Y. Aa	Ba	<u>bA</u>	BA	bB
Z. 3A	3B	<u>33</u>	B3	BB

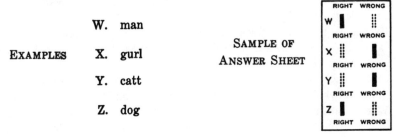

SAMPLE OF ANSWER SHEET

Mechanical Reasoning

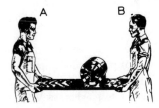

A   B

X

Which man has the heavier load?

(If equal, mark C.)

Space Relations

Decide which figure can be made from the pattern at the left.

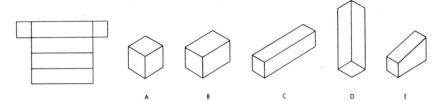

A   B   C   D   E

Spelling

Indicate whether the word is spelled correctly or incorrectly.

EXAMPLES

W.   man

X.   gurl

Y.   catt

Z.   dog

SAMPLE OF
ANSWER SHEET

	RIGHT	WRONG
W	▮	⫶
X	⫶	▮
Y	⫶	▮
Z	▮	⫶

Language Usage

Indicate which part of the sentence contains an error.

EXAMPLE

SAMPLE OF ANSWER SHEET

Ain't we / going to the / office / next week / at all.

A   B   C   D   E

A	B	C	D	E
▮	⫶	⫶	⫶	▮

The authors recommend administering the entire battery of eight tests so that the pattern of scores can be considered when counseling the student. Total testing time is slightly over 3 hours, with time limits varying from 6 to 30 minutes per test.[1] The

[1]The latest revision also includes an optional Career Planning Questionnaire.

tests can be administered by the classroom teacher, are printed in a reusable booklet, and utilize separate answer sheets, permitting hand or machine scoring.

Consistency and validity[2]   The corrected split-half reliability coefficient was computed for all subtests except CSA; since CSA is speeded, an alternative forms reliability estimate was used. Data from various sex and grade (8–12) groups show that the large majority of the corrected split-half reliability coefficients are over .90 on all subtests. Long-term stability data are not yet available for the new forms, but data from previous forms showed r's of .58–.87 over a period of 3 years (from grades 9 to 12). The coefficient of equivalence for Forms S and T is not reported, a strange oversight considering the completeness of the consistency, validity, and normative data.

Because the pattern of test scores is considered important when counseling students, the intercorrelations between tests become of paramount importance. The intercorrelations between tests vary widely, with the largest number falling in the .51–.69 range. In general, CSA is the most independent test, whereas VR correlates with all others (except, of course, CSA). Thus, although the separate tests are by no means independent (nor do the authors claim them to be), neither are they so highly related as to be considered all measures of the same ability.

Over the years, an abundance of validity data has been collected for the DAT. The bulk of the data presented involves prediction of grades in specific high school courses. Although any attempt to summarize these data necessarily involves oversimplification, several trends are apparent:

1. Grades in the common high school courses are best predicted by VR, NA, and LU, and by the VR + NA composite.
2. VR + NA is usually the best predictor of grades. In the core areas—English, Math, Science, Social Studies, History, and Languages—the median validity coefficients generally are in the .50s.
3. By and large, course grades are predicted by the corresponding test; for example, VR and LU are the best predictors of English grades, NA of math grades, and LU in language courses.
4. In less academic courses, such as art and industrial arts, there is some, but far from overwhelming, support for the differential validity of the DAT tests.
5. When results are considered on a school-by-school basis, there is a wide range of validity coefficients. For example, the validity of the VR + NA composite ranged from zero to the .80s when predicting English and math grades in different schools. The DAT data clearly illustrate the situation-specific nature of validity data and reinforce the need for evaluating the validity of a test in each specific situation.
6. The validity coefficients are slightly higher for girls than for boys, a trend that has been observed in a variety of situations (Seashore, 1962).

[2]Since Forms S and T are new, most of the validity data apply to studies conducted using previous forms of the test. However, similar results might be expected from the revised forms.

Other types of validity data are less prevalent. Some of the data presented show that the predictive accuracy of the DAT decreases only slightly over a period of several years. Evidence is also presented showing that DAT scores are often highly correlated (for example, .70–.80) with scores on achievement test batteries administered either concurrently with or after the DAT. Finally, several large-scale follow-up studies indicate that students who obtain different amounts of post–high school education and/or enter different occupations can be discriminated on the basis of their (high school) DAT scores; however, the difference appears to be as much a function of the level of DAT scores as the pattern of scores.

Score interpretation   In many ways the DAT procedures are a model for the interpretation of test scores. Normative data are presented for large representative samples of high school students with separate norm tables available for each grade (8–12) and sex grouping and for fall and spring testings. On CSA, a highly speeded test, there are even separate norms depending on what type of answer sheets were utilized. Percentile rank and stanine conversion tables are available. When scores are reported, raw scores are translated into percentile ranges to emphasize the fact that each score contains some measurement error and to caution the user against overinterpretation. Normal percentile charts are used to present the test scores graphically (see Figure 10.6). Note that the profile is constructed so that significant differences on two tests are indicated by nonoverlapping bars. Finally, the test authors stress the value of collecting local validity data and suggest use of expectancy tables to present normative-validity data.

Evaluation   The DAT is a well-constructed test of abilities that has been demonstrated to predict academic success and that counselors think has significance for vocational and educational guidance. The test construction process illustrates a blending and balancing of practical and theoretical concerns. Administration and scoring procedures are simple and straightforward, and reliability is high. Validity data are abundant and although most of the data concern prediction of academic grades, it is in this area that the test will find greatest use. Normative and interpretive data are excellent. Only one concern clouds the picture. The DAT is a multiaptitude battery, and the justification for such batteries is that the component tests will measure independent traits and be differential predictive. Neither of these has been firmly established by the available data.

Other Multiaptitude Batteries

The DAT typifies the approach to and problems encountered in the development of a multiaptitude battery. However, there are several other batteries that, because of their special features, deserve at least brief mention. These include the SRA[3] Primary Mental Abilities, the Flanagan Aptitude Classification and Industrial Tests,

[3]SRA refers to Science Research Associates, one of the major test publishers.

Figure 16.2 Examples of items on FACT Inspection and Assembly tests. Sample and practice items pictured copyright 1953, John C. Flanagan. Reprinted by permission of the publisher, Science Research Associates, Inc.

A. Inspection

Task is to identify parts having flaws — that is, ones that do not match first part in row.

SAMPLE PROBLEMS

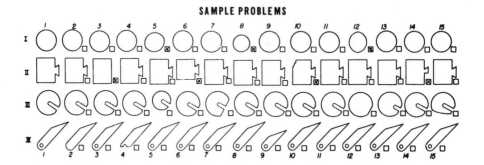

B. Assembly

Task is to indicate which completed part can be made by assembling component parts.

PRACTICE PROBLEMS

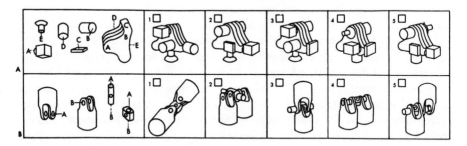

and the General Aptitude Test Battery. The reader who desires more information on these or other multiaptitude batteries should consult Buros (1972), Super (1958), Super and Crites (1962), and the individual test manuals.

The Primary Mental Abilities   The PMA is important historically because it was developed from Thurstone's pioneering research on the structure of abilities and was the first multifactor battery. The current revision has five levels, covering K–12 grade range, with four or five tests at each grade level. The tests are designed to measure readiness to learn—both overall and in specific courses. The factors measured include: Verbal Meaning—the ability to deal with words and verbal concepts; Number Facility—facility in doing simple numerical tasks; Spatial Relations—ability to visualize and conceptualize; Reasoning—the ability to think logically; and Perceptual Speed—ability to distinguish sizes and shapes. The Verbal Meaning, Number Facility, and Spatial Relations Tests occur at each level; Perceptual Speed is tested only at younger ages (grades K–6), and Reasoning at older age levels (grades 4–12).[4]

The reviews of the PMA have been somewhat critical. Perhaps the lesson to be drawn from the PMA is that results of basic research cannot be routinely translated into a workable test. Or, as Super has more picturesquely phrased it, "The pioneer who blazes the trail and builds the first log cabin does not necessarily build a good house for the city that later develops around the site of his cabin" (Super, 1958, p. 90).

The Flanagan Aptitude Classification and Industrial Tests   Both the DAT and PMA were designed for school age children and emphasize those abilities that underlie academic performance. Flanagan's tests,[5] in contrast, were explicitly designed to tap abilities that are important in successful occupational performance. Systematic job analyses were conducted to identify elements that are common to a number of jobs and related to successful job performance. Tests were then constructed to measure these job elements, using content that was directly relevant to the occupational world. For example, the *Inspection* test requires the subject to compare pictures of small parts and identify ones having imperfections (see Figure 16.2). Or, to use another example, the *Assembly* test consists of a picture of a number of disassembled parts followed by a series of pictures of completed parts; the subject's task is to choose the completed object that can be made from the disassembled parts. On other tests in the battery (for example, Arithmetic and Vocabulary) the content is not as specifically vocational.

The critical questions concerning a test such as the FACT are: (1) Does the use of vocationally relevant materials produce a more valid battery? (2) Do the tests show differential validity? Although the rationale of the test and the author's experience lend credence to the test's validity claims, at present one must return a Scotch verdict regarding the validity claims: not proven.

The General Aptitude Test Battery   In contrast to the multiaptitude discussed previously, the GATB, which was developed by the U.S. Employment Service (USES) for use by employment counselors in State Employment Service offices, includes several performance measures. Two of the nine factors measured—Finger Dexterity and Manual Dexterity—utilize performance tests; the other seven factors (Intelligence, Verbal Aptitude, Numerical Aptitude, Spatial Aptitude, Form Perception, Clerical Perception, and Motor Coordination) are measured by conventional paper-and-pencil tests. In all, the GATB includes 12 tests requiring approximately 2½ hours of testing time.

[4]Two of Thurstone's original factors, Word Fluency and Memory, are not represented in the current battery.

[5]There are two separate, though overlapping, test batteries: The Flanagan Aptitude Classification Test (a battery of 16 tests) and the Flanagan Industrial Tests (18 tests).

The GATB has several distinctive features besides utilization of performance measures. For one, it was designed for use in pre-employment counseling of high school students and adults seeking employment. That is, its major purpose is to provide a basis for job placement and referral. Also, an extensive program of research, including longitudinal studies, is being carried out by the USES to increase the pool of validity and interpretive data. The paradigm used in the majority of these studies involves identifying the aptitudes needed in a given occupation and then establishing the minimum test scores needed for successful job performance. This approach uses a multiple cutoff strategy, an approach some testing experts feel to be less desirable than multiple regression (cf. Chapter 9). Finally, the speeded nature of the tests and the lack of a mechanical comprehension test are limitations of a battery designed for use in employment counseling.

Evaluation of Multiaptitude Batteries

Multiaptitude tests, like any class of tests, vary widely among themselves; thus any overall evaluation will be subject to numerous qualifications. However, consideration of several fundamental questions will serve to put these tests in perspective. First, are multiaptitude tests based on any explicit rationale? Multiaptitude tests are based on the assumption that human performance can be described by a relatively small number of basic abilities. Many of the tests are based on a further assumption: The appropriate strategy for identifying these traits is factor analysis. Thus multiaptitude tests are based on a specific, clearly defined rationale.

Second, have the desired technical standards of test construction been attained? Although there are wide differences among the tests, it is clear that highly adequate levels of consistency and sufficient normative data can be obtained (for example, the DAT).

Third, do the multiaptitude tests cover a wide range of abilities? The batteries discussed covered from four to twenty-odd abilities. In some cases (such as the DAT and PMA), coverage was limited to academically related abilities that can be measured by paper-and-pencil tests; others (such as FACT) have a broader coverage of skills and use more ingenious formats. Especially for vocationally oriented batteries, more performance and motor tests would be desirable.

Fourth, do the tests measure "pure" factors? By and large the answer is no, but this reflects a deliberate choice by test constructors. Since many important abilities are factorially complex, and abilities tend to correlate positively, test constructors are faced with a choice between measuring psychometrically pure factors and measuring less pure, more complex, and probably more meaningful abilities. Most test constructors have opted for the latter alternative.

Finally, do the tests demonstrate differential validity? This is the central issue; yet, here, support for the multiaptitude approach is the weakest. Although the empirical evidence shows that single tests within multiaptitude batteries, or combinations of tests, can predict specific educational outcomes, there is little strong evidence that the tests are differential predictive—either in terms of different tests predicting different outcomes or by increasing predictive accuracy by using patterns of scores. The validity of multiaptitude tests in predicting vocational criteria is even less well established. In short, multiaptitude tests, even when well constructed and technically sound, have not clearly demonstrated the ability to accomplish their stated goal—that of being differential predictive.

MEASURES OF SPECIFIC APTITUDES AND ABILITIES

Multiaptitude batteries attempt to measure a wide range of abilities within the context of a single, integrated test battery. As indicated earlier, there is another approach to measuring abilities: building separate tests to measure each specific aptitude or ability. In this section we shall discuss examples of this approach. Some of the tests we shall consider focus on abilities germane to an academic setting; others tap occupational and vocational skills. In either case, the test constructor has concentrated on measuring a specific ability rather than attempting to provide a broad picture of abilities.

Using this approach has both advantages and limitations. The major advantage of constructing specific aptitude tests is that the ability of concern can be measured in more depth. That is, by concentrating on a single ability, one can probe its various facets in more detail. And since the test is usually developed for a specific purpose or situation, it should be a more valid indicator for that particular situation. On the other hand, such an approach can lead to overspecificity and lack of generality. Then, too, if a test user wishes to measure several abilities, he will have to develop his own test battery by combining several existing tests. In some ways this is good, in that he can pick the most relevant tests for his purposes rather than accepting an existing battery. But this may require developing a new battery for each person or situation. Furthermore, since the various tests will have been developed on different populations, normative data will not be comparable, and thus there will be interpretation problems, especially when scores on various measures are compared.

Creativity

An area of continuing interest in psychology and education is creativity (see, e.g., Getzels and Jackson, 1962; Barron, 1963, 1968, 1969; MacKinnon, 1962; Taylor and Barron, 1963; Torrance, 1962; Torrance and Myers, 1970; Vernon, 1970; Wallach and Wing, 1969; Cattell and Butcher, 1968; Nichols, 1972; Guilford, 1968). Some of the interest has been generated because creativity is an important element for people in certain occupations (for example, artists, research scientists); other interest has been directed toward the study of creativity as an intellectual ability; and yet other interest has been directed toward creativity as a problem-solving method. Research strategies have been of two general types: Some studies have concentrated on the personal characteristics and background experiences that typify creative persons, and others have attempted to study the creative process.

Defining the construct of "creativity" or "creative behavior" is an exercise in convergent and discriminant validity. The various skills and functions proposed as manifestations of creativity not only must be intercorrelated (convergent validity), they also must be distinct from other abilities, particularly intelligence (discriminant validity). There is general agreement that in order for a behavior to be indicative of creativity, or a test classed as a measure of creativity, responses must be produced rather than just selected from among available alternatives. Operationally, the subject is required to think divergently, to produce a number of responses to a specified stimulus situation; for example, he might be asked to indicate all the possible uses of a brick. A second essential element of creative behavior is that the responses be, in some sense, original.[6] Although some writers appear to accept all original responses as being of equal value, most writers insist that the response be useful or relevant so as to eliminate obviously absurd responses. There is also disagreement as to the role personality and motivational variables should play in the definition. As a working definition to guide test construction, creativity can be viewed as the ability to think divergently, to produce a large number and variety of original responses to a stipulated stimulus situation.

Tests of creativity   The search for characteristics that identify creative persons and pleas for identification and training of creative talent have far outstripped the development of tests for measuring creativity. However, several tests have been developed. In addition, parts of established tests (for example, Word Fluency measures) are sometimes considered to be indices of creativity. Some of the tests developed from Guilford's structure of the intellect model, particularly those that measure aspects of divergent thinking, can be classed as tests of creativity. Examples would include Guilford's tests of Word Fluency (rapid listing of words containing a given letter), Ideational Fluency (naming things or objects that belong in the same class), Associational Fluency (producing synonyms), Alternative Uses (listing possible uses for an object, other than its normal uses), and Consequences (listing the various possible consequences of a given act). Note that these tests all require verbal responses. Other tests in the model require figural responses, for example, the Making Objects tests, which involve drawing specified objects utilizing a specified set of stimulus designs. Others, though requiring pictorial responses, are primarily conceptual tasks. For example, the Match Problems tests is based on an illustrated design made of matchsticks; the subject must remove a certain number of matchsticks to produce a new design.

In contrast to Guilford's tests, which were an outgrowth of his research program, Torrance has developed creativity tests in an educational context. As a consequence, the tests measure creativity as it might be complexly expressed in a natural setting (a school). Nevertheless, there is a high degree of similarity between the two tests.

The *Torrance Tests of Creative Thinking* are divided into two major sections: Thinking Creatively with Words and Thinking Creatively with Pictures. The tests

[6]Barron has pointed out that a response can be original in at least two ways: It can be original in the normative sense of not occurring frequently, or it can be new to a given individual, occurring to him for the first time. Creativity tests utilize the former definition.

are structured as games or activities tests and are presumed to be applicable from kindergarten through graduate school, although certain modifications are made for younger children. Thinking Creatively with Words consists of a variety of activities. Three are based on a single sketch, with the subject's task being to list the questions he would ask to find out what is happening in the picture, guess the possible causes of the action in the sketch, and guess the possible consequences of the action pictured. Other activities require suggesting improvements for a toy, suggesting unusual uses for a common object, asking questions about the same common object, and guessing the consequences of an improbable action. Scoring is on three dimensions: fluency (number of relevant responses), flexibility (variety of response classes), and originality. Thinking Creatively with Pictures consists of three tasks: utilizing a colored shape to construct an original picture, sketching objects using pairs of specified irregular lines (see Figure 16.3), and constructing designs either from pairs of parallel lines or circles. These tests are scored on the basis of fluency, flexibility, originality, and elaboration.

Figure 16.3   Example of an item similar to those on Torrance's Thinking Creatively with Pictures. See text for explanation.

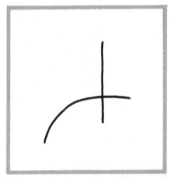

Evaluation   Certain problems are apparent on creativity tests. For example, both the Torrance and Guilford tests are time-limited measures. Scoring, of course, cannot be completely objective. However, data show that trained scorers using a scoring manual can attain acceptable levels of scorer reliability. Still, the reliability of creativity tests are lower than desirable, especially for individual scores. Normative data are limited. Guilford's test construction procedures ensure that his tests will have both factorial and discriminant validity. However, correlations with other tests and socially relevant criteria are generally lacking. Torrance's tests, in contrast, have been related to a variety of criteria, but his research has lacked the systematic nature of Guilford's. Consequently, no clear pattern of validity results has emerged. Thus, although several creativity tests are available for research use, the tests have not yet reached the stage of development that allows for meaningful interpretations of individual scores.

Another important question, which is not restricted to any one test, involves the relationship between creativity and intelligence. Many people believe that intelligence and creativity are unrelated. However, the data indicate that creativity and intelligence are correlated if we study the entire range of intellectual ability. However, given persons of above average intelligence, intelligence and creativity are essentially uncorrelated (Butcher, 1968). Furthermore, studies (e.g., Getzels and Jackson, 1962) of high-ability high school students have shown that students who score high on creativity measures but lower on intelligence tests perform as well on many academic tasks as individuals who score high on intelligence tests and lower on creativity. The data can be summarized in two statements. First, above-average intelligence is necessary for creativity. However, the converse is not true, or, in other words, high intelligence is a necessary but not sufficient condition for creativity. Second, in many situations, equivalent performance levels can be obtained by using intelligence (convergent thinking) or creativity (divergent thinking).

Musical and Artistic Abilities

Tests of musical and artistic ability can be considered together because many of the same problems are encountered in both areas. For example, in both music and art one can clearly distinguish between appreciation and performance. It is one thing to be able to paint a picture, throw a pot, or cast a statue; it is another to be able to understand and appreciate a work of art. The two skills are not necessarily highly intercorrelated: Many persons can evaluate the merit of a work of art but are themselves able to produce only stereotyped works. Consequently, tests of the two types of skills must be quite different. Similarly, music appreciation and the ability to play an instrument (or sing) are distinct abilities.

A second common element is the difficulty in predicting success in artistic and musical activities. These difficulties take several forms. For one, even experts often disagree dramatically when rating the quality of a given performance or the merit of a particular musical or artistic work. This problem is exacerbated when we try to compare diverse modes of expression. To illustrate, can level or skill in playing an instrument be directly compared with singing ability? Then, too, in musical and artistic fields, more so than in many other occupations, ''success'' seems to be a function of a particularly fortuitous combination of ability, training, hard work, personality factors, the availability of opportunities to perform, the correspondence of one's performing style and the current mood, and breaks and luck.

Appreciation tests are best exemplified in the artistic areas. The format of most tests is quite similar: The test taker is presented with representations of two works of art—one a work of proven and judged merit, the other the same or similar object in slightly modified form—and is asked to indicate which work is aesthetically superior. Aesthetic sensitivity is measured by the extent to which the examinee can select the appropriate response. Data suggest that scores do discriminate between relevant groups (for example, artists and art teachers obtain higher scores than do other persons) but these differences may result from either selection practices or training in art, or both.

Standardized tests of both musical and artistic abilities generally assess only component skills rather than attempt to measure complex performance skills. Thus, for example, the *Seashore Measures of Musical Talents* measures skills such as pitch, rhythm, timbre, loudness discrimination, and tonal memory. In the pitch test the subject indicates which of two tones is higher (or lower) in pitch; the rhythm test requires the subject to compare two rhythm patterns and judge whether they are similar or different. Performance tests in art typically require the examinee to produce drawings under restricted conditions (for example, using a set of irregular lines as part of a picture). Scoring, requiring quality ratings, is subjective and often unreliable.

Tests of artistic and musical skill would seem to be prime candidates for a threshold approach to interpretation. That is, low scores indicate lack of necessary skills, thus indicating that chances for attaining success are virtually nonexistent. (A person who has trouble discriminating between tones will never learn to play the violin well.) However, because of the myriad of factors that determine artistic or musical success, performance above the threshold level would indicate only that the person has the minimal level of necessary ability.

Vocational Aptitudes

Most of the tests discussed in this chapter have measured abilities or aptitudes that are particularly relevant in academic settings. However, the concept of aptitude is much broader, covering vocational and occupational aptitudes as well (cf., for example, parts of the DAT and FACT). Certainly intellectual aptitudes, such as verbal and numerical reasoning, are important determiners of vocational success, especially in occupations requiring extensive academic preparation. Yet there are other aptitude measures that focus on vocationally related skills.

The major factor that defines this class of tests is an emphasis on the prediction of vocational rather than academic criteria. Consequently, item content represents job components more closely than do items on scholastic aptitude tests. For example, although vocabulary tests may be good measures of academic aptitude, rarely does actual course work include vocabulary exercises. In contrast, the ability to visualize objects as they are rotated in space or make perceptual discriminations may be an essential job component as well as a basis for test items. In other words, vocational tests frequently are *job samples*. And, because job performance, and even its component elements, may require complex acts, tests designed to predict job performance usually are factorially complex.[7]

Whereas scholastic aptitude tests measure cognitive skills, vocational aptitudes include both cognitive skills and motor and manipulative abilities. Consequently, although many vocational aptitude tests use a paper-and-pencil format (for administrative and scoring ease), they are not restricted to this format. Furthermore, many tests have restrictive time limits, either because speed is an essential element

---

[7]In an extensive series of studies, Fleishman (1964, 1972) has identified eleven perceptual-motor and nine physical proficiency factors. The perceptual-motor factors are multilimb coordination, control precision, response orientation, reaction time, speed of arm movement, rate control, manual dexterity, finger dexterity, arm-hand steadiness, wrist-finger speed, and aiming. The physical proficiency factors are static strength, dynamic strength, explosive strength, trunk strength, extent flexibility, dynamic flexibility, gross body coordination, gross body equilibrium, and stamina.

in successful job performance or because the basic task is so simple that the only meaningful way to discriminate between individuals is in terms of their speed of response.

Examples of vocational aptitude tests   An example of a vocational aptitude test using a paper-and-pencil format is the Bennett Mechanical Comprehension Tests, the test from which the DAT Mechanical Comprehension section was derived. This test measures the ability to understand physical principles expressed through practical situations (see Figure 16.1). Studies have shown that scores on the Bennett are unrelated to intelligence (in homogeneous groups), are relatively unaffected by training in physics, and show large sex differences in performance. Scores do predict success in a variety of training programs and on a variety of jobs—for example, mechanics, machine operators, foremen, inspectors, machine testers, and toolmakers (Super and Crites, 1962). Because the test measures understanding of principles, it is most appropriate for predicting success on skilled technical jobs and semiskilled jobs involving the use of complex machinery.

Another vocationally relevant ability that can be assessed by paper-and-pencil tests is spatial visualization—the ability to visualize two- and three-dimensional objects as they are rotated, manipulated, or changed in some manner. For example, on the *Minnesota Paper Form Board* the stimulus consists of several geometric pieces; the test taker is asked to select, from among several alternatives, the geometric design that can be made by assembling the pieces. The DAT Spatial Relations test uses a slightly different task. Note that these tests require mental, rather than physical, manipulation of the object. Studies have shown that spatial ability is positively related to intelligence and predicts performance in occupations such as art, engineering, toolmaking, and inspection (Super and Crites, 1962).

A quite different ability that also can be assessed by paper-and-pencil tests is clerical aptitude. Tests of this ability (for example, The Minnesota Clerical Test and the Clerical Speed and Accuracy section of the DAT) might equally well be called tests of perceptual speed and accuracy, since they assess the ability to note details quickly and accurately. The typical format requires comparing pairs of names or numbers; the task is to indicate whether the two elements are identical or different (in any respect). Clerical tests are probably the best example of a pure speed test. The tests are speeded because the skill tested is so simple that almost anyone could attain 100 percent accuracy given sufficient time; however, people differ widely in the speed with which they can perform the task. Clerical aptitude tests predict success in clerical and inspection jobs, particularly routine ones (Super and Crites, 1962). In addition, they also have frequently been found to predict success in academic courses.

Other vocational aptitude tests, particularly those measuring manipulative and dexterity skills, use performance tasks. As an illustration, consider the *Purdue Pegboard.* This test is designed to measure two types of dexterity: arm-and-hand and finger dexterity. The test apparatus consists of a board with two parallel rows of holes drilled down the center and a set of shallow trays at one end; the trays contain metal pins, collars, and washers. The test consists of four separately timed portions:

(1) placing pins in the holes, one at a time, with the right hand; (2) the same task using the left hand; (3) the same task using both hands simultaneously; and (4) assembling pin-washer-collar-washer combinations using both hands. The test would seem to be a promising selection aid for assembly, packing, and other precise manipulative jobs; however, few validity data are available (Super and Crites, 1962). Other tests of manipulative abilities involve tasks such as placing cutouts into a form board and manipulating objects with a tweezers or other tools.

The tests discussed are all standardized measures published by testing companies and designed for use in both counseling and selection. The armed services and many individual companies have developed their own tests to aid in selecting among applicants and placing workers in positions. Being designed for a particular job, these tests are often better job samples than standardized tests, which necessarily are more general. They can also make more extensive use of apparatus.

Proficiency tests   The vocational tests discussed in the previous paragraphs can properly be called aptitude tests since they measured broad skills and are used to predict occupational success. An ability approach to testing vocationally related skills can also be used; that is, we could measure whether an individual has already developed the necessary knowledge and skills to perform in an occupation. Note that the emphasis here is on current skills; we are interested in whether the person currently has the skills necessary to perform the job or task. Such tests are called proficiency or competency tests.

Proficiency tests can be used in various ways. One obvious use is in selection and placement. That is, an employer can administer a competency test to determine whether an applicant possesses the abilities necessary to perform a particular job. The tests could also be used to determine eligibility for promotion to a higher job classification. A related use is for certification, such as in professional specialties (such as medical specialties, CPA) or skilled trades. And, with the increasing emphasis on continuing education, many colleges are using proficiency exams as a basis for awarding credit for skills developed through nontraditional educational experiences.

An example of competency testing is the National Occupational Competency Testing Program (ETS, 1973). This program was instituted because it was recognized that many skilled craftsmen had developed high levels of skill through experience on their jobs. Certification of these skills would be valuable for several purposes, including awarding college credit and as a basis for certifying the occupational proficiency of prospective teachers of vocational subjects in community and junior colleges. Tests have been developed for 24 specialities in 13 industrial areas (including auto mechanics, plumbing, architectural drafting, printing, quantity food cooking, cabinet making, and millwork). Each test consists of a 3-hour written test plus a 4- to 6-hour performance section.

Obviously, the crucial step in developing any proficiency exam is identification of the knowledge and skills necessary for satisfactory performance in the occupation. This can be accomplished by a thorough job analysis. Written items and performance tasks are then developed to measure these skills. Because of the nature of the occupations, performance tests generally will be an integral part of the assessment procedure. Besides developing appropriate items, the other major problem is establishing the competency level—that is, the minimal level of skill needed for certification of competency. This mastery (competency) level can be set logically or, preferably, empirically.

Evaluation   Any general statements about the validity of vocational aptitude tests must be qualified since, as might be expected, validity coefficients are highly situation-specific (Ghiselli, 1966; Super and Crites, 1962). It is clear, however, that validity coefficients of vocational aptitude tests used to predict vocational criteria are generally lower than those for intelligence or scholastic aptitude tests predicting academic criteria. It is also clear that prediction generally is better when the criterion is performance in a training program rather than on-the-job performance.

Because scores on vocational aptitude tests often correlate with other relevant variables (such as intelligence and education), the relative contribution of vocational aptitude measures to predictive efficiency should be assessed in terms of their incremental validity. However, this procedure is infrequently used. Similarly, studies using multivariate prediction models and moderator variables are only now beginning to appear. Harking back to Dunnette's warning that the idea of *the* criterion is a gross oversimplification (Dunnette, 1966), studies should attempt to predict specific job behaviors. Finally, in business and industrial situations where personnel decisions often are on an accept-reject basis, and the contribution of a worker (potentially) can be assessed in dollar terms, it is surprising to find so little validity data expressed as decision-making accuracy or utility indices.

It is also necessary to distinguish between predicting future performance (predictive validity) and predicting present performance (concurrent validity). That is, in some circumstances an employer may want to hire a worker who, over the long run and with the appropriate training, will be an asset to his company. In other situations he may have a job that needs to be done immediately, and consequently he needs someone who currently possesses the skills to do the job. In the former case we are interested in predictive validity and require an aptitude measure; in the latter case we are interested in concurrent validity and an ability or proficiency measure. The situation is further complicated by the fact that vocational aptitudes and abilities vary as a function of the maturity and experience of the subject (Fleishman, 1972). Thus even though two persons may have the same test score, one person's score may represent the limits of his ability whereas the other's score may represent a still-developing ability. These scores would, of course, have different implications. Again we have an illustration of the necessity for interpreting test scores in the context of their relationship to other variables.

PROBLEMS IN MEASURING APTITUDES AND ABILITIES

At this point we shall review some of the major problems encountered when measuring aptitudes and abilities, and suggest some ways in which these problems might be overcome. We shall consider three major problem areas: the fact that abilities change, testing of minority groups, and the question of how other factors interact with abilities to determine performance. The first problem arises because abilities change with age and can be modified by appropriate training. Testing minority groups can present a problem because persons in these groups often do not have the same background experiences, and thus opportunities to develop their abilities, as does the middle-class individual. The third problem reflects the fact that performance in any situation is determined by a multiplicity of factors.

Changes in Ability

It is obvious, to even the most casual observer, that abilities change with age. Perhaps the most dramatic changes occur during childhood and adolescence. During this period almost all skills and abilities increase rapidly. (This fact is reflected in the use of age- and grade-equivalent scores on ability and achievement tests.) Not only do abilities increase during earlier years, they also decline in later life. Thus, if one were to plot intellectual development as a function of age, he would obtain a somewhat S-shaped curve (see Figure 16.4). This curve shows rapid growth during childhood, followed by a slower increase in adolescence and the early adult years. Mental ability then appears to reach a maximum in the early adult years, remains constant through middle age or later, and then declines.

Figure 16.4 presents an oversimplified picture, for several reasons. One is that the shape of the curve will depend on the ability being tested. Some abilities, particularly speeded and perceptual tasks, peak and decline relatively early. Others, particularly more complex reasoning skills, develop more slowly and decline less readily[8] (see Figure 16.5). Thus, rather than making general statements about the growth and decline of abilities, we must always refer to the growth curve for a spe-

Figure 16.4 The mental growth curve. After Guilford (1967) and Thurstone and Ackerson (1929).

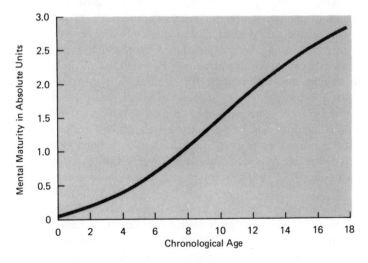

[8]Compare Cattell's concept of fluid and crystallized intelligence.

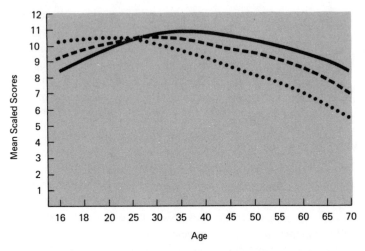

Figure 16.5 Change in abilities with age. Lines show scores on three WAIS subtests. Solid line = vocabulary; dashed line = similarities; and dotted line = picture arrangement. (Adapted from Wechsler. *The Measurement and Appraisal of Human Intelligence,* 1958.)

cific ability. The growth curve is also affected by the experiences of the particular person. This is particularly apparent with the decline of abilities. If an ability is constantly used, its decline will be less rapid. For example, the decline in the ability to do arithmetic computations will be pronounced if a person does not use this skill, whereas it will remain high, or even increase, in people who practice the skill.

Not only is the rate of growth different at various ages, the organization of abilities changes with age (see, e.g., Reinert, 1970; Horn, 1970). We have already referred to this phenomenon when we noted that intelligence tests measured different skills at various age levels. During the preschool years the tests measured perceptual skills; in later years the emphasis was on verbal reasoning abilities. These changes in emphasis reflect differences in experiences at various ages as well as changes associated with physiological and neurological development.

If an individual has not been exposed to the appropriate experiences and training, he obviously cannot develop an ability. However, we might be able to provide him with training that will increase his abilities. The evidence would seem to indicate that specific training is unlikely to affect measures of broad, general abilities, such as IQs or scores on scholastic aptitude tests in a significant way unless the training is intensive and long-lasting (Jensen, 1969; CEEB, 1965). However, more specific abilities, particularly ones that can be learned through formal education, are modifiable by specific training. There is also abundant evidence (see, e.g., Fleishman, 1972) that perceptual and motor abilities can be modified by training.

Although abilities can change as a result of maturation and specific training, the empirical evidence shows that most abilities are relatively stable, even over long periods of time. Why is this so? When considering this question, keep in mind that most evidence of stability refers to the relative position of individuals. That is, although intellectual abilities increase with age, a person's relative position compared to his agemates remains relatively constant. Why? One reason is that similar skills are tested at each age. Thus, persons who have high ability can build on this foundation and remain ahead while people whose ability is weak continue to lag behind. Another reason is the consistency of the environment. Large changes in ability tend to occur as a consequence of large changes in one's environment. Since, for most people, the environment remains relatively stable, at least when considered in the context of the wide variety range of possible environments in a society, we would expect their abilities to remain relatively unchanged. Then, too, as Ferguson (1954) has pointed out, ability tests tend to measure overlearned skills. That is, we measure skills that are so well established that little change can be expected.

What is the practical implications of the fact that there are changes in ability? The obvious implication is that we must always consider the developmental level and past experiences of an individual when interpreting his scores on ability measures. His score indicates his level of development at the time of measurement. Whether this represents the maximal level of his development or only a stage in the developmental process will depend on his age and previous experience.

Testing Minority Groups

Throughout our discussion we have emphasized that ability tests measure performance at a given point in time and that the level of performance will be, at least in part, a function of the person's experiences prior to testing. In other words, an individual must have had the opportunity to learn a skill, if he is to be expected to demonstrate it. This fact becomes of particular importance when testing individuals who have had limited opportunities to learn. In our society these people usually are members of minority groups (such as blacks, Chicanos, American Indians) and persons from lower socioeconomic classes.

There are differences in the average score obtained by various minority groups on aptitude tests. For example, on the average, blacks score about one standard deviation below the mean of whites on intelligence tests. There are also social class differences on many specific learning tasks and abilities (Jensen, 1968). So, too, there are sex differences in abilities; for example, males score higher on mechanical ability tests and females on tests of perceptual speed and accuracy. (For a comprehensive review, see Anastasi, 1965; Macoby and Jacklin, 1974; or L. Tyler, 1965).

Given these differences, what can and should we do? For some people, the answer is to not use standardized tests with members of minority groups. They argue that as the tests were developed primarily (if not entirely) on middle-class white populations, and minority group members score lower, the tests are obviously inappropriate and thus should not be used. This is one extreme view. At the other extreme, we could use the tests and interpret them as we would for any other person. This approach makes sense when, and only when, we want to compare an individual to his immediate potential competitors and/or want to determine whether the individual possesses some crucial minimal level of skill. For example, a (valid) reading comprehension test will indicate the student's level of reading ability and predict how well he will do if he enrolls in a course requiring reading skill. This is true whether the student is white or black. Or, to use another example, when hiring persons for a job requiring mechanical ability, we should select the persons scoring highest on a mechanical ability test, regardless of their sex. In other words, as a measure of current status, or for comparisons at a given time, the test may provide useful information.

When we take a longer range view, the problem becomes more complicated. One reason that members of the minority group score lower is that they have not had the essential background experiences. How can we handle this? One approach that has been suggested is to develop separate norms for each (minority) group. Rather than comparing, say, blacks to white norms, we would compare their performance to other blacks; that is to other persons having similar experiences and opportunities for learning. The rationale behind this approach is, of course, to compare an individual to others who have had the same opportunities to develop the skill. A variation of this approach has been used for years: providing separate sex norms for males and females on tests where there are pronounced sex differences.

The approaches discussed above may facilitate accurate interpretation of scores but do not remedy the basic problem—the lack of opportunity to learn. This can only be accomplished by providing training and experiences to persons who are in any way disadvantaged, so that they have an opportunity to learn. The provision of compensatory education, of course, extends well beyond the measurement questions. One aspect, however, is particularly relevant—that is, test-taking skills. In some cases the reason for poor test performance may not be lack of opportunity to learn the skill, it may be not knowing how to demonstrate the ability on a test. In other words, an individual may lack test-taking skills. In this situation, we need to provide persons with experiences in test taking. The Psychological Corporation has developed a set of exercises, called the Test Orientation Procedure, designed to familiarize people with the skills and procedures of test taking. The goal is to decrease the impact of test-taking skills (in this case, lack of them) on test performance, thus providing a more accurate measurement of ability.

Other Factors Determining Performance

One of the truisms of psychology is that behavior is determined by multiple causes. In terms of ability testing, this means that abilities are only one factor in determining performance; interests, values, personality characteristics, motivation, and a myriad of other factors also are important. Moreover, few jobs or academic courses are so simple or specific that only one ability is required. Furthermore, situational factors are important; that is, demands and requirements vary widely, even on presumably similar jobs or courses. The moral is obvious: When trying to predict performance, one must consider more information than just abilities. In addition, we must recognize that there are various ways to attain the same performance level—that is, that people will use different abilities to attain the same level of performance. Or, as Gough has phrased it, psychologists must recognize that there is "no one true path to grace."

The need to incorporate diverse sorts of data has been recognized in various ways. One approach is the use of test batteries, either *ad hoc* batteries or multiple-aptitude batteries, such as the DAT. In addition, many batteries that once measured only cognitive abilities now include personal and vocational preference data in their assessment procedure. For example, both of the major college admissions programs (CEEB and ACT) now include questionnaire data concerning the student's academic and vocational plans. And the DAT has recently added a Career Planning Program as a supplement to the testing program. The information derived from these questionnaires can be used in conjunction with the test scores in educational and vocational planning.

From the researcher, the problem is to determine what variables determine success, and their relative contribution (importance). Since situations (for example, jobs, schools, courses) vary widely, this must be determined in each particular setting. The usual research strategy is multiple regression (see Chapter 10). The typical test user probably will not have the time or the resources to conduct such studies; however, he should familiarize himself with the relevant research literature so he will understand what factors are likely to determine success in settings similar to the one in which he is working.

Some New Approaches

To conclude our discussion of measures of maximal performance, let us look briefly at some recent developments in the measurement of abilities.

One development has been the increased flexibility in testing procedures brought about by advances in technology. For example, it is now possible to administer tests by computers and other electronic devices (Atkinson, 1968). Computers can present prose material, graphs, and other pictorial representations. Of more importance, however, is the fact that a computer can be programmed to score responses and make decisions regarding sequences of items. That is, when a student responds to a particular item, the computer can score the item, integrate other information about the student (such as stage of learning and past performance) and select, from among various possibilities, the next item to be presented. In essence, the computer has been programmed to prescribe a test.

A closely related application is sequential testing (Weiss, 1974). A sequential test is similar to the branching format described above, but is more limited in scope. The crucial characteristic of a sequential test is that the response to each item determines what item will be administered next. The test usually starts with an item of moderate difficulty. If a student passes the first item, he is given a more difficult item; if he fails, he is given an easier item. A similar procedure is followed throughout the test. This format adapts the testing to the student's performance and requires fewer items than a conventional test.

A second approach is to consider different types of abilities. One that is currently been receiving intense interest is cognitive styles (see, e.g., Kogan, 1971; Messick, 1970). Cognitive styles are methods of perceiving, remembering, and thinking, and of apprehending, transforming, and using information. They differ from abilities in that abilities are concerned with level of skill whereas cognitive styles emphasize the manner and form of processing information (Kogan, 1971). Thus, in many ways, they represent a middle-ground between abilities and personality factors. Kogan reviewed the literature on nine cognitive styles (including field dependence-independence, reflection-impulsivity, cognitive complexity-simplicity) and concluded that they can be measured reliably and are relatively independent of ability factors. One thrust of the research in progress is to determine how these styles affect how material is learned.

Finally, two recent articles have been concerned with the nature of abilities, suggesting that our traditional ways of conceptualizing abilities may not be the most fruitful approach. Estes (1974) attempted to integrate learning theory with ability measurement. His major point was that knowing a person's score on an ability test tells us little about the learning processes that led to the score. Thus he suggests the development of measures that more directly indicate the nature of the learning process used. Glaser (1972), in contrast, looked more to the use of ability tests. His concern was that aptitudes should be defined in terms of the type of performances or learning they predict. That is, we should first determine the nature of learning tasks, and then develop tests that predict success in these types of learning. Both are suggesting a more developmental view of abilities.

SUGGESTED FURTHER READING FOR PART IV

Anderson, R. How to construct achievement tests to measure comprehension. *Review of Educational Research,* 1972, *42*, 145–170.

Argues that comprehension can best be measured by well-constructed multiple-choice items, particularly ones presenting new examples.

Block, J. E. (Ed.) *Mastery learning.* New York: Holt, Rinehart and Winston, 1971.

Papers describing the mastery approach to teaching and testing; a basic reference in the area.

Bloom, B. S., Hastings, T., & Madaus, G. F. *Handbook on formative and summative evaluation of student learning.* New York: McGraw-Hill, 1971.

The theory and practice of the mastery approach; includes extensive number of sample items in various subject areas; an excellent book and reference.

Brown, F. G. *Measurement and evaluation.* Itasca, Ill.: F. E. Peacock, 1971.

An introduction to the construction and use of tests in education.

Butcher, H. J. *Human intelligence: Its nature and assessment.* New York: Harper Torchbooks, 1973.

An introductory but broad-range survey of the nature of intellectual abilities. (Originally published by Methuen, 1968.)

Ebel, R. *Essentials of educational measurement.* Englewood Cliffs, N.J.: Prentice-Hall, 1972.

The best presentation of the more traditional approach to educational measurement; many examples of items; an excellent reference.

Estes, W. K. Learning theory and intelligence. *American Psychologist,* 1974, *29*, 740–749.

Suggests that ability tests indicate status but do not tell how testee arrived at performance level; thus argues for more integration of testing and learning theories.

Fleishman, E. A. On the relation between abilities, learning and human performance. *American Psychologist,* 1972, *27,* 1017–1032.

Describes his research on the structure of perceptual and motor abilities and their relation to skill acquisition and task performance.

Glaser, R. Individuals and learning: The new aptitudes. *Educational Researcher,* 1972, *1* (No. 6), 5–13.

Argues that aptitude tests should be constructed so as to provide a more specific and direct indication of learning potential.

Goslin, D. A. *The search for ability.* New York: Russell Sage Foundation, 1963.

Describes role of standardized tests in American society and discusses social consequences of test use.

Horn, J. L. Intelligence: Why it grows, why it declines. *Transaction,* November 1967, 23–31.

A clear introduction to Cattell's concepts of fluid and crystallized intelligence.

Hunt, J. McV. (Ed.) *Human intelligence.* New Brunswick, N.J.: Transaction Books (E. P. Dutton), 1972.

Series of papers on the nature, measurement, and utilization of intellectual abilities.

Klein, S. P., & Hart, F. M. Chance and systematic factors affecting essay grades. *Journal of Educational Measurement,* 1968, *5,* 197–206.

A study illustrating some of the persistent problems involved in grading essay exams.

Lindvall, C. M., & Nitko, A. J. *Measuring pupil achievement and aptitude.* (2d ed.) New York: Harcourt Brace Jovanovich, 1975.

An introduction to measuring educational achievement; emphasis on using tests to facilitate instruction.

McClelland, D. C. Testing for competence rather than for "intelligence." *American Psychologist,* 1973, *28,* 1–14.

A critical evaluation of intelligence tests with suggestions for improvements in measuring intellectual ability.

McNemar, Q. Lost: Our intelligence. Why? *American Psychologist,* 1964, *19,* 871–882.

A defense of the usefulness of the concept of general intelligence.

Mehrens, W. A., & Lehmann, I. J. *Standardized tests in education.* (2d ed.) New York: Holt, Rinehart and Winston, 1975.

An introduction to use of standardized tests in educational settings; discussion of problems, and many good illustrations of commonly used tests.

Taylor, I. A., & Getzels, J. W. (Eds.) *Perspectives in creativity.* Chicago: Aldine, 1975.

A survey of the current status of research on creativity described in papers by leading researchers.

Thorndike, R. L. (Ed.) *Educational measurement.* (2d ed.) Washington, D.C.: American Council on Education, 1971.

The most comprehensive discussion of measurement in education with chapters by leaders in the area.

Wiseman, S. (Ed.) *Intelligence and ability.* Baltimore: Penguin Books, 1967.

A collection of classic papers in the history of the measurement of mental abilities.

PART V

MEASURES OF TYPICAL PERFORMANCE

Earlier we made a distinction between two broad classes of tests: those that measure maximal performance and those that measure typical performance. This distinction was based, in part, on the set that the test taker adopted when responding to the test items. On maximal performance tests, test takers are instructed to do their best, to try to obtain the highest possible score; on measures of typical performance they are asked to indicate their usual or habitual reactions. As might be expected, different types of tests fall into the two classes. The types of tests discussed in Part IV of this book—ability, achievement, and aptitude tests—were all maximal performance tests. In contrast, measures of interests, attitudes, values, and personality characteristics are usually typical performance tasks. These will be discussed in this part of the book.

When measuring typical performance we encounter certain problems that are absent, or at least less pronounced, when measuring maximal performance. In a broad sense we can say that the major problem is to ensure that our measurement actually reflects typical performance. For example, when measuring extraversion we want to know whether the test taker typically acts in an extraverted manner. Most people are extraverted at certain times and in certain situations. Thus, if asked to respond as an extraverted person would, they could do so. But this is not what we want to measure; we want to determine how the person usually behaves. Thus we have to construct our measures so as to ensure that responses indicate typical behaviors.

A closely related problem is that of response biases. Many people, either consciously or unconsciously, adopt a particular set when answering personality items. For example, a premed student, when taking an interest inventory, might answer items as he believed a physician would answer them rather than express his true interests. Consequently, here too we must develop ways to identify and/or control such response biases.

We shall also consider three other problems inherent in personality measurement. One is the definition of the traits to be measured. Since personality encompasses such a broad range of behaviors, different theorists focus on different aspects of personality, and terms are often only vaguely defined, the problem of what is being measured becomes crucial. A second problem involves the effects of the testing on the individual being tested. More so than in other areas of testing, in personality assessment the testing process may actually change the person's responses and/or his behavior. Finally, we shall consider the ethical issues involved in personality measurement, particularly the question of whether personality assessment constitutes an invasion of an individual's privacy.

In our discussion we shall consider three general approaches to measuring typical performance. The first is by means of self-report inventories. In this method the test taker is presented with a large number of statements that describe interests, attitudes, feelings, and behaviors; his task is to indicate whether or not the statements describe him. The basic assumption of this method is that the individual himself is in the best position to observe and report on his behavior and reactions. The major problem, of course, is that he may not present an unbiased report.

There are several ways to construct scales for self-report inventories. Three widely used methods will be discussed in detail. Logical keying (also called *a priori* or intuitive keying) involves nothing more than selecting items that appear to reflect the trait being measured. As might be expected, this results in obvious scales, which are open to dissimulation. In the second approach, empirical (or external) keying, items are selected on the basis of their relationship to some external criterion. For example, interest scales are developed by comparing the responses of people in different occupations, and personality scales are developed by identifying responses that typify certain classes of people. In homogeneous (or internal) keying, scales are developed by clustering items that are highly intercorrelated. In many ways logical keying is the analog of content validity, empirical keying the analog of criterion-related validity, and homogeneous keying the analog of construct validity.

The second general approach to personality assessment is through projective techniques. The basic assumption of projective techniques is that a person will respond to an unstructured or ambiguous situation in accord with his personality structure. Thus stimuli (items) are usually ambiguous, unstructured, and/or incomplete, and the test taker's task is to place some structure, meaning, or interpretation on the stimulus. From these responses, the psychologist makes inferences about the person's personality structure and dynamics.

The third major approach is situational tests. Here the test taker is placed in a "real-life" or contrived situation and his behavior is observed and rated. Because scores on situational tests are often ratings, rating errors must be taken into account when performance is interpreted. And, though they are more realistic, situational tests are usually more costly than other methods of personality assessment. Although we will be discussing situational tests as measures of typical performance, you will be able to see readily how they could be used to measure maximal performance.

As with our discussion of maximal performance tests, in our discussion of typical performance tests we shall make no effort to survey existing tests. Rather, we shall present a small number of examples, ones that clearly point out some principle of test construction or a problem encountered in personality measurement.

17

SELF-REPORT INVENTORIES

Our original distinction between measures of maximal and typical performance emphasized the purpose of the measurement and the test taker's set. That is, on maximal performance measures the goal is to obtain an indication of the test taker's best possible performance, on typical performance measures we are interested in his habitual or usual performance. Thus, on maximal performance tests, the test taker was instructed to do his best, to obtain the highest possible score; on typical performance tests, he is instructed to report his typical reactions or behavior.

The two types of tests also differ along several other dimensions. One is the types of behavior measured. Maximal performance measures are concerned with cognitive functions (skills, abilities, knowledge), whereas typical performance measures focus on interests, feelings, attitudes, and reactions. Then, too, on maximal performance tests there is usually an external criterion or basis for determining what are correct and incorrect answers. In contrast, on typical performance measures, the keyed response usually represents the predominant response tendency of some designated group. This does not mean scoring is any less objective, only that the basis for keying responses is different.

Although typical performance tests measure diverse types of behaviors (interests, attitudes, feelings about oneself), we shall use the generic term "personality" to refer to the domains measured by typical performance measures.

Approaches to Personality Measurement

More than other areas of psychological and educational testing, personality measurement is characterized by a variety of approaches. The reasons for this diversity are several. Personality, as usually defined, encompasses a broad and heterogeneous area and includes a plethora of concepts and constructs (see, e.g., Hall and Lindzey, 1970). And, historically, the personality area has been the subject of much theorizing, with different theories leading to different approaches to both the definition and measurement of central concepts. Nevertheless, three distinct approaches to personality measurement can be identified: self-report methods, projective methods, and situational methods.[1] We shall discuss each method briefly here, and then consider each in more detail later.

Self-report methods   One method of measuring personality characteristics is to have an individual describe or characterize himself. He may be presented with a list of adjectives and asked to check the ones that describe his personality; he may be asked whether a series of statements describe him; he may be asked to report his usual reactions to a situation, or to indicate his attitudes, interests, or values. The common element in these situations, and in all self-report techniques, is that the individual provides a description or report of his own behavior and/or reactions.

The basic assumption behind this approach is quite simple: The individual is in the best position to observe, describe, and report upon his own behavior. After all, you are the only person that is within your skin 24 hours of a day, 365 days of the year; you are always present to observe your own behavior. Any observer would not be privy to all aspects of your life. He could not know your attitudes or reactions to certain events, your thoughts, and your reasons for taking certain actions, although he could ask you about them or infer them from your overt behavior. In short, only you can observe yourself in all situations; thus you can base your report on the widest possible range of observations.

A corollary of the assumption, that the person will report his behavior in an unbiased manner, rests on less solid ground. Many personality theories, in fact, imply that the person will present a somewhat biased picture of himself. Thus, when constructing and scoring self-report techniques, it becomes necessary either to eliminate the opportunity to present a biased report or to identify the degree to which such tendencies operate. In fact, much effort in developing personality tests and

[1] We shall use the terms "method" and "technique" interchangeably; e.g., projective method or projective technique.

much of the controversy over the value of personality measures is directly related to this issue.

Of the many possible methods that could be used to elicit a person's description of himself, the most widely used is the *personality inventory*. An inventory consists of a relatively large number of statements, such as:

> I frequently get headaches.
> I enjoy competitive games.
> New and different experiences excite me.
> People often expect too much of me.

The test taker responds true (or agree, or some other variation) to the statement if the item describes or characterizes him, and false (or disagree) if the statement does not describe him. Because all persons respond to the same set of questions, an inventory can be likened to a standardized interview. Although other writers stress various characteristics of the inventory approach (for example, "objective" scoring) we shall use the term in the dictionary sense; that is, an inventory is a detailed listing of objects or events. This view stresses the broad coverage and multi-item format of the inventory approach.

Rather than using descriptive statements or phrases, an inventory might be composed of a list of adjectives (for example, honest, pigheaded, intelligent, aggressive, obnoxious, simpleminded, loving) with the test taker's task being to check those adjectives that describe him. Such tests are, not surprisingly, called *adjective check lists*. Another approach has the student check those problems, from a list of problems, that pertain to him. Another approach uses statements of possible attitudes towards persons or events (for example, "Blacks are inferior to whites"), with the test taker indicating his agreement with the expressed attitude. Although *attitude scales* are constructed in a different manner than personality inventories (that is, with systematic attempts to scale items) they are a type of self-report.

Self-report techniques are often referred to as objective personality tests. If we follow our previous usage of objectivity as referring to recording and scoring procedures, self-report techniques are objective measures. However, if, in addition, we consider that responses to the items are not unbiased, that they reflect personal needs and characteristics, a subjective or projective element clearly enters into the measurement (Meehl, 1945).

Projective methods   Projective techniques present the test taker with ambiguous stimuli and ask him to interpret or impose some structure upon them. This methodology follows from the projective hypothesis that states that an individual, when confronted with an ambiguous stimulus situation, will impose a structure on the stimulus that reflects his particular personality organization. Thus by knowing how a person interprets and structures ambiguous stimuli we can infer something about his personality.

An example of a projective technique, which is familiar to most persons, is the Rorschach Method (Ink Blot test). The Rorschach consists of a series of designs that resemble ink blots; the test taker's task is to tell what he sees in the blots. Here, obviously, the stimuli have no inherent meaning; therefore, any meaning must be supplied by the subject, the meaning he projects into the blots. Another widely used variety of projective method is the Thematic Apperception Test (TAT). The TAT consists of a series of semiambiguous pictures showing persons engaged in various activities; the test taker's task is to construct a story describing the characters and action. Another approach is the sentence completion test. Here, sentence stems such as "My greatest failure was . . ." serve as stimuli, and the task is to complete the sentence.

Situational methods   In the third general class of personality assessment methods, the common requirement is that the individual is placed in a situation that calls for some action or reaction, his behavior is observed and/or recorded, and a rating is made of the personality characteristics displayed. For example, several persons might be brought together and instructed to devise a plan for an advertising campaign. By observing how the persons interact with each other, how they present their ideas, how their ideas are accepted by other members of the group, who emerges as a leader, how they handle assignments, and other relevant behaviors, an observer could rate the persons along several personality dimensions (for example, leadership, sociability, effectiveness of expression, dominance, cooperativeness).

A widely used, perhaps overused, situational method is the interview. Although we usually think of one person interviewing another, it is possible to have several interviewers (as in a press conference or selection boards) and/or several candidates being interviewed simultaneously by one interviewer. The interview procedure itself can vary from a highly structured sequence of questions to an open-ended encounter that follows the interests of the participants. So, too, ratings or evaluations resulting from interviews may vary from quantitative ratings on well-defined dimensions to global, qualitative evaluations.

Before discussing each approach in detail, let us briefly look at some of the major problems in personality assessment.

Some Problems Peculiar to Personality Measurement

In most respects the measurement of maximal performance is quite straightforward. Such is not the case with typical performance measures. To cite only several of the more obvious problems, in personality assessment the test taker may not be clear what characteristics are being measured or how scores will be interpreted. There is also more opportunity for responses to be distorted or items to be misinterpreted and, because expression of personality characteristics may be more situation-specific than on ability measures (Mischel, 1968), the problems of item sampling loom larger.

What is being measured?   Aptitude and ability tests assume a trait model and the purpose of the measurement is to establish an individual's scale position for each trait measured. An analogous approach can be used in personality measurement. Since each individual's pattern of trait scores will differ from every other individual's, each individual will have a unique personality structure (cf. Allport, 1955). However, we usually consider only one trait, or a small number of traits, at one time. If, however, we cluster individuals on the basis of the similarity of their trait patterns we have a *typology,* with "types" being defined by the similarity of their scores on various traits. Note that this typology does not involve mutually exclusive types; rather, it is a typology formed by using a multidimensional trait model.

An objection to the trait approach is that it is too static to represent adequately the dynamic nature of personality. Although there is no doubt that any measurement procedure will necessarily "freeze" personality at a given point, it is difficult to ascertain exactly what a dynamic measurement of personality would entail. If by dynamic is meant changing over time, then repeated testings combined sequentially (similar to combining frames to produce movement in a motion picture) could represent the dynamic nature of personality. If by dynamic is meant some complex configuration, then we would have to resort to complex multivariate methods of analysis.

On self-report inventories another sort of question can be raised. If a person responds "yes" to the item "I frequently have headaches," how shall we interpret his response? We can, of course, accept the statement at face value as an accurate report. Or should we accept the response only as the second best source of information about the individual, the best source being direct observation? Or, should we view the response as an interesting bit of verbal behavior and determine the meaning of the response by empirical studies? (Meehl, 1945). In this view, what is important are the behavioral correlates of making the particular response. This third viewpoint is espoused by persons supporting the empirical keying of personality inventories (see below). In this approach the meaning of response is determined by what the response signifies; that is, by its empirical correlates.

Does the measurement process affect the individual?   One feature that distinguishes psychological measurement from physical measurement is the degree to which the measurement process may affect the object (person) being measured. In the measurement of maximal performance it is recognized that the test may affect the test taker's behavior, but this effect frequently occurs only after the testing is completed. For example, a student finding that he cannot answer many of the questions on an exam may vow to study harder in the future. There are exceptions, however, as when a student experiences failure in the early part of a test and, consequently, gives up and does not try on the remaining items. (It is precisely for this reason that it was suggested that tests begin with several easy items.)

Tests of typical performance appear to be more susceptible to changes produced by the testing situation. It is not uncommon for a counselee who has just taken a test to tell the counselor "You know, when I started to think about my interests when taking that interest inventory, I decided that I really don't like engineering after all." But there are also effects that influence responses to the test items. For example, when confronted with items that force them to think about themselves, some people become defensive; others are unwilling to say other than pleasant and socially desirable things about themselves.

If these reactions carry over outside the testing situation, the person has literally been changed by the testing. If they are manifested only on the test and do not carry over outside the test, the validity of the test becomes questionable.

Response sets and styles   On maximal performance tests the only ways to distort scores are to not respond, deliberately select wrong answers, or guess. On typical performance tests, however, the situation is more complex. For example, the test taker may alter his responses in an attempt to picture himself in a more (or less) desirable light than would honest responding. Or, the test taker may attempt to present a particular picture of himself—for example, as being aggressive, sociable, having the interests of physicians, or being very religious. Such attempts to respond so as to present a particular picture of oneself are referred to as *response sets*.

When the test taker adopts a particular response set he responds as he thinks a person with the particular characteristics he is trying to emulate would respond. When items are ambiguous or subtle (in the sense that their keying is not obvious) this will be more difficult than when the meaning and scoring of the item is obvious. Yet the evidence is overwhelming that test takers do adopt response sets and that these sets do affect their scores (see, e.g., Rorer, 1965; Longstaff, 1948; A. Edwards, 1957; Berg, 1967; Jackson and Messick, 1958). The test constructor thus must devise means of identifying and/or controlling this tendency to dissimulate.

To illustrate a response set, we will consider social desirability. A. Edwards (1957, 1967) has shown that personality items can be ranked, with high reliability, along a dimension that indicates whether the statement is considered socially desirable or undesirable.[2] For example, the statement "I am an intelligent and creative person" would almost certainly be judged as highly desirable, whereas the statement "I often have temper tantrums when something doesn't go my way" would almost certainly be rated as socially undesirable. By having judges rate items on social desirability, we could obtain a social desirability scale value for each item and/or develop a social desirability scale.

Edwards' contention was that people respond to items on personality inventories not only in terms of their actual behavior and characteristics, but also in terms of the social desirability of the items. When confronted with the item, "I have strange and peculiar thoughts," the test taker's response will be determined both by whether he has what he considers to be strange and peculiar thoughts *and* by the perceived social desirability of the item, in this case its extreme undesirability. As would be expected, items that are rated as being socially desirable are endorsed with greater frequency than items rated as being socially undesirable; in fact, there is a very high positive correlation between the social desirability rating of a item and the probability of its being endorsed.

---

[2]Edwards (1957) has defined social desirability as the proportion of people who will say an item describes them. Thus, it is a normative description. He also considers social desirability to be a unitary dimension.

The results of the research on social desirability have been given widely divergent interpretations; from the conclusion that the major source of variance in certain personality test scores can be attributed to the social desirability response set to the view that saying undesirable things about oneself is an essential aspect of many personality syndromes (see, e.g., Block, 1965; A. Edwards, 1957, 1959; Rorer, 1965).

Response sets, such as social desirability, are dependent upon the content of the item. That is, a test taker cannot alter his responses to produce the desired picture unless he can see the relationship between the item content and the probable keying of the item. In addition to content-dependent response sets, various content-independent response tendencies, or *response styles,* have been identified. Examples include the tendency to select some response when unsure of the corect response (guessing), the tendency to agree with a statement when having no informed basis for agreeing or disagreeing (acquiescence), and the tendency to avoid extreme responses (central tendency). Note than an essential condition for manifestation of a response style is that the test taker has no rational way of choosing between responses, usually because the item is ambiguous, meaningless, or difficult. In these situations it is postulated that the test taker will respond, not at random, but in accord with a particular response style. Note, also, that response styles may operate on tests of maximal performance as well as tests of typical performance; for example, when unsure of the correct response to true-false items, most people respond true.

Since Cronbach (1946, 1950) first voiced concern over the effects of response tendencies, there has been a plethora of research studies. Like the studies of response sets, different investigators have reached widely divergent conclusions (compare, e.g., Jackson and Messick, 1958, and Rorer, 1965). In a comprehensive review, Rorer (1965) concluded that response styles seldom explain more than 20 percent of the variance in scores; that there is no reason to believe that respondents rely on response styles on objective personality, interest, and attitude inventories; and that response styles are easily alterable and test-specific. Nevertheless, the search for viable response styles goes on and we must be aware of the possible effects of response tendencies when constructing and interpreting tests.

Item sampling   One final problem should be briefly noted, that of obtaining a large and representative sampling of items. When measuring achievement, abilities, and aptitudes, the content/skill universe is relatively well-defined and items can be scaled in terms of difficulty. If items are sampled from various areas and at varying difficulty levels, a test can be constructed (using relatively few items) that will accurately estimate how the individual would perform in the universe being sampled.

In measuring typical performance the situation is more complex. The traits being measured are broad, frequently heterogeneous, and often not clearly defined. The variety of possible stimuli is exceedingly large (e.g., Edwards and Walsh, 1963, report a pool of 3000 personality items; there are more than 18,000 adjectives in the English language to describe personality). Because people seem to respond to the nuances of personality items, minor differences in content and wording often produce large differences in response rates. And, since behavior is multiply determined, to sort out the effects of any given variable requires a large number of items. The designation "typical performance" also implies that the behavior measured occurs in a wide variety of situations. Thus, the number of items on personality tests usually is much larger than on maximal performance test; in fact, most personality inventories consist of several hundred items.

SCALE CONSTRUCTION STRATEGIES

The common element in all self-report techniques is that the test taker serves as the observer and reporter of his own behaviors, attitudes, or feelings. However, several other characteristics also typify self-report techniques: The measuring instrument is usually an inventory; the format is of the paper-and-pencil type; several traits are measured simultaneously by different scales; scoring is normative; and appropriate procedures must be built into the test to control the action of response sets and styles.

Because the interpretation of any score depends upon the manner in which the scale was constructed and because several distinct approaches to scale construction are used on self-report inventories, we shall consider three scale construction strategies in detail: rational (or *a priori*) methods, empirical keying, and homogeneous keying. After we have discussed these test construction strategies, we shall illustrate how they have been applied in the construction of extant personality inventories.

Logical Keying

One approach to scale construction, which was used on most earlier instruments, is to assign items to scales on theoretical or rational bases. In practice, this means once the test constructor has decided on the trait to be measured, he writes items that *appear* to measure that trait. For example, a scale measuring "introversion" would probably be composed of such items as the following:

> I blush easily.
> At a party, I introduce myself to people I do not know.
> I prefer small parties with friends to large gatherings.
> Reading is one of my favorite activities.

Keying of the items would be on rational bases only. Although there might not be universal agreement regarding the keying of any single item, the scale construction procedure favors items whose keying is obvious. (Note, you probably could easily tell what response to each of the sample items would be scored for introversion.)

The construction of a personality inventory often begins in this manner, by writing items that appear to bear a relationship to the trait being measured. But this approach must be treated as only a beginning, since items that appear to measure a given trait may not, in fact, measure that trait. Also, a test composed only of obvious items would be exceedingly prone to distortion and dissimulation. In short, logically keyed inventories are of limited value.

Empirical Keying

In the second approach, items are selected on the basis of their empirical relationship with a criterion measure. The first step in this procedure is to select a (criterion) group that displays the characteristic or trait to be measured. Suppose, for example, that we were interested in leadership. (Assume that leadership is, in fact, a trait.)[3] After defining what we mean by leadership, our next step would be to identify a group of persons who can be considered as leaders. One possible approach would be to define leaders as people who have been elected to offices in certain organizations. Thus, if we were dealing with a high school population, we might define our criterion group (leaders) as including class officers, student council representatives, captains of athletic teams, and presidents of major clubs and organizations.

The next question is: What characteristics differentiate the leaders from other students? To answer this question requires at least two things: a pool of stimuli (items) and a comparison group composed of persons who are not leaders. To collect a pool of items we might consult textbooks and studies of leadership behavior, ask peers and other judges to list qualities they think describe leaders, and review other tests measuring leadership and related traits. From these sources we could then write or select a pool of potential items. As nonleaders we might use participants in athletics and clubs or a cross-section of the student body, excluding those students designated as leaders. We would then administer the items to both groups. To determine which items differentiated between leaders and nonleaders, we would look at the proportion of students in each group who answered each item in a particular manner.

Suppose that we follow the procedure described and obtain the following hypothetical results:

	Proportion responding "true"		
Item	Leaders	Others	Difference
I would rather give than follow directions	.75	.37	.38
People often ask my advice	.36	.32	.04
I like to listen to classical music	.28	.07	.21
I frequently have headaches	.09	.12	−.03

Which items distinguish the leaders from other persons? Although there are differences between the two groups on all four items, only the first and third items show

---

[3]Note that although we say leadership "ability," what we are interested in measuring is the person's habitual or usual behavior in leadership situations. That is, we are interested in the characteristics that distinguish leaders—how the person typically behaves, not whether he knows how a leader behaves. In other words, we are interested in the personal characteristics and behaviors that typify leaders.

relatively large differences. Thus, these two items would be included on the leadership scale and the second and fourth items discarded.[4] Note, also, that although the results for the first and fourth items might have been predicted, we probably would have expected the second item also to show a difference; yet because there was no difference, the item would be eliminated. Conversely, although there is no logical grounds for expecting leaders to prefer classical music more than other persons, they did; thus, this item would be included on the leadership scale.

By using similar procedures with a large number of items, a scale could be developed. The method of item selection guarantees that the scale will have concurrent validity; that is, since each item selected discriminates between the groups, a combination of these items will also differentiate the groups. And by repeating the procedure using the same pool of items but different criterion groups, a multiscale test could be developed, with each scale measuring a particular criterion or trait.

Two aspects of the procedure deserve especial mention. First, inasmuch as items are keyed to a particular criterion group, the nature of the criterion group will be reflected in the scale. In our example, leaders were defined as persons holding certain offices. But is this an adequate definition of leadership? Does election to an office really constitute leadership? Even granted that the persons selected are leaders, is the group representative of all leaders? If a different definition of leadership is used, or if the criterion group does not adequately reflect the stipulated definition, the scale will not be completely appropriate. In other words, whenever using empirically keyed scales, score interpretations will be relative to the original criterion group.

A related concern is the generalizability of the scale. The test construction procedure has guaranteed that the scale will have concurrent validity. But will it predict criteria other than membership in the original criterion group? Does the test make any theoretical sense? Such questions can only be answered by further study of the test. Whereas the first question is a straightforward empirical question, the second is more complicated. Because the items were chosen on empirical bases, their theoretical importance was irrelevant. Yet if we wish to use tests to measure constructs in a theory, we have to be able to make theoretical sense out of empirical results. An important consideration then becomes how to integrate seemingly meaningless results (for example, the fact that leaders like classical music) into the theoretical network. We have, in short, an exercise in construct validity.

Homogeneous Keying

A third strategy for scale development is based on the view that only homogeneous scales can be used to measure psychologically meaningful variables. That is, the *sine qua non* in scale construction is that the scale must be homogeneous. Thus, when scales are being developed, items not correlating with the other

---

[4]The present discussion has been simplified so as to emphasize the basic logic of the procedure. There are a variety of more sophisticated statistical methods that could be used in item selection. In addition, items would be included on a test only if they attained a desired level of statistical significance.

scale items are eliminated because they are considered to be measuring a different trait or construct. Only those items that correlate with other items in the scale are retained.

The scale development process proceeds as follows. First, a large number of items are administered to an appropriate standardization group—usually a representative sample of the population in which the test will be used. The intercorrelations among items are then subjected to some analytic procedure that clusters items into homogeneous groups (for example, factor analysis). These homogeneous item groupings form the basis of a scale. The content of the items comprising the scale give meaning (and a name or label) to the scale. Here we assume that the analytic procedure will identify measurable dimensions; if a proposed construct is not represented by a cluster of items, the construct is presumed not to exist.

The process of homogeneous keying results in unidimensional scales that have some construct validity. Whether the scales have criterion-related validity is another question, one that can be answered only by empirical data. Although psychologists who advocate homogeneous keying feel that the scale construction procedure ensures that scales will measure important dimensions, more empirically oriented persons will demand empirical proof of the scale's validity. So, too, psychologists who prefer homogeneous keying demand that the empiricist explain the meaning of their scales. In short, the difference between empirical and homogeneous keying is in the methods, data preferences, and research styles.

Combining Strategies

Logical, empirical, and homogeneous keying represent three major approaches to the construction of scales for self-report personality inventories. Although the rational approach is no doubt the weakest, all approaches use rational methods when selecting items in the earliest stages of test construction. That is, items are included in the pool of potential items only if there is some rationale for doing so.

Perhaps the optimal test construction strategy is a combination of empirical and homogeneous keying. In this approach, homogeneous scales would first be constructed. These homogeneous keys would then be validated against empirical criteria, and those items that did not demonstrate empirical validity would be eliminated. The final scale would, thus, be both homogeneous and empirically valid—thereby, hopefully, being both practically and theoretically useful.

In many situations, some particular property of test items may be of such importance that it must be controlled by the construction process. To illustrate, Edwards concluded that the social desirability variable has such pervasive importance that any acceptable personality scale must assure that its influence is controlled. Thus in constructing his personality inventory, he attempted to eliminate the influence of the social desirability variable by adopting a forced-choice format (that is, the test taker must choose between two equally desirable, or equally undesirable, alternatives). Although he developed scales that measured psychologically meaningful constructs, the entire test construction process was dominated by the desire to control the effects of the social desirability.

EXAMPLES OF SELF-REPORT INVENTORIES

We shall now turn to a consideration of some specific tests and inventories that exemplify the various approaches to scale construction. We will show how the approach was used in the development of the test, describe the test that resulted, and briefly discuss the validity, usefulness, and limitations of the test. Because of the obvious deficiencies of scales developed on purely *a priori* bases, we will not discuss tests developed by purely logical methods. The reader should be aware, however, that many of the earliest personality inventories (some of which, unfortunately, are still available on the market) utilized this mode of test construction.

The Strong-Campbell Interest Inventory

That men and women who work in different occupations have different abilities, interests, attitudes, and personality characteristics is a well-documented fact. Because the measurement of vocational interests—the preferences, likes, and dislikes of persons in various occupational and vocational groups—illustrates many of the problems in personality measurement, it will be used as a jumping-off point for our discussion.

Approaches to the measurement of interests   Before constructing an instrument for measuring vocational interests, the test constructor must make three fundamental decisions. First, he must decide which approach to interest measurement he will follow. Second, he must decide whether to measure interest in specific occupations or in broad vocational areas. And, third, if he chooses the inventory approach, he must decide between empirical and homogeneous keying. Let us consider each decision briefly.

Vocational interests can be measured in at least four different ways (Super and Crites, 1962). One approach would be to study *stated interests* by asking each individual what occupations he was interested in and using his response as the measure of interest. Or we could consider his *manifest interests* by observing how the person actually spends his time. Thus, if a student spent countless hours collecting rocks, his manifest interest would be in geology. A third approach, called *tested interests*, attempts to derive an indication of interests from scores on standardized achievement tests—the assumption being that a person will learn and retain more information about areas of high interest. A fourth approach asks the test taker to express his liking or preference for a wide variety of vocationally related activities. That is, we take an inventory of his vocational and occupational preferences; hence, the label *inventoried interests*. Almost all instruments that measure vocational interests fall within this fourth category.

A second decision is whether to measure interests in specific occupations or in broad vocational areas. If one opts for the former approach, the inventory would have scales measuring interest in, say, medicine, law, real estate sales, psychology, elementary school teaching, and other occupations. Using the latter approach would result in scales covering broad vocational areas—for example, scientific, mechanical, artistic, sales, or linguistic interests. In other words, we can adopt a rather broad-gauged or narrow-gauged approach.

A third dimension is the method of scale construction and item keying. The approach may be logical, with items assigned to scales on a rational, *a priori* basis; empirical, with items assigned to scales on the basis of their observed relationship to some criterion; or homogeneous, with items assigned to scales on the basis of their intercorrelations. Each of these approaches has been applied to the development of interest inventories, with the empirical method appearing to predominate at this time.

The choice of the Strong-Campbell Interest Inventory[5] as a starting point for our discussion of empirically keyed inventories was made for several reasons: First, the Strong was one of the first inventories to use empirical keying and is backed by research and use extending over half a century (see, e.g., Darley and Hagenah, 1955; Campbell, 1971; Strong, 1955); second, the use of occupational criterion groups is meaningful to most persons; and third, since the Strong is widely used, many readers may have taken the test and thus they have some familiarity with the material discussed.

The SCII   The first form of the test appeared in 1927 and the latest revision was published in 1974. The inventory originally had both Men's and Women's forms. However, the 1974 revision, called The Strong-Campbell Interest Inventory, is a "neuter" form, appropriate for both men and women. As research has shown that vocational interests of most persons do not stabilize until the age of 17 or 18, or later (21–25), the test is primarily for adults. However, since the reading level of the SCII is at a sixth grade level, it can be administered to younger persons. Whether it should be is another question.

The SCII consists of 325 items divided into seven sections (see Table 17.1). On the majority of the items, the test taker responds by indicating whether he likes, is indifferent to, or dislikes a particular activity; however, some items require a ranking. The inventory is untimed, with the median time for completing the blank being approximately 25 to 35 minutes. Scores are available on 124 Occupational Scales, 23 Basic Interest Scales, 6 General Occupational Themes, and several special scales. Because of the number of items and scales, special machine scoring is necessary. (Several private test-scoring agencies contract to score answer sheets for a fee.)

The most common use of the Strong is for counseling high school and college students regarding their vocational plans. It may seem absurd that a person would have to take an interest test to find out his interests; however, with limited work experiences, misperceptions of jobs, and the inability to view oneself objectively, an inventory can often clarify interests. Although the SCII can be utilized for selection and placement, both in academic and business settings, the fact that it can be faked (see, e.g., Longstaff, 1948) would seem to dictate caution when using the

[5]The Strong-Campbell Interest Inventory (SCII) is the latest revision of the test formerly called the Strong Vocational Interest Blank (SVIB).

TABLE 17.1   Types of items on the Strong-Campbell Interest Inventory.

Part I. *Occupations* (131 items; respond L (Like), I (Indifferent to), or D (Dislike))
   Sample items: Actor/Actress, Advertising Executive, Architect

Part II. *School Subjects* (36 items; L-I-D)
   Sample items: Algebra, Art, Philosophy

Part III. *Activities* (51 items; L-I-D)
   Sample items: Adjusting a carburetor, Making a speech

Part IV. *Amusements* (39 items; L-I-D)
   Sample items: Golf, Playing chess, Jazz or rock concerts

Part V. *Types of People* (24 items; L-I-D)
   Sample items: Emotional people, Babies, Nonconformists

Part VI. *Preferences between Two Activities* (40 pairs)
   Sample items: Airline pilot—Airline ticket agent, Dealing with things—Dealing with people, Having a few close friends—Having many acquaintances

Part VII. *Your Characteristics* (14 items; yes-no)
   Sample items: Win friends easily, Have patience when teaching others

test in this manner. Needless to say, interest inventories should be used in conjunction with other information—for example, abilities, achievement, and values —when counseling students regarding vocational choices.

Occupational scales   Occupational scales on the SVIB were developed by comparing the interests of men working in a given occupation to those of men in general.[6] Scores measure the similarity of a person's interests to those of workers in various occupations. The procedure for developing scales illustrate the empirical keying method. The first step was to select criterion groups. Although the exact bases for selection varied somewhat between scales, in general the criterion group for each occupation was composed of about 300 men aged 25 to 55, who had been employed in the occupation at least three years (thus ensuring that they were at least minimally successful on their job), and who indicated that they liked their work. Next, the items were administered to the criterion groups, and their responses were compared to the responses of a group of men in general. If an item differentiated between men in general and men in the occupation, it was included on the scale for that occupation.

After a scale was developed by item analysis procedures, the responses of the criterion group and of men in general were scored on the resultant occupational key to ensure that the scale did, indeed, differentiate betweem the two groups. If the groups were separated satisfactorily, norms and scores were established. The standard score system (with $\bar{X} = 50, s = 10$) uses the criterion group as the norm-

[6]On scales normed on women, the comparison group would be women in general. In either case, the group is composed of people in other scored occupations. Thus, it is not a representative sample of the population, rather is biased towards higher level occupations.

ing group. Thus, a score of 50 is the mean of the distribution of scores of persons in an occupation, a score of 60 is one standard deviation above the occupational mean, and so on.

The question may well be raised as to how effective this scale development procedure was; that is, to what extent can men in general and men employed in a given occupation be separated? Data from earlier forms indicated a median overlap of about 30 percent. In general, professional-level occupations, which have relatively few practitioners, can be differentiated better than the more popular occupations.

As mentioned previously, the composition of the criterion groups defines the dimension being measured. The criterion groups used on the SVIB varied in size, method of selection, and how well they represented the profession. Although many samples are of recent origin, some are based on smaller, older, less representative groups. Although this might seem to be a weakness of the test, Campbell (e.g., 1965, 1966a, 1966b) has shown that occupational interest patterns have not changed as much over the years as one might believe. Then, too, scales can be, and are, continually revised using better occupational samples.

Finally, the perceptive reader may have already deduced that there is no reason that the scale development procedure cannot be extended to the problem of differentiating specialties within occupations. And, in fact, *specialty scales* have been developed for at least two occupations: psychology and medicine. Specialty scales are developed by contrasting the responses of men in different specialty areas of an occupation with those of the average practitioner of the occupation (note: *not* men in general). Thus, for example, it is possible to differentiate between industrial, clinical, counseling, and experimental psychologists.

Other scales   The empirically keyed occupational scales formed the basis on the earlier versions of the Strong. However, in later editions, other types of scales have been added. These are the Basic Interest Scales, the General Occupational Themes, and several administrative and special scales.

The *Basic Interest Scales* were formed by clustering items that were highly intercorrelated; that is, they are homogeneously keyed scales. These scales represent broader occupational areas (such as Agriculture, Science, Teaching, Sales) than do the Occupational Scales. They would seem to be most useful in directing students' interests toward particular occupational areas and when counseling with students whose interests have not fully crystallized. These scales focus more on the liking of the content of various occupational areas, whereas the occupational scales are based on both content and other aspects of an occupation.

The Basic Interest Scales were normed on a general norm group, which included both men and women. Thus, a standard score of 50 represents the average of people in general (not of people in a specific area, as on the Occupational Scales). However, people in occupations falling with the interest area tend to score about one standard deviation (8–10 points) above the population average. Scores do not change much with age; an exception being the Adventure scale, on which young boys score higher than adult men.

The *General Occupational Themes* scales first appeared in the latest edition and are the broadest of the various types of interest scales. They were derived from Holland's (1973) theory of vocational interests. In essence, Holland suggests that there are six idealized occupational types, each based on a constellation of interest-personality types. Holland believes that each type of person seeks out a different type of occupational environment. Thus, the tenor of any occupation is determined by the personality characteristics of the workers as well as its skill requirements. Like the Basic Interest Scales, norming was on a general population sample. And also like the Basic Interest Scales, scores on the General Occupational Themes can be used to direct students' attention to more specific interest areas or occupations.

The remaining scales of the inventory are either administrative indices, used to spot people who misunderstood the directions or otherwise responded in an atypical manner, or special scales. One of the special scales, Academic Orientation (AOR), discriminates between students at varying educational levels. On this scale, college freshmen average around 40, college graduates about 50, and Ph.D.s about 60. The occupational Introversion-Extraversion (IE) scale reflects preferences for working in settings involving extensive contact with other people (e.g., education, social service jobs), with low scores representing the extroverted end of the scale. Both provide useful supplementary information in some counseling cases.

The profile   To aid interpretation, scores are presented as a profile (see Figure 17.1). Within each type, scales are grouped according to their intercorrelations, with scales that are highly intercorrelated being grouped together. The shaded area on each scale represents "average" scores, a type of chance or baseline range. Note that, in addition to numerical (standard) scores, score ranges have been given descriptive labels—on the Occupational Scales, very similar, similar, average, dissimilar, very dissimilar. Scores in the similar and very similar range indicate that the test taker's preferences are like those of people in the occupation. In contrast, scores in the dissimilar and very dissimilar range, indicate little congruence with the interests of people in the occupation.[7]

Interpretation of the profile can be quite complex. We must consider patterns of scores as well as scores in particular occupations or interest areas. Some of the reasons for considering patterns are illustrated by the following points: (1) Not all occupations are represented by scales. To obtain an indication of a person's interest in a nonrepresented occupation we could consider his scores in related occupations (the group the occupation would fall in) and on the relevant Basic Interest Scales. (2) Since there are various ways of performing any occupation and various jobs within an occupation, the pattern of scores may give a clue to the specialty or type of position to be considered. For example, a combination of high interests in Psychology and social service occupations (S-coded occupations) might indicate

[7]Inasmuch as standard scores are based on the distribution of scores of persons in an occupation, approximately 70 percent of the people in an occupation will score in the similar or very similar range (scale score of 45 or higher) and only 1 percent will score in the dissimilar or very dissimilar range (scale score of 25 or lower).

Figure 17.1 The Strong-Campbell Interest Inventory profile. Reprinted by permission of Stanford University Press.

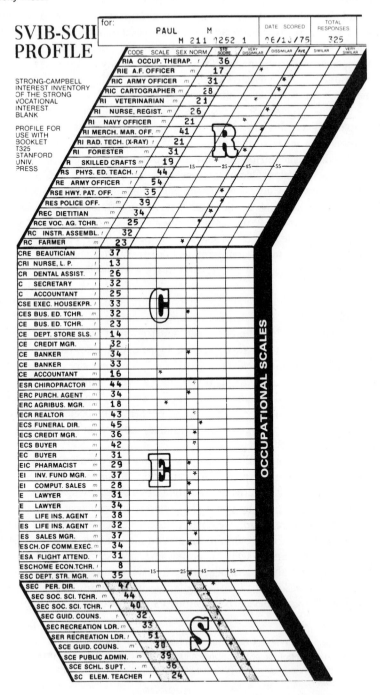

Figure 17.1 (cont.)

INFREQUENT RESPONSES	AOR	IE	OCCUPATIONS LP	IP	DP	SCHL SUBJECTS LP	IP	DP	ACTIVITIES LP	IP	DP
19	26	41	31	26	43	17	50	33	35	43	22

	STANDARD SCORE FOR:	RESULTS
GENERAL OCCUPATIONAL THEMES	**R** THEME	53 THIS IS AN AVERAGE SCORE.
	I THEME	41 THIS IS A LOW SCORE.
	A THEME	47 THIS IS AN AVERAGE SCORE.
	S THEME	53 THIS IS AN AVERAGE SCORE.
	E THEME	56 THIS IS AN AVERAGE SCORE.
	C THEME	48 THIS IS AN AVERAGE SCORE.

BASIC INTEREST SCALES

SCALE	STD. SCORE	VERY LOW	LOW	AVERAGE	HIGH	VERY HIGH
AGRICULTURE	52					
NATURE	49	30	35 40	45 50 55	60 65	70
ADVENTURE	59					
MILITARY ACTIVITIES	45					
MECHANICAL ACTIVITIES	48					
SCIENCE	38					
MATHEMATICS	35					
MEDICAL SCIENCE	49					
MEDICAL SERVICE	43					
MUSIC/ DRAMATICS	37					
ART	49					
WRITING	45					
TEACHING	55					
SOCIAL SERVICE	51					
ATHLETICS	63					
DOMESTIC ARTS	39					
RELIGIOUS ACTIVITIES	37					
PUBLIC SPEAKING	63					
LAW/ POLITICS	56					
MERCHANDISING	53					
SALES	52	30	35 40	45 50 55	60 65	70
BUSINESS MGMT	55					
OFFICE PRACTICES	41					

clinical or counseling psychology, whereas Psychology interests combined with high interests in physical sciences would be more compatible with experimental psychology. (3) A preponderance of high scores in the several related occupations reinforces that the person's interests are in that area. (4) Low scores indicate areas in which the individual's interests are definitely dissimilar to persons currently employed in the field. (5) The relative scatter of scores—whether there are pronounced likes and dislikes or whether most scores are near the average—gives an indication of the relative strengths of various interests. (For further discussion of the interpretation of SVIB profiles, with case studies, see Campbell and Strong, 1966; Zytowski, 1973; or Layton, 1958.)

Research results The SVIB-SCII has been one of the most widely studied personality measures. These studies have, in general, been on the occupational scales (and on earlier SVIB forms). To survey this literature is beyond the scope of this book (see, e.g., Campbell, 1971), so we shall only indicate some of the types of questions that have been asked and some of the answers that have been given.

How stable are SVIB scores? Scale scores are consistent over short periods (median r_{xx}'s over .90) and remarkably consistent over longer periods. In what must surely rate as one of the longest-term retest studies, Strong (1955) found a median r of .67 over a 22-year interval! If we ask at what age interests tend to stabilize, the answer is usually at around 20 (Darley and Hagenah, 1955; Strong and Campbell, 1966).

A related question concerns the stability of occupational characteristics; that is, do the interests of persons employed in given occupations change over time? In a series of ingenious studies, Campbell (1965, 1966a, 1966b) found that the interests of individuals holding the same position have not changed greatly over time. For example, he tested persons holding the same position in particular banks in 1934 and 1964, thirty years apart, and found their interests to be remarkably similar. These data seem to fly in the face of the view that occupational requirements are rapidly changing.

What is the relationship between interests and other characteristics? Although there is some relation between interests and ability, these two variables are only moderately related (r's rarely over .30). Similarly, studies of the relationship between interests and personality measures have shown some consistent patterns, but the magnitude of the correlations is almost always low. Nor have interest scores been found to correlate highly with academic or vocational success or satisfaction.

When, then, do SVIB scores predict? The empirical scale construction strategy guarantees that the scales will discriminate between people in various occupations. Other data suggest that persons select, enter, and remain in occupations that are compatible with their interests as measured by the SVIB (Strong, 1943, 1955; Layton, 1960; Campbell, 1971). However, McArthur (1954) has shown that the predictive effectiveness varies with social class; the SVIB predicted better for middle- than upper-class students. There also is some evidence (Berdie, 1960; Kelly and Fiske, 1951) that the SVIB can significantly add to predictive ability in academic situations.

Can the interests of nonprofessional men be measured? Most SVIB-SCII scales are for professional, semiprofessional, and business occupations; few scales deal with other types of occupations. For many years little success was obtained in measuring the interests of nonprofessional men. The reason seems to be that the interests of persons in professional occupations are more clear-cut than the interests of skilled and semiskilled workers. However, Clark and his associates (Clark, 1961), working with Navy enlisted men's specialties, have developed an inventory measuring interests of occupations other than professions (see below).

A similar situation obtains when measuring the vocational interests of women; that is, the interests of women have been harder to measure than those of men in professions. Although there were women's forms in the earlier editions of the Strong, they were limited in scope (that is, covered fewer occupations). The main reasons were that the majority of women had family- or child-centered interests and few occupations (except for some traditional ones such as elementary teaching and nursing) attracted large numbers of women. The latter fact, particularly, made it difficult to obtain sufficient normative data. But, as we have indicated, the SCII now is "neuter" and the same form is administered to both men and women. However, the norm groups on the Occupational Scales are still based on either male or female samples.

Summary   We have devoted a large amount of space to the SVIB-SCII. Why? One reason is that it is a well-established and widely-used test that has been intensively studied. Another reason is that the Occupational scales, which formed the core of early editions of the test, clearly illustrate the process of empirical keying. In addition, other scales illustrate different methods of keying—for example, the Basic Interest Scales were developed by homogeneous keying. Thus, you can see how various types of scales are constructed, interpreted, and used. Then, too, the SCII represents a blending of psychological theory, psychometric considerations, and the need to develop an instrument that has practical usefulness in counseling settings. Finally, the test has been frequently revised, each time incorporating the latest psychological and psychometric knowledge and research results into the revisions.

The Minnesota Multiphasic Personality Inventory: An Empirically Keyed Personality Inventory

Just as work on group intelligence tests and interest inventories began around the time of World War I, so did the development of personality inventories. During the period between World War I and World War II a number of personality inventories were developed, the best known of which, the Bernreuter Personality Inventory and the Bell Adjustment Inventory, are still used. The inventories of this era were, by and large, keyed by *a priori* methods, measured only one or a few dimensions, and lacked empirical validity evidence. Then a major landmark in the development of self-report personality inventories occurred with the publication of the *Minnesota Multiphasic Personality Inventory* (MMPI) in 1942. The MMPI has so influenced the course of personality measurement and research since its publication that we will look in detail at what is unique about this instrument.

Development of the MMPI   The authors of the MMPI hoped to developed a new kind of personality inventory—"an objective instrument for the 'multiphasic' assessment of personality by means of a profile of scales" (Hathaway, 1960, p. vii). By multiphasic they meant an instrument that would measure many facets of personality simultaneously (in contrast to the limited number of traits measured by tests available at that time). Furthermore, they hoped to include only empirically developed scales that could be used for diagnostic purposes.

The basic procedure used was empirical keying. Criterion groups were composed of persons classified into one of the then prevalent psychiatric diagnostic categories—for example, hysterics, hypochondriacs, psychopaths, schizophrenics. Members of each criterion group were carefully selected to represent unambiguous manifestations of the syndrome being studied. Responses of the criterion group members were compared to the responses of a normal sample[8] to select those items that differentiated between normals and members of the diagnostic group. Both validation and cross-validation samples were used. Responses of criterion group members were also contrasted with responses of patients hospitalized for physical complaints. This procedure was used because an item might differentiate between normals and a criterion (psychiatric) group but really be discriminating only between hospitalized and nonhospitalized persons. However, if the item also discriminated between persons hospitalized for mental and for physical complaints, it could be assumed to be tapping an essential aspect of the psychiatric disorder.

The item pool consisted of a wide variety of descriptive statements taken from other inventories, textbook descriptions, psychiatric case write-ups, medical records, and self-descriptions. The content of these items was related to areas such as general health; neurologic, physical, and physiological symptoms; family and marital relations; religious, sexual, and social attitudes; morale and affect; obsessions, compulsions, delusions, hallucinations, and phobias. Typical items are of the form:

> I frequently find myself worrying about something.
> At times I feel like smashing something.
> I am happy most of the time.
> I cry easily.
> I am afraid when I look down from a high place.

Subjects respond yes, no, or cannot say (?), depending on whether or not the statement described them.

The process of developing and purifying the scales varied somewhat for each scale. Suffice it to say that the technique involved comparing the response frequencies of the criterion groups with those of the various normal groups. (For a detailed description see Dahlstrom et al., 1972 and 1975.) Eight diagnostic scales were originally developed. The criterion groups, and thus the scale names, being:

---

[8]Various normal groups were used. The basic one was hospital visitors, which turned out to be a fairly good sample of the adult population. However, other groups (for example, college students) were used in certain norming operations.

hypochondriasis (Hs), depression (D), hysteria (Hy), psychopathic deviate (Pd), paranoia (Pa), psychasthenia (Pa), schizophrenia (Sc), and hypomania (Ma). Since each scale was developed independently, some items are scored on more than one scale.

Validity scales   One of the major innovations of the MMPI was the incorporation of scales to identify various test-taking attitudes. These are called *validity scales* since deviant scores on these scales invalidate the rest of the scores or, at least, call their validity into question. One of the indices, the *?* or *Cannot Say* scale is simply a count of the number of omitted items. If a large number of items are omitted, the test may be discarded or the test taker may be asked to complete the test; a small number of omissions are generally neglected and the test scored as usual.

On personality inventories, some persons will try to present themselves in the best possible light. To identify these people, a *Lie (L) scale* was constructed. The items on the L scale are virtues that few mortals possess, at least in the degree indicated by the items (such as: I do not always tell the truth; Once in a while I put off until tomorrow what I ought to do today; At times I feel like swearing). Persons who answer many of the items in the keyed direction either are trying to present a good impression or are very moral (in the conventional and straight-laced sense) persons. The items are quite obvious to any one with much sophistication.

Just as there are situations in which a person might want to present a good impression, there also are situations in which a person might want to appear more disturbed or give a poorer impression—for example, to increase the probability of being accepted into therapy, to avoid an onerous assignment. These persons can sometimes be detected by their scores on the *F scale,* a scale consisting of items that are infrequently answered in one direction (for example, I have nightmares every few nights; My soul sometimes leaves my body; Someone has been trying to poison me). However, high scores can also be obtained by people who do not understand the testing process, by answering randomly, and by people who are truly disturbed.

The fourth validity index, the *K scale,* consists of items that are susceptible to distortion or faking. The scale was developed in an attempt to reconcile MMPI scores with psychiatric diagnoses for several subsets of individuals whose MMPI scores did not typify their behavior (see Meehl and Hathaway, 1946). Persons scoring high on the K scale tend to be defensive and deny personal inadequacies and problems of self-control; low scores indicate a willingness to say socially undesirable things about oneself. Thus a low score may be indicative of "faking bad" (but also seems to be a good prognostic sign for psychotherapeutic success) whereas high scores may represent "faking good." Correcting certain of the diagnostic scales with the K score seems to increase the validity of the diagnostic scales; thus K corrected scores are used on certain of the clinical scales.

One further method of identifying possible invalid scores should be mentioned. Because the items comprising each scale were selected empirically, some items do not bear any logical relationship to the label of the scale. For example, the item "I often feel as if things were not real" could probably be identified as being on the Sc scale, whereas the item "I enjoy children" would not seem to bear any obvious relation to any diagnostic category. The former item is obvious, the latter one subtle. For a diagnostic scale, two subscales thus can be constructed: one of obvious items and the other of subtle items. If a scale is scored on both subsets of items, differences in scores would provide another method of detecting dissimulation.

The inventory   The inventory consists of 550 items. Although the MMPI can be administered in card form (each item being printed on a separate card with the subject sorting the cards into piles), the usual format has the items listed in a booklet, with responses made on a separate answer sheet. No time limit is used and, since the reading level is very low, an adult should be able to complete the MMPI in less than an hour. The inventory is typically scored on the validity scales (L, F, K), the eight clinical scales (discussed previously), plus several other scales: most frequently, masculinity-femininity (Mf), and social introversion-extraversion (Sie). Scores are converted to a T score scale (standard scores with $\bar{X} = 50$ and $s = 10$) based on a normal group (see Figure 17.2).

Reliability estimates for the MMPI scales, as is true of most personality measures, are lower than reliabilities on measures of maximal performance. For example, retest reliabilities range from .60 to .90 over short periods (a month or less) with normal subjects. The reliabilities decrease over longer time periods, but do not seem to be noticeably lower for deviant groups. Although the MMPI scales were not designed to be homogeneous scales, internal consistency estimates of .90 and higher have been obtained for several of the scales.

The MMPI has proved to be a fertile item pool for persons wishing to construct special scales. More than 200 scales have been developed from the item pool, bearing such diverse labels as anxiety (several scales), ego strength, academic achievement, impulsivity, originality, pharisaic virtue, and ulcer personality. There is nothing to prevent an investigator from choosing a criterion group having certain characteristics, having them take the MMPI, and comparing their responses to the norm group, thus developing a new scale. From the proliferation of scales, it appears that the MMPI has kept a number of psychologists busy building new scales.

Interpretation of MMPI scores   Even though the diagnostic scales were constructed empirically, it soon became apparent that using the MMPI solely as a diagnostic sorting device was a tremendous waste of information. The item pool of the MMPI was too rich to be used for so limited a purpose. Furthermore, it also became apparent that to make maximum use of the information provided, scores would have to be interpreted, not by treating each scale individually, but in terms of patterns of scores.

To interpret scores configurally requires specifying rules and procedures for arranging and summarizing the pattern of scores. To facilitate the interpretation, each scale was given a number and profiles were coded as a sequence of numerals corresponding to the rank ordering of scale scores. This procedure (of referring to

Figure 17.2 The Minnesota Multiphasic Personality Inventory Profile. Copyright 1948, The Psychological Corporation, New York, N. Y. All rights reserved.

The Minnesota Multiphasic Personality Inventory

Starke R. Hathaway and J. Charnley McKinley   Scorer's Initials_____

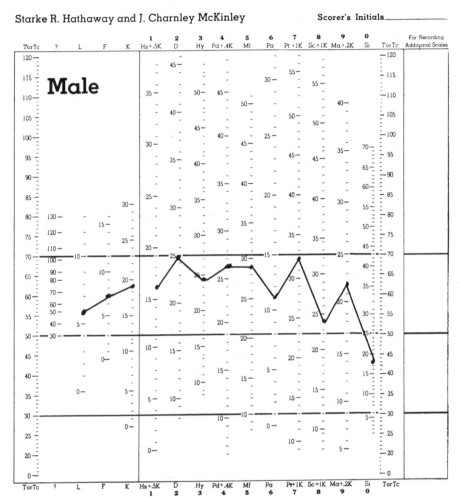

scales by number rather than name) also focuses attention on the broader meaning of the scale, not just the label derived from the original criterion group.

Several alternative coding systems are available—the distinction between them being primarily in the complexity of the symbolization used. One simple system uses only the two highest scale scores to form the code. Thus, a profile with the highest score on scale 4 (Pd) and the second highest score on scale 9 (Ma) would be classified "49." Slightly more complex systems use a combination of the three highest scales and the lowest scale; for example, a code might be 498-2. Highly complex systems use various symbols to indicate the absolute level of scores and which scores differ by only one point.[9] Coding permits objective classification of MMPI profiles—by similarity of profile codes—and thereby enables one to search for behavior patterns that typify a particular profile code, thus providing a basis for interpreting scores on the test.

It would not be unfair to say that many of the major advances in the objective interpretation of personality test scores have resulted directly from attempts to interpret the MMPI. One of the first approaches was the Atlas approach (Hathaway and Meehl, 1951). The *MMPI Atlas* consists of a collection of MMPI profiles, arranged by profile codes, with each profile being followed by a brief narrative description of the characteristics of the person whose profile was presented. The test user could look in the Atlas for examples of profiles with similar coding, read the personality descriptions, and get a flavor of the behavior characterizing persons having that particular profile pattern. The Atlas approach suffers, however, from the limitations of being an anecdotal approach. As a source of hypotheses about expected behaviors, however, it is a valuable interpretive aid.

As use of the MMPI expanded, a folklore of interpretation clues developed based on patterns of profile scores. Thus, a profile with scales 1 and 2 coded highest was said to indicate a neurotic pattern with depression and probably pain and/or somatic complaints; if scale 8 was significantly higher than scale 7, the indication was that the person was psychotic rather than neurotic; the relation of scores on scales 3 and 4 was said to indicate the amount of libidinal energy; and so on. Some of these folklore interpretations were supported by hard data, others were the distillation of clinical experience, and others probably represented severe cases of selective retention. Because of their unsystematic nature, these proposed interpretations lacked many of the requisites for being acceptable scientific knowledge.

What was needed were more systematic data regarding the characteristics of persons obtaining certain patterns of MMPI scores; or, as Meehl phrased it, what was needed was a good cookbook (Meehl, 1956). Good cookbooks (or codebooks, as they came to be known) would be empirically derived; would be based on a representative, or at least specifiable, population; and would summarize the characteristics of persons having a given MMPI profile that differentiated them from other persons (see Table 17.2). Because there are many possible MMPI patterns, and data must be available for a number of people having the same profile in order to ensure stable results, the development of a cookbook requires tremendously large samples. However, several cookbooks have been developed (e.g., Drake and Oetting, 1959; Marks and Seeman, 1963; Marks, Seeman, and Haller, 1974). With the advent of computers, the entire process has been further mechanized. That is, scoring rules and codebook data can be stored in a computer. The item responses can be put into the computer, which will score the test and look up the appropriate codebook entry, then print a verbal interpretation of the score.

---

[9]Note that three different levels of measurement are used: Scale scores, being standard scores, are on an interval scale; codes are on rank order scales, and thus represent ordinal measurement; and profile categories are on a nominal scale.

TABLE 17.2   An example of a codebook entry.

The description below illustrates the type of description that would be provided by a codebook or a computerized MMPI interpretation program.

The test results appear to be valid. He has followed the instructions and seems to have answered truthfully. There is no sign of undue defensiveness.

The client tends to be tense, overanxious, and impulsive. He has a high energy level and is aroused quite easily. He may find it difficult to stick to tasks, especially those assigned by others. Although he will probably be outgoing and sociable, he may lack consideration and judgment. He is quite concerned about what others think of him. His performance on a job or task may be erratic. He will frequently ask for reassurance that he is proceeding correctly. However, because he is impulsive, he may continue to make mistakes, particularly foolish ones. He will be more concerned with finishing a job, and others' evaluation of his performance, than with his own standards of success. He may be easily swayed by other people's opinions.

The codebooks represent another step towards objective interpretation of personality test scores; whether it is a step in the right direction depends upon whether you believe that interpretation of personality test scores can be an objective procedure or whether it must rely on the clinician's intuitive judgment.

Some research questions   As with the Strong, the research on the MMPI is so voluminous that it would be impossible to summarize it in a few pages (see, e.g., Dahlstrom et al., 1975; Butcher, 1969). So we shall only select several illustrations of the type of research questions that have been investigated.

Which of the available methods of summarizing and interpreting MMPI profiles is most valid? This question is often raised in conjunction with the clinical versus statistical prediction issue. These studies have generally compared the accuracy with which various coding methods, from simple to complex, can classify profiles as psychotic or neurotic. The most comprehensive studies (e.g., Goldberg, 1965b; Meehl, 1959) have shown that: (1) actuarial methods are more accurate than clinical judgment; and (2) the simpler actuarial methods are generally as accurate as the more complex, configural models.

A second set of research studies revolves around the question of the process clinicians go through in interpreting profiles and making diagnoses. This area of investigation was sparked by the writings of Sarbin (1944) and Meehl (1954). The types of questions raised include: What cues do clinicians use in making interpretations? How much information must be presented before the clinician can make a stable and/or valid judgment? How accurate are clinicians in their judgment? Can clinicians be trained to be more accurate or make better use of the available cues? Although the research designs utilized to study this problem have been quite sophisticated, the results of the studies have been disappointing if one expected judges to agree among themselves, to be accurate predictors or become more accurate with training, or to make use of complex configural clues. One could summarize the evidence, somewhat irreverently, by stating that clinicians tend to use rather simpleminded approaches and, when it comes to simpleminded approaches, the computer and statistical formulas are better than the human brain (Goldberg, 1968; Kleinmutz, 1975).

A third group of studies has centered on the question of what the MMPI scales measure. Welsh (1956) factor-analyzed the MMPI scales and found two major factors: the first was an anxiety, or general emotional disturbance, factor; and the second appeared to be a denial, repression, and lack of self-insight factor. Other researchers have attempted to interpret these general factors in terms of response sets but cannot seem to agree on what the set is, some feeling that it is social desirability, others feeling that it is acquiescence. Still others (e.g., Rorer, 1965; Block, 1965) feel that the variance in MMPI scores is primarily "true" variance, representing substantive differences between individuals, rather than response set components.

Contributions of the MMPI   The MMPI is one of the most widely used, if not the most widely used, self-report personality inventory. It is used as a diagnostic aid, as a screening device, as a counseling and psychotherapeutic tool, and as a research instrument. It is used for both decision-making and descriptive purposes. Its wide usage attests to the fact that many psychologists consider it to be both valid and useful in both clinical and research settings. But the MMPI is also important for its influence on the development of personality assessment. No other test has influenced objective personality assessment procedures as much as the MMPI.

What then are its major contributions? For one, the MMPI demonstrated that personality measurement could be an objective, empirically based procedure. Previously, personality measures had used *a priori* scoring keys or, at best, had used statistical criteria based on item distribution properties. The MMPI, in contrast, incorporated scales derived by empirical methods. Second, the MMPI included validity scales to control distortion. Although several previous tests had made passes at validity keys, the MMPI was the first to incorporate validity scales as an integral part of the testing (and interpretation) procedure. Third, research on the MMPI demonstrated that not only could the process of test construction be empirical and objective, so also could the test interpretation process. The development of coding systems, atlases, configural scoring rules, and cookbooks all represented attempts to objectify the interpretation process. Fourth, and by no means least, the MMPI has provided a large item pool that has been used for development of further scales and in research projects of various sorts. Particularly important is the fact that new scales could be developed without changing the stimulus situation for the test taker, thus increasing the comparability of results obtained in different settings.

Other Empirically Keyed Instruments

We have discussed the Strong Vocational Interest Blank and the Minnesota Multiphasic Personality Inventory at length to illustrate the process of constructing, validating, and interpreting an empirically keyed inventory. We shall now briefly discuss two empirically keyed instruments that differ from the SVIB and MMPI in some crucial respects. Again, our coverage will be illustrative rather than comprehensive.

The California Psychological Inventory   One of the most frequently heard complaints about the MMPI concerns its "pathological" nature. In many ways the California Psychological Inventory (CPI) can be considered an MMPI for normal personality. The CPI consists of 480 statements, including some MMPI items, that are presented in a format similar to the MMPI. In contrast to the MMPI, however, the CPI scales are designed to measure dimensions of normal personality—for example, dominance, sociability, tolerance, achievement via independence, flexibility. The 18 scales are grouped into four categories: measures of poise, ascendancy, and self-assurance; measures of socialization, maturity, and responsibility; measures of achievement potential and intellectual efficiency; and measures of intellectual and interest modes.

The majority, though not all, of the scales were developed by empirical methods. For example, the Dominance scale was validated (1) by its ability to differentiate between groups of students rated as "most" and "least" dominant by teachers and/or principals, and (2) by correlating dominance scores with the ratings of dominance by peers or psychologists. In short, scales were validated against "real-life" social criteria. The goal was to develop scales that would measure important and socially relevant personality dimensions. This, then, is the important aspect of the CPI; it illustrates that empirical keying procedures can be applied to measuring "normal" personality.

Kuder Occupational Interest Survey   The Occupational Interest Survey (OIS) is one of several interest inventories developed by G. F. Kuder, who has been a major contributor to the field of interest measurement. Although the OIS more closely parallels the SVIB than do Kuder's earlier inventories, it differs from the SVIB in several fundamental respects. One is that the items are presented in a triad format, and the test taker's job is to select the activity that he most prefers and the one he least prefers from among the three alternative statements. This is essentially a forced-choice procedure, and it lets one triad do the work of three separate items. A typical triad might be:

   a. write a story about a sports event
   b. play in a baseball game
   c. teach children to play a game

The test taker responds by indicating which activity he most prefers and which he least prefers. This enables all possible pairs of items to be compared.

The second major difference is that the OIS is scored on a different set of occupational scales than the SVIB, although there is some overlap between occupations scored on the two inventories. The fact that the same occupations appear on both inventories should not, however, be taken as an indication that occupational scales with the same label measure the same things, since Zytowski (1968) has shown that the correlations between supposedly comparable scales are often low. In addition, the OIS can be scored on scales representing educational majors as well as occupational groups (see Figure 17.3).

A third basic difference between the OIS and the SVIB is in the derivation of scale scores. Both inventories use empirical keys based on the similarity of an individual's responses to those of men in an occupational group. However, scores on the OIS represent the correlation between the individual's interests and the interests of men in various occupations (Kuder, 1963, 1966; Zytowski, 1973). The comparison of the individual to the criterion group is thus direct on the OIS, avoiding the problems associated with selecting an appropriate men-in-general group. Although extensive research has not yet been published, Kuder claims that this procedure significantly reduces classification errors.

Many other empirically keyed personality inventories could be discussed. By and large, they represent variations on the inventories already discussed (perhaps being designed for a different age level or to measure a different set of traits), rather than illustrating fundamentally different approaches to personality measurement (see Appendix B and Buros, 1971, 1974). Thus we shall turn to another approach to personality measurement: homogeneously keyed inventories.

Homogeneous Keying of Inventories

The inventories discussed thus far have, with few exceptions (for example, the SCII Basic Interest Scales), been criterion-centered. That is, they were empirically keyed. Thus, an item was retained on a scale if it predicted the criterion measure. Formal personality theory played little, if any, role in item selection, and the homogeneity of the resultant scale was irrelevant.

But, as was mentioned previously, one can take other approaches to scale development. One attack sets homogeneity as the prime requirement of any scale and, consequently, the test construction process is designed to ensure that the completed scale will be homogeneous (Nunnally, 1967). The dimensions measured may be specified before the test construction process starts or scales may be allowed to emerge from the empirical data. The item selection procedure is based on procedures for clustering intercorrelated items. In all instances, the goal is to develop a scale that is homogeneous (unidimensional).

To illustrate, consider the hypothetical example of constructing a scale to measure interest in mechanical activities. The first step would be to collect or write items which, on *a priori* grounds, appeared to measure mechanical interests. These items would then be administered to a representative sample of individuals, responses recorded, and item intercorrelations computed. Items that did not correlate highly with the other items, or the total scale score, would be eliminated. The entire process would be repeated on another sample to cross-validate the item statistics. In this way, a pure (homogeneous) scale could be developed.

The actual scale development process might, of course, vary from this ideal paradigm. For example, if a factor analysis indicated that the items measured more

Report of Scores   Kuder Occupational Interest Survey   (FORM DD)

NAME _____ LOCATION _____ DATE OF SURVEY _____

OCCUPATIONAL SCALES — WOMEN

Accountant	Secretary	
Bank Clerk	Social Case Worker	XXX
Beautician	Social Worker, Group	
Bookkeeper	Social Worker, Medical	
Bookstore Manager	Social Worker, Psychiatric	XXX
Counselor, High School	Social Worker, School	
Dean of Women	Stenographer	
Dental Assistant	X-Ray Technician	
Department Store Saleswoman		
Dietitian, Administrative		
Dietitian, Public School		
Florist		
Home Demonstration Agent		
Home Ec Teacher, College		
Interior Decorator		
Lawyer		
Librarian		
Math Teacher, High School		
Nurse		
Nutritionist		
Occupational Therapist		
Office Clerk		
Physical Therapist		
Primary School Teacher		
Psychologist		
Psychologist, Clinical		
Religious Educ Director		
Sci Teacher High School		

COLLEGE MAJOR SCALES — WOMEN

- Art & Art Education
- Biological Sciences
- Elementary Education
- English
- Foreign Languages
- General Social Sciences
- History
- Home Economics Education
- Mathematics
- Music & Music Education
- Nursing
- Psychology
- Religious Education

OCCUPATIONAL SCALES — MEN

Occupation	Score
Acc't, Certified Public	.47
Architect	.58
Automobile Mechanic	.19
Automobile Salesman	.33
Baker	.40
Banker	.36
Barber	
Bookkeeper	.34
Bookstore Manager	.55
Bricklayer	.28
Building Contractor	.31
Buyer	.40
Carpenter	.23
Chemist	.46
Clothier, Retail	.41
Counselor, High School	.51
County Agricultural Agent	.34
Dentist	.37
Department Store Salesman	.45
Electrician	.25
Engineer, Civil	.44
Engineer, Electrical	.38
Engineer, Heating/Air Cond	.41
Engineer, Industrial	.40
Engineer, Mechanical	.41
Engineer, Mining & Metal	.44
Farmer	.28
Florist	.39

Occupation	Score
Forester	
Insurance Agent	.47
Interior Decorator	.58
Journalist	.19
Lawyer	.33
Librarian	.40
Machinist	.36
Mathematician	.33
Math Teacher, High School	.34
Meteorologist	.55
Minister	.28
Nurseryman	.31
Optometrist	.40
Osteopath	.23
Painter, House	.46
Pediatrician	.41
Personnel Manager	.51
Pharmaceutical Salesman	.34
Pharmacist	.37
Photographer	.45
Physical Therapist	.25
Physician	.44
Plumber	.38
Plumbing Contractor	.41
Podiatrist	.40
Policeman	.41
Postal Clerk	.32
Printer	.28
Psychiatrist	.39

Occupation	Score
Psychologist, Clinical	.35
Psychologist, Counseling	.33
Psychologist, Industrial	.55
Psychology Professor	.51
Radio Station Manager	.52
Real Estate Agent	.61
Sales Eng, Heating, Air Cond	.21
Sci Teacher, High School	.51
School Superintendent	.40
Social Case Worker	.43
Social Worker, Group	.53
Social Worker, Psychiatric	.42
Statistician	.46
Supv/Foreman, Industrial	.36
Travel Agent	.27
Truck Driver	.49
Television Repairman	.48
University Pastor	.34
Veterinarian	.35
Welder	.43
X-Ray Technician	.39
YMCA Secretary	.36

COLLEGE MAJOR SCALES — MEN

Major	Score
Agriculture	.54
Architecture	.53
Biological Sciences	.50
Business: Acc't & Finance	.52
Business & Marketing	.41
Business Management	.41
Economics	.36
Engineering, Chemical	.40
Engineering, Civil	.43
Engineering, Electrical	.55
Engineering, Mechanical	.56
English	.53
Forestry	.57
History	.31
Mathematics	.45
Physical Sciences	.20
Political Science & Govt	.32
Premed, Pharm & Dentistry	.54
Psychology	.31
Religious Education	.22

V 50

M .39	S .31		
MBI .32	F .39		
W .55	D .46		
WBI .38	Mo .48		

Figure 17.3 The Kuder Occupational Interest Survey profile. Copyright 1964, Science Research Associates, Inc.

than one factor, the test constructor would have to decide whether to include scales for the several factors or retain only items measuring the factor of prime concern. If several scales were being developed simultaneously, the procedures used must ensure both the homogeneity of each individual scale and that the several scales were not highly intercorrelated. This method of scale development assumes that constructs can be measured along a single dimension.

Kuder Vocational Preference Record   Since the SVIB is the classic example of an empirically keyed interest inventory, the Kuder Vocational is the prototype of a homogeneously keyed interest inventory. Like the other Kuder inventories, the items are presented in triads. Unlike the SVIB and Kuder OIS, which assess interest in specific occupations, the Kuder Vocational measures interest in broad vocational areas. Thus, it is appropriately used in situations in which the concern is with identifying broad areas of interest, rather than choosing a specific occupation; for example, with junior high and high school students.

The process of scale construction proceeded as follows. After an item pool had been developed, *a priori* item keys were constructed. Thus, for example, all items that appeared to measure literary interests were included on one scale, all items denoting scientific interests on another, and so on. The items were then administered to an experimental sample, and items that did not correlate with the total score on the *a priori* key were eliminated. By this procedure the scoring keys were made more homogeneous. These analyses resulted in the scrapping of some *a priori* scales and the restructuring of others. Analogous procedures were used to add scales. The present form of the test (Form C) consists of ten scales—Outdoor, Mechanical, Computational, Scientific, Persuasive, Artistic, Literary, Musical, Social Service, and Clerical.

Although the scale construction procedure guarantees that the scales will be homogeneous, it raises some problems when interpreting scores. Because responding to the inventory items requires a choice between alternatives that are scored on different scales, any response will increase the score on one scale but consequently limit the maximal possible score on another scale. Thus the sum of the raw scale scores, over all scales, will be the same for each person. Therefore, scores on the Kuder-Vocational are *ipsative,* not normative.

How are ipsative scores to be interpreted? The scoring procedure on the Kuder (or on any ipsative scale) ranks interests in terms of their relative strength within the individual but gives no indication of the absolute strength of any interest. Thus, a person with intensive interests in several areas will have his intense interests cancel each other out. Conversely, an individual who is generally indifferent but has one strong interest will score very high in that area. Furthermore, we must consider the general interest level in mechanical and clerical areas. For example, since the average male probably has stronger interests in mechanical than clerical activities, the same percentile rank on the two scales would not necessarily indicate comparable levels of interest (see, Bauernfeind, 1962; or Katz, 1962, 1965). Thus, in spite of the fact that the scale development procedures on the Kuder Vocational make logical sense and produce homogeneous scales, interpretation of scores is not as simple as it might seem at first glance.

Other Self-Report Inventories

In this section we shall discuss three inventories whose special characteristics make them worthy of special comment: a test designed to control a major response set; a test designed to measure interests of nonprofessional men; and a test for masculinity-femininity.

Edwards Personal Preference Schedule   The Edwards Personal Preference Schedule (EPPS) is a self-report personality inventory, consisting of 225 items in forced-choice format. It is scored on 15 scales corresponding to Murray's need categories (see Figure 17.4). Whether the EPPS, in fact, adequately measures the dimensions that it supposedly taps is an open question (see reviews in Buros, 1965, 1971), but one that is of secondary importance for our purposes. Of primary importance is the fact that the EPPS was designed to control the effects of one of the major response sets, social desirability.

Edwards, it will be recalled, showed that there was a high correlation between the rated social desirability of an item and the probability of endorsement of that item. This finding cast doubt on the validity of all self-report inventories by opening the possibility that the test takers were responding not solely to the content of a test item but also to its social desirability. Thus scores on, say, the MMPI might as readily be interpreted as measures of the test taker's willingness to say socially

Figure 17.4   The Edwards Personal Preference Schedule profile. Reproduced by permission. Copyright 1954, © 1959 by The Psychological Corporation, New York, N. Y. All rights reserved.

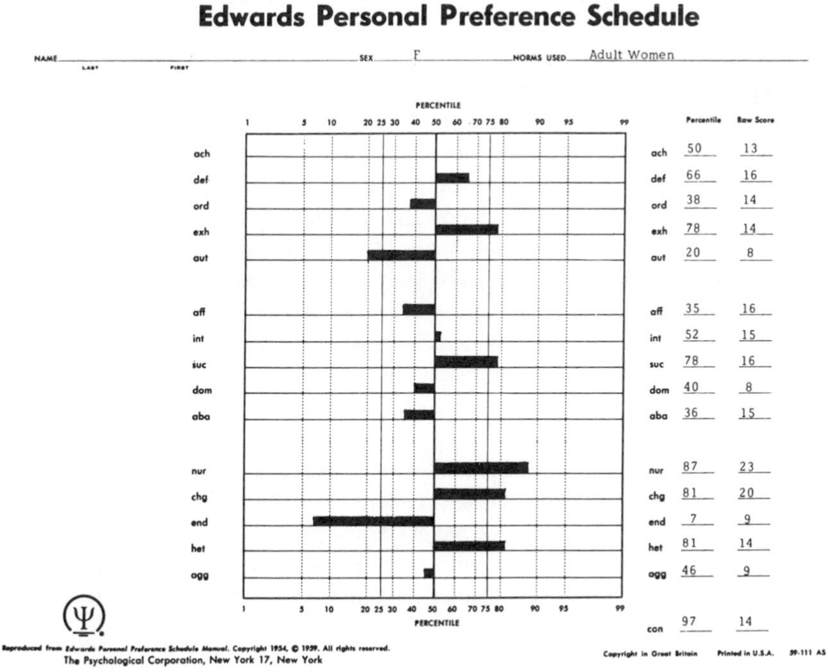

Edwards Personal Preference Schedule

undesirable things about himself. The test constructor, consequently, must decide how to control for this possibility and ensure that the scale scores reflect trait differences rather than differences attributable to the social desirability variable.

Edwards reasoned that the best way to control social desirability was to force the test taker to choose between two equally desirable (or undesirable) alternatives, each of which measured different traits. By pairing alternatives having the same rated social desirability but measuring different traits, the test taker must respond on the basis of item content (as both statements in the pair are equally desirable or undesirable). Thus, confronted with the choice between two equally desirable alternatives, for example,

> I like to help my friends when they are in trouble.
> I like to do my very best in whatever I undertake.

or two equally undesirable alternatives, for example,

> I feel depressed when I fail at something.
> I feel nervous when giving a talk before a group.

the test taker will respond primarily on the basis of content. Of course, on any particular item, one statement may be more socially desirable for a given individual than the other but, averaging over all items on the test, the effects of social desirability should cancel out.

By this procedure of constructing items by systematically pairing alternatives with similar social desirability ratings but representing different traits (needs), Edwards constructed an inventory that presumably eliminated the influence of social desirability. How well did he succeed in attaining his goal? The preponderance of evidence seems to indicate that although the influence of social desirability is much less on the EPPS than on the typical personality inventory, its influence has by no means been completely eliminated.

Two other important consequences of Edwards' attempt to control social desirability by use of a forced-choice format should be mentioned. First, utilization of the forced-choice format necessarily resulted in ipsative scores, thereby introducing complications into both the interpretation and statistical analyses of the scores. And, second, concentration on controlling the effects of the social desirability variable evidently resulted in less care being devoted to item selection, with the only apparent criterion for inclusion being the logical relation of the item content to one of Murray's need categories. Thus it appears that in test construction, as in other endeavors, when one attempts to maximize one value he frequently sacrifices another.

Minnesota Vocational Interest Inventory   In the discussion of interest research, we mentioned that one of the difficult tasks in interest measurement has been to develop scales that measured the interests of nonprofessional men. However, Clark and his associates (Clark, 1961), working with Navy enlisted men, were able to develop such an inventory, the Minnesota Vocational Interest Inventory (MVII). The MVII, as it finally evolved, consists of 158 triadical items, e.g.:

Repair electrical wiring.

Fix a clogged drain.

Check for errors in a copy of a report.

with the test taker indicating which of the three activities he likes best and which of the three he would most dislike to do. Thus the item format is similar to the Kuder inventories.

Although there are a number of notable features about the MVII, two are most important. One is that he did succeed in identifying the interests on nonprofessionals. The other is that the MVII has two sets of scoring scales: Occupational Scales and Homogeneous Scales. The Occupational Scales were developed by empirical keying methods similar to those used on the SVIB; the basic procedure being to contrast the responses of men in a particular occupation (for example, baker, printer, carpenter, painter, truck driver, machinist, electrician) with the responses of tradesmen in general. Note that the basic comparison group, tradesmen in general, is different from the men-in-general group used on the SVIB, which was composed of men in professional occupations. But, in both cases, the item selection procedures were similar and the comparison group was composed of persons working in occupations at the same occupational level as the occupations being keyed.

The MVII also may be scored on a number of Homogeneous or Area Scales. Here the procedure for keying responses was similar to other homogeneous scales, items that were intercorrelated being placed on the same scale. Nine Homogeneous Scales were developed (see Figure 17.5). Although one might expect that the homogeneous keys and the occupational keys would be quite independent, the empirical data (Clark, 1961; Barnette, 1973) show that each homogeneous key is highly correlated with at least one occupational scale. For example, the Mechanical homogeneous key correlates high positively with the occupational keys for Truck Mechanic, Sheet Metal Worker, and Plumber, and high negatively with Retail Sales Clerk, Stock Clerk, Tabulating Machine Operator, and several other occupational keys.

The Bem Androgyny scale   One particularly messy area of personality research has been the measurement of psychological masculinity-femininity (MF). MF scales typically measure the interests, preferences, and values of males and females. That is, scales are developed by selecting items that differentiate between the "average" man and "average" woman. For example, if more women than men express interest in classical music, preferences for classical music would be scored "feminine." The result is a scale with feminine interests at one end and masculine at the other.

Recently Bem (1974) suggested that this approach is inappropriate because it forces persons to one or the other end of the scale, whereas many people may have both masculine and feminine characteristics. Thus she developed a test with separate scales for masculinity and femininity. The items on the scale are adjectives that were placed on either the masculine or feminine scale on the basis of the ratings of judges. That is, adjectives that were seen as more typically masculine were placed

Figure 17.5   The Minnesota Vocational Interest Inventory profile. Reproduced by permission. Copyright © 1965 by The Psychological Corporation, New York, N.Y. All rights reserved.

NAME _____   AGE _____ SEX __M__ DATE _____

MINNESOTA VOCATIONAL INTEREST INVENTORY

	OCCUPATIONAL SCALES	STD. SCORE[a]
1	BAKER	53
2	FOOD SERVICE MANAGER	50
3	MILK WAGON DRIVER	45
4	RETAIL SALES CLERK	40
5	STOCK CLERK	50
6	PRINTER	38
7	TAB. MACHINE OPERATOR	36
8	WAREHOUSEMAN	43
9	HOSPITAL ATTENDANT	36
10	PRESSMAN	23
11	CARPENTER	37
12	PAINTER	34
13	PLASTERER	37
14	TRUCK DRIVER	36
15	TRUCK MECHANIC	27
16	INDUSTRIAL EDUC. TEACHER	15
17	SHEET METAL WORKER	31
18	PLUMBER	24
19	MACHINIST	22
20	ELECTRICIAN	19
21	RADIO-TV REPAIRMAN	24
22		
23		
24		
25		

(scale: 0   10   20   30   40   50   60)

a. SCORES ABOVE 60 ARE PLOTTED AS 60.
NEGATIVE SCORES ARE PLOTTED AS ZERO.

AREA SCALES	STD. SCORE
H-1 MECHANICAL	42
H-2 HEALTH SERVICE	50
H-3 OFFICE WORK	55
H-4 ELECTRONICS	46
H-5 FOOD SERVICE	69
H-6 CARPENTRY	50
H-7 SALES-OFFICE	54
H-8 "CLEAN HANDS"	58
H-9 OUTDOORS	47

STANDARD SCORES
(scale: 20   30   40   50   60   70   80)

SEE OTHER SIDE FOR EXPLANATION

on the masculine scale. The test taker indicates, on a 7-point scale, whether an item describes him. Thus, he receives two scores: one on masculinity and one on femininity. Thus, it is possible for a person to score high on both scales—that is, have the interests of both sexes.

In addition, an *androgyny* score can be obtained by comparing scores on the M and F scales. People whose scores are similar are androgynous and have the characteristics of both sexes. Persons whose scores differ widely are sex-typed. The test promises to be useful in studies of sex differences and sex role development.

Evaluation of Self-Report Inventories

Having looked at a number of examples[10] of personality inventories, albeit in a cursory fashion, we might ask: What does it all mean? Can personality be measured by self-report inventories? To be consistent with our view that validity is the most important characteristic of any test and that validity is situation-specific would dictate a response that such questions are essentially unanswerable. And in one important sense they are: The test user must always evaluate any test in light of the particular requirements of the particular situation (see, especially, Mischel, 1968). Nevertheless, certain recurring themes appeared throughout our discussion. We shall review these by asking several questions.

Does the self-report approach to the construction of personality measures work? If by this question is meant, "Can inventories based on self-reports be constructed?", the answer is obviously yes, for many have been constructed. If the question means, "Can the self-report format be adapted to the measurement of a wide variety of traits or aspects of personality?", the answer is again yes, since self-report inventories have been developed to measure vocational interests, psychiatric syndromes, normal personality, cognitive styles, and values— everything from schizophrenic tendencies to interest in baking, from religious values to psychopathic tendencies, from aggression to nurturance. If the question is rephrased to mean, "Do the inventories measure the basic components of an individual's personality?", no answer can be given. Instead, one must ask, what is meant by "basic components"? If, like some factor analysts, one means well-documented factors, then the answer is yes; if, like some personality theorists, you mean some intangible underlying motivating agent, then the answer is "probably not."

Do self-report personality inventories attain the desired standards of consistency and validity? The evidence shows that the consistency of personality measures—be it stability, equivalence, or internal consistency—is generally lower than on other types of measures. But is this a function of the phenomenon we are dealing with or the mode of measurement? There is evidence that well-constructed inventories can meet rigorous standards of internal consistency and stability (for example, Strong's 18-year follow-up). Validity is another question. In most cases the appropriate method of establishing validity is construct validity, and construct validity can neither be established overnight nor be summarized by a single index. Certainly, there is evidence showing that scores on personality inventory do relate to a variety of other variables. However, in the large majority of instances the relationships are disappointingly low.

What is the relationship between personality measurement and personality theory? With several exceptions, tests developed to reflect a particular theory have not been epitomes of good test construction methodology and, conversely, the most rigorous test construction methods have been adopted by persons whose philosophic viewpoint approaches dust-bowl empiricism. Personality inventories have, of

---

[10]We have not discussed certain types of tests, such as adjective and problem check lists. For examples, see Appendix B or Buros (1971, 1974).

course, been used to test concepts in, and deductions from, personality theory, but too often the tests used have been accepted uncritically, been developed on an *ad hoc* basis, or have been used for purposes for which they were not designed. In short, the relation between personality theory and personality measurement is far from the desired level.

Have empirical correlates of personality inventory scores been established? If anything is certain in personality measurement it is that scores on the widely used personality inventories have been, or will be, correlated with practically any variable imaginable. For example, the Seventh Mental Measurements Yearbook lists 3300 references for the MMPI, and 1100 for the SVIB; and the Edwards PPS had well over 300 references in the first 10 years after its publication. So there is no doubt that there is a plethora of data; the problem is making any sense out of the data. Since much of the data are situation-specific, collected on particular samples in a particular place at a particular time for a particular purpose, rather than as part of systematic attempts to understand the meaning of a particular test or test score, the data are almost impossible to comprehend. One can only admire the attempts made to summarize the data on particular tests—attempts like those of Dahlstrom et al. (1972, 1975) for the MMPI, Campbell (1971) for the SVIB, Super and Crites (1962) for a variety of tests, and some of Buros' reviewers.

What impact do response sets, response styles, and faking have on inventory scores? In spite of concentrated research and attempts at control, it is clear that the effects of these variables have not been completely eliminated from any of the extant inventories. Although the identification of the direction and amount of possible dissimulation (as in the MMPI validity scales) and incorporation of these data into the test interpretation process is a desirable step, adoption of a test format that would eliminate their effects would be an even more desirable solution. The most systematic attempt to accomplish this end (Edwards' work) has been only partially successful. Furthermore, since much of the research on these variables has involved only intratest measures and not extratest variables, it is impossible to ascertain definitely whether their effects are test-specific or represent broader personality traits. But, without doubt, response sets and styles do influence test scores and faking of personality inventories is possible.

Is empirical or homogeneous keying a more effective approach to construction of self-report inventories? To answer this question, of course, requires another question: more effective for what purpose? There is no question but that empirically keyed tests (such as the MMPI and SVIB) are more widely used, receive stronger support from the research literature, and have had a greater impact on personality assessment. These conclusions hold in spite of the fact that the homogeneously keyed instruments, theoretically, should possess the advantages of an empirically keyed instrument plus have the advantage of providing homogeneous, and hence hopefully more readily interpretable, scores. The reasons for the failure of the homogeneously keyed instruments is unclear; one possible reason is that the existing inventories do not tap all the relevant factors. Ideally, of course, the instrument should include items that are *both* empirically and homogeneously keyed, not in the sense of the scales on the SCII or MVII, but in the sense that the items included on a scale have surmounted both empirical and homogeneous selection hurdles.

Are different item formats differentially effective? For the most part, constructors of items for self-report personality inventories have not been noticeably creative, relying primarily on two basic item formats: statements requiring an agree-disagree response, and/or a forced-choice between two or more alternatives. Although the latter approach has certain benefits in controlling irrelevant variables, it also leads to ipsative scores and, consequently, problems in analyzing and interpreting scores. Thus lacking any persuasive argument based on differential reliability and/or validity, there may be some slight advantage for the simpler yes-no approach. One would hope, however, the test constructors might show more ingenuity in attempting to develop new item formats. To cite only one example of what might be done, Goldberg has experimented with an item format that requires the respondent to indicate whether he has engaged in an activity in the past (say, climbing a mountain or telling off a teacher), what his subjective reaction to the experience was (did he like it or dislike it?), and what the probability is that he will engage in the activity in the future. This format not only provides a large amount of response data from a single stimulus item, it also allows for the analysis of response patterns.[11]

Finally, for what practical purposes can self-report inventories be used? Because of the openness of self-report inventories to faking and other varieties of dissimulation, they should be used only in circumstances in which the test taker will treat the test as a measure of typical performance. The empirical data certainly support the use of interest inventories in vocational counseling and planning, and, if used with caution, in educational and vocational placement. The more traditional personality inventories exhibit such low relationships with real-life criteria that their use for purposes other than hypothesis building and to make statements about the general characteristics of groups seems quite tenuous.

[11]For example, what is indicated by the response pattern: "I have done it, I liked it, but I won't do it in the future" or the pattern: "I have done it, I didn't like it, but I would do it again"?

18

PROJECTIVE AND SITUATIONAL MEASURES

In many ways, self-report personality inventories follow the same psychometric tradition as do achievement and ability tests. This is seen most clearly by the emphasis on objectivity and standardization. The testing procedures and scale construction methodology also parallel those of maximal performance tests, differing primarily in the test content and the criteria used to validate scores—that is, in the dimensions measured.

There have been several major criticisms of "objective" personality measurement. One has to do with the emphasis on empirical keying. The emphasis on scale construction methodology has, in many cases, relegated personality theory to a subsidiary role. That is, how a trait is measured has seemed, at least to some people, to be more important than what is measured. The types of measuring instruments discussed in this chapter—projective and situational tests—by and large are more theory-based. Although Lindzey (1961, p. 108) has stated "most work with projective techniques has been carried out with little serious attention to psychological theory,'' this conclusion reflects test constructors' general lack of concern with personality theory rather than a specific fault of projectives. Without doubt, projective techniques are more theory-based than are personality inventories.

Another criticism of self-report techniques has been that they are too atomistic, that they focus on the independent dimensions of personality rather than attempting to present an integrated, dynamic picture. Although there have been attempts to integrate data from various individual scales (see the discussion of profile in-terpretation of the SCII and MMPI), this criticism undoubtedly has much validity. The approaches discussed in this chapter adopt a more wholistic view. As we shall see, however, this presents some problems, especially for those concerned with the normative aspects of personality measurement.

Finally, personality inventories have been criticized because they represent measurement in an artificial situation. What is needed, critics suggest, are as-sessments obtained in more real-life, naturalistic settings. Rather than ask how a person would react, critics argue, we should observe how a person actually does react. This, of course, implies that the assessment situation should be as similar to a real-life setting as possible. Situational methods, and behavioral assessments in particular, are designed to meet this criticism.

Thus in this chapter we shall be discussing methods of measuring personality that are based on a somewhat different methodology than self-report inventories. Or perhaps we should say that they represent a different focus or emphasis. In short, these methods represent attempts to provide a more global picture of personality from reactions in more naturalistic settings.

PROJECTIVE METHODS

The term ''projection,'' when applied to projective methods, is used in a general sense to denote the process by which the characteristics of the individual—his personality structure—influence the ways in which he perceives, organizes, and interprets his environment and experiences. These influences are best seen (and measured) when an individual encounters new and/or ambiguous situations (stimuli).

The implication for test construction is obvious: To study personality, one should present an individual with new and/or ambiguous stimuli and observe how he reacts and structures the situation. From his responses we can then make inferences concerning his personality structure. The crucial requirements are that the stimulus situation lack definitive structure and that the test taker be given wide latitude in his mode of response; unduly restricting his response options would, in effect, be structuring the task.

Not all authors agree that these are the essential features of projective methods. Lindzey (1961), for example, after surveying the various definitions of projective techniques, concluded that the hallmarks of projective techniques were their sen-sitivity to unconscious or latent aspects of personality, the multiplicity of responses permitted the subject, the fact that several personality dimensions are measured simultaneously, the subject's unawareness of the purpose of the testing,[1] and the richness of the response data elicited. In addition, certain other characteristics frequently are noted, but are not of prime importance: the ambiguity of the stimulus, the use of holistic analyses, the evocation of fantasy responses, and the fact that there are no correct or incorrect responses.

Rather than haggling further over a definition, we shall describe several widely used projective methods. After reading these descriptions, the reader can decide for himself which dimensions are fundamental and which are incidental.

The Rorschach Method

Perhaps no other psychological test is as well known, has intrigued the layman as much, or caused as much division of opinion among psychologists as the Rorschach Method. The test consists of ten cards, each of which contains an amorphous design resembling an inkblot (see Figure 18.1). All of the designs are symmetrical and printed on a white background; half are in shades of gray and black, others are gray plus color, and others are completely chromatic.

Since the stimuli are ambiguous, how the test taker structures and responds to the cards—that is, what he "sees" in the blots—represents his projection of meaning into the stimuli. These projected meanings, in turn, are used as the basis for making inferences about his personality structure and dynamics.

The use of "inkblots" as stimuli illustrates an important aspect of projective testing: the unimportance of item content. The only requirement is that the stimulus be unstructured but capable of having a structure imposed upon it. The inkblots are, of course, essentially meaningless; yet because they resemble and suggest real objects, they are capable of being structured, allowing the subject to project meaning onto them. Thus they are ideally suited to serve as stimuli, even though they have no inherent meaning.

Administration, scoring, and interpretation   Administration of the Rorschach typically occurs in two stages. During the first stage the test administrator presents the cards, one at a time, in a set order. The subject is instructed to report what the blots resemble or suggest to him. The examiner records the subject's responses and keeps a record of several other aspects of performance—for example, the latency of the first response to each card, the total time spent on a card, how the card is turned. The second stage of the administration is an inquiry. In this stage the subject goes through the cards a second time, commenting upon the features of the blots that caused him to have a particular response. The administrator may actively question the subject during the inquiry, seeking to clarify his responses. The test obviously is administered individually.

There are several approaches to scoring the Rorschach. In general, in all systems it is agreed that certain dimensions—such as location, determinant, and content—

---

[1] Awareness is a relative term. A person may be aware that he is being tested, but not know what is being measured and/or how his scores will be used. In this connection we might mention Kelly's (1958) classic definition: An objective test is one where the test taker tries to guess what the examiner is thinking; a projective test is one where the examiner tries to guess what the test taker is thinking.

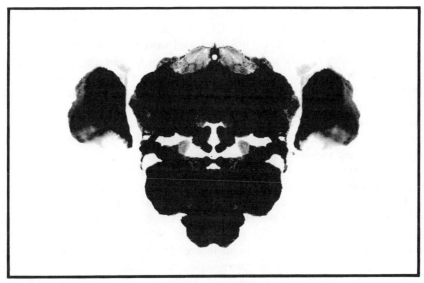

Figure 18.1   An inkblot similar to those used in the Rorschach Method

should be scored, but there is disagreement on exact scoring techniques, the relative emphases to be given each score, and the other dimensions scored. *Location* refers to the portion of the blot used as the basis of the response. It can vary from use of the whole blot, through use of a major detail, to use of minor details of the blot, or even use of white background space. *Determinants* refer to which aspects of the blot determined the response: the shape or form, shading or texture, coloring, and whether movement was perceived. *Content,* of course, refers to the category the percept falls into—for example, a human, details of humans, an animal, a plant. Every response is scored on all three dimensions: location, determinant, and content.

These scores, plus other data (for example, total number of responses, reaction times, various ratios between scores, whether the responses were popular or original) are combined into a *psychogram.* From this point, intepretation becomes a highly individualized matter. Some clinicians rely on actuarial patterns and signs; others proceed on a completely intuitive basis. Some emphasize the pattern of scores; others emphasize individual responses. Some pay particular attention to content; others pay little attention to the content. It is at this point, consequently, that the Rorschach loses its objectivity. Although actuarial validity data could be developed, these have not become popular because of certain statistical problems (Cronbach, 1949)—for example, different numbers of responses are given by different subjects—and because many Rorschach users feel that statistical treatment destroys the dynamic and holistic nature of the interpretation.

Validity   Although the literature is replete with studies utilizing the Rorschach, the validity of the method is often questioned. Opinions range from the view that the Rorschach's validity is beyond question to the view that it is a worthless instrument.

The reasons for these differences of opinion are numerous. The statistical problems with scores, for one, render much of the validity data meaningless or at least inconclusive. Then, too, since control of relevant variables is difficult, the results of any study are open to various interpretations. Third, because the test presumably measures unconscious motivating factors, and criterion measures reflecting these factors are not available, direct validity evidence is lacking. Conversely, some Rorschach advocates consider studies of the relationship between Rorschach scores and objective criterion measures to be trivial. And fourth, although the test is supposed to reflect basic personality structures, changes in the testing situation affect the subject's responses (Masling, 1960).

Because interpretations of Rorschach scores are highly individualized, studies are actually validating a particular examiner's interpretation of the Rorschach.[2] That is, the test and examiner are confounded and validation of the test per se is impossible. For example, suppose that Dr. Chiaroscuro looks at Rorschach psychograms of students at Waterman College and identifies the students needing counseling. Any study relating his diagnoses to an independent criterion will, in essence, be validating Dr. Chiaroscuro's interpretation of the Rorschach, not the test. What validity should be attributed to the good doctor and what to the test is an unanswerable question. To validate Rorschach scores one would, of course, have to relate psychogram scores to the criterion directly, without the examiner's interpretation.

Modifications   As would be expected with an instrument as popular as the Rorschach, there have been various modifications of the method. Some of these have been designed to permit group administration, whereas others have attempted to make the scoring more objective. The major modification is the Holtzman Inkblot Test (Holtzman, 1959, 1961; Hill, 1972). Holtzman's test differs from the Rorschach in several ways: There are many more cards; the subject is allowed only one response per card; scoring is restricted to a small number of important dimensions; quantitative scoring weights are used; and several forms of the test have been developed. These changes result in reliable scores, avoid many of the statistical problems inherent in the Rorschach, and simplify administration while retaining many of the desirable projective features of the original test.

The Thematic Apperception Test

On a continuum measuring the degree of structure, self-report inventories would fall at the high structure end and projective methods at the unstructured end. But projectives vary among themselves in degree of structure. While the Rorschach presented the test taker with a highly ambiguous stimulus situation and permitted wide latitude in response, the Thematic Apperception Test (TAT) presents the

[2]The confounding of test scores and their interpretation occurs whenever scores are combined subjectively. The problem is more obvious, however, on projectives because scoring rules are less well-defined.

Figure 18.2   A card similar to those used on the Thematic Apperception Test.

subject with a more structured stimulus and response situation. However, the TAT does not approach the restraints imposed by self-report techniques.

The TAT consists of a set of 20 cards, 19 of which picture scenes varying in content and ambiguity—typically of people engaged in some activity—and one blank card (see Figure 18.2). The cards are presented to the subject, one at a time, and he is requested to make up a story about the card. This story should include details such as what is happening, who the people involved are, what actions have preceded the scenes, what will happen, and what the actors are thinking and feeling. The examiner plays a relatively passive role, giving the initial instructions and recording responses.

The basic rationale of the test depends heavily on the mechanism of identification. The major assumption is that the test taker will identify with one of the characters in the scene, particularly the hero or central actor. Since the stimuli on the TAT generally involve people pursuing various activities, the test has more face validity and more apparent relevance to the life of the test taker than does the Rorschach.

As with the Rorschach, there are several scoring systems. The original scoring system emphasized analysis of the needs of the main actor and the environmental presses that impinge upon him; an emphasis that followed directly from Murray's (1938) theory of personality. Other scoring systems are variations of Murray's approach, differing in the role of structural (noncontent) variables, the unit of analysis, and the inferences made. In general, the various scoring and interpretation systems rely heavily on an analysis of the thematic content of the stories, with structural properties playing a relatively minor role.

The exact content (that is, cards used) varies with the age and sex of the subject. Thus, some flexibility in adapting the test to the subject is possible. Special sets of cards have also been developed for use with various groups—for example, blacks and children (the Children's Apperception Test). Other sets have been developed to measure particular personality variables, such as McClelland's use (McClelland et al., 1953) of modified TAT cards for the study of achievement motivation. Several other tests use the same general principles as the TAT, such as the Blacky Pictures and the Make-A-Picture-Story Test.

Determining the validity of the TAT is a difficult task. The first question one has to answer is whether the stories actually reflect the test taker's personality or whether they are only stereotypic reactions to the situations pictured.[3] Even assuming this, can we assume that the test taker identifies with the "hero"; that the hero's problems, reactions, and pressures acting upon him reflect aspects of the test taker's life? Lack of agreement on a single scoring and interpretation system complicates the task. And, since the test is designed primarily to provide a general description of personality, the ubiquitous criterion problem looms large. Hence, acceptable validity data remain difficult to find.

Other Projective Methods

Although the Rorschach and TAT, and their modifications, are the most common projective techniques, a number of other approaches can also be used. One is the *word association technique*. On word association tests, the examiner reads a list of words and the subject responds with the first word that comes into his mind. As might be expected, the ideal stimulus words are ones that permit a wide variety of associations, some of which have diagnostic significance. By analyzing the pattern of responses, recurrent themes, hesitations in responding, and other signs, inferences about personality dynamics are made. Although most interpretations are based on content analysis, empirically keying methods can be applied to word association tests. For example, a scale to identify depressed individuals could be developed by identifying responses that occur more frequently in protocols of depressed persons than in normals. Although they are simple, rapid, and easy to administer, word association tests do not produce the variety or richness of response found on other projective methods.

Another well-known method is the *sentence completion test*. These tests typi-

---

[3]This is analogous to the social desirability response bias on personality inventories.

cally consist of sentence stems, with the subject's task being to complete the sentence in his own words (see examples on page 357). As on word association tests, ideal stems are ones that can be completed in several ways and deal with diagnostically relevant topics. Scoring usually is subjective, stressing content analysis, but can be objective. Sentence completion tests are easily administered and scored, but, more so than most projective techniques, do not disguise their purpose from the test taker.

A third type of projective method, *figure drawings,* have been used for the assessment of both cognitive and personality characteristics. The simplest form of this technique requires the test taker to draw a person; more complex versions require the subject to draw several persons or draw a person in relation to other objects. Scoring and interpretation, though more objective than on most projective techniques, are far from standardized. However, most systems rely on the characteristics of product (the drawing), the method of attack, and comments made by the individual, either spontaneously or in response to the examiner's inquiry. Since the test content is universal, the technique can be applied in almost any group. Thus it is often used in cross-cultural studies, with retarded children, and with children having language handicaps.

Finally, several projective methods can be subsumed under the label *expressive methods.* These include role-playing techniques and psychodrama, where subjects act out a particular role or part, and play techniques, where a child is presented with a variety of objects and asked to play with them in a particular manner. There are also picture completion and arrangement tests, where the examinee constructs a story, either by completing or arranging pictorial or cartoonlike materials; reproduction techniques, such as the Bender-Gestalt, that require the subject to remember and reproduce designs; and tests involving manipulation and interpretation of designs. In short, almost any unstructured situation can be used as stimulus material.

Evaluation of Projective Methods

Is the widespread, though presumably decreasing (Thelen et al., 1968), use of projective methods justified by the validity evidence? Do projectives accomplish their stated aims? Is any information provided by projectives that is not obtainable by other methods? Are there particular situations in which projective methods are most useful? Can responses to projective methods be faked?

Before considering these validity questions, one might ask a prior question: Are projective methods tests? A test, you will recall, was defined as a systematic procedure for measuring a sample of (an individual's) behavior. For the current purposes the crucial phrase is "systematic procedure"; in other words, standardization.

By and large, the content of projective techniques is as standardized as that of other tests. The administrative procedures, though more flexible than those on standardized aptitude and achievement tests and self-report personality inventories, are comparable to the procedures used on individual intelligence tests. However, when it comes to scoring procedures, trouble often arises. With a couple of notable exceptions (e.g., Holtzman's Inkblot Test), scoring procedures are either un-standardized and/or there is disagreement between several alternative scoring systems. Hence, if we adhere to a literal interpretation of the definition, projective methods are not tests.[4]

The lack of standardized scoring procedures has other important consequences. Without quantifiable scores, consistency estimates cannot be made. Without objective scoring, adequate normative data cannot be developed. (A weakness of almost all projective methods is the lack of adequate normative data.) And, without adequate normative data, interpretation of scores must be idiographic, rather than normative or nomothetic.

In personality measurement the basic concern is construct validity. Here we encounter an impenetrable barrier. If projective techniques measure basic components of personality, and if these facets are, by definition, unconscious (thus inaccessible to observation and measurement), then one can never directly validate a projective method. Several indirect lines of evidence, however, can be brought to bear. For example, if a projective method (or any other personality test) measures "basic" traits, scores should be relatively unaffected by ephemeral conditions associated with the particular test administrator, the conditions of test administration, slight changes in the stimulus materials or responding mode, or transient states of the test taker. Yet all of these factors influence responding on projective techniques. Also, dissimulation is possible on projective methods. Thus, whatever projectives measure, they are not pervasive, immutable aspects of personality structure.

Proceeding to a different level of analysis, and ignoring the fact that any interpretation will reflect a test by examiner interaction, we can ask whether the holistic descriptions, such as obtained from projective methods, are valid? Here we encounter an interesting phenomenon, called *the Barnum effect,* which must be taken into account when determining the validity of holistic personality descriptions. The Barnum effect suggests that by relying on vague statements and going with the base rates, one can produce a personality description having superficial validity. For example, consider the following personality description:

> Although not brilliant, the subject is well above average in intelligence with a streak of creativity. Many of his talents go unnoticed by other people, but when he sets his mind on a task, he does an excellent job. Although his moods are generally fairly even, he has periods of the blues and, at other times, has boundless energy and accomplishes a great deal in a short period. He is fair in his dealings with other persons. He is quite sociable, generally liking the company of other people, but there are times when he would rather be alone.

Most people would probably accept this statement as being a reasonably good description of their personality. The main point is not that such descriptions can be prepared without the aid of test scores, which is true. The point is that in situations

---

[4]The APA Standards suggest that even self-report personality measures be referred to as inventories, rather than tests. (APA, 1974, Principle B1.1.1, p. 13.)

in which scoring and interpretive processes are ill-defined, and holistic descriptions are used (as is typically the case with projectives), such statements frequently are presented as interpretations of test scores. Because of the vagueness of the interpretive procedures and the generality of the description, it is impossible to establish direct links between specific test scores or signs and specific descriptive statements. Yet, the apparent validity of the description suggests that the test is valid.

What sort of evidence do projective techniques provide that is not available from other methods of measuring personality? One presumed advantage of projective measures was the richness of responses generated, and, consequently, the variety of dimensions tapped. However, one would be hard put to find a variable measured by a projective technique that has not also been measured by more objective methods. The question then becomes: Do projectives assess these variables more validly or efficiently? Here, no definitive evidence is available, nor will there likely be any until the scoring problems of projectives are overcome.

Thus, what can we conclude about the value of projective methods? Judged by the standards of classical psychometric theory, projective methods would be rated as unacceptable—as instruments that should be drummed out of the arsenal of psychological tests. Yet many clinicians apparently find them useful. Can so many people be wrong? Possibly. But one can also defend the alternative view that classical testing approaches are limited, that there are several other possible approaches to knowing what another person is like, and that projectives constitute one of these other classes. One also cannot ignore the fact that, whereas other methods divorce the test from the interpreter, intepretation of projective methods involves an examiner-test interaction, opening the possibility that different dynamics may be involved. For example, the testing procedure may provide the examiner with clues to the examinee's personality that he could not obtain in any other way. Yet, the validity of these clues is open to scientific test, and projective methods frequently failed the test.

SITUATIONAL METHODS

Self-report and projective methods measure reactions in a contrived, somewhat artificial testing situation. Although a testing situation possesses certain definite advantages (for example, control of irrelevant variables by standardized conditions), it is still one step removed from "real life." Thus, interpretations of behaviors and responses exhibited on tests are open to the criticism that the subject's behavior might have been different in a more natural, real-life situation. We can partially vitiate this argument by establishing the relationship between test performance and external criteria. However, failure to find a significant relationship between a test-defined variable and an external criterion measure always has at least two explanations: (1) There is, in fact, no relationship between the two variables; or (2) the test does not measure the variable it is designed to measure.

The need for the testing situation to be as natural as possible is particularly critical when measuring typical performance. Ideally, we would study the behavior a person (typically) exhibits, not his reports of how he does or would behave. To illustrate, suppose that we want to determine how effective a supervisor a worker will be. One possible approach would be to administer a test whose items present a variety of supervisory problems. He might respond to the test as a measure of maximal performance, choosing the responses that he knows represent acceptable supervisory practices, rather than selecting the alternative that describes how he would react. Or if his previous experience offered no basis for making a choice, or for some reason he distorts his responses, his score will not indicate how he would actually act if given the job of supervisor. In either case we would not obtain an indication of his most probable (that is, typical) behavior. An alternative approach might be better. For example, we could have him serve as supervisor for a period of time, either on the job or in a simulated job situation. This latter approach would be a situational test.

Dimensions of Situational Methods

Situational methods can be classified or described along a number of dimensions. First, and most important, is whether the assessment situation is natural or contrived. The subject's performance in a natural situation may be observed, or the assessment may be made in a specially designed or simulated situation. In either case, the performance measure would probably be a rating made by a trained observer. Ratings of football players on the basis of their game performance are an example of use of a natural situation; ratings of performance in a leaderless group discussion represent an artificial or contrived setting.

A second dimension involves the subject's awareness that he is being observed and/or rated. In natural situations he may or may not be aware that he is being evaluated; in contrived situations he will almost certainly be aware that he is being observed. Of course, the fundamental question is not whether the subject is aware he is being observed and rated; the basic question is whether this awareness affects his behavior. If it does, we do not observe his typical behavior. Although one might argue that as we are constantly being evaluated (for example, on our jobs or as a student, by family and friends), additional observations should have little effect. But most persons, knowing they are being observed, will try harder to put their best foot forward. Therefore, when a person knows he is being evaluated, the test may be a measure of maximal performance rather than one of typical performance.

Situational methods also vary widely in scope, format, and purpose. The assessment process may cover several days, or be based on a few minutes' observation. It may provide a global assessment, an intensive personality description, or a rating on a single trait. The procedure may be applied to several individuals simultaneously (in some cases, performance being a group effort) or each individual may be tested separately.

Finally, there is the question of what is an appropriate performance measure. Although objective performance (outcome) measures can be used on many situational tests, particularly when measuring maximal performance, in most cases scores will be ratings by trained observers. The rater will observe such things as the individual's approach to the problem, his interactions with other individuals (if a group assessment), and his reactions to stress or failure. On the basis of these observations, he will rate the individual on the relevant dimensions.

Examples of Situational Methods

Situational tests generally are both expensive and time-consuming. Consequently the only one that is used to any extent is the simplest and least costly, the interview. The other examples discussed have not received widespread use, but illustrate approaches that have been used in special situations.

The interview   The interview[5] is one of the most widely used, if not the most widely used, assessment technique. You probably have been interviewed many times—for example, when applying for college or a job. Although an interview usually is a one-to-one situation, there are a number of possible variations on this traditional procedure. A *panel interview* involves one person being confronted by a panel of interviewers. This procedure has the obvious advantage of decreasing repetition that would occur if each member of the panel interviewed the candidate individually. Another variation is the *stress interview,* where the interviewer attempts to subject the interviewee to stress by constant probing, asking personal and embarrassing questions, trying to confuse the interviewee, and other similar techniques. The purpose of this type of interview is to see how the subject reacts under anxiety-producing conditions, the presumption being that this will give a more valid assessment than a nonstressful situation.

In evaluating interviews, several questions are of prime importance: Can reliable ratings be obtained from an interview? Is any information obtained from interviews that cannot be obtained by other methods? What is the validity of the interview as an assessment tool?

It is well known that different interviewers often arrive at widely divergent conclusions after interviewing the same candidate. One reason is lack of standardization: Not only do different interviewers cover different topics, they also look for different qualities in an individual. So, too, the interviewee may react differently to various interviewers. The reliability of interview judgments can be increased by structuring interviews so that the same topics are covered by all interviewers, and the traits to be rated and the rating procedure are clearly specified. Given reliable ratings, we encounter a second question: Does the interview provide information that cannot be obtained by other methods? Factual information and estimates of personality traits can be collected more economically in other ways (for example, by application blanks and self-report inventories, respectively). Thus, the maximal payoff will be attained by concentrating on social behavior and information that would particularly qualify or disqualify the person (for example, speech problems, unique abilities or accomplishments). Finally, evidence shows that interview ratings

[5]We shall consider only interviews used for diagnostic and evaluative purposes; other uses, such as in counseling interviews, will not be considered here.

decrease validity as often as they increase it. The main reason for this finding is that interviewers overemphasize the particular traits they think are important.[6] Still interviews continue to play a major role in many assessment procedures, apparently because everyone feels that he is an excellent judge of other people.

Indirect tests   Some methods might best be described as indirect tests. By indirect we mean that the test serves primarily as a vehicle for observing the subject's behavior, not as end in itself. An example is the *leaderless group discussion.* In this technique a group of persons are brought together and asked to discuss some (usually controversial) topic. In other situations, they may be asked to devise a plan of operations (for example, a sales campaign), to construct some object or device, or to solve a problem (for example, how to cross a natural barrier, such as a stream or canyon, using only selected materials). Although success in completing the task may be scored, the focus is usually on characteristics displayed in attacking the problem—ones such as perseverance and leadership.

An assumption when using indirect tests is that observations based on performance in lifelike situations will produce more valid scores. Yet a perceptive subject will almost certainly recognize the situation for what it is, deduce what traits are being rated, and alter his behavior. Indirect tests, therefore, can easily become maximal performance situations.

The OSS Assessment   One of the most intensive assessments ever conducted was that done by the Office of Strategic Services during World War II (OSS Assessment Staff, 1948). In order to select personnel for intelligence-related assignments, a three-day assessment procedure was developed. Groups of candidates were brought to an assessment center and subjected to a wide variety of assessment techniques, including paper-and-pencil tests, stress interviews, problem-solving exercises, and numerous ingenious situational tests. Performance on these tasks was rated by the Assessment Staff (which included psychologists, physicians, and military officers), and ratings were also obtained from peers. On the basis of these ratings, a formulation of the personality structure of each individual was developed and a prognosis of his success on OSS assignments made. Because of the nature of the criterion, a systematic validity study was largely precluded. Because of the time and expense of such an approach, and its doubtful validity (Vernon, 1964), similar procedures are used only with highly sensitive positions and for research purposes (Barron, 1963; MacKinnon, 1962).

The In-Basket Test   An interesting example of an attempt to assess candidates' job performance is the *In-Basket Test* (Frederiksen et al., 1957). Variations of the test have been constructed for several occupations, including school administrators and military officers. In each case the person is provided with a variety of materials (organizational charts, technical reports, surveys, and memoranda) that provide background knowledge of the situation. He is then presented with materials that

[6]See the discussion of clinical prediction in Chapter 9.

might be found in the "in-basket" on his desk and is asked to take action on these matters. For example, a school administrator might have to decide whether to hire (or fire) a particular teacher, how to handle children who damaged some school property, plan a campaign for a school bond issue, decide on the adoption of new texts, plan how to handle teachers' demands for higher salaries, and so on. He can handle each problem by making a decision, requesting further information, deferring action until a later date, assigning the job to a subordinate, or in any other manner he could use on the job. Decisions will be made on the basis of his repertoire of job skills, taking into consideration the characteristics of the particular situation (as described in the background materials). Scoring is on a variety of dimensions, involving both process and outcome, but stresses general styles or patterns of handling administrative tasks. The nature of the In-Basket Test makes it suitable as a training device as well as a selection test.

Evaluation of Situational Tests

One obvious disadvantage of situational tests is their cost. They involve large amounts of both the candidates' and raters' time, can be applied to only one or a few candidates simultaneously, require trained judges to observe and rate performance and, often require expensive materials. The fundamental question is, however, not their absolute cost but whether their advantages justify the additional costs. We would probably have to conclude that any increase in validity does not overbalance the additional costs. This conclusion would hold even considering that the technique is generally employed only when selecting personnel for jobs in which a mistake in judgment can involve great costs (for example, military officers, school superintendents, CIA agents). In these cases a costly selection device might well repay its costs. On the other hand, these techniques may be used for training as well as assessment.

Another weakness of situational techniques is that they generally rely on ratings. Since ratings are subject to various types of errors, they often are not as reliable or valid as would be desired. (For a more complete discussion of ratings, see pp. 408–411).

Third, the distinction between maximal and typical performance often becomes blurred with situational measures. As should be obvious, many situational tasks can be used to measure maximal performance (for example, whether the candidate can develop an advertising campaign or find a way to cross the river). This is not what concerns us. What does is that knowing he is being evaluated, a candidate may adopt a maximal performance, rather than a typical performance, set. Unless his maximal and typical behavior are the same, we will not be measuring what we want to measure.

Finally, how do we synthesize and express the results of the assessment? Situational tests generally involve measurement along more than one dimension, with scores combined to produce an integrated picture of the individual. If the end product of this combination is a global personality description, direct predictions of specific behaviors may not be possible. If, on the other hand, the data are expressed as a series of specific predictions, an integrated picture will not be obtained. In either case, the problem is to find an appropriate method of combining the various scores (see Chapter 9). This problem is further complicated by the fact that the data (that is, scores and ratings) often have undesirable statistical properties (for example, they are unreliable, have a limited range of values, are expressed on an ordinal scale). In short, many of the most difficult problems in psychological measurement are encountered when synthesizing data from situational tests.

OTHER APPROACHES TO MEASURING TYPICAL PERFORMANCE

Having presented three major approaches to the measurement of typical performance, we now turn to a discussion of four other methods that are used in certain situations. Three of the approaches share many features in common with situational methods. Direct behavioral assessments are advocated by persons who support a behavioristic approach to psychology. Unobtrusive measures are designed for situations in which awareness of being observed might significantly alter certain essential characteristics of the situation or the person's response. The third approach, ratings, can be viewed as either a method of obtaining scores (as on situational tests) or as an assessment method in its own right. The fourth approach, attitude scaling, is designed for the particular problem of ascertaining opinions. Although attitude scaling is in many ways similar to self-report inventories, the methods of scale construction are different enough to warrant separate consideration.

Behavioral Assessment

To a psychologist with behavioristic leanings, the approaches to measurement we have been discussing seem inappropriate (cf. Mischel, 1968). Behaviorists would argue that the concepts of traits as characteristics of an individual that guide and direct his reactions have no meaning unless we can specify the behavioral referents. Even if traits are viewed in a more limited sense (as they are in this book) as a summary label applied to intercorrelated behaviors, the behaviorist would point out several problems. One is the situation-specific nature of many relations involving traits. Another is the apparent ease with which trait scores can be modified by changing the testing conditions. These facts suggest to the behaviorist that the focus of measurement is wrong. Rather than focus on characteristics of the individual, behaviorists argue that we should look to the environmental conditions associated with the individual's behavior.

Perhaps an illustration will clarify the difference between the trait and behavioristic approaches. Suppose a student tells a counselor that he gets tense, nervous, and uptight on exams and, consequently, obtains low grades. A counselor using the trait approach would concentrate on assessing characteristics of the student that might relate to his problem—for example, his degree of anxiety, attitudes towards school, personality characteristics. The behavioral assessment approach, in contrast, would focus on specifying the conditions under which the student became anxious. In other words, we would look for the situational conditions that are present whenever the student became anxious. His assessment would also focus on specifying, in behavioral terms, the students' behaviors or reactions to these conditions. In short, the goal is to specify the stimulus and response contingencies in the anxiety-provoking situations.

There are several other salient characteristics of the behavioral assessment approach. One is an emphasis on direct measures of behavior, rather than reports of behaviors. An interesting example is provided by the study of phobias. Suppose that an individual is afraid of high places. To measure the degree of fear, the behaviorist might actually measure how high off the ground an individual will venture. Or, if a person is afraid of snakes, he would measure how closely the individual will approach a snake.

Since the goal is to change the individual's behavior, once the conditions associated with the undesired response are identified the behavioral counselor will alter the conditions and observe what changes occur in the individual's behavior. Here, again, he will rely on direct behavior measures of both the stimulus situation and the client's behavior. If one type of stimulus change does not produce the desired behavior in the client, he will try another. Another way of looking at this procedure is that the goal of measurement is to provide a basis for prescribing environmental changes.

In summary, the behaviorist position emphasizes that behavior is a function of stimulus conditions. To change behavior, you must change the stimulus situation. Measurement enters into the process only to provide a precise description of the stimulus conditions and client behaviors.

Unobtrusive Measures

One of the major problems in personality measurement is that the measurement process may affect the test taker's behavior and, in turn, the results obtained from the measurement. In other words, measurement is *reactive* (Webb et al., 1966). Reactive effects can be manifested in various ways. For one, awareness of being tested may cause the subject to view himself in a different manner (the "guinea pig" effect). Or the subject may select a particular role or set in an attempt to meet what he views to be the experimenter's demand. Or the measurement process may actually produce changes in the subject's view of himself. Finally, the subject may adopt certain response sets or styles. In each case, the test taker reacts to the measurement process and changes his behavior.

Because these reactive tendencies alter the individual's behavior or responses, they may result in invalid or distorted responses. The question then becomes: Can we measure behavior by methods that are not reactive? In their book, Webb et al. (1966) describe a number of ingenious ways of obtaining information nonreactively. They call these measures *unobtrusive* because they do not in any way intrude upon the performance.

One obvious method is to use archival records. For example, to study a sales ability, we could look at production records; to study "accident proneness," we could look at accident records. Usually, of course, other demographic information is available that helps us interpret the performance. For the salesman, we could use biographical and experience data from his employment records. For the driver, we might have demographic data from his insurance application, and possibly, his arrest record for traffic violations. The point is that a wide variety of data are available in archival sources.

One problem in observational studies is that many crucial phenomena do not occur on any predictable schedule. Thus, we have to take them as they occur. Even systematic observation, unless involving continuous monitoring, may miss the phenomena. Analysis of retrospective records allows for the identification of patterns and frequency of these critical and important behaviors. However, being retrospective, we cannot study the behavior as it occurs.

Another approach is simply to observe people's behavior. For example, if we wanted to study people's reactions to minority groups, we could observe social contacts. We might, for example, have a black worker sit at a table in a company cafeteria and observe whether other employees will sit with him and/or engage him in conversation. Or we might observe people to determine how they spent their working time. In one study, Thrush (1957) periodically observed counselors to see how they were spending their time—for example, in counseling interviews, working on research, writing case notes, reading, teaching a class. He used a procedure called *time sampling,* which involves making observations on a prearranged random schedule. This procedure assures both that observations will occur at various times during the working day and that the subject, even if aware of being observed, cannot anticipate when he will be observed.

Rating Scales

In our discussion of situational tests, we mentioned that scores were usually ratings. That is, trained judges observed the individual and assigned him a score (rating). Although rating scales differ in format, they all have the same goal: assigning a numerical value to the individual's performance along a continuum. The score may be a point on the continuum or one of a set of ordered categories (Guilford, 1954).

What are the ways in which rating scales differ? For one, ratings may be based on observations in a natural setting or in a more contrived, testlike situation. Second, ratings may be of specific behaviors or of global characteristics. Ratings on the various dimensions may be combined into an overall score, or each dimension may be considered individually. There also are wide differences in the degree of inference required. Although ratings of specific behaviors can be quite objective, global ratings often involve a high degree of inference and subjectivity. Third, an individual may rate himself or be rated by an expert judge, his supervisor, or peers. And, fourth, the format and procedures used will vary between methods (see Guilford, 1954, or Kerlinger, 1973).

Types of rating scales   The type of rating scales most people are familiar with is the *graphic rating scale*. On these scales, the rater is presented with a series of ordered categories and asked to check which one best describes the person being rated (see Figure 18.3a). The category descriptions may be estimates of magnitude or qualitative behavior descriptions. The descriptions may have numerical scale values; scales having numerical values are referred to as numerical rating scales. In any case, numerical values are assigned before the ratings are analyzed. Since graphic rating scales are simple and straightforward, they are widely used.

On *standard rating scales* the categories represent preestablished levels of performance. These standards are usually expressed in the same terms as the object being rated. For example, on man-to-man rating scales, these scale points are people who exemplify a particular level of the trait being rated. The rater's task is to judge which scale point (standard) is most similar to the person being rated. Although developing such a scale is more difficult than developing a graphic rating scale, the rating procedure is more direct and less ambiguous.

A *checklist* is nothing more than the name implies. The rater is presented with a list of adjectives, terms, or descriptions and instructed to check the ones exhibited by the person being rated (see Figure 18.3b). The rating is either yes-no (present-absent), not on a continuum. Scores are usually derived by counting the number of descriptive terms checked.

Scales used to describe college and high school environments represent a variation of the checklist approach. For example, Pace's (1963, 1967) *College and University Environment Scales* (CUES) consists of 150 statements that describe college environments (see Figure 18.3c). Students, or other observers, indicate which of the statements describe the college. By summing across raters, we can determine which items best describe a particular college. In addition, items are grouped into five scales labeled Practicality, Community, Awareness, Propriety, and Scholarship. The CUES, thus, provides a description of a college as perceived by its students. By comparing the CUES scores from various colleges, a prospective student can obtain a picture of the differing atmospheres of various colleges (see Figure 18.4).

Forced-choice rating scales involve comparative rather than absolute ratings. The rater is presented with various possible descriptions and must choose the one that best typifies the person or object being rated (see Figure 18.3d). This procedure is designed to eliminate certain rating errors (see below) and, thus, presumably, result in more valid ratings.

One widely used variation of the forced-choice procedure is the *Q sort* (Stephenson, 1953). In this procedure, the rater is given a number of descriptive statements and asked to sort them in piles (from most to least typical). The rater can place only a certain number of statements in each category so as to produce a normal distribution of ratings. That is, only a few statements can be placed in the extreme categories and many in the middle categories.

Rating errors   In spite of their apparent directness and simplicity, rating scales are subject to numerous errors, which reduce their reliability and validity. Some people

Figure 18.3 Examples of types of rating scales

(a) *Graphic rating scale*
Compare the quality of the student's classwork with that of other students in his major.

1	2	3	4	5	6	7
One of the weakest students			An average student			One of the very best students

(b) *A Checklist rating form*
Which of the following terms describes the student:

__Intelligent   __Friendly   __Puts things off
__Hard-working   __Self-centered   __Creative
__Conscientious   __Lacks motivation   __A leader

(c) *Items from the* CUES
Students are generally quite friendly on this campus. (T F) There is a lot of pressure to obtain high grades. (T F)

(d) *Forced-choice rating scale*
Can the student best be described as:
__Creative   __Hard-working   __Cooperative

tend to rate people too strictly (error of severity), whereas others are very easy in their ratings (error of leniency). Another problem is the tendency of some people to avoid extreme judgments and, consequently, to use only the middle points of the scale (error of central tendency error). When rating several traits, two other types of errors often occur. One is letting an overall opinion of an individual influence specific ratings (halo effect); the other is assigning similar ratings to traits that the rater considers to be related (logical error). These, and several other less common errors, plague ratings.

What then can be done to minimize the effects of such rating errors? Most important is make certain that the dimensions to be rated and the points on the rating scale are clearly defined. This can best be accomplished by using behaviorally stated descriptions that require observations and little inference. This approach also implies that ratings should be of specific behaviors, with global ratings, if desired, being formed from combinations of specific ratings. Second, train raters thoroughly before having them make their ratings. And, third, make sure that the raters have ample opportunity to observe the behavior in question before making a rating.

One final question might be mentioned: What characteristics should be rated? Ideally, ratings should be made only on characteristics that, through validity studies, have been shown to be important. And, because ratings are subject to numerous errors, they should be used only when more objective data is not available. Still, how do we know what behaviors to study originally? Flanagan (1954) has suggested one method. He pointed out that what distinguishes between good and poor workers is how they handle certain critical situations. Thus he suggested that

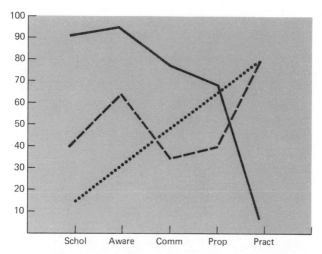

Figure 18.4 CUES scores at various types of colleges. The data show the CUES scores in a sample of 10 highly selective liberal arts colleges (solid line), 20 general universities (dashed line), and 10 teacher education colleges (dotted line). The scales are Scholarship, Awareness, Community, Propriety, and Practicality (from Pace, 1967).

we start by collecting incidents that represent particularly good or poor performance (for example, how a physician handled a particular emergency or what a worker did when his machine failed). These critical incidents, then, would be the behaviors to be given most importance in ratings.

Attitude Scales

Most of the procedures discussed have focused on the behaviors and/or feelings of the individual. That is, they were measuring enduring characteristics (traits) of an individual. Attitude scales, in contrast, focus on an individual's thoughts, perceptions, feelings, and behaviors toward a cognitive objective (Kerlinger, 1973). That is, they represent attitudes towards a particular referent.

Attitude scales are also constructed in a different manner than inventories (see Guilford, 1954; Dawes, 1972; or A. Edwards, 1957). The most important point of difference is that a conscientious attempt is made to scale responses. Rather than logically assigning weight to each response, empirical scaling procedures are used to determine the scale value for each response. The exact scaling procedure will vary on different scales.

On one type of attitude scale, called a *Likert scale,* the subject is presented with a series of stimulus items, all of which are considered to be of equal value. He responds by indicating his degree of agreement (or disagreement) to the item, usually along a 5- or 7-point scale (see Figure 18.5a). The responses to each item are summed and an average is taken. This average represents the individual's scale position regarding his attitude towards the object in question.

On another type of scale, the *Thurstone scale,* items are scaled before they are

Figure 18.5 Examples of attitude scale items

(a) *Likert Scale item*
Capital punishment should be used for crimes such as armed robbery.
Strongly agree
Agree
Undecided
Disagree
Strongly disagree

(b) *Thurstone scale items*
Capital punishment should be used for all crimes where a person is killed or threatened to be killed. (6.3)
Capital punishment should be used only for treason or killing a police officer. (4.1)
Capital punishment should never be used. (0.3)
(Note: Scale values, in parentheses, would not appear on the test; they are included here for illustration only.)

administered. This scaling usually is based on the opinions of expert judges. Items are selected to represent different scale points. The respondent indicates his agreement or disagreement with each item (see Figure 18.5b). His score is the average scale value of the items he endorses.

A third type of scale, the *Guttman scale,* also scales items prior to administration. Guttman scales are designed to measure a single dimension. Ideally, items are selected so that a person who agrees with an item falling at a given scale point will also agree with all items falling between that point and the end of the scale. This produces a unidimensional scale. As might be expected, such scales are extremely difficult to construct.

Attitude scales are subject to many of the same types of errors as rating scales. In addition, there is the problem of the relation between attitudes and actions. Just because a person holds a particular attitude toward a type of person, object, or institution is no guarantee that he will behave in accordance with his attitude. For example, there is evidence that people's attitudes towards minority groups do not parallel their actual behavior in interactions with minority group members.

In behavioral sciences, Likert scales are used most frequently. One reason, no doubt, is that they are easier to construct. However, in addition, they generally yield scores that are as reliable and valid as those derived from the other types of scales.

ISSUES IN PERSONALITY MEASUREMENT

Having described the major approaches to measuring typical performance, we shall now consider some of the important issues in personality measurement. The term *issues* (defined as points in question) was deliberately chosen, since in personality measurement many fundamental questions remain without definite answers. Although many of the issues concern technical psychometric points, significant social issues are also raised by personality measurement. In the long run, the development and direction of personality assessment may be more influenced by these social and political issues than by the more mundane technical issues.

Psychometric and Theoretical Issues

Throughout this section we have mentioned particular tests, or approaches to test construction, that did not meet the technical standards for consistency, validity, and normative data outlined earlier in the book (and in the APA *Standards*). At this point it would be well to review and evaluate the current status of personality testing in regard to some of the more important questions.

Standardization   One of the stipulated requirements of a psychological test was standardization of content, administrative procedures, and scoring. If a test is not standardized, its procedures cannot be replicated. Consequently, scores on two administrations of the test (either to the same or different individuals) cannot be directly compared, nor can scores be interpreted normatively. Although the content of some personality meaures may be varied slightly to suit the needs of a particular individual or situation, by and large the content is quite well standardized. Similarly, administrative procedures are generally relatively standardized. It is in scoring procedures that many personality measures fall short. Projective methods, in particular, seem prone to use of unstandardized and subjective scoring methods. Although some persons may argue that standardizing scoring procedures decreases flexibility of the method, unstandardized scoring procedures preclude normative interpretations. This would seem to be of greater consequence than the loss of flexibility.

Norms   Even among measures having standardized scoring procedures, a common weakness of personality measures is the lack of adequate normative data. Part of the problem stems from disagreement over what constitutes an appropriate norm group for a personality test. Should it be a sample of the general population? Or should a norm group include only persons of the same sex, age, and/or socioeconomic level? On most personality measures, general population norms are desirable. Readily available populations, such as students, are not representative of the general population; thus they cannot be used to define a meaningful normative group.[7] And, because of the nature of the test, enlisting volunteers may be difficult. In short, obtaining general population norm groups is a difficult and expensive operation.

Consistency   Scores on personality measures are generally less stable than scores on measures of maximal performance. Whether these results are primarily attributable to the measurement procedures or the traits being measured is an unsettled question (cf. Mischel, 1968). Few personality tests are published with equivalent

[7]This is in contrast to the situation with achievement and scholastic aptitude tests, in which the captive population is usually the most appropriate norm group.

forms; thus the ability to draw equivalent samples of items from personality domains remains essentially untested. Although empirically keyed scales generally are factorially complex, homogeneous personality scales have been developed. Studies also indicate that scores on personality measures are relatively susceptible to even slight variations in testing conditions, item wording, and short-term fluctuations within the individual (see, e.g., Mischel, 1968; Rorer, 1965). In summary, personality measures are generally less consistent than would be desirable. Thus, individual scores should be interpreted with due caution.

There is another aspect of the consistency problem, another way of viewing personality measurement, which may help explain the lack of success in measuring personality characteristics. This is the trait-state distinction. In our discussion, we have considered tests as measuring dimensions of stable individual differences (traits). This was true for both maximal and typical performance measures. However, on some personality dimensions, responses vary over time. These dimensions are more properly called states. For example, we might ask a person whether he is frequently or generally depressed (a trait measurement) or whether he is depressed now (a state measurement). The implication is that measurements of states, even though done accurately and precisely, will not produce high predictive value, inasmuch as the person's state will vary at different times.

Dissimulation   It is clear that responses on personality tests reflect both item content and response biases. This is true of projective and situational tests, as well as self-report techniques. What, then, can be done to minimize the effects of these variables? At least three approaches are possible. First, structure the testing situation so that the test taker is not motivated to dissemble. The most effective method is also the simplest: Enlist his cooperation by explaining the purpose of the testing and how his scores will be used. Second, include dissimulation indices on the test so that you can assess the degree of bias. And, third, establish empirical relations between test scores and extratest criteria. This will allow the meaning of the score to be determined, independent of the dynamics determining the score.

Validity   Personality measures can best be conceptualized as signs. That is, the behavioral domain sampled generally is not well defined, nor are appropriate external criteria readily apparent. In some cases, particularly with projective techniques, the variables measured are defined so as to preclude meaningful external criteria. Thus in personality measurement we are concerned with construct validity. And even here, because of hazy definition of variables, one often has to make broad leaps of faith to accept certain measures as valid reflections of the underlying construct. What, for example, is an appropriate criterion measure for a measure of flexibility or dominance?

A closely related problem is the issue of the appropriate unit of analysis. Self-report techniques measure several relatively independent dimensions or traits and, in so doing, have been criticized by advocates of holistic analyses. The latter claim that analyzing personality in a piece-by-piece fashion necessarily fragments and destroys the phenomena being studied. In reply, proponents of the trait approach insist that scientific measurement occurs only when dimensions are treated individually. Although there is no reason why both approaches cannot be used (after all, gross and microscopic anatomy are both respectable subjects), psychologists usually defend one or the other. Perhaps, the question should be rephrased: What is the appropriate way to combine scores? In answer to this question, the trait camp would say collect scores on individual traits, then synthesize them into an overall view; the holistic camp would emphasize synthesis, with specific reactions being deduced from the general personality picture.

We can also address the question of comparative validity. This question has at least three aspects. First, how does the validity of personality measures compare with that of achievement and aptitude tests? Second, which of the general approaches to personality measurement is most valid? And, third, within a given approach, which specific technique is most valid? Of course, since validity is situation-specific, any answer to these questions will reflect the trends of the evidence rather than give a definitive answer applicable to all situations.

The first question has several answers. Looking at the absolute magnitude of validity coefficients, one would conclude that validity generally is lower for personality tests than for other types of measurement. Yet, because different situations and criteria are involved, one cannot conclusively state that personality measurement is inherently less valid than the measurement of aptitudes and achievement. If we look at incremental validity, we find that there are few situations in which the addition of personality variables significantly increases predictive accuracy over measures of maximal performance. However, the situations in which tests are typically used as predictors (such as academic success or job performance) are ones in which the criteria are heavily weighted in favor of intellectual skills.

The author's conclusion in regards to the second question should be obvious from the amount of space devoted to the three major approaches. However, one could argue that this only reflects the author's bias toward the traditional psychometric approach to validity. Granted; but until alternative methods of assessing the effectiveness of measurement procedure are developed, these are the only acceptable standards available. Finally, in spite of the theoretical advantages of homogeneous keying, the hard evidence supports empirical keying as the better method of keying self-report inventories.

Psychological theory Although there is a close relationship between personality measurement and psychometric theory, there is not as close a relationship between personality measurement and substantive personality theory. Some of the tests described have had their roots in a particular theory—for example, the Edwards PPS and TAT in Murray's need-press theory and the Rorschach in psychoanalytic theory. Otherwise, personality measures in general, and empirically keyed self-report inventories in particular, have only fleeting connections with personality theory. When convenient, various investigators have used particular scales to measure theoretical constructs. However, systematic attempts to build tests measuring the basic constructs of a given theory, or attempts to build a theory of personality around a particular test, are few and far between.

Social Issues

Although there has been some reaction against ability and aptitude tests, mainly on the grounds that they have a "middle-class" bias and thus discriminate against persons from culturally disadvantaged backgrounds, most people consider these tests, when used properly, to be impartial methods of assessing competence. The major complaints in these domains are often not with tests per se (except, possibly, intelligence tests), but with the consequences of test use.[8] In the realm of personality testing, however, there has been a reaction against the idea of testing itself. One view is that personality tests invade an individual's privacy. In particular, items about certain subjects—usually politics, religion, and sex—have come under fire (Berdie, 1971). Another view is that use of personality measures, particularly in personnel decisions, rewards conformity and penalizes individuality—again, an unwarranted use of tests.

As in many controversies, the issues are complex and no simple prescription or decreee will ameliorate the situation. For one, the invasion of privacy is often confused with the improper use of tests. Misuse of personality measures is relatively common, in spite of attempts at control by a formal code of ethics (APA, 1973) and by standards controlling the distribution of tests (APA, 1966, 1974). One type of misuse occurs when persons untrained in the use of a particular technique nevertheless use it in applied psychological work. Another type of misuse involves applying a test in situations in which its validity has not been demonstrated. For example, the author once encountered a situation in which cutting scores on a personality inventory were used as a basis for admitting students into a teacher training program. The cutting scores used represented one psychologist's judgment of the acceptable score range; no objective evidence of the relationship between test scores and success, either in the program or as a teacher, was ever collected. Whether such practices are unethical or stupid, or both, is a moot point. The major concern is that such practices may result in decisions that may be harmful to the individual who takes the test.

But assuming that some, at least presumptive, validity data are available, we can still ask whether personality measurement does invade privacy. Here the issue becomes a legal as well as a psychological one, for in our society the question of what constitutes the limits of privacy will ultimately be determined by legal and legislative action.[9] Legal rulings are necessary because, although we all supply personal information in many situations, individuals differ in what they consider a reasonable request. Where one person may feel that a request for certain personal information may be unreasonable and invade his privacy, to another person the same request may seem reasonable, or even innocuous. The disagreement is in where to draw the line.

One approach to deciding where to set the limits would be to stipulate certain

---

[8]This issue will be discussed in more detail in Chapter 21.

[9]Bills placing restrictions on the use of tests have been considered in Congress, and several recent court decisions have restricted the use of tests.

categories of requests (for example, information about sexual and religious activities and attitudes) as being invasions of privacy in all circumstances. The main disadvantage of this approach, from the social scientist's view, is that these sensitive areas are frequently the ones that provide the most meaningful data. Another approach would be to allow questions about these areas to be raised only in certain situations—for example, as part of medical treatment or examination. Such an approach would discount empirical validity as being a meaningful concept. A third approach is to restrict use of personality measures to certain professions or to persons possessing certain qualifications (for example, psychiatrists or licensed psychologists). Here we would ignore the differing competencies of persons within the same occupation and introduce the question of which professional group should control personality assessment. Thus any arbitrary restrictions will not be wholly acceptable or effective.

Perhaps the key to the issue is found in the fact that people often react negatively to personality assessment because they either do not understand how the test will be used or do not feel that they have any role in deciding how the results will be used. In short, the test is threatening because the situation is ambiguous. If the purposes and uses of the test are known, the objections often vanish. For example, most counselors have encountered students who adamantly refuse to take an interest or personality inventory but who, after having the purposes of the testing explained to them, have no further objections. The moral for the test user is obvious.

The issues discussed in the preceding paragraph have direct relevance for the legal aspects of the invasion-of-privacy issue. For only if the test taker understands the nature of the test and how the results will be used can he make an informed decision as to the value of the test for himself. If he understands the purpose of the test, he can decide whether the test will invade his privacy, and then give (or withhold) his *informed consent* to the testing.[10] If he gives his informed consent he is, in essence, saying that he does not believe that the testing will invade his privacy.

[10]For further information, see *Privacy and Behavioral Research* (1967), Ruebhausen and Brim (1966), and the *American Psychologist* (November 1966).

SUGGESTED FURTHER READING FOR PART V

Butcher, J. N. (Ed.) *Objective personality assessment: Changing perspectives.* New York: Academic Press, 1972.
   Papers critically examining the current status of personality measurement; emphasis on the MMPI.
Dawes, R. M. *Fundamentals of attitude measurement.* New York: Wiley, 1972.
   Brief technical and theoretical discussion of the process of measuring attitudes.
Edwards, A. L. *The measurement of personality traits by scales and inventories.* New York: Holt, Rinehart and Winston, 1970.
   An introduction to the methodology of constructing personality scales; a quantitative approach.

Goldberg, L. Some recent trends in personality assessment. *Journal of Personality Assessment,* 1972, *36*, 547–560.

A readable but provocative discussion of the current status of personality measurement.

Harmon, L. W. Sexual bias in interest measurement. *Measurement and Evaluation in Guidance,* 1973, *5*, 496–501.

Addresses the question of possible sexual bias in interest inventories.

Hase, H. D., & Goldberg, L. R. Comparative validity of different strategies for constructing personality inventory scales. *Psychological Bulletin,* 1967, *67*, 231–248.

An empirical comparison of several methods of constructing personality scales.

Holt, R. R. *Assessing personality.* New York: Harcourt Brace Jovanovich, 1971.

A relative brief, readable introduction to personality measurement.

Jackson, D. N., & Messick, S. (Eds.) *Problems in human assessment.* New York: McGraw-Hill, 1967.

A comprehensive collection of articles on many aspects of personality measurement.

Kerlinger, F. N. *Foundations of behavioral research.* (2d ed.) New York: Holt, Rinehart and Winston, 1973.

Chapters 28 to 34 describe a variety of methods for observing and measuring typical performance; good blend of methodology and applications.

Mischel, W. *Personality and assessment.* New York: Wiley, 1968.

Argues that personality theorists should pay less attention to the measurement of traits and more to situational effects.

Rorer, L. The great response-style myth. *Psychological Bulletin,* 1965, *63*, 129–156.

Review of the evidence of the effects of response sets and styles in personality measurement.

Semeonoff, B. (Ed.) *Personality assessment.* Baltimore: Penguin Books, 1966.

Collection of writings of the major personality theorists and researchers; good historical perspective.

Wiggins, J. S. *Personality and prediction: Principles of personality assessment.* Reading, Mass.: Addison-Wesley, 1973.

Introductory text, particularly strong on prediction models and methodology.

Zytowski, D. G. (Ed.) *Contemporary approaches to interest measurement.* Minneapolis: University of Minnesota Press, 1973.

Description of the construction and use of the major interest inventories.

PART VI

USING PSYCHOLOGICAL AND EDUCATIONAL TESTS

Up to this point we have discussed the basic psychometric characteristics of tests (measurement, consistency and validity, scores and norms) and the various types of tests (measures of maximal and typical performance). Although at times we did mention practical uses of tests, this was not the main focus. In this last part of the book we shall discuss, albeit briefly, some practical aspects of testing. Thus, in many ways this part will be a review and reorganization of the material presented previously.

Chapter 19 is primarily a discussion of how tests can be used in four common situations—school testing programs, counseling, personnel selection and placement, and research. Again, we shall present several practical examples rather than attempt a thorough coverage. In each situation we shall first consider why tests are used and what information they might provide, and then give an illustration. The emphasis throughout will be on the decisions to be made, the practical constraints in the situation, and what information is provided by the tests. When reading each example you should ask yourself: Why are tests being used? What information is provided by the tests? And, how will this information be used in the decision-making process?

Chapter 20 focuses on the process of selecting and evaluating tests. In other words, assuming that you want to use a test, how do you decide which test to use? We will start by reviewing the basic questions that you should ask yourself before beginning your search, then consider the various sources that can be used to locate published tests. After you have located potentially useful tests, your next task is to evaluate each one to determine which best fits your needs. Thus in the second half of the chapter we will discuss the process of evaluating a test, presenting several possible formats for evaluations. Throughout the chapter we will emphasize that as each situation is in many ways different so, too, will our testing requirements differ. In short, no one test is best for all purposes; we must pick the test that best fits the particular situation.

The last chapter (Chapter 21) will be an assessment of the current status of educational and psychological testing. In this chapter we shall point out some of the current and persistent problems in measurement—be they psychometric, practical, or social—and discuss some of the approaches which are being developed to attack these problems. Finally, we shall go out on the proverbial limb and make some predictions about the future course of educational and psychological testing.

19

APPLICATIONS OF EDUCATIONAL AND PSYCHOLOGICAL TESTS

In earlier chapters we have approached psychological and educational testing from two directions. First we considered the logical and statistical foundations of testing as they are expressed in the concepts of consistency and validity and through normative data. Then we considered three major classes of tests: achievement tests, ability and aptitude tests, and personality measures. In this chapter we shall approach testing from a third direction by looking at some situations in which tests frequently are used. In the previous chapters we have focused on particular (types of) tests and have, in essence, said that a particular test can do certain jobs. In this chapter the focus will be reversed; we shall take a problem situation and ask which kinds of tests will provide relevant information.

To attempt to cover all possible situations would be a mammoth undertaking.[1] So, rather than attempt an exhaustive treatment, we shall restrict our discussion to four areas: education, business and industry, counseling and

[1]The use of tests in education is covered by Bauernfeind (1969), Dressel (1961), Ebel (1972), Lindquist (1951), Mehrens and Lehmann (1975), and Thorndike (1971a). The best discussion of using tests in counseling is by Goldman (1971). Surveys of vocational tests have been done by Ghiselli (1966) and Super and Crites (1962).

guidance, and research. Our goal will not be to indicate what particular tests are best; rather we will seek to illustrate (1) how the problem is defined, (2) what relevant information tests might provide, (3) how this information might be used, (4) what practical constraints may be operating in the situation, and (5) what social and ethical implications are involved.

Before turning to specific illustrations, it would be well to review several points that become particularly relevant when we move from the hypothetical realm of the textbook into the "real world." In a broad, and very real sense, many of these points can be classed as ethical issues, since they concern the responsible use and interpretation of tests and test data and the considerate and humane treatment of the test taker.

First, and most important, the use of tests should be based on empirical data.[2] That is, a test should not be used as a decision-making aid until validity studies have indicated that the test is valid in the particular situation. This procedure is, however, unfeasible in many circumstances, usually because decisions have to be made immediately, whereas conducting a study, particularly obtaining criterion data, takes time. Thus, use of the test often must be instituted without confirming data. In this case, however, one should concurrently begin collecting validity data and if, at any point, it becomes evident that the test is not doing the intended job, its use should be discontinued.

If he lacks validity data obtained in the situation in which the test is to be applied, the test user has to be guided by results of empirical studies conducted in similar settings. Thus, for example, in selecting a test to aid in choosing students for a Ph.D. program in Psychology, one could search for predictors that have exhibited validity in graduate programs in Psychology at other universities. The more similar the programs (for example, curricular emphases, type of students admitted), the higher the probability that the test will be valid in the new setting.

When evaluating validity data in applied situations, one must keep several principles in mind: (1) The value of any predictor is determined by comparison to the predictive efficiency of other available techniques and/or to the base rates. That is, we are interested in a test that can improve on the present methods of prediction. (2) The search for valid predictors should not be limited to psychological tests. In many situations other variables—such as peer ratings, biographical information, job or educational histories—may be better predictors. If they are, they should be used rather than the test. (3) One must consider the circumstances in which the validity data were collected, particularly the motivation of the testees and any unique characteristics of the situation or criterion.

In practical situations we also run into the distinction between the validity of the test for groups of persons and for a given individual. Validity data are always based on the performance of groups of persons. Even with a highly valid predictor, incorrect decisions will be made for a number of individuals. From the viewpoint of the test user (the institution or company using the test) these incorrect decisions are

---

[2]Recent court decisions and federal guidelines require that employment tests have demonstrated validity.

regrettable but unavoidable. For the individual test taker the impact of the decision is more direct, often being the difference between being hired or not or being allowed to enter a given educational program or not. However, since no objective technique for evaluating tests has yet been devised that does not depend on group data, evaluation must be based on group data.

The discussion in the previous paragraph serves to emphasize another point: When tests are applied in the solution of practical problems, the test user must be concerned with the social consequences of the testing program. Not only must he be concerned with the undesirable effects that would occur as a consequence of using an invalid test, he must also be alert to the possibility that a seemingly valid test may unfairly discriminate[3] against certain groups of persons.

For example, suppose in considering all applicants for a job that one finds a high positive relationship between predictor test scores and the criterion measure of job success. In addition, suppose that a particular subgroup of applicants (for some reason) scores relatively low on the test but, if given the opportunity, can perform the job satisfactorily. In this case, use of test scores as a basis for selection would systematically discriminate against individuals in the subgroup and they would not be hired, even though they could do the job. Many people feel that such a situation occurs in the employment (and education) of certain minority groups within this country. They would argue that blacks may be denied employment or access to higher education, not because it has been shown that they cannot succeed but because they obtain low scores on the selection tests and consequently are not even allowed the opportunity to try.

Keeping these considerations in mind, let us now turn to some more specific examples of the application of psychological tests.

SCHOOL TESTING PROGRAMS

We shall begin by considering school testing programs. This starting point is particularly appropriate because tests have been more widely used in the planning and evaluation of educational processes than for any other purpose. Afterwards we shall look at the use of tests in counseling, in selection and placement, and in research.

Each year several hundreds of millions of standardized tests are administered in the United States, most of them in public schools (Goslin, 1963; Mehrens and Lehmann, 1969, 1975). Most frequently these are achievement batteries and scholastic aptitude or group intelligence tests, but interest and personality inventories and special aptitude tests may also be administered.[4] The testing program may be administered by an individual school or the local school district, or it may be part of a coordinated statewide testing program.

---

[3]All tests are designed to discriminate, in the sense that they differentiate between people having varying degrees of a trait or skill. Test constructors attempt to develop tests that do not discriminate on irrelevant bases—for example, age, sex, or race.

[4]We shall not consider uses of classroom tests here (see Chapter 13).

Functions of a Testing Program

School testing programs are designed to provide information regarding the characteristics of individual students or groups of students (for example, a class, a school, or a school system). Sometimes test scores will be used directly in the making of educational decisions—for example, to place students in various sections of classes. Other times the effect may be more indirect, as when data regarding the average achievement level of students in a school system stimulates the school board to revise the educational program. Unfortunately, in too many situations, test results are just filed away and not used.

In all cases, tests should not be used unless they help answer educationally relevant questions. What, then, are some of these questions? Although the number of potential questions is virtually limitless, some of the more important are:

1. Is the child ready to begin a formal educational program? Is he ready to begin instruction in a particular subject (such as reading)? Can instruction be conducted in a reasonably efficient manner with children at this stage of development? (These are all readiness questions.)
2. What has the child learned? This question may be asked in very broad terms (general educational development) or in terms of a limited subject matter area; the focus may be on development to a particular point in time or learning within a specific time period. For example, what did the child learn in third grade?
3. Which students should be placed in each of various sections of a course, tracks, or curriculum?
4. How effective was a given course or unit of instruction?
5. Which students should be admitted to a particular school? Because of universal education through adolescence, this question usually arises only in higher education.
6. What skills, abilities, interests and personality characteristics does the student have that will be important in his educational and vocational planning? This is the guidance or counseling function of tests.
7. What factors are hindering the student's learning progress?

Although asking the appropriate questions and selecting tests that can answer these questions are undoubtedly the most important steps in the development of a testing program, several other considerations are also important. Since education is a cumulative process, continuity and articulation is needed from level to level. So, too, with testing programs. It is not enough that the tests provide an indication of achievement or ability at a given point in time; they should also provide a basis for comparing performance at different grades or times. Generally, but not necessarily, this means that the same test series will be administered at several grade levels. Then, too, because schools operate within time and budget limitations, one must consider the time and cost requirements of any proposed testing program.

Developing a School Testing Program

Given these general guidelines, each school must translate them into operational procedures. Frequently, a committee consisting of representatives from the central administration, school principals, guidance counselors, and classroom teachers recommends areas to be covered by the testing program. Considering the nature of the students and the educational philosophy and organization of the school system, the committee outlines the testing program. The committee may also select particular tests or delegate this task to someone in the system who is a testing "expert"— for example, a counselor or school psychologist. In either case the goal is to develop a testing package that will provide the maximal amount of usable information with a minimum amount of testing.

Let us first consider the primary grades. There are a number of arguments against extensive testing in the primary grades; for example, the contention that teachers' close contact with students allows them to judge progress accurately; students' limited reading ability; and problems of test administration and scoring (for example, separate answer sheets cannot be used at this level). However, the development of reading ability is so important in the primary grades that reading progress should be assessed by a measure independent of teachers' judgments. Thus standardized reading tests are usually administered, at least yearly, during the primary grades.

Many schools administer an achievement battery periodically during elementary and junior high years. Balancing the advantages of frequent testing against administrative considerations, administering a battery every other year—say, in the third, fifth, seventh, and ninth grades—would seem to be reasonable. To provide continuity and allow for the measurement of growth, the same battery should be used at all levels. So that the test results will be of maximal use in educational planning, the battery should be administered early in the fall. Then teachers can use test scores, along with other information, to design programs both for individuals and classes. Particularly at younger ages, the battery should emphasize skills rather than content. Another valuable procedure would be to administer an achievement battery covering the basic academic areas during the junior year of high school. Scores could be used both to evaluate the school program and to provide information for use in counseling students regarding their future educational plans.

What about aptitude and intelligence tests? The current trend is to deemphasize aptitude measures. However, there are several points at which a measure of academic aptitude may provide useful information for academic advising. One is the transition from elementary school to junior high. Thus, a scholastic aptitude test might be administered to all sixth grade students. Another point is when planning high school programs for individual students. One way would be to administer a multiaptitude test during the ninth or tenth grade, using the scores in educational and vocational planning. Finally, students planning to go to college will probably take one of the national college admission tests; however, arrangements for these tests are made by the national agencies, working through the local schools.

Although personality and interest inventories may provide valuable information in certain circumstances (for example, in counseling students), many schools do not have an across-the-board administration of such inventories. If they do, it probably involves use of interest inventories at the junior high or high school level.

The program we have outlined is hypothetical, and is only one of many possible programs. Furthermore, the program outlined is minimal; many experts would argue that we have not included enough testing (see, e.g., Bauernfeind, 1969; Mehrens and Lehmann, 1973, 1975). Particularly, many people would suggest measuring achievement every year and making more extensive use of intelligence and scholastic aptitude tests. Our approach has been to restrict testing to the minimum amount needed to answer basic educational questions. If more testing of an individual or group is needed, it can always be done on an *ad hoc* basis.

Interpretation of Test Scores

Let us assume that a school has developed a testing program. Now three further questions must be answered: Who interprets the test scores? To whom will test scores be interpreted? How will the scores be interpreted?

Consider first the question of who will interpret the test scores. Whether a given individual possesses the competencies to interpret a particular test depends on the type of test, to whom the results will be reported, and how the results need to be interpreted. At the least complex level, achievement batteries generally can be interpreted by classroom teachers. This is not to say that classroom teachers can interpret scores on these tests without any training. Rather, with a minimum amount of training, the classroom teacher can understand the meaning of the scores and communicate this information to parents and other interested parties. To interpret achievement test scores adequately the teacher must understand: (1) the nature and content of the test; (2) the relation of the test to local goals; (3) the composition of the various norm groups used, particularly the difference between local and national norms; and (4) the implications of the various scores. Of course, all the information he has about the student's background, experience, interests and goals should be brought to bear when interpreting scores of each individual student.

The interpretation of scores on aptitude measures requires more sophistication than the interpretation of achievement test data but, again, this can be done by the classroom teacher, given appropriate training. Perhaps the single most important point to stress concerning the interpretation of intelligence and aptitude test scores is that these tests do not provide immutable indices of inherited abilities but rather are an index of the present level of developed abilities. There is also a constant temptation to use aptitude scores to estimate potential achievement and then compare this estimate with the student's actual achievement. A common practice is to label a student as an "underachiever" or "overachiever," a procedure that may both be technically unsound (Thorndike, 1963) and damaging to the educational process (see, Rosenthal and Jacobsen, 1968; Mercer, 1973). It should also go without saying that, because of the widespread misunderstanding of the nature of intelligence tests, interpretation of scores on these tests requires a high degree of both technical knowledge and tact. To simply report the scores may be threatening to the student or his parents or give him undue confidence, depending on the score; playing down the test results is also unfair to the student, preventing him from clearly understanding his own abilities and limitations.

Individually administered intelligence tests and personality and interest measures should be interpreted only by persons with specific training in their interpretation—for example, counselors and school psychologists. Although interest inventories are sometimes administered and interpreted by classroom teachers as part of a unit on careers, such practices are not to be condoned, since these instruments are not as simple to interpret as they might appear at first blush (see Chapter 17). In all circumstances, training of teachers and administrative staff in the use and interpretation of tests should be supervised by a staff member (for example, the counselor) who is thoroughly trained in psychological and educational measurement.

The second question concerns who should have access to test scores and to whom test scores should be interpreted. Although few people would argue with the right of teachers and other school personnel to have access to the test scores of individual students, a surprisingly large number of school officials object to test scores (particularly scores on intelligence, aptitude, and personality measures) being interpreted to students and their parents. Sometimes the objection is only to providing exact scores, the implication being that these scores will be misused and misinterpreted. In other cases the objection is to providing any test scores to the students and their parents. One cannot argue with the fact that test scores may be misunderstood (Can a young child really understand the implications of an achievement test score, let alone a score on an aptitude or intelligence test?) or misused (Parents may use the scores as a ''club'' to force the child to work harder). Yet, since parents have the ultimate responsibility for the child's education and development, it is hard to justify not interpreting scores to parents. One would also be hard put to justify keeping scores from children, especially older children, solely on the basis that the scores might be misused or misinterpreted. Actually this issue is now, in many ways, moot, since recent congressional legislation has opened all official school records (including test scores) to inspection by students and parents.

The issue can be further clarified by consideration of the third question: How should test scores be reported and interpreted? Persons who are trained and sophisticated in test usage—for example, counselors and school psychologists—certainly can be expected to apply necessary cautions and draw the correct implications from scores. Scores on achievement tests should be reported to teachers, parents, and students in a readily understandable score system—such as percentiles—or in broad qualitatively defined categories (such as high, above average, average, below average, low). Because scores on intelligence and scholastic aptitude tests can arouse emotional reactions, they should be interpreted to parents and children individually, by trained personnel. So should scores on personality and interest inventories.

Another aspect of this question is: What norms should be used as the basis for test interpretation? Since the normative data provided by the test publisher will undoubtedly be based on national samples, the question involves the desirability of using local norms. In almost all situations the advantages of local norms outweighs the difficulty and expense of developing local data. Thus, local normative data should be used in conjunction with the national normative data in test interpretations. In addition, whenever feasible, both norm-referenced and criterion-referenced interpretations should be provided.

To summarize, tests can provide useful data to aid individuals and school personnel in making educational decisions; tests should not be administered unless they will answer educationally relevant questions; and, once tests have been administered, scores should be made available to all persons who can profitably use the information to further the student's educational development.

USING TESTS IN COUNSELING

In school testing programs, the same test battery was administered to all members of a particular group. The use of tests in counseling, in contrast, illustrates how a testing program can be tailored to fit a particular individual.

Testing may serve various purposes in the counseling process. Sometimes test results are used to confirm the client's ideas about his skills, abilities, or personality characteristics. For example, a high school student planning to study engineering in college may take an interest test to confirm that his interests are, in fact, compatible with engineering. Conversely, a student enrolled in an engineering program who has little interest in his courses might use scores on an interest inventory to confirm his hunch that his interests are not similar to those of other engineering students. Test scores may also be used to provide an estimate of the counselee's probable success in a particular educational or vocational area. Thus scores on a scholastic aptitude test may indicate that the client's chances of obtaining a B average at the local junior college are 50-50 but only 5 in 100 at the state university. He can then take this information into account when making college plans. Or scores on a mechanical aptitude test might be used when discussing the possibility of entering an auto mechanics training program.

Tests can also be used to ensure that important skills, interests, and personality traits are not overlooked. Many persons take vocational interest inventories, not because they do not have any idea of their interests, but because their experience with occupations is so limited that they do not have a basis for assessing their interest in many occupational areas. The test scores may point out areas that otherwise may have been overlooked. In other cases, test scores may be used to stimulate discussion and self-exploration. Many persons find it difficult to talk about their own abilities, limitations, plans, and aspirations because they are unsure about their own abilities or do not know how to express their feelings. Oftentimes, communication is facilitated if the person can reflect his ideas against some other estimate, such as a test score.

Tests are also used for purposes that are of more direct concern to the counselor than the client. For example, test scores may be used for diagnostic purposes, to provide clues as to the nature, severity, and causes of the client's problems. In clinical settings this is perhaps the major function of tests. Thus, the MMPI might be administered to aid the counselor in determining the severity and dynamics of a client's discomfort. Finally, tests may be used in research on the counseling process. For example, a special test battery might be administered at various stages in the counseling process to evaluate the progress of the client or the effectiveness of counseling.

Most of the counseling uses of tests can be categorized as hypothesis building or diagnostic. The latter function is illustrated by the counselor's use of tests to understand a client; the former when the client uses test scores to build constructs about his personality structure and plan future courses of action. In essence, the client hypothesizes, ''I have the necessary academic ability and interests similar to physicians; therefore, I will plan to go to medical school.'' The validity of his hypothesis (that he will succeed in medical school and as a physician) can only be ascertained with time.

It is also important to note that much of the information provided by tests in counseling situations often can be obtained in other ways—from clients' statements about themselves, from counselors' estimates of client traits, and from formal records. However, tests provide a more objective, and frequently more efficient, method of collecting the same data. They also allow for interindividual comparisons. Thus, the contribution of tests is in their objectivity and normative function.

The Case of B.H.

To illustrate the use of tests in counseling we shall discuss in detail one particular counseling case. This particular illustration was selected because a wide variety of tests were used at various points in the counseling process to serve several different functions. Thus, the case illustrates many of the potential uses of tests in the counseling process.

Background   The client, B.H., was a 30-year-old, married college freshman who was referred to the Counseling Center by a physician. The client had complained of nervous and digestive troubles. The physician, feeling that these symptoms were reactions to academic pressures, prescribed medicine to relieve the physical complaints, then referred the student to the Counseling Service for help in ameliorating his educational problems. In the initial interview the client stated that his teachers had always considered him dumb and a behavior problem. Consequently, he was shuffled from school to school, and finally dropped out of high school. He entered the army and, after completing his duty, obtained a high school diploma at a night school. He then spent 10 years in a series of sales jobs, but never progressed far, losing promotions because of his lack of education and differences with his boss. Finally, he entered college. His original curriculum choice was Business Administration but, because of low grades in a required math course, he was thinking of changing majors. The counselor described B.H. as being pleasant and easy to talk to, but also vocationally and educationally naive, and obviously under a great deal of tension.

At this point the counselor looked at B.H.'s scores on a series of tests he had taken as part of the admission process to the University. On a scholastic aptitude test, the School and College Ability Test (SCAT), his total score was at the 50th percentile and his verbal score at the 88th percentile, but his quantitative score was only at the 12th percentile. His performance was also below average (30th to 40th percentile) on achievement tests in science and social studies. On an English test, his total score placed him at the 51st percentile compared to freshmen, with percentile ranks on the various subtests being: Vocabulary 77, Reading Speed 22, and Reading Comprehension 55.

Taken at face value, the total score on the SCAT and the English test indicated that B.H.'s ability was average for college students. However, the relatively high verbal and vocabulary scores, combined with lower scores in several content areas (science, social studies, and numerical) suggested restricted knowledge in several basic fields. Furthermore, his reading speed was slow. The pattern of test scores was interpreted by the counselor as indicating that B.H. had average academic ability but that he would be handicapped by his poor precollege preparation and slow reading speed. Thus, he would probably have to spend more time than the average student on reading assignments and frequently would have to do supplemental work to fill in gaps in his knowledge. These problems were further complicated by his long absence from an academic situation, his negative attitudes toward himself as a student and toward education, and financial problems and family commitments.

Counseling Since B.H.'s grades were placing him in scholastic jeopardy, the counselor and client decided to work first on academic problems, assigning vocational plans and personal problems a secondary role for the moment. And because the meaning of scores on a scholastic aptitude test might be somewhat ambiguous for such an atypical freshman as B.H., they decided to administer an individual intelligence test. A study habits inventory was also administered to spot weaknesses in his study techniques.

On the WAIS, B.H. obtained a Verbal IQ of 117, a Performance IQ of 110, and a Full Scale IQ of 115, with his highest scores on the Comprehension and Vocabulary subtests. The counselor interpreted these scores as confirming B.H.'s ability to do college-level work, and that his skills were concentrated in the verbal areas.

Study habits were investigated by the Brown-Holtzman Survey of Study Habits and Attitudes. This inventory contains scales measuring the ability to plan and organize work, study techniques, and attitudes towards teachers and education. However, the counselor ignored these scores and used B.H.'s responses to individual items to point out specific weaknesses in study techniques and as the basis for a discussion of methods of improving study habits.

His study techniques improved and he was able to maintain a B− average. Because of his weaknesses in mathematical and quantitative areas, coupled with his apparent strength in verbal areas (both confirmed by test scores), he decided not to major in Business Administration. However, he was unable to choose another major. Furthermore, his personal problems still prevented him from making optimal use of his abilities. To facilitate discussion of both these problems, the counselor and client decided that B.H. would take two interest inventories, the Strong and the Kuder, and a personality inventory.

The counselor first considered the MMPI profile. Consulting the *MMPI Atlas,* the Codebook for college students, and other sources, the counselor interpreted

TABLE 19.1 B.H.'s scores on the Kuder Preference Record—Vocational.

SCALE	P.R.
Outdoor	1
Mechanical	46
Computational	24
Scientific	27
Persuasive	91
Artistic	74
Literary	74
Musical	88
Social Service	30
Clerical	35

B.H.'s scores as typifying a restrained, tense, controlled, somewhat depressed person who was partially immobilized by his conflict. Although quite passive, he was fighting to break out of his restraints and conflicts, both by intrapsychic processes and by acting out. This interpretation served both as a diagnostic guide to the counselor and as a basis for the discussion in the counseling interviews. (The resultant counseling regarding personal problems extended over several dozen interviews and will not be discussed in detail here.)

The picture obtained from the interest inventories was far from sharp. The highest score on the Kuder was the Persuasive area, which Kuder describes as indicating a liking for meeting and dealing with people and for promotion and selling (see Table 19.1). Actors, radio announcers, and salesmen typically obtain high scores in this area. Other high areas were Musical, Artistic, and Literary. The Strong VIB profile (Figure 19.1) was relatively flat, with the highest scores being in music (Musician key), sales (group IX), and verbal occupations (group X). The high scores in musical areas reflected an avocational interest, and B.H. rejected sales occupations because of his previous experiences in these occupations.

After discussing these results, B.H. decided to enroll in courses in several areas that emphasized verbal skills (history, literature, political science, sociology, speech) to see if any of the courses particularly stimulated his interest. In the course of this exploration, B.H. became interested in speech courses, particularly courses in radio. His grades improved significantly, to high B's, and his tension and emotional problems decreased. He continued in school until he obtained a master's degree in Speech, and is now manager of a radio station in a small city. His job allows him to make use of his verbal skills (through announcing, news writing, program planning, and so on), as well as his avocational interest in music, and also makes some use of his sales and business background, without directly involving selling.

Points Illustrated by the Case

The case of B.H. illustrates several points concerning the use of tests in counseling. First, the tests were chosen to provide a unique set of information about a

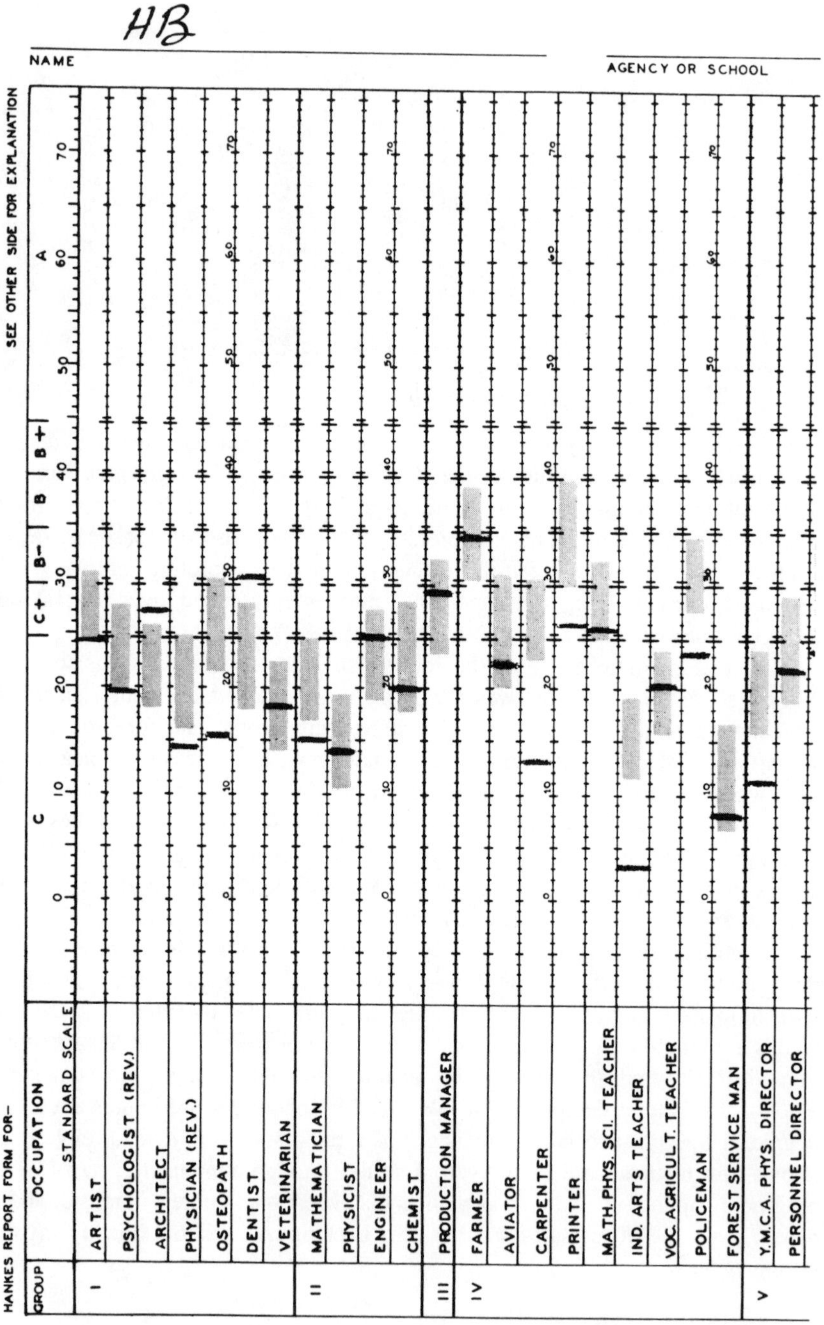
STRONG VOCATIONAL INTEREST TEST-MEN
SEE OTHER SIDE FOR EXPLANATION
HANKES REPORT FORM FOR-
HB
NAME
AGENCY OR SCHOOL
GROUP
OCCUPATION
STANDARD SCALE
C
C+
B-
B
B+
A
0
10
20
30
40
50
60
70
I
ARTIST
PSYCHOLOGIST (REV.)
ARCHITECT
PHYSICIAN (REV.)
OSTEOPATH
DENTIST
VETERINARIAN
II
MATHEMATICIAN
PHYSICIST
ENGINEER
CHEMIST
III
PRODUCTION MANAGER
IV
FARMER
AVIATOR
CARPENTER
PRINTER
MATH. PHYS. SCI. TEACHER
IND. ARTS TEACHER
VOC. AGRICULT. TEACHER
POLICEMAN
FOREST SERVICE MAN
V
Y.M.C.A. PHYS. DIRECTOR
PERSONNEL DIRECTOR

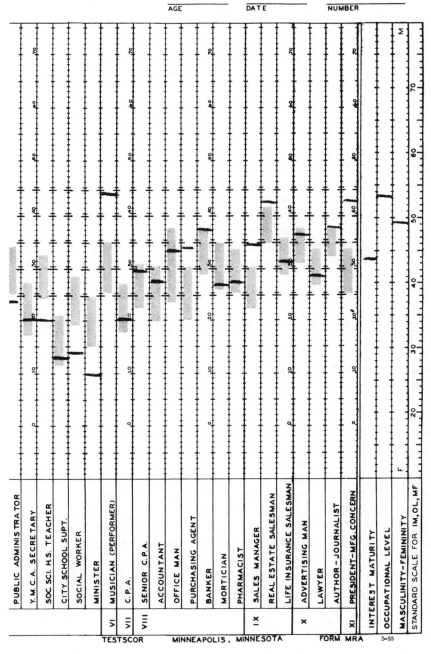

Figure 19.1 B.H.'s Strong Vocational Interest Blank profile. Copyrighted by the Board of Trustees of the Leland Stanford Junior University and published by Stanford University Press.

particular person (although a few test scores were obtained from an admissions testing battery). Second, the test results were used to focus on the individual—his characteristics, plans, strengths, and limitations. Third, the client had a hand in choosing the tests; he and the counselor jointly decided what sort of information was needed. This decision determined what class of tests (for example, interest inventories, scholastic aptitude tests) would be administered; the counselor, of course, selected the specific tests. Fourth, all test scores were interpreted to the client. Fifth, there is no clear-cut method to judge whether the tests provided any useful information. Even though B.H. appeared to make an appropriate vocational choice, too many variables were operating to attribute the choice to information provided by any particular test score. Finally, test scores were used for a variety of purposes: to confirm previous information, to develop hypotheses about appropriate choices, for diagnostic purposes, to guide specific actions (how to improve study habits), and to stimulate self-exploration.

It should also be noted that, in some ways, tests were used atypically. Certainly, a larger than average number of tests were administered, primarily because other sources of information were not available; for example, data on academic ability and achievement were unavailable because of the 12-year gap between high school and college. The use of item responses rather than subtest scores (as on the Brown-Holtzman), while not an infrequent occurrence, is a somewhat atypical practice. But, in general, the case shows how tests can facilitate the counseling process.

USING TESTS IN BUSINESS AND INDUSTRY

Many uses of psychological tests in business and industry involve personnel decisions—for example, selection among applicants, placement of workers on jobs, and determining whether a worker is qualified for promotion. Tests may be used in either of two ways: (1) to measure the individual's abilities and characteristics in order to make a prediction of his performance on the new job, or (2) as proficiency measures to establish whether the individual possesses the knowledge and skills outlined in the job specifications.

Tests are also used in training programs, both as criterion measures and as learning experiences (for example, the In-Basket Test). In addition, psychological tests may be used when studying jobs, to determine the abilities and characteristics that typify workers on various jobs and how these characteristics influence the way the job is performed. And, although the process generally occurs in other settings, vocational counseling is directed toward occupational selection and placement.

In our discussion we shall focus on a particular use of tests in business and industrial settings—the selection and placement of personnel. We shall follow the views of Dunnette (1963, 1966) and, to a lesser extent, those of Cronbach (Cronbach, 1970; Cronbach and Gleser, 1957, 1965).

Personnel Decisions

The use of psychological tests as decision-making aids is particularly appropriate for two types of personnel decisions: selection and placement. Selection, it will be recalled, refers to the situation in which there are more applicants than positions, and the goal is to select the most qualified applicants. In the placement situation, however, the number of applicants and positions are equal, and the goal is to assign workers optimally to positions. When companies hire large numbers of workers, the selection and placement processes may be handled jointly. That is, there will be various positions open, and many applicants are (minimally) qualified for more than one position. The personnel manager must select the most qualified workers and, at the same time, fill each of the open positions.

In performing this dual task, the personnel manager may adopt one of several possible strategies. At first glance, it might appear that all he has to do is hire the best qualified worker for each position; however, the situation is not quite that simple. On the one hand, a particular applicant might be the best qualified person for each of several positions. The question then becomes: To which position shall he be assigned? On the other hand, few applicants may be highly qualified for a particular position. In this situation, the question is: Which of the applicants can fill the position at a minimally satisfactory level? Thus, the personnel manager must adopt a strategy that maximizes the overall level of performance on all jobs.[5] This will necessarily mean that some applicants will be placed in jobs other than the one for which they are best qualified, whereas in other cases the job will be filled by other than the most highly qualified individual.

Note that this strategy optimizes assignments from the standpoint of the company, not necessarily for any individual. Although one might adopt a counseling viewpoint and argue that each individual should be allowed to work at a position that best utilizes his particular skills and abilities, within the confines of a particular company this approach is never completely possible. The worker, however, does have the option of accepting the position offered, even if it does not make optimal use of his talents, or looking elsewhere for employment, hopefully finding an employer that will offer him a position that better utilizes his talents.[6]

Some constraints   Within the general framework described above, the decision maker (for example, the personnel manager) has to operate within a further set of constraints and considerations, the most apparent being the size and nature of the applicant pool. If the number of acceptable applicants (that is, persons who are at least minimally qualified) is less than the number of positions open, either more applicants must be recruited or some positions must be left unfilled. If the number of acceptable applicants approximates the number of positions, his task is primarily placement, not selection. If the number of acceptable applicants exceeds the number of open positions, some selection can take place. The skills and characteristics of persons applying for positions will, of course, also influence the effectiveness of the placement procedures. When many applicants are highly skilled, the average job performance of the workers hired will be higher than if a majority of workers are

[5]In our discussion we shall assume that appropriate criteria of success have been identified and that the tests used have been validated. For a discussion of the procedures used, see Dunnette (1966).

[6]An interesting and provocative discussion on the utilization of talent can be found in an article by Wolfle (1960).

only minimally qualified. Finally, if the pool of applicants is small but a position does not have to be filled immediately, the chances of hiring a well-qualified applicant will, of course, be increased.

A second set of considerations involves the evaluation of the effectiveness of selection. Usually one thinks of performance as being evaluated in terms of objective measures of productivity—for example, units produced or dollar volume of sales. But this approach is oversimplified, since it neglects situational and environmental variables that may influence productivity. For example, the nature of a salesman's territory may have a greater effect on his productivity than does his selling ability; production on an assembly line may be determined by the rate set by other workers and/or the speed of the line. Thus, supervisor's ratings of job performance are often used, but these, too, are open to a variety of biasing effects (see Chapter 18).

An alternative approach (Dunnette, 1966) focuses on job elements or skills, rather than an overall outcome measure, thereby minimizing the effects of situational variables. This approach recognizes that different persons may perform the same job in different ways (by using different skills or job elements). It also recognizes the interaction of situational factors with job skills. Regardless of which approach is adopted, the effectiveness of the selection and/or placement program can be evaluated only with reference to a particular criterion.

A closely related problem is whether performance is to be evaluated immediately or at some time in the future. If a junior executive needs a typist to handle his correspondence, his evaluation will be based on her immediate performance. The performance of the junior executive, however, will probably be evaluated in terms of his contribution to the company over a longer period. In the broader sense, we are concerned with a distinction between training and job performance. If a position requires skills that are relatively uninfluenced by specific training, then persons who already possess the necessary skills must be hired. If, on the other hand, the needed skills can be developed through a training program, then persons who have the potential to acquire the necessary skills can be selected.

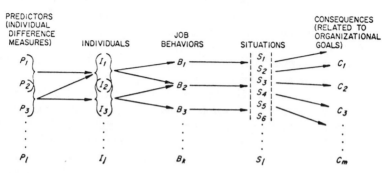

Figure 19.2   Dunnette's model for test validation and selection research. (Figure 6–1, p. 105, in M. D. Dunnette, *Personnel selection and placement.* Belmont, Calif.: Wadsworth Publishing Company, Inc., 1966.)

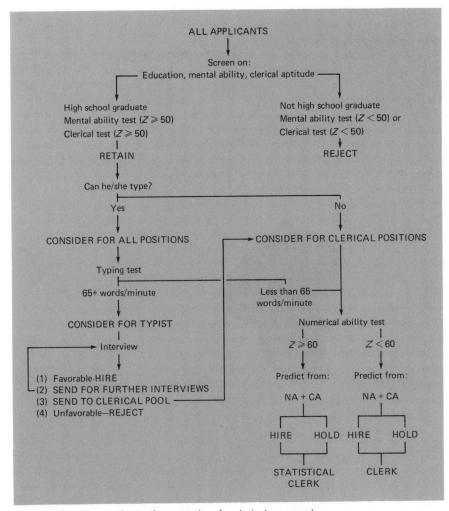

Figure 19.3 Diagram of selection procedure for clerical personnel

A Model for Selection Research

Much of the previous discussion can be summarized by a model (see Figure 19.2) for selection research and test validation proposed by Dunnette (1963, 1966). In contrast to the typical, more simplified model, which relates predictor scores to a criterion measure, Dunnette's model includes five elements and stresses the many possible interactions between these elements. In short, different strategies must be used for different subgroups of individuals, different tests, different jobs, and different situations.

The first element in the model (at the extreme left) is the various possible predictors. These may be tests, physical characteristics, biographical data, educational or work history, interviewer's ratings, or any other predictor variable. These predictors are then applied to the individual applicants. But since different predictors may be available or desirable for different individuals, the same predictors will not necessarily be used for all individuals. These various measures are used to predict specific job behaviors. Here again, the arrows remind us that different job behaviors may be salient for different individuals. Specific job behaviors are predicted, rather than some overall measure of success, in order to minimize situational effects. Adoption of this approach should also increase predictive validity, as clearly defined and specific behaviors are predicted. The interaction of the situational effects (fourth column) with job behaviors determine on-the-job performance (labeled consequences in the model).

Dunnette's model is an improvement over the traditional model in several ways. It takes into account situational effects and emphasizes studying behaviors in the actual job context. It stresses the need to study actual job behaviors rather than predicting overall job success, a procedure that Dunnette feels may mask important behaviors and skills. It also takes into account the fact that different persons may perform the same job in different ways by making use of different skills.

An Example of a Selection and Placement Program

To illustrate how tests can be used in a selection/placement program we shall consider a hypothetical example. Suppose that a company employing a large number of female clerical workers in three different clerical job classifications—typist, clerk, and statistical clerk—plans to open a new branch office. The company has conducted an extensive series of job analyses and validation studies in its other offices and, on the basis of these studies, has established minimal performance levels for each job, and has identified the variables that best predict performance on each of the jobs. These variables form the basis of the selection procedure; cutting scores have been determined by previous research.

Because there is overlap in the requirements for each job, all applicants are originally placed in one pool. As a first step, each applicant fills out an application blank and takes a short paper-and-pencil mental ability test and a clerical ability test. All applicants who are high school graduates and obtain scores equivalent to the average high school senior ($Z = 50$) on the mental ability and clerical test remain in the pool of potential applicants; all others are terminated at this point.[7] Applicants who can type also take a typing test; those who cannot type are retained for consideration as clerks or statistical clerks. Those applicants who meet the minimum typing requirements (65+ words per minute) are retained in the typist pool; the others are considered for clerical positions. Note at this point that we have two groups of applicants (typist and clerk–statistical clerk) and that screening has been done on the basis of biographic information (education), tests of mental and clerical ability, and a proficiency measure (the typing test). Note also that the first step was a selection step (that is, some applicants were eliminated), whereas the second step

[7]We are using standard scores in the example; thus the average score is represented by $Z = 50$.

(typing) only classified applicants into potential job grouping and did not result in anyone's being dropped from further consideration.

Consider now the first pool: the potential typists. As the next step in the selection process, applicants are interviewed by the person who would be their supervisor. He has four options: (1) hire as a typist, (2) not hire the applicant but recommend interviews by other supervisors for a similar position, (3) recommend that the applicant be placed in the pool of clerical applicants, or (4) recommend that the applicant not be considered for employment with the company. These procedures are shown in the left-hand column of Figure 19.3.

Those applicants remaining in the clerical pool are given a test of numerical ability. Those scoring well above average (that is, $Z = 60$) are considered for the position of statistical clerk; the others are considered for positions as clerks. Within each group the remaining candidates are ranked on the basis of their predicted job performance. The prediction for statistical clerks is made on the basis of their scores on the numerical and mental ability tests; the predictions for clerks are made from scores on the mental ability and clerical tests. Applicants are offered jobs in the order of their ranking (predicted criterion scores). Those who remain after all positions are filled are told that they will be contacted if an opening develops. Of course, if there is a continual flow of applicants, some later applicants will rank higher and thus will be offered jobs before persons who applied earlier but scored lower.

Several facets of the process should be especially noted: (1) The process was sequential in nature. (2) Certain stages involved selection decisions and others involved placement decisions. (3) Various sources of information were used, including tests, interviews, biographical data, and proficiency measures. (4) In some circumstances, a person not hired for one position was considered for another position. (5) Not all applicants went through the same procedures. (6) The interaction of the individual and situational characteristics was recognized; for example, each manager was allowed to hire a typist who met his particular requirements. (7) For one job (typists) the final hiring decision was based on a supervisor's preference; for other jobs it was based on a statistical prediction of on-the-job performance.

Even this presentation has greatly oversimplified the actual procedures. For example, the procedures followed in determining the validity of the process (and its components steps) were not described. Nor was there any discussion of how the criteria of job performance was developed, how the predictor tests were selected, and why the particular cutting scores were used. Nor was there any indication of the utility of the procedure. Since our goal was to present only an overview, an example of how tests might be used in selection and placement, such details were eliminated from the discussion. The reader who wishes to pursue these topics in more depth is advised to consult Dunnette's (1966) excellent book.

USING TESTS IN RESEARCH

By now it should be obvious that tests play an important role in psychological and educational research. (See, for example, our previous discussions of clinical judgment, intellectual structure, and Barron's Ego Strength scale.) In validation studies, tests are used to predict some criterion of interest. In other research, tests are used to measure a variable or construct of interest. For example, a psychologist interested in the effects of anxiety on learning might use a self-report inventory to measure anxiety. Other psychologists investigate the relationships between performance on various tests in order to learn more about the structure of abilities or personality organization.

We have chosen as examples two somewhat atypical uses of tests—atypical in the sense that the focus is not on the performance of individual students. The first is the National Assessment of Educational Progress, a program designed to determine what U.S. students of various ages know and can do. The other, the International Studies of Educational Achievement, explores the differential achievement in various countries and the factors relating to this differential achievement.

The National Assessment of Educational Progress

You have probably read articles that suggest that present-day students have learned much more than their parents did at the same age. About as frequently, you see articles that suggest that today's students are not as well prepared as those of previous generations, especially in basic subjects (see, e.g., Kline, 1974). Which view is correct? No one knows. One reason is that there is no baseline data to compare achievement at different times. The National Assessment of Educational Progress was designed to provide information on the knowledge, skills, and attitudes of American children and young adults (Committee on Assessing the Progress of Education, 1968; Tyler, Merwin, and Ebel, 1966; Womer, 1970a, 1970b). Because the focus is on providing baseline data, individual scores are not reported; in fact, each person takes only parts of the test battery.

The total battery consists of ten tests (Literature, Science, Social Studies, Writing, Citizenship, Music, Mathematics, Reading, Art, and Vocational Education), representing areas taught in most schools. Within each area, objectives were developed and items written to measure these objectives. Although some questions measure knowledge (for example, name the U.S. Senators from your state), the emphasis is on understanding and applications (for example, being able to select a balanced diet or tell the consequences of disturbing a given ecological system). In addition to paper-and-pencil items, exercises involved observations, interviews, questionnaires, performance tests, and sample productions.

The exercises were administered to students at four age levels: 9, 13, 17, and young adults (26–35). At each age level, some items were designed to be ones that practically all subjects could answer correctly, some that about half the students could answer correctly, and some that only the ablest students could answer correctly.

The primary goal of the Assessment is to measure change. This will be accomplished by repeating each test every several years. By not releasing all the items, some items can be repeated in following testing. The results of the two testings can be compared to see if performance has increased or decreased. Although there will be no analyses of scores of individual students or schools, comparisons will be made by geographic region, size and type of community, sex, race, and the educational background of the student's home.

Analysis of individual items has provided some interesting data. For example, 9 of 10 nine-year-olds can name the President but only 3 percent of the 17-year-olds know that cans are made chiefly of iron. More valuable, however, are analyses of the trends in the data. As might be expected, "book learning" increases with age. However, when comparing 17-year-olds and young adults the pattern becomes more complex. For example, in Science, 17-year-olds do better on items involving material learned in formal educational settings. In contrast, young adults do better on items where learning occurs through practical experience. This finding suggests that school learning may be different from real-life learning. Or, to cite another interesting finding, young adults are more willing than younger children to admit that they do not know an answer.

To summarize, the National Assessment will provide two types of data: what students of various ages know and can do and how these knowledges and skills change over time.

The International Studies of Educational Achievement

The goals of a series of studies conducted by the International Association for the Evaluation of Educational Achievement are to develop standard measures of educational achievement, describe the achievement level in various countries, and identify the factors that account for cross-national differences in achievement.

The first study (Husén, 1967) involved achievement in mathematics. In this study 133,000 students in 20 countries were tested; one group tested was 13-year-old students, the other students in the last preuniversity year. Besides achievement test scores, data were collected on student, teacher, and school characteristics.

The second phase of the study, the Six Subject Survey, covers Science (Comber and Keeves, 1973), Literature (Purves, 1973), Reading Comprehension (Thorndike, 1973), English and French as Foreign Languages, and Civic Education. Approximately 258,000 students in 20 countries (including several undeveloped nations) will be tested. The target populations include 10-year-olds, 14-year-olds, and students in the last year of precollege education.

When looking at the results of such studies, most people probably look first at the rank of their country. However, these rankings can be misleading. One problem, of course, is developing tests that are applicable in all nations. Although this is comparatively simple in mathematics, it is more difficult in areas like reading. Another problem is the different curricular emphases in the various countries. A third, and perhaps most difficult, problem is sampling students, particularly at older age levels. Consider the fact that U.S. high school seniors scored relatively low on the Mathematics, Science, and Reading Comprehension tests. What does this mean? On face value it might seem that the U.S. schools are not doing a good job. On the other hand, more than 70 percent of the children of this age are in school in the United States, whereas in other countries only one in 10 may be in school. As students who are in school are likely to be the most able, the U.S. standing may reflect our policy of open access to education.

Other interesting information is being obtained from analyses of demographic data. For example, among U.S. students, performance on the Reading Comprehension test was correlated (r's in the .30s) with mother's education, socioeconomic level of the home, and the amount of reading resources in the home. In other countries, these correlations ranged from zero to .50, indicating that different factors promote achievement in different nations.

Both the National Assessment and the International Study show that important information can be obtained from testing programs, information that can be used to improve education without reporting scores for individual students.

SUMMARY AND RECAPITULATION

At this point, let us review some of the important points made by our examples. The most obvious, and important, is that every situation will be different. Thus, the prospective test user must always start by considering the purposes of the testing. What does he want to measure? Why? What information should the tests provide? What sort of decisions will be made? What role will tests have in the process? And so on.

After he has answered these questions, he can develop operational procedures; that is, select the particular tests and/or measuring instruments he will use (see Chapter 20). Hopefully, these will be the ones that will provide the most reliable and valid information for his purposes. Unless a well-developed testing program is already in operation, he will probably select tests that have proved to be useful in other similar situations. But, as we have repeatedly pointed out, these tests may not work as expected. Thus, we should always collect validity data in our particular situation.

It should also be obvious that, in any situation, there will be a number of practical constraints. Some of these are financial, others concern personnel, and others involve time. In most practical situations, to be useful, results must be obtained within a limited time period. Although it would be desirable to develop and thoroughly validate a testing program before applying it, often we will have to evaluate our procedures as we proceed. Also, use of certain tests or procedures may not be feasible because we do not have personnel trained to administer and interpret them. Consequently, we often have to rely on simpler, perhaps less valid, procedures. Our goal should always be to use the best possible methods, given the practical constraints.

Finally, in practical situations, conflicts may arise because we are serving two publics: the individuals being tested and the organization doing the testing. In some cases, such as in counseling and therapy, concern for the client is clearly paramount. In contrast, in selection and placement the testing program is designed to benefit the employer, not the applicant. The goal of the program is to increase the productive efficiency of the company or organization. Hopefully, the program could be of some benefit to the individual; for example, if we give each applicant feedback on his performance (indicating his strengths and limitations) he may be better able to direct his future job hunting. The point is that most practical situations are designed for the benefit of either the tester or the test taker, not both.

In some cases, the testing relationship can benefit both parties. Consider college admissions testing. The student's ACT or SAT scores provide the college with useful information regarding the students' qualifications. If, in return, the college provides an applicant with data on the average ability of its students, he can compare himself with other students attending the school, and make an informed decision as to whether he should attend the college. Hopefully, more testing situations can be structured so as to be mutually beneficial.

20

SELECTING AND EVALUATING TESTS

Throughout this book we have discussed the basic requirements of a "good" test. These characteristics and requirements have been treated individually and somewhat abstractly. For the majority of readers the problem of greatest concern will be applying these principles, when the need arises, to selecting or evaluating a test. This chapter will focus on these problems. Thus it will be, in part, a review and summary of the material in previous chapters.

Two separate, but related, problems will be considered. The first is selecting the test[1] that best fits one's purposes from among the myriad of published tests. The second is evaluating a given test that has, on some basis, been chosen for consideration.

In most situations the first step is to select one or a small number of tests from among the available tests. We generally have certain general requirements in mind (for example, type of test, age or educational level of the test takers) and the task is to identify tests that meet these

---

[1]We shall use the term "test" (in the singular), even though more than one test may be considered.

requirements. After the search has been narrowed to a few tests, we can evaluate each test and select the one that best meets our requirements.

SELECTING A TEST

To narrow the field of potential tests, the test user should consider the purpose of the testing, the characteristics of the group being tested, practical limitations, and potential interpretation problems. Using these dimensions will reduce the potential pool of tests to a manageable number, thus allowing a detailed review of the best prospects.

Factors in Test Selection

The first and most important question to be asked is: What (trait) is to be measured and for what purpose? If we are interested in measuring achievement in mathematics, we can immediately eliminate all other types of tests; if we are interested in vocational interests, we can limit our search to vocational interest inventories; and so on. Our delineation here may be very broad (mathematics) or quite narrow (plane geometry).

We must also consider the purpose of the testing. For example, is the test to be used for selection? As a diagnostic device? Specifying the purpose indicates what format and types of scores will be appropriate. If, for example, an English grammar test is needed to place students in various sections of an English course, a test with comprehensive content coverage would be required, but one summary score would be sufficient. However, if the grammar test were to be used for diagnostic purposes, we would need a test that covered the various areas of grammar and provided separate scores of each subarea.

A second consideration is the nature of the group tested. Are we testing adults or children? Groups with particular educational or cultural backgrounds? People with particular handicaps or special abilities? Since tests are developed for certain age, educational, and cultural groups, knowledge of the characteristics of the group to be tested will further limit the number of possible tests. Thus, knowing that we need a grammar test limits our search; moreover, the additional requirement that the test be appropriate for junior high students further limits the field of potential tests.

The particular characteristics that will be relevant in any situation will, of course, depend on the particular situation and the purpose of the testing. These characteristics, in general, are the same as those considered in forming norm groups—for example, age, education, socioeconomic status, and level of particular skills (such as reading ability). Whenever test performance varies as a function of some characteristic, that characteristic should be considered when selecting the test.

Practical considerations   There are also practical limitations that must be taken into account. One is *time*. Usually we are not able or willing to devote unlimited time to testing. For example, an employer may use a test only if it can be administered in a half hour; an instructor may require a test that can be administered within one class period; a college admissions test may have to fit into a half-day testing session. Probably the most common limitation is the need for tests given in public schools to conform to class schedules. In this situation, the test must be able to be administered within one class period, or a multiple of a class period, or must have subtests that can be administered within a single class period.

A second practical consideration is *cost*. Users must choose tests that fit their budgets. These costs include not only test booklets and answer sheets but also scoring and reporting expenses. Costs can be minimized in many ways; for example, using separate answer sheets and staggered testing sessions can reduce the number of test booklets required. We must also take into account indirect costs, including staff time to prepare, administer, and interpret the test, and any special equipment or facilities needed.

A third consideration is *staffing*. One reason for the popularity of paper-and-pencil tests is that they can be administered by an educated layman, given minimal training. Other tests, such as individual intelligence tests, require specially trained administrators. Both the need for trained administrators and for individual administration increase costs.

An often overlooked factor is the need for staff who are competent to interpret the test results. Too frequently, people assume that because a test is simple to administer, it also can be interpreted by almost anyone. This is not the case, even with the least complex test. Test interpretation is more than reporting scores to an individual. For effective interpretation, one must understand both the test and the test taker, and possess communication and counseling skills (see Chapter 11 and Goldman, 1971).

These practical constraints must be placed in perspective. Rather than being hard-and-fast determinants, they are better viewed as flexible guidelines. Certainly, practical considerations are much less important than the technical quality of the test. Also, practical limitations sometimes are more apparent than real. Of all the considerations involved in selecting tests, practical ones are least important.

Ethical considerations   A closely related concern is the problem of establishing ethical standards for the use of tests. Professional organizations whose members frequently use tests (for example, the American Psychological Association, the American Personnel and Guidance Association, the National Council on Measurement in Education, and the American Educational Research Association) all have explicit codes and/or implicit standards regarding the construction, use, and interpretation of psychological tests. These ethical principles are phrased in quite general terms, have no legal standing, and are applicable only to members of the particular organization. They do, however, exert some control over test usage.

In addition, the *Standards for Educational and Psychological Tests and Manuals* make suggestions regarding the qualifications required to administer and properly interpret tests. The 1966 revision listed three levels of tests:

> Level A. Tests or aids that can adequately be administered, scored and interpreted with the aid of the manual and a general orientation to the kind of institution or organization in which one is working (e.g., achievement or proficiency tests).

Level B. Tests or aids that require some technical knowledge of test construction and use, and of supporting psychological and educational fields such as statistics, individual differences, psychology of adjustment, personnel psychology, and guidance (e.g., aptitude tests, adjustment inventories applicable to normal populations).

Level C. Tests and aids that require substantial understanding of testing and supporting psychological fields, together with supervised experience in the use of these devices (e.g., projective tests, individual mental tests). (APA, 1966, p. 10)

The 1974 revision of the *Standards* makes many more explicit recommendations regarding the qualifications necessary to use and interpret various types of tests. However, the basic point is clear: There are various types and uses of tests, and different qualifications are needed when using the various types of tests.

Whether these standards prevent tests from getting into the hands of incompetent users is problematical, since the proper distribution of test materials, depends both upon the ability of the user to assess his own capabilities and the marketing policies of the test publishers. They do, however, recognize that the tests require various levels of sophistication and training of their user, and provide guidelines for restricting the use of tests to individuals competent to administer them.

What Tests Are Available?

Having identified the type of test needed, and the practical constraints, the next step is to locate the tests that fit our specifications. In most cases the best place to start the search will be with one of the standard reference books.

There are two basic reference books, both edited by Oscar K. Buros. One, *Tests in Print II* (Buros, 1974) is a comprehensive bibliography of tests used in education, psychology, and industry.

Although some confidential and restricted tests (for example, the SAT and GRE) are included, most of the almost 2500 tests listed are available to qualified users. The tests are listed by type, thus allowing the test user to focus his search. Each entry includes the title of the test, the examinees, and level for which the test was designed (for example, grades 4–6), the author, publisher, publication date, parts or subtests, scores, and comments (for example, "new form available annually," "for research use only"). In addition, each entry is cross-referenced to other categories of test within *Tests in Print* and to the *Mental Measurements Yearbook.*

The main use of *Tests in Print* is to determine whether any published tests are available in a given category. Thus, it is an excellent starting point. Its major weakness is that it is a listing that provides only minimal information regarding a test. Thus, one will always have to consult other sources for more detailed information.

The Mental Measurements Yearbooks   The other major reference is also edited by Buros. The *Mental Measurements Yearbook* is not an annual publication—but rather a series, with volumes issued every several years. The sixth edition was published in 1965, the seventh in 1972, and the eighth is being prepared. The

Yearbooks have three major objectives: (1) to provide a readily available, comprehensive, up-to-date bibliography of tests and sources of information about test construction, validation, and use; (2) to encourage more sophisticated and higher-quality critical evaluations and appraisals of tests and testing practices; and (3) to encourage publication of fewer, but better, tests. The first purpose has been accomplished by the *Yearbooks* themselves and the second encouraged by the high critical standards of the *Yearbook* reviews. Unfortunately, the third goal has not yet been attained.

The *Yearbooks* are the test users' bible. The entry for each of the tests in the seventh edition includes the test title; author, publisher and publication date; groups for which the test is intended; part scores, levels, forms; method of scoring; cost; time, both working time and total administration time; pages; and an indication of whether reliability and validity data are available (see Figure 20.1). There is also a bibliography on the test, and cross-references to other editions of the *Yearbook*.

Although this descriptive material is of great value, the heart of the *Yearbook* is the critical reviews of tests. Not every test is reviewed, but reviews are given of the more important, widely used new and revised tests. These reviews vary in length from a few paragraphs to several pages. They are frankly critical and evaluative. About half of the tests are reviewed by more than one person, with reviews written from different perspectives. For example, a French test might be reviewed by a psychologist, who would focus on the technical quality of the test, and by a French teacher, who would evaluate the content and coverage of the test.

The *MMY* also includes reviews of books about testing, a directory of periodicals that publish articles on testing and measurement, a directory and index of test publishers, and several indices (by test name, title, classification).

For comprehensiveness and critical evaluations there is no single source to match the *Yearbooks*. Not only does the descriptive information enable the user to determine whether a test meets his requirements, but the reviews provide expert opinions on the merits and limitations of the test. All test users should become familiar with this reference.

Other sources of information Textbooks on psychological and educational testing provide descriptions and evaluations of various tests. Depending on the purpose of the text, the coverage may be superficial or detailed, comprehensive or limited to a particular area. Examples on books that thoroughly cover an area are Super and Crites' (1962) *Appraising Vocational Fitness,* Mehrens and Lehmann's (1975) *Standardized Tests in Education,* and Zytowski's (1973) *Contemporary Approaches to Interest Measurement.* There are also books devoted to a single test.

Psychological and educational journals provide another source of information. A few journals (for example, *Journal of Educational Measurement, Measurement and Evaluation in Guidance,* and *Journal of Counseling Psychology*) periodically publish test reviews. Several other publications (for example, the *Review of Educational Research* and the *Annual Review of Psychology*) periodically include

Figure 20.1 A page from the Mental Measurements Yearbook. From *The Sixth Mental Measurements Yearbook,* O. K. Buros, Ed. (Highland Park, N.J.: The Gryphon Press, 1965), p. 456.

origin and not of a kind likely to be useful to an American user. A reference is made to the use of the test in the measurement of mental deterioration. Two references in French are given to deterioration studies.

Until the publishers produce evidence that this test is equal or superior to the many non-verbal tests published in the United States, it has little to commend it for use in guidance situations. The fact that it is a test of a single item type may make it useful for certain factor analytic studies.

[455]

★**Deeside Non-Verbal Reasoning Test: English-Welsh Bilingual Version.** Ages 10–12; 1961–63; 2 forms: test 1 ('61), test 2 ('63), (16 pages); separate mimeographed manuals for test 1 ['61, 17 pages], test 2 ['63, 19 pages]; distribution restricted to directors of education; 25s. per 25 tests; 7s. 6d. per manual; postage and purchase tax extra; 37–38(60) minutes; W. G. Emmett; George G. Harrap & Co. Ltd. *

[456]

*****Doppelt Mathematical Reasoning Test.** Grades 16–17 and employees; 1954–63; IBM; Form A ('54, 4 pages); manual ('58, 10 pages); bulletin of information ('63, 36 pages); revised procedures for testing center operation ('63, 8 pages); distribution restricted and test administered at specified licensed university centers; scoring and reporting handled by the local center; examination fee to centers: $1 per examinee; fees to examinees are determined locally and include reporting of scores to the examinee and to 3 institutions or companies designated at the time of testing; additional score reports may be secured from the publisher at a fee of $1 each; 50(60). minutes; Jerome E. Doppelt; Psychological Corporation. *

REFERENCES

1. SCHWARTZ, MILTON M., AND CLARK, F. EUGENE. "Prediction of Success in Graduate School at Rutgers University." *J Ed Res* 53:109–11 N '59. * (*PA* 35:1223)
2. ROEMMICH, HERMAN. "The Doppelt Mathematical Reasoning Test as a Selection Device for Graduate Engineering Students." *Ed & Psychol Meas* 21:1009–10 W '61. *

W. V. CLEMANS, *Director, Test Department, Science Research Associates, Inc., Chicago, Illinois.*

The *Doppelt Mathematical Reasoning Test* contains 50 problems that differ from the usual pattern for multiple choice questions in that there are no stems. The task facing the examinee is defined once for the entire set in the directions which state:

Each problem in this test consists of five mathematical figures or expressions. Four of these have something in common which is not shared by the remaining one. You are to choose the *one* figure or expression which does *not* belong with the other four and mark the letter corresponding to your choice in the proper place on the answer sheet.

None of the problems involves mathematics **beyond the usual secondary school level.** The test can be easily administered to large groups or to individuals.

The manual states that the test "was designed primarily as an aid in the selection of students for graduate work" and that it "may also be useful in the classification and assignment of college graduates applying for positions in industry which require mathematical reasoning."

Correlations of the DMRT with faculty ratings or grades for three groups of 41, 57, and 109 graduate students taking mathematics suggest that the test may have some value for selecting graduate students. The coefficients obtained were .52, .71, and .43, respectively. Similar coefficients are reported for 28 graduate students in chemistry and 26 undergraduates in a psychometrics course, but a coefficient of only .32 was found for 29 medical students. This latter finding is hardly significant, but is the only coefficient reported for a criterion group whose course work is not primarily quantitative. The Psychological Corporation supplies summaries of five studies reported by independent investigators that tend to corroborate the claim that the test relates to measures of success in graduate study in mathematics or statistics. Apparently no systematic approach has been made to determining how valuable the test is for graduate students in other areas. Validity data for industrial criteria have not yet been supplied.

In the norms section of the manual percentile equivalents are given for five small student samples ranging in size from 102 to 145 students selected from 15 colleges and universities. The groups consisted of senior psychology students, medical students, psychology majors, education majors, and graduate students taking courses in statistics. Percentile equivalents are also given for a group of 388 engineers from one industrial organization.

Reliability coefficients were computed for each of the six groups using the odd-even approach and the Spearman-Brown formula. The coefficients range from .78 to .85. The author points out that the lowest values were found for the most homogeneous groups. He fails to point out, however, that the three groups yielding the highest reliability coefficients (all .85) not only had the largest standard deviations but also the lowest means. This phenomenon suggests to this reviewer that the higher values may have been due to speeded-

reviews of testing and measurement. Studies using tests are published in a large number of journals.[2] One can search for studies using the test under consideration and/or studies of similar tests and problems. The main disadvantage of journals as information sources is, of course, that the information is diffused throughout many issues of many journals.

Most colleges and universities, and many public school systems, have persons on their staffs who are knowledgeable about testing. In addition, there are psychologists who work for public or private agencies or in business and industry, or who are in private practice. These persons generally can suggest appropriate tests, direct the test user to information sources, or suggest persons or agencies that can help with his testing problem.

For the most detailed information about a particular test, one should contact the test publisher. Each publisher prints a catalog of the tests they publish, which can be used to locate possible tests. Of more interest, however, is the fact that publishers also provide *specimen sets* of most tests. A specimen set (which usually can be obtained for a minimal fee) consists of a copy of the test, the answer sheet, scoring key, and technical and interpretive manuals. The potential test user can study these materials and evaluate the content, administration, and technical quality of the test.

Summary   When searching for an appropriate test, you may investigate any or all of the sources mentioned. Probably the most efficient procedure is to start with *Tests in Print* and the *Mental Measurements Yearbooks,* then look to sources such as journals and textbooks. Once the field of potential tests has been narrowed to a small number, the test user should obtain specimen sets and use them as a basis for a detailed study of the tests.

Sometimes no test will be found that meets your requirements. In this situation you have several alternatives. One is to look for another (nontest) method of obtaining the relevant data. Or certain of your original requirements might be changed, or relaxed. A third possibility is to construct a new test to meet your requirements. Since test construction is both time-consuming and expensive, this is usually the least feasible alternative.

EVALUATING A TEST

Let us assume that several tests appear to meet the general requirements. The task then becomes to evaluate these tests and select the best one for the particular situation. These evaluations are usually made using the materials in the specimen set. The content and coverage of the test can be ascertained by studying the individual items; the test takers' task from the test, answer sheet, and administrative directions; and the technical adequacy from the test manual.

[2]For example, the *Journal of Applied Psychology, Journal of Counseling Psychology, Personnel and Guidance Journal, Measurement and Evaluation in Guidance, Journal of Educational Measurement, Educational and Psychological Measurement, Personnel Psychology, American Educational Research Journal, Journal of Educational Psychology,* and *Reveiw of Educational Research.*

The *test manual*[3] is the basic source of information about the construction and standardization of the test. It should contain detailed information regarding the procedures used in selecting and constructing the test items, directions for administration and scoring, normative data, reliability and validity data, and any other information that aids in the interpretation of the scores obtained from the test. In short, the test manual should provide all the data necessary to evaluate the administrative and psychometric aspects of the test. Thus, obtaining and studying the test manual is the most important step in choosing and evaluating a test.

Two Considerations

When evaluating any test, two overriding considerations must constantly be kept in mind. First, one must adopt a skeptical and critical attitude when evaluating any test. Remember, test publishing is a business and, as such, will try to present its products in the most favorable light. In particular, one must be on guard not to be overwhelmed by sheer amounts of data. Instead, you should constantly ask: Why were the data collected? Were the proper controls maintained? What do the data mean? In short, you should consistently and rigorously hold to the standards and principles discussed in previous chapters.

The second major consideration is that the test will be used in a particular situation, with a particular group of persons, for a specific purpose. Thus, we are looking for the test that will be most appropriate for this particular purpose. This may, or may not, be a test that has proved valuable for other related purposes or in other, presumably similar, situations. Even though there are certain factors that are relevant to the evaluation of any test, there will also be certain requirements specific to each individual situation. In other words, no test will be best in all situations. In more technical terms, there is a test-situation interaction. Thus, even a well-constructed test may be inappropriate in a given situation. Therefore, in evaluating a test one must always consider the specific, unique aspects of the situation in which the test will be used.

Formats for Evaluating Tests

As with techniques of studying, singing styles, and golf putting stances, there is no one format or procedure for evaluating a test. Any individual who consistently evaluates tests will, in time, develop his own format and procedures, emphasizing the characteristics of tests that he thinks most important. There are, however, common elements that must be included in any test evaluation.

The standards for educational and psychological tests There have been several attempts to designate standards for evaluating tests in some systematic manner. The most comprehensive of these is the *Standards for Educational and Psychological*

---

[3]Many tests have several manuals, most frequently one for test users (concerned with administration, scoring, and interpretation) and one covering more technical aspects (scale construction, reliability, validity, and norming).

Figure 20.2 An excerpt from the *Standards for Educational and Psychological Tests and Manuals.* (Washington, D.C.: American Psychological Association, 1966).

C1. The manual should report the validity of the test for each type of inference for which it is recommended. If its validity for some suggested interpretation has not been investigated, that fact should be made clear. ESSENTIAL

C1.1. Statements in the manual about validity should refer to the validity of particular interpretations or of particular types of decision. ESSENTIAL

[Comment: It is incorrect to use the unqualified phrase "the validity of the test." No test is valid for all purposes or in all situations or for all groups of individuals. Any study of test validity is pertinent to only a few of the possible uses of or inferences from the test scores.

If the test is likely to be used incorrectly for certain areas of decision, the manual should include specific warnings. For example, the manual for a writing skills test states that the test apparently is not sufficiently difficult to discriminate among students "at colleges that have selective admissions."]

C1.2. Wherever interpretation of subscores, score differences, or profiles is suggested, the evidence in the manual justifiying such interpretation should be made explicit. ESSENTIAL (Also see B4.4.)

[Comment: One aptitude test manual indicates the difficulties involved in computing the statistical significance of differences between scores in a profile. In an effort to cope with this problem a convenient method of approximating the significance of plotted differences is provided. Cautions and limitations of this type of profile interpretation are suggested.]

C1.21. If the manual for an inventory suggests that the user consider responses to separate items as a basis for personality assessment, it should either present evidence supporting this use or call attention to the absence of such data. The manual should warn the reader that in-

ferences based on responses to single items are subject to extreme error, hence should be used only to direct further inquiry, as, perhaps, in a counseling interview. ESSENTIAL

C2. Item-test correlations should not be presented in the manual as evidence of criterion-related validity, and they should be referred to as item-discrimination indices, not as item-validity coefficients. ESSENTIAL

[Comment: It is, of course, possible to make good use of item-test correlations in reasoning about construct validity. However, such correlations are not, in themselves, indicators of test validity; they are measures of internal consistency.]

Content Validity

C3. If a test performance is to be interpreted as a sample of performance or a definition of performance in some universe of situations, the manual should indicate clearly what universe is represented and how adequate is the sampling. ESSENTIAL

[Comment: Some consideration should be given to the adequacy of sampling from both the appropriate universe of content and the universe of behaviors that the items are intended to represent. For example, the manual of a test of achievement in American history might not only describe the item types used and the coverage of the subject matter, but also should describe to what extent responding to the test items serves as an adequate sample of the examinee's attainment of such skills as critical reading of historical material, including evaluation of evidence, analysis of cause and effect relationships, and whatever other behaviors are considered to be "achievement in American history."]

C3.1. When experts have been asked to judge whether items are an appropriate

Tests and Manuals (APA, 1954, 1966, 1974). This pamphlet was prepared by three major professional organizations: the American Psychological Association, the American Educational Research Association, and the National Council on Measurement in Education. It was designed as a guide to test users and constructors in evaluating test manuals and test usage.

The *Standards* cover three major areas. The first involves standards for tests, manuals, and reports. Subareas are concerned with the dissemination of information, aids to interpretation, directions for administration and scoring, and scores and norms. This section is primarily concerned with ways of communicating information about the test to the test user. The second major section is concerned with standards for research studies of reliability and validity. The third section focuses on the use of tests, considering such factors as qualifications of test users, choosing tests, administration and scoring, and the interpretation of scores.

Within each section are a number of general principles (standards) and subprinciples. These are classified on three levels: essential, very desirable, and desirable. The essential recommendations, of course, represent the minimum amount of information that should be presented about the test. Along with the recommendations are appropriate explanatory comments and examples (see Figure 20.2). The *Standards* is an excellent reference for use in evaluating a test; every test user should own, study, and constantly use this reference.

A suggested format   Figure 20.3 shows a format, in outline form, that the author has found useful in evaluating tests. This guide, as any other, should be treated as a minimum, as a series of essential questions. In any particular evaluation, other questions may also be asked; what these additional questions are will depend on the type of test, the proposed use, and the group tested. For example, if a test is too long or comprehensive, the prospective user might want to know the answers to such questions as: Is there any way the test can be split? Can certain sections be eliminated? What effect will this have on validity? Will the scores obtained from the revised test be comparable to those obtained using the entire battery?

The Evaluation Process

The evaluation will cover various areas, utilizing information obtained from various sources. General information (time, scores, age level, forms, and so on) can be obtained from reference sources (e.g., Buros). This information can be confirmed, and missing data supplied, from the test manual. Next we study the test itself, focusing on the format and layout and on the content and coverage of the individual items. Here some reference will have to be made to the manual, to determine the rationale and method of selecting items. After study of the test itself, we turn to the psychometric characteristics of the test—its reliability, validity, scores, and norms. Data for these sections will come primarily from the test manual. The manual will also provide the information regarding administration and scoring. Finally, we take into account any other information, from the test publisher's

Figure 20.3 A suggested format for evaluating a test

1. General Information
   Title:
   Author:
   Publisher:
   Publication date:
   Forms and levels (Equivalent forms available?):
   Manual and other technical aids:
2. Purposes and Uses
   Purpose as stated by author:
   Other purposes/uses implied by author:
   Other purposes/uses reported in literature:
3. Practical Considerations
   Direct costs (booklets, answer sheets, scoring, etc.):
   Indirect costs:
   Time (working time, total administrative time):
4. Format and Layout
   General editorial quality (printing, paper, format, readability, etc.):
   Arrangement of items and subsections/parts:
   Appeal to layman (face validity):
   Test takers' ease of comprehension and response:
5. Items and Their Coverage
   Basis of item selection:
   Coverage (especially, over- and underrepresented areas):
   General quality of items (complexity, ambiguity, control of response
       sets, etc.):
   Variety of item formats:
   Item difficulty:
6. Consistency
   Evidence (amount and quality) on various types of consistency:
       equivalence:
       stability:
       equivalence and stability:
       internal consistency:
   Factors influencing reliability and magnitude of their effect:
   Reliability of subtest scores (if applicable):
   Reliability of difference scores (if applicable):
   Standard error of measurement (total, subtest/scales):
   Consistency for different groups of subjects:
7. Validity
   Evidence (amount and quality) of:
       content validity:
       construct validity:
       criterion-related validity (note especially criteria; incremental
       validity):

Figure 20.3   (continued)

What traits the test measures   (construct validity, homogeneity, discriminant validity):

Validity of subtest/part scores:

Confidence in predictive ability for groups, for individuals:

Generalizability of validity data to other groups, situations:

8. Scores and Norms

Norm groups (how many? clearly defined? size? sampling? recency? broken down by appropriate classes?) :

Will local norms be needed?

Scales used to report scores:

Any interpretative aids available?

Information on subtest scores:

9. Administration and Scoring

Individual or group administration:

Qualifications for test administrator:

Apparatus, equipment needed for administration:

Instructions for administration (for administrator, for test taker, to control response biases) :

Timing, amount and ease:

How scored? (hand, machine; ease of scoring)

Directions for scoring (Scoring objective? If scoring subjective, what evidence for agreement between scorers? What scoring aids? Who can score test?) :

10. Other Information

Comments by reviewers/users:

Test part of series or battery:

Any auxiliary services available/provided (research, scoring) :

material or outside sources (e.g., Buros, test reviews) that may be relevant to our evaluation.

Once the evaluation has been completed, the test user must make a decision. If he has been evaluating only one test, he must decide whether it looks promising enough to use. If he has been evaluating several tests, he must choose between them (or possibly reject them all). Reaching this decision is a rational, judgmental process, similar to that involved in determining the content validity of the test. The test user must weigh the advantages and limitations of the various tests in question, make a decision, and then proceed on the basis of that decision.

The evaluative procedure does not end at this point. Because each testing situation is unique, it is impossible to predict with absolute certainty that the test chosen will, in fact, work. Thus a tryout in an actual situation is essential. Preferably, a preliminary tryout should be conducted before the test is put into widespread or routine use. Ideally, a tryout would involve the use of several tests with a sample of persons from the population that will be used later, with the final selection being based on the results of the tryout. If a tryout is not feasible, a test should be adopted tentatively and its usefulness constantly reviewed and evaluated. In all circumstances, the value of a test will not be determined until validity data, based on studies of the test in the actual situation, are available.

SUMMARY

To summarize, the process of selecting and evaluating tests is a systematic, rational process consisting of the following steps:

1. Outline your general considerations—the purpose of the testing, characteristics of the group being tested, practical constraints.
2. Determine what tests are available.
3. Obtain information about the tests from texts, journals, and reference books. Using these data, select the several most promising tests.
4. Obtain samples (specimen sets) of these tests.
5. Do your own detailed evaluation of the test, keeping in mind the unique requirements of your particular situation. On the basis of this evaluation, make your selection of the test or tests to be used.
6. If possible, conduct an experimental tryout.
7. Put the test into use. Evaluate its effectiveness.

The need for holding to rigorous critical standards of evaluation and for continual evaluations cannot be overstressed. If at any point in the procedure the test fails to meet your criteria, its use should be discontinued and other tests or procedures substituted.

21
PROBLEMS
AND
TRENDS

Having described the process of test construction, the basic concepts of testing, and the varieties and uses of tests, we will complete the book by considering some of the major problems and trends in the utilization of psychological and educational tests. As a framework for this discussion, we will first summarize some of the most important principles presented in the previous chapters.

A test has been defined as a systematic procedure for measuring a sample of behavior. Systematic procedures insure that irrelevant variables will be controlled and that all persons will take the test under equivalent conditions. Thus, scores of different individuals can be compared. As a test is a measuring instrument, certain requirements regarding the establishment of scale units must be met; however, most psychological tests approximate an interval scale. And as only a sample of the relevant behavior (domain) is measured, statements made about an individual's total repertoire of behavior or about the existence of underlying traits necessarily will be inferential.

Remember also that a test measures only developed skills, the characteristics of the test taker at a given point in time. Thus, an individual's score on a test will be a function of inherited characteristics, learning, and life experiences prior to the test, as well as the conditions of the testing session. Although when interpreting scores we usually assume that, at least within broad limits, the testees have had comparable prior experiences, this assumption cannot be verified from the test itself. Therefore, while scores from a single testing session may provide useful predictive data, an adequate understanding of the developmental processes that resulted in the individual obtaining a particular score will require information from other sources.

Tests serve three broad functions—as predictors, as samples, and as signs. A test functions as a predictor when it is used to forecast some qualitatively different behavior, as when a scholastic aptitude test is used to predict college grades. As a sample it represents (samples) a clearly defined content or behavior domain; classroom exams are a clear illustration of this function. A test serves as a sign when it points out the nature of the (still incompletely defined) behavioral domain being sampled; an intelligence test, for example, helps define what is meant by intelligence. In many ways, these three functions parallel the notions of criterion-related, content, and construct validity. Furthermore, they roughly parallel the three major types of tests: Aptitude tests are predictors, achievement tests are samples, and personality tests are signs.

Useful mathematical models have been developed to define the concepts of reliability, homogeneity, and validity. The most widely used model is the trait or individual differences model. This model is useful with tests designed to discriminate between individuals; it must be modified when applied to criterion-referenced tests. A number of procedures and formulas for computing the various forms of the reliability and validity indexes have been developed from this model.

The central concept in testing is validity. Validity has been defined as the extent to which the test measures a trait, characteristic, or outcome. As validity is situation specific, a distinction can be made between the validity of a test in a particular situation (its usefulness) and the validity of the test in measuring some psychological variable (trait). A main thesis of this book is that a test is useful to the extent that it provides additional information over-and-above that provided by other methods or measures. In other words, incremental validity, broadly conceived, is the basic index of the effectiveness of a test.

The interpretation of test scores requires a combination of validity and normative data. A mere indication of where an individual's score falls within a particular norm group is rarely, if ever, valuable without supporting validity data. Thus, normative data expressed in outcome terms (for example, through expectancy tables) is generally more meaningful than other kinds of normative data. Although most normative data is expressed as norm-referenced scores—where an individual's performance is compared to the performance of a group of his peers—under some conditions scores can be expressed in criterion-referenced terms—by comparison to some absolute or ideal standard. However, as we have pointed out, many criterion-reference scores have implicit normative bases.

SOME PROBLEMS IN EDUCATIONAL
AND PSYCHOLOGICAL TESTING

It should be apparent that testing is not without its problems. In several places we have mentioned the deficiencies of current practices and procedures, and the reader undoubtedly has questioned other assumptions or procedures. The problems discussed below are particularly critical or pervasive; other, more specific problems could as easily have been included.

Availability of Tests

The procedures for distributing testing materials and the ethical guidelines related to qualifications of test users (APA, 1974, 1975) do not completely prevent unqualified persons from gaining access to tests. More importantly, there is no guarantee that unqualified persons will not use tests to make decisions about individuals or evaluate the effectiveness of a program. Control of access to test materials rests primarily with test publishers, however, for the current standards are without legal force or other sanctions. Most publishers do take steps to ensure that only qualified persons can purchase tests. However, a completely effective control mechanism, which does not unduly restrict qualified users, has not yet been developed. Perhaps more stringent controls over the distribution and use of tests should be instituted.

Another problem is that the number of well-constructed standardized tests is limited in many important areas. For example, only recently have tests of creativity appeared; testing of writing skills is still in a relatively primitive stage, and tests of logical and critical thinking, motivation, and many personality characteristics are virtually nonexistent. In other areas only one or two even minimally acceptable tests are available. Furthermore, most standardized tests are limited to a paper-and-pencil, multiple-choice format. Thus, in both content and format, the testing arsenal is limited and could well be expanded.

On the other hand, there is no effective way to remove out-of-date and invalid (or unvalidated) tests from the market. As long as enough persons buy a test to make publication profitable, the test will be published. Oscar Buros, when instituting the *Mental Measurements Yearbooks,* hoped that publication of critical reviews of tests would expedite the removal of poor tests from the market; this effort, he feels, has not succeeded (Buros, 1968). Ideally, test users would identify their deficiencies and not purchase them, thus making their publication unprofitable and forcing the publisher to revise the test or withdraw it from circulation. Unfortunately, such an ideal has not been realized; in fact, getting prospective teachers, counselors, personnel men, and other potential test users to take courses in educational and psychological measurement is in itself somewhat of a problem.

Psychometric Problems

A relatively neglected area of testing research is the study of the effects of environmental, situational, and personal variables on test performance. Too often test scores are naively interpreted as precise indexes of immutable psychological traits. But studies have shown conclusively that test performance is a function of numerous variables (see, for example, Mischel, 1968). Thus, if test scores are to be interpreted accurately, the effects of personal and situational variables must be thoroughly understood. Knowledge of the effects of these variables is particularly critical when test scores serve to define theoretical constructs.

Validity   As validity is, in many ways, the central issue in psychological testing, any problems in the conceptualization and/or application of validity studies will be especially crucial. The failure to consider base rates in determining validity has been discussed in detail. Criterion problems, both conceptual and practical, have been mentioned, as has the fact that the several possible validity indexes may not agree with each other. The fundamental problem, however, is that the concept of validity is an amalgam of practical and theoretical considerations, and never completely separates the two (Ebel, 1961; Loevinger, 1957). Furthermore, the 40-odd types of validity proposed in the literature defy the neat tripartite classification described in the *Standards for Educational and Psychological Tests*.

A second problem is the level of predictive accuracy attained by present tests. For example, when predicting academic performance from scholastic aptitude test scores, validity coefficients generally cluster around .50 to .60 (Hills, 1971; Lavin, 1965). Utilization of multiple predictors (for example, personality measures in addition to ability measures) usually increases predictive accuracy only slightly. Predictions of nonacademic outcomes are no more accurate (Ghiselli, 1966). Furthermore, this level of predictive accuracy has been essentially constant over several decades, even when new tests or analytic methods have been used. Although there may be certain dangers associated with a high level of predictive accuracy (see Goslin, 1963; Young, 1961), present tests and methods account for less than half of the criterion variability, certainly far from an optimal level. Perhaps newer analytic models (for example, moderators, differential prediction, Dunnette's validation model) may improve predictive accuracy.

As validity data are situation specific, applying results obtained in one situation to another, even presumably comparable situation always involves some risk. Development of procedures for grouping similar situations would reduce this risk and increase the probability that the validity data will generalize (see Cronbach, Gleser, Nanda, & Rajaratnam, 1972). Then, too, as validity evidence is based on the performance of groups of individuals, the meaning of an individual score is always somewhat ambiguous; that is, does the testee follow the general trend or is he the exception?

The question of the optimal method to combine (predictor) scores is also still open. Although actuarial methods have proven to be more accurate than clinical methods in many circumstances—for example, when a personality description rather than a specific prediction is the desired outcome—actuarial methods generally are not applicable. (Codebooks are obvious exceptions.) A set of standard rules and procedures for deriving descriptions and classifications would be helpful. Predictability may also be increased perhaps by the further development and adaptation of more powerful methods for comparing individuals to a group (for example, discriminant analysis); by multivariate techniques that establish the relationship between several predictors and several criterion measures simultaneously; and by techniques of differential prediction and placement (Cronbach and Gleser, 1965; Horst, 1964).

The model   The traditional model for conceptualizing test scores is an individual differences model. As long as the purpose of the testing is to discriminate between individuals, the model is appropriate. However, when testing focuses on something other than individual differences—as in mastery and criterion-referenced tests—the traditional model may not be adequate.

Other problems and limitations are encountered when studying consistency. Typical reliability measures consider variation over only several of the relevant dimensions: Consistency over time and forms is recognized, while consistency over situations and persons is not. Thus a broader concept of reliability may be needed. (cf. Cattell, 1964; Cronbach, Gleser, Nanda, & Rajaratnam, 1972). And, as we have noted, the classical reliability model encounters problems when dealing with mastery and change scores. Even though an individual differences model, it is concerned with the average or typical person. For example, the weights associated with each variable in a multiple regression equation are identical for all individuals. However, in some circumstances the optimal procedure might be differentially weighting the various predictors for each individual. In other words, the general model could be improved by incorporating procedures that identify atypical persons (that is, persons for which the model is not applicable) and then take into account those individual characteristics through differential weighting or other procedures.

One can also question the practice of using tests (and other measures) to predict future performance. Here our concern is not with the accuracy of prediction, an issue previously discussed, but with the idea of prediction. The reason for predicting is, of course, to maximize the fit between the individual and the treatment applied—for example, to ensure that those persons chosen to enter a training program are the ones who are most likely to profit from that program.[1] But if, as some people have argued, the very act of predicting may influence the outcome—that the test scores might be part of a self-fulfilling prophecy—then persons predicted to succeed, by virtue of the prediction, have a higher probability of success. Superficially, such predictions would be valid, but in actuality their validity would be spurious and illusory. At a different level, one must be concerned with the possible side-effects of excessive reliance on prediction and preselection. Some gross manifestations include possible creation of an elite group based on test-taking ability, loss of motivation and hope, and reward for potential rather than performance.

Social Consequences of Testing

The topic of the previous paragraph was the (possible) social consequences of testing. By identifying and optimally utilizing talent, testing is generally beneficial,

---

[1]The phrase "profit from" can have various meanings, depending upon how the criterion is defined. For example, the goal might be to maximize (1) the number of persons attaining mastery level, or (2) the average gain in knowledge or skill.

but it may have undesirable side-effects. While there is no doubt that tests are a fairer and more accurate indices of ability than many other procedures that have been used as selection devices (for example, skin color, identity of one's parents, wealth, social or political influence) still they may perpetuate certain undesirable practices and attitudes.

Ebel (1964), for example, has identified four possible consequences of educational testing, consequences that critics of testing have implied might result from testing programs. First, testing may place on the child a stamp of intellectual status—whether superior, mediocre, or inferior—and influence self-esteem, decrease motivation (if scores are low), and consequently help determine adult social status. Second, testing may lead to a narrow conception of ability or to the pursuit of a single goal, thus reducing the diversity of talent in society. Third, testing may place test publishers in the position of determining educational content. And, fourth, testing may encourage inflexible, impersonal, and mechanical methods of appraisal, thereby reducing human freedom.

In his article, Ebel points out that these arguments are based more on opinion than hard data, and are more criticism of how tests are used than criticisms of tests themselves. He also points out that there are consequences of not testing: Encouragement and rewarding of individual efforts and achievement would be more difficult; it would be harder to evaluate programs and identify excellence; opportunities would be awarded less on other bases (for example, social influence) than merit; and decisions would be based on less adequate evidence.

In summary, Ebel suggests several ways that the use of tests could be improved. One is to use tests to identify strengths and weaknesses and thereby help students improve their performance, rather than using tests primarily to identify and label present status. Second, by developing tests in many different areas we would foster the idea that a wide variety of talents are important in our society. Third, we should communicate the results of the tests to the individuals concerned so they can make plans on the basis of solid evidence. And, fourth, we should decrease the emphasis on using tests to make decisions about other people and encourage their use as a basis for helping individuals make their own decisions about their life plans and goals.

Testing special groups   Over the past decade or two, a question of concern has had to do with the proper use of tests with various atypical subgroups within the population. In the 1960s the concern was primarily with blacks, other ethnic minority groups, and the culturally deprived; in the 1970s the emphasis has shifted to a concern with women. Two related factors have contributed to this trend. One is the fact that minority group members often score lower on certain types of tests. A plausible explanation for this is that members of the minority group perform more poorly because they lack the background experiences necessary to develop the skill being tested. The other set of issues revolves around the use of these test scores in making social and educational decisions. This is more of a political and legal question.

Consider first the situation where, on the average, members of a particular ethnic or cultural minority group score low on a test. How can we proceed? One suggestion is not to administer the test. This procedure has the disadvantage of forcing reliance on other sources of information, sources that may be less accurate. Another solution is to develop separate tests for each particular group. While such an approach will tell how a person in the particular subgroup compares with others of similar background it does not allow for comparisons with broader groups; thus this approach is of limited usefulness. A third approach has been to concentrate on identifying and measuring skills that are so basic that every member of society must master them and put less emphasis on more specialized skills, ones that are important for only certain segments of society. This approach implies that remedial programs should be designed to provide the experiences necessary to develop these crucial skills (compensatory education programs and Head Start are examples). A fourth approach is to attack the problem through normative data. One way is to be sure that minority groups are proportionally represented in any norm group. Another approach is to develop separate normative data for each minority group, thus providing several methods of interpreting scores.

At another level, we can approach the problem through the test interpretation process. We have already indicated one way–that of developing several different norm groups. Another, perhaps better method is to focus on the implications of scores. That is, to recognize that a given score may mean different things if obtained by a member of a minority group or by a white, middle-class individual. Mercer's studies (1973) of the classification of mentally retarded children provide a good illustration of this approach. Her data, it will be recalled, indicated that the same IQ had different implications for classifying a child as mentally retarded in black or Chicano groups than in white groups.

In the 1970s questions have arisen about possible sex bias in tests. Here the major concern has been with the possible sex stereotyping in tests. For example, surveys of achievement tests have shown that many more items use masculine referents than feminine ones (Tittle, 1973). However, there is no data which shows that this bias affects performance on tests. Also of concern has been the possible sexual stereotyping fostered by interest inventories (Harmon, 1973). One result of this concern has been the development of a ''neuter'' form of the Strong-Campbell Interest Inventory. But as we have seen, even the neuter form does not avoid all problems of sex bias as scores on most scales are compared to either a male or female norm group. The problem, of course, is that, due to conditioning, males and females have different occupational average interests.

From a psychometric point of view, when considering the desirability of separate tests or norms for various subgroups, two questions must be faced. First, to assume that there are no differences between groups—say between males and females—is to prejudge the question. That is, to take this approach requires assuming that, in fact, the groups do not differ. But, given present methods, the question of whether the groups differ is unanswerable. Second, whether separate tests or norms are needed depends on the question to be answered. If we want to compare an individual to persons with similar background and experience, separate norm groups will suffice; however, if we want to compare an individual to a broader group, separate norm groups will not be sufficient. For example, it may be useful to know that a child from a disadvantaged home reads better than other children from similar homes. However, if we want to compare his reading ability to all children he may compete with, a broader norm group will be needed. Thus, having both types of normative data will be necessary.

Finally, we must keep in mind that certain decisions may be made regardless of what the test scores tell us. Suppose that children from a particular minority group perform differently on a test than white, middle-class children. Suppose also that we have evidence that these differences affect what they will learn in school. We might suggest that children from the two groups be placed in different types of schools or classes. However, the school board or legislature may decide that it is more important that children from various groups attend the same schools than to maximize educational achievement. In this case, assignment to schools would be made on the basis of social and political considerations, rather than psychological data.

Privacy   Finally, there is the issue of the invasion of privacy. Even if a test is valid and provides useful information, it may do so at the cost of intruding upon an individual's privacy. A question of concern then becomes whether the advantages of testing are sufficient to justify such an intrusion. Sometimes unobtrusive measures (E. J. Webb et al., 1966) can be substituted for psychological tests, thus avoiding the appearance of excessive probing. In all cases, however, the test takers' reactions to the testing must be considered.

WHAT'S IN THE FUTURE?

In the course of this book we have paid little attention to the history of psychological testing, considering it more important to present basic principles and procedures. However, at this point, we will take the perhaps foolhardy step of predicting some trends that might be expected in educational and psychological testing in the coming years.[2] Actually, we are not being that rash, as many of these trends have already begun to emerge.

Some Major Trends

One trend will be a decreasing emphasis on aptitude tests and an increasing emphasis on achievement, ability, and proficiency tests. That is, there will be greater concern with developed skills and demonstrated competence. One reason is the reaction against the determinism and elitism implied by aptitude tests; another is the recognition that past performance is usually the best predictor of future performance. Also important are federal regulations and court rulings that state that tests cannot be used in employment unless they measure components of the job, again implying we should measure present abilities rather than potential performance.

[2]For another set of predictions see Thorndike (1971b).

This does not mean that aptitude tests will disappear. Rather, they will come to resemble more closely achievement tests due to added emphasis on developed skills; consequently long-range predictive ability will become only one criterion in developing tests. Moreover, new definitions of aptitude—such as Estes's (1974) and Glaser's pleas (1972) for relating aptitudes more closely to learning and instructional theory—may be adopted as guides to test construction.

Similarly, less use will be made of personality measures in situations involving personnel or educational decisions. This change will result from two separate forces. First, the validity of personality measures as decision-making aids has not been demonstrated and, second, there has been increased concern with the ethical questions (invasion of privacy, for example) that arise in connection with their use. However, personality measures will continue to be used extensively in counseling and research, perhaps with increasing frequency.

A second major trend concerns the use of tests in the educational process. Here the emphasis is shifting from the use of tests solely to evaluate students to the utilization of test data to improve instruction and to evaluate instructors and instructional methods. This new orientation toward improved instruction is illustrated by several examples: the emphasis on formative evaluation; the feedback provided by test publishers through item analysis data that allows schools to determine if their objectives have been attained; major research programs such as the National Assessment of Educational Progress and the International Studies of Achievement; and the suggestions of Glaser (1972), Estes (1974), and Carver (1974) regarding different types and focuses of tests. The trend toward the use of tests in the evaluation of instruction is shown by the increasing emphasis on accountability. And, of course, the major focus of the mastery, task analysis (Gagné, 1970) and behavioral objectives approaches to education is on the improvement of instruction.

Another important example is the shift in emphasis on achievement tests from norm-referenced to criterion-referenced scores. As computer-assisted instruction and other methods of individualized instruction give promise of enabling more students to attain a wide range of educational skills, so too emphasis has shifted from measuring differences between students (the individual differences of norm-referenced approach) to measuring the individual's mastery of the course objectives (the criterion-referenced approach).

Third, new types of tests will appear. Some of these will be excursions into areas not previously tapped by psychological tests—for example, measures of complex cognitive skills and styles. Equally as noticeable will be changes in the format of tests. Rather than being limited to paper-and-pencil formats, tests can now be administered by television, computer, and tape recorder. The computer will probably be the single most important influence on further testing. Already used for the rapid scoring and norming of standardized tests, the computer has, among other things, made national testing programs feasible; built model item and test score distributions that can be used to study the assumptions of psychometric theory; and made possible the application of complex methods of combining and analyzing test scores. But, more importantly, new test formats are now possible through use of the computer. An ideal instrument for administering a sequential test, the computer allows more individualized test taking. Instead of all students taking the identical items in the same order, responses to one item determine which of several possible items will be administered next. By choosing a particular sequence to maximize discrimination, sequential tests allow for both efficiency and individualization of testing.

A fourth trend will be the reconceptualization of some of the basic concepts in psychological testing. Some of these reformulations will arise out of the realization that present conceptions are limited (for example, Cattell's and Cronbach's reconceptualization of reliability and validity). Other reassessments will result from an attempt to explain research data; from the realization that the present models do not satisfactorily handle certain types of data (criterion-referenced and change scores, for example); and, finally, from the availability of computers, which allow for more complex analyses than were previously feasible. These factors, combined with more critical looks at the goals and functions of testing and with the increasing interaction of testing with experimental psychology, should lead to the reformulation of many old concepts and persistent problems.

Fifth, there will be increasing concern with the social consequences of testing. No longer will a psychologist be able to administer a test, make decisions on the basis of the test scores, and not worry about the consequences to the individual or society (see, for example, Cronbach, 1975). As this problem has been discussed several places previously, it need not be repeated here. However, it should be emphasized that the concern with social consequences will be broad, involving questions such as the optimal utilization of talent within society, and ethical issues arising whenever distinctions among people are made.

One tangible piece of evidence of the increasing concern with the social consequences of testing is the court decisions concerning use of tests in employee selection. Another is the moratoria on testing proposed (and implemented) by several colleges and school systems. Another is the attempt to develop tests that are more appropriate for minority groups and for both males and females. All of these point to an increasing concern with the consequences of testing.

A Final Word

In this book we have tried to accomplish several goals: to present the basic concepts of psychological measurement, to indicate how tests are developed and used, to identify factors that influence test performance and show how these factors operate, and to illustrate the variety of psychological and educational tests. But, more importantly, we have attempted to develop a critical attitude, so that when confronted with the need to select or interpret a test you will approach the task with deliberate caution, carefully weighing the multitude of factors that must be considered. No book can completely prepare you for this task; it can only be developed by continual study of and experience in the development, validation, and use of educational and psychological tests. Thus, this book is but a beginning.

We believe that in many situations tests provide useful information, information which could not be obtained from other sources. We are also not unaware of the consequences that result from the use, both proper and improper, of tests. However, the fact remains that decisions frequently have to be made about individuals. In these circumstances, we should use the best information available. If it can be obtained from test scores, then tests should be used; if some other method provides better information then tests should not be used. What is important is that we evaluate the effectiveness of the various methods (i.e., sources of information) and look at the consequences of adopting each approach. To proceed in ignorance or to throw out less-than-perfect methods (as tests are) and substitute even less perfect methods are not the answers. The only rational approach is to make informed decisions based on critical evaluations of all options, then apply the selected procedure fairly, objectively, and as humanely as possible.

Finally, in a discussion that has focused on the methods of educational and psychological testing, it is easy to overlook the most important point: It is not the test that is of prime importance, it is the individual who takes the test. Test scores may influence decisions that will alter the course of the individual's life. Therefore, when using tests, our foremost concern must always be with the effects of the testing on the person. Keeping this fact in mind will be the greatest single deterrent to misuse of tests.

SUGGESTED FURTHER READING FOR PART VI

Anastasi, A. Psychology, psychologists and psychological testing. *American Psychologist,* 1967, *22*, 297–306.

A consideration of some of the major objections to psychological tests and the relation of tests to psychological theory.

Astin, A. W., & Panos, R. J. The evaluation of educational programs. Chapter 20 in R. L. Thorndike (Ed.), *Educational measurement* (2d ed.), Washington, D.C.: American Council on Education, 1971.

Description of how tests can be used to evaluate educational programs; excellent brief introduction.

Buros, O. K. The story behind the Mental Measurement Yearbooks. *Measurement and Evaluation in Guidance,* 1968, *1*, 86–95.

A description of the history and development of the MMYs by their author.

College Entrance Examination Board Commission on Tests. *Righting the balance.* New York: College Entrance Examination Board, 1970.

A critical review of the CEEB program. Recommends that test users be aware of their obligation to communicate information back to test takers.

Cleary, T. A. et al. Educational uses of tests with disadvantaged students. *American Psychologist,* 1975, *30*, 15–41.

Review of the literature and consideration of the issues involved when testing disadvantaged students. Must reading for anyone concerned with testing disadvantaged students.

Coffman, W. E. (Ed.) *Frontiers of educational measurement and information systems.* Boston: Houghton Mifflin, 1973.

Report of a conference concerned with various innovative programs in educational measurement.

Cronbach, L. J. Evaluation for course improvement. *Teachers College Record,* 1963, *64*, 672–683.

Discussion of how tests can be used to improve the instructional process.

Dunnette, M. D. *Personnel selection and placement*. Belmont, Calif.: Wadsworth, 1966.

Best brief introduction to the use of tests in business and industry; emphasis on measuring job components.

Ebel, R. L. The social consequences of educational testing. *College Board Review,* Winter 1964, 10–14. (Also in Proceedings of the 1963 Invitational Conference on Testing Problems, Princeton, N.J.: Educational Testing Service, 1964.)

A classic paper considering the consequences of testing and not testing.

Glaser, R., & Nitko, A. J. Measurement in learning and instruction. Chapter 17 in R. L. Thorndike (Ed.), *Educational measurement* (2d ed.), Washington, D.C.: American Council on Education, 1971.

Excellent discussion of newer models for using measurement to facilitate and improve instruction.

Goslin, D. A. Standardized ability tests and testing. *Science,* 1968, *159*, 851–855.

Discussion of issues involved in standardized testing; written for general audience.

Thorndike, R. L. Educational decisions and human assessment. *Teachers College Record,* 1964, *66*, 103–112.

Nontechnical discussion of the advantages of using tests as aids in educational decision making.

Tyler, R. W., & Wolf, R. M. (Eds.) *Critical issues in testing*. Berkeley, Calif.: McCutchan, 1974. (A National Society for the Study of Education Publication.)

Critical examination of major issues in testing—for example, testing minority groups, grouping students, criterion-referenced testing, evaluating instruction, and testing and privacy.

Wesman, A. G. Intelligent testing. *American Psychologist,* 1968, *23*, 267–274.

Discussion of the nature of intelligence and implications for its measurement; written for a general audience.

Willtrock, M. C., & Wiley, D. E. (Eds.) *The evaluation of instruction*. New York: Holt, Rinehart and Winston, 1970.

Series of papers relating to various aspects of the problems in evaluating instruction; a basic reference in this area.

Appendix A

AREAS OF THE NORMAL CURVE WITH COMPARABLE PERCENTILE RANKS AND STANDARD SCORES

Consider a normal distribution of scores with the area within the curve equal to 1.0000 units:

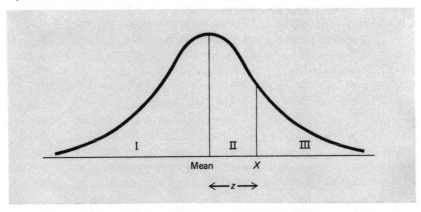

Under these circumstances certain constant relationships hold; the most important of these for psychological testing are tabled below.

Column A lists the normal deviate (z), the deviation of an obtained score (X) from the mean in standard deviation units, i.e.:

$$z = \frac{X - \text{Mean}}{s} = \frac{x}{s}$$

z, of course, can be either positive or negative depending upon whether the obtained score falls above or below the mean.

Column B indicates the proportion of area of the curve that falls between the mean and the corresponding z (i.e., area II in the figure).

Column C indicates the proportion of the area in the larger section when the distribution is divided at point z (i.e., areas I + II in the figure). When z is positive, this will be the proportion of the area falling below point z; when z is negative, this will be the proportion falling above point z.

Column D gives the area in the smaller section (i.e., area III in the figure); this area equals (1 − the value in column C).

Column E is the percentile rank associated with z when z is positive.

Column F gives the corresponding percentile rank when z is negative.

Column G gives the standard score, Z, (where $Z = 50 + 10z$) when z is positive.

Column H gives Z for the corresponding negative value of z $(-z)$.

(A)	(B)	(C)	(D)	(E)	(F)	(G)	(H)
	Area mean	Area larger	Area smaller	\multicolumn{2}{c}{Percentile}	\multicolumn{2}{c}{Z}
z	to z	portion	portion	$+z$	$-z$	$+z$	$-z$
0.00	.0000	.5000	.5000	50	50	50	50
0.05	.0199	.5199	.4801	52	48		
0.10	.0398	.5398	.4602	54	46	51	49
0.15	.0596	.5596	.4404	56	44		
0.20	.0793	.5793	.4207	58	42	52	48
0.25	.0987	.5987	.4013	60	40		
0.30	.1179	.6179	.3821	62	38	53	47
0.35	.1368	.6368	.3632	64	36		
0.40	.1554	.6554	.3446	66	34	54	46
0.45	.1736	.6736	.3264	67	33		
0.50	.1915	.6915	.3085	69	31	55	45
0.55	.2088	.7088	.2912	71	29		
0.60	.2257	.7257	.2743	73	27	56	44
0.65	.2422	.7422	.2578	74	26		
0.70	.2580	.7580	.2420	76	24	57	43
0.75	.2734	.7734	.2266	77	23		
0.80	.2881	.7881	.2119	79	21	58	42
0.85	.3023	.8023	.1977	80	20		
0.90	.3159	.8159	.1841	82	18	59	41
0.95	.3289	.8289	.1711	83	17		
1.00	.3413	.8413	.1587	84	16	60	40
1.05	.3531	.8531	.1469	85	15		
1.10	.3643	.8643	.1357	86	14	61	39

(A)	(B) Area mean to z	(C) Area larger portion	(D) Area smaller portion	(E) Percentile $+z$	(F) Percentile $-z$	(G) z $+z$	(H) z $-z$
1.15	.3749	.8749	.1251	87	13		
1.20	.3849	.8849	.1151	88	12	62	38
1.25	.3944	.8944	.1056	89	11		
1.30	.4032	.9032	.0968	90	10	63	37
1.35	.4115	.9115	.0885	91	9		
1.40	.4192	.9192	.0808	92	8	64	36
1.45	.4265	.9265	.0735	93	7		
1.50	.4332	.9332	.0668	93	7	65	35
1.55	.4394	.9394	.0606	94	6		
1.60	.4452	.9452	.0548	95	5	66	34
1.65	.4505	.9505	.0495	95	5		
1.70	.4554	.9554	.0446	96	4	67	33
1.75	.4599	.9599	.0401	96	4		
1.80	.4641	.9641	.0359	96	4	68	32
1.85	.4678	.9678	.0322	97	3		
1.90	.4713	.9713	.0287	97	3	69	31
1.95	.4744	.9744	.0256	97	3		
2.00	.4772	.9772	.0228	98	2	70	30
2.05	.4798	.9798	.0202	98	2		
2.10	.4821	.9821	.0179	98	2	71	29
2.15	.4842	.9842	.0158	98	2		
2.20	.4861	.9861	.0139	99	1	72	28
2.25	.4878	.9878	.0122	99	1		
2.30	.4893	.9893	.0107	99	1	73	27
2.35	.4906	.9906	.0094	99	1		
2.40	.4918	.9918	.0082	99	1	74	26
2.45	.4929	.9929	.0071	99	1		
2.50	.4938	.9938	.0062	99	1	75	25
2.55	.4946	.9946	.0054	99.5	0.5		
2.60	.4953	.9953	.0047	99.5	0.5	76	24
2.65	.4960	.9960	.0040	99.6	0.4		
2.70	.4965	.9965	.0035	99.6	0.4	77	23
2.75	.4970	.9970	.0030	99.7	0.3		
2.80	.4974	.9974	.0026	99.7	0.3	78	22
2.85	.4978	.9978	.0022	99.8	0.2		
2.90	.4981	.9981	.0019	99.8	0.2	79	21
2.95	.4984	.9984	.0016	99.8	0.2		
3.00	.4987	.9987	.0013	99.9	0.1	80	20

Appendix B

EXAMPLES OF COMMERCIALLY PUBLISHED TESTS

NOTE: This listing is designed to illustrate the variety of commercially published tests available. It is not intended to be exhaustive—for example, achievement tests in specific subject-matter areas and tests of specific vocational abilities are not included. Nor should this listing be considered as a recommendation for these particular tests. The reader who is interested in obtaining further information about a particular test should consult the *Mental Measurements Yearbook* or test publishers' catalogs. For a comprehensive listing of published tests, see the *Mental Measurements Yearbook* or *Tests in Print.* Each listing includes the name of the test, the publisher, and a one-sentence description of its coverage, age range, and intended uses.

Intellectual Development: General

Bayley Scales of Infant Development (Psychological Corporation). Assesses mental and psychomotor development of children aged 2½ or younger.

Culture Fair Intelligence Tests (Institute for Personality and Ability Testing). Nonverbal items designed to reduce effects of verbal, cultural, and educational factors; three series, ages 4 to adult.

Goodenough-Harris Drawing Test (Harcourt Brace Jovanovich). Nonverbal test; adaptation of Draw-a-Man Test.

McCarthy Scales of Children's Abilities (Psychological Corporation). Assesses verbal, perceptual, and psychomotor development of children aged 2½ to 8½.

Peabody Picture Vocabulary Test (American Guidance Service). Wide-range picture vocabulary test; ages 2½ to adult.

Progressive Matrices (Psychological Corporation). Nonverbal test using problems presented as abstract pictures and designs; age 8 or older.
Stanford-Binet Intelligence Scale (Houghton-Mifflin). See text for description.
Wechsler Adult Intelligence Scale (Psychological Corporation). See text for description.
Wechsler Intelligence Scale for Children (Psychological Corporation). See text for description.
Wechsler Preschool and Primary Scale of Intelligence (Psychological Corporation). See text for description.

Group Intelligence and Scholastic Aptitude Tests

Academic Promise Test (Psychological Corporation). Measures verbal, numerical, and abstract reasoning abilities and language usage; outgrowth of the DAT; grades 6 to 9.
American College Testing Program (ACT). See text for description.
Analysis of Learning Potential (Harcourt Brace Jovanovich). Measures both numerical and verbal abilities; five levels, grades 1 to 12.
California Test of Mental Maturity (California Test Bureau/McGraw-Hill). Items measuring both language and nonlanguage, including numerical, abilities; six levels, kindergarten to adult; available in both regular and short forms.
Graduate Record Examination (Educational Testing Service). Used for graduate school admissions; measures both verbal and quantitative reasoning; separate achievement tests; restricted.
Henmon-Nelson Tests of Mental Ability (Houghton-Mifflin). Usual variety of items; 4 levels, kindergarten to grade 12; also college edition.
Kuhlmann-Anderson Tests (Personnel Press). Eight levels, kindergarten to grade 12; lower levels tap variety of skills, higher levels primarily verbal and quantitative.
Lorge-Thorndike Intelligence Test (Houghton-Mifflin). Verbal and nonverbal skills, including pictorial and numerical items; eight levels, grade 3 to college; also separate college edition.
Miller Analogies Test (Psychological Corporation). Very difficult test of verbal reasoning ability; used for graduate school admissions; restricted.
Minnesota Scholastic Aptitude Test (W. L. Layton). Test of verbal abilities—vocabulary, verbal reasoning, reading comprehension; high school and college level.
Otis-Lennon Mental Ability Test (Harcourt Brace Jovanovich). Verbal comprehension and reasoning, abstract reasoning, numerical reasoning; six levels, kindergarten to grade 12.
Scholastic Aptitude Test (Educational Testing Service). The College Board's admissions test; see text for description; restricted.
School and College Ability Tests, Series 2 (Cooperative Tests, Educational Testing Service). Verbal and quantitative reasoning; four levels, grades 4 to 14.
Short Test of Educational.Ability (Science Research Associates). Verbal, numerical, and abstract reasoning; kindergarten to grade 12.
Wesman Personnel Classification Test (Psychological Corporation). Verbal and numerical; for selection of clerical, sales, supervisory, and managerial employees.

Achievement Batteries

Adult Basic Learning Examination (Harcourt Brace Jovanovich). Measures basic learning of adults in four areas—Reading, Spelling, Arithmetic Computation, and Problem Solving; items focus on everyday situations; three levels (comparable to grades 1 to 12).

California Achievement Tests (California Test Bureau/McGraw-Hill). Tests of knowledge and understanding in Reading (Vocabulary, Comprehension), Arithmetic (Reasoning, Fundamentals), and Language (Mechanics, Spelling); five levels, grades 1 to 14.

Comprehensive Tests of Basic Skills (California Test Bureau/McGraw-Hill). Covers Reading (Vocabulary, Comprehension), Language (Mechanics, Expression, Spelling), and Arithmetic Skills (Computation, Concepts, Applications); also has a Study Skills sections; four levels, grades 2 to 12.

Iowa Tests of Basic Skills (Houghton-Mifflin). Covers Vocabulary, Reading Comprehension, Language Skills, Arithmetic Skills, and Work-Study Skills; generally several subtests for each part. Various forms, grades 1 to 9.

Iowa Tests of Educational Development (Science Research Associates). Emphasis on critical thinking, analysis, and applications; major sections are Reading (Comprehension, Vocabulary), Language Arts (Usage, Spelling), Mathematics, Social Science, Sciences, Use of Sources of Information; grades 9 to 12.

Metropolitan Achievement Tests, 1970 edition (Harcourt Brace Jovanovich). All levels cover basic language (e.g., word knowledge, reading, spelling) and math skills (e.g., computations, concepts, problem solving); upper levels contain science and social studies tests. Six levels, kindergarten to grade 9.

Sequential Tests of Educational Progress, Series II (Cooperative Tests, Educational Testing Service). Tests cover English Expression, Reading, Mechanics of Writing, Mathematics Computation, Math Basic Concepts, Science, and Social Studies; four levels, grades 4 to 14.

SRA Achievement Series (Science Research Associates). Battery for grades 1 to 4 covers Reading, Arithmetic, and Language Arts; for grades 4 to 9 includes Reading, Language Arts, Math, Social Studies, Sciences, and Uses of Sources; for Reading, Language Arts, and Math/Arithmetic there are several subtests.

Stanford Achievement Tests (Harcourt Brace Jovanovich). See text for description.

Tests of Academic Progress (Houghton-Mifflin). Covers Social Studies, Composition, Science, Reading, Math, and Literature; three forms, grades 9 to 12.

Achievement Tests: Individual, Diagnostic, Readiness

Advanced Placement Exams (College Board, Educational Testing Service). See text for description.

College Level Examination Program (Educational Testing Service). See text for description.

Cooperative English Tests (Cooperative Tests, Educational Testing Service). Tests of Reading Comprehension (vocabulary, level, speed) and English Expression (effectiveness, mechanics); two levels, grades 9 to 14.

Davis Reading Tests (Psychological Corporation). Measures level and speed of comprehension; two levels, grades 8 to 13.

Diagnostic Reading Scales (California Test Bureau/McGraw-Hill). Covers areas such as word recognition, oral reading, silent reading, auditory comprehension, and phonics (six areas); grades 1 to 8 and retarded readers in grades 9 to 12.

Durrell Listening-Reading Series (Harcourt Brace Jovanovich). Survey reading and listening tests; three levels, grades 1 to 9.

Gates-MacGinitie Reading Tests (Teachers College, Columbia). Vocabulary and comprehension, speed and accuracy; six levels, grades 1 to 9; also readiness tests for kindergarten and grade 1.

Individual Pupil Monitoring System—Mathematics (Houghton-Mifflin). Criterion-referenced test based on specified behavioral objectives; grades 1 to 8; separate test for each grade level.

Metropolitan Readiness Tests (Harcourt Brace Jovanovich). Tests of Word Meaning, Listening, Matching (visual perception), Alphabet, Numbers, and Copying; kindergarten and grade 1.

Metropolitan Reading Tests (Harcourt Brace Jovanovich). Word Knowledge and Reading subtests; four levels, grades 2 to 9.

MLA–Cooperative Foreign Language Tests (Cooperative Tests, Educational Testing Service). Tests in five languages—French, German, Italian, Russian, and Spanish; each covers Listening, Speaking, Reading, and Writing; high school and college levels.

Nelson-Denny Reading Test (Houghton-Mifflin). Vocabulary and Reading (comprehension and rate); grades 9 to adult.

Prescriptive Mathematics Inventory (California Test Bureau/McGraw-Hill). Criterion-referenced test used for diagnosis and prescription; both traditional and modern math; three levels, grades 4 to 8; similar test available in reading.

SRA Modern Math Understanding Test (Science Research Associates). Covers three areas—foundations, operations, and geometry and measurement; each area includes items testing knowledge, comprehension, application, and problem solving; three levels, grades 1 to 9.

Stanford Diagnostic Arithmetic Test (Harcourt Brace Jovanovich). Two levels, grades 2 to 8; lower level (grades 2.5–4.5) gives 13 scores in three areas—concepts, computations, and number facts; upper level (4.5–8.5) gives 16 scores in five areas—concepts, computations, fractions, decimals, and number facts.

Stanford Diagnostic Reading Test (Harcourt Brace Jovanovich). Tests Reading Comprehension, Vocabulary, Syllabication, Auditory Skills, Phonetic Analysis, and Rate of Reading; two levels, grades 2 to 8.

Tests of Achievement in Basic Skills—Mathematics (Educational and Industrial Testing Service). Criterion-referenced items covering skills, computation, and applications; four levels, grades 2 to 12.

NOTE. The subtests on achievement batteries usually can be purchased and used as separate tests.

Aptitude and Ability Tests and Batteries

Academic Promise Tests (Psychological Corporation). Outgrowth of the DAT; tests Verbal, Numerical, Abstract Reasoning, and Language Usage; grades 6 to 9.

Boehm Tests of Basic Concepts (Psychological Corporation). Pictorial items measuring mastery of basic concepts needed in early school work (e.g., size and positional relations); kindergarten to grade 2.

Differential Aptitude Tests (Psychological Corporation). See text for description.

Flanagan Aptitude Classification Test (Science Research Associates). Sixteen tests measuring job related aptitudes (e.g., Inspection, Assembly, Patterns, Coding, Tables); grades 9 to adult.

Flanagan Industrial Tests (Science Research Associates). Eighteen tests covering aptitudes important in supervisory, technical, office, and factory jobs; tests similar to FACT. High school and adults.

Frostig Developmental Test of Visual Perception (Consulting Psychologists Press). Measures abilities such as eye–motor coordination, figure–ground discrimination, form constancy, spatial relations, and position in space; ages 3 to 8.

Fundamental Achievement Series (Psychological Corporation). Tests of basic literacy for adolescents and adults; measures skills required for job competence; Verbal and Numerical sections.

General Aptitude Test Battery (U.S. Training and Employment Services). Twelve tests with 9 scores—intelligence, verbal, numerical, spatial, form perception, clerical perception, motor coordination, finger dexterity, manual dexterity; also screening procedure for reading comprehension and orientation exercises to give test-taking practice; used for vocational counseling of students in grades 9 to 12 and adults.

Illinois Test of Psycholinguistic Abilities (University of Illinois). Measures language, perceptual and memory skills in auditory and visual modes; 12 scores; ages 2 to 10.

Personnel Tests for Industry (Psychological Corporation). For adults applying for factory and maintenance jobs; paper-and-pencil tests of Verbal and Numerical abilities plus Oral Directions Test.

Primary Mental Abilities (Science Research Associates). Five levels, kindergarten to grade 12; tests Verbal Meaning, Number Facility, Spatial Relations, Perceptual Speed (K–6 only), Reasoning (4–12 only).

The Short Employment Tests (Psychological Corporation). Five-minute tests for clerical applicants; Verbal, Numerical, and Clerical tests.

Torrance Tests of Creative Thinking (Personnel Press). See text for description.

Vocational Interests and Values

Kuder General Interest Survey (Science Research Associates). Measures interests in ten, broad job families (e.g., Mechanical, Science, Outdoor, Clerical); grades 6 to 12.

Kuder Occupational Interest Survey (Science Research Associates). Scores on specific occupations and college majors; see text; grades 11 and 12 and adults.

Kuder Vocational Preference Record (Science Research Associates). Scores on ten broad areas, as in the General Interest Survey; college and adults.

Minnesota Vocational Interest Inventory (Psychological Corporation). See text for description.

Ohio Vocational Interest Survey (Harcourt Brace Jovanovich). For vocational planning; items based on work activities; 24 scales; grades 8 to 12.

Strong-Campbell Interest Inventory (Stanford University Press). See text for description.

Vocational Preference Inventory (Consulting Psychologists Press). Six occupational/personality types based on Holland's theory—Realistic, Intellectual, Social, Conventional, Enterprising, and Artistic.

Work Values Inventory (Houghton-Mifflin). Covers 15 values related to work (e.g., Intellectual Stimulation, Relations with Associates, Job Security, Variety); grades 7 to adult.

Personality: Self-Report

Adjective Check List (Consulting Psychologists Press). Standard list of 300 adjectives; can be scored on 24 scales.

California Psychological Inventory (Consulting Psychologists Press). See text for description.

Edwards Personnel Preference Schedule (Psychological Corporation). See text for description.

Eysenck Personality Questionnaire (Educational and Industrial Testing Service). Three basic dimensions of personality—Psychoticism (tough-mindedness), Extraversion, and Neuroticism (emotionality).

IPAT Anxiety Scale (Institute for Personality and Ability Testing). Brief measures of five dimensions of anxiety; adolescents and adults.

Minnesota Counseling Inventory (Psychological Corporation). For use in counseling high-school students; three areas of adjustment and four modes of adjusting.

Minnesota Multiphasic Personality Inventory (Psychological Corporation). See text for description.

Omnibus Personality Inventory (Psychological Corporation). Fourteen scales covering intellectual values, attitudes, social-emotional adjustment, and modes of responding (e.g., Thinking Introversion, Autonomy, Practical Outlook, Social Extraversion); college.

Sixteen Personality Factors Questionnaire (Institute for Personality and Ability Testing). Based on Cattell's research; 16 scales (e.g., Assertiveness, Emotional Maturity, Impulsiveness, Self-Sufficiency, Tension); adults; also editions for high-school and elementary levels.

State-Trait Anxiety Inventory (Consulting Psychologists Press). For research studies on anxiety; measures Anxiety Proneness (trait) and Current Level of Tension (state).

Study of Values (Houghton-Mifflin). Often referred to as Allport-Vernon-Lindzey Study of Values; measures 6 basic motives—Theoretical, Economic, Aesthetic, Social, Political, and Religious; high school, college, and adult.

Personality: Projective

Bender-Gestalt (Western Psychological Services, Psychological Corporation). Also called Bender Visual Motor Gestalt Test; various forms; task is to reproduce designs; measures perceptual and intellectual functioning; ages 4 and over.

Holtzman Inkblot Test (Psychological Corporation). See text for description.

Rorschach Method (Grune & Stratton). See text for description.

Thematic Apperception Test (Harvard University Press). See text for description.

Other Typical Performance Measures

Barron Welsh Art Scale (Consulting Psychologists Press). Measure of artistic preferences, used in creativity research; task is to indicate preferences for black-and-white drawings; age 6 and over.

College and University Environment Scales (Educational Testing Service). See text for description.

Stern Environment Indices (Psychological Research Center). Scales measuring 30 environmental presses (e.g., Achievement, Affiliation, Emotionality–Placidity, Nurturance); grades 9 to college, adults.

Survey of Study Habits and Attitudes (Psychological Corporation). Commonly referred to as the Brown-Holtzman Survey of Study Habits and Attitudes; tests Delay Avoidance, Work Methods, Teacher Approval, Educational Acceptance; high school and college.

Vineland Social Maturity Scale (Psychological Corporation). Age scales measuring development of social competencies.

REFERENCES

Allport, G. W. *Becoming*. New Haven, Conn.: Yale University Press, 1955.

American College Testing Program. *Assessing students on the way to college*. (vol. 2) Iowa City: American College Testing Program, 1972.

American Psychological Association. Technical recommendations for psychological tests and diagnostic techniques. Washington, D.C.: American Psychological Association, 1954.

American Psychological Association. Standards for educational and psychological tests and manuals. Washington, D.C.: American Psychological Association, 1966.

American Psychological Association. Ethical principles in the conduct of research with human participants. *American Psychologist,* 1973, *28,* 79–80.

American Psychological Association. Standards for educational and psychological tests. Washington, D.C.: American Psychological Association, 1974.

American Psychological Association. Standards for providers of psychological services. *American Psychologist,* 1975, *30,* 685–694.

Anastasi, A. The nature of psychological "traits." *Psychological Review,* 1948, *55,* 127–138.

Anastasi, A. Heredity, environment and the question "How." *Psychological Review,* 1958, *65,* 197–208.

Anastasi, A. *Psychological testing.* (2d ed.) New York: Macmillan, 1961.

Anastasi, A. (Ed.) *Individual differences.* New York: Wiley, 1965.

Anastasi, A. Psychology, psychologists, and psychological testing. *American Psychologist,* 1967, *22,* 297–306.

Anastasi, A. *Psychological testing.* (3d ed.) New York: Macmillan, 1968.

Anastasi, A. On the formation of psychological traits. *American Psychologist,* 1970, *25,* 889–910.

Anderson, J. E. The prediction of terminal intelligence from infant and preschool tests. Thirty-ninth Yearbook, National Society for the Study of Education, 1940, Part I, 385–403.

Anderson, R. C. How to construct achievement tests to assess comprehension. *Review of Educational Research,* 1972, *42,* 145–170.

Anderson, R. C., & Faust, G. W. *Educational psychology.* New York: Dodd, Mead, 1973.

Anderson, S. B., Ball, S., Murphy, R., & associates. *Encyclopedia of educational evaluation.* San Francisco: Jossey-Bass, 1974.

Angoff, W. H. Scales, norms, and equivalent scores. Chapter 15 in R. L. Thorndike (Ed.), *Educational measurement* (2d ed.). Washington, D.C.: American Council on Education, 1971. (a)

Angoff, W. H. (Ed.) *The College Board Admission Testing Program.* New York: College Entrance Examination Board, 1971. (b)

Angoff, W. H. Criterion-referencing, norm-referencing, and the SAT. *College Board Review,* Summer 1974, 2–5; 21.

Angoff, W. H., & Ford. S. F. Item-race interaction on a test of scholastic aptitude. *Journal of Educational Measurement,* 1973, *10,* 95–106.

Astin, A. V. Standards of measurement. *Scientific American,* June 1968, 50–62.

Astin, A. W. Criterion-centered research. *Educational and Psychological Measurement,* 1964, *24,* 807–822.

Astin, A. W., & Panos, R. J. The evaluation of educational programs. Chapter 20 in R. L. Thorndike (Ed.), *Educational measurement* (2d ed.). Washington, D.C.: American Council on Education, 1971.

Atkinson, R. C. Computerized instruction and the learning process. *American Psychologist,* 1968, *23,* 225–239.

Atkinson, R. C. Teaching children to read using a computer. *American Psychologist,* 1974, *29,* 169–178.

Ausubel, D. P. & Robinson, F. G. *School learning.* New York: Holt, Rinehart and Winston, 1969.

Balma, M. J. The concept of synthetic validity. *Personnel Psychology,* 1959, *12,* 395–396.

Barnette, W. L., Jr. The Minnesota Vocational Interest Inventory. Chapter 4 in D. G. Zytowski (Ed.), *Contemporary approaches to interest measurement.* Minneapolis: University of Minnesota Press, 1973.

Barron, F. *Creativity and psychological health.* Princeton, N.J.: Van Nostrand, 1963.

Barron, F. *Creativity and personal freedom.* Princeton, N.J.: Van Nostrand, 1968.

Barron, F. *Creative person and creative process.* New York: Holt, Rinehart and Winston, 1969.

Bauernfeind, R. H. The matter of "ipsative" scores. *Personnel and Guidance Journal,* 1962, *41,* 210–217.

Bauernfeind, R. H. *Building a school testing program.* (2d ed.) Boston: Houghton Mifflin, 1969.

Bayley, N. Behavioral correlates of mental growth: Birth to thirty years. *American Psychologist,* 1968, *23,* 1–17.

Bechtoldt, H. Construct validity: A critique. *American Psychologist,* 1959, *14,* 619–629.

Bem, S. L. The measurement of psychological androgyny. *Journal of Consulting and Clinical Psychology,* 1974, *42,* 155–162.

Bennett, G. K., & Doppelt, J. E. Test Orientation Procedure. New York: The Psychological Corporation, 1967.

Bennett, G. K., Seashore, H. G., & Wesman, A. G. Manual for the Differential Aptitude Tests. (4th ed.) New York: The Psychological Corporation, 1966.

Berdie, F. S. What test questions are likely to offend the general public? *Journal of Educational Measurement,* 1971, *8,* 87–93.

Berdie, R. F. Validities of the Strong Vocational Interest Blank. In W. L. Layton (Ed.), *Strong Vocational Interest Blank: Research and uses.* Minneapolis: University of Minnesota Press, 1960.

Bereiter, C. Some persisting dilemmas in the measurement of change. Chapter 1 in C. W. Harris (Ed.), *Problems in measuring change.* Madison: University of Wisconsin Press, 1963.

Berg, I. A. (Ed.) *Response set in personality assessment*. Chicago: Aldine, 1967.

Berliner, D. C., & Cahen, L. S. Trait-treatment interaction and learning. Chapter 3 in F. N. Kerlinger (Ed.), *Review of Research in Education, 1*. Itasca, Ill.: F. E. Peacock, 1973.

Birnbaum, M. H. Reply to the Devil's Advocate: Don't confound model testing and measurement. *Psychological Bulletin, 1974, 81,* 854–859.

Black, H. *They shall not pass*. New York: William Morrow, 1963.

Block, J. *The challenge of response sets*. New York: Appleton, 1965.

Block, J. H. (Ed.) *Mastery learning*. New York: Holt, Rinehart and Winston, 1971.

Block, J. H. (Ed.) *Schools, society, and mastery learning*. New York: Holt, Rinehart and Winston, 1974.

Bloom, B. S. *Stability and change in human characteristics*. New York: Wiley, 1964.

Bloom, B. S. Mastery learning. Chapter 4 in J. H. Block (Ed.), *Mastery learning*. New York: Holt, Rinehart and Winston, 1971.

Bloom, B. S. Time and learning. *American Psychologist, 1974, 29,* 682–688.

Bloom, B. S., et al. Taxonomy of educational objectives. *Handbook I: Cognitive domain*. New York: David McKay, 1956.

Bloom, B. S., Hasting, J. T., & Madaus, G. F. *Handbook on formative and summative evaluation of student learning*. New York: McGraw-Hill, 1971.

Borgen, F. H., & Harper, G. T. Predictive validity of measured vocational interests with black and white college men. *Measurement and Evaluation in Guidance, 1973, 6,* 19–27.

Bornmuth, J. R. *On the theory of achievement test items*. Chicago: University of Chicago Press, 1970.

Bowers, J. The comparison of GPA regression equations for regularly admitted and disadvantaged freshmen at the University of Illinois. *Journal of Educational Measurement, 1970, 7,* 219–225.

Bracht, G. H. Experimental factors related to aptitude-treatment interactions. *Review of Educational Research, 1970, 40,* 627–645.

Brim, O. G., Jr., Glass, D. C., Neulinger, J., & Firestone, I. J. *American beliefs and attitudes about intelligence*. New York: Russell Sage Foundation, 1969.

Brogden, H. E. On the interpretation of the correlation coefficient as a measure of predictive efficiency. *Journal of Educational Psychology, 1946, 37,* 65–76.

Brogden, H. E. A new coefficient: Application to biserial correlation and to estimation of selective efficiency. *Psychometrika, 1949, 14,* 169–182.

Brown, F. G. *Principles of educational and psychological testing*. Hinsdale, Ill.: Dryden Press, 1970.

Brown, F. G. *Measurement and evaluation*. Itasca, Ill.: F. E. Peacock, 1971.

Brown, F. G., & Scott, D. A. Differential predictability in college admissions testing. *Journal of Educational Measurement, 1967, 4,* 163–166.

Buros, O. K. (Ed.) *The sixth mental measurements yearbook*. Highland Park, N.J.: Gryphon Press, 1965.

Buros, O. K. The story behind the Mental Measurements Yearbooks. *Measurement and Evaluation in Guidance, 1968, 1,* 86–95.

Buros, O. K. (Ed.) *Personality tests and reviews: I*. Highland Park, N.J.: Gryphon Press, 1970.

Buros, O. K. (Ed.) *The seventh mental measurements yearbook*. Highland Park, N.J.: Gryphon Press, 1972.

Buros, O. K. (Ed.) *Tests in print: II*. Highland Park, N.J.: Gryphon Press, 1974. (a)

Buros, O. K. (Ed.) *Personality tests and reviews: II*. Highland Park, N.J.: Gryphon Press, 1974. (b)

Burt, C. Inheritance of general intelligence. *American Psychologist,* 1972, *27,* 175–190.

Butcher, H. J. *Human intelligence: Its nature and assessment.* New York: Harper & Row, 1973. (Originally published, 1968.)

Butcher, J. N. (Ed.) *MMPI: Research developments and clinical applications.* New York: McGraw-Hill, 1969.

Butcher, J. N. (Ed.) *Objective personality assessment: Changing perspectives.* New York: Academic Press, 1973.

Campbell, D. P. The vocational interests of American Psychological Association presidents. *American Psychologist,* 1965, *20,* 636–644.

Campbell, D. P. Stability of interests within an occupation over 30 years. *Journal of Applied Psychology,* 1966, *50,* 51–56. (a)

Campbell, D. P. The stability of vocational interests within occupations over long time spans. *Personnel and Guidance Journal,* 1966, *44,* 1012–1019. (b)

Campbell, D. P. *Handbook for the Strong Vocational Interest Blank.* Stanford, Calif.: Stanford University Press, 1971.

Campbell, D. T. Recommendations for APA test standards regarding construct, trait, and discriminant validity. *American Psychologist,* 1960, *15,* 546–553.

Campbell, D. T., & Fiske, D. W. Convergent and discriminant validation by the multitrait–multimethod matrix. *Psychological Bulletin,* 1959, *56,* 81–105.

Campbell, D. T., & Stanley, J. C. Experimental and quasi-experimental designs for research on teaching. In N. L. Gage (Ed.), *Handbook of research on teaching.* Skokie, Ill.: Rand McNally, 1963.

Carroll, J. B. A model of school learning. *Teachers College Record,* 1963, *64,* 723–733.

Carver, R. P. Two dimensions of tests: Psychometric and edumetric. *American Psychologist,* 1974, *29,* 512–518.

Cattell, R. B. The three basic factor analytic research designs: Their interrelations and derivates. *Psychological Bulletin,* 1952, *49,* 300–304.

Cattell, R. B. Theory of fluid and crystallized intelligence: A critical experiment. *Journal of Educational Psychology,* 1963, *54,* 1–22.

Cattell, R. B. Validity and reliability: A proposed more basic set of concepts. *Journal of Educational Psychology,* 1964, *55,* 1–22.

Cattell, R. B. Are I.Q. tests intelligent? *Psychology Today,* March 1968, 56–62.

Cattell, R. B., & Butcher, H. J. *The prediction of achievement and creativity.* Indianapolis: Bobbs Merrill, 1968.

Child, D. *The essentials of factor analysis.* New York: Holt, Rinehart and Winston, 1970.

Clark, K. E. *The vocational interests of nonprofessional men.* Minneapolis: University of Minnesota Press, 1961.

Cleary, T. A. Test bias: Prediction of grades of negro and white students in integrated colleges. *Journal of Educational Measurement,* 1968, *5,* 115–124.

Cleary, T. A., Humphreys, L. G., Kendrick, S. A., & Wesman, A. Educational uses of tests with disadvantaged students. *American Psychologist,* 1975, *30,* 15–41.

Coffman, W. E. On the validity of essay tests of achievement. *Journal of Educational Measurement,* 1966, *3,* 151–156.

Coffman, W. E. Essay examinations. Chapter 10 in R. L. Thorndike (Ed.), *Educational measurement.* (2d ed.) Washington, D.C.: American Council on Education, 1971.

Coffman, W. E. (Ed.) *Frontiers of educational measurement and information systems.* Boston: Houghton Mifflin, 1973.

Cole, N. S. Bias in selection. *Journal of Educational Measurement,* 1973, *10,* 237–255.

College Entrance Examination Board. Effects of coaching on Scholastic Aptitude Test scores. New York: College Entrance Examination Board, 1965.

College Entrance Examination Board, Commission on Tests. *Report of the Commission on Tests*. (2 vols.) New York: College Entrance Examination Board, 1970.

College Entrance Examination Board. *Bulletin of information*. New York: College Entrance Examination Board, 1971.

Comber, L. C., & Keeves, J. P. *Science education in nineteen countries: An empirical study*. New York: Wiley, 1973.

Committee on Assessing the Progress of Education. How much are students learning? Plans for a National Assessment of Education. New York: Committee on Assessing the Progress of Education, 1968.

Cronbach, L. J. Response sets and test validity. *Educational and Psychological Measurement*, 1946, *6*, 475–494.

Cronbach, L. J. Statistical methods applied to Rorschach scores: A review. *Psychological Bulletin*, 1949, *46*, 393–429.

Cronbach, L. J. Further evidence on response sets and test design. *Educational and Psychological Measurement*, 1950, *10*, 3–31.

Cronbach, L. J. Coefficient Alpha and the internal structure of tests. *Psychometrika*, 1951, *16*, 297–334.

Cronbach, L. J. *Essentials of psychological testing*. (2d ed.) New York: Harper & Row, 1960.

Cronbach, L. J. Course improvement through evaluation. *Teachers College Record*, 1963, *64*, 672–683.

Cronbach, L. J. How can instruction be adapted to individual differences? In R. M. Gagné (Ed.), *Learning and individual differences*. Columbus, Ohio: Charles Merrill, 1967.

Cronbach, L. J. *Essentials of psychological testing*. (3d ed.) New York: Harper & Row, 1970.

Cronbach, L. J. Test validation. Chapter 14 in R. L. Thorndike (Ed.), *Educational measurement*. (2d ed.) Washington, D.C.: American Council on Education, 1971.

Cronbach, L. J. Five decades of public controversy over mental testing. *American Psychologist*, 1975, *30*, 1–14.

Cronbach, L. J., & Furby, L. How should we measure "change"—Or should we? *Psychological Bulletin*, 1970, *74*, 68–80.

Cronbach, L. J., & Gleser, G. C. Assessing similarity between profiles. *Psychological Bulletin*, 1953, *50*, 456–473.

Cronbach, L. J., & Gleser, G. C. *Psychological tests and personnel decisions*. Urbana: University of Illinois Press, 1957.

Cronbach, L. J., & Gleser, G. C. *Psychological tests and personnel decisions*. (2d ed.) Urbana: University of Illinois Press, 1965.

Cronbach, L. J., Gleser, G. C., Nanda, H., & Rajaratnam, N. *The dependability of behavioral measurements*. New York: Wiley, 1972.

Cronbach, L. J., & Meehl, P. E. Construct validity in psychological tests. *Psychological Bulletin*, 1955, *52*, 281–302.

Cronbach, L. J., & Merwin, J. C. A model for studying the validity of multiple-choice items. *Educational and Psychological Measurement*, 1955, *15*, 337–352.

Cronbach, L. J., Rajaratnam, N., & Gleser, G. C. Theory of generalizability: A liberalization of reliability theory. *British Journal of Statistical Psychology*, 1963, *16*(2), 137–163.

Cronbach, L. J., & Snow, R. E. *Aptitudes and instructional methods*. New York: Irvington, 1975.

Cureton, E. E. et al. The multi-aptitude test. New York: The Psychological Corporation, 1955.

Cureton, L. W. The history of grading practices. *Measurement in Education* (NCME), May 1971, 1–8.

Dahlstrom, W. G., Welsh, G. S., & Dahlstrom, L. E. *An MMPI Handbook. Vol. I: Clinical interpretation.* Minneapolis: University of Minnesota Press, 1972.

Dahlstrom, W. G., Welsh, G. S., & Dahlstrom, L. E. *An MMPI handbook. Vol. II: Research applications.* Minneapolis: University of Minnesota Press, 1975.

Darley, J. G., & Hagenah, T. *Vocational interest measurement: Theory and practice.* Minneapolis: University of Minnesota Press, 1955.

Darlington, R. B. Another look at "culture-fairness." *Journal of Educational Measurement,* 1971, *8,* 71–82.

Darlington, R. B., Weinberg, S. L., & Walberg, H. J. Canonical variate analysis and related techniques. *Review of Educational Research,* 1973, *43,* 433–454.

Das, J. P. Structure of cognitive abilities: Evidence for simultaneous and successive processing. *Journal of Educational Psychology,* 1973, *65,* 103–108.

Das, J. P., Kirby, J., & Jarman, R. F. Simultaneous and successive syntheses: An alternative model for cognitive abilities. *Psychological Bulletin,* 1975, *82,* 87–103.

Davis, F. B. Item selection techniques. Chapter 9 in E. F. Lindquist (Ed.), *Educational measurement.* Washington, D.C.: American Council on Education, 1951.

Davis, F. B. *Educational measurements and their interpretation.* Belmont, Calif.: Wadsworth, 1964.

Davis, J. A. Non-apparent limitations of normative data. *Personnel and Guidance Journal,* 1959, *37,* 656–659.

Dawes, R. M. *Fundamentals of attitude measurement.* New York: Wiley, 1972.

Dawes, R. M. Graduate admissions variables and future success. *Science,* 1975, *187,* 721–723.

Dawes, R. M., & Meehl, P. E. Mixed group validation. *Psychological Bulletin,* 1966, *66,* 63–67.

Drake, L. E., & Oetting, E. R. *An MMPI codebook for counselors.* Minneapolis: University of Minnesota Press, 1959.

Dressel, P. L. & associates. *Evaluation in higher education.* Boston: Houghton Mifflin, 1961.

Drever, J. *A dictionary of psychology.* (rev. ed.) Baltimore: Penguin Books, 1964.

DuBois, P. H. *A history of psychological testing.* Boston: Allyn & Bacon, 1970.

Dunnette, M. D. A modified model for test validation and selection research. *Journal of Applied Psychology,* 1963, *47,* 317–323.

Dunnette, M. D. *Personnel selection and placement.* Belmont, Calif.: Wadsworth, 1966.

Dunstan, M. R. Using educational measurement for educational change. Chapter 9 in W. E. Coffman (Ed.), *Frontiers of educational measurement and information systems.* Boston: Houghton Mifflin, 1973.

Ebel, R. L. Must all tests be valid? *American Psychologist,* 1961, *16,* 640–647.

Ebel, R. L. Content standard test scores. *Educational and Psychological Measurement,* 1962, *22,* 15–25.

Ebel, R. L. The social consequences of educational testing. *College Board Review,* Winter 1964, 10–14.

Ebel, R. L. *Measuring educational achievement.* Englewood Cliffs, N.J.: Prentice-Hall, 1965.

Ebel, R. L. The value of internal consistency in classroom examinations. *Journal of Educational Measurement,* 1968, *5,* 71–73.

Ebel, R. L. *Essentials of educational measurement.* Englewood Cliffs, N.J.: Prentice-Hall, 1972.

Educational Testing Service. Multiple-choice questions: A closer look. Princeton, N.J.: Educational Testing Service, 1963.

Educational Testing Service. ETS builds a test. Princeton, N.J.: Educational Testing Service, 1965.

Educational Testing Service. Competency tests help tradesmen earn academic credit. *ETS Developments,* Fall 1973, 1; 5.

Edwards, A. J. *Individual mental testing: I. Mental tests.* New York: Intext, 1971.

Edwards, A. J. *Individual mental testing: II. Measurement.* New York: Intext, 1972.

Edwards, A. J. *Individual mental testing: III. Research and interpretation.* New York: Intext, 1975.

Edwards, A. L. *The social desirability variable in personality assessment.* New York: Holt, Rinehart and Winston, 1957.

Edwards, A. L. Social desirability and personality test construction. In B. M. Bass & I. A. Berg (Eds.), *Objective approaches to personality assessment.* Princeton, N.J.: Van Nostrand, 1959.

Edwards, A. L. The social desirability variable: A review of the evidence. In I. A. Berg (Ed.), *Response set in personality assessment.* Chicago: Aldine, 1967.

Edwards, A. L. *The measurement of personality traits by scales and inventories.* New York: Holt, Rinehart and Winston, 1970.

Edwards, A. L. *Statistical analysis.* (4th ed.) New York: Holt, Rinehart and Winston, 1974.

Edwards, A. L., & Walsh, J. A. Relationships between various psychometric properties of personality items. *Educational and Psychological Measurement,* 1963, *23,* 227–238.

Englehart, M. D. What to look for in a review of an achievement test. *Personnel and Guidance Journal,* 1964, *42,* 616–619.

English, H. B., & English, A. C. *A comprehensive dictionary of psychological and psychoanalytic terms.* New York: David McKay, 1958.

Estes, W. K. Learning theory and intelligence. *American Psychologist,* 1974, *29,* 740–749.

Faller, J. E. Precision measurement of the acceleration of gravity. *Science,* 1967, *158,* 60–67.

Ferguson, G. A. On learning and human ability. *Canadian Journal of Psychology,* 1954, *8,* 95–112.

Fincher, C. Is the SAT worth its salt? *Review of Educational Research,* 1974, *44,* 293–305.

Flanagan, J. C. The critical incident technique. *Psychological Bulletin,* 1954, *51,* 327–358.

Fleishman, E. A. *The structure and measurement of physical fitness.* Englewood Cliffs, N.J.: Prentice-Hall, 1964.

Fleishman, E. A. On the relation between abilities, learning, and human performance. *American Psychologist,* 1972, *27,* 1017–1032.

Frederiksen, N. et al. The In-Basket Test. *Psychological Monographs,* 1957, *71*(9).

Gage, N. L. (Ed.) *Handbook of research on teaching.* Skokie, Ill.: Rand McNally, 1963.

Gagné, R. Instructional variables and learning outcomes. UCLA Symposium on Problems in the Evaluation of Instruction, 1967.

Gagné, R. *The conditions of learning.* (2d ed.) New York: Holt, Rinehart and Winston, 1970.

Getzels, J. W., & Jackson, P. W. *Creativity and intelligence.* New York: Wiley, 1962.

Ghiselli, E. E. Differentiation of individuals in terms of their predictability. *Journal of Applied Psychology,* 1956, *40,* 374–377. (a)

Ghiselli, E. E. Dimensional problems of criteria. *Journal of Applied Psychology,* 1956, *40,* 1–4. (b)

Ghiselli, E. E. The prediction of predictability. *Educational and Psychological Measurement,* 1960, *20,* 3–8. (a)

Ghiselli, E. E. Differentiation of tests in terms of the accuracy with which they predict for a given individual. *Educational and Psychological Measurement,* 1960, *20,* 675–684. (b)

Ghiselli, E. E. Moderating effects and differential reliability and validity. *Journal of Applied Psychology,* 1963, *47,* 81–86.

Ghiselli, E. E. *Theory of psychological measurement.* New York: McGraw-Hill, 1964.

Ghiselli, E. E. *The validity of occupational aptitude tests.* New York: Wiley, 1966.

Glaser, R. Instructional technology and the measurement of learning outcomes. *American Psychologist,* 1963, *18,* 519–521.

Glaser, R. Adapting the elementary school curriculum to individual performance. Proceedings of the 1967 Invitational Conference on Testing Problems. Princeton, N.J.: Educational Testing Service, 1968.

Glaser, R. Individuals and learning: The new aptitudes. *Educational Researcher,* June 1972, 5–13.

Glaser, R., & Nitko, A. J. Measurement in learning and instruction. Chapter 17 in R. L. Thorndike (Ed.), *Educational measurement.* (2d ed.) Washington, D.C.: American Council on Education, 1971.

Gleser, G. C., Cronbach, L. J., & Rajaratnam, N. Generalizability of scores influenced by multiple sources of variance. *Psychometrika,* 1965, *30,* 395–418.

Goldberg, L. R. Grades as motivants. *Psychology in the Schools,* 1965, *2*(1), 17–24. (a)

Goldberg, L. R. Diagnosticians versus diagnostic signs: The diagnosis of psychosis versus neurosis from the MMPI. *Psychological Monographs,* 1965, *79*(9). (b)

Goldberg, L. R. Simple models or simple processes? Some research on clinical judgments. *American Psychologist,* 1968, *23,* 483–495.

Goldberg, L. R. Some recent trends in personality assessment. *Journal of Personality Assessment,* 1972, *36,* 547–560.

Goldman, L. *Using tests in counseling.* (2d ed.) New York: Appleton, 1971.

Goodenough, F. L. *Mental testing.* New York: Holt, Rinehart and Winston, 1949.

Goslin, D. A. *The search for ability.* New York: Russell Sage Foundation, 1963.

Goslin, D. A. *Teachers and testing.* New York: Russell Sage Foundation, 1967.

Goslin, D. A. Standardized ability tests and testing. *Science,* 1968, *159,* 851–855.

Guilford, J. P. *Psychometric methods.* (2d ed.) New York: McGraw-Hill, 1954.

Guilford, J. P. The structure of the intellect. *Psychological Bulletin,* 1956, *53,* 267–293.

Guilford, J. P. Three faces of intellect. *American Psychologist,* 1959, *14,* 469–479.

Guilford, J. P. *The nature of human intelligence.* New York: McGraw-Hill, 1967.

Guilford, J. P. *Intelligence, creativity, and their educational implications.* San Diego: Robert Knapp, 1968.

Guttman, L. A basis for analysing test–retest reliability. *Psychometrika,* 1945, *10,* 255–282.

Hall, C. S., & Lindzey, G. *Theories of personality.* (2d ed.) New York: Wiley, 1970.

Harman, H. H. *Modern factor analysis.* Chicago: University of Chicago Press, 1967.

Harmon, L. W. Sexual bias in interest measurement. *Measurement and Evaluation in Guidance,* 1973, *5,* 496–501.

Harrell, T. W., & Harrell, M. S. Army General Classification Test scores for civilian occupations. *Educational and Psychological Measurement,* 1945, *5,* 229–239.

Harris, C. W. (Ed.) *Problems in measuring change.* Madison: University of Wisconsin Press, 1963.

Hase, H. D., & Goldberg, L. R. Comparative validity of different strategies for constructing personality inventory scales. *Psychological Bulletin,* 1967, *67,* (Eds.) 231–248.

Hathaway, S. R. Foreword to W. G. Dahlstrom & G. S. Welsh (Eds.), *An MMPI Handbook.* Minneapolis: University of Minnesota Press, 1960.

Hathaway, S. R., & Meehl, P. E. *An atlas for the clinical use of the MMPI*. Minneapolis: University of Minnesota Press, 1951.

Hays, W. L. *Statistics for the social sciences*. (2d ed.) New York: Holt, Rinehart and Winston, 1973.

Helmstadter, G. C. *Principles of psychological measurement*. New York: Appleton, 1964.

Henryssen, S. Gathering, analyzing, and using data on test items. Chapter 5 in R. L. Thorndike (Ed.), *Educational measurement*. (2d ed.) Washington, D.C.: American Council on Education, 1971.

Herrnstein, R. I.Q. *Atlantic,* September 1971, 43–64.

Hill, E. F. *The Holtzman Inkblot techniques: A handbook for clinical application*. San Francisco: Jossey-Bass, 1972.

Hills, J. R. The effect of admissions policy on college grading standards. Atlanta: Office of Testing and Guidance, University System of Georgia, Research Bulletin 63-5, 1963.

Hills, J. R. Use of measurement in selection and placement. Chapter 19 in R. L. Thorndike (Ed.), *Educational measurement*. (2d ed.) Washington, D.C.: American Council on Education, 1971.

Hively, W., Patterson, H. L., & Page, S. H. A "universe-defined" system of arithmetic achievement tests. *Journal of Educational Measurement,* 1968, *5,* 275–290.

Hoffmann, B. The tyranny of multiple-choice tests. *Harpers,* March 1961, 37–44.

Hoffmann, B. *The tyranny of testing*. New York: Macmillan, 1962.

Hoffman, P. The paramorphic representation of clinical judgment. *Psychological Bulletin,* 1960, *57,* 116–131.

Hoffman, P. J. Assessment of the independent contribution of predictors. *Psychological Bulletin,* 1962, *59,* 77–80.

Holland, J. L. *Making vocational choices: A theory of careers*. Englewood Cliffs, N.J.: Prentice-Hall, 1973.

Holt, R. R. Clinical and statistical prediction: A reformulation and some new data. *Journal of Abnormal and Social Psychology,* 1958, *56,* 1–12.

Holt, R. R. *Assessing personality*. New York: Harcourt Brace Jovanovich, 1971.

Holtzman, W. H. Objective scoring of projective techniques. In B. M. Bass & I. A. Berg (Eds.), *Objective approaches to personality assessment*. Princeton, N.J.: Van Nostrand, 1959.

Holtzman, W. H. *Inkblot perception and personality*. Austin: University of Texas Press, 1961.

Horn, J. L. Some characteristics of classroom examinations. *Journal of Educational Measurement,* 1966, *3,* 293–295.

Horn, J. L. Intelligence: Why it grows, why it declines. *Trans-Action,* November 1967, 23–31.

Horn, J. L. Organization of data on life-span development of human abilities. Chapter 16 in L. R. Goulet & P. B. Baltes (Eds.), *Life-span developmental psychology*. New York: Academic Press, 1970.

Horst, P. A. A technique for the development of a differential prediction battery. *Psychological Monographs,* 1964, *68*(9).

Horst, P. A. *Psychological measurement and prediction*. Belmont, Calif.: Wadsworth, 1966.

Howe, M. J. A. *Understanding school learning*. New York: Harper & Row, 1972.

Hoyt, C. Test reliability obtained by analysis of variance. *Psychometrika,* 1941, *6,* 153–160.

Hoyt, D. P. The relationship between college grades and adult achievement. *ACT Research Reports,* 1965, No. 7.

Hunt, J. McV. *Intelligence and experience*. New York: Ronald, 1961.

Hunt, J. McV. (Ed.) *Human intelligence.* New Brunswick, N.J.: Transaction Books (E. P. Dutton), 1972.

Husén, T. (Ed.). *International study of achievement in mathematics.* (2 vols.) New York: Wiley, 1967.

Jackson, D. N., & Messick, S. Content and style in personality assessment. *Psychological Bulletin,* 1958, *55*, 243–255.

Jackson, D. N., & Messick, S. (Eds.) *Problems in human assessment.* New York: McGraw-Hill, 1967.

Jacoby, L. L. Test-appropriate strategies in retention of categorized lists. *Journal of Verbal Learning and Verbal Behavior,* 1973, *12*, 675–682.

Jaeger, R. M. The national test-equating study in reading (The anchor test study). *Measurement in Education* (NCME), Summer 1973, 1–8.

Jensen, A. R. Social class, race and genetics: Implications for education. *American Educational Research Journal,* 1968, *5*, 1–42.

Jensen, A. R. How much can we boost IQ and scholastic achievement? *Harvard Educational Review,* 1969, *39*, 1–123.

Jensen, A. R. The effect of race of examiner on the mental test scores of white and black pupils. *Journal of Educational Measurement,* 1974, *11*, 1–14.

Jessor, R., & Hammond, K. R. Construct validity and the Taylor Anxiety Scale. *Psychological Bulletin,* 1957, *54*, 161–170.

Jones, L. V. The nature of measurement. Chapter 12 in R. L. Thorndike (Ed.), *Educational measurement.* (2d ed.) Washington, D.C.: American Council on Education, 1971.

Katz, M. Interpreting Kuder Preference Record-Vocational scores: Ipsative or normative? Paper presented at the annual meeting of the American Personnel and Guidance Association, 1962.

Keats, J. A. Test theory. *Annual Review of Psychology,* 1967, *18*, 217–238.

Kelly, E. L. *Assessment of human characteristics.* Belmont, Calif.: Brooks/Cole, 1967.

Kelly, E. L., & Fiske, D. W. *The prediction of performance in clinical psychology.* Ann Arbor: University of Michigan Press, 1951.

Kelly, G. A. The theory and technique of assessment. *Annual Review of Psychology,* 1958, *9*, 323–352.

Kerlinger, F. N. *Foundations of behavioral research.* New York: Holt, Rinehart and Winston, 1965.

Kerlinger, F. N. *Foundations of behavioral research* (2d ed.) New York: Holt, Rinehart and Winston, 1973.

Kerlinger, F. N., & Pedhazur, E. J. *Multiple regression in behavioral research.* New York: Holt, Rinehart and Winston, 1973.

Klein, S. P., & Hart, F. M. Chance and systematic factors affecting essay grades. *Journal of Educational Measurement,* 1968, *5*, 197–206.

Kleinmuntz, B. The computer as clinician. *American Psychologist,* 1975, *30*, 379–387.

Kline, M. *Why Johnny can't add.* New York: Vintage, 1974. (Originally published, St. Martin's Press, 1973.)

Kogan, N. Educational implications of cognitive styles. Chapter 10 in G. S. Lesser (Ed.), *Psychology and educational practice.* Glenview, Ill.: Scott, Foresman, 1971.

Kuder, G. F. A rationale for evaluating interests. *Educational and Psychological Measurement,* 1963, *23*, 3–12.

Kuder, G. F. The Occupational Interest Survey. *Personnel and Guidance Journal,* 1966, *45*, 72–77.

Kuder, G. F., & Richardson, M. W. The theory of estimation of test reliability. *Psychometrika*, 1937, *2*, 151–160.

Lavin, D. E. *The prediction of academic performance*. New York: Russell Sage Foundation, 1965.

Layton, W. L. Counseling use of the Strong Vocational Interest Blank. Minneapolis: University of Minnesota Press, 1958.

Layton, W. L. The Strong Vocational Interest Blank: Research and uses. Minneapolis: University of Minnesota Press, 1960.

Lindquist, E. F. (Ed.) *Educational measurement*. Washington, D.C.: American Council on Education, 1951.

Lindvall, C. M., & Nitko, A. J. *Measuring pupil achievement and aptitude* (2d ed.) New York: Harcourt Brace Jovanovich, 1975.

Lindzey, G. *Projective techniques and cross-cultural research*. New York: Appleton, 1961.

Livingston, S. A. Criterion-referenced applications of classical test theory. *Journal of Educational Measurement*, 1972, *9*, 13–26.

Loevinger, J. A systematic approach to the construction and evaluation of tests of ability. *Psychological Monographs*, 1947, *61*(4).

Loevinger, J. Objective tests as instruments of psychological theory. *Psychological Reports, Monograph Supplement 9*, 1957, *3*, 635–694.

Longstaff, H. P. Fakability of the Strong Interest Blank and Kuder Preference Record. *Journal of Applied Psychology*, 1948, *32*, 360–369.

Lonner, W. J. The SVIB visits German, Austrian, and Swiss psychologists. *American Psychologist*, 1968, *23*, 164–179.

Lord, F. M. Do tests of the same length have the same standard error of measurement? *Educational and Psychological Measurement*, 1957, *17*, 510–521.

Lumsden, J. The construction of unidimensional tests. *Psychological Bulletin*, 1961, *58*, 122–131.

Lyman, H. B. *Test scores and what they mean*. (2d ed.) Englewood Cliffs, N.J.: Prentice-Hall, 1971.

MacKinney, A. C. The assessment of performance change: An inductive example. *Organizational Behavior and Human Performance*, 1967, *2*, 56–72.

MacKinnon, D. W. The nature and nurture of creative talent. *American Psychologist*, 1962, *17*, 484–495.

Maccoby, E. E., & Jacklin, C. N. *The psychology of sex differences*. Stanford, Calif.: Stanford University Press, 1974.

Mager, R. F. *Preparing instructional objectives*. Palo Alto, Calif.: Fearon, 1962.

Magnusson, D. *Test theory*. Reading, Mass.: Addison-Wesley, 1967.

Marks, P. A., & Seeman, W. *The actuarial description of abnormal personality: An atlas for use with the MMPI*. Baltimore: Williams & Wilkins, 1963.

Marks, P. A., Seeman, W., & Haller, D. L. *The actuarial use of the MMPI with adolescents and adults*. Baltimore: Williams & Wilkins, 1974.

Masling, J. The influence of situational and interpersonal variables in projective testing. *Psychological Bulletin*, 1960, *56*, 65–85.

Matarazzo, J. *Wechsler's measurement and appraisal of adult intelligence* (5th ed.) Baltimore: Williams & Wilkins, 1972.

McArthur, C. Long-term validity of the Strong Interest Test in two subcultures. *Journal of Applied Psychology*, 1954, *38*, 346–353.

McCall, R. B., Hogarty, P. S., & Hurlburt, N. Transitions in infant sensorimotor development and the prediction of childhood IQ. *American Psychologist,* 1972, *27*, 728–749.

McCall, W. A. *How to measure in education.* New York: Macmillan, 1922.

McClelland, D. C. Testing for competence rather than for "intelligence." *American Psychologist,* 1973, *28*, 1–14.

McClelland, D. C., Atkinson, J. W., Clark, R. A., & Lowell, E. L. *The achievement motive.* New York: Appleton, 1953.

McHugh, R. B. The interval estimation of a true score. *Psychological Bulletin,* 1957, *54*, 73–78.

McNemar, Q. Lost: Our intelligence. Why? *American Psychologist,* 1964, *19*, 871–882.

Meehl, P. E. The dynamics of "structured" personality tests. *Journal of Clinical Psychology,* 1945, *1*, 296–303.

Meehl, P. E. Configural scoring. *Journal of Consulting Psychology,* 1950, *14*, 165–171.

Meehl, P. E. *Clinical versus statistical prediction.* Minneapolis: University of Minnesota Press, 1954.

Meehl, P. E. Wanted: A good cookbook. *American Psychologist,* 1956, *11*, 263–272.

Meehl, P. E. When shall we use our heads instead of the formula? *Journal of Counseling Psychology,* 1957, *4*, 268–273.

Meehl, P. E. A comparison of clinicians with five statistical methods of identifying psychotic MMPI profiles. *Journal of Counseling Psychology,* 1959, *6*, 102–109.

Meehl, P. E., & Hathaway, S. R. The K factor as a suppressor variable in the MMPI. *Journal of Applied Psychology,* 1946, *30*, 525–564.

Meehl, P. E., & Rosen, A. Antecedent probability and the efficiency of psychometric signs, patterns, or cutting scores. *Psychological Bulletin,* 1955, *52*, 194–216.

Mehrens, W. A., & Lehmann, I. J. *Standardized tests in education.* New York: Holt, Rinehart and Winston, 1969.

Mehrens, W. A., & Lehmann, I. J. *Measurement and evaluation in education and psychology.* New York: Holt, Rinehart and Winston, 1973.

Mehrens, W. A., & Lehmann, I. J. *Standardized tests in education.* (2d ed.) New York: Holt, Rinehart and Winston, 1975.

Mercer, J. *Labelling the mentally retarded.* Berkeley: University of California Press, 1973.

Messick, S. The criterion problem in the evaluation of instruction: Assessing possible, not just intended outcomes. In M. C. Wittrock & D. E. Wiley (Eds.), *The evaluation of instruction.* New York: Holt, Rinehart and Winston, 1970.

Michael, W. B. Aptitudes. In C. W. Harris (Ed.), *Encyclopedia of educational research.* New York: Macmillan, 1960, pp. 59–63.

Michael, W. B. et al. The description of spatial-visualization abilities. *Educational and Psychological Measurement,* 1957, *17*, 185–199.

Mischel, W. *Personality and assessment.* New York: Wiley, 1968.

Mosier, C. I. Batteries and profiles. In E. F. Lindquist (Ed.), *Educational measurement.* Washington, D.C.: American Council on Education, 1951.

Munday, L. Predicting college grades in predominantly Negro colleges. *Journal of Educational Measurement,* 1965, *2*, 157–160.

Murray, H. A. *Explorations in personality.* New York: Oxford University Press, 1938.

Nicholls, J. G. Creativity in the person who will never produce anything original and unique: The concept of creativity as a normally distributed trait. *American Psychologist,* 1972, *27*, 717–729.

Nunnally, J. *Psychometric theory.* New York: McGraw-Hill, 1967.

OSS Assessment Staff. *Assessment of men.* New York: Holt, Rinehart and Winston, 1948.

Overall, J. E., & Woodward, J. A. Unreliability of difference scores: A paradox for measurement of change. *Psychological Bulletin,* 1975, *82*, 85–86.

Pace, C. R. College and University Environment Scales: Technical manual. Princeton, N.J.: Educational Testing Service, 1963.

Pace, C. R. Analyses of a national sample of college environments. University of California at Los Angeles, 1967.

Page, E. B. Grading essays by computer. In the Proceedings of the 1966 Invitational Conference on Testing Problems. Princeton, N.J.: Educational Testing Service, 1967, pp. 87–100.

Payne, D. A. *The assessment of learning: Cognitive and affective.* Lexington, Mass.: Heath, 1974.

Pinneau, S. R. *Changes in intelligence quotient from infancy to maturity.* Boston: Houghton Mifflin, 1961.

Popham, W. J., & Husek, T. R. Implications of criterion-referenced measurement. *Journal of Educational Measurement,* 1969, *6*, 1–9.

Privacy and behavioral research. Washington, D.C.: Government Printing Office, 1967.

Purves, A. C. *Literature education in ten countries.* New York: Wiley, 1973.

Rasch, G. An item analysis which takes individual differences into account. *British Journal of Mathematical and Statistical Psychology,* 1966, *19*(1), 49–57.

Reinert, G. Comparative factor analytic studies of intelligence throughout the human life-span. Chapter 17 in L. R. Goulet & P. B. Baltes (Eds.), *Life-span developmental psychology.* New York: Academic Press, 1970.

Richardson, M. W., & Kuder, G. F. The calculation of test reliability coefficients based on the method of rational equivalence. *Journal of Educational Psychology,* 1939, *30*, 681–687.

Ricks, J. H., Jr. Local norms: When and why. New York: The Psychological Corporation, Test Service Bulletin, No. 58, 1971.

Rohwer, W. D., Jr., Ammon, P. R., & Cramer, P. *Understanding intellectual development.* Hinsdale, Ill.: Dryden Press, 1974.

Rorer, L.G. The great response-style myth. *Psychological Bulletin,* 1965, *63*, 129–156.

Rothkopf, E. Z., & Bisbicos, O. Selective facilitative effects of interspersed questions on learning from written materials. *Journal of Educational Psychology,* 1967, *58*, 56–61.

Rosenthal, R., & Jacobson, L. *Pygmalion in the classroom.* New York: Holt, Rinehart and Winston, 1968.

Rowley, G. L. Which examinees are most favored by the use of multiple-choice tests? *Journal of Educational Measurement,* 1974, *11*, 15–23.

Ruebhausen, O. M., & Brim, O. G., Jr. Privacy and behavioral research. *American Psychologist,* 1966, *21*, 423–437.

Sarason, S. B., Davidson, K. S., Lighthall, F. F., Waite, R. R., & Ruebush, B. K. *Anxiety in elementary school children.* New York: Wiley, 1960.

Sarbin, T. R. The logic of prediction in psychology. *Psychological Review,* 1944, *51*, 210–228.

Schrader, W. B. A taxonomy of expectancy tables. *Journal of Educational Measurement,* 1965, *2*, 29–35.

Scriven, M. The methodology of evaluation. In R. Tyler et al., Perspectives on curriculum evaluation. Chicago: Rand McNally, 1967. AERA Monograph Series on Curriculum Evaluation, no. 1.

Seashore, H. G. Methods of expressing test scores. New York: The Psychological Corporation, Test Service Bulletin, No. 48, 1955.

Seashore, H. G. Women are more predictable than men. *Journal of Counseling Psychology*, 1962, *9*, 261–270.

Seashore, H. G., & Ricks, J. H., Jr. Norms must be relevant. New York: The Psychological Corporation, Test Service Bulletin, No. 39, 1950.

Sechrest, L. Incremental validity: A recommendation. *Educational and Psychological Measurement*, 1963, *23*, 153–158.

Semeonoff, B. (Ed.) *Personality assessment*. Baltimore: Penguin Books, 1966.

Skinner, B. F. *The technology of teaching*. New York: Appleton, 1968.

Stanley, J. C. Reliability. Chapter 13 in R. L. Thorndike (Ed.), *Educational measurement*. (2d ed.) Washington, D.C.: American Council on Education, 1971.

Stanley, J. C., & Porter, A. C. Correlation of Scholastic Aptitude Test scores with college grades for negroes versus whites. *Journal of Educational Measurement*, 1967, *4*, 199–218.

Stephenson, W. *The study of behavior: Q-technique and its methodology*. Chicago: University of Chicago Press, 1953.

Stevens, S. S. Mathematics, measurement, and psychophysics. In S. S. Stevens (Ed.), *Handbook of experimental psychology*. New York: Wiley, 1951.

Strong, E. K. *Vocational interests of men and women*. Stanford, Calif.: Stanford University Press, 1943.

Strong, E. K. *Vocational interests 18 years after college*. Minneapolis: University of Minnesota Press, 1955.

Strong, E. K., & Campbell, D. P. Manual for the Strong Vocational Interests Blanks. Stanford, Calif.: Stanford University Press, 1966.

Super, D. E. The use of multifactor tests in guidance. Washington, D. C.: American Personnel and Guidance Association, 1958.

Super, D. E., & Crites, J. O. *Appraising vocational fitness*. New York: Harper & Row, 1962.

Tatsuoka, M. Multivariate analysis in educational research. Chapter 9 in F. N. Kerlinger (Ed.), *Review of research in education; 1*. Itasca, Ill.: F. E. Peacock, 1973.

Taylor, C. W., & Barron, F. *Scientific creativity: Its recognition and development*. New York: Wiley, 1963.

Taylor, H. C., & Russell, J. T. The relationship of validity coefficients to the practical effectiveness of tests in selection: Discussion and tables. *Journal of Applied Psychology*, 1939, *23*, 565–578.

Taylor, I. A., & Getzels, J. W. (Eds.) *Perspectives in creativity*. Chicago: Aldine, 1975.

Terman, L. M., & Merrill, M. A. *Measuring intelligence*. Boston: Houghton Mifflin, 1937.

Terman, L. M., & Merrill, M. A. *Stanford-Binet Intelligence Scale: Manual for the third revision, form L-M*. Boston: Houghton Mifflin, 1960.

Thelen, M. H., Varble, D. L., & Johnson, J. Attitudes of academic clinical psychologists toward projective techniques. *American Psychologist*, 1968, *23*, 517–521.

Thomas, C. L., & Stanley, J. C. Effectiveness of high school grades for predicting college grades of black students: A review and discussion. *Journal of Educational Measurement*, 1969, *6*, 203–215.

Thorndike, R. L. Reliability. In E. F. Lindquist (Ed.), *Educational measurement*. New York: American Council on Education, 1951.

Thorndike, R. L. *The concepts of over- and under-achievement*. New York: Bureau of Publications, Teachers College, Columbia University, 1963.

Thorndike, R. L. Educational decisions and human assessment. *Teachers College Record*, 1964, *66*, 103–112.

Thorndike, R. L. (Ed.) *Educational measurement*. (2d ed.) Washington, D.C.: American Council on Education, 1971. (a)

Thorndike, R. L. Educational measurement for the seventies. Chapter 1 in R. L. Thorndike (Ed.), *Educational measurement*. (2d ed.) Washington, D.C.: American Council on Education, 1971. (b)

Thorndike, R. L. *Reading comprehension education in fifteen countries*. New York: Wiley, 1973.

Thorndike, R. L., & Hagen, E. P. *Ten thousand careers*. New York: Wiley, 1959.

Thorndike, R. L., & Hagen, E. P. *Measurement and evaluation in psychology and education*. (2d ed.) New York: Wiley, 1961.

Thorndike, R. L., & Hagen, E. P. *Measurement and evaluation in psychology and education*. (3d ed.) New York: Wiley, 1969.

Thrush, R. S. An agency in transition: The case study of a counseling center. *Journal of Counseling Psychology*, 1957, *4*, 183–189.

Thurstone, L. L., & Ackerson, L. The mental growth curve for the Binet tests. *Journal of Educational Psychology*, 1929, *20*, 569–583.

Tilton, J. W. The measurement of overlapping. *Journal of Educational Psychology*, 1937, *28*, 656–662.

Tittle, C. K. Sex bias in educational measurement: Fact or fiction. *Measurement and Evaluation in Guidance*, 1973, *6*, 219–226.

Torrance, E. P. *Guiding creative talent*. Englewood Cliffs, N.J.: Prentice-Hall, 1962.

Torrance, E. P., & Myers, R. E. *Creative learning and teaching*. New York: Dodd, Mead, 1970.

Travers, R. M. W. (Ed.) *Second handbook of research on teaching*. Chicago: Rand McNally, 1973.

Tyler, L. *The psychology of human differences*. (3d ed.) New York: Appleton, 1965.

Tyler, R. W., Merwin, J. C., & Ebel, R. L. Symposium: A National Assessment of Educational Progress. *Journal of Educational Measurement*, 1966, *3*, 1–17.

Tyler, R. W., & Wolf, R. M. (Eds.) *Critical issues in testing*. Berkeley, Calif.: McCutchan, 1974.

Vernon, P. E. *Personality assessment: A critical survey*. London: Methuen, 1964.

Vernon, P. E. (Ed.) *Creativity*. Baltimore: Penguin Books, 1970.

Vernon, P. E. *Structure of human abilities*. New York: Barnes & Noble, 1971.

Wallace, J., & Sechrest, L. *The nature and study of psychology*. Itasca, Ill.: F. E. Peacock, 1973.

Wallach, M. A., & Wing, C. W. *The talented student: A validation of the creativity–intelligence distinction*. New York: Holt, Rinehart and Winston, 1969.

Wang, M. W., & Stanley, J. C. Differential weighting: A review of methods and empirical studies. *Review of Educational Research*, 1970, *40*, 663–705.

Watts, G. H., & Anderson, R. C. Effects of three types of inserted questions on learning from prose. *Journal of Educational Psychology*, 1971, *62*, 387–394.

Webb, E. J., Campbell, D. T., Schwartz, R. D., & Sechrest, L. *Unobtrusive measures: Nonreactive research in the social sciences*. Chicago: Rand McNally, 1966.

Webb, S. C. Measured changes in college grading standards. *College Board Review*, 1959, No. 39, 27–30.

Webster's New World Dictionary (College Ed.) Cleveland: World, 1966.

Wechsler, D. Manual for the Wechsler Adult Intelligence Scale. New York: The Psychological Corporation, 1955.

Wechsler, D. *The measurement and appraisal of adult intelligence*. Baltimore: Williams & Wilkins, 1958.

Wechsler, D. Intelligence defined and undefined: A relativistic approach. *American Psychologist,* 1975, *30*, 135–139.

Weiss, D. J. Strategies of adaptive ability measurement. Minneapolis: University of Minnesota, Department of Psychology, 1974.

Weitz, J. Criteria for criteria. *American Psychologist,* 1961, *16*, 228–231.

Welsh, G. S. Factor dimensions A and R. In G. S. Welsh & W. G. Dahlstrom (Eds.), *Basic readings on the MMPI in psychology and medicine.* Minneapolis: University of Minnesota Press, 1956.

Wesman, A. G. Comparability vs. equivalence of test scores. New York: The Psychological Corporation, Test Service Bulletin, No. 53, 1958.

Wesman, A. G. Double-entry expectancy tables. New York: The Psychological Corporation, Test Service Bulletin, No. 56, 1966.

Wesman, A. G. Intelligent testing. *American Psychologist,* 1968, *23*, 267–274.

Wesman, A. G. Writing the test item. Chapter 4 in R. L. Thorndike (Ed.), *Educational measurement.* (2d ed.) Washington, D.C.: American Council on Education, 1971.

Wiggins, J. S. *Personality and prediction: Principles of personality assessment.* Reading, Mass.: Addison-Wesley, 1973.

Wine, J. Test anxiety and direction of attention. *Psychological Bulletin,* 1971, *76*, 92–104.

Wiseman, S. (Ed.) *Intelligence and ability.* Baltimore: Penguin Books, 1967.

Wittrock, M. C., & Wiley, D. E. *The evaluation of instruction.* New York: Holt, Rinehart and Winston, 1970.

Wolfle, D. Diversity of talent. *American Psychologist,* 1960, *15*, 535–545.

Womer, F. B. The National Assessment of Educational Progress: Concept and organization. *ERIC Capsule,* Winter 1970, 1–7. (a)

Womer, F. B. National Assessment says. *Measurement in Education* (NCME), October 1970, 1–8. (b)

Young, M. *The rise of the meritocracy.* Baltimore: Penguin Books, 1961.

Young, R. K., & Veldman, D. J. *Introductory statistics for the behavioral sciences.* (2d ed.) New York: Holt, Rinehart and Winston, 1972.

Zytowski, D. G. Relationships of equivalent scales on three interest inventories. *Personnel and Guidance Journal,* 1968, *47*, 44–49.

Zytowski, D. G. (Ed.) *Contemporary approaches to interest measurement.* Minneapolis: University of Minnesota Press, 1973.

NAME INDEX

SUBJECT INDEX